The Lifespan

The Lifespan

Fourth Edition

Guy R. Lefrançois

University of Alberta

Wadsworth Publishing Company
Belmont, California
A Division of Wadsworth, Inc.

Education Editor: Suzanna Brabant
Editorial Assistant: Kate Peltier
Production Editor: Angela Mann
Managing Designer: Kaelin Chappell
Print Buyer: Barbara Britton
Art Editor: Donna Kalal
Permissions Editor: Peggy Meehan
Designer: Paula Shuhert
Copy Editor: Tom Briggs
Photo Researcher: Marty Kongsle
Technical Illustrators: Kathryn Werhane, Steve Markovich
Cover Illustrator: Yan Nascimbene
Compositor: Thompson Type
Printer: Rand McNally, Taunton

Printed in the United States of America

2 3 4 5 6 7 8 9 10 — 97 96 95 94 93

Library of Congress Cataloging-in-Publication Data
Lefrançois, Guy R.
    The lifespan / Guy R. Lefrançois. — 4th ed.
      p.   cm.
    Includes bibliographical references and indexes.
    ISBN 0-534-17778-6 (alk. paper)
    1. Developmental psychology.   I. Title.   II. Title:
    Lifespan.
BF713.L44   1993
155 — dc20   92-30607

DEDICATED

To my grandparents and all the old people without whom
we would not be here today.

To my children and all the young people without whom
we will not be here tomorrow.

Brief Contents

Contents

Know then thyself,
presume not God to scan;
The proper study of
Mankind is Man.

Alexander Pope,
Essay on Man

The dwarf sees farther than the giant, when he has the giant's shoulders to stand on.

Samuel Taylor Coleridge,
The Friend

3 Genetics and Context 77

Sir Roger told them, with the air of a man who would not give his judgment rashly, that much might be said on both sides.

Joseph Addison,
Spectator, Vol. 1

Nature is often hidden;
sometimes overcome;
seldom extinguished.

Francis Bacon,
Of Nature in Men

4 Prenatal Development and Birth 109

I wish either my father or my mother, or indeed both of them, as they were in duty both equally bound to it, had minded what they were about when they begot me.

Laurence Sterne,
Tristram Shandy

Part II: Infancy 147

Language was not powerful enough to describe the infant phenomenon.

Charles Dickens,
Nicholas Nickleby

When the first baby laughed for the first time, the laugh broke into a thousand pieces and they all went skipping about, and that was the beginning of fairies.

James Matthew Barrie,
Peter Pan

Part III: Early Childhood 223

7 Physical and Cognitive Development: Early Childhood 225

G₀ directly — see what she's doing, and tell her she mustn't.

Punch, 1872

Every time a child says "I don't believe in fairies," there is a little fairy somewhere that falls down dead.

James Matthew Barrie,
Peter Pan

More than either, it [England] resembles a family, a rather stuffy Victorian family, with not many black sheep in it but with all its cupboards bursting with skeletons. It has rich relations who have to be kow-towed to and poor relations who are horribly sat upon, and there is a deep conspiracy about the source of the family income. It is a family in which the young are generally thwarted and most of the power is in the hands of irresponsible uncles and bedridden aunts. Still, it is a family.

George Orwell,
England, Your England

Part IV: Middle Childhood 295

9 Physical and Cognitive Development: Middle Childhood 297

"I dare say you haven't had practice," said the Queen. "When I was your age, I always did it for half an hour a day. Why, sometimes I've believed as many as six impossible things before breakfast."

    Lewis Carroll,
    Through the Looking-Glass and What Alice Found There

See the happy moron,
He doesn't give a damn,
I wish I were a moron,
My God! perhaps I am!

Anonymous,
Eugenics Review, 1929

A traveler at Sparta, standing long upon one leg, said to a Lacedaemonian: "I do not believe you can do as much." "True," said he, "but every goose can."

Plutarch,
Laconic Apothegms

Part V: Adolescence 375

11 Physical and Cognitive Development: Adolescence 377

Everybody worships me, it's nauseating.

Noel Coward,
Present Laughter

Live as long as you may, the first twenty years are the longest half of your life.

Robert Southey,
The Doctor

Part VI: Early Adulthood 449

We think so because other people think so,
Or because — or because —
after all we do think so,
Or because, we were told
so, and think we must
think so,
Or because we once thought so,
and think we still think so,
Or because having thought so,
we think we will think so.

Henry Sidgwick,
Lines Composed in His Sleep

Give me chastity and continence, but not yet.

St. Augustine,
Confessions

Part VII: Middle Adulthood 523

15 Physical and Cognitive Development: Middle Adulthood 525

I am convinced digestion is the great secret of life.

Sydney Smith,
in a letter to Arthur Kingslake

Happiness in marriage is entirely a matter of chance.

Jane Austen,
Northanger Abbey

Part VIII: Late Adulthood 581

17 Physical and Cognitive Development: Late Adulthood 583

It is always the season for the old to learn.

Aeschylus,
Fragments

18 Social Development: Late Adulthood 615

I keep looking back, as far as I can remember, and I can't think what it was like to feel young, really young.

John Osborne,
Look Back in Anger

Part IX: The End 639

19 Dying and Grieving 641

I silently laugh at my own
    cenotaph,
And out of the caverns of
    rain,
Like a child from the womb,
    like a ghost from the
    tomb,
I arise and unbuild it again.

        Percy Bysshe Shelley,
        The Cloud

Topical Arrangement of Contents

Preface

Edmonton, Alberta

Fall 1992

Dear Reader,

The Lifespan is an academic text. Its purpose is to lay before you, in simple language, the concepts and preoccupations of lifespan developmental psychology, to present clearly and accurately the field's most important discoveries, its controversies, its puzzles, and its promises. The substance of *The Lifespan* is contemporary research in human development; its sources include psychology, biology, medicine, education, anthropology, philosophy, genetics, and demography; its function is to teach.

But teaching is more than simply telling. It isn't enough simply to gather and organize the facts of a discipline and squeeze them between two covers. Good teaching also requires motivating, illustrating, explaining, relating, evaluating, perhaps even inspiring.

The Lifespan tries to be a good teacher. It illustrates and compares; sometimes it wonders; occasionally it is awed or puzzled or even frightened—although mostly it is hopeful. Sometimes it even pauses to tell tales about old people or infants, to intrigue with accounts of feral children or the misbehaviors of delinquent adolescents, to alarm with instances of social injustice or environmental atrocity.

Coverage and Organization

The Lifespan, Fourth Edition, divides human development into nine parts. The introductory section outlines the subject, discusses research methods and theories, explores gene–environment interaction, and traces prenatal development. The seven middle sections deal systematically with physical, cognitive, and social development in each major chronological division of the lifespan: infancy; early and middle childhood; adolescence; and early, middle, and late adulthood. A final section discusses death and grief.

Although the organization in this edition remains systematically chronological, chapters can be read independently rather than sequentially. For those who prefer a topical approach, chapters are organized so that it is relatively simple to rearrange them by topics using the detailed thematic table of contents included on pages xxxi–xxxv.

Special Features

A number of elements have been incorporated into *The Lifespan* to make it a better teaching and learning tool: chapter outlines; end-of-chapter main-point summaries and annotated readings; and an end-of-text glossary of important words, bold-faced when they are first discussed in the text. In addition, there are many figures, concept-summarizing tables, and other graphics to simplify and summarize textual material, as well as a large number of new *interactive* graphics and tables to involve the student more directly. Short, primarily graphic features labeled "At a Glance" summarize and highlight important information through photographs, figures, and brief explanations. There are no lengthy boxed inserts in this edition. These are too often hurdles that present serious problems for the student who must decide whether boxed material is so important that it has to be set aside and highlighted—or so unimportant that it was not given a place in the regular text. In this text, important material is emphasized in context—and there is no unimportant material.

What's New in the Fourth Edition?

The Lifespan, Fourth Edition, recognizes more clearly than previous editions its underlying and integrating themes. The most important of these is a new emphasis on the importance of interactions and relationships within context. Accordingly, it includes more contextual/ecological research and theory—for example, new sections on Bronfenbrenner and Vygotsky in Chapter 2, and expanded sections on family, peers, school, culture, and other systems throughout. Other important themes include the following: (1) Development is a lifelong process; it does not end with adolescence. (2) Focusing on processes is more important for understanding development than focusing on states or stages. (3) Developmental influences are bidirectional: The individual affects the environment even as the environment affects the individual. (4) Genes and context interact in complex ways throughout the lifespan. (5) Each of us is unique; the average individual is a myth, a convenient invention.

This edition has been thoroughly updated (over 400 new, mostly very recent references). New or significantly expanded topics include sections on contextual and open systems, self-efficacy, AIDS, children's rights, family violence, child abuse, date (acquaintance) rape, gender roles, self-worth, fragile X syndrome, avoidance-prone (shy kid) temperament, the impact of VCRs and videogames, and others. And Wadsworth has again prepared a complete and magnificent arsenal of guides, aids, test items, and so on, for use with *The Lifespan*.

Acknowledgments

This text owes much to many. There are historical debts to Richard Greenberg and Ken King, the production and copy editors who worked on the previous editions, the reviewers, students and professors, and many others. . . .

The fourth edition of *The Lifespan* owes less historical debts to Suzanna Brabant, education editor; Angela Mann, production editor; Tom Briggs, copy editor; Kaelin Chappell, designer; Donna Kalal, art editor; Marty Kongsle, photo researcher; and Mark B. Alcorn, University of Northern Colorado; William R. Fisk, Clemson University; Phyllis A. Heath, Central Michigan University; Joan M. Jones, University of Wisconsin, Milwaukee; Lynn Katz, University of Pittsburgh; Fayneese Miller, Brown University; and Karen H. Nelson, Austin College, reviewers for this fourth edition. Although I am solely responsible for all the ~~good things~~ errors, omissions, and stupidities in this text, your positive influence is considerable. I thank each of you.

I thank also George Semb, JoAnn Hinton, Alexandra Gikalov, Melinda Kuti, and Lisa Walsh, for writing the accompanying Study Guide and Instructor's Manual for this fourth edition.

There are many others to whom I am grateful; some of you know who you are. To each, my heartfelt thanks.

Sincerely,

The Lifespan

Winslow Homer: *The Herring Net*, 1885, oil on canvas, 30⅛" × 48⅜". Mr. and Mrs.
Martin A. Ryerson Collection 1937.1039. © 1989 The Art Institute of Chicago. All
rights reserved.

Forward, forward let us range,

Let the great world spin for ever down the
ringing grooves of change.

Alfred Lord Tennyson,
Locksley Hall

PART

I

The Beginning

Change is what human development is all about—enormous, fantastic change. Change, yet continuity. First, we are a speck in a mother's womb, insignificant and microscopic; soon, a wailing infant, unfamiliar with the world, helpless and totally dependent; next, a burgeoning child exploring the mysteries of time and space, yet still awed by magic and enchanted by fairies; then, an adolescent practicing the secrets of love and logic, at once sophisticated and naive; now, an adult, vigorous and powerful, but no longer able to see elves and other mystical things; and before we know it, we ease into our last age. Through all these changes, our sense of who we are, of our *selves*, endures.

The four chapters in "The Beginning" are about the things we need to know to understand this change and continuity. The first and second chapters lay out the subject, its methods, its most important theories; the third explores complex gene–context interactions that account for change; and the fourth traces the course of prenatal human development.

There is much to consider if we are to understand ourselves in a world that "spins for ever down the ringing grooves of change."

CHAPTER 1

Studying the Lifespan

"Begin at the beginning," the King said gravely, "and go on till you come to the end: then stop."

Lewis Carroll, *Alice in Wonderland*

"No," Alice might have retorted had she been telling the story this book must tell. "It's not so simple, your Majesty."

True, it isn't nice to say no to a king. But the beginnings of stories such as the one *The Lifespan* must tell are not always apparent. If we begin at what seems like the beginning—at conception—and plod along until what looks like the end—death—the stage will not have been set and we may be left wondering what our characters are doing and why.

So before we get to the very beginning, we must set the stage. But when we get to the end, we *will* stop.

This Text

Describing how infants, children, adolescents—and even adults—become progressively more familiar with the world is a large part of what *The Lifespan* is about.

The text is divided into nine major sections. The introductory section comprises four chapters: Chapter 1 defines what lifespan developmental psychology studies and describes its most important methods for discovering useful information. Chapter 2 introduces some of the major theories psychologists use to organize and understand this information. Chapter 3 discusses how genes and environment interact to influence development. And Chapter 4 describes the mechanics and mysteries of prenatal development and birth.

The middle seven sections are arranged chronologically: infancy; early childhood; middle childhood; adolescence; and early, middle, and late adulthood. The first chapter in each of these sections describes physical and intellectual change; the second discusses emotional and social development. The final section looks at dying (see Table 1.1).

To help your study, each chapter is preceded by a detailed outline; and each is followed by a summary of the main points in the chapter and a brief list of readings for additional information and opinion.

Lifespan Developmental Psychology

Psychology* is a general term for the science that studies behavior and thinking. **Developmental psychology** is concerned specifically with changes that occur over time. Accordingly, **lifespan developmental psychology** is the discipline that studies changes that occur from conception through adulthood and that looks at the processes and influences that account for these changes.

The Lifespan Perspective

Lifespan developmental psychology is a relatively new area of interest. During the century or so since the beginning of scientific psychology, most studies of human development focused on infancy, childhood, and, to a lesser extent, adolescence. True, even close to the beginning, there was some interest in adulthood and aging. A French mathematician by the name of Quetelet wrote a book about aging as far back as 1835, and, in 1922, G. S. Hall also published a major book on aging—a feat for which he is sometimes referred to as one of the founders of the study of aging. But the view of human development that long dominated psychological research, and that is still widely influential, is dramatically different from the contemporary *lifespan view*.

Development Is Continuous.
This traditional view of human development is, in some ways, quite simple. It holds that almost all important developmental changes occur between conception and adolescence, and that after adulthood is reached, little happens that might be of concern to a developmental psychologist. According to this view, adulthood is a stable period—a lengthy period of little change eventually followed by the declines of old age.

We now know that this traditional view of development is inaccurate and misleading. The more current lifespan view of development recognizes that important

---

*Boldfaced terms are defined in the Glossary at the end of the book.

T A B L E 1.1

Divisions of the Lifespan in This Text

Period/Part	Approximate Ages	Chapters
I. The Beginning	—	1. Studying the Lifespan 2. Theories of Lifespan Development 3. Genetics and Context 4. Prenatal Development and Birth
II. Infancy	Birth to 2 years	5. Physical and Cognitive Development 6. Social Development
III. Early Childhood	2 to 6–7 years	7. Physical and Cognitive Development 8. Social Development
IV. Middle Childhood	6–7 to 11–12 years	9. Physical and Cognitive Development 10. Social Development
V. Adolescence	11–12 to 19–20 years	11. Physical and Cognitive Development 12. Social Development
VI. Early Adulthood	20 to 40–45 years	13. Physical and Cognitive Development 14. Social Development
VII. Middle Adulthood	40–45 to 65–70 years	15. Physical and Cognitive Development 16. Social Development
VIII. Late Adulthood	65–70 years onward	17. Physical and Cognitive Development 18. Social Development
IX. The End	—	19. Dying and Grieving

changes occur at all ages throughout the lifespan. In fact, as Basseches (1984) notes, the lifespan view is rooted in the suggestion that the changes that occur in adulthood are similar in magnitude to those of earlier developmental periods. Hence the single most important characteristic of the lifespan view of human development is the recognition that both children and adults are developing organisms *throughout* life, that development does not cease with the beginning of adulthood.

Maturity Is Relative. If development continues through adulthood, it cannot easily be described in terms of a predetermined final state. What is important to the developmental psychologist is not the state so much as the *process*. We do not stand still long enough for our states of competence or readiness to endure. We continue to change, to struggle, to move toward new states of readiness, new competencies. The infant who

suddenly recognizes the meaning of the word *mother* is still a long way from a complete understanding of either words or mothers. Similarly, the 30-year-old who succeeds in resolving an emotional dilemma by finding someone to love and be loved by may be far from having learned to solve other emotional problems.

Accordingly, terms such as *mature*, as a description of a finally reached state of readiness or competence, have little place in the lifespan view of development. Maturity, like so many other states, is relative: We can be mature in certain areas but not in others. And even as we reach a state of relative maturity, we continue to change. To be a person is to change.

Change is what human development is about. Emphasis on the ongoing and never-ending processes of change — on the dynamism of the developmental process — is one of the things that distinguishes the contemporary lifespan view from an older and more restricted view of development.

Development Occurs in Context. Another characteristic of the lifespan view of human development is its recognition of the importance of *context*, or what is termed **ecology**.

As a general term, *ecology* refers to the science that studies the relationship between organisms and their environment (*oikos* is the Greek word for "home"; the suffix *-logy* means "the study of"). As a more specialized term in developmental theory, *ecology* refers primarily to the social context in which behavior and development occur. Thus, ecological approaches to understanding and explaining development pay a great deal of attention to the individual's social environment, and to the changing relationships between the individual and the environment. The key concept of this approach, Bronfenbrenner (1977b) insists, is development of the individual *in that individual's specific social context or ecology*. As Kegan (1982) notes, the emphasis is no longer simply on how the child constructs the world but also on how the world constructs the child. And the adult.

Developmental Influences Are Bidirectional. A final important characteristic of contemporary approaches to the study of human development is a stronger recognition of the **bidirectionality** of influences in the developmental process. Not only are children influenced by social context (which includes parents, siblings, peers, teachers, and so on), but in turn they influence their environment. For example, what parents do can have a pronounced and dramatic effect on their children. Genie, a girl whose parents confined her to a tiny bedroom, never speaking with her or allowing anyone else to interact with her, was, in the end, rather dramatically different from you or me (Curtiss, 1977). But influence is bidirectional. The effects of Genie's surroundings (her "context" or "ecology") are clearly apparent when we look at the pathetic, undernourished, nonverbal child that she grew to be. But even here, there is evidence of bidirectionality of influences. For example, Genie's confinement, arranged and insisted upon by her father, also meant that her father forbade her brother to visit her or to play with her. On those rare occasions when it was necessary for the brother to feed his little sister, he was ordered to approach her on hands and knees, like a dog. Perhaps he might be allowed to bark and growl a little, but he was not, under any circumstance, to speak with her. And if she didn't shovel her mushy food into her mouth

as fast as humanly possible, he was to rub her face in the dish and take it away.

We can only speculate about the effect that this might have had on the brother's personality. Or on that of the mother. But more about Genie in Chapter 3.

A Brief Summary

Belsky, Lerner, and Spanier (1984) summarize the most important beliefs that underlie current approaches to studying the lifespan:

- Children and adults are constantly developing, as are families, societies, and cultures. Development does not stop at any given point but continues throughout life.

- Influences in development are bidirectional. Children change their parents and other aspects of their environments even as the environment changes children.

- Not only do parents and children influence one another, but also they, in turn, are greatly affected by the social context in which they are embedded.

As will become increasingly apparent as you progress through this text, these beliefs are tremendously significant for contemporary lifespan developmental research. Among other things, they are reflected in a shifting of interest from the individual in isolation to the individual as part of a complex social system (ecological orientation). They also are apparent in increased attention to the ways in which the individual affects surrounding systems as well as the ways in which systems affect the individual. And, finally, they are evident in a shifting of our focus from describing states to investigating processes — that is, a shifting of concern from the static to the dynamic.

A Short History

Lifespan development is a recent area of psychological interest. Its most obvious roots can be found in the study of children. And the scientific study of children, too, is not very old. In fact, most of its development belongs to this century. At least some of the reasons for this long delay in the development of a science of child study have to do with attitudes toward children that appear to have been prevalent throughout much of human history.

The attitudes toward children reflected in this text are warm, positive, interested, sympathetic, concerned . . . all the good things we think of as characteristic of our enlightened 20th century. It has not always been so. In fact, even today it isn't always so.

Before the 18th Century

Nature has been stingy with her ancient records. There are vast gaps in our knowledge about the origins of plants and animals, long series of missing links about which we can only guess.

Unfortunately, we don't fare all that much better with human history, even when the questions we ask don't deal with very ancient events. There are few reliable records of what life might have been like for a child prior to what have sometimes been called the "print" cultures. When Ariès (1962) studied the lives of medieval children, he was forced to put together fragments from a variety of sources — 16th- and 17th-century paintings, school and university regulations, and Doctor Heroard's description of the upbringing of the French king Louis XIII. The result is a fascinating but not entirely reliable account.

In the Middle Ages, Ariès informs us, childhood did not exist as we know it. Early paintings depict children as miniature adults. True, there was a period of dependency early in the child's life, a period during which the infant needed a parent or some other care-giver to survive. Sadly, however, a vast number didn't survive. Ariès describes one scene in which a mother has just given birth to her fifth child. She is depressed; there had not been enough food and clothing before. What will it be like now? The neighbor consoles her: "Before they are old enough to bother you," she says, "you will have lost half of them, or perhaps all of them" (Ariès, 1962, p. 38).

The implication clearly is that the children's dying is somehow preferable to the burdens of caring for them. And the inference is that the mother is not strongly attached to the child. Hence there is little need to worry that it might suffer or die. And if it did die, it might simply be buried in the yard like a dog or a cat (Ariès, 1962) — additional evidence of parental in-

difference. Those children who did manage to survive would be expected to be working long before what we now consider adulthood — or even adolescence. You see, the medieval child, Ariès tells us, did not have a childhood — at least, not a prolonged childhood. Just those few short years of dependence, and then direct entry into the world of adults. In the Middle Ages, teen marriages were the rule rather than the exception.

This admittedly incomplete sketch of medieval childhood reflects a cold, callous, unfeeling attitude toward children. We don't know for certain how accurate it is, but we do know that it omits exceptions, and as a result, it exaggerates — as do many historical accounts. We know there were many exceptions, that many children were much loved and tenderly reared.

Did the number of exceptions increase with the passage of time?

The 18th and 19th Centuries

In the 18th and 19th centuries, written and printed records became more common as literacy slowly spread through the world. Accordingly, accounts of attitudes toward children are far more reliable than those for earlier periods. Sadly, in some ways, they are no less shocking. Laws and courts had not yet begun to grant children any rights or any protection; by today's standards, child-rearing practices were often cruel and unforgiving; and child labor flourished throughout Europe and North America.

The 18th Century.   History contains some shocking instances of abuse and cruelty toward children, much of which went unnoticed and unpunished. The examples that we know best are perhaps more flagrant than others; some of these were brought to justice. For example, in 1761, the British courts sentenced Anne Martin to two years in Newgate Prison. Her crime? She habitually poked out the eyes of the children she took begging with her; it increased their success — and hers. Aha, you say, the courts did offer some protection to children! True, but it was skimpy protection indeed. As Pinchbeck and Hewitt (1973) point out, Anne Martin's case was unusual in that the children whose eyes she removed were somebody else's. Had they been her own, it is likely that no one would have paid any attention. Parents could generally treat their own children any way they wanted.

Contrasting attitudes toward children are reflected in 18th-century (William Hogarth, left) and 19th-century (Mary Cassatt, opposite) art.

The courts also were not above severely punishing children for infractions of laws. Siegel and White (1982) report the case of a 7-year-old girl who stole a petticoat, surely not that terrible a crime. Still, she was brought to trial, convicted, sentenced—and hanged!

Eighteenth-century attitudes toward children are apparent not only in the ways courts treated them but also in the ways parents treated them. In the crowded slums of 18th-century European cities, thousands of parents bore children whom they promptly abandoned in the streets or on the doorsteps of churches and orphanages. Foundling homes were established through-

out Europe to care for these children, but the majority died in **infancy** (before the age of 2). Indeed, until the turn of that century, even if a child were not abandoned, chances of surviving until the age of 5 were less than one in two (Kessen, 1965).

This was true not only in Europe but in the United States as well. Bakwin (1949) cites evidence that, with few exceptions, children in infant homes (asylums) in the United States prior to 1915 died before the age of 2. In the face of this tragic mortality rate, is it surprising that parents were reluctant to become emotionally attached to their children?

The 19th Century.

The 19th century brought some improvement in the status of children in Europe, and abandonments decreased drastically. Unfortunately, this change resulted less from increasing love and concern for children than from their economic value. At that time, for example, children were widely used in British coal mines. Most of these mines were underground, and the tunnels that led to them were often no more than about two feet in height, poorly ventilated, and sometimes covered with three or four inches of water. Children were especially valuable in these mines because they were small enough to crawl through the tiny tunnels, dragging baskets loaded with coal behind them using a "girdle and chain." The Seventh Earl of Shaftesbury (his name was Anthony Ashley Cooper) described the blisters and the wounds that resulted from this device, the injuries and diseases children suffered in the mines, the physical and mental abuse, the beatings. He begged the British House of Commons to pass a bill that would set age 13 as a minimum for male employment in the coal mines, and that would completely prohibit the employment of females underground. Following considerable debate, and in spite of strong opposition, a bill prohibiting females from working underground was passed. But the House was moved by the argument that children whose fathers were miners were more likely to profit from an education in the mines than from a "reading" education; boys could continue to work in the mines as long as they had reached the age of 10.

Conditions in North America were, in some instances, not vastly different from those in some parts of Europe. Children were used in large numbers in factories and cotton mills, in fields and shops. But profound social and economic forces would soon change all that.

The 20th Century

The murder of infants, we are told, was not uncommon in ancient times (DeMause, 1975). And, as we saw, abandonment and various forms of child use and abuse have been common until very recently. Our contemporary attitudes toward—and treatment of—children, however, are vastly different. Or are they?

Age Distribution Projections

At the turn of this century, almost 100 of every 1,000 children died in infancy, but until 1972, birthrates remained at a high rate of *natural increase* (that is, parents more than replaced themselves). Now, infant mortality has been reduced to about 10 per 1,000, but since 1972, birthrates have been below replacement at between 14 and 16 per 1,000. However, the population continues to grow, largely as a result of increased life expectancy. In 1920, life expectancy in the United States was 54 years; it is now about 75. At present in the United States, there are about 50 percent more people under the age of 5 than over the age of 75. By the year 2000, numbers should be approximately equal.

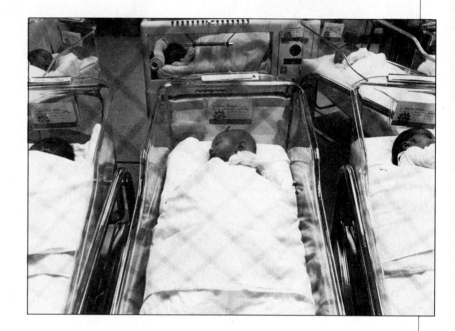

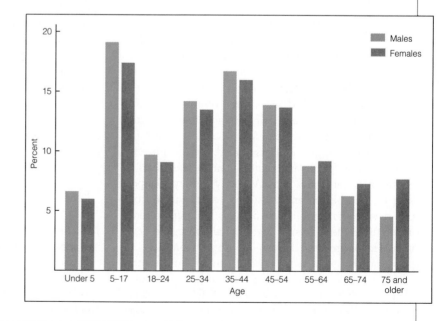

Figure 1.1 Projected age distribution of the U.S. population, by sex, in the year 2000. (Based on U.S. Bureau of the Census, 1988, p. 15.)

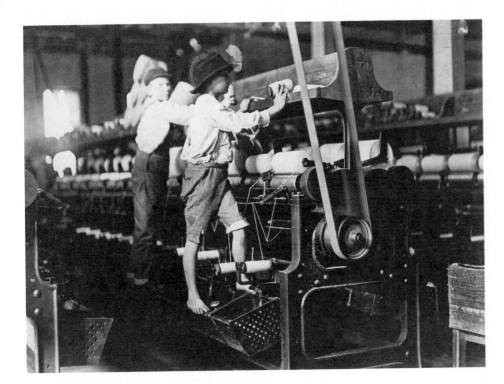

The scientific study of children is a relatively recent undertaking. Where infant mortality is high or where children are highly prized for their economic value, they are perhaps less likely to be loved and studied. Under those circumstances, they are also more likely to be exploited in child labor, as in this early 20th-century cotton mill in Georgia. Note the bare feet dangerously close to the turning spindles, and the completely exposed and unguarded belt and pulley system.

The Industrialized World. In the industrialized world, we no longer abandon children for fear they will prove too much of an economic burden. Nor do we send them into mines and factories. The recognition of childhood as a distinct period, coupled with increasing industrialization and scientific advances, led to organized "child saving" movements, especially in the early 20th century. "For the first time in history," writes Culbertson (1991), "children were accorded basic rights as individuals to preservation of health and life, education, freedom from working in the adult labor force, and protection within the judicial system" (p. 8). (See Interactive Table 1.2.)

Children's rights are geared toward providing optimal, growth-fostering conditions for them, says Caldwell (1989). They are rights of *protection* rather than rights of *choice*: They protect children from labor, from incarceration, from abuse.

This hardly means that all is perfect for the Western industrialized world's children. In fact, some observers believe that there is much that is far from well. For one thing, the family is rapidly falling apart, Bronfenbrenner (1977a) tells us. Divorce rates have increased dramatically in recent decades, so that close to half of all

INTERACTIVE TABLE 1.2

Children's Boric Rights

▶ *A 1979 proclamation of the United Nations asserts that every child has certain rights, listed below. Can you find examples of violations of some of these rights in a current newspaper or magazine?*

- adequate medical care
- adequate nutrition
- affection, love, and understanding
- education
- the opportunity for play and recreation
- a peaceful environment
- the opportunity to develop individual abilities

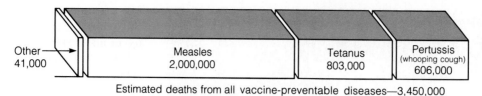

Estimated deaths from all vaccine-preventable diseases—3,450,000

Figure 1.2 Estimated number of deaths in children under age 5 from vaccine-preventable diseases. (Based on UNICEF information presented in Grant, 1986, p. 3.)

children spend an average of six years in a one-parent family. In 90 percent of these families, the mother is the single parent (U.S. Bureau of the Census, 1990). In addition, demographic (population) changes have resulted in smaller families, reduced birthrates, larger numbers of childless couples, and a greater proportion of young adults (resulting from previous increases in birthrates) and of elderly people (resulting from medical advances). Another important change, the effects of which are discussed in detail in Chapter 10, is associated with the role of television in people's lives—and especially in the lives of children.

Some argue that the net effect of these changes is that modern Western societies are less child-centered than had been anticipated. Packard (1983), for example, offers the chilling thought that childhood today may be a terribly lonely experience. Among other things, childhood in our times brings with it a high probability of being looked after by a series of strangers, most likely outside the child's home. It includes, as well, the probability of losing a father or a mother for much of childhood—or at least of losing some of their interest and attention, and perhaps some of their affection as well. There is also the possibility of major readjustments if one or the other of the parents remarries, particularly if stepsiblings are brought into the family. And, especially in one-parent families, there is the likelihood of poverty. In the United States in 1989, more than one third of those who lived below the poverty level were under 16—some 11.5 million children (U.S. Bureau of the Census, 1991).

There was a time, not very long ago, when the things that most children feared were highly predictable: pain, death, spinach, darkness, and things that go bump in the night. The 1980s added some new fears: concern over whether the parents will divorce; apprehension related to being left alone; trauma associated with the likelihood of having to make new adjustments. And the aloneness that is thrust on many of today's children can also bring new sources of loneliness.

But lest this paint too bleak a picture, let me hasten to point out that these challenges and changes don't overwhelm all children, and are not always a source of loneliness or despair. For many, they may be challenges that result in strength rather than in weakness. Keep in mind, too, that these changes have little do with the lives of many children.

The Developing World. Obviously, not all children were murdered in those very dark ages we call antiquity. Nor were all children abandoned through the Middle Ages—or ignored or abused until they died and then were buried in the back yard or in the garden. The children of Europe's 18th and 19th centuries weren't all forced into the coal mines, and North American's children weren't all driven into the cotton fields and the textile factories. Even then, there were warm, loving parents. Historical accounts are typically painted with very broad strokes, the vividness of the colors exaggerated. We tend to concentrate on single themes and ignore what doesn't fit.

Sometimes we do the same thing when history is not to blame. The 20th century, we say piously, is characterized by a loving and helping attitude toward children. We are tempted to assume that in our enlightenment we have corrected most of the evils of a more ignorant age. The assumption is naive, misleading, and dangerous.

The 20th century, too, has its share of ignorance, of cruelty, of needless pain and suffering. In some third world countries such as India, for example, as many as 100 or more infants out of every 1,000 born alive subsequently die, a rate that is perhaps ten times higher than that of such countries as the United States or Canada. Even in relatively rapidly developing countries such as Mexico, infant mortality rates are still five times higher than in the United States (Alba & Potter, 1986). The French newspaper *Le Monde* reports United Nations data indicating that some 8,000 infants die each day from measles, tetanus, and whooping cough—and

Infant Survival

Infant mortality rates in the United States have now been reduced to about 10 per 1,000. However, infant mortality rates in many parts of the nonindustrialized world sometimes continue to exceed 100 per 1,000 live births in the first year of life, a figure comparable to that for the United States at the turn of the century. Each year, more than 15 million of the world's infants die from *preventable* causes. Almost one quarter of these die from diarrheal dehydration; another 2 million die from measles. Education, vaccination, and improved health care could dramatically reduce infant mortality.

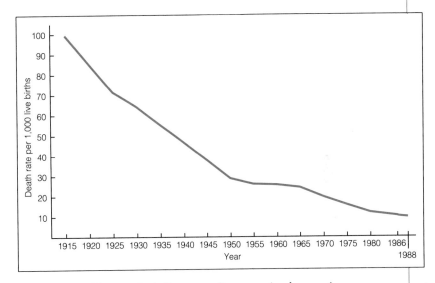

Figure 1.3 Changes in infant mortality rates (under age 1, per 1,000 live births) in the United States, 1915–1988. (Based on U.S. Bureau of the Census, 1991, p. 77.)

another 7,000 from diarrheal dehydration. Pneumonia adds significantly to this total, and starvation more than doubles it. As a result, even in 1990 more than 30,000 children die each day from preventable causes ("Le monde au chevet," 1990). That's about 15 million preventable child deaths a year (see Figure 1.2).

At a theoretical level, solutions for these social crimes are simple and technically possible: Vaccine-preventable diseases require immunization; nutrition-related suffering and dying can be alleviated through a redistribution of vast surpluses of food; and diarrheal infection can be lessened through sanitation, and its

effects can be countered through oral rehydration therapy (ORT). (ORT involves an attempt to increase the infected child's fluid intake, and to replace essential salts.) And the effects of each of these causes of infant and child death—vaccine-preventable diseases, diarrheal infection, and poor nutrition—can be lessened enormously through something as simple as breast-feeding. Incidence of diarrhea among breast-fed infants is far lower than among bottle-fed infants ("Breast milk prevents disease," 1984). In addition, breast milk provides infants with a degree of immunity to various other diseases as well as with nutritious food in hygienic conditions (David & David, 1984). (Clearly, these arguments for breast-feeding are not entirely relevant in developed societies where malnutrition, poor sanitation, and gastrointestinal infections are less common.) Unfortunately, breast-feeding has declined significantly in some developing areas (see Figure 1.4).

Not surprisingly, one of the important factors in infant mortality is the mother's education. There is, according to Levine (1987), a growing consensus that female schooling can be a direct *cause* of reductions both in birthrate and in infant death. An analysis of information collected by the World Bank from some 99 different third world countries shows a very strong correlation between the proportion of a country's females enrolled in primary schools and infant mortality rates some 22 years later (Caldwell, 1986). These data reveal that even incomplete primary schooling often leads to smaller families and to the loss of fewer children, even where sanitation, nutrition, and medical care have not improved noticeably.

Sadly, in most developing countries, and especially Africa, fewer than 50 percent of all children enroll in primary schools. And even at this level, dropout rates are extremely high, quality of education is very low, and the relative cost of education is high (Tsang, 1988). As Grant (1986) points out, "it is the poor, those whose need is greatest, who have the least surplus of resources—of money, time, energy, health, knowledge, and confidence—to invest in improvements. That is the catch-22 of poverty . . . and so the cycle goes on" (p. 41).

But the cycle needn't go on forever. Nutrition, education, immunization, and medical care can break it. (See Table 1.3 for a summary of historical trends in the treatment of children.)

A More Global Context

Our contexts—our social and physical environments—are clearly important in determining our development. Being born in a wooden hut in the rain forests of the Amazon Basin must surely lead to a very different life than being delivered by a private doctor on a New York estate. But our world is changing remarkably rapidly. Most of our villages are no longer isolated. Telephones, computers, satellites, television, airplanes, transnational corporations—these bind us in a shrinking global village. "Today's realities," writes Greer (1991), "dictate that what happens in the rain forests of

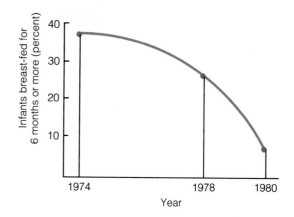

Figure 1.4 Decline in breast-feeding, São Paulo, Brazil, 1974–1980. (Based on UNICEF information presented in Grant, 1986, p. 25.)

South America is as relevant to us as the unification of Germany. . . . In today's society, the economy of Japan affects the financial stability of the world. . . . Today's world has at last become the global village so long envisioned" (p. 198).

Global Environmental Change. "The universality of a child in need," Greer writes, "is perhaps the greatest unifier of all" (p. 199). But, sadly, there is another global unifier. It has to do with negative changes that affect our entire globe. Most of us have grown up believing that the world's bounties would never run out, that no matter what we did, nature would always clean up after us.

We were wrong. Some of the effects of human actions—burning fossil fuels, deforestation, emission of substances like carbon dioxide gas, methane, and chlorofluorocarbons (used mainly in refrigeration and air-conditioning and in electronics production)—are perhaps irreversible. These greenhouse gases increase the earth's temperature and deplete the ozone layer so that ultraviolet radiation is no longer effectively screened (Turner et al., 1991). Ultraviolet radiation damages our immune system, destroying its ability to fight infection and disease; it is also linked directly to skin cancer, the incidence of which has doubled in less than a decade (Pawlik, 1991). And the most vulnerable among us are the children.

If we don't change our actions, perhaps the children of a future world will be driven indoors by the sun.

What does global environmental change have to do with psychology and with lifespan development? A

TABLE 1.3

Six Historical Trends in the Treatment of Children★

Antiquity	Little evidence of strong parental attachment; occasional infanticide socially acceptable.
Middle Ages	Poverty and emotional indifference lead to widespread abandonment of infants; very high infant mortality rates.
Renaissance	Ambivalent attitude toward children.
18th Century	Industrialization contributes to widespread use of children as manual laborers in factories, mines, fields, shops.
19th Century	Child labor continues to flourish; beginnings of important medical and educational changes.
20th Century	Child-centered, especially in the industrialized world; concern with the rights and plights of children. But there are still many instances of abuse, starvation, exploitation, and unnecessary mortality.

★ Note that although these trends and attitudes are descriptive of some cultures and of some families during the periods in question, they are sometimes not very general. Clearly, although infanticide might once have been acceptable under some circumstances, no society permitted all its infants to be killed. Similarly, even at the height of the period of child labor in the 18th century, there were many well-cared-for children who played and went to school and had carefree childhoods in loving homes.

Source: Based in part on DeMause, 1975.

great deal. Tomorrow's world is being shaped by global environmental change (Lévy-Leboyer & Duron, 1991); environmental change results from human behavior; and human behavior is psychology's main concern.

Psychology's challenge, says Stern (1992), is to bring about changes in environmentally significant behaviors. Basically, we can respond in two ways: (1) We can take actions to prevent or slow negative change (like limiting deforestation and fuel consumption), or (2) we can respond by adapting to change (by developing ultraviolet screens and drought-resistant food-crops, or by staying indoors).

Or we can do absolutely nothing.

Pioneers in Developmental Psychology

As noted previously, the study of the human lifespan as a scientific undertaking is a relatively recent enterprise whose historical roots are closely linked with profound changes in our attitudes toward children. In addition, current demographic changes, especially those associated with the aging of Western industrialized societies (largely as a result of reduced birthrates and increased longevity), have contributed to a shift in focus from the preadult years to the entire lifespan (see Figure 1.5).

Early Pioneers

Closely associated with the intellectual movements linked to changing attitudes toward children were such individuals as John Locke and Jean-Jacques Rousseau.

Locke. Locke, writing in the late 17th century, argued that the child is essentially a rational creature, born with few predispositions, whose mind is comparable to a blank slate (*tabula rasa*) upon which experience writes messages. The child described by Locke is a passive recipient of knowledge, information, and habits, and is highly responsive to rewards and punishments. In Locke's (1699) words, "If you take away the Rod on one hand, and these little Encouragements which they are taken with, on the other, How then

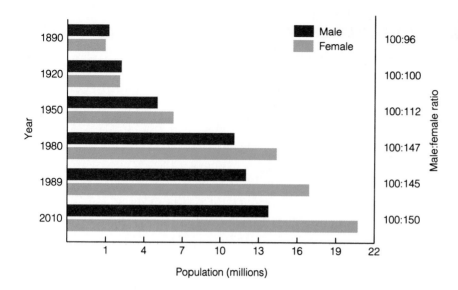

Figure 1.5 Changes in the U.S. population above age 65 since 1890. (Based on U.S. Department of Commerce, 1980, and U.S. Bureau of the Census, 1991, p. 17.)

(will you say) shall Children be govern'd? Remove Hope and Fear, and there is an end of all Discipline."

Rousseau. In contrast, Rousseau's child, immortalized in his book *Emile*, is active and inquiring. Furthermore, this child is not a "blank slate," neither good nor bad until the rewards and punishments of experience exert their influence, but innately good—a "noble savage." Rousseau (1911) insists that if children were allowed to develop in their own fashion, untainted by the corruption and evil in the world, they would be undeniably good when grown: "God makes all things good; man meddles with them and they become evil."

Locke's and Rousseau's ideas have led to fundamentally different conceptions of childhood. Locke's description of the child as a passive creature, molded and shaped by the rewards and punishments of experience, has a close parallel in learning-theory descriptions of development (for example, the work of Skinner and Bandura, described in Chapter 2). Rousseau's view of an active, exploring child purposefully interacting with the environment is illustrated in the work of Jean Piaget (also described in Chapter 2 and elsewhere in this text).

Later Pioneers

Although the *science* of developmental psychology owes much to early "child philosophers" like Rousseau and Locke, its beginnings are usually attributed to the first

systematic observations and written accounts of children. Preyer's detailed observations of his own children are generally considered among the first significant studies in child development (Preyer, 1888–1889), as is Darwin's (1877) biography of his son.

Hall. Hard on the heels of these two pioneers followed G. Stanley Hall (1891), who became the first president of the American Psychological Association. Hall was profoundly influenced by Darwin's theories of evolution. "Ontogeny recapitulates phylogeny," he informed his colleagues, summarizing in one short phrase his conviction that the development of an individual in a species parallels the evolution of the entire species. As evidence for this theory, Hall described the evolution of children's interests in games, noting how these seem to correspond to the evolution of human occupations and life-styles. The child is, in sequence, interested in games corresponding to each of the following: tree-dwelling (for example, climbing on chairs and tables); living in caves (crawling into small spaces, making tiny shelters with old blankets); a pastoral existence (playing with animals); an agricultural life (tending flowers and plants); and finally industrialization (playing with vehicles).

Hall pioneered the use of the questionnaire for studying children. He questioned children at great length, attempting to discover something of their behavior and their thoughts. Often, he presented his questionnaires to adults, asking them to remember what they had felt and thought as children. And always, he summed, tabulated, averaged, and compared the results

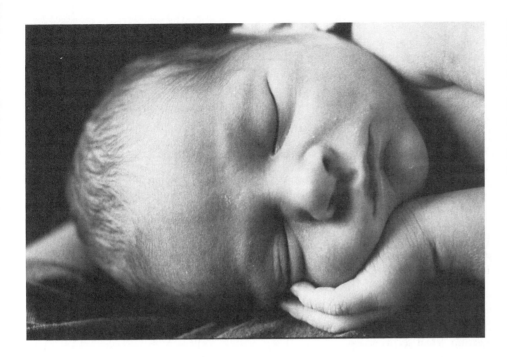

Early 18th-century philosophers saw in the child either, as Locke said, a passive creature with a mind comparable to a blank slate or, as Rousseau speculated, a noble savage fundamentally good unless corrupted by society.

of his questionnaires, serving as an important pioneer in the application of scientific procedures in the study of human development.

Watson. Another pioneer of child psychology was John B. Watson, who introduced an experimental, learning theory–based approach to the study of development. Following his influence, as well as B. F. Skinner's, this model dominated child study through the early part of the 20th century. It was a model that looked for the causes of developmental change among the rewards and punishments of the environment and viewed the child as the passive recipient of these influences.

Recurring Questions

Several important questions have served as recurring themes in developmental psychology and guided much of its research and theorizing. The Locke–Rousseau question is one of them:

- Is it best to view the child as an active, exploring organism, discovering or inventing meaning for the world, as Rousseau argued?

Or is it more useful to emphasize, as did Locke, the effects of rewards and punishments on a more passive recipient? Most contemporary developmental psychologists do not adhere passionately to one or the other point of view as did Locke and Rousseau. However, the predominant current view is of an active, exploring child (Rousseau's view), while recognizing the importance of reward and punishment.

- What are the relative effects of genetics and of environments on the developmental process?

This question has been the source of one of the greatest controversies in psychology: the **nature–nurture controversy**. Extreme points of view on this issue maintain either that the environment is solely responsible for whatever we become (nurture) or that genetic background (nature) determines the outcome of development. Although neither of these extreme positions is completely valid, the issue continues to be debated and is discussed in some detail in Chapter 3.

- Is development a continuous, relatively uninterrupted process, or does it consist of separate stages?

As for most of the recurring questions in lifespan development, there is no simple answer. **Stages** in developmental psychology are typically defined as separate, sequential steps in the evolution of abilities, understandings, or competencies, these steps being closely related to age. As we will see in the next chapter, many important developmental theories are stage theories (for example, Piaget or Freud). But as we will also see, it has been difficult to identify abilities or competencies that *invariably* develop in a fixed, predictable sequence appearing at a predetermined age. We do not develop like caterpillars: cocoon to butterfly to egg to cocoon to butterfly, each stage undeniably different from the one preceding or following. Nevertheless, stage theories are useful in organizing the *facts* of human development and in helping us understand and talk about them.

- Is development invariably positive? Does all developmental change represent an improvement in abilities or other characteristics?

The answer seems clear: Age brings some obvious decline in certain physical characteristics such as strength, speed, and stamina, as well as in the functioning of senses such as vision and hearing (even as it brings inevitable death, which, at least in one sense, represents decline). But what is not clear is whether it is also accompanied by inevitable decline in intellectual functions such as remembering or solving problems. And if there is decline in these areas, how bad is it? Can it be avoided or lessened? As is discussed in some detail in Chapter 15, these questions are a source of controversy—perhaps not only because some of the answers are not particularly pleasant but also because they sometimes contradict our logic, our research, or our intuition.

Basic Beliefs

Lifespan developmental psychology is much more than a handful of questions with controversial and contradictory answers. There are also a number of widely held beliefs about some of the important characteristics and causes of human development. Many of these are discussed in an earlier section, "The Lifespan Perspective." Because of their importance, they are listed briefly here.

- Change does not stop at adulthood but continues through the entire lifespan.
- The causes of development are to be found in the *interaction* of environmental and genetic factors (rather than in their *separate* effects).

- Development occurs in a specific historical and ecological context, and is profoundly influenced by that context. Observations that are valid in one context may not be valid in another.
- Some common threads appear to run through the developmental paths that different individuals take. These commonalties allow developmental psychologists to describe stages or phases and to make generalizations.
- At the same time, there are pronounced individual differences among individuals, differences that are most apparent where context and genetic history are very different.
- Change is what human development is all about. The quest to describe and understand changes that occur with age and experience is based on the belief that some of the factors that influence change are identifiable and their effects predictable.

Some Definitions

Important concepts in the study of the lifespan include growth, maturation, and learning. Put another way, to develop is to grow, to mature, and to learn.

Growth ordinarily refers to physical changes, which are primarily quantitative because they involve addition rather than transformation. Such changes as increasing height and enlargement of the nose are examples of growth.

Maturation describes changes that are relatively independent of the environment. These changes are often attributed to heredity. In almost all aspects of human development, however, maturation and learning interact. Learning to walk, for example, requires not only that the child's physical strength and muscular coordination be sufficiently mature but also that there be opportunities to learn the various skills involved.

Learning is defined as the result of experience rather than as a maturational process. All changes in behavior resulting from experience are examples of learning, provided these changes are not simply the temporary effects of drugs or fatigue.

In summary, **development** is the total process whereby individuals adapt to their environment. Because we adapt by growing, maturing, and learning, these are all aspects of development. The main difference between learning and development is simply that learning is concerned with immediate, short-term ad-

TABLE 1.4

Important Definitions

Psychology	The science that studies human thought and behavior.
Developmental Psychology	Division of psychology concerned with changes that occur over time, and with the processes and influences that account for these changes.
Development:	
Growth	Physical changes; primarily quantitative.
Maturation	Naturally unfolding changes, relatively independent of the environment (for example, pubescence — the changes of adolescence that lead to sexual maturity).
Learning	Relatively permanent changes in behavior that result from experience (rather than from maturation, fatigue, or drugs).

aptation, whereas development refers to gradual adaptation over a period of years. (See Table 1.4 for a summary of important definitions.)

Methods of Studying the Lifespan

Observers of human development may focus on natural events, such as children playing in a park; they may collect information on less naturally occurring events, such as old people being interviewed; or they may collect experimental observations. In addition, lifespan research may often be described as *longitudinal* (following the same subjects over a period of time) or *cross-sectional* (using a cross section of different subjects at one point in time). Each of these approaches is described in the following sections. Note that these categories are not mutually exclusive. For example, a lifespan study might be experimental and longitudinal or cross-sectional simultaneously.

Observation

Observation is the basis of all science. The study of the lifespan always begins with observation — naturalistic and nonnaturalistic.

Naturalistic Observation.
Observations are termed *naturalistic* when people are observed without

interference in natural rather than contrived situations — for example, on the playground or in school. Psychologists who observe children and write **diary descriptions** of their behavior are making use of naturalistic observation. Similarly, those who describe continuous sequences of behavior (**specimen descriptions**), specific behaviors only (**event sampling**), or behaviors during specified time intervals (**time sampling**) are using naturalistic observations (Wright, 1960; see also Table 1.5). In each of these naturalistic methods, the hope is that the observation will not affect the subject's behavior. In naturalistic observation, it is important that the investigator be a detached observer.

Time and event sampling are often used together. Time sampling specifies when observations will be made; event sampling specifies what will be observed. For example, if an investigator wanted to determine whether a new approach to teaching encourages student participation, a combination of time and event sampling would be appropriate. During specified intervals over a number of days (time sampling), the investigator would record instances of student participation (event sampling). Subsequently, observed participation before and after introduction of the new teaching method would be compared.

Nonnaturalistic Observation.
In nonnaturalistic observations, the investigation affects the subject's behavior Nonnaturalistic observations are sometimes called *clinical* if they use interviews or questionnaires. If they attempt to manipulate or change the environment, they are termed *experimental*. Experiments are described in the next section.

TABLE 1.5

Naturalistic Methods of Observing Children

Method	Description	Main Uses
Diary description	Fairly regular (often daily or weekly) descriptions of important events and changes.	Detecting and understanding major changes and developmental sequences.
Specimen description	Detailed descriptions of sequences of behavior, detailing all aspects of behavior during sequence.	In-depth study of individual children, not restricted to only one or two predetermined characteristics.
Time sampling	Specific behaviors are recorded during short but regular periods of time.	Detecting and assessing changes in specific behaviors over time.
Event sampling	Specific behaviors (events) are recorded during observation, and others are ignored.	Understanding the nature and frequency of specific behaviors (events).

Source: Based in part on *Handbook of Research Methods in Child Development* by H. F. Wright (Ed.), 1960, New York: John Wiley.

In practice, the methods used by those who investigate development are determined by the questions they want to answer. Some questions can best be answered with one approach; others with another. And some questions, of course, lend themselves to more than one approach. If you are interested in knowing whether children have more affection for cats than for dogs, you might simply compare the number of children who have dogs with the number who have cats (naturalistic observation). Alternatively, you might ask a sample of children which they like best (interview technique). Or you might arrange for different children, alone and in groups, to meet different cats and dogs—also alone and in groups (experimental approach)—and assess their reactions (through simple visual observation or perhaps by measuring their heart rates and other physiological functions).

Notice that each of these approaches might lead to somewhat different answers for the same questions. Perhaps there are more cats than dogs in the homes of your subjects—many parents think cats are less demanding—but children really like dogs better. And maybe, even if they do like dogs better, more children would be afraid of dogs than of cats because strange dogs are more frightening than are strange cats. Thus it's important to keep in mind as you go through some of the studies described in this text that conclusions are sometimes partly a function of research methods; they

might have been different had the investigation been conducted differently.

In many cases, the study of the lifespan involves a combination of methods rather than a single method. Experiments typically require observations. Hence, interviews and questionnaires are often part of an experiment.

Experiments

Science's most powerful tool for gathering useful observations is the experiment. An **experiment** is distinguished from other observations in that it requires deliberately and systematically manipulating some aspect of a situation to detect and measure the effects of doing so. In an experiment, the observer controls certain **variables**—termed **independent**—to investigate their effect on other variables—termed **dependent**. For example, in an experiment designed to investigate the relationship between two teaching methods and the development of language skills, the experimenter can manipulate (control) the variable teaching method by arranging for the use of teaching method A with one group of students and teaching method B with a second group. In addition, if we are to have faith in the results of the experiment, subjects must be assigned to methods A or B *randomly* to guard against the possibility that students in one group might have some systematic advantage over students in the other.

In this illustration, teaching method is the independent variable; it is under the experimenter's control. Measures of the subjects' language skills are a dependent variable. The experimenter's **hypothesis** (scientific prediction) is that the independent variable (teaching method) will affect the dependent variable (language skills).

Experimental procedures often involve the use of experimental groups and control groups. **Experimental groups** are ordinarily made up of subjects who are treated in some special way. In this case, the goal is usually to discover whether the special treatment (independent variable) has a predictable effect on some outcome (dependent variable). To ensure that any changes in the dependent variable are due to the treatment, it is often necessary to use a second group — the **control** (or *no-treatment*) **group**. This second group must be as similar as possible to the experimental group in all relevant ways. The effect of the special treatment is then assessed by comparing the two groups with respect to some outcome (dependent variable) after the experimental group has been given the treatment.★

A careful, well-controlled experiment *that can be replicated* is science's only reliable method for discovering causes and effects. Experiments that cannot be replicated — that is, that lead to different conclusions on different occasions — tell us nothing about causes and effects. Science pays little attention to things that happen only once.

Example of an Experiment.   According to a theory of emotions developed by Carroll Izard (1977), expressions of emotion by one member of a *dyad* (two people interacting) can elicit similar emotions in the other member. The theory also argues that feelings are powerful human motivators that can lead to predictable kinds of behaviors. For example, emotions associated with interest might lead to exploration, play, learning, or other sorts of *approach* behaviors; in contrast, sadness typically leads to a slowing or cessation of exploration or play or to other kinds of *avoidance* behaviors.

Considerable evidence supports and clarifies this theory with respect to adults and children. However,

relatively little work has been done with infants, partly because of difficulties involved in identifying and measuring infant emotions.

In an experiment conducted by Termine and Izard (1988), thirty-six 9-month-old infants were brought into a laboratory on two separate occasions (nonnaturalistic observation). On both occasions, they were placed in high chairs directly in front of their mothers, and their behaviors and facial expressions, as well as those of their mothers, were videotaped for later analysis. In one experimental manipulation, mothers were instructed to show *sadness* by recalling a sad incident, talking about it, and making a sad face. After two minutes of sad expression and vocalization, an experimenter entered and presented the infant with a series of toys, all of which were removed three minutes later. During this period, mothers were reminded at 30-second intervals, by earphones, to continue to look sad and to occasionally say something like "I feel so sad today."

In the other experimental manipulation, the same infants were brought into an identical situation except that mothers were now instructed to sound and look *joyful*. Half the infants were exposed to the sad situation first; the other half to the joy situation first.

This experiment permits a comparison of the effects of two sets of independent variables (sad expressions and expressions of joy) on a set of dependent variables (infant responses to both their mothers and toys). Three hypotheses were examined: (1) Infants would show more joy in the joy situation and more sadness in the sad condition; (2) infants would look at their mothers less in the sad condition (an avoidance behavior), and more in the joy situation (an approach behavior); and (3) infants would play more in the joy than in the sad condition.

Measures of infant emotions — the extent to which they looked at their mothers and their play behavior — were obtained by having two trained observers analyze videotapes of each session. A **blind procedure** was used; that is, the observers were unaware of the experimental condition to which each infant had been exposed. As is explained later, this is an important safeguard against the possibility that the observer's expectations might affect experimental outcomes.

Analysis of the results supports the investigators' principal expectations. First, infants in the joy condition expressed more joy; those in the sad condition, more sadness. Not surprisingly, infants in the sad condition also displayed more anger, perhaps because, as Termine

---

★This is only one of a large variety of experimental designs (arrangements) that are employed in psychological research. For others, see Ray and Ravizza (1985).

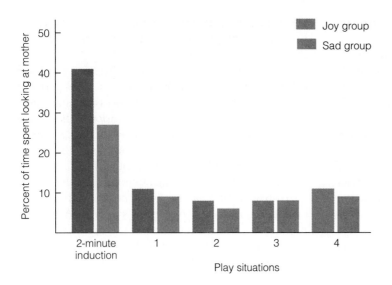

Figure 1.6 Infants whose mothers acted sad were more likely to avoid looking at them than were infants whose mothers displayed joy. (Based on Termine & Izard, 1988, p. 226.)

and Izard (1988) suggest, anger and sadness are related emotions.

Second, as is shown in Figure 1.6, infants in the sad condition looked at their mothers significantly less during the initial two minutes, while the mothers were actively attempting to induce an emotional state. After the presentation of toys, the infants in both groups looked at their mothers only briefly.

Finally, infants in the joy condition played more with the toys than did infants in the sad condition (see Figure 1.7).

A single experiment does not *prove* anything. In fact, a whole battery of related experiments might not *prove* much either; absolute fact is a rare luxury in science. Still, experiments such as this, carefully controlled and replicated, are, as we have noted, science's only reliable way of investigating cause-and-effect relationships. They are science's best source of information, the foundation for its most logical and useful conclusions. But there are many situations in which experiments are not possible, or in which they would be quite unethical. In some of these situations, **correlational studies** might be used.

Correlational Studies

Many developmental studies proceed as follows: Researchers decide to investigate the sources (causes) of specific characteristics; people with these characteristics

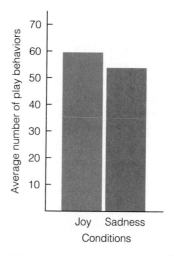

Figure 1.7 Average (mean) frequency of play in joy and sadness conditions. (Play includes mouthing, manipulation, and naming.) (Based on Termine & Izard, 1988, p. 277.)

are identified; a comparison group *without* these characteristics is also identified; an attempt is then made to obtain historical information about these people (home environment, presence or absence of a father, intelligence, similar characteristics in biological ancestors, and so on). Researchers compare the two groups with respect to these historical variables. In the end, a relationship (correlation)★ will be found to exist between specific historical variables and present characteristics, or no relationship will be found.

Through studies such as these, research has established relationships between variables such as poverty and delinquency, or between the personality characteristics of parents and those of children. Many such studies are described in this text. They are called *retrospective* studies because they try to establish relationships by looking *backward* at the person's history (*retro* means "backward") to see how factors in the individual's past affect present behavior.

One caution is extremely important here. One of the most common errors in the interpretation of research results stems from the apparently logical but false assumption that if two events are related (correlated), one causes the other. Some studies have demonstrated, for example, that children from disadvantaged homes (low socioeconomic level, low parental education, low academic aspirations, and so on) often do less well in school than children from more advantaged backgrounds. Does this mean that home background *causes* low or high achievement? No. At best, correlational studies show relationships or their absence; they do not establish causation. It is possible that home background is related to nutrition, nutrition to intelligence, intelligence to achievement, and hence home background to achievement.

These comments should not be interpreted to mean that correlational studies should be avoided and that only experiments should be conducted. Not only are correlational studies often highly informative (when interpreted cautiously), but experiments are often impossible for practical and ethical reasons. Consider, for example, an experiment designed to investigate the effects of poverty. Such an experiment would require that investigators assign randomly selected (or highly similar) children to precisely defined conditions of wealth or poverty at some critical and presumably early stage in their lives, and that these children be examined and compared later—hardly an ethical undertaking.

★A *correlation* is a statistical measure of relationship. It is usually expressed as a number ranging from +1.00 (a perfect *positive* relationship—as one variable increases, so does the other), through 0 (no relationship), to −1.00 (a perfect *inverse* relationship—as one variable increases, the other decreases).

Longitudinal and Cross-Sectional Studies

There are two approaches to the study of human development: the longitudinal and the cross-sectional. A **longitudinal study** observes the same subjects over a period of time; a **cross-sectional study** compares different subjects of different developmental levels at the same time. For example, there are two ways of investigating the different rules used in games played by 2-year-old and 6-year-old children. One is to observe a group of 2-year-olds at play and four years later repeat the same procedure with the same children. This is the longitudinal approach, which, for this purpose, is more time-consuming than necessary. The same study might simply look at groups of 2- and 6-year-old children at the same time and compare them directly.

Advantages and Disadvantages.
Cross-sectional and longitudinal approaches are both essential for studying human development. Each approach has its strengths, and each has weaknesses and limitations. For some questions, a longitudinal approach is best. If, for example, investigators wish to discover whether intelligence test scores for a given individual change with age or remain stable, they need to observe the same individual at different times. This question could not be answered by a cross-sectional approach. A cross-sectional approach cannot give us information concerning changes that occur over time within a single individual because it looks at each individual only once. Put another way, cross-sectional research is insensitive to intraindividual change.

Among the problems associated with longer-term longitudinal research are its higher cost, the possibility that instruments and methods may become outdated before completion or that some of the research questions will be answered in some other way, and the tremendous amount of time sometimes required (Harway, Mednick, & Mednick, 1984). Often, an experiment must be designed to go beyond the lifetime of a single investigator (or team of investigators), particularly if it is intended to examine most or all of the human lifespan. This is the case with the Terman study of giftedness that began in the early 1920s and continues today (Terman et al., 1925). This kind of study encounters an additional problem related to subject mortality. The death of subjects not only reduces the size of samples but also may serve to bias the results. For

TABLE 1.6

Methods of Studying Lifespan Development

Observation	The basis of all science. Observation is naturalistic when subjects are observed without interference in natural rather than contrived situations. Naturalistic observation may involve time or event sampling, diary descriptions, or specimen descriptions (see Table 1.5). Nonnaturalistic observation may be clinical when it involves structured interviews or questionnaires.
Experiments	Science's most powerful means of gathering observations. They involve systematic attempts to manipulate the environment to observe what the effects of specific independent variables are on given dependent variables.
Correlational Studies	Examinations of relationships among two or more variables. A correlation exists when changes in one variable are accompanied by systematic changes in another (for example, during childhood, increasing age is correlated *positively* with increasing strength). The existence of a correlation is necessary but *insufficient* for inferring causality.
Longitudinal Studies	Where the same subjects are followed over a period of time.
Cross-Sectional Studies	Where subjects of different ages are studied at one point in time.

example, if individuals of a certain personality type die younger than do others, a longitudinal assessment of personality change might reveal some significant changes with old age when, in fact, such is not the case. As a hypothetical illustration, if aggressive people die before those who are not aggressive, we might be led to believe that people become less aggressive as they age.

Perhaps the most serious limitation of longitudinal studies is that they must frequently assume that currently valid measures will be equally valid later. This problem is particularly evident in longitudinal studies of vocabulary growth, intelligence, and related variables where rapidly changing cultural conditions may significantly affect the appropriateness of the measures used. Cross-sectional studies sometimes suffer from a similar problem, which stems from their assumption that children at one age level now are comparable to children at that age level at another time. With respect to intelligence, for example, drastic improvements in educational experiences and perhaps in television fare can affect children sufficiently over time that measures of intelligence obtained at one time cannot easily be compared with measures obtained earlier.

Many of the problems associated with longitudinal research (for example, subject mortality, higher cost, greater time requirement, changing contexts in the lives

of subjects) apply only to *longer*-term research. But not all longitudinal research is long-term. For example, longitudinal studies of infant development might span only weeks, or perhaps only days or hours. However, because human development spans a huge spread of years, much of our longitudinal research necessarily is long-term. (See Table 1.6 for a summary of research methods.)

Sources of Variation: Age, Time, and Cohort. Cross-sectional and longitudinal studies look at three separate sources of variation: (1) changes related to age, (2) influences related to the time of testing, and (3) the influence of the cohort (Schaie, 1983a). Of these, age and cohort are the most important. Nesselroade and Baltes (1984) argue that for most developmental research, the effects of time of measurement are usually trivial.

A **cohort** can be described as a group of individuals who were born within the same range of time. The 1980 cohort includes all those who were born during the year 1980. A cohort is, therefore, of a specific size and composition initially. It does not normally increase in size but rather decreases as members die, until it has completely disappeared. Its composition also changes gradually in other ways. For example, because men die sooner than women, the male:female ratio of a cohort usually changes over time. Similarly, racial composition might also change as a result of different mortality rates.

What is most important for the lifespan psychologist is that members of a single cohort may be subject to experiences very different from those to which members of other cohorts are exposed. For example, cohort groups such as that of my grandmother date to the turn of this century and include people who were born into a world without radios, automobiles, televisions, or computers. These obvious cohort-related influences might be important in attempting to understand why an 80-year-old person in 1994 might be quite different from an 80-year-old in 2024 or in 1944. Less obvious cohort-related influences would also include changes in medical practices (including the general use of a variety of inoculations, for example), nutrition, recreation, work roles, morality, and so on. Because of these influences, cohorts might be very different in some important ways.

One of the serious problems developmental researchers have faced has been the difficulty in attempting to separate the effects of age and cohort. In both longitudinal and cross-sectional research, age and cohort effects become confounded. Consider, for example, the apparently simple question of whether performance on intelligence tests changes with age. A cross-sectional method for answering this question would require administering intelligence tests to a number of different groups of subjects—say, a group of 20-year-olds and one of 70-year-olds—and comparing their performance. But what would it mean if differences were found among these groups—if, for example, 70-year-olds scored higher than 20-year-olds? Would it mean that intelligence increases with age or, at least, that 70-year-olds are more intelligent than 20-year-olds?

Perhaps, and perhaps not. The problem, as we noted earlier, is that a cross-sectional design confounds age with cohort. That is, a cross-sectional design uses samples that, because they are of different ages at the same time, are by definition different cohorts. And with a simple cross-sectional design there is no way to tell whether differences found between groups are related to their different ages, to the different experiences that might be associated with different cohorts, or to both.

Would a longitudinal design answer the question more accurately? Such a design would require that the same subjects be tested when they are 20, 25, 30, and

so on, and that scores for each individual be compared across all age ranges. What if there are differences now? Could we confidently assert that these are related to age and that we have established that intelligence changes in such and such a way as individuals age? Perhaps not. One of the problems with longitudinal research is that only one cohort is used throughout the study. As a result, developmental changes identified in such research are not always universal. They might result from something specific to the history of the cohort; they might also be due to the time at which the testing occurred.

Sequential and Time-Lag Designs

One way of overcoming these important research problems is to use **sequential designs** (Schaie, 1965). This involves taking sequences of samples at different times of measurement. One well-known sequential design is the **time-lag study** in which different cohorts are compared at different times. For example, a time-lag study might compare 10-year-olds in 1993 with 10-year-olds in 1995, 1997, and 1999. Because these subjects are the same age when tested but were born in different years, they belong to different cohorts. Consequently, observed differences among the groups might reveal important cohort-related influences.

An Illustration.   An excellent example of a sequential design is the 28-year longitudinal study conducted by Schaie and associates (see Figure 1.8). The study began in 1956 as a simple cross-sectional investigation of differences in intellectual functioning among groups of individuals ages 25–67. Schaie (1983b) soon realized, however, that a cross-sectional design would not answer important questions about changes that occur within individuals. Accordingly, seven years later he retested as many of the original samples as he could and also selected a second series of samples ages 25–74 (those who had been 67 in 1956 were now 74). A third group was added seven years later (1970); this group included a sample of 81-year-olds because the oldest samples in the 1956 and 1963 samples were now 81. A fourth sample was added in 1977 and a fifth in 1984. Because samples were selected at seven-year intervals, subjects are grouped by cohort and by age in clusters seven years apart—that is, ages 25, 32, 39, 46, 53, 60, 67, 74, 81, and 88. Results of this study are discussed in Chapter 15.

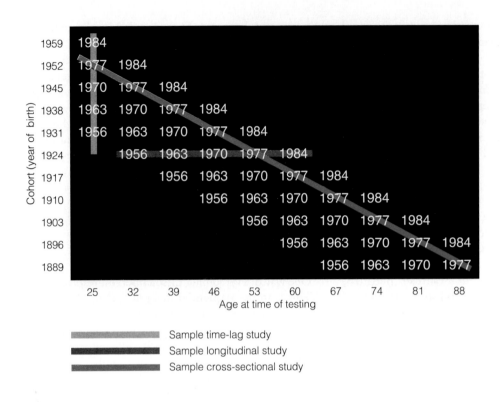

Figure 1.8 Schematic representation of the sequential design used in the Seattle Longitudinal Study. The years in the table indicate times of measurement. Vertical columns represent possible time-lag studies (different cohorts, different times of measurement, same age); horizontal rows represent longitudinal studies (the same cohort examined at up to five points in time); and diagonals represent cross-sectional studies (as many as nine cohorts examined at a single point in time). (Based on Schaie, 1965, 1983a, 1986.)

Criteria for Evaluating Lifespan Research

Truth in psychology, as in most disciplines, is relative. The validity of conclusions derived from research can seldom be judged absolutely right or wrong but must instead be interpreted in terms of usefulness, clarity, logical consistency, and **generalizability**. Of all these criteria, perhaps generalizability is the most important. Too often, results of a research project apply only to the situation in which they were obtained. The value of conclusions that can't be generalized is limited.

Sampling

Research in psychology tries to reach conclusions that are generalizable to entire populations — that is, to entire collections of individuals (or objects or situations) with similar characteristics. In most cases, the populations that are of interest to the researcher are too large to be investigated in their entirety. What the investigator does, instead, is select a sample from this larger population, carefully chosen to represent the entire population. It would be difficult, for example, to obtain valid information concerning the moral beliefs and behaviors of American children by observing a sample of subjects from San Francisco or Boston alone. If the results are to be generalized to the entire population, subjects should represent all major geographical areas in the nation. In addition, all nationalities, major religious groups, socioeconomic levels, occupations, and ages should be represented in proportions similar to the entire population. One of the simplest and most effective ways of ensuring that this is the case is to select subjects at random from the population.

Memory

Studies of the ages at which girls experience their first menstrual period (**menarche**) have often had to rely

▶ Subject   Male, age 75; retired
              schoolteacher.
              (on children growing up)

....

" *It's going to be a lot different for kids growing up now compared to my day. Just take a few examples like television, which we didn't have. Kids know things now that we didn't even teach when I first started. In some ways, they have to be a lot more intelligent. But in other ways they're sure not. Maybe they don't read as much as we did because they don't have enough time left over even if they don't have a long list of chores like most of us did. Another thing is their morals are going to be a lot different too. Lots of the things we thought were wrong, nobody even cares about anymore.* "

on the memories of women for whom the event may not be entirely recent; investigations of the ages at which children first walk or talk sometimes base their conclusions on the memories of mothers. Unfortunately, human memory is far from perfect. Not only does it forget but it also distorts — sometimes in predictable ways, sometimes not.

Honesty

Having to rely on the honesty of subjects is a serious problem with questionnaire and interview data, especially when highly personal areas are being researched. Comparisons of contemporary adolescent sexual behavior with behavior that was characteristic of adolescents several generations ago are typically unreliable primarily for this reason. Given prevailing attitudes toward sexual behavior, it is not unreasonable to suppose that today's adolescent may be more honest about sexual behavior than the adolescent of the 1930s might have been.

Experimenter Bias

Some research indicates that experimenters sometimes inadvertently bias the results of their experiments in the direction of their expectations (see, for example, Rosenthal & Jacobson, 1968a). One effective way to guard against experimenter bias is the **double-blind procedure**. This requires simply that the experimenters and examiners, as well as the subjects, not be aware of the expected outcomes of the research or of which subjects are experimental subjects and which are members of the control group. Recall that a *blind* procedure was used by Termine and Izard (1988) in their study of the effect of joy and sadness on infants.

Subject Bias

Subject bias may also have an effect on the outcome of an experiment. In a highly publicized experiment, two psychologists (Roethlisberger & Dickson, 1939) compared ways to increase productivity among workers in the Hawthorne plant of the Western Electric Company in Chicago. In successive experiments, the workers were subjected to shorter and longer working periods, to better and poorer lighting conditions, to long and short periods of rest, to work incentives such as bonuses, and to other conditions. Under most of these conditions, productivity apparently increased. This observation led to the conclusion that if subjects are aware they are members of an experimental group, performance may improve simply because of that fact.

Although the "Hawthorne effect," as it is now called, is usually accepted as fact in social science research, its existence has not been well established — in spite of the Hawthorne experiments just described. Following a careful reexamination of the original experiments and interviews with some of the people who were involved at that time, Rice (1982) found little evidence of a Hawthorne effect. He reports that productivity did not increase in many of the experiments but that later reports of the study usually concentrated on only experiment in which there was a marked improvement over the 5-year course of the study. In this particular experiment, workers (all women) were paid according to the productivity of the entire group (as they were throughout this factory). Because there were only seven or eight women in the group, individual productivity would have a noticeable effect on the pay received by each woman. Accordingly, when several

In North American societies, fewer than 1 in 20 of the very old are in retirement homes or other institutions, which makes it difficult for researchers to obtain large, representative samples of the elderly.

of the experimental group members proved to be slower than the average, the other women became unhappy; as a result, the slower workers were dropped from the group. Under these circumstances, is it any wonder that the experimental group's performance should improve?

Some Special Problems

Problems involving inadequate sampling, memory distortions, questionable honesty, and experimenter or subject bias may affect research in all areas of psychology. In addition, lifespan research is faced with a handful of unique problems. One such problem, already mentioned, is that of comparing different cohorts. Many lifespan questions concern important changes that occur with advancing age or that follow major transitions. Identifying and investigating these changes often require the comparison of different cohorts. It is often difficult to determine whether observed differences are due to changes that occur with age or simply reflect different cohort experiences.

A second problem specific to lifespan research is related to difficulties experienced in obtaining large, representative samples. Because most children are in schools for a large part of their childhood and are therefore easily accessible to researchers, this problem

applies much less to them than it does to older subjects. In fact, approximately only 5 percent of the very old★ are in retirement homes and other institutions for the aged. Unfortunately, this relatively small number of individuals serves as the subject group for an overwhelming majority of studies of the aged. Accordingly, investigators must be concerned about whether these subjects are actually representative of others not living in institutions. They must also always keep in mind that as people become older, they may also become less representative. That is, there may be something special that allows 90-year-olds to live so long. Death does not always select at random.

The use of institutionalized individuals in psychological research poses an additional problem relating to research ethics. First, not all elderly people are capable of informed consent; second, there are sometimes subtle forms of coercion involved in research with those in institutions. Some might feel pressured into participat-

---

★Although "very old" is uncomfortably vague, our studies and theories of aging have not yet provided us with terms that are specific and widely understood to discriminate among older age groups as the terms *neonate, infant, toddler, child,* and *adolescent* distinguish among those who are younger. In this context, the "very old" are over 80.

INTERACTIVE TABLE 1.7

Checklist for Evaluating Developmental Research

▶ *When you read lifespan research, you should ask yourself a number of questions in addition to "Are the research questions important, or are they merely trivial?" and "Do the answers really matter?" The following checklist can serve as a guide.*

Sampling	Is the sample a good representation of the population to which the observations and conclusions are meant to apply?
Ecosystem	Is there something special or unique about the social, cultural, or historical context in which observations are made? Do the characteristics of the context *in interaction with* the characteristics of the individuals reduce the generalizability of the findings?
Memory	Does the investigation have to rely on human memories? Has the possibility of systematic or random distortion been taken into account?
Honesty	Does the validity of the observations depend on the honesty of subjects? Do they have a reason to distort facts consciously or unconsciously?
Experimenter or Subject Bias	Is there a possibility that experimenter or subject expectations might have influenced observations?

ing simply by being members of a group; others might volunteer to please their attendants or to ensure favorable treatment. (See Interactive Table 1.7 for a checklist for evaluating developmental research.)

The Mythical Average

A word of caution is appropriate at this point. This book deals largely with so-called average individuals — with the normal processes of conception, fetal growth, birth, infancy, childhood, adolescence, adulthood, old age, and death. It describes typical behavior and characteristics throughout the lifespan, and it discusses theoretical explanations of normal patterns of development. *But there is no average child, let alone adult!* The concept is a convenient invention, a necessary creation if we are to speak coherently of human development. Bear in mind that each person is a unique individual, that each will differ from the average, and that no one theory will account for all behavior. We are incredibly more complex than any description provided by even the most complex of theories. A theory — and a book — can deal only with the objective details of human behavior, not with its essence.

Main Points

1. *Lifespan developmental psychology* is concerned with understanding and explaining changes that occur between conception and death. *The Lifespan* is organized chronologically.

2. The traditional view of human development was that all major, positive developmental changes occur before adulthood. The contemporary lifespan perspective recognizes that change continues

throughout the lifespan, that maturity is a relative and changing state, that it is important to consider the context (*ecology*) of human development, and that developmental influences are bidirectional.

3. There is evidence that in medieval times the concept of childhood did not exist as we know it, that parent-child attachment was indifferent, and that infant mortality was very high. Through the 18th and 19th centuries, child labor flourished, and child-rearing practices were often harsh and cruel by current North American standards. The 20th century brought increasing concern with the social, physical, and intellectual welfare of children, especially in the industrialized world.

4. About 15 million children die of preventable causes each year, primarily from malnutrition, vaccine-preventable diseases such as measles and tetanus, and diarrheal dehydration.

5. Among early pioneers in the scientific study of human development were John Locke (*tabula rasa*) and Jean-Jacques Rousseau ("noble savage"). Later pioneers included Charles Darwin (child biography and evolution), G. Stanley Hall ("ontogeny recapitulates phylogeny"), and John B. Watson (we become what we are as a function of our experiences).

6. Among the recurring themes in studies of the lifespan are questions relating to whether heredity or environment has more influence, whether development is continuous or progresses in discrete stages, and whether development is primarily linear and characterized initially by increments followed by inevitable decline in the later stages of life.

7. Important beliefs concerning the characteristics and causes of human development are that development occurs throughout the lifespan; the causes of change are to be found in the *interaction* of genetic and environmental forces; development is profoundly influenced by historical and social context; there are commonalities in the development of different individuals, and also marked variations among individuals; and some of the factors that influence change are identifiable, and their effects predictable.

8. Development is the total process by which individuals adapt to their environment. It includes maturation (genetically programmed unfolding), growth (quantitative changes), and learning (changes due to experience).

9. Observation is the basis of all science. Naturalistic observation occurs when individuals are observed without interference (diary descriptions—regular, often daily, descriptions of interesting observations; specimen descriptions—descriptions of continuous sequences of behavior; event sampling—recordings of specified, predetermined behaviors; and time sampling—recordings during predetermined time intervals. Nonnaturalistic observations may be clinical (involve the use of questionnaires or interviews) or experimental (involve the deliberate manipulation of the environment).

10. In an experiment, the investigator randomly assigns subjects to groups and controls relevant variables to determine whether independent variables (those controlled) affect dependent variables (outcomes). Experiments are useful for investigating cause-and-effect relationships. Correlational studies look at relationships among variables and provide useful information relating to cause-and-effect relationships, although *a correlation is not proof of causation.*

11. Longitudinal studies examine the same individuals at different periods in their lives; cross-sectional studies compare different individuals at the same time. Longitudinal studies, if they are long-term, may be more costly and time-consuming and may suffer from problems relating to subject (or experimenter) mortality and the eventual obsolescence of experimental methods and instruments.

12. Cross-sectional studies are useful for comparing groups of different ages at one time but provide little information about intraindividual changes. Longitudinal studies are sensitive to intraindividual changes, but because they typically involve a single cohort, it is difficult to determine whether the changes they identify are related to the age of the subjects or are specific to the time of testing or the cohort or both.

13. A cohort is a group of individuals born during a single timespan and often subject to a variety of unique influences that might account for important differences between them and members of other cohorts. Attempts to reduce the confounding of age and cohort in developmental research have led to *sequential* research designs—so called because they involve the selection of a sequence of samples. The time-lag study is a sequential design in which different cohorts are compared at different times

with age held constant. It allows investigators to identify important cohort-specific effects.

14. A population is the entire group in which the investigator is interested (for example, all North American children or all children with statistically improbable names). A sample is a representative subset of a population.

15. The validity and reliability of research results are subject to the influences of sample size and representativeness, subject memory and honesty, experimenter and subject biases, and cohort-related experiences.

16. The average individual is a conceptually useful invention but does not exist.

Further Readings

The following book by Kegan is an intriguing, superbly written approach to human development. Its central theme is that we are *meaning-making* organisms. Our lives are directed by behaviors that organize the world in meaningful ways, and that make us meaningful to others (as in "Hamlet *meant* a lot to Ophelia"):

Kegan, R. (1982). *The evolving self: Problem and process in human development.* Cambridge, MA: Harvard University Press.

Books by Belsky, Lerner, and Spanier, and by Bronfenbrenner are excellent examples of lifespan emphases on ecological (contextual) influences in development:

Belsky, J., Lerner, R. M., & Spanier, G. B. (1984). *The child in the family.* Reading, MA: Addison-Wesley.

Bronfenbrenner, U. (1979). *The ecology of human development: Experiments by nature and design.* Cambridge, MA: Harvard University Press.

Moving descriptions of changes in the status of children throughout history are provided by Ariès:

Ariès, P. (1962). *Centuries of childhood: A social history of family life* (R. Baldick, Trans.). New York: Knopf. (Originally published 1960.)

The following is a short book on science and its methods. It includes a number of useful suggestions for conducting experimental research as well as for writing research articles:

Ray, W. J., & Ravizza, R. (1988). *Methods toward a science of behavior and experience* (3rd ed.). Belmont, CA: Wadsworth.

Not everyone believes that science is the only, or even the best, way of knowing. For a provocative and sometimes challenging view of science and our conception of reality, see:

Pearce, J. C. (1971). *The crack in the cosmic egg.* New York: Fawcett.

CHAPTER 2

Theories of Lifespan Development

"Now what I want is facts. Teach these boys and girls nothing but Facts. Facts alone are wanted in life. Plant nothing else, and root out everything else. . . . Stick to Facts, Sir!"

Charles Dickens, *Hard Times*

It is a fact that Sylvia Knobbler once drowned three cats in a gunnysack into which she had dropped a cast-iron skillet stolen from Mike's Hardware and Dry Goods Limited. It is also a fact that she was arrested five times in a 3-week period while in the act of stuffing various items into oversized coat pockets or inside her blouse.

These are facts. The judge weighed them and pronounced his judgment. "The girl's a kleptomaniac," he said. "That's why she steals things."

He was dead wrong. Maybe Sylvia was a kleptomaniac, but that is *not* why she stole things. Kleptomaniac is just a label, a name. To assume that naming something explains it is a common error called the *nominal fallacy*. To explain behavior, we need more than the labels that the facts suggest.

The facts of developmental psychology are the observations we make—the replicable, objective observations that are the basis of the discipline. But isolated facts do not necessarily lead to understanding; they don't often allow us to make predictions or to affect the outcomes of development. We need to go beyond facts, Mr. Dickens.

This Chapter

We need to build theories. That's what this chapter is about: theories that lifespan theorists have built to explain and elaborate their *facts*. Theories that allow us to go *beyond* the facts.

A **theory** is essentially a description and explanation of observations. A theory can be so specific and simple, says Kuhn (1970), that it attempts to explain only a single relationship. My grandfather's belief that drinking wild mint tea prevents colds is one such theory. The belief that kleptomaniacs are people whose left-handed mothers got pregnant on the night of a new moon in October is another.

Most of the theories that are important in the study of lifespan development are more general. They consist of collections of statements intended to organize and explain related observations. For example, this chapter deals with theories designed to explain normal and abnormal personality development (Freud and Erikson); theories intended to explain how we learn and how we respond to the consequences of our behaviors (conditioning and social-learning theories); theories that look at the development of mental capacities and processes (Piaget's cognitive theory; information processing theory); theories concerned with the influences of culture and language on development (Vygotsky's sociocultural theories); and theories that look at the influences of biology on behavior (sociobiology and ethology). Each of these theories suggests different explanations for Sylvia Knobbler's behavior, and each might lead to a different kind of understanding.

Functions of Theories

The purpose of theories is to explain. Explanation is important because if we can explain something, we might also be able to make predictions about it, and we might be able to control certain outcomes. If we can explain Sylvia's compulsion to steal, for example, we might have been able to predict it beforehand. And we might even have been able to eradicate this compulsion or change it into something else, like an urge to sing arias from Italian operas.

Not only do theories have a very practical aspect, they also are one of science's primary guides for doing research. In large part, it is a theory—sometimes crude, sometimes elegant and refined—that tells the researcher where to look for a cure for cancer, what the cure will look like when it is found, and how it might be used. In the same way, psychology's theories tell the researcher where and how to look for personality or cognitive change in the lifespan; they also indicate why it might be important to look for that change.

Evaluating Theories

Why, you might ask, must there be a variety of theories if a theory is simply an explanation of facts? One reason is that different theories may be used to explain quite different facts. And even the most general theories of development are not all based on the same observations.

Theorists *select* observations that need to be explained. Furthermore, given the same set of observations, not all theorists will arrive at the same explanations. And, finally, fact (or truth) is no less elusive in developmental psychology than it is elsewhere. Our observations are often relative. They are more or less accurate depending on the precision of our observation (or measurement); they often apply only in specific circumstances and sometimes for specific individuals; and they are colored by our beliefs and expectations. As Scarr (1985) put it, "We do not discover scientific facts; we invent them" (p. 499). Nor do we always generalize appropriately. And it is on generalizations that our theories are based.

We cannot easily determine whether a theory is right or wrong, say Wellman and Gelman (1992); but we can evaluate it in terms of its usefulness.

Thomas (1992) suggests several criteria that might be used to judge a theory. A theory is better, he says, if it (1) accurately reflects the facts, (2) is expressed in a clearly understandable way, (3) is useful for predicting future events as well as explaining past ones, (4) is applicable in a practical sense (that is, has real value for counselors, teachers, pediatricians, and so on), (5) is consistent within itself rather than self-contradictory, and (6) is not based on numerous assumptions (unproven beliefs).

A good theory should also be thought-provoking and should have *heuristic* value—that is, it should be useful in our quest for knowledge. It should lead to new ideas, new discoveries, or new applications. And it should provide satisfying explanations, says Thomas (1992).

Models in Lifespan Development

Imagine that you have just been presented with this problem: Your psychology instructor has brought into class a small thing inside a larger glass container. You don't know what this small thing is. Your task is to decide what the best way would be to discover all that you can about this thing. Think about the problem for a moment before reading on.

Is there enough information presented so that you can make some reasonably intelligent suggestions? Consider, now, what the nature of your suggestions might be had I written, "Your instructor has brought into class a small animal inside a glass cage," or "Your instructor has brought into class a small piece of machinery inside a glass box," or "Your instructor has brought into class a strange new fruit in a glass container." Why is the task of investigating the object so much easier in the last three cases? Simply because you have been presented with information that allows you to classify the object in terms of a something about whose properties and functioning you already know a great deal. You have, in your view of the world, a mental **model** of what animals, fruits, and machines are like.

Psychologists investigating human development are, in some ways, in the same position as a student presented with a *thing*. At first, it is difficult to know what questions would be the best ones to ask. But if we could look at development in terms of something more familiar, many questions, not to mention a few answers, might suggest themselves. And that is, in effect, the starting point of all systematic investigation. We begin with a metaphor—a comparison. We say, this is *like* that, and it might therefore work in the same way as that. The *that* serves as our model.

Machine–Organism Models

In developmental psychology, there are two basic models that underlie many of our theories: the organismic and the mechanistic (Fischer & Silvern, 1985), with a third, the contextual, rapidly becoming more influential.

The **organismic model** assumes that it is useful to view people as though they are like active organisms; the **mechanistic model** assumes that it is more useful to view people as though they are like machines. In the first instance, the model is primarily *active*; in the second, the model is *reactive*.

These models are very important in the development of theory. In effect, they suggest what the theorist will investigate and what the resulting theory will look like. An organismic view (Jean Piaget's, for example) will describe development as a process resulting from self-initiated activities and will look for regularities in behavior in order to understand the wholeness and unity of the organism. In contrast, a more mechanistic view (early behaviorism, for example) will describe development as a process resulting from reactions to external events and will search for the machinelike predictability that might result, given sufficient knowledge about how the machine reacts to external forces.

Both the mechanistic and the organismic models emphasize *stages* that follow one another in predictable sequence. Accordingly, they are concerned with the *outcomes* rather than the *processes* of development. But much of development is not highly linear and predictable, says Steenbarger (1991): Human behavior is more complex than simple stage theories imply. It is profoundly influenced by the situations in which people find themselves; and it reflects continually changing *interactions* between individuals and their environments. Put another way, human development reflects the influence of context (Kleinginna & Kleinginna, 1988).

A Contextual or Ecological Model

The **contextual** (or *ecological*) **model** emphasizes the role of society, culture, and family, and recognizes the importance of the historical period in which the individual develops, as well as the importance of events that are unique to the individual (Bronfenbrenner, 1989).

The contextual model shares characteristics of both the organismic and the mechanistic models. It is organismic in that it sees development as the product of organism–environment interaction and because it looks for universal principles that might be useful for describing development (Lerner, 1985). It is mechanistic in that it is concerned with the influence of the environment on the developing organism.

One of the important characteristics of a contextual model is that it is based on an open systems view of human development (Bertalanffy, 1950). An **open system** is one that depends on interaction (in contrast to a *closed* system, which is completely predictable and totally unaffected by its environment). Thus an open system is constantly open to change. It is a system that is fundamentally dependent on its context, and that adapts continually as a function of interacting with its context. Accordingly, it is impossible to predict precisely what the final adaptation will be in an open system.

All biological, psychological, and social systems are open systems, says Valsiner (1987). Hence all developmental research ideally should be based on models that take into consideration interaction between the person's characteristics and characteristics of the environment.

The contextual or ecological model is exemplified in Bronfenbrenner's *ecological systems theory* and in Vygotsky's *social-cognitive* theory, both of which are described later in this chapter. It is also the model that is most apparent throughout this text, which, with Bronfenbrenner, views lifespan development as the progressive adaptation of active, growing human beings to changing environments. Our emphasis is on understanding development as an interactive process involving individuals with different characteristics in a range of different ecological systems or contexts. Thus the emphasis on the importance of the family, school, peers, siblings, and other significant aspects of context. Thus, too, the emphasis on the importance of the social and interactive nature of the processes of development.

At this point, you might ask which of these models is correct. The answer is simple: The question is irrelevant. The models are simply metaphors—comparisons. You might as well ask whether "The moon was a ghostly galleon, tossed up on cloudy seas" is more accurate than "That orbed maiden with white fire laden / Whom mortals call the moon." Metaphors are apt and useful or they are clumsy and useless. We might judge our poetic metaphors in terms of the images and feelings they arouse; we can judge our scientific metaphors only in terms of their usefulness.

Table 2.1 summarizes these three metaphors (or models). The remaining pages of this chapter describe five major groups of developmental theories. Note how each reflects the influence of one or more of these basic underlying metaphors.

Psychoanalytic Approaches: Freud

Psychoanalytic theory reflects Sigmund Freud's basic assumption that the most important causes of human behavior and personality are deep-seated, usually unconscious forces within individuals—hence organismic. Freud believed that these forces, some of which lead to conflict between desires and conscience, are at the root of mental disorders. Hence therapists (psychoanalysts) can help restore mental health, argued Freud, by help-

TABLE 2.1

Three Basic Models in Developmental Psychology

	Organismic	Mechanistic	Contextual
Metaphor	A biological organism	A machine	A plastic—strong, resilient, but responsive
Perception of Person	Sees individual as active, self-directed	Sees individual as reactive, responsive to environment	Sees individual as active and reactive
Developmental Process	Tends toward final adult stage, describable in terms of adult thought structures (logical characteristics of adult thought)	Described in terms of learning and problem solving; no clearly described end goal	Involves universal principles influenced by the individual's specific social, historical, and personal context
Theories	Age-related stage theories emphasizing similarities of thought at each level	Theories emphasizing the continuity of development	Theories emphasizing the interaction of age, historical variables, important life events, culture, and other aspects of context
Emphasis	Attention to similarities	Attention to individual differences	Attention to similarities; recognition of context-related differences
Theorists	Jean Piaget; Sigmund Freud	Early behaviorism	Richard M. Lerner; K. Warner Schaie; Gisela Labouvie-Vief; M. Basseches; also contemporary behaviorists

ing patients understand unconscious drives and resulting conflicts. Among the techniques he found most useful for this—techniques that soon became part of standard psychoanalytic procedure—were free association; the analysis of dreams and of the unintended use of words and expressions (popularly referred to as *Freudian slips*), both of which were assumed to reflect unconscious desires or fears; and painstaking analysis of childhood experiences—especially those of a sexual or traumatic (intensely frightening) nature.

Not surprisingly, the principal usefulness of Freudian psychoanalytic theory has been for the treatment of mental disorder. However, much of the theory is developmental. And although the most important beliefs of psychoanalytic theory are no longer an important part of current developmental theories, their historical importance and their influence on the thinking of later theorists justifies their inclusion here. The following sections present an abbreviated account of this complex, sometimes bewildering, but always fascinating view of the development and machinations of human personality.

While going through these brief sections, keep in mind that Freudian theory is very much a product of the Victorian era in which it was developed—an era that, by contemporary standards, was one of extreme sexual repression and masculine domination. These cultural factors greatly influenced Freud's theory and are reflected in the importance he gave sexual motives and behaviors, and in the masculine orientation of the theory. Much of what Freud initially thought about development applied primarily to male children, and to females only as a sometimes very hasty and incomplete afterthought (Gilligan, 1982).

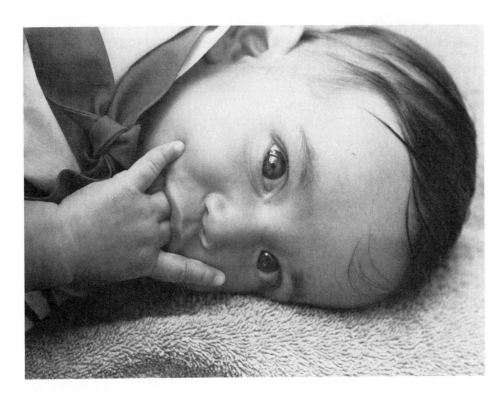

The newborn infant, says Freud, has a simple, undeveloped personality consisting largely of innate urges and desires. In the earliest stage of personality development, the *oral* stage, the infant is preoccupied with the mouth and with sucking. Sucking, Piaget agrees, is one of the infant's earliest and most effective means of exploring the world. So is looking.

Basic Ideas

Among the most fundamental Freudian ideas is the notion that human behavior, and consequently the direction that personality development takes, derives from two powerful tendencies: the urge to survive and the urge to procreate (Roazen, 1975). The survival instinct has long been of secondary importance because it is not usually endangered by our environments. (The Freudian term for environment is *reality*.) The urge to procreate, however, is constantly discouraged and even prevented; this accounts for the tremendous importance of sexuality in Freud's description of human development.

Sexuality, however, is a very broad term in Freud's writings. It means not only activities clearly associated with sex but also other behaviors and feelings, such as affection and love, and perhaps such actions as eating, thumb-sucking, smoking, and others. Sexual urges are so important in Freud's system that they are given a special term — **libido**. The libido is the source of energy for sexual urges; accordingly, the urges themselves are referred to as *libidinal urges*. However, the satisfaction of sexual impulses need not involve the sexual regions of the body.

Three Levels of Personality

Id. According to Freud, the newborn infant has a simple, undeveloped personality, consisting of primitive, unlearned urges that will be a lifetime source of what he called *psychic energy*, the urges and desires that account for behavior. Freud's label for the child's earliest personality is **id**. The urges that define id are mainly sexual.

The Freudian infant is all instincts and reflexes (unlearned tendencies), a bundle of energy seeking, almost desperately, to satisfy urges that are based upon a need to survive and to procreate. An infant has no idea of what is possible or impossible, no sense of reality, no conscience, no internal moral rules that control behavior. The most powerful urge at this stage is to seek immediate satisfaction of impulses. A child who is hungry does not wait. *Now* is the time for the nipple and sucking!

Ego. Almost from birth, the child's instinctual urges come into abrupt collision with reality. The hunger urge (linked with survival) cannot always be satisfied immediately. The *reality* of the situation is that the mother is often busy elsewhere and the infant's satis-

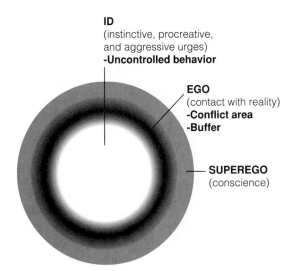

ID
(instinctive, procreative,
and aggressive urges)
-Uncontrolled behavior

EGO
(contact with reality)
-Conflict area
-Buffer

SUPEREGO
(conscience)

Figure 2.1   The Freudian conception of the three levels of personality: id, ego, and superego. The id, consisting of instinctual urges, develops first. The ego and the superego (conscience) develop later. In normal personality development, the ego acts as a buffer between the id and superego, which are in conflict with each other. Personality disorders may arise from unrestricted conflict when the ego fails to mediate successfully.

faction has to be delayed or denied. Similarly, the child learns that defecation cannot occur at will; parental demands conflict with the child's impulses. This constant conflict between the id and reality develops the second level of personality, the ego.

The **ego** grows out of a realization of what is possible and what is not; it is the rational, or cognitive, level of human personality. It comes to include the realization that delaying gratification is often a desirable thing, that long-term goals sometimes require the denial of short-term goals. Although the id wants immediate gratification, the ego channels these desires in the most profitable direction for the individual. Note that the levels of personality represented by the id and the ego are not in opposition. They work together toward the same goal: satisfying the needs and the urges of the individual.

Superego.   The third level of personality, the superego, sets itself up in opposition to the first two. **Superego** refers to the moral aspects of personality. Like

the ego, the superego develops from contact with reality, although it is more concerned with social than physical reality. The development of the superego, or **conscience**, does not occur until early childhood. Freud assumed that it resulted principally from a process of identifying with (trying to be like) parents, particularly the like-sexed parent. To *identify* in a Freudian sense is to adopt values, beliefs, and behaviors. By identifying with their parents, children learn the religious and cultural rules that govern their parents' behaviors. These rules then become part of the child's superego. Since many religious rules, as well as many social and cultural rules, oppose the urges of the id, the superego and the id are generally in conflict. Freud assumed that this conflict accounts for much deviant behavior.

In summary, Freud's theory establishes three levels of personality: the id, the ego, and the superego (see Figure 2.1). The first is the source of energy or motivation, deriving from instincts for survival and procreation. The ego is reality oriented and intervenes between the id and the superego to maintain a balance between the id's urges and the superego's rules. It is as if the id were continually saying, "I want that banana split supreme right now; I want to be caressed immediately; I want that Lambourghini today; I want to punch that guy's lights out," while the superego protests, "Don't you dare; deny your desires; thou shalt not steal; fighting is a sin." And the ego, seated between these warring forces, attempts to make peace: "Have you considered eating only at mealtime and with some moderation? Chew a piece of gum instead. Maybe you should take a bus. As for that idiot, let the courts handle it. You can watch. How would that be?"

Psychosexual Stages

Freud's account of the development of the three levels of personality is a description of development. His ideas are also relevant for understanding the motivational changes that occur as an individual develops. Freud divides changes in motivation into a sequence of stages that are distinguishable by the objects or activities necessary for the satisfaction of the individual's urges during each stage. The labels for each stage reflect changes in the areas of sexual satisfaction as the child matures.

The **oral stage** lasts through infancy (approximately to 18 months). It is characterized by the infant's

According to Freud, the moral aspect of personality (the superego) develops largely as a result of the child identifying with parents—and especially with the like-sexed parent. To identify with someone is to try to become like him or her in important ways, not only in behavior but also in values and ideals. This little lad may already have begun to learn something about the importance of reading—as well as about what it is important to read.

preoccupation with the mouth and with sucking. During this first stage, the child's personality consists mainly of id. Children seek constantly to satisfy their urges and are incapable of deliberately delaying gratification.

Toward the end of the first year, the area of sexual gratification shifts gradually from the oral to the anal region. According to Freud, in the early part of the **anal stage** the child derives pleasure from bowel movements. Later in this stage, the child acquires control of sphincter muscles and may then derive considerable pleasure from withholding bowel movements to increase anal sensation. Both of these behaviors oppose the mother's wishes. As a result of these conflicts, the child begins to develop an ego—a sense of reality, an awareness that some things are possible while others are not, coupled with the ability to delay gratification to some extent.

The third stage, which lasts roughly from ages 2 to 6, is labeled **phallic**, not only because the zone of sexuality has shifted from the anal to the genital region but also because the phallus (the male genital) is of primary importance in the sexuality of girls as well as boys. Whereas gratification had been obtained earlier

by sucking or by expelling or withholding feces, children now often masturbate (manipulate their genitalia).

Normal development now takes the male child through the **Oedipus complex**, when his increasing awareness of the sexual meanings of his genital area leads him to desire his mother (and to wish unconsciously to replace his father). For girls ages 4–6, there is the **Electra complex**, in which a girl's sexual feelings for her father lead her to become jealous of her mother.

The resolution of the Oedipus complex marks the transition from the phallic stage to the period of sexual **latency** that follows. The period of latency (ages 6–11) is marked by a loss of sexual interest and a continued **identification** with the like-sexed parent (attempts to be like the object of identification in terms of beliefs and values). In this way, the child begins to develop a superego.

Following this lengthy period of sexual neutrality, the child enters the stage of adult sexuality, the **genital stage** (at around age 11). During this period, the child begins to establish the sorts of heterosexual attachments that characterize normal adult sexual relationships. Also during this last developmental stage, the superego (con-

TABLE 2.2

Freud's Stages of Psychosexual Development

Stage	Approximate Ages	Characteristics
Oral	0–18 months	Sources of pleasure include sucking, biting, swallowing, playing with lips. Preoccupation with immediate gratification of impulses. Id is dominant.
Anal	18 months to 2–3 years	Sources of sexual gratification include urinating and expelling, as well as retaining, feces. Id and ego.
Phallic	2–3 to 6 years	Child becomes concerned with genitals. Source of sexual pleasure involves manipulating genitals. Period of Oedipus or Electra complex. Id, ego, and superego.
Latency	6–11 years	Loss of interest in sexual gratification. Identification with parent of same sex. Id, ego, and superego.
Genital	11 onward	Concern with adult modes of sexual pleasure, barring fixations or regressions.

science), which has previously been rigid and almost tyrannical, normally becomes progressively more flexible and less rigid with increasing maturity. (See Table 2.2 for a summary of Freud's stages of psychosexual development.)

Defense Mechanisms

An overview of Freud's theories would be incomplete without a consideration of **defense mechanisms**—the irrational and sometimes unhealthy methods many people use to compensate for their inability to satisfy the demands of the id and to overcome the anxiety that accompanies the continual struggle between the id and the superego. Defense mechanisms are invented by the ego in its role as a mediator between the id and the superego; they are the ego's attempt to establish peace between the two so that the person can continue to operate in an apparently healthy manner. Defense mechanisms are particularly important for understanding disturbed personalities, although they are not at all uncommon in the lives of those who have no clearly recognizable disturbances. It is only when people rely on them excessively that defense mechanisms become unhealthy. (See Interactive Table 2.3 for some examples of common defense mechanisms.)

Freud in Review

Freud paints a dark and somewhat cynical picture of human nature: Primitive inherited forces over which we have no control drive us relentlessly toward the satisfaction of instinctual urges and bring us into repeated conflict with reality. From the moment of birth, our most basic "selves"—our *ids*—react with fear and anxiety. We fear that our overpowering urges to survive (and eventually to procreate) will not be satisfied, and we suffer from the anxiety that accompanies that fear. This *trauma of birth* is, according to Freud, the forerunner of all our adult anxieties.

Hofer (1981) describes Freud's theory as one of the most comprehensive and influential of all human psychological theories. There is little doubt that its direct impact on our attitudes toward children and child rearing is considerable. More than anyone else, Freud was responsible for making parents realize how important

INTERACTIVE TABLE 2.3

Some Freudian Defense Mechanisms

 Can you think of additional examples of each?

Mechanism	Example
Displacement: A suppressed behavior appears in a more acceptable form.	A potential murderer hunts predatory animals or becomes a mercenary soldier.
Reaction formation: Behavior is the opposite of what the individual would like it to be.	A woman loves an unobtainable man and behaves as though she dislikes him.
Intellectualization: Behavior is stripped of its emotional concomitants.	A man who loves his aunt too dearly treats her with extreme consideration, kindness, and devotion but convinces himself that he is motivated by duty and not by love.
Projection: People come to believe that their own undesirable feelings or inclinations are more descriptive of others than of themselves.	A man who is extremely jealous of another and unconsciously wishes him harm believes it is others who have those feelings.
Denial: Reality is distorted to make it conform to the individual's wishes.	A heavy smoker is unable to give up the habit and decides that there is no substantial evidence linking nicotine with human diseases.
Repression: Unpleasant experiences are stored deep in the subconscious mind and become inaccessible to waking memory.	A soldier comes very close to death but remembers no details of the event.

the experiences of the early years can be. The significance of Freudian theory, however, is not limited to its direct impact on parents, educators, doctors, and others; it includes the tremendous influence it has had on the development of other theories (for example, those of Erikson and Bowlby). However, many of Freud's students and followers have not accepted the theory entirely.

Freud's theory is clearly weak from a scientific point of view, based as it is on a limited number of observations collected by a single individual (Freud himself), and not subjected to any rigorous analysis. In addition, it uses difficult and important terms and concepts, such as *unconscious*, in confusing and ambiguous ways; it leads to contradictory predictions; and it places excessive emphasis on sexual and aggressive impulses (Rothstein, 1980).

In spite of these criticisms, Freud's theorizing is an immensely rich basis for understanding human personality. In summarizing the contributions of psychoanalysis, Kegan (1982) notes that it remains the single most

important guide for mental health practitioners in clinics and in hospitals. Ironically, however, its status in academic psychology is relatively minor. In contrast, theories such as Piaget's cognitivism are an ongoing source of debate and research in academic circles, but these theories have remarkably little influence on the application of psychology in the real world.

Psychoanalytic Approaches: Erikson

Freud's influence can be found among the many theories developed by some of his followers. Perhaps the most important of these for understanding lifespan human development is Erik Erikson's (1956, 1959, 1961, 1968). It draws heavily from Freud's work but also departs from it in several important ways.

For Erikson, development involves resolving important conflicts by acquiring new competencies. For example, as children learn that they can carry out some of the behaviors they intend, they develop a sense of autonomy that surmounts earlier doubts and fears.

Recall that Freud's primary emphasis was on the role of sexuality (libido) and on the importance of conflicts involving id, ego, and superego in determining personality and mental health. In contrast, Erikson downplays the importance of sexuality and of psychodynamic conflicts, and instead emphasizes the importance of the child's social environment. His theory is a theory of **psychosocial** rather than **psychosexual** development. It is more *contextual* than Freud's.

A second departure from Freudian theory is Erikson's emphasis on the role of the ego rather than the superego. As a result, the theory is more positively oriented, being concerned with the development of a healthy ego (of **identity**, in Erikson's terms) rather than with the resolution of powerful internal conflicts. This concern with the healthy personality describes a third important difference between his work and that of Freud.

Psychosocial Stages

Erikson describes human development in eight stages, the first five of which span infancy, childhood, and adolescence; the last three describe adulthood. Each of Erikson's stages involves a basic conflict, brought about primarily by a need to adapt to the social environment.

Resolution of this conflict results in the development of a sense of competence. Although Erikson's first five stages closely parallel Freud's psychosexual stages in terms of ages, his descriptions and his emphases are quite different. The stages are described briefly here; they are covered in more detail in Chapters 12, 14, 16, and 18.

Trust Versus Mistrust. One of the most basic components of a healthy personality is a sense of trust. This sense of trust toward oneself and toward others develops in the first year of life (Erikson, 1959). The infant is initially faced with a conflict between mistrust of a world about which little is known and an inclination to develop a trusting attitude toward that world. The most important person in the infant's life at this stage is the primary caregiver—usually the mother. Successful resolution of the conflict between trust and mistrust depends largely on the infant's relationship with this caregiver and on the gradual realization that the world is predictable, safe, and loving. If the world is unpredictable and the caregiver rejecting, the infant may, according to Erikson, grow up to be mistrustful and anxious.

Autonomy Versus Shame and Doubt. During this stage, corresponding to Freud's anal stage, children begin to realize that they are the authors of their own actions. Initially, the child does not deliberately act upon the world but reacts to it. Sucking, for example, is not engaged in when the child *intends* to suck, but rather when appropriate stimulation is provided. With the recognition that they can carry out some of the behaviors they intend, children develop a sense of autonomy. This autonomy, however, is threatened by children's inclination to avoid responsibility for their own actions, to go back to the comfort and security that characterized the first stage (Erikson, 1961). But children experience shame and doubt at this inclination.

If the child is to successfully resolve this conflict and develop a sense of autonomy, it is important that its parents encourage attempts to explore and provide opportunities for independence. Overprotectiveness can lead to doubt and uncertainty in dealing with the world later.

Initiative Versus Guilt.

By the age of 4 or 5, children have resolved the crises of autonomy; in short, they have discovered that they are somebody. During the next stage, they must discover who it is that they are (Erikson, 1959). True to his Freudian orientation, Erikson assumes that children seek to discover who they are by attempting to be like their parents. During this stage, they establish a wider physical environment, made possible by their greater freedom of movement. Their sense of language becomes sufficiently advanced for them to be able to ask many questions and understand some of the answers; it also permits them to imagine all sorts of possibilities about themselves. With their increasing exploration of the environment, children need to develop a sense of initiative with respect to their behaviors. They are autonomous as well as responsible for initiating behavior.

Because the central process involved in resolving the initiative versus guilt conflict is one of identification, parents and the family continue to be the most important influences in the child's development. It is important for them to encourage the young child's sense of initiative and to nurture a sense of responsibility.

Industry Versus Inferiority.

The fourth developmental phase, corresponding to Freud's latency period, is marked by the child's increasing need to interact with and be accepted by peers. It now becomes crucial for children to discover that their selves, their identities, are significant, that they can do things—in short, that they are competent. Children now avail themselves of opportunities to learn things they think are important to their culture, hoping that by so doing they will become someone. Successful resolution of this stage's conflict depends largely on the responses of significant agencies—especially schools and teachers—to the child's efforts. Recognition and praise are especially important in developing a positive self-concept. If the child's work is continually demeaned, seldom praised, rarely rewarded, the outcome may well be a lasting sense of inferiority.

Identity Versus Identity Diffusion.

Erikson's fifth developmental stage, corresponding to the beginning of Freud's genital period and dealing directly with the period ordinarily referred to as adolescence, involves the development of a sense of identity. Here, Erikson's emphasis on the ego becomes most evident. The development of a strong sense of identity implies the development of a strong ego—hence Erikson's expression *ego identity*. The crisis implicit in this stage concerns a conflict between a strong sense of *self* and the diffusion of **self-concepts**.

At a simple level, the formation of an identity appears to involve arriving at a notion not so much of who one is but rather of who one can be. The source of conflict resides in the various possibilities open to the child—possibilities that are magnified by the variety of models in the environment. Conflict and doubt over the choice of identity lead to what Erikson terms *identity diffusion*. It is as though adolescents are torn between early acceptance of a clearly defined self and the dissipation of their energies as they experiment with a variety of roles. The development of identity during adolescence is discussed in Chapter 12.

Adulthood.

Erikson's description of development does not end with adolescence but continues through the entire lifespan. He describes three additional psychosocial conflicts that occur during adulthood and old age, and that require new competencies and adjustments. The first of these, *intimacy and solidarity versus isolation*, relates to the need to develop intimate relationships with others (as opposed to being isolated) and is particularly crucial for marital and parental roles. The second, *generativity versus self-absorption*, describes a need to assume social, work, and community responsibilities that will be beneficial to others (that will be generative), rather than remaining absorbed in the self. And the

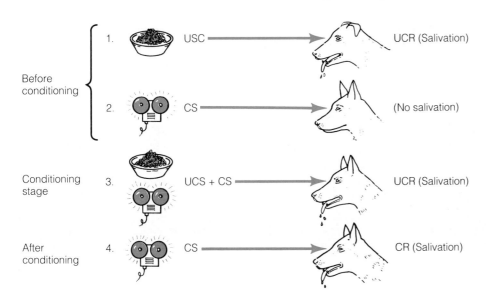

Before conditioning

1. USC → UCR (Salivation)

2. CS → (No salivation)

Conditioning stage

3. UCS + CS → UCR (Salivation)

After conditioning

4. CS → CR (Salivation)

Figure 2.2 Classical conditioning. In (1), an unconditioned stimulus leads to an unconditioned response, whereas in (2), a conditioned stimulus does not lead to the same response. In (3), the unconditioned stimulus is paired with the conditioned stimulus a number of times so that eventually the conditioning stimulus alone elicits the original response, as in (4).

old infant named Albert. To demonstrate the effectiveness of classical conditioning in producing emotional reactions, each time the experimenter presented Little Albert with the rat, an accomplice made a loud noise behind Albert. As was expected, the poor infant was very frightened. After repeating the procedure seven times, Watson and Rayner simply presented the rat without making any noise. Now, as soon as Albert saw the rat, he was terrified and began to whimper, attempting desperately to crawl away. Unfortunately, Little Albert left the hospital before Watson could cure him of his fear. A conditioning procedure could have been used for that as well (M. C. Jones, 1974).

Although Watson and Rayner's experiment with Albert is more systematic and deliberate than most situations in which we acquire emotional responses, the results can be generalized. There is considerable evidence that emotional reactions do transfer from one situation to another. People who react with fear to the sound of a dentist's drill are not fearful because the *sound* of the drill has been responsible for any pain they have felt in the past. But the sound of the drill has previously been associated with pain and has thus acquired the capability of eliciting reactions associated with pain.

Operant Conditioning

A classical conditioning model is sometimes useful for explaining the learning of simple behaviors that occur in response to specific stimuli. As Skinner (1953, 1957,

1961) notes, however, a great many human behaviors or responses are not **elicited** by any obvious stimuli but appear instead to be **emitted** by the organism, for whatever reason. In Skinner's terms, an emitted behavior is an **operant**; an elicited response is a **respondent**. Skinner's major work is an attempt to explain how operants are learned.

The simplest explanation of **operant conditioning** is that the *consequences* of a response determine how likely it is to be repeated. Behaviors that are reinforced tend to be repeated; those that are not reinforced (or that are punished) are less likely to occur again (see Figure 2.3). This is very different from saying that learning will occur as a function of the pairing of stimuli regardless of consequences. When Little Albert reacted with fear to the rat, it was not because his fear responses led to pleasant consequences but because the rat was paired with some other fear-producing situation.

Reinforcement. **Reinforcement** is whatever increases the probability of a response recurring. A **reinforcer** is the stimulus that reinforces; reinforcement is the *effect* of a reinforcer. Positive reinforcement is one kind of reinforcement; negative reinforcement is the other. Both negative and positive reinforcement *increase* the probability that a response will occur. The difference between the two is that **positive reinforcement** is effective as a result of a **reward** being added to a situation after the behavior has occurred, whereas **negative reinforcement** is effective through the removal of an unpleasant stimulus. A simple way of

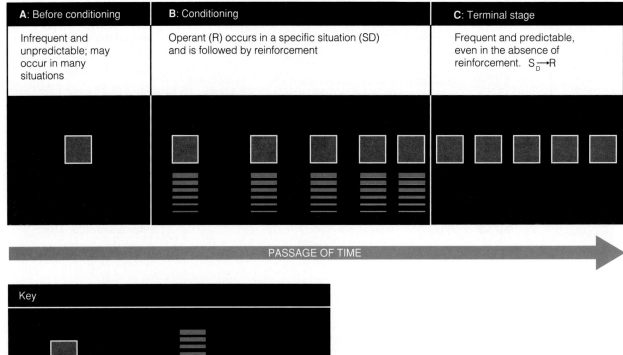

A: Before conditioning	**B**: Conditioning	**C**: Terminal stage
Infrequent and unpredictable; may occur in many situations	Operant (R) occurs in a specific situation (SD) and is followed by reinforcement	Frequent and predictable, even in the absence of reinforcement. $S_D \rightarrow R$

PASSAGE OF TIME

Key

Operant (R)   Reinforcement

Figure 2.3 Schematic model of operant conditioning. In (A), the operant behavior alone is not rewarded. In (B), conditioning begins. The operant behavior takes place by chance; it is immediately reinforced. It occurs again, by chance or deliberately, and the reinforcement is repeated. As the time line chart shows, repetition becomes more and more frequent as the learner catches on. Eventually, the operant behavior continues even without reinforcement at the terminal stage (C).

remembering the difference between the two is to remember that positive reinforcement involves a *reward* for behavior; negative reinforcement involves *relief* from something unpleasant.

Unfortunately, real-life situations are more complicated than this black-and-white terminology suggests. Subjective judgments such as "pleasant" and "unpleasant," although they make our understanding simpler, are misleading. Reinforcement and punishment have to do with *effects* rather than perceived pleasantness. Thus a parent or teacher who keeps "punishing" a child but who observes that the punished behavior becomes more rather than less frequent may well be reinforcing that behavior—or something (someone?) else is. Similarly, on occasion, a teacher's

praise of a student's behavior will lead to a drastic reduction of that behavior. Reinforcement? No. By definition, this is **punishment**. The important point is that pleasantness and unpleasantness are subjective. In contrast, reinforcement and punishment are objective phenomena defined in terms of increases or decreases in the frequency of behavior.

Punishment.   Whereas reinforcement, whether positive or negative, serves to make a response more likely, punishment does not.

There are several different kinds of punishment. The kind that we usually think of first involves a clearly unpleasant consequence. Being beaten with a hickory stick or having one's hair pulled are examples of this

	Pleasant	Unpleasant	No consequences
Added to the situation	*Positive reinforcment:* Louella is given a jelly bean for being "good"	*Punishment:* Louella has her nose tweaked for being "bad"	*Extinction:* Louella's behavior has no apparent effects, and is ignored
Removed from the situation	*Punishment:* Louella has her jelly beans taken away for being "bad"	*Negative reinforcement:* Louella's nose is released because she says "I'm sorry"	

Interactive Figure 2.4 The four alternatives that define punishment and reinforcement, and a fifth where behavior has no apparent consequences — with examples. Were you ever punished or reinforced in these ways? Can you think of specific examples?

kind of punishment. Another kind involves taking away something that is pleasant. Being prevented from watching television (what psychologists refer to as a *time out* procedure) and having to give up something desirable, such as money or privileges (called *response-cost* punishment), are examples of this kind of punishment. Another possibility, of course, is that a behavior will not have consequences, and will simply cease to be emitted (will be *extinguished*). Distinctions among the various kinds of reinforcement and punishment are illustrated in Interactive Figure 2.4. As the illustration makes clear, both may involve pleasant or unpleasant stimuli, but whether these stimuli are added to or removed from the situation determines their effect. It is worth repeating that reinforcement and punishment are defined by their effects.

Behavioristic Approaches in Review

Learning-theory explanations for human development emphasize the role of the environment in shaping our personalities and our behaviors. Unlike psychoanalytic approaches, they are not concerned with psychodynamic conflicts and other hidden causes of behavior, and unlike the more cognitive approaches, which we discuss next, they pay relatively little attention to concepts such as *understanding* and *knowing*. Instead, they focus on the role of reinforcement and punishment and

on the extent to which behavior can be shaped by its consequences.

One of the main criticisms of these approaches is that they are poorly suited to explain what are referred to as *higher mental processes* — for example, thinking, feeling, analyzing, problem solving, evaluating, and so on. Their emphasis, and their principal usefulness, relates to actual behavior rather than to thinking and feeling.

A second criticism of behavioristic approaches is that to the extent that they emphasize the machinelike qualities of human functioning, they rob us of those capabilities that we consider most human — our ability to think and imagine, and our ability to exercise significant personal control over our own behaviors. In brief, critics have claimed that in its attempts to reduce behavior to a handful of understandable and observable stimuli and responses, behaviorism *dehumanizes* us.

Although these criticisms may be valid for older, more extreme interpretations of behaviorism, they are less pertinent for more current positions. For example, Bijou (1989) notes that whereas Watson's theory describes an essentially passive organism, contemporary behaviorism sees the individual "as *always* being in an interactive relationship with the environment" (p. 68). In his words, the individual is "adjustive" rather than simply reactive. However, Bijou's contemporary behaviorist does not view our ability to think, to imagine, or to feel as a *cause* of behavior. Bijou labels these cognitive activities *implicit interactions*. The primary concern of the behaviorist is not so much these implicit,

We are products of our surroundings—of our contexts. According to Bandura's social-learning theory, much of our behavior is a function of observing the behavior of others. Through observational learning (imitation), we not only learn specific behaviors (such as how to salute) but also acquire complex beliefs about right and wrong (such as notions about honor and duty and patriotism).

hence unobservable, interactions as it is the more observable interactions between stimuli and responses. Bijou cautions, however, that insofar as the contemporary behaviorist views people as adjustive rather than simply reactive, the environment is given a less important role in determining behavior. The causes of behavior, he claims, will be found not in the environment alone, but rather in all the factors that are involved in a person's interactions, including past interactions.

On a more positive note, behavioristic approaches to development are sometimes very useful not only for understanding developmental change, but also for controlling it. The deliberate application of conditioning principles to change behavior (termed **behavior modification**) has proven extremely useful in a variety of settings including the classroom and psychotherapy.

Theories, we should remember, are inventions whose purpose is to simplify, to explain, sometimes to predict. Unlike traditional religions, they don't have to be accepted, or rejected, in their entirety. Elements from different theories can sometimes be combined to produce new theories, new insights, that go far beyond the original theories. A case in point is Albert Bandura's theorizing, which, in some ways, serves as a transition between behaviorism and cognitivism.

Social Cognitive Theory

At one level, Bandura's (1977, 1986) is a **behavioristic theory** of imitation based on the assumption that much important learning involves models of various kinds that act as social influences on the child. At another level, it is a **cognitive** theory in that it recognizes the importance of our ability to think, to symbolize, to ferret out cause-and-effect relationships, to anticipate the outcomes of behavior. There is no doubt, Bandura (1977) assures us, that reinforcement controls much of our behavior. But it does not control us blindly. Its effects depend largely on our awareness of the relationship between our behavior and its outcomes. As Bruner (1985) points out, reinforcement often occurs long after the behavior it follows — as happens, for example, when you study for an examination. In such cases, it isn't reinforcement (or the possibility of punishment) that affects behavior directly so much as your ability to anticipate the consequences of behavior.

Bandura's social-learning theory is a theory of **observational learning** (or **imitation**). It can be summarized simply as follows:

- Much human learning and behavior is a function of observing the behavior of others or of symbolic models such as fictional characters and television or folk heroes.

- Imitation is often reinforced.

- Observational learning can therefore be explained largely through operant conditioning principles.

The Processes of Observational Learning

Bandura (1986) emphasizes that the effects of models are due largely to their *informative function*. From observing models, we learn not only how to do certain things but also what the consequences of our behaviors are likely to be. Accordingly, there are four distinct processes involved in observational learning.

First, there are *attentional processes*. Clearly, children are not likely to learn very much from a model if they pay no attention to important aspects of that model's behavior. Whether they will attend, Bandura informs us, depends partly on the value of the model's behavior (Is it important for the observer to be able to swear like that? Throw a ball in that way? Cock his head in just that fashion?). It also depends on other factors such as the distinctiveness of the behavior, its prevalence, and its complexity, as well as on such things as the motor and perceptual capacities of the observer and previous reinforcement for imitation.

Second, not only are there attentional processes involved, but also *retentional processes*. The child must attend and then be able to remember. According to Bandura, this implies being able to represent mentally, either in terms of images or words.

Third, there must also be appropriate *motor reproduction processes*. In order to imitate, the observer must be able to translate what has been retained (represented mentally) into actual behavior. This might require certain motor and physical capabilities, as well as the ability to monitor and correct one's own behavior.

Finally, in observational learning, as in all learning, there must be relevant *motivational processes*. In the absence of appropriate motivation (reasons for behavior), many behaviors that are observed and potentially learned will not be performed. In this connection, learning theorists make an important distinction between acquisition and performance. Much is acquired (learned, in other words) that does not become part of behavior. (See Figure 2.5 for a summary of Bandura's theory of observational learning.)

Manifestations of Observational Learning

The term *model* may refer to an actual, and perhaps very ordinary, person who does something, and whose behavior serves as a guide, a blueprint, or perhaps an inspiration for somebody else. A model might also be **symbolic**. Symbolic models include books, oral or written instructions, pictures, mental images, cartoon or film characters, television programs, and so on.

The Modeling Effect.
Bandura and Walters (1963) describe three different effects of imitation on learning. The first, the learning of novel behavior, is labeled the **modeling effect**. One example of the modeling effect is the learning of some aspects of language. That the rain forest people of the Cameroon speak their own language and not Chippewa is evidence that they model the language that surrounds them. (There is much more to language learning than simply imitation, however; see Chapters 5 and 7.)

The Inhibitory-Disinhibitory Effect.
The effects of imitation are also found in the **inhibitory effect** (the suppression of deviant behavior) and the **disinhibitory effect** (the appearance of previously suppressed deviant behavior). These effects are usually the result of punishment or rewards to the model for engaging in deviant behavior. Consider the hypothetical case of a teenager from an upstanding, conservative, middle-class family whose friends have recently discovered marijuana. The behavior is deviant by the child's own standards, but the amount of reinforcement (in terms of social prestige, acceptance by the group,

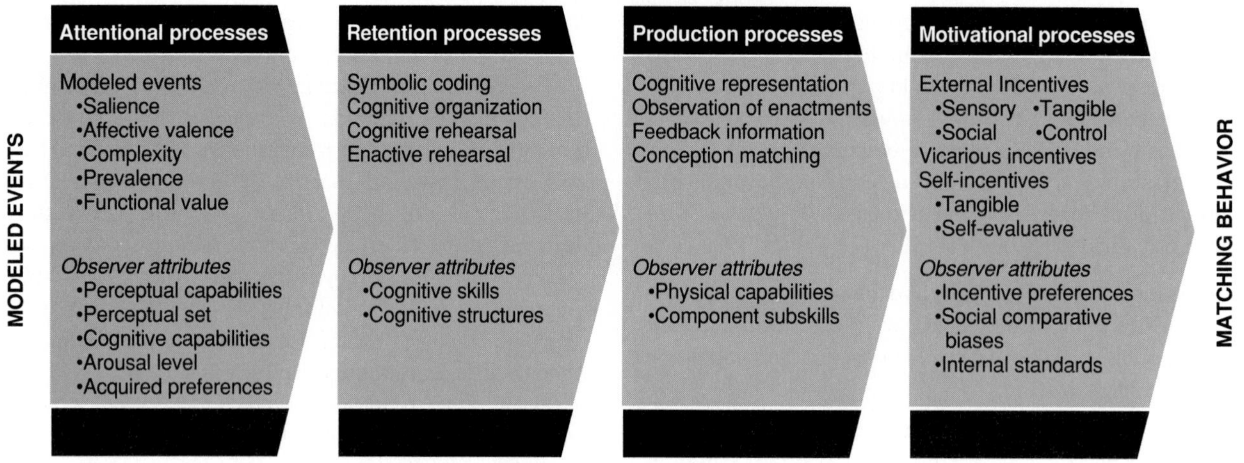

Figure 2.5 Subprocesses governing observational learning in Bandura's social cognitive theory. (From Albert Bandura (1989). Social cognitive theory. In Ross Vasta (Ed.), *Annals of Child Development*, Vol. 6, p. 16. JAI Press. Reprinted by permission of the publisher.)

and so on) that others appear to derive from smoking marijuana may well *disinhibit* this behavior in the child. There is really no new learning involved, as there is in modeling, but merely the disinhibition of previously suppressed behavior. If this teenager later observes members of her peer group punished by law, parents, or school authorities, or experiences ill effects from the drug, she might cease engaging in this behavior. Again, no new learning is involved, although a change in behavior does result from the influence of models; thus this change illustrates the *inhibitory* effect.

The Eliciting Effect. A third effect of imitation is the **eliciting effect**, in which the learner's behavior is not identical to the model's, or deviant or novel, but is simply related to it. It is as though the model's behavior suggests some response to observers and therefore *elicits* that response. For example, a child "acting up" in school may *elicit* related but not identical misbehaviors among classmates. (See Interactive Table 2.6 for a summary of the effects of imitation.)

Self-Efficacy

Theories in psychology, as elsewhere, are not often static, unchanging things—unless the theorist has lost interest, moved on to other issues, or died. But even then, if the theory is at all compelling or important,

INTERACTIVE TABLE 2.6

Three Effects of Imitation

▶ *Can you provide specific examples of each?*

Modeling	Acquiring *new* behavior as a result of observing a model
Inhibitory-disinhibitory	Ceasing or starting some *deviant* behavior as a result of seeing a model punished or rewarded for similar behavior
Eliciting	Engaging in behavior related to that of a model

there will be others who will chew at it, who will try to change its shape to fit new facts and to answer new questions.

Albert Bandura's theorizing is a case in point. His early ideas stemmed directly from a behavioristic orientation. Thus his imitation-based theory of social learning attempted to explain the complex effects of modeling in terms of rewards and punishments, either actual or anticipated. But when a behavioristic theorist speaks of *anticipating*, of *imagining* the consequences of a behavior, that theorist has moved a long way beyond traditional behaviorism. There is little room for imagining among the objective, observable, and measurable stimuli, responses, and reinforcement schedules of the behaviorist. Thus Bandura's social-learning theory has become progressively more *cognitive* (more concerned with *knowing, understanding, thinking,* and other mental processes). It gives an increasingly important role to the *informative* function of models. It is what the observer imagines and anticipates that is fundamentally important in learning through imitation.

Recently, Bandura's research and theorizing has taken yet another turn—one that is even more clearly cognitive and that is often referred to as *social cognitivism* (Bandura, 1981, 1986; Evans, 1989). It has to do with what is termed **self-referent** thought—thought that relates to our *selves*, our own mental processes. Among other things, self-referent thought deals with our estimates of our abilities, with our notions about how capable and how *effective* we are in our dealings with the world and with others. And a very specific term has been coined to describe our estimates of our effectiveness: **self-efficacy**.

Definition.   In a nutshell, efficacy signifies competence in dealing with the environment. The most *efficacious* people are those who can most effectively deal with a variety of situations even when these situations are ambiguous or highly stressful. Thus self-efficacy has two separate but related components: (1) the skills required for the successful performance of a behavior, and (2) the individual's beliefs about personal effectiveness. From a psychological point of view, it is not so much the skills component that is important, but rather the person's own evaluations of personal efficacy. *Self-efficacy* is the term that refers more precisely to the judgments we make about how *efficacious* we are likely to be in given situations. Among the most important of all the different aspects of self-knowledge, Bandura insists, is our conception of personal efficacy.

Implications of Self-Efficacy Judgments.   Our judgments about our personal effectiveness are extremely important determiners of what we do and don't do. In fact, in some situations, self-efficacy may be a better predictor of behavior than relevant skills are (Schunk, 1984). Under most circumstances, children—and adults—do not seek out and undertake activities in which they expect to perform badly.

Judgments of personal efficacy affect not only our choices of activities and settings but also the amount of effort we are willing to expend when faced with difficulties. The stronger an individual's perceptions of efficacy, the more likely that individual is to persist, and the greater the effort expended will be. But if notions of self-efficacy are not highly favorable, difficult activities may be abandoned after very little effort and time.

Finally, perceived self-efficacy influences our thoughts and emotions. Those whose judgments of their effectiveness is low are more likely to evaluate their behaviors negatively and to see themselves as being inadequate. Related to this, Cowen and associates (1991) found that children with the more favorable self-efficacy judgments were more resilient, more resistant to stress.

Sources of Efficacy Judgments.   Judgments of personal efficacy, Bandura (1986) suggests, stem from several sources. First are the direct effects of behavior. Whether we succeed must surely have some effect on our estimates of how efficacious we are. However, the inferential processes involved are not always simple and linear. The individual who is mostly successful does not invariably arrive at highly positive judgments of self-efficacy; nor does lack of success always correspond to negative judgments. As Weiner (1980) points out, success—or lack of success—can be attributed to a number of factors. Some of these, such as ability and effort, are under personal control, and reflect directly on the efficacy of the individual. Others, such as luck or the difficulty of the task, are not under personal control and do not, therefore, have very direct implications for judgments of self-efficacy. Some individuals are prone to attribute the outcomes of their behaviors to factors over which they have control. Dweck (1975) refers to these people as *mastery-oriented*. Others are more likely to attribute their failures and successes to luck or to the task being too difficult or too easy. Dweck describes these individuals as being characterized by *helplessness* rather than by a mastery orientation (see Chapter 10).

One source of influence for judgments of personal efficacy, then, are personal accomplishments and especially individual judgments about the causes underlying these accomplishments. A second influence is vicarious (secondhand); it comes from observing the performance of others. Even as children, we judge how effective we are partly by comparing ourselves to others. The most informative comparisons we can make are those that involve others whose performance is similar to ours.

A 12-year-old who demolishes his 6-year-old brother in a game of skill and intelligence learns very little about his personal effectiveness. Similarly, if he, in turn, is blown away by his father, he may not have learned much more—except, perhaps, a touch of humility.

A third source of influence on self-judgments, Bandura (1986) argues, is persuasion: "You can do it. We know you can. Sing for us. We love the way you sing." Persuasion, depending on the characteristics of the persuader and on the relationship between persuader and "persuadee," can sometimes change an individual's judgments of self-efficacy and lead that individual to attempt things that would not otherwise be attempted—or not to attempt them: "They're just flattering you. Please don't sing."

The fourth source of influence on judgments of self-efficacy is the person's **arousal** level. *Arousal* is a big word with a lot of meanings. In this context, its most important meaning is alertness or intensity of immediate emotional reaction. Whether arousal will have positive or negative effects on the individual's self-judgments may depend largely on experiences the individual has had in situations of high or low arousal. Some people find that moderately high arousal helps their performance; others react in the opposite way. For example, the fear that precedes speaking in public may be seen as helpful by some speakers and as highly negative by others.

In summary, there are four separate sources of influence that can affect the individual's judgments of self-efficacy. Bandura (1986) labels these *enactive* (based on the outcome of the individual's own actions); *vicarious* (based on comparisons between the person's performance and the performance of others); *persuasory* (the result of persuasion); and *emotive* (the result of arousal or emotion).

Development of Self-Efficacy.   After watching Superman as a child, did you ever think you could put on a cape and actually fly? Many young children do. They don't have a very good notion of their personal capabilities. Their self-judgment, and their corresponding self-guidance, is less than perfect. As a result, without external controls, they would often be in danger of severely hurting themselves. Instead of imposing on themselves the internal self-judgment "*I* can't do that," they require the external judgment "*You* can't do that."

The sense of personal control over behavior that is essential for judgments of personal efficacy begins to develop very early in infancy. Some of its roots lie in the infant's discovery that looking at the mother makes her look back in return, that smiling or crying draws her attention, and that waving a hand makes her smile. Later, as infants start to move around freely, they begin to learn more about the *effects* of their behaviors—and also more about their *effectiveness* as "behavers." Language provides them with a means to analyze and think about themselves and a means to symbolize and anticipate the consequences of their behaviors.

In the early stages, Bandura (1986) informs us, the most important source of information for the development of self-referential thought is the family. Soon, however, peers begin to increase in importance. Now the behavior of others, as well as their response to our behavior, is factored into our personal estimates of our efficacy. Eventually, schools, too, exert their powerful influences. Teachers tell us a great deal about how well—or how badly—we can do things. So, too, does the response of our classmates—and the response of our parents to the evidence we bring home of our worthwhileness in school, of our intelligence, of our ability to do the things that teachers require.

And so it continues throughout life. In adolescence, we are faced with new tasks, new challenges, and so on throughout adulthood and into old age. At every step, these new challenges require new competencies and new behaviors—and new judgments of personal effectiveness.

Among the judgments of efficacy that are perhaps most important to the individual at all stages of life are those that have to do with our ability to capture the attention, the interest, the affection of others. As Kegan (1982) argues, we strive to *mean* something. We want people to pay attention to us, to like us, to want to be with us, listen to us, do things with us. Put another way, we need to feel that we are capable of eliciting these feelings on the part of others—that we are *socially effective*. Hence the central role of self-efficacy judgments in our lives. And in our happiness.

A Cognitive Approach: Piaget

Psychoanalytic theorists are concerned primarily with personality development; behavioristic theorists emphasize behavior and its consequences; and a third group of theorists focus on the intellectual (cognitive) development of children. **Cognition**, my dictionary informs me, is the art or faculty of knowing. Cognitive theorists are concerned with how we know—that is, with how we obtain, process, and use information. Flavell (1985) suggests there are two main orientations in the study of cognitive processes: the information-processing approach and Piaget's approach. The information-processing approach is concerned mainly with memory processes—processes such as deriving information, abstracting, sorting, organizing, analyzing, and retrieving. Piaget's approach deals with the same basic questions but is more interested in the developmental aspects of cognition. That is, it looks at how the child's interaction with the environment leads to the progressive development of cognitive abilities.

Important aspects of Piaget's theory are introduced briefly in this section. More specific details of the theory, and the contributions of information-processing approaches, are discussed in Chapters 5, 7, 9, and 11, which deal chronologically with the child's cognitive development.

Basic Piagetian Ideas

Piaget was trained as a biologist rather than a psychologist. Consistent with his early training, he began his study of children by posing two of the fundamental questions of biology: (1) What is it that enables organisms to adapt to their environments and survive? and (2) What is the most useful way of classifying living organisms?

The questions of biology can be rephrased and applied to the development of children: (1) What are the characteristics and capabilities of children that allow them to adapt to their environments? and (2) What is the most useful way of classifying or ordering child development? Piaget's answers for these two questions, developed over an extraordinarily prolific career spanning more than six decades (he died in 1980 at the age of 84), are the basis for his theory.

Assimilation and Accommodation Permit Adaptation.
The newborn infant that Piaget describes is in many ways a helpless little organism, unaware that the world out there is real, with no storehouse of thoughts with which to reason, no capacity for intentional behaviors, no more than a few simple reflexes. But infants are much more than this. They are also

remarkable little sensing machines that seem to be naturally predisposed to acquiring and processing a tremendous amount of information. They continually seek out and respond to stimulation. As a result, the sucking, reaching, grasping, and other reflexes that were present at birth become more complex, more coordinated, and, eventually, more purposeful. The process by which this occurs is **adaptation**. And to answer the first of the biology questions as simply as possible, assimilation and accommodation are the processes that make adaptation possible.

Assimilation involves responding to situations in terms of activities or knowledge that have already been learned or that are present at birth. For example, an infant is born with the capability to suck—with a sucking **scheme**, in Piaget's terms (sometimes called *schema*, pluralized as *schemata*). The sucking scheme allows the infant to assimilate a nipple to the behavior of sucking. Similarly, a child who has learned the rules of addition can assimilate a problem such as 2 + 2 (can respond appropriately in terms of previous learning). Often, however, our understanding of the world is insufficient to deal with the present situation. The newborn's sucking scheme is adequate for ordinary nipples but does not work for fingers and toes; the preschooler's understanding of number is sufficient for keeping track of toys but is inadequate for impressing kindergarten teachers. Changes are required in information and behavior. These changes define **accommodation**. In short, assimilation involves reacting on the basis of previous learning and understanding; accommodation involves a change in understanding. The interplay of assimilation and accommodation leads to adaptation. (See Chapter 5 for a further illustration of these concepts.)

Development Can Be Ordered in Stages.
The second of biology's questions asks what is the most useful way of organizing and classifying child development. Piaget's answer is found in his description of the stages through which each child passes. There are four major stages in this description, each marked by strikingly different perceptions of the world and by different adaptations to it. Each is the product of learning that occurred in earlier stages, and each is a preparation for the next stage.

Note that although Piaget's theory is most easily explained and understood in terms of stages, he nevertheless viewed development as a *continuous* process of successive changes. Development does not consist of abrupt, clearly recognizable changes like steps on a

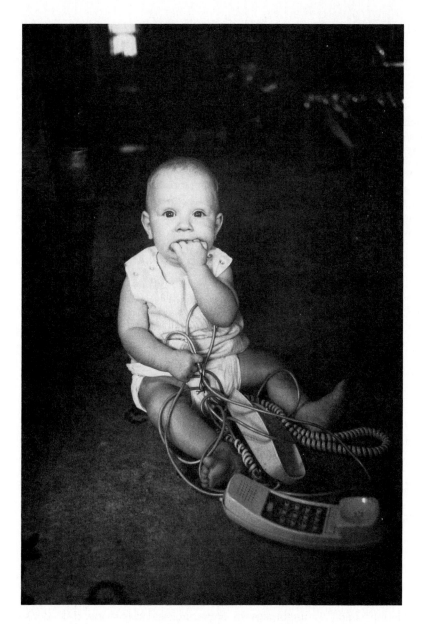

For the sensorimotor infant, the world derives its existence and its meaning from actions that can be performed on it. Thumbs, fingers, entire hands, and even telephones are there to chew, suck, smell, taste, and sometimes look at.

stairway; it is more like a gradual incline. Although cognitive development moves along relatively smoothly, it is useful, and simpler, to divide it into stages. Doing so allows us to compare behaviors and capabilities that are characteristic of different levels, and sometimes leads to discoveries about the processes underlying change. Note, too, that the ages Piaget assigned to each stage are simply average ranges reflecting the behaviors of upper-middle-class Swiss children through the middle of the 20th century. Children from different cultural contexts and with different characteristics sometimes pass through these stages much earlier or much later than Piaget's norms would suggest.

The Stages

Piaget's major stages are summarized very briefly here, and discussed in more detail in Chapters 5, 7, 9, and 11.

Sensorimotor Period.   The first two years are labeled the **sensorimotor period** because during this period the child understands the world largely through immediate action and sensation. For the infant, the world exists *here and now*. It is real only when it is being acted upon and sensed. When the ball is not being chewed, looked at, or touched, it doesn't exist. Only toward the end of the second year do children finally realize that objects are permanent and have an identity of their own — that they continue to exist when they are out of sight. Also, toward the end of the first 2 years, the child begins to acquire language and progresses slowly from a sensorimotor to a more cognitive intelligence (see Chapter 5).

Preoperational Thinking.   Following the acquisition of language, the child enters the period of **preoperational thought** (ages 2–7) — a period marked by an excessive reliance on perception rather than on logic. Piaget's well-known *conservation* experiments illustrate this well. In one of these experiments, for example, children are shown two like-sized glasses that contain equal amounts of water. The experimenter then pours the contents of one glass into a tall, thin tube — or, alternately, into a low, flat dish. Do they still have the same amount, or does one now have more than the other? Preoperational children, relying on the appearance of the two containers, almost invariably think the tall tube has more because it is higher (or less because it is thinner) — or that the flat dish has more because it is "fatter" (or less because it is shorter). Even when they realize that the water could be poured back into the original container so that the two would then be equal, preoperational children continue to rely on perception (on actual appearance) rather than on reasoning (see Chapter 7 for more details).

Concrete Operations.   The major acquisition of the next period of development is the ability to think operationally (ages 7 or 8 to 11 or 12). An **operation** is a thought — what Piaget called an internalized or *mental* action. Mental actions are governed by certain rules of logic. These rules permit the concrete-operations child to laugh at the ridiculous simplicity of a conservation problem. Of course there is the same amount of water in both containers, because none has been added or taken away, one misleading dimension is compensated for by the other (it is taller but thinner), and the act of pouring the water from one container to

the other can be reversed to prove that nothing has changed. The concrete-operations child is capable of this kind of logic. But it is a logic that is tied to real, concrete objects and events. The child is still unable to reason logically about hypothetical situations or events and cannot go from the real to the merely possible or from the possible to the actual. Thought is bound to the real world, the concrete — hence the label **concrete operations** (see Chapter 9).

Formal Operations.   When children finally liberate themselves from the restrictions that have bound them to the concrete world, they enter the last stage of cognitive development — **formal operations**, which is characterized by the ability to manipulate abstract ideas. During this stage, which begins around age 11 or 12 and ends at 14 or 15, the child's thought becomes as logical as it will ever be; it is the culmination of a decade of preparation (see Chapter 11). (See Table 2.7 for a summary of Piaget's stages of cognitive development.)

Piaget in Review

Development, says Piaget, is best described as the emergence of progressively more logical forms of thought that become increasingly effective in freeing children from the present and allowing them to use powerful symbols to understand and to manipulate the environment. According to the theory, the major characteristics of thinking in each of the four developmental stages influence all aspects of children's understanding of the world, including their notions of space, time, number, reality, causality, and so on.

A theory such as Piaget's is considerably easier to evaluate objectively than are the psychoanalytic approaches because it makes specific predictions about how children function intellectually at different age levels. An enormous number of these predictions have been tested by researchers. In general, this research confirms Piaget's initial findings with respect to the order of stages, although it is clear that the ages at which different children reach specific stages can vary considerably.

Also, it appears that Piaget vastly underestimated the information-processing capabilities of infants and young children (Flavell, 1985). However, this is due less to weaknesses in the theory than to Piaget's lack of instruments and procedures sensitive enough to detect

TABLE 2.7

Piaget's Stages of Cognitive Development

Stage	Approximate Age	Some Major Characteristics*
Sensorimotor	0–2 years	Intelligence in action World of the here and now No language, no thought in early stages No notion of objective reality
Preoperational	2–7 years	Egocentric thought Reason dominated by perception Intuitive rather than logical solutions Inability to conserve
Concrete operations	7 to 11–12 years	Ability to conserve Logic of classes and relations Understanding of number Thinking bound to concrete Development of reversibility in thought
Formal operations	11–12 to 14–15 years	Complete generality of thought Propositional thinking Ability to deal with the hypothetical Development of strong idealism

*   Each of these characteristics is detailed in appropriate sections of Chapters 5, 7, 9, and 11.

the infant's cognitive capacities. For example, studies that need to detect the infant's responsiveness to stimulation often use sophisticated instruments that measure changes in heart and respiration rates, movements of the eyeballs, changes in pupil size, brain wave activity, and so on — all instruments not available to Piaget in the 1920s and 1930s.

Another weakness in Piaget's theorizing is that he overestimated the importance of motor activity in the infant's cognitive development and underestimated the importance of perception, especially visual perception (Bullinger, 1985). Others criticize the theory because it says little about individual differences among children, about the factors that might account for those differences, or about what can be done to promote intellectual development. In addition, the theory's language and concepts are sometimes difficult, and it isn't always clear that terms such as *assimilation* and *accommodation* add significantly to our understanding of human behavior. In spite of these weaknesses, Piagetian theory has been the most dominant cognitive developmental theory of this century, and it continues to have a profound influence on current research and practice.

Beyond Piaget

One additional weakness of Piaget's theorizing — and one especially important for our purposes — is that it assumes that development ceases with adolescence. Although Piaget recognized that the abilities that characterize formal operations, the final developmental stage, are not always achieved during adolescence — or even in adulthood — he describes no further developmental stages.

Not surprisingly, a number of other theorists have attempted to elaborate on and extend Piaget's views. Some, often collectively referred to as *neo-Piagetians*, have argued that Piaget's stages should be replaced with more global descriptors, perhaps with broad developmental *levels* rather than specific stages (for example, Fischer & Silvern, 1985; Case, 1985). The stages, they reason, are not very universal, transitions between them are not clear, and there are sometimes wide variations in the responses of a single child to problems that appear to require the same underlying logic. Hence the need for a rethinking of stages.

Others, responding to the lack of any description of adult cognitive development in Piaget's system, have attempted to extend his thinking to the adult years (for example, Arlin, 1975; Basseches, 1984).

A growing number of theorists and researchers, moved perhaps by this age's increasing interest in the processes by which we come to know our *selves* (as knowers, rememberers, doers, and creators of meaning), also have been busy inventing new ways of viewing the processes and the products of lifespan human development. Some of these views are labeled *information processing* (Anderson, 1980; Chi & Glaser, 1980), some deal with *social cognition* (Bandura, 1989), and some are concerned with *self* (or *ego*) development (Kegan, 1982; Loevinger, 1987). All are dealt with in greater detail at appropriate places in this text (see the Index for specific page references).

Biological and Ecological Approaches

Biological approaches to understanding human development stress the importance of innate, predetermined behavior patterns or tendencies. These approaches often stem from research conducted with animals, in which genetic influences are sometimes more readily apparent than they are among humans.

Ecological approaches emphasize the importance of the individual's context—hence the importance of the environment. But for contemporary ecological theorists, it is not so much the context as the interaction between the person's characteristics and specific characteristics of the environment that are important. As Bronfenbrenner (1989) insists, the most useful ecologically oriented model is one that takes the environment into account jointly with the person, and that looks for processes to explain changes in development—hence the label *process–person–context* model.

This section looks at Bowlby's biologically based approach to human development; at sociobiology, which attempts to uncover the biological basis of social behaviors; at Vygotsky's cultural-historical approach;

and at Bronfenbrenner's ecological systems theory, which emphasizes the importance of the accommodation between changing human beings and changing aspects of their environments.

Ethology and Bowlby's Attachment Theory

The importance of biology (of heredity) in determining animal behavior has long been accepted. I accept without question that my English setter is good at sniffing out certain potent-smelling birds precisely because she *is* an English setter. I would not expect the same behavior of Id, our rather useless, but aptly named, cat. Even if their early experiences had been identical, I still would not expect Id to enjoy walking at my heels or to drool at the prospect of a cold swim in a reedy pond. You see, we know that many of the behaviors and habits characteristic of nonhuman animal species are not acquired solely through experience. A moth does not fly into a flame because it has learned to do so; dead moths don't fly. We can therefore assume that the attraction light has for a moth, like the overpowering urge of a goose to go south or a salmon to swim up a specific river, is the result of inherited tendencies.

Are we, in at least some ways, like moths and salmon? If so, what are our flames? Our rivers?

Ethologists (scientists whose principal concern is with studying behavior in natural situations) think that yes, we are a little like moths. And although the flames that entice us might be less obvious than those that draw the moth, they are perhaps no less powerful.

Lorenz's (1952) studies of imprinting in ducks and geese were among the first to draw parallels between inherited animal behavior and humans. **Imprinting** is the tendency of newly hatched geese (or chickens, ducks, and related birds) to follow the first moving object they see during a **critical period**, which occurs shortly after hatching. The period is *critical* because exposure to the same moving object (a *releaser*) before or after this period does not ordinarily result in the appearance of the same imprinted behavior (see Figure 2.6).

Although the search for imprinted behaviors among humans has not led to the discovery of behaviors as obvious as "following" among geese, some theorists argue that ethology's emphasis on genetic contributions to behavior is important, especially when

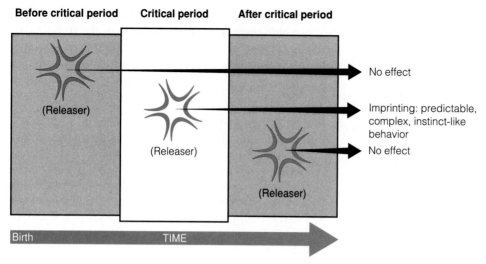

Figure 2.6 A model of imprinting. Under appropriate environmental conditions, exposure to a releaser during the critical period leads to imprinting, which is manifested in predictable behaviors in response to specific environmental conditions. Imprinting does not occur if a releaser is not present or if the releaser is presented too early or too late.

human social relationships are also taken into account (Hinde, 1989). Other theorists, such as John Bowlby (1979, 1980, 1982), believe that there are important links between the findings of ethologists and the development of attachment between mother and infant. Bowlby's research with young infants suggests we have a natural (inherited) tendency to form emotional bonds with our mothers or with some other permanent caregiver. Such bonds, Bowlby argues, would clearly have been important for the infant's survival in a less civilized age. The need for them is evident in the infant's attempts to maintain physical contact, to cling, and to stay in visual contact with the mother (Bowlby, 1969). It is also apparent in the effects of separating mother and infant—effects that are marked by "emotional distress and personality disturbance, including anxiety, anger, depression, and emotional detachment" (Bowlby, 1979, p. 127).

In Bowlby's view, early attachment to a mother (or some other permanent caregiver) is so crucial that in its absence, the infant is likely to suffer emotional problems and to experience great difficulty in establishing emotional bonds with others. A number of studies reviewed by Ainsworth (1979) provide tentative evidence that infants who are securely attached to their mothers often have an advantage over what are termed "anxiously attached" infants (see Chapter 6).

Although researchers have not identified specific critical periods during which a mother (or other caregiver) *must* be present for the infant to form strong attachment bonds, many speak of a **sensitive period**. According to Bowlby, this sensitive period spans the first 6 months of life. Although attachment behaviors (clinging, looking) tend to be directed indiscriminately toward anyone in the early months, by the age of 6 months, infants who have been given the opportunity to do so will have formed strong bonds with their mothers. Abrupt disruptions of these bonds after the age of 6 months can be extremely distressing (see Chapter 6). However, in the normal course of development, the bonds become less intense as the child matures. Although the mother usually remains the dominant figure until well into the third year of life, by then the child will experience progressively less anxiety during her temporary absences and will have formed important attachments with others.

Bowlby's Attachment Theory in Review

Although Bowlby's ethological theory provides an intriguing biological explanation for mother–infant attachment, it is not without critics. Many feel that he has overemphasized the role of the mother and neglected that of the father. But, as Ainsworth (1979) points out, Bowlby has emphasized the role of the mother primarily because she is typically the principal caregiver. In fact, his theory is quite compatible with the belief that in the absence of the mother, the father or some other caregiver may substitute for her.

A more serious criticism of Bowlby's theory concerns his belief that failure to form strong attachments during infancy is related to later adjustment problems and to difficulties in establishing loving relationships in adulthood. If this were always true, children who are raised without contact with their mothers for prolonged periods (in institutions or even in day-care centers or foster homes) should experience problems. Research suggests, however, that this is not the case. For example, in a longitudinal study that compared home-raised infants with those raised in day-care centers, Kagan, Kearsley, and Zelazo (1978) found no systematic differences between these two groups even on measures of attachment to their mothers.

What these criticisms point out most clearly is that the concepts and the language of animal imprinting are not always entirely appropriate for understanding human behavior. Human attachment is not as predictable as is "following" in geese; nor is there as definite a *critical* period during which the appropriate stimulus must be presented if the behavior is to appear. In addition, the implications of not forming an attachment bond with a mother (or other caregiver) early in life are not as clear for an infant as for a gosling. The gosling that fails to imprint on its mother is likely to become lost and perish; our infants often fare better. (See Chapter 6 for a more detailed discussion of attachment and bonding.)

Sociobiology

Bowlby is only one of a large number of theorists interested in applying knowledge of biology (and, more specifically, of genetics and evolution) to an understanding of human development and behavior. A group of ethologically oriented scientists are attempting to explain the development of all social behavior in terms of genes. These researchers call themselves *sociobiologists*. Led by such people as E. O. Wilson (1975, 1976), they argue that science has neglected the role of heredity in

determining many of the behaviors that we attribute to our environments and upbringing. **Sociobiology** is defined as "the systematic study of the biological basis of all social behavior" (Wilson, 1975, p. 4). Its most striking and controversial belief is that human social behavior is the product of a lengthy evolutionary history — that it is therefore genetically based. We are altruistic, sociobiologists argue, because helping others contributes to the group's survival. In much the same way as altruism might be explained by reference to the "selfishness" of genes (it is, after all, genetic material that survives), sociobiological theory can be used to explain maternal love, sexual mores, aggression, spitefulness — indeed, the entire range of human social behaviors.

Sociobiology in Review

Not surprisingly, sociobiological theory has provoked considerable controversy and reaction. Critics have been quick to point out that the theory is highly speculative and is based on a handful of assumptions that not only have not been tested but are probably untestable in any case (Eckland, 1977). As Mazur (1977) notes, the theory is premised on the assumption that behaviors occur because they increase the genetic survival of a group (or the probability that genetic material will survive). How do we know this is so? Because the behavior occurred. Why did the behavior occur? Because it increases average genetic survival. This type of circular reasoning offers no hope of proof. To validate the theory, it would be necessary to establish the presence of "altruistic" genes, for example, by some means unrelated to the behaviors these genes are intended to explain. That has yet to be done.

This does not mean that genetics are therefore irrelevant to understanding human behavior. In fact, as is made clear in Chapter 3, our genes are fundamentally involved in everything we do. What it does mean is that science has not yet succeeded in showing that specific genes, or combinations of genes, directly cause specific individual behaviors. The fundamental error in sociobiological theory has to do with level of explanation. Evolutionary theory, the basis of sociobiology, is designed to explain variation at broad zoological levels such as classes, orders, families, or species (Plomin, 1987). It can rarely predict individual behaviors.

Culture and Ecology

Ethologists (and sociobiologists) emphasize the importance of biological or genetic contributions to development; ecologically oriented theorists stress the importance of culture or context. However, the differences between ethological and ecological positions frequently have more to do with different emphases than with different beliefs. Most theorists readily accept that both ecological (cultural or environmental) influences and biological tendencies are intimately involved in determining human development. In Hinde's (1989) words, "the futility of a dichotomy between the biological and social aspects of human nature is now generally recognized." It is still true, however, that many theories continue to emphasize one at the expense of the other. Vygotsky and Bronfenbrenner present approaches that are, in some ways, a synthesis of the two orientations.

Vygotsky's Cultural-Historical Approach

The Russian psychologist L. S. Vygotsky was a major force in Soviet psychology by the time he was 28; that was in 1924. Sadly, 10 years later, he died of tuberculosis. But many of his ideas, old as they may be, still seem fresh and important.

Among the most central of Vygotsky's ideas is the belief that human development is fundamentally different from the development of animals. Why? Because humans can use tools and symbols; as a result, they create cultures. And cultures have a vitality, a life of their own. They grow and change; and they exert a very powerful influence on their members. They determine the end result of competent development—the sorts of things that its members have to learn, the ways they should think, the things they are most likely to believe. As Bronfenbrenner (1989) puts it, we are not only culture producing, but culture-produced.

Several underlying themes run through Vygotsky's theorizing. One, just mentioned, has to do with the centrality of culture in human development; a second deals with the functions of language; and a third relates to the developing child's relationship with the environment—a relationship Vygotsky described as the *zone of proximal growth*. We look at each of these briefly.

Culture. Culture, Vygotsky insists, is what most clearly separates us from animals. It is the manifestation of our ability to think and to invent symbol systems (Vygotsky, 1986). It permits humans to have a history, and perhaps a future as well.

There is an important distinction, says Vygotsky, between *elementary* mental functions and *higher* mental functions. Elementary functions are our natural, unlearned capacities. They are evident in the newborn's ability to attend to human sounds and to discriminate among them. They are apparent in the ability to remember the smell of the mother, or in the capacity to coo and gurgle, and to scream and cry. In time, however, these elementary capacities are gradually transformed into higher mental functions—that is, they change from natural, unlearned functions to more sophisticated, learned behaviors and capacities. This transformation, which is absolutely fundamental to human development, is made possible through language.

The Role of Language. Language, after all, is what makes thinking possible, Vygotsky asserts (see Wertsch, 1985). During the preverbal stage of development, the child's intelligence is much like that of, say, an ape. It is purely natural, purely practical—elementary, in other words. But language changes all that.

Vygotsky describes three forms of language that develop sequentially; each has different functions. The first, *social* (or external) *speech*, is common until around the age of 3. The most primitive form of speech, its function is largely to control the behavior of others (as in "I want candy!") or to express simple concepts.

Egocentric speech dominates the child's life between ages 3 and approximately 7. This type of speech is a sort of bridge between the social speech of the preceding period and the more internal (inner) speech of the next period. Egocentric speech often serves to control the child's own behavior, but is often spoken out loud. For example, young children often talk to themselves as they are trying to do something: "Push. Okay, now turn. Turn. Turn . . . push . . ."

Inner speech is our private self-talk—what James (1892) called our stream of consciousness. According to Vygotsky, inner speech is what makes thought possible. It is the basis of all higher mental functioning (see Table 2.8).

Zone of Proximal Growth. Language is a cultural invention. It is one of the most important ways in which the environment, the child's context, influences and shapes the course of development. For

TABLE 2.8

Vygotsky's Theory of the Role of Language

Stage	Function
Social (external) (*to age 3*)	Controls the behavior of others; expresses simple thoughts and emotions
Egocentric (*3–7*)	Bridge between external and inner speech; serves to control own behavior, but spoken out loud
Inner (*7 onward*)	Self-talk; makes possible the direction of our thinking and our behavior; involved in all higher mental functioning

Vygotsky, development is a function of the interaction between culture and the child's basic biological capacities and maturational timetables. But, insisted Vygotsky, it is the environmental context (the culture) that is most important—not biological maturation (Valsiner, 1987). Development (or growth) takes place when environmental opportunities and demands are appropriate for the child. In a sense, the environment *instructs* the child in the ways of development. But the instruction is effective only if the child's biological maturation and present developmental level are sufficiently advanced. For every child, says Vygotsky, there is a zone of proximal growth—a sort of potential for development (Belmont, 1989). Demands that are in advance of this zone—in other words, that are beyond the child's capacities—are ineffective in promoting growth. Similarly, demands that are too simple are wasteful.

In summary, Vygotsky's developmental theory underscores the role of culture, and especially of its most important invention, language. The zone of proximal development—sort of a label for developmental potential—expresses Vygotsky's belief in the interdependence between the processes of child development and the resources that cultures provide (Valsiner, 1987). A second approach that also emphasizes the importance of context–person interaction is Bronfenbrenner's.

Bronfenbrenner's Ecological Systems Theory

Psychological, biological, and social systems are *open* systems, we noted earlier in this chapter. This means that their existence depends on interaction and that they are constantly subject to change as a function of interaction. The Piagetian infant, born with a small number of reflexes, adapts and changes as a function of interacting with the environment—in Piaget's terms, as a result of assimilating and accommodating. It is infant–environment interaction that results in the notion that objects are permanent, that symbols represent, that quantities can be added and subtracted, that a fine and elegant logic governs physics and chemistry.

Bronfenbrenner refers to the interaction of the individual with the environment as the *ecology of human development* (also the title of his 1979 book). Here is the cornerstone of his theory, expressed in his own words in what he labels *definition I* (Bronfenbrenner, 1989):

> The ecology of human development is the scientific study of the progressive, mutual accommodation, through the life course, between an active, growing human being, and the changing properties of the immediate settings in which the developing person lives, as this process is affected by the relations between these settings, and by the larger contexts in which the settings are embedded. (p. 188)

The emphasis in this theory is clearly on understanding development as an interactive function of the person and the environment. That is, Bronfenbrenner's ecological system is not *out there* in the environment, but is to be found in interactions. Hence the Bronfenbrenner model has three components: the person, the context in which behavior occurs, and the processes that account for developmental change. It is, in Bronfenbrenner's words, a *process–person–context* model. And development is simply the processes through which "properties of the person and the environment interact to produce constancy and change in the characteristics of the person" (p. 191).

One of the basic principles of Bronfenbrenner's ecological systems theory is that differences in intellectual performance between different groups are a function of interacting with different cultures or subcultures, which may be characterized by different types of cognitive processes. It follows that a person's cognitive competence is always culturally relative. A very intelligent, well-adapted native of the Cameroon jungle would not necessarily function very intelligently in downtown Chicago. But then a Chicago lawyer might quickly lose her bearings—and perhaps her marbles—in the Cameroon jungle.

Not only are we influenced by our contexts, but we also influence them in turn. If infant Ronald cries more than is expected, he may change some significant aspects of the environment with which he interacts. His mother may come running sooner than she otherwise would; his nurse might become more irritable, more impatient; his father might pay more, or less, attention to him; his siblings might openly resent his intrusion in the family; even the dog might be annoyed. And each of these changing aspects of context might, in turn, alter Ronald's behavior. That his mother runs to soothe his cries might encourage his crying even more. But now, perhaps the mother senses what is happening and comes more slowly, more reluctantly, and again the interaction changes. Thus the mother's personality and her beliefs about child rearing interact with Ronald's personality, and his behavior, in a constantly changing, *open ecological* system. There is always an interplay between the person's characteristics and those of the environment, says Bronfenbrenner: "The one cannot be defined without reference to the other" (p. 225). He also makes the point that some characteristics (termed *developmentally instigative*) are more important than others in influencing contexts. Temperament, size or appearance, age, sex, race, developmental handicaps, and many other factors tend to provoke important reactions—hence changes—in context. These, in turn, affect the individual.

One of Bronfenbrenner's important contributions to the study of child development lies in his description of the parameters of the context in which development occurs. The ecological system of which he speaks consists of interactions with four different levels of context. From nearest (most proximal) to most remote, these are the microsystem, the mesosystem, the exosystem, and the macrosystem.

- **Microsystem**. Interactions that occur at an immediate, face-to-face level define the microsystem. The complex patterns of behaviors, roles, and relationships within the home, the school, the peer group, the workplace, the playground, and so on, are the microsystem component of the individual's ecological system. Most important within the microsystem are the personality characteristics, the attitudes, the customary behaviors, and so on, of *other people* in these contexts. The interaction of Ronald's crying with the behaviors of mother, father, siblings, and dog illustrates what is meant by a microsystem. Everybody in a microsystem influences everybody else.

- **Mesosystem**. In turn, microsystems may influence one another in important ways. For example, the home does not exist in isolation from other elements of the microsystem. How parents treat children is influenced by schools, by teachers, perhaps by the church. Similarly, homes and churches influence schools, and schools' treatment of children reflects some of these influences. Interactions between elements of the microsystem that include the developing person define what is meant by the mesosystem.

- **Exosystem**. Interactions between an element of the microsystem that ordinarily includes the developing child and an element of the wider context that does not include the child define the exosystem. For example, interactions between the school and such formal trappings of contemporary contexts as legal or welfare systems, or between the home and federal taxation departments, are exosystem interactions that might have important influences on the child. Also, interactions among less formal contexts such as fishing buddies or colleagues and mother or father are potentially significant exosystem interactions.

- **Macrosystem**. All the interactive systems—micro-, meso-, and exo-—that characterize cultures (or subcultures) define the macrosystem. Macrosystems are describable in terms of beliefs, values, customs, expected behaviors, social roles, status assignments, life-styles, religions, and so on, as these are reflected in interactions among systems. In Bronfenbrenner's (1989) words, the macrosystem "may be thought of as a societal blueprint for a particular culture, subculture, or other broader social context" (p. 228). Macrosystems may be identified in terms of such things as common beliefs, values, resources, goals, life-styles, and ambitions.

Macrosystems can change over time, and sometimes these changes are very significant for the developing individual. For example, within the last few decades of this century, there have been profound changes in family employment patterns (from one to two wage-earners), in family structure (from two- to one-parent families), in child-rearing styles (from home-rearing to other child-care options), in age of marriage (from younger to older), in age of childbearing (also from younger to older), in range of expected school attendance (from quasi-compulsory kindergarten to quasi-expected postsecondary). Clearly, many of these macrosystem changes impact directly on the microsystems of which the child is a part—the family, the home, the school. (See Table 2.9.)

Bronfenbrenner's Ecological Systems Theory in Review

Although most contemporary developmental theorists pay lip service to the importance of taking context, person, and interaction into account, many researchers continue to operate within more traditional models. Two such models have dominated much of our thinking and research. One says that the causes of developmental change are to be found primarily within the individual; the other insists that the individual's environment is a more important cause of change. It is, of course, the old nature–nurture debate (about which we say more in the next chapter).

The model that underlies our thinking is tremendously important to our research and our conclusions. One model says that if Johnny turns out to be an unmanageable scoundrel, we should look for the cause and the explanation in his temperament and his personality characteristics; the other says we should look to his environment. But neither of these models says that we should look at how Johnny's characteristics influence his environment, and at how, in turn, his environment influences him. Neither insists that the cause is to be found in the progressive changes in the *interactions* that take place between Johnny and his al-

---

TABLE 2.9

Levels of Context in Bronfenbrenner's Ecological (Open) Systems Theory

Level	Type of Interaction
Microsystem	Child in immediate, face-to-face interaction
Mesosystem	Relationships between two or more microsystems
Exosystem	Linkages and relationships between two or more settings, one of which does not include the child
Macrosystem	The totality of all other systems, evident in the beliefs, the options, the life-styles, the values, the mores of a culture or subculture

---

coholic mother, his overworked and indifferent teachers, his peers (the microsystem). Neither suggests that the aborted love affair between Johnny's mother and his tee-ball coach is of consequence (the mesosystem). Neither is concerned with interactions that might have occurred between Johnny's mother and her employer leading to a reduction in her pay and chronic disgruntlement (the exosystem). Neither asks the researcher to look at how society's encouragement of the changing structure of the family impact on Johnny's well-being (the macrosystem). That they do not ask these questions is a weakness of some of our traditional approaches to understanding child development; that Bronfenbrenner's ecological systems theory does pose these questions is among its strengths.

But that is also among its weaknesses. Explanations based on ecological systems theory require the analysis of an almost infinite number of highly complex interactions. Identifying these interactions, observing and quantifying them, sorting out relationships among them, teasing out reciprocal influences between individuals and their micro-, meso-, and exosystems, and determining how changing cultural values and options impinge on the individual—these are difficult tasks. But perhaps if we chew at them long enough, we may find that they are not impossible. Bronfenbrenner's ecological systems theory at least suggests where we should begin.

Humanistic Approaches

Had I spoken of Piaget or Freud, of Skinner or sociology, of ethology or ecology in my grandmother's kitchen, the old lady would have listened politely. She was always polite. But in the end, she would probably have said, "That's theory. It's all very nice, but what about Frank?" Why Frank? Simply because he was a unique child—as we all were (or are). And although there is little doubt that Freud, Skinner, and Piaget might each have had something very intelligent, and perhaps even useful, to say about Frank's habits of stealing chicken eggs, writing poetry, and dancing little jigs in mudholes, they would have been hard pressed to convince my grandmother that they knew more about Frank than she did. My grandmother was a humanist.

Humanistic psychologists are concerned with the uniqueness of the individual. A prevalent humanistic notion is that it is impossible to describe the environment, much less a person, in a truly meaningful way because the important features of the environment are particular to each individual. To understand the behavior of others, one must attempt to perceive the world as they see it—from the perspective of their knowledge, experiences, goals, and aspirations (Rogers, 1951). Such an orientation does not imply that it is impossible to understand human nature or human behavior generally, although it renders the task more difficult. It does imply, however, that understanding human behavior in a general sense may be of relatively little value for understanding the behavior of one person. As noted earlier, the individual is one, not an average. There is no average person.

Humanistic concerns with the uniqueness of the individual do not lend themselves easily to the formulation of theories that are both highly specific and widely applicable. But they do suggest an attitude toward people, and toward the process of developing, that is of tremendous potential value to those concerned with human welfare. Humanistic orientations tend to personalize (to humanize?) our attitudes toward others; they restore some of the dynamism of the developmental process that our more static and more complex theories might otherwise remove.

Abraham Maslow (1970), one of the individuals closely associated with the humanistic movement in psychology, was primarily concerned with the development of the healthy personality. Fundamental to his position is a belief that we are moved by two systems of needs (Maslow, 1970). The **basic needs** are physiological (food, drink) and psychological (security, love, esteem). The **metaneeds** are higher-level needs. They manifest themselves in our desire to know, in our appreciation of truth and beauty, and in our tendencies toward growth and fulfillment (termed *self-actualization*) (see Figure 2.7). Alternately, these two groups of needs are sometimes labeled *growth needs* (metaneeds) and *deficiency needs* (basic needs). The basic needs are termed deficiency needs because when they are not satisfied, individuals engage in behaviors designed to remedy this lack of satisfaction. (For example, hunger represents a deficiency that can be satisfied by eating.) The metaneeds are termed growth needs because activities that relate to them do not fulfill a lack but lead toward growth.

These needs are assumed to be hierarchically arranged in the sense that the metaneeds will not be attended to unless the basic needs are reasonably well satisfied. In other words, we pay attention to beauty, truth, and the development of our potential when we are no longer hungry and unloved (at least not terribly so). Put more simply, hunger for food is more compelling than hunger for knowledge. But keep studying—this is important.

Chief among Maslow's metaneeds, and most important for understanding human development, is **self-actualization**. By his own admission, the term is difficult to define (Maslow, 1970). He suggests that it is characterized by the absence of "neurosis, psychopathic personality, psychosis, or strong tendencies in these directions" (1970, p. 150). On the more positive side, he claims that self-actualized people "may be loosely described as [making] full use and exploitation of talents, capacities, potentialities, etc." (p. 150). And

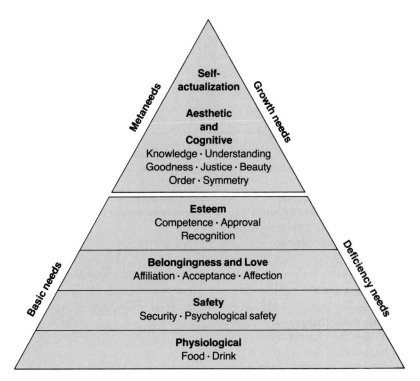

Figure 2.7 Maslow's hierarchy of needs.

the reinforcement—the satisfaction associated with true self-actualization—comes from within rather than without. In contrast, satisfaction of lower-level needs, such as those associated with *esteem*, is associated with external sources of reinforcement (approval and recognition). Using this loose definition, Maslow searched among 3,000 college students and found only one person he considered to be actualized (although there were several dozen "potentials").

Self-actualization is best described as a process that guides the direction of development rather than as a state we can attain. The view that people are directed by a need *to become* (to actualize) and that the process of actualization is essentially positive and self-directed presents an important contrast to the more mechanistic, more passive, and less inner-directed theories that we have considered thus far. And although humanistic theory does not address itself to the specifics of the developmental process, it might in the end serve to explain facts that are not easily explained by other theories.

A Final Word About Theories

We began this chapter by insisting that facts and theories are not worlds apart in terms of "truthfulness"— that theories are intended as explanations of facts. From these explanations, scientists strive for understanding, for prediction, and sometimes for control. But theories do more than explain facts. As Scarr (1985) notes, they guide our invention of "facts" and give them meaning. Theories lead us to accept certain things as true — specifically, those things that fit our beliefs and expectations. By the same token, theories also lead us to ignore contradictory or apparently irrelevant observations.

Table 2.10 summarizes the approaches to developmental theory discussed in this chapter. As so often happens, history will inform us later about the fruitfulness of these approaches.

TABLE 2.10

Approaches to Developmental Theory

Approach	Representative Theorist	Major Assumptions (theoretical beliefs)	Key Terms
Psychoanalytic	Freud	Individual is motivated by instinctual urges that are primarily sexual and aggressive.	Id, ego, superego, psychosexual, fixation, regression
	Erikson	Child progresses through developmental stages by resolving conflicts that arise from a need to adapt to the sociocultural environment.	Competence, social environment, developmental tasks, psychosocial
Behavioristic	Watson, Skinner	Changes in behavior are a function of reinforcement and punishment.	Reinforcement, punishment, stimuli, responses
Social cognitive	Bandura	Observational learning leads to developmental change; our ability to symbolize and to anticipate the consequences of our behavior is fundamental, as are our estimates of our self-efficacy.	Imitation, modeling, eliciting, self-efficacy
Cognitive	Piaget	Child develops cognitive skills through active interaction with the environment.	Stages, assimilation, accommodation, adaptation, scheme
Biological	Bowlby, Wilson	Social behaviors have a biological basis understandable in evolutionary terms. The formation of attachment bonds is one example.	Attachment bonds, biological fitness, survival value, altruistic genes, sensitive period
Ecological systems	Bronfenbrenner	The ecology of development is the study of accommodations between a person and the environment, taking the changing characteristics of each into account.	Open systems, ecology, microsystem, mesosystem, exosystem, macrosystem
Humanistic	Maslow, Rogers	All individuals are unique but strive toward the fullest development of their potential.	Self, positive growth, metaneeds, self-actualization

Main Points

1. A theory is a collection of statements intended to organize and explain important observations. Theories are best evaluated in terms of usefulness rather than truthfulness. They should reflect "facts," be understandable, and be useful for predicting events as well as for explaining the past.

2. Models are metaphors that underlie theories. The organismic model describes people as active, functioning biological organisms; the mechanistic view stresses the reactive, machinelike predictability of human functioning; the contextual model emphasizes the influence of historical variables, life events, and other aspects of context.

3. Freud's theory is based on the assumption that among the most important causes of behavior are deep-seated, unconscious forces that can be discovered and understood through techniques such as free association, dream analysis, and the analysis of childhood experiences.

4. The newborn child is all libido (instinctual urges). The label *id* is applied to the level of personality concerned solely with the gratification of urges — urges that are primarily sexual in Freud's view. Conflict between the id (instinctual urges) and reality develops the *ego* — the aspect of personality concerned with finding ways for the id to satisfy its basic urges. Later in the course of development, the *superego* forms as an offshoot of the ego. It represents social and cultural taboos and restrictions that are imposed on an individual's instinctual urges and is often called *conscience*.

5. Freud describes development as a progression through five stages: the oral, the anal, the phallic, a period of latency, and the genital stage. Each is differentiated from the others primarily by the areas of the child's body that are the principal sources of sexual gratification at that time.

6. Freud's theory reflects the sexual repression and the masculine domination of the Victorian era in which he lived. For this reason, and also because of its scientific and methodological weaknesses, it has sometimes been severely criticized. However, its monumental contributions to the development of psychological thinking have also been acknowledged.

7. According to Erikson's psychosocial, ego-oriented theory of child development, the child progresses through a series of stages characterized by basic conflicts, the resolution of which results in the appearance of new capabilities and attitudes. Erikson's stages, in order, are trust versus mistrust, autonomy versus shame and doubt, initiative versus guilt, industry versus inferiority, identity versus identity diffusion, intimacy versus isolation, generativity versus self-absorption, and integrity versus despair.

8. Havighurst describes development in terms of a series of requirements that are placed on individuals by their society. These provide a rough index of developmental maturity.

9. Behavioristic (learning-theory) approaches to development focus on immediate behavior and on environmental forces that affect behavior. The most important concepts for these theories are conditioning and imitation.

10. In classical conditioning, a neutral stimulus (conditioned stimulus, or CS) is paired with a second stimulus (unconditioned stimulus, or UCS) that reliably brings about a response (unconditioned response, or UCR) until presentation of the CS by itself is sufficient to bring about the response (now termed a conditioned response, or CR).

11. Operant conditioning changes the probability of a response occurring as a function of its consequences. A reinforcer is whatever increases the probability of a response occurring; reinforcement is the effect of a reinforcer. Positive reinforcers increase the probability of a response as a function of being added to a situation; negative reinforcers have the same effect when they are taken away from a situation. Punishment, unlike negative reinforcement, does not ordinarily increase the probability of a response, but has the opposite effect. It might add something unpleasant or remove something pleasant.

12. Observational learning theories explain socialization as a function of imitating models (which can be symbolic as well as actual people). Bandura describes four processes involved in observational learning: attentional processes (wherein important aspects of the model's behaviors are attended to), retentional processes (wherein the observer mentally represents, in images or words, what has been observed and stores it in memory), motor reproduction processes (which make possible the performance of the observed behavior), and motivational processes (which lead to actual performance rather than simply acquisition without performance).

13. Three manifestations of observational learning include the learning of new responses (modeling effect), the suppression or reappearance of deviant behaviors (inhibitory–disinhibitory effect), and the emission of behaviors similar but not identical to that of the model (eliciting effect).

14. Self-referent thought has to do with our estimates of our selves, our capabilities, our effectiveness. *Self-efficacy* refers specifically to judgments about personal effectiveness. Notions of self-efficacy are important in determining the behaviors we undertake, the amount of effort we are willing to expend on a given task, and our feelings about ourselves.

15. Judgments of self-efficacy derive from four sources: enactive (based on the outcome of our own behaviors), vicarious (based on comparisons between the self and similar others), persuasory (the result of persuading, cajoling, pleading, bribing by others), and emotive (the function of arousal or high emotion).

16. Piaget's theory describes cognitive development (*cognition* refers to knowing or understanding) in terms of adaptation resulting from interaction with the environment through using activities already in the child's repertoire (assimilation) and changing activities to conform to environmental demands (accommodation).

17. Piaget describes the child's cognitive development in terms of sequential progression through four major stages: sensorimotor (world of here and now; intelligence in action), preoperational (egocentric thought; perception-dominated; intuitive rather than logical), concrete operations (logical thought operations applied to real objects and events), and formal (propositional thinking; potentially logical thought; hypothetical, idealistic reasoning).

18. Biological approaches to development look at the role of biology (heredity) in determining development and behavior; ecological approaches emphasize the importance of interaction in changing contexts; ethologists are biologically oriented scientists who study behavior in natural situations.

19. Bowlby has adapted some of the concepts and principles of ethology (specifically, of imprinting) to explain the development and importance of the attachment bond that forms between mothers (or other principal caregivers) and their infants.

20. Sociobiologists are concerned with the biological basis of social behavior and try to explain behaviors such as altruism and aggression in terms of their survival value for a related group of individuals.

21. Bronfenbrenner's ecological systems theory looks at the interaction and progressive mutual accommodation between the growing child and changing environmental contexts. It is a process–person–context model where context is described in terms of four levels: the microsystem (the child in face-to-face interaction with, for example, family members or teachers), the mesosystem (interactions among contexts in the child's microsystem such as, for example, between parents and teachers), the exosystem (interactions between one of the child's microsystem contexts and another context with which the child does not ordinarily interact), and the macrosystem (the totality of all contexts relevant to the child's life, and identifiable in terms of the major characteristics of a culture or a cultural subgroup).

22. Humanistic theory is concerned with the uniqueness of the individual child and with the development of human potential. Maslow is an important representative of humanistic concerns.

23. People are incredibly more complicated than this chapter might suggest, but they are easier to understand within the context of the more organized systems provided here than within the context of our more naive intuitions.

Further Readings

Freud and Piaget were voluminous writers. It is often easier and sometimes more valuable to use secondary sources for information about their theories. The following are particularly useful starting points:

Baldwin, A. L. (1980). *Theories of child development* (2nd ed.). New York: John Wiley.

Brill, A. A. (Ed.). (1938). *The basic writings of Sigmund Freud*. New York: Random House.

Ryce-Menuhin, J. (1988). *The self in early childhood*. London: Free Association Books. (See especially Chapter 11 for an account of Freud.)

Singer, D. G., & Revenson, T. A. (1979). *A Piaget primer: How a child thinks*. New York: International Universities Press.

Thomas, R. M. (1992). *Comparing theories of child development* (3rd ed.). Belmont, CA: Wadsworth.

Wadsworth, B. J. (1989). *Piaget's theory of cognitive and affective development* (4th ed.). New York: Longman.

The first of the next two references is an excellent summary of Bandura's social-cognitive theory. The second is a fascinating and insightful view of the theorist and a remarkably clear exposition of his beliefs:

Bandura, A. (1986). *Social foundations of thought and action: A social cognitive theory*. Englewood Cliffs, N.J.: Prentice-Hall.

Evans, R. I. (1989). *Albert Bandura: The man and his ideas—a dialogue*. New York: Praeger.

For a clear account of Vygotsky's life and theories, see:

Kozulin, A. (1990). *Vygotsky's psychology: A biography of ideas*. New York: Harvester Wheatsheaf.

Maslow's humanistic psychology is well explained in:

Maslow, A. H. (1970). *Motivation and personality* (2nd ed.). New York: Harper & Row.

An excellent introduction to the role of biology in development is presented by:

Hofer, M. A. (1981). *The roots of human behavior: An introduction to the psychobiology of early development*. San Francisco: W. H. Freeman.

For more detailed information about Bronfenbrenner's ecological systems theory, see either the following book or, for a more recent account, the relevant chapter in the Vasta book referenced below:

Bronfenbrenner, U. (1979). *The ecology of human development*. Cambridge, MA: Harvard University Press.

Loevinger's book is an excellent general summary and comparison of most of the major theoretical approaches discussed here. The collection edited by Vasta is an authoritative exposition of important current theoretical positions in child development:

Loevinger, J. (1987). *Paradigms of personality*. New York: W. H. Freeman.

Vasta, R. (Ed.). *Annals of child development (Vol. 6)*. Greenwich, CT: JAI Press.

CHAPTER 3

Genetics and Context

All the goodness of a good egg
cannot make up for the badness
of a bad one.

Charles Anderson Dana,
The Making of a Newspaperman

My grandmother once made an omelette that proved Charles Anderson Dana right. Most of her eggs were fine, one wasn't, and the resulting omelette was horrible. It was as though the bad egg won.

An omelette is a useful analogy for this chapter, which deals with the *nature–nurture* puzzle. The nature–nurture puzzle is a little like the omelette puzzle.

An omelette, you see, is not just eggs, milk, salt, pepper, and whatever else you might put into it. It's all of these things mixed together *and cooked*. Put another way, an omelette results from the *interaction* of a mixture of ingredients. Mixing and heating is what makes the interaction possible.

We can say something quite similar about heredity and environment: Heredity is a little like the ingredients of an omelette, and the environment acts a little like an oven. Different people inherit different ingredients. There are good eggs and bad eggs — or at least different eggs. So our omelettes are not likely to be exactly the same.

This Chapter

Unfortunately, the situation with **heredity** and **environment** is far more complex than might be suggested by this simple analogy; the analogy does not *solve* the nature–nurture puzzle.

How does science begin to solve a puzzle such as this? How does it determine what mixture of ingredients and what conditions of heat and other circumstances will make the very best omelette?

One argument runs something like this: For those human characteristics that are determined primarily by genetic factors, changes in the environment should have little effect. By the same token, vastly different environments should have profound effects on characteristics that depend largely on nurture. Thus eye color should not change whether a person is reared by natives

in the Amazon jungle, by Ihalmiuts in Greenland, or by Americans in Boston. But the individual's speech will be vastly different in each of these environments.

One way, then, of beginning to sort out and understand the interaction of heredity and environment is to look at individuals with similar genetic backgrounds — say, identical twins, whose genetic similarity is perfect. Investigators can examine the outcomes of the developmental process when each member of the pair is raised in a highly similar environment (twins who are brought up in the same home) or in a highly different environment (twins who are reared apart). Another possibility is to look at fraternal twins, whose genetic similarity is about 50 percent — roughly that of any other pair of siblings — but whose environments might be nearly as similar as those of identical twins reared together. Still another alternative is to look at individuals who are adopted, and to compare them with their adoptive parents, their natural parents, their biological siblings, and their adoptive siblings. Examples of each of these approaches, together with the most important findings of this research, are summarized in this chapter.

Development in Context

In an attempt to understand things, we often simplify them. For example, we treat environment and heredity as though they are separate forces even when we know they are very closely linked. We think of our genes as something within us, unaffected by what is out there; and we view the environment as something that is out there, separate from us. These views are misleading:

> Humans did not evolve in habitats; they were *of* them, like other animals. . . . An animal's habitat is the temperature of the air next to its skin, the rainfall dampening the dust beneath its feet and its cycle through the seasons, the height of the mountains and the depth of the winters, the salt in the earth and the oxygen in the air. By day a habitat sucks up energy from the sun; by night it gets hungry and eats its own tail. A habitat is *alive*. It moves. It runs away from you or snaps at your hooves. It gets to the food before you do, or it paces nearby while you eat. It may steal your meal, your portion of the energy, from under your nose, or it waits in your gut and steals it later.

A habitat is dynamic. It is more than the physical environment and the sum of the organisms that live and die in its boundaries; it is the conflicts and interdependencies that bind them together. A habitat doesn't stand still while you evolve to master it. It evolves too. (Johanson & Shreeve, 1989, p. 260)

We, too, are *of* habitats. We are part of our own ecologies. Our characteristics have an effect on our surroundings; and, undeniably, our surroundings have an effect on us.

The evolutionist is concerned with changes that occur in a species over eons—changes that define **phylogeny**. The developmentalist is concerned with changes that occur in a single individual during the course of one lifetime; these changes define **ontogeny**.

The study of human development is the study of the sequence of changes that transpire from the moment we are conceived to the moment we die. We cannot understand these changes without also beginning to understand the influences that shape us.

Gene–Context Interactions

Among early attempts to shed light on questions about how heredity and environment influence us are fascinating accounts of children who have allegedly been abandoned in the wilds. Some of these children, legend and folklore inform us, were found by wild animals, taken into their lairs and dens, and raised as their own (hence the term **feral children**, meaning wild children). The wild behavior of these children is strong evidence, Singh and Zingg (1942) argued, that the special qualities that make us human are not inherited, but have to be learned. But the evidence is not at all convincing. As Dennis (1941a, 1941b, 1951) points out, there is not a single fully documented case of a child having been raised by a wild animal. The evidence is entirely anecdotal. Most of the feral children, Dennis argues, have traits in common with mentally retarded or brain-damaged children—and most were likely mentally retarded when abandoned. In fact, that might well have been why they were abandoned in the first place. Hence no reliable conclusions can be drawn from stories of wild children.

But there are other accounts of abandoned children that are more reliable. One is the story of a little girl, initially nameless but who later came to be known as Genie. Genie was not abandoned in the wilds, but in a small upstairs bedroom in her own home. Except for brief periods when she was still a toddler, Genie would not leave her room from the age of 20 months until she was almost 14—nearly 12 years!

Genie's room was barren and completely unfurnished save for a small crib completely covered with wire mesh, and an infant "potty." The little girl was left alone in this room, day after day, week after week, year after year—alone and naked, with a sturdy leather harness strapped to her body and fastened to the potty so that she was forced to sit on it hour after hour. At night, when she wasn't simply left on the potty, she would be stuffed into a sleeping bag that had been specially made to restrain her, much like a straightjacket, and placed inside the crib, completely imprisoned within the wire mesh. On occasion, someone, usually her father, would come in and feed her—almost always either baby food, soupy cereal, or a soft-boiled egg. Her father insisted that contact with her be minimal and that no one speak to her, so feeding times were extremely rushed; whoever fed her simply stuffed as much food as possible into her mouth. If she spit some of it out, her face would be rubbed in it. And if she whimpered or made some other noise, perhaps with her potty or her crib, her father would come in and beat her with a stick. Nor did he ever speak to her. Instead, he pretended he was a dog, barking and growling at her, and sometimes scratching her with his fingernails. If he just wanted to threaten her, he would stand outside her door and make his most vicious dog noises.

When Genie was 13½ years old, following an especially violent fight with the father, the mother finally took her and left. Shortly after that, Genie was discovered, charges were filed against the parents, and Genie was brought into a hospital. Genie's father committed suicide on the day he was to be brought to trial (see Curtiss, 1977, for more complete details).

Two Models

From a psychological point of view, Genie's story is important because it provides evidence relevant to the heredity–environment issue. Simply stated, the issue concerns the relative contributions of our genes (heredity or nature) on the one hand, and of our experiences (environment or nurture) on the other. If the question were merely one of determining which of these two forces is responsible for this characteristic or that one—or for a certain percentage of this characteristic and a different percentage of that one—cases such as that of Genie and other abandoned children would provide us with useful information. Whatever characteristics these children share with others who are brought up in more "normal" environments, we would assume to result from genetic influences; and whatever "human" characteristics they failed to develop, we would attribute to environmental forces. Thus we might separate the relative contributions of each to our development.

But the issue is not quite so simple. It concerns, as Anastasi (1958) put it, not what? or how much? but *how*?

Nor is the answer very simple. In fact, there are at least two sorts of answers reflecting two different points of view (Overton, 1973): the additive and the interactive. The additive point of view assumes that the effects of heredity and environment are, in a sense, additive. That is, heredity accounts for a certain percentage of the variation in a characteristic, environment for the remainder. This is the model that has governed the work of researchers such as Jensen (1968), who argues, for example, that approximately 80 percent of the variation in measured intelligence is accounted for by genetic factors, with the remaining 20 percent influenced by the environment.

The interactive model, currently the more favored of the two models, argues that heredity and environment do not influence development in a linear, additive way, but instead *interact*. And the interaction is not always simple and highly predictable.

Interaction

Take something as simple as water and temperature. We know that water and temperature interact to form ice; but can we understand the hardness of ice, its taste, its effect on our skin, solely by understanding temperature and water? And is it not true that steam also results from the interaction of water and temperature? The interaction becomes more complex, but it still appears linear and predictable: More heat equals steam; less heat equals ice. Even here, however, interaction is not quite so simple. With changes in air pressure, the interaction of water and temperature changes. Now an

even higher or lower temperature is required for the same effect.

So, too, with heredity, environment, and human behavior—interaction is not a simple additive affair. Relative contributions of heredity and environment may change with age, might be different in different environments, and might vary from one individual to another. Furthermore, quite apart from their interactive role in influencing developmental outcomes, genes and environment can influence each other directly (Lerner, 1991). What we know of evolution makes it clear, for example, that gene combinations that underlie adaptive behaviors are more likely to survive in our genetic pools; those that are maladaptive have a poorer chance of surviving. Thus does the environment influence genes. It is perhaps not so obvious, but no less true, that genes can also influence environment. For example, a study of 700 pairs of twins reported by Plomin (1987) and his associates provides strong evidence of a close relationship between genetic influence and measures of environmental factors. This relationship, Plomin argues, may come from two sources. First, parental characteristics that are themselves genetically influenced might determine important aspects of a child's environment. For example, high-IQ parents might provide more books for their children, might enroll them in a variety of courses, might take them on field trips, and so on. Second, children's characteristics that are genetically influenced might have a direct bearing on their environments. For example, parents might provide different experiences (hence different environments) for high-IQ children.

The story of Genie provides one example of the complexity of gene–environment interaction specifically in the area of language development. Obviously, the acquisition of language is made possible by our genes. Not only have we been endowed with vocal cords, tongues, mouths, ears, brains, and other structures that make the production and the identification of speech sounds possible, but we also seem to be predisposed to acquire language early in our lives. Genie, who was not exposed to language during this sensitive early period (roughly, the early preschool years) had not learned to speak or to understand others. When she was later exposed to a normal language environment, as well as to direct language tuition, she managed to develop a small vocabulary and to acquire a limited, though uncertain, grasp of elementary language-production rules. But, as Curtiss (1977) points out, her development of language was far from normal.

As we saw in Chapter 2, Bronfenbrenner's ecological systems theory is based squarely on the notion that both the characteristics of the person *and* those of the context need to be taken into account. We return to the ecology of human genetics and human contexts later in this chapter; first, a look at the mechanics of heredity.

The Mechanics of Heredity

The mechanics of heredity are complex and still somewhat bewildering. But they can be simplified.

Ova, Sperm, and Conception

Human life begins with the joining of the mother's **ovum (egg cell)** and the father's **sperm cell**. For life to occur, this union is necessary. And because two people of opposite sexes are involved, it ordinarily requires a physical union between a male and a female as well—ordinarily, but not always. Conception is also possible with **artificial insemination**, a clinical procedure wherein the father's sperm is introduced directly into the mother. If viable, the father's sperm is typically used; at other times, donor sperm may be used, either alone or combined with the father's, so that the identity of the biological father may never be clear. Another possibility is conception outside the mother's body, either in another woman's body or *in vitro* (literally, "in glass"). The fertilized egg can then be implanted in the mother to develop as it normally would. Surrogate mothering is yet another possibility. A final medical solution for childlessness involves the use of fertility drugs—that is, drugs whose effects typically stimulate the production of mature ova. In these cases, pregnancy usually comes about as a result of the male–female union to which we referred earlier in this section.

None of these procedures is a certain solution for all childless couples, nor are they a *cure* for the causes of childlessness. Currently, the average success rate of most North American fertility clinics is about 10 percent.

A single ovum is released by a mature woman usually once every 28 days (usually between the 10th and the 18th days of her menstrual cycle). Sometimes, however, two or more eggs are released at once or a single fertilized egg divides, thus making multiple births possible.

Interestingly, all of the woman's ova are present in her ovaries at birth—perhaps as many as a million of them. These are primitive and immature, and more than half of them atrophy before **puberty** (the beginning of sexual maturity). Of those that remain, about 400 will mature and be released between puberty and **menopause** (cessation of menstruation). In contrast, a man produces several billion sperm a month (200 million or 300 million every four days or so) and usually continues to produce them from puberty until death.

The ovum is the largest cell in the human body (about 0.15 millimeter in diameter—about half the size of each period on this page). The sperm cell is one of the smallest cells in the body (0.005 millimeter in diameter). What the sperm cell lacks in size is made up by the length of its tail—fully 12 times longer than the main part of the cell to which it is attached. It is this long tail that enables the sperm to swim toward the ovum.

Protein, DNA, Chromosomes, and Genes

The egg cell and the sperm cell, called **gametes**, are the immediate origins of new life. Not only do they give rise to the development of a new human, they also carry the instructions or blueprints that determine what physical characteristics the individual will inherit.

The basis of all human life—the living, functioning cells of which we are composed—can be reduced to complicated molecules called **proteins**. These, in turn, are made up of different *amino acids*, of which there are approximately 20, arranged in an astounding number of combinations and sequences. Specific combinations determine the nature and function of the proteins they make up. In turn, these combinations and sequences are determined by a special code contained in a substance called *deoxyribonucleic acid*, or **DNA**. This substance consists mainly of four components that are arranged in different sequences of pairs in a structure termed a *double helix* (see Figure 3.1). In effect, this arrangement of DNA components is the blueprint or genetic code that determines our heredity.

All normal cells in our body contain identical genetic information. That is, all have the same assortment

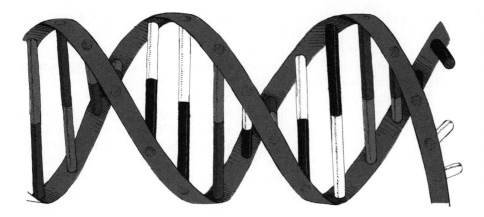

Figure 3.1 DNA molecules are arranged in sequences of pairs in a spiraling, double-helix structure. Genes, labels for carriers of specific hereditary information, can be thought of as locations or addresses on a segment of the DNA molecule.

of DNA molecules—the same genetic code. These DNA molecules are located on rodlike structures called **chromosomes**. Every human body cell has 23 pairs of these chromosomes.

The smallest units of heredity, which are defined by particular types and combinations of DNA molecules, are called **genes**. It's useful to think of genes as specific locations or segments of DNA molecules that contain instructions for a protein.

Body Cells and Sex Cells

There are two types of cells in our bodies: body cells and sex cells. Body cells each contain an identical complement of 23 pairs of chromosomes, each with identical sequences of DNA molecules. We have inherited one member of each pair of chromosomes from our mothers and the other member from our fathers—in other words, 23 chromosomes from each of our parents, for a total of 46 chromosomes. The division of body cells involves what is called **mitosis**—a process that results in genetically identical pairs of cells.

Unlike body cells, mature sex cells (sperm and ova) contain only 23 chromosomes rather than 23 pairs (46 chromosomes). This is because the gametes (sex cells) result from a special kind of cell division termed **meiosis** that results in daughter cells that have only half the number of chromosomes of the parent cell.

Note that when chromosome pairs in the parent cell divide to form mature sperm or ova, they do so randomly. That is, individual members of chromosome pairs wind up in any of a mind-boggling number of different possible combinations—in fact, some 2^{23} dif-

ferent possibilities. And because two parents are involved, the total number of different individuals that can result from a single human mating is an almost meaningless number—over 60 *trillion*. And that figure does not even take into account that during meiosis, segments of chromosomes sometimes "cross over" and exchange places, thereby further multiplying the number of possible combinations.

So should we be amazed that we are so much like our parents and siblings? Not really. You see, in these 60 trillion theoretically possible combinations, there will be a vast amount of redundant information. And much of that redundant information is absolutely fundamental to our humanity. Among other things, it is expressed in the fact that most of us have a single head, two eyes, a brain with a marvelously developed cortex, limbs, digits, and on and on.

But genetics, which is the science of heredity, deals less with our sameness than with our variability. It is concerned with the chemistry and the biology that account for differences among individuals of the same species. And one very noticeable and very important difference among individuals is sex.

Sex Chromosomes

Of the 23 chromosomes in each sperm and each ovum, one, labeled the **sex chromosome**, determines whether the offspring will be male or female. (The other 22 chromosomes are labeled **autosomes**.) As shown in Interactive Figure 3.2, the father produces two types of sperm, one with a larger sex chromosome, labeled X, and one with a smaller sex chromosome,

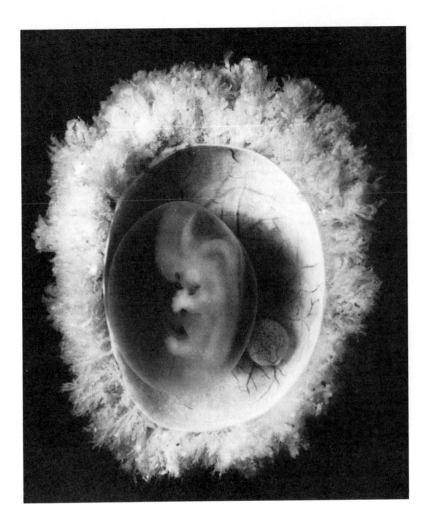

Human fetus at 48 days. A genetic pattern has been carried through the parents' chromosomes, creating a child with some but not all of its parents' characteristics.

labeled Y. If the sperm that fertilizes the ovum contains an X chromosome, the offspring will be a girl; if the sperm cell contains a Y chromosome, the result will be a boy. Because the mother produces only X chromosomes, only the father's sperm determines the sex of the offspring.

Genes

Recall that the units of heredity carried by the chromosomes are called genes. Chromosomes contain between 20,000 and 100,000 genes (Snyder, Freifelder, & Hartl, 1985). These genes, either in pairs or in complex combinations of pairs, determine our potential for inherited characteristics. There are, for example, pairs of

genes that correspond to eye color, hair characteristics, and virtually every other physical characteristic of an individual. In addition, other combinations of genes appear to be related to personality characteristics such as intelligence—although the ways in which genes affect personality are perhaps not as obvious or as easily measured as the ways in which they affect physical characteristics.

A simple explanation of gene functioning involves dominance and recessiveness. From studies of animals and plants (particularly fruit flies and peas), as well as from observations of human and other animals, scientists have discovered that certain members of pairs of genes are **dominant** over their corresponding members. When a dominant gene is paired with a corresponding **recessive** gene, the characteristics corresponding to the dominant gene will be manifested in

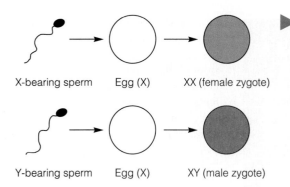

Interactive Figure 3.2 In this figure, there is a clue to a fact of which Henry VIII was sadly ignorant as he beheaded a succession of wives for *failing to give him a son*. Can you figure it out before continuing? If the xygote (fertilized egg) contains an X spermatozoon, the result is a girl. If the zygote contains a Y spermatozoon, the result will be a boy. What did Henry VIII not know? The mother produces only X chromosomes; only the father can produce the Y sex chromosome. Hence, the father's sperm determines whether the offspring will be male or female.

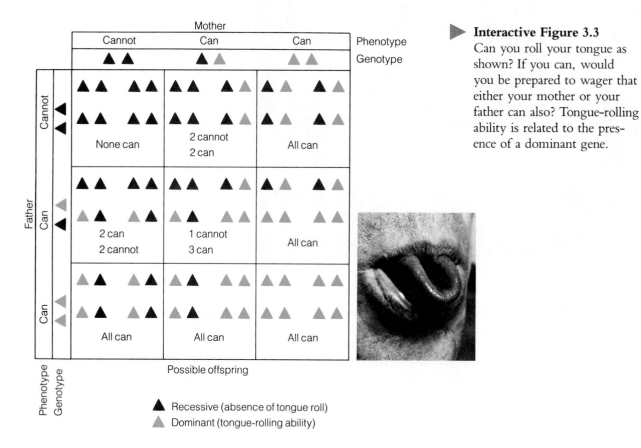

Interactive Figure 3.3 Can you roll your tongue as shown? If you can, would you be prepared to wager that either your mother or your father can also? Tongue-rolling ability is related to the presence of a dominant gene.

the individual. We know, for example, that the gene for normally pigmented skin is dominant over the gene for albinism (unpigmented skin). Hence, an individual who inherits a gene for normal skin from one parent and one for albinism from the other will have pigmented skin. A true albino (an individual with completely unpigmented skin) has inherited a recessive gene for unpigmented skin from *each* parent. It follows, as well, that two albino parents will inevitably produce albino children. (See Interactive Figure 3.3 for an illus-

Parents and their children often look very much alike because they have in common certain genes related to physical characteristics. However, the complexity of the processes by which the genes are transmitted and the astronomical number of combinations possible make it very difficult to predict the nature and extent of family resemblance before the fact.

tration of a characteristic related to the presence of a dominant gene.)

If human genetics were limited to the effects of single pairs of genes and their relative dominance or recessiveness, genetics would be far simpler. In fact, however, many characteristics are functions of an undetermined number of pairs of genes acting in combination. In addition, genes are seldom completely dominant or recessive under all circumstances. Some genes appear to be dominant over a specific gene but recessive with respect to another. Furthermore, the material of which genes consist occasionally undergoes *mutation* — change that may be brought about through X rays, mustard gas, drugs, or other causes.

Genotype and Phenotype

Your genetic makeup is your **genotype**. It consists of all the genes you have inherited from your parents. Your manifested characteristics define your **phenotype**. That is, phenotype is what you see — what is on the outside; genotype is hidden, and has to be inferred from phenotype — or what can sometimes be determined through an examination of the matter of which genes are composed.

It's possible to make accurate inferences about genotype with respect to characteristics determined by recessive genes, but not for those determined by dominant genes. Normally, for example, the gene for brown eyes is dominant over that for blue eyes. Therefore we can infer that individuals whose phenotype (manifested characteristics) includes blue eyes must have two recessive genes for blue eyes (genotype). On the other hand, the genotype for brown-eyed individuals cannot be inferred with certainty from their phenotype since they might have two dominant genes for brown eyes or a dominant gene for brown eyes and a recessive gene for blue eyes (see Figure 3.4). As we noted, however, the effects of genotype on phenotype are not quite so simple. In fact, most human characteristics, including eye color, are often the result of combinations of genes (polygenesis). The effects of polygenetic determination, as Plomin (1987) points out, are not either-or (for example, either blue or brown), but include a whole range of possibilities. Thus individuals are not simply blue- or brown-eyed, but can also have eyes that are green or hazel or blue-green, or a variety of other related shades.

According to Plomin, three conclusions summarize the relationship between genotype (inherited genetic structure) and phenotype (manifested character-

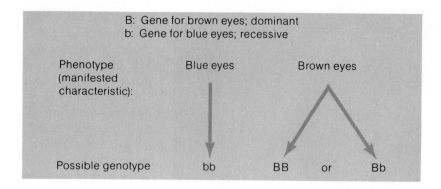

Figure 3.4 Phenotype (manifested characteristic) is influenced by genotype (chromosomal makeup); but genotype cannot always be determined from the phenotype. A brown-eyed individual might have a recessive gene for blue eyes or two genes for brown eyes.

istics). First, genetic differences (genotype) clearly lead to phenotypic differences. Second, characteristics that are influenced by more than one gene tend not to be dichotomous (black or white), but are distributed in a manner that approximates what is referred to as the **normal curve** (a bell-shaped curve where the majority of cases cluster near the average, with fewer and fewer cases deviating further and further from the average). Third, the environment also has an important effect on manifested characteristics.

Reaction Range and Canalization

In fact, for some characteristics, the environment makes a great deal of difference (language learning, for example); for others, it makes little apparent difference (eye color, for example). That is, some manifested characteristics seem to correspond much more closely than others to underlying genetic material. In Waddington's (1975) terms, they are more highly **canalized**. Strongly canalized characteristics are less affected by environmental forces. Thus, for a highly canalized characteristic, phenotype corresponds closely to genotype. Eye color is a highly canalized characteristic; it typically corresponds to genotype and is unaffected by experience. In contrast, many complex intellectual abilities (the ability to learn to speak several languages, for example) do not appear to be highly canalized but result from specific experiences.

Described in evolutionary terms, canalization may be seen as a genetic tendency toward predictable regularity. This predictable regularity ensures that individuals of one species will be much more similar than dissimilar.

Figure 3.5 is Waddington's (1975) *epigenetic landscape*, an analogy he uses to illustrate canalization. In this illustration, genetic forces are the canals that run down the landscape; the tilt of the figure represents environmental forces; and the ball represents some characteristic of the developing organism. Where the ball ends up represents the final state of the characteristic.

The analogy makes several important points. First, shifts (different tilts) in the environment can change the ball's path and dramatically affect the final outcome. Second, for highly canalized traits (deeper channels) greater environmental forces (changes in tilt) will be needed to affect the final outcome. And third, subtle environmental forces are more likely to significantly affect the course of development early (top of the figure) rather than later in development (bottom of the figure, where all channels are deeper).

Even for highly canalized characteristics, phenotype (manifested characteristics) seldom results only from predetermined genetic influences; it is usually influenced by environmental factors as well. That is, **epigenesis**, the unfolding of genetically influenced characteristics, is brought about by the interaction of genes and environment (Gottlieb, 1991). In a sense, it is as though genetic influences (genotypes) make possible a range of different outcomes, with some being more probable than others. As these genetic influences interact with context, the outcomes become manifest (phenotypic). Gottesman (1974) introduces the concept of reaction range to illustrate this. Simply stated, the reaction range for a particular characteristic includes all the possible outcomes for that characteristic given variations in the nature and timing of environmental influences. It is the existence of a reaction range for any given characteristic that makes it possible

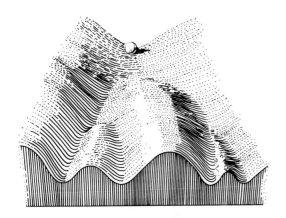

Figure 3.5 Waddington's epigenetic landscape, a graphic analogy depicting the interaction between environmental and genetic forces. Genetic forces are represented by the valleys and contours of the landscape; they make certain outcomes more probable than others. Environmental forces are represented by changes in the tilt of the landscape. (Based on Waddington, 1975.)

for the same genotype to give rise to very different outcomes (different phenotypes). By the same token, highly similar phenotypes need not reflect identical genotypes.

In conclusion, there are two important points to keep in mind. First, the effects of heredity and environment are interactive rather than additive. Second, a range of possibilities is implicit in your genotype. Some of these possibilities are more probable than others. They are, in a sense, protected by your genes. These traits are referred to as being more highly canalized than others.

Molecular Genetics

Genotype (genetic makeup) need not always be inferred from phenotype. The techniques of molecular genetics make it possible to examine chromosomes directly, to look at sequences of DNA molecules, to identify their specific chemical components, and to locate chemical segments that correspond to genes.

How is this done? Among important new techniques that have come out of molecular genetics, and specifically out of recombinant DNA research, is the use of certain *enzymes* (proteins that catalyze biochemical reactions); these enzymes cut through sequences of DNA, in effect, producing microscopic DNA fragments. Where two individuals have identical DNA sequences, the length of the resulting fragments will be exactly the same; but if the sequences are different, the resulting fragments will be of different lengths (called *restriction fragment length polymorphisms*, or RFLPs). Thus RFLPs (pronounced "rifflips") allow geneticists to identify genes on specific chromosomes that are associated with the presence or absence of some observable characteristic. These genes are termed **marker genes**. Plomin (1987) reports that marker genes have been discovered for all chromosomes. Some examples are the location of marker genes for Huntington's disease, for some forms of schizophrenia (Loehlin, Willerman, & Horn, 1988), and for manic depression (Egeland et al., 1987; Baron et al., 1987).

For traits that result from the effects of a large number of genes, it is possible to use a series of RFLPs to begin to sort out genetic contributions. The approach is complex but incredibly promising. It brings with it the possibility not only of discovering the location and composition of DNA sequences that underlie human defects as well as human strengths but also perhaps of correcting defective genes, or, at the very least, of identifying their presence early—perhaps even before conception.

By March 1989, some 4,550 genes had been identified. A massive federally funded genetics project is now underway in the United States. Its goal is eventually to provide a complete genetic map of the human being—a map of what is termed the **genome**, the complete set of genetic instructions contained in our cells ("The Gene Hunt," 1989).

The ethical implications of success in this endeavor are staggering. Not only might it be possible to correct genetic defects, but it might also be possible to predict accurately the outcome of different gene pairings. What happens next? Does medicine play God? Do governments *engineer* genes to produce the kinds of people they want? Do chromosomal tests become mandatory? Do they become part of our government-mandated "identity," like Social Security numbers? Only time will tell.

Genetic Defects

In addition to their role in influencing the course of normal development, genes are also sometimes responsible for certain diseases and defects. In most cases, these disorders are linked with *recessive* rather than *dominant* genes. The reason for this is simple: Any abnormality that is linked with a dominant gene will always be manifested in all carriers and will have relatively little chance of being passed on to offspring (particularly if it leads to early death). In contrast, abnormalities that are linked to recessive genes will be manifested only when the carrier has inherited the two related recessive genes. Many individuals may be carriers of a single recessive gene for some abnormality without manifesting the abnormality. Likewise, their offspring will not manifest the abnormality unless *both* parents carry the relevant recessive gene *and* each passes it on to the offspring.

The risk of genetic disorders among the children of biologically related parents is considerably higher than for children whose parents are not related. This is simply because if genetic disorders linked to a recessive gene are present in a family, matings among family members will have a higher probability of producing offspring with a pair of the recessive gene (or gene groupings) in question. In contrast, if a member of this family, who is a carrier of the recessive gene, mates with someone outside the family who does not carry the gene, there is only one chance in four that the offspring will inherit the gene, and no chance that this offspring will manifest the disorder (because the gene is recessive). Thus continued matings among individuals who are not biologically related may, over a period of generations, eventually succeed in eradicating or greatly reducing the incidence of the recessive gene in question. By the same token, continued matings among members of a family in which the gene is initially widespread might lead to a proliferation of the gene and a corresponding increase in the manifestation of the disorder it underlies.

Huntington's Disease

Most very serious or fatal genetic disorders, as we have just noted, are linked with recessive genes; if they were associated with dominant genes, all carriers would be affected and would either die before having children or would be aware of the risks involved and refrain from parenthood. One exception to this general rule, however, is **Huntington's disease** (also called Huntington's chorea), which is both fatal and associated with a dominant gene. It is still present because it does not ordinarily manifest itself until the age of 30 or 40. When it does appear, it leads to rapid neurological deterioration and eventual death.

Until recently, there was no way to determine whether a given individual carried the dominant gene for Huntington's disease. Thus, an individual with cases of Huntington's among parents, uncles and aunts, siblings, or grandparents could only wait to see whether the disease would eventually strike. Using the RFLP technology described earlier, geneticists have now succeeded in locating the gene for the disorder, thus making it possible to detect its presence (or absence) before it becomes manifest. Eventually, it might also be possible to replace this defective DNA sequence with a normal gene spliced to a harmless virus (Loehlin, Willerman, & Horn, 1988).

Sickle-Cell Anemia

Sickle-cell anemia is a genetic disorder linked to a recessive gene. Approximately 10 percent of all blacks in the United States (and a much lower proportion of whites) carry the recessive gene for this disorder (see Figure 3.6). These 10 percent are **heterozygous** for this gene (have one normal and one abnormal gene); another 0.25 percent are **homozygous** (carry two defective genes). Effects of the defective gene are clearly apparent in abnormally shaped red blood cells (sickle-shaped rather than circular), which multiply as a function of lack of oxygen (see Figure 3.7). Individuals who are homozygous for this gene often die in childhood or are severely ill throughout life. Those who are heterozygous for the gene are ordinarily healthy except in conditions of low oxygen, such as at high altitudes; here they may become quite ill, indicating that the normal gene is not completely dominant.

PKU

Phenylketonuria, or **PKU**, is another genetic defect associated with the presence of two defective recessive genes. In an individual suffering from PKU, the liver enzyme that is responsible for breaking down phenyl-

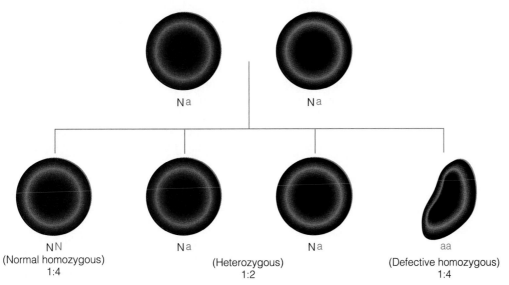

Na   Na

NN
(Normal homozygous)
1:4

Na

(Heterozygous)
1:2

Na

aa
(Defective homozygous)
1:4

Figure 3.6 An illustration of recessive gene action in the determination of sickle-cell anemia. Parents are heterozygous; that is, they possess one normal (*N*) and one defective (*a*) gene, and will therefore not suffer from the disease. A child born to these parents will have 1 chance in 4 of not carrying the defective gene, 1 chance in 2 of being heterozygous, and 1 chance in 4 of possessing two defective genes and therefore suffering from sickle-cell anemia.

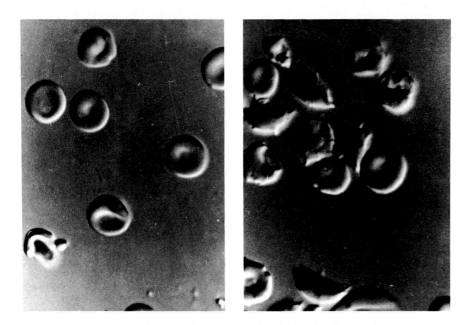

Figure 3.7 On the left, normal oxygenated red blood cells; on the right, sickle cells.

alanine into usable substances is absent or inactive. At birth, the infant appears completely normal, but the continued buildup of phenylalanine, which makes up approximately 5 percent of the weight of proteins, leads to progressive mental retardation and brain seizures. Fortunately, however, PKU can easily be detected in the newborn, and its onset can be prevented by providing the child with a special diet low in phenylalanine (Springer, 1982). This is a striking example of developmental plasticity in the face of a strongly canalized tendency. Although PKU is clearly associated with a pair of defective genes, the disorder is brought about through diet and can also be prevented through diet.

Other Genetic Defects

Nearly 2,000 other genetic defects have now been identified and catalogued (McKusick, 1986). Among them is **Tay–Sachs disease**, a disorder linked to recessive genes. This enzyme disorder results in the brain's inability to break down certain fats. Eventually, these fats build up, preventing neural transmission and leading to the degeneration of brain cells. Affected individuals commonly die before age 3. Tay–Sachs disease can be detected before birth but cannot yet be prevented or cured.

Muscular dystrophy, a degenerative muscular disorder of which there are a variety of forms, is, in many of its forms, linked to a recessive gene or is multifactorial. It usually involves an inability to walk, and may lead to death. Similarly, some forms of **diabetes**, an insulin deficiency disease, are associated with recessive genes, as are neural tube defects. **Neural tube defects** may take the form of *spina bifida*, in which the spine remains open at the bottom, or of *anencephaly*, in which portions of the skull and brain are absent. Neural tube defects often lead to severe retardation or death. Although genetically linked, the causes of these defects are multifactorial. They generally develop very early in pregnancy (as early as the first week), and can be detected by means of the **AFP test**—a test that looks at the level of *alphafetoprotein* in the mother's blood. If this substance is present in concentrations higher than usual, further tests such as ultrasound or fetoscopy (described later) are performed to determine whether there is a neural tube defect. In some jurisdictions, AFP screening is routine or even mandatory (as are tests for PKU).

In addition to a large number of medical conditions that are clearly genetically linked, there is increasing evidence of a genetic basis for at least some manifestations of emotional and behavioral problems such as alcoholism, depression, anorexia nervosa, infantile autism, and schizophrenia (Loehlin, Willerman, & Horn, 1988). Specific genes have been located for some of these conditions. But because their causes are multifactorial, they are highly susceptible to environmental influence.

Chromosomal Disorders

Genetic defects are linked to specific recessive or dominant genes, or to a combination of genes; they may also be related to certain environmental conditions. **Chromosomal disorders**, on the other hand, are associated not with specific genes but with errors in chromosomes. Many of these errors result from improper divisions and recombinations during meiosis.

Down Syndrome

Down syndrome is the most common of chromosomal birth defects. It affects approximately 10 percent of all children institutionalized for mental retardation and 1 in 750 live births (Snyder, Freifelder, & Hartl, 1985). Some Down syndrome children have characteristic loose folds of skin over the corners of the eyes, producing an Oriental appearance; hence the now uncommon label *mongolism*.

Mental retardation is common among Down syndrome children. Their developmental rates often lag behind normal, and their language development is often retarded. Not all children are equally affected.

Children suffering from Down syndrome have an extra chromosome (chromosome 21, as it is numbered by geneticists)—three rather than a pair—hence, the alternative medical label of Trisomy 21. Most cases of Down syndrome are due to failure of the 21st pair of chromosomes to separate (*nondisjunction*). Hence, the resulting gamete (sex cell) has an extra copy of the chromosome. When this gamete combines with the other gamete during fertilization, the resulting zygote has an extra 21st chromosome. A smaller number of cases are caused by *translocation* of chromosome 21 material to another chromosome (Emery, 1984).

Since nondisjunction of the 21st chromosome typically occurs during meiosis of the ovum rather than of the sperm, Down syndrome is usually associated with the mother rather than the father. The probability of producing a child with Down syndrome is linked with the age of the mother. The incidence ranges from 1 in 1,500 for mothers ages 15–24 to 1 in 38 for mothers over 45 (Brock, 1982). The age of the father, too, appears to be linked to the incidence of the defect, with fathers older than 55 having a 20–30 percent greater chance of fathering children with Down syndrome (Erikson & Bjerkedal, 1981). In these instances, disjunction failure occurs during meiosis of the sperm rather than the egg.

The extra 21st chromosome that is present in Down syndrome has led to an important discovery with respect to **Alzheimer's disease**, some forms of which appear to be inherited. Alzheimer's, which is discussed in some detail in Chapter 17, is a serious illness that typically occurs between the ages of 40 and 80 or older, and involves nerve fibers in the brain becoming coated with amyloid filaments. Investigators noticed that middle-aged individuals with Down syndrome typically display the same development of amyloid filaments as Alzheimer's patients. Further research revealed that the gene that underlies the production of amyloid is located on the 21st chromosome (Goldgaber et al., 1987). At least in some cases, it appears that Alzheimer's may result from a defective gene on the 21st chromosome.

Turner's Syndrome

A relatively large, though infrequent, number of chromosomal defects are linked to the sex chromosome. Of these, *Turner's syndrome* affects 1 out of 5,000 female children (Thompson, 1975). These children are born with a missing sex chromosome (designated as 45, X, rather than as 46, XX; the "45" indicates the total number of chromosomes). Most such children are aborted spontaneously; those who survive typically have underdeveloped secondary sexual characteristics, although this is not evident until puberty (Money, 1975). Possible symptoms of the disorder include swelling in the extremities that disappears with age — leaving

loose folds of skin (webbing), particularly at the neck, fingers, and toes — and dwarfism. Mental ability is usually normal. Injection of the sex hormone *estrogen* prior to puberty is sometimes helpful in bringing about greater sexual maturation (Timiras, 1972).

Klinefelter's Syndrome

Klinefelter's syndrome is a chromosomal aberration linked to the sex chromosome. It involves the presence of an extra X chromosome in a male child (thus 47, XXY). It is considerably more common than Turner's syndrome (1 out of 400 males; Thompson, 1975) and is marked by the presence of both male and female secondary sexual characteristics. Children suffering from this disorder typically have small, undeveloped testicles, more highly developed breasts than is common among boys, high-pitched voices, and little or no facial hair after puberty. Treatment with the male sex hormone, *testosterone*, is often effective in enhancing the development of masculine characteristics and in increasing sex drive (Johnson et al., 1970). Without such treatment, many children suffering from Klinefelter's syndrome remain infertile throughout life.

XYY Syndrome

Males with an extra Y chromosome (47, XYY), sometimes referred to as "super males" because they possess one extra male chromosome, are characteristically tall; frequently, they are also of lower than average intelligence. Some evidence has linked this syndrome with criminality, following the observation that considerably more of the tall men in prisons are of the XYY type than is true of tall men in the general society (see, for example, Telfer et al., 1968). The theory is that the extra chromosome is linked with greater aggressiveness and hence greater tendencies toward violent crimes. In fact, the syndrome was first discovered among prisoners with violent histories; among them the incidence is between 2 and 12 percent, while only 0.1 percent of the normal population has the syndrome (Jarvik, Klodin, & Matsuyama, 1973). The conclusion that the XYY syndrome is linked with criminality remains tentative, however (Falek, 1975). Certainly, not all XYY individuals manifest undue aggression. In fact, Witkin and associates (1976) found that imprisoned XYY individuals were more often guilty of nonviolent crimes. Kalat (1981) suggests that one reason many of these individuals are in jail may be their lower intelligence rather than their greater aggressiveness.

Fragile X Syndrome

Fragile X syndrome is a condition in which the X sex chromosome is abnormally compressed or even broken. Although it can also occur in females, it is far more common among males, accounting for between 5 and 7 percent of retarded males (Zigler & Hodapp, 1991). Interestingly, many females with fragile X syndrome are of normal intelligence. That can also be the case with males, but is less common.

Unlike Down syndrome in which mental retardation is typically apparent very early in life, fragile X individuals often manifest no symptoms of retardation until puberty (Silverstein & Johnston, 1990). Between the ages of 10 and 15, however, there is frequently a marked decline in intellectual functioning.

Other Sex-Linked Defects

Fragile X syndrome is a sex-linked defect; the genes that underly its manifestation are located on the X chromosome. This chromosome is also the site for genes relating to various other defects such as night-blindness, baldness, and hemophilia. Each of these defects is associated with recessive genes; and each, like the fragile X syndrome, is more often manifested among males than females. Why? Simply because females who inherit the defective gene on one of their two X chromosomes often have the corresponding *normal* gene on the other chromosome. As a result, they are *carriers* of the defective gene, but they do not manifest it (since it is recessive). Males, on the other hand, have only one X chromosome; the other sex chromosome is a Y. In many cases, the normal dominant gene that would counter the effect of the recessive gene for one of these disorders is not present on the Y chromosome. Accordingly, males manifest conditions like hereditary baldness (and the fragile X syndrome) far more often than do females. Yet the gene is passed on from mother to son—not from father to son (since the father always passes on a Y chromosome to his sons, and the mother always passes on the X chromosome).

Fetal Diagnosis

More than 3,000 chromosomal aberrations and other disorders can now be detected in the fetus as a result of advances in medical knowledge and technology (Emery, 1984). There are four principal techniques for fetal diagnosis.

In **amniocentesis**, a thin, hollow needle is inserted into the amniotic fluid surrounding the fetus, allowing the physician to obtain fluid containing fetal cells. An examination of chromosomes in these cells can reveal chromosomal abnormalities. In addition, the blood type of the fetus can be detected, as can the chemical composition of the amniotic fluid; these may provide evidence relating to other diseases that might affect the unborn child. Because the procedure involves a slight risk of infection, it is commonly employed only in those cases in which the mother is older and where there is a probability of fetal abnormality or other complications. Amniocentesis is not usually performed before the 15th or 16th week of pregnancy, and does not yield results for approximately three to four weeks (Raeburn, 1984).

In **chorion biopsy** (also called *chorionic villus sampling*, or *CVS*), a plastic tube is inserted through the vagina to withdraw a small sample of the chorion, which is a precursor of the placenta and contains the same genetic information as does amniotic fluid. The advantage of a chorion biopsy over amniocentesis is that it can be performed as early as seven weeks after conception. In addition, it yields results faster than does amniocentesis (within one week). If these results lead to a decision to terminate the pregnancy, this can be accomplished more simply and more safely in the first trimester of pregnancy. Amniocentesis, as we saw, does not provide results until well into the second trimester of pregnancy.

Chorion biopsy procedures are somewhat more experimental than amniocentesis and carry a slightly higher risk of complications. Neither is used routinely.

Ultrasound (sometimes called *sonogram*) is among the least harmful and least traumatic of techniques currently available for fetal diagnosis. It is also the method of choice to prove the presence of a living fetus. It provides the most exact means for estimating fetal age, for detecting the exact position of the fetus, for discerning changes in fetal position, for detecting multiple pregnancies, and for identifying growth disorders and malformations. Ultrasound images of the fetus in "real time" make it possible to see the beginnings of fetal activity, including such behaviors as thumb sucking. They also allow the physician to examine bone structure, assess the length of bones, determine relationships among the size and growth of various bodily structures, and even count fingers and toes (Galjaard, 1982). Ultrasound is always employed with amniocentesis or chorion biopsy to guide the physician.

Fetoscopy is a surgical procedure that allows the physician to *see* the fetus. It is used mainly to obtain samples of tissues from the fetus itself, the most important being blood. Fetoscopy can provide the physician with a tremendous amount of information about the status of the fetus. Because it is a more exacting surgical procedure than amniocentesis and carries higher risks, it is most likely to be used where the probability of defects or disease is high.

Although amniocentesis, chorion biopsy, ultrasound, and fetoscopy are powerful tools for detecting possible abnormalities in offspring, not all risks can be eliminated by these means. When family background and abnormalities in one or both of the parents as well as in siblings indicate a higher-than-chance probability of some defect, parents and physicians may be faced with decisions involving serious ethical questions. In these situations, genetic counseling offers a valuable service.

Genetic Counseling

Genetic counseling is a branch of medicine and of psychology that attempts to provide advice and information to physicians and parents. Such counseling typically attempts to assess the probability of a defect's occurring, its likely seriousness, the extent to which it can be treated and even reversed, and the best courses of action to follow once a decision has been made about whether to have a child. In many instances, genetic counseling will occur prior to conception and might take into account the age and health of the mother as well as the presence of genetic abnormalities in ancestors and siblings. In other cases, genetic counseling will occur after conception (see Table 3.1). Genetic counsel-

ing may be involved in deciding whether to have an abortion (see Figure 3.8).

In spite of the growing availability of genetic counseling, there is still relatively widespread lack of knowledge on the part of both physicians and potential clients. In addition, psychological barriers such as fear of genetic disease, social stigma attached to such diseases, and values that stress God's will, as well as financial considerations, serve to limit the use of genetic counseling and to reduce its effectiveness even when it is available.

Prenatal fetal diagnosis also presents some potential for abuse. For example, in the Ganxiao district of the province of Hubei in northern China, as elsewhere in China, parents take tremendous pride in male children. Accordingly, government regulations limiting parents to a single child have led to the widespread killing of baby girls. In addition, many parents are having the sex of the fetus determined before birth so that female fetuses can be aborted. As a result, by 1983 there were five boys for every girl under age 5 in the Ganxiao district ("China fears sexual imbalance," 1983).

Studying Gene–Context Interaction

Genesis refers to the beginning; it refers, as well, to development or unfolding. Our genes are aptly named: They are clearly our beginnings. But they are more than simply beginnings; in interaction with our contexts, they are also involved in guiding our development. "Genes do not by themselves produce structural or functional characteristics," says Lerner (1991, p. 27). Instead, they *interact* with context to produce change.

Earlier, we looked at Waddington's epigenetic landscape. The most important point this analogy makes is this: All genetically influenced characteristics, whether or not they are highly canalized (highly probable), can be influenced by context. Waddington's analogy of canalization, say Turkheimer and Gottesman (1991), underlines the interdependence of genes and experiences. The current emphasis in genetic research is on finding out how context and genes work together. Keep in mind that genetic and environmental forces do not compete; rather, they work together to increase the individual's adaptation (Cairns, Gariépy, & Hood, 1990).

TABLE 3.1

Probability of Some Common Genetic Defects

Genetic Defect	Incidence (per 1,000 population)	Sex Ratio (M:F)	Normal Parents Having a Second Affected Child (%)	Affected Parent Having an Affected Child (%)	Affected Parent Having a Second Affected Child (%)
Asthma	3.0–4.0	1:1	10	26	—
Cerebral palsy	2.0	3:2	1	—*	—
Cleft palate only	0.4	2:3	2	7	15
Cleft lip and/or cleft palate	1.0	3:2	4	4	10
Club foot	1.0	2:1	3	3	10
Congenital heart disease (all types)	5.0	1:1	1–4	1–4	10
Diabetes mellitus (juvenile, insulin-dependent)	2.0	1:1	6	1–2	—
Dislocation of hip	0.7	1:6	6	12	36
Epilepsy ("idiopathic")	5.0	1:1	5	5	10
Manic-depressive psychosis	4.0	2:3	10–15	10–15	—
Mental retardation (of unknown cause)	3.0–5.0	1:1	3–5	10	20
Profound childhood deafness	1.0	1:1	10	8	—
Schizophrenia	1.0–2.0	1:1	10	16	—
Spina bifida (neural tube defect)	3.0	2:3	5	4	—

* —means no data.

Source: Adapted from *Elements of Medical Genetics* (6th ed.) by A. E. H. Emery. Edinburgh and London: Churchill-Livingstone, 1983. Used by permission.

Historical Family Studies

One way to investigate gene–context interaction is to look at differences and similarities among members of families. Why? Simply because family members share some genes. As Plomin (1987) points out, there is 100 percent genetic similarity between pairs of identical twins, approximately 50 percent similarity among siblings who share both parents, and somewhere around 25 percent similarity among siblings who share only one parent. In actuality, however, what is called *assortative* mating—the tendency of mates to select each other on the basis of similarity—increases genetic relatedness even more.

It is the high degree of genetic relatedness among members of families that led Francis Galton, Charles Darwin's cousin, to conclude that intelligence is largely hereditary. He had noticed that most of England's outstanding scientists came from a small number of families. Not very good research, surely. Even if Galton's

Abortion Rates in the United States

The rate of legal abortions in the United States increased dramatically between 1972 and 1980 but has since leveled off. It is probable that the number of *illegal* abortions declined as legal abortions became more widely available. However, the legal availability of abortion remains an extremely controversial issue. In the United States, the highest abortion rate is for teenagers, ages 15–19; they account for more than one-quarter of all abortions. The abortion rate for black women is about twice as high as for white women (U.S. Bureau of the Census, 1988, p. 70).

Figure 3.8 Legal abortions in the United States (per 1,000 women ages 15–44), 1972–1987. (Based on U.S. Bureau of the Census, 1991, p. 71.)

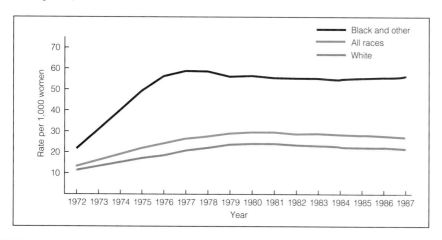

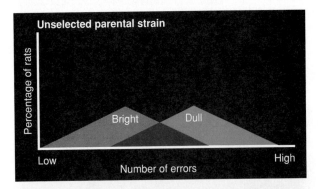

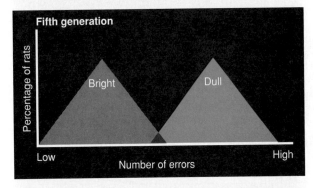

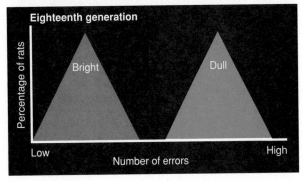

observations were entirely accurate, they don't prove his point. An environmentalist might argue, for example, that the reason these families produced outstanding scientists was simply that they provided children with environments conducive to the development of genius. Still, Galton was convinced of the heritability of intelligence, and argued that parents should be selected for favorable genetic characteristics—a practice termed **eugenics**.

Animal Studies

Gene–environment interactions can sometimes be studied more easily with animals than with humans. First, certain physiological measurements are possible with animals but not with humans (brain dissections, for example). Second, animal environments can be controlled far more completely than can human environments (in terms of environmental stimulation, food, social contacts, and so on). Third, animal matings can be controlled precisely, and many generations can be produced and studied within a relatively short period of time. Not so with humans.

There are, of course, some serious limitations of animal studies in this area, not the least of which is the difficulty of generalizing findings from animals to humans. This text is about the human lifespan; we mention rats and other animals only in passing.

A classical study of genetic influence in rats is that of Tryon (1940), who began by having his rats learn a maze to test their intelligence. Fast learners were then mated with other fast learners, and slow learners were paired with other slow learners. After only 18 generations, there was no longer any overlap between the groups. The dullest rats among the bright group were now brighter than the smartest of the dull group. And vice versa (see Figure 3.9).

Figure 3.9 An approximate representation of Tryon's successful attempt to produce maze-bright and maze-dull rats through selective breeding. After 18 generations of selective breeding, the dullest of the bright rats were brighter than the brightest of the dull group, and vice versa. (From Tryon, 1940, p. 113.)

Other animal studies have demonstrated it is possible to breed different strains of the same species that are predictably different in some identifiable characteristic. For example, in only a few generations mice can be bred for aggression, emotionality, preference for alcohol, and other characteristics (see Cairns, Gariépy, & Hood, 1990). In much the same way, various "personality" characteristics have been developed in different breeds of dogs: fierceness and fighting ability in pit bull terriers; vigilance in German shepherds; obstinacy and contrariness in the Lefrançois hound.

But even in rats and dogs and other nonhuman animals, genetics by itself tells little of the story. Consider, for example, the case of the song thrush, which dearly loves to eat snails. This bird grabs the snail in its beak and smashes the shell against a rock by means of a rapid, sideways motion of its head, back and forth, back and forth (Weisfeld, 1982). This appears to be a genetically influenced behavior since the European blackbird, a close relative of the song thrush that also loves to eat snails, doesn't seem to be able to learn the same smash-the-snail's-shell behavior. But it is also an environmentally influenced behavior since the young song thrush doesn't instinctively know how to smash a snail shell, but learns to do so largely by trial-and-error during a critical period early in its life. If it's not given an opportunity to learn during this critical period, it goes through life never knowing how to eat a snail properly, the way other song thrushes do it.

What investigations such as these illustrate most clearly is the complexity of gene–environment interaction, even for behaviors we might assume to be entirely genetically based. In addition, animal studies suggest that behaviors having important adaptive functions become more probable through succeeding generations. Since these behaviors have to do with biological adaptation and the survival and propagation of species, they are typically related to feeding, rest, defense, reproduction, or elimination (Weisfeld, 1982). Are there similar, genetically ordained behaviors among humans?

Some researchers think so. These behaviors, they argue, are common to all members of the species — hence common to all human cultures. In addition, they occur in the absence of experiences that might otherwise explain their acquisition. Weisfeld (1982) suggests these genetically programmed behaviors might include such things as the infant's distress at being separated from the mother or other caregiver (more about this in Chapter 6); the tendency of mothers in all cultures to hold their infants on the left side, whether or not they are right-handed; various facial expressions that have identical meanings everywhere (such as the human smile, which occurs in blind as well as in sighted infants); and human vocalizations, which are initially identical in deaf and in hearing infants.

Intervention Studies

Another way of studying gene–environment interactions is through various kinds of interventions. It is possible, for example, to deprive certain individuals of important experiences, and to measure the effects of this deprivation. Another possibility is to enrich the individual's environment, to provide special experiences.

An early study by Sherman and Key (1932) provides tentative evidence of the effects of intervention. The study compared the intelligence test scores of groups of isolated children (the Mountain children) with those of a control group in a more normal environment (the Briarsville children). Most of the Mountain children had been exposed to very little schooling, and came from homes devoid of newspapers, magazines, most forms of reading material, or any consistent source of contact with the outside world. Briarsville children had been exposed to normal schooling and had access to the offerings of the wider culture through newspapers and so on. Results of the comparison are shown in Figure 3.10. Note that the Briarsville children performed significantly better than the Mountain children on all three measures of intellectual performance.

Sherman and Key argue that these differences reflect the effects of environmental pressures. Is that the only, or even the best, explanation? Probably not. We don't know, for example, whether the parents of these children were comparable in terms of intelligence; none were tested. It is possible that the parents who chose to isolate themselves in the mountains were less intelligent than those who lived closer to the cultural mainstream. It's also possible that they were more intelligent.

There is an abundance of more recent and better controlled interventions. One example is Project Head Start, a massive, federally funded American program designed to alleviate, through intervention, some of the possible disadvantages of being born and raised

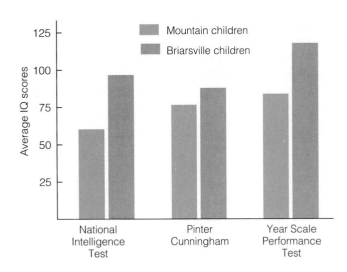

Figure 3.10 Comparisons between Mountain children and Briarsville children on some measures of intelligence.

in homes less advantaged economically, socially, and intellectually.

There have been more than 2,000 different Head Start programs (Zigler & Freedman, 1987). Many of these lasted only a few hours a day, and many did not expose children to systematic, well-thought-out experiences. Not surprisingly, some evaluations of Head Start have concluded that intelligence is perhaps not as malleable as had been hoped (see Lazar et al., 1982). In general, however, the evidence is that higher-quality programs are effective in increasing measured intelligence, and that children exposed to such programs often do better in subjects such as mathematics. In addition, there are usually improvements in more-difficult-to-measure areas such as social functioning (Zigler & Freedman, 1987).

Studies of Twins

"If I had any desire to lead a life of indolent ease," Stephen Jay Gould tells us, "I would wish to be an identical twin, separated at birth from my brother and raised in a different social class. We could hire ourselves out to a host of social scientists and practically name our fee. For we would be exceedingly rare representatives of the only really adequate natural experiment for separating genetic from environmental effects in humans" (1981, p. 234).

Why is this so? Because identical twins are genetically identical; they result from the splitting of a single zygote, a fertilized ovum. This segmentation results in

two fertilized eggs, each with an identical genetic makeup, producing **identical (monozygotic) twins.** The other type of twins, **fraternal** or **dizygotic,** results from the fertilization of two *different* egg cells by two *different* spermatozoa. This is possible only when the mother produces more than one egg and results in twins who are no more alike genetically than ordinary **siblings**.

Unfortunately for research, the incidence of twins is relatively low—approximately 1 in every 86 births. Furthermore, identical twins are much rarer than fraternal twins—perhaps 1 in 300 births in North America. The precise causes of twin births are not known, although heredity appears to be a factor, because twins are found relatively frequently in some families and not at all in others. Also, older parents are more likely to have twins than are younger parents (Ernst & Angst, 1983).

Intelligence. Many studies of twins have looked at correlations for intelligence test scores. Recall from Chapter 1 that a correlation is a measure of relationship usually expressed in numbers ranging from 0 to plus or minus 1. A high *positive* correlation—say, +0.75 to +1.00—means that if one twin has a low intelligence test score, the corresponding twin is likely to have a low score also (or both are likely to have high or mediocre scores). A high *negative* correlation—say, -0.75 to -1.00—means that a high score for one would be associated with a low score for the other.

Bouchard and McGue (1981), Scarr and Kidd (1983), Loehlin, Willerman, and Horn (1988), and others have summarized some of the correlations of studies

Twins occur rarely in human births—approximately 1 in every 86 births. Identical twins are rarer—perhaps 1 in 300 or so births among caucasians and far fewer among the Chinese or Japanese. Twins provide researchers with an excellent opportunity to separate the effects of heredity and environment. Triplets, such as the Koralja trio, who are Jersey City policemen, are even rarer than twins.

of twins. In general, the average correlation for intelligence test scores for identical twins is above +0.80, while that for fraternal twins is below +0.60. If members of identical and fraternal twin pairs have had similar environments, these correlations are evidence that measured intelligence is influenced by heredity. Related to these studies is the observation that with decreasing genetic similarity, there is a corresponding decrease in similarity between intelligence scores. Figure 3.11 is a summary of a number of correlations for intelligence test scores.

These data also support the belief that contexts influence intelligence. Since most sets of identical twins have more similar environments than do cousins or siblings, the higher correlation between various intelligence measures for identical twins may be due at least partly to their more nearly identical environments. And the difference between identical twins reared together and those reared apart is additional evidence that environment influences development. Figure 3.11, for example, reports correlations of +0.67 and +0.85, respectively, for identical twins reared apart and those reared together. Because these twins are genetically identical, environmental forces are clearly important.

It is also revealing that as identical twins grow up, their phenotypes (manifested characteristics) become less similar; but, of course, their genotypes remain identical. Apparently, the interaction of these identical genotypes with somewhat different contexts leads to progressively more dissimilar developmental outcomes (McCartney, Bernieri, & Harris, 1990).

Personality. Twin studies also provide evidence that a host of personality characteristics are strongly influenced by genetic factors (Plomin, 1989). In an Australian survey of 3,810 pairs of adult identical and fraternal twins, for example, Martin and Jardine (1986) found high correlations for personality characteristics such as anxiety, depression, conservatism, and introversion/extroversion. Similar results have also been reported in a survey of American adult twins (Pogue-Geile & Rose, 1985).

Perhaps more striking is the finding that some mental disorders have a genetic basis. For example, Gottesman and Shields (1982) found that of 28 pairs of identical twins there was 42 percent concordance for schizophrenia—that is, 42 percent of all schizophrenic members of twin pairs had a schizophrenic twin. The concordance between members of fraternal twin pairs was only 9 percent, from a sample of 34 pairs.

Studies of adopted children and studies of mental disorders among related family members also confirm the finding that some forms of schizophrenia as well as manic-depression have a genetic component (Loehlin,

No. of Correlations	34	3	3	8	41	69	2	32	4	2	4	5	6	8	8	16
No. of Pairings	4,672	65	410	982	5,546	26,473	203	8,433	814	200	1,176	345	369	758	1,397	3,817
Median Correlation	.85	.67	.73	.475	.58	.45	.24	.385	.22	.35	.145	.29	.31	.19	.18	.365

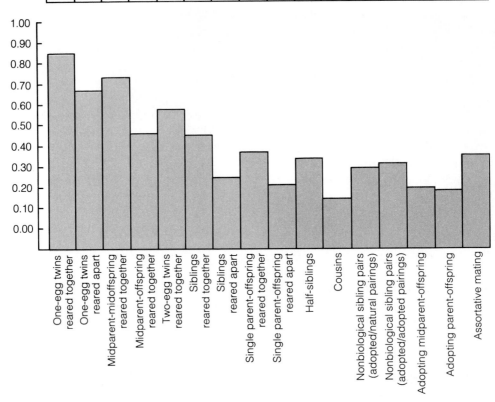

Figure 3.11 Median correlation coefficients for intelligence test scores from a large number of studies. The high correlation for identical twins shows the strong genetic basis of measured intelligence. The greater correlation for siblings or twins reared together compared with those reared apart supports the view that environmental forces are also important in determining similarity of intelligence test scores. (From T. J. Bouchard and M. McGue (1981). "Familial Studies of Intelligence: A Review." *Science 212*, 1055–1059. © 1981 by the AAAS. Used by permission of the AAAS and the author.)

Willerman, & Horn, 1988). Similarly, there appears to be little doubt that heredity is often involved in the onset of alcoholism, and, as we saw earlier, it is also implicated in at least some forms of such disorders as Alzheimer's disease, infantile autism (a schizophrenia-like disorder first apparent in early infancy), and even anorexia nervosa.

Adopted Children Studies

Adopted children studies are another rich source of information about the interaction of contexts and biology. Where it is possible to obtain information about biological as well as adoptive parents, and about natural and adopted children, these studies permit a wide range

TABLE 3.2

IQ Correlations in the Texas Adoption Project

Correlation Pairing	Number of Pairs	Observed Correlations
Share genes only:		
Adopted child × biological mother	297	0.28
Share environment only:		
Adopted child × adoptive mother	401	0.15
Adopted child × adoptive father	405	0.12
All unrelated children	266	0.18
Share genes and environment:		
Natural child × adoptive mother	143	0.21
Natural child × adoptive father	144	0.29
Natural child × natural child	40	0.33

Source: From "The Texas Adoption Project," by J. M. Horn, 1983, *Child Development*, pp. 268–275. © 1983 by the Society for Research in Child Development, Inc. Reprinted by permission.

of comparisons that make it easier to untangle the interaction of genes and context.

In the Texas Adoption Project, which began in 1973, investigators have access to data that include physical as well as cognitive measures of the adopted children's biological mothers (and sometimes fathers as well), in addition to similar measures for the children themselves, their adoptive parents, and other "natural" children in the adoptive home (Horn, 1983; Loehlin, 1985; Willerman, 1979). This makes it possible to compare relationships between adopted children and their biological mothers with those between the adopted children and their adoptive mothers. Furthermore, these relationships can also be compared with those that exist between the adoptive parents and their natural children. In other words, the design of this study makes it possible to look at correlations where the members of a pair have common genes but different environments (adopted children and their biological mothers); where members of a pair share an environment but are genetically unrelated (adopted children and their adoptive parents); and where there is some commonality with respect to both genes and the environment (adoptive parents and their natural children).

Some of the results of the Texas Adoption Project are summarized in Table 3.2. What is most striking about these findings is that the correlation between adopted children and their biological mothers is higher than that between the adopted children and their adoptive parents — a finding that has been replicated in other studies as well (Turkheimer, 1991). Also, the relationship between adopted children and their biological parents is about the same as that between adoptive parents and their own children in spite of the fact that the adopted children are not raised by their own parents. Eysenck (Eysenck & Kamin, 1981) claims this is strong evidence that genetics is the principal determiner of variation in intelligence. It should be noted, however, that these correlations are very low; they do not, by themselves, account for very much variation in intelligence. But, as geneticists would be quick to point out, the degree of genetic relatedness between a child and a natural parent is not nearly as high as that between siblings, and even less than that between identical twins.

Several other studies of adopted children, many of them employing longitudinal designs, have begun to contribute significantly to our knowledge of the ways in which heredity and environment interact to determine changes during the course of development. One of the Minnesota Adoption Studies, for example, found that black children adopted into white homes performed as well on IQ tests as the "natural" white children in these homes (Scarr & Weinberg, 1983). Black children adopted into white homes had higher average intelligence test scores than their biological parents. Significantly, however, their measured intelligence was more closely related to that of their biological than their adoptive parents. What this means is that if the biological parents were ranked according to measured IQ, and then their children were ranked in the same way, the correspondence between the two rankings would be high (the correlation would be high). Put another way, variations in measured intelligence are more easily explained in terms of genetics than environment (Plomin, 1989). Clearly, however, no explanation that does not consider the interaction of the two can be complete.

An Illustration of Gene–Context Interaction

A dramatic illustration of context–person interaction is found in Elder, Nguyen, and Caspi's (1985) analysis of the effects of the 1930s Great Depression on children's lives. The analysis is based on a longitudinal study of 167 children born in 1920 and 1921, who were therefore in the second decade of their lives during the depression. Earlier investigations of these children had suggested that the severe economic hardships of the depression had profound effects on the lives of parents and children (Elder, 1974). Fathers seemed to be most affected, probably because they were usually the ones who lost their jobs and consequently their ability to provide for their families as they had before. As a result, many women and older children were forced to work. These changes, says Elder (1979), increased the tendency for some fathers to become punitive and perhaps exploitive, and for others to become more rejecting and indifferent. In contrast, mothers, for whom loss of the husband's job would be an economic but not a personal blow, seemed relatively unaffected. Their relationships with their children did not change in very noticeable ways.

In a later analysis of some of this earlier data, Elder and associates (1985) looked at the effects of the depression on the experiences and lives of adolescents, paying particular attention to sex and physical attractiveness.

The analysis indicates that, like younger children, many adolescents suffered during the depression, and that their relationships with parents changed in systematic ways. For example, boys' perceptions of the power and attractiveness of their fathers tended to decline whereas their peers became more appealing. This was especially true in the more deprived homes where boys were even more likely to stress the importance of being with peers and to diminish the importance and influence of the father. Interestingly, however, adolescent boys did not appear to suffer in terms of confidence, aspirations, and positive self-concept. In contrast, girls tended to lower their aspirations and their self-esteem, and to experience increased moodiness and unhappiness.

Elder and associates (1985) found that these negative effects, which were more serious for girls than for boys, were not linked so much to economic hardships as to the rejecting behavior of the fathers. But what is most striking is that the least attractive girls suffered most. In the researchers' words, "If girls were unattractive, family hardship accentuated fathers' overly demanding, exploitive behavior . . . [but] only when girls were rated as unattractive" (p. 371). In fact, they report, in some cases, economic hardship actually increased the extent to which fathers were warm and supportive of their *attractive* daughters, sacrificing and going out of their way to provide for them.

The lesson to be learned from such studies is clear: If we are to understand the development and the lives of people, we must take into account the contexts in which they are born and live. In Bronfenbrenner's terms, the interactions that define our changing ecologies are fundamentally important. They need to be considered at a variety of levels: the microsystem (for example, in this study, the adolescent in interaction with father, mother, peers), the mesosystem (for example, family interactions with school or with the adolescent's workplaces), the exosystem (for example, the father's changed relationship with his work setting), and the macrosystem (for instance, the dramatic changes in social and economic conditions that defined the Great Depression). And at each level — and perhaps especially that of the microsystem — the researcher has to take into consideration the characteristics of the individuals involved. In this study, for example, sex is clearly an important factor; furthermore, girls' physical attractiveness is especially important in influencing the father's behavior.

An ecological approach to understanding development not only emphasizes the importance of the interactions that define the child's ecological system, but underscores as well the importance of the characteristics of individuals and settings in interaction. And it provides a framework for beginning to understand how characteristics that have a strong genetic basis (physical appearance, for example) can influence interactions in systems that are also influenced by environmental factors (such as economic conditions, for instance).

The Continuing Controversy

When Snyderman and Rothman (1987) questioned 1,020 American scholars, researchers, and theorists, they found that most believed that intelligence is inherited to a significant degree. This, of course, does not contradict the fact that all human characteristics are influenced by the interaction of genes and changing contexts.

So what is the controversy? Essentially, it's still the same old nurture–nature question—the question of whether certain traits are influenced primarily by heredity or only by the environment, and of how important each is. It's a controversy that stems from an extreme and often emotional belief that we are—or at least should be—equal. And if we are equal, then it cannot be that Jill has an assortment of genes highly likely to lead to charm and intelligence and grace while Mikey starts his life with an assortment of genes that propel him blindly toward low intelligence or schizophrenia.

Or can it? Science suggests that yes, our genes are different, and yes, we have different probabilities of reaching certain outcomes. But science also tells us that genes, by themselves, determine little. They simply underlie potential, making some outcomes more probable than others. Even in the face of highly probable (highly canalized) outcomes, environmental forces can lead to surprising and wonderful things.

Plasticity

That is the essence of Gottesman's (1974) concept of reaction range of which we spoke earlier. Reaction range is the range of possibilities implicit in our genes. It includes all the outcomes possible for any given characteristic, taking into account variations in the timing and nature of environmental influences.

What the concept of reaction range recognizes is our plasticity. *Plasticity*, or adaptability, is one of our most fundamental characteristics. But, as Lerner (1987) notes, our malleability does have limits. It is as though our genetic makeup, our biology, sets a range of possible outcomes. Ultimately, it is the complex interplay between our contexts and our characteristics that gradually shapes our developmental paths. If, for example, we are attractive adolescent females, perhaps events like great economic depressions will affect us far less than if our genetic makeup has made us physically unattractive (Elder, Nguyen, & Caspi, 1985). The ecologies defined by our face-to-face interactions (in what Bronfenbrenner calls microsystems) always reflect our personal characteristics as well as the characteristics of the contexts with which we are interacting. The processes are complex, the systems are "open," and our developmental outcomes are never completely predictable.

The Stern Hypothesis

The concept of human plasticity is simplified by Stern (1956) in what he calls the "rubber band hypothesis" (see Figure 3.12):

> The genetic endowment in respect to any one trait has been compared to a rubber band and the trait itself to the length which the rubber band assumes when it is stretched by outside forces. Different people initially may have been given different lengths of unstretched endowment, but the natural forces of the environment may have stretched their expression to equal length, or led to differences in attained length sometimes corresponding to their innate differences and at other times in reverse of the relation. (p. 53)

Put somewhat more simply, some of us have short bands (the initial length of the band corresponds to inherited potential for being intelligent); others have longer bands. Some environments (good ones?) stretch bands a great deal; others hardly stretch them. Long bands, of course, stretch to great lengths more easily than short bands. Given the right environment, a short

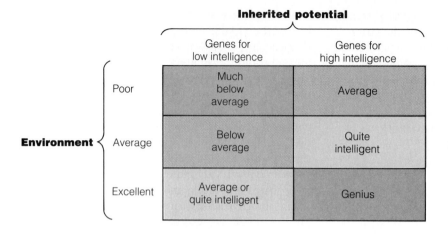

Inherited potential

	Genes for low intelligence	Genes for high intelligence
Poor	Much below average	Average
Average	Below average	Quite intelligent
Excellent	Average or quite intelligent	Genius

(Environment)

Figure 3.12 The Stern hypothesis, an example of gene–environment interaction. Individuals with different inherited potentials for intellectual development can manifest a wide range of measured intelligence as a function of environmental forces.

band might in the end be longer than one that was initially quite long—and vice versa.

Do highly demanding environments break bands? Do old bands become frayed and brittle? Do bands stretch more easily when new? Unfortunately, analogies are simply comparisons. They provide no answers for questions such as these.

There is a myth, says Weinberg (1989), that if something is genetic, it is fixed. In fact, however, genes merely establish a range of possibilities—Gottesman's reaction range. One of the dangers when considering the effects of heredity and environment is to assume that heredity determines only by limiting our possibilities. And while this point of view is at least partly accurate (no amount of nutrition would have been likely to make me 7 feet 3, allowing me to become a basketball star), it is nevertheless true that while we can do little about genetics, we still have considerable control over the environment. It is certainly far more optimistic to adopt a point of view that, with Gould (1981), emphasizes the flexibility and uniqueness made possible by our biological natures. In spite of our tremendous similarities, you and I are really quite different.

The Future

Molecular genetics, as we saw earlier, is a rapidly developing and tremendously exciting field. Almost daily, there are new discoveries. Science is at the threshold of being able to detect genetic weaknesses, as well as strengths, from the very earliest moments of life. It is at the threshold, too, of altering genetic messages, of rewriting the code to enhance the possibilities implicit in our genetic ranges. Our mushrooming knowledge of cell biology at the molecular level is opening new doors into the vast and almost uncharted world of genetic engineering. Recombinant DNA techniques now make it possible for scientists to use bacteria to reproduce specific sequences of genetic material. The results include new medications, new refining and manufacturing processes, and new products.

Science is breaking the code. It is learning to read the messages that direct the arrangements of the amino acids that, in turn, define the structure and function of the protein molecules that are the fundamental units of our biological lives.

There are ethical issues involved here—important ethical issues. Some have to do with the potential dangers of experiments that can, theoretically, produce new forms of life, the consequences of which cannot really be imagined because the nature of that life may be unknown before its creation.

Other issues have to do with the morality of altering genetic codes, with the ethics of decisions relating to creating or ending life, with the legality and morality of surrogate mothering and artificial insemination, maybe even with the very definition of life. Perhaps in another decade these issues will have become more important than the science that gave them birth, and another new discipline will have arisen to deal with them.

Science has not yet unraveled the combined effects of heredity and environment in its efforts to understand how and why we become who we are. Will hours of dedicated practice make a prodigy of this boy? How important is it that his family be rich with musicians? That his ancestors have startled ancient kings and queens with their talent?

Main Points

1. We think of our genes as being within us, and of contexts as out there, each totally separate from the other. But each changes as a function of the other. Developments made possible by our genes (language) nevertheless depend on context (not being abandoned).

2. The additive view with respect to gene–environment contributions to human development assumes that genes contribute a certain percentage, and environment the remainder. The interactive model assumes a more complex relationship between genes and environment, such that neither alone accounts for anything.

3. Conception, the beginning of life, ordinarily requires a physical union between male and female, or may be achieved through artificial insemination, *in vitro* fertilization, or the use of another woman as a surrogate, either to carry a fetus to term or to produce an embryo that can be removed and placed in a "host" mother.

4. The bases of biological life are protein molecules whose function is determined by the arrangement of the 20 or so amino acids of which they are composed. In turn, arrangements of the amino acids are determined by a special genetic code contained in sequences of deoxyribonucleic acid (DNA) molecules located on rodlike structures called chromosomes. The hereditary basis of life resides in the ovum (egg cell) and in the sperm cell, each of which contains half the number of chromosomes found in ordinary human body cells. In the chromosomes are the carriers of heredity, the genes.

5. Only the father can produce a Y sex chromosome, while both mother and father produce X chromosomes. The presence of a Y chromosome in the

fertilized egg determines that the offspring will be male; two X chromosomes determine a female.

6. Genes, in pairs or in combinations of pairs, interact with the environment to influence certain characteristics. In major gene determination, characteristics corresponding to *dominant* genes will be manifested in the individual except where two recessive genes are paired.

7. Genetic makeup is *genotype*; phenotype refers to manifested characteristics. Manifested characteristics that typically correspond closely to underlying genetic makeup are said to be highly canalized. Reaction range refers to the range of possibilities implicit in genotype. The nature of the characteristics manifested is a function of gene–environment interaction, within the limits of the trait's reaction range. Waddington's epigenetic landscape presents an analogy for understanding gene–environment interaction.

8. Molecular genetics, which looks at the structure and function of genes, has succeeded in locating a large number of marker genes—specific segments of DNA that are associated with some identifiable characteristic. Many genetic defects (approximately 2,000 have been identified) are associated with recessive genes and will therefore not be manifested unless the individual inherits the genes (or gene combinations) from both parents. The same is not true of defects associated with dominant genes.

9. Huntington's disease (a fatal neurological disorder) is caused by a dominant gene. Sickle-cell anemia (the reduced ability of red blood cells to obtain oxygen), PKU (an enzyme disorder that sometimes leads to mental retardation), Tay–Sachs disease (another enzyme disorder leading to brain degeneration and death), and some forms of muscular dystrophy (a degenerative muscular disorder), diabetes (a sugar-processing disorder), and neural tube defects are all examples of genetic disorders associated with recessive genes.

10. Chromosomal disorders result from errors in chromosomes rather than from defective genes. They include Down syndrome (Trisomy 21) and disorders associated with errors in sex chromosomes such as Turner's syndrome (linked to an absent sex chromosome); XYY syndrome (super males), af-

fecting men only; Klinefelter's syndrome, affecting men with an extra X chromosome (XXY); and fragile X syndrome (often linked with mental retardation).

11. Some genetic abnormalities and fetal diseases can be detected prior to birth by means of amniocentesis (analysis of amniotic fluid withdrawn through a needle), chorion biopsy (analysis of preplacental tissue), fetoscopy (a surgical procedure sometimes employed to obtain fetal blood or skin samples), or ultrasound (use of sonar techniques to detect physical characteristics as well as fetal movement).

12. Intervention studies such as Sherman and Key's work with the Mountain and Briarsville children, and investigations of the effects of preschool programs such as Head Start, indicate that the environment influences characteristics such as intelligence. The fact that identical twins reared together are more similar than those reared apart corroborates these findings. However, with higher genetic relatedness, individuals are in general more similar—a finding that illustrates the importance of biology.

13. Studies of adopted children typically report higher (although modest) correlations for measured intelligence between biological mothers and the children they have given up for adoption than between the adopted children and their adoptive mothers (and/or fathers).

14. Elder's study of the differential impact of the Great Depression on the lives of attractive and less attractive girls illustrates how biology (attractiveness) and the environment can interact to influence development. It is useful to emphasize the plasticity of, rather than the limits implicit in, our genes.

15. The Stern hypothesis presents a summary of the evidence relating to the nature–nurture controversy by stating that genetic endowment is like a rubber band that assumes its final length (the actual performance of an individual) as it interacts with the environment. Implicit in this summary is the notion that it is easier to stretch a long band than one that was short to begin with.

16. The possibilities implicit in recombinant DNA technology and in various other facets of genetic engineering give rise to important legal, moral, and ethical issues.

Further Readings

For a fascinating and tragic account of an abandoned child, see:

Curtiss, S. (1977). *Genie: A psycholinguistic study of a modern-day wild child*. New York: Academic Press.

The following is a comprehensive summary of current research on the inheritability of intelligence, personality characteristics, and psychopathologies such as schizophrenia, alcoholism, and Alzheimer's disease:

Loehlin, J. C., Willerman, L., & Horn, J. M. (1988). Human behavior genetics. *Annual Review of Psychology, 39*, 101–133.

Eysenck and Kamin present two of the more extreme points of view in the classical nature–nurture debate in:

Eysenck, H. J., & Kamin, L. (1981). *Intelligence: The battle for the mind*. London: Macmillan.

Stephen Jay Gould's aptly titled book presents a fascinating account of the history of mental measurement and a strong indictment of historical and sometimes current beliefs concerning IQ and its heritability:

Gould, S. J. (1981). *The mismeasure of man*. New York: W. W. Norton.

The first chapter of the following book is a somewhat advanced but intriguing look at the application of genetics to a study of the lifespan:

Baltes, P. B., Featherman, D. L., & Lerner, R. M. (1988). *Lifespan development and behavior* (Vol. 8). Hillsdale, NJ: Erlbaum.

CHAPTER 4

Prenatal Development and Birth

"Who was your mother?"
"Never had none!" said the child, with another grin.
"Never had any mother? What do you mean? Where were you born?"
"Never was born!" persisted Topsy.
"Do you know who made you?"
"Nobody, as I knows on," said the child, with a short laugh. "I 'spect I grow'd."

Harriet Beecher Stowe,
Uncle Tom's Cabin

No, child, you didn't just "grow'd"; something started you. And you clearly had a mother. In your day, there was seldom any doubt about who the mother was—although there might have been some uncertainty about the father.

Things are no longer so clear-cut as more and more women turn to artificial insemination and surrogate mothering. In fact, under some circumstances, they are so unclear that even the highest courts in the land are hard-pressed to determine maternity. Ms. Anna M. Johnson, for example, agreed to bear a child for Mark and Crispina Calvert in exchange for $10,000 ("Court to Decide," 1992). The Calverts later had a disagreement with the surrogate mother, and both parties sought legal custody of the child. The issue is complex: The child was conceived from Mark Calvert's sperm and Crispina Calvert's ovum; Ms. Johnson was then artificially inseminated with the fertilized ovum and bore the child to term. Who is the natural mother? Who is entitled to be the legal mother?

Not the surrogate mother, the California appellate court decided, agreeing with an earlier New Jersey Supreme Court ruling. Because surrogate mothers are not biologically related to the fetus, said the court, they cannot be considered either *natural* or *legal* mothers. The decision is under appeal.

Where does that leave the growing numbers of single women who turn to artificial insemination to produce children not as surrogate mothers, but for themselves ("Babies Without Dads," 1992)?

This Chapter

Sometimes artificial insemination involves donor sperm but uses the mother's ova, fertilized in the body or outside (*in vitro*). In such cases, the mother is also a biological parent. But in cases such as Ms. Johnson's, both sperm and ovum are donated, and the woman who carries the child serves as a host rather than a biological parent.

In all cases, however, after **conception** the fetus develops in a predictable fashion. The function and structure of each of the body's cells is largely preordained by the genetic material in the 23 pairs of chromosomes in the fertilized egg. But even here, as in all of life, development is always subject to a variety of influences.

This chapter traces the normal course of prenatal development from conception through birth, looks at some of the factors that can affect the fetus, and describes childbirth.

Detecting Pregnancy

Women find it useful to be able to detect **pregnancy** before the actual birth of the baby. In the absence of chemical tests or a professional medical examination, there are few certain indications of pregnancy before the later stages of **prenatal development**. However, there are some less certain signs such as cessation of **menses** (menstruation), morning sickness, changes in the breasts, and **quickening** (movement of the fetus). Most of these symptoms do not occur very early in pregnancy. Cessation of menses is not usually noticed until at least two weeks of pregnancy have passed, because conception ordinarily occurs approximately two weeks after the last menstrual period. Nor is this a certain sign of pregnancy—many other factors may be its cause. Morning sickness, although it affects approximately two-thirds of all pregnant women, does not ordinarily begin until two weeks after the missed period and can easily be mistaken for some illness. Breast enlargement and soreness, and darkening of the aureoles, are highly subjective and quite unreliable symptoms. Quickening, the movement of the fetus in the womb, is not noticeable by the mother until the fourth or fifth month, and by then most reasonably

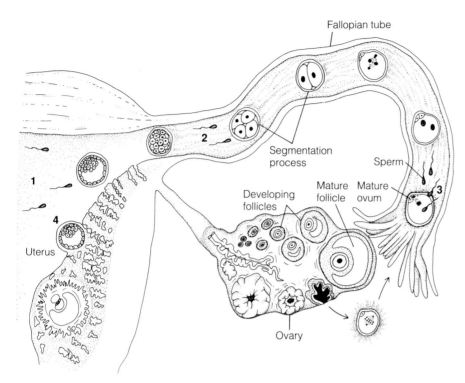

Figure 4.1 Fertilization and implantation. At (1), millions of sperm cells have entered the vagina and are finding their way into the uterus. At (2), some of the spermatozoa are moving up the fallopian tube (there is a similar tube on the other side) toward the ovum. At (3), fertilization occurs. The fertilized ovum drifts down the tube, dividing and forming new cells as it goes, until it implants itself in the wall of the uterus (4) by the seventh or eighth day after fertilization.

intelligent women have realized for some time that they are pregnant.

In addition to these probable signs of pregnancy, there are some more *positive* signs, such as the ability to hear fetal heartbeats with a **stethoscope**. Similarly, if fetal movements can be detected by feeling the abdomen, or sometimes simply by looking at it, one can be fairly confident that a fetus is present. Other methods for determining the presence of a fetus are to x-ray the mother to detect its outline, to feel it manually through the abdominal walls, or to use ultrasound, a high-frequency sonic device that provides a representation of the fetal outline.

Several decades ago, the surest early medical test of pregnancy required the aid of a virgin rabbit, a frog, a mouse, or some other unfortunate creature. Fortunately for virgin rabbits and mice, the medical sciences seldom stand still very long. Chemical pregnancy tests have now been devised for in-home use and are readily available in kit form. These kits detect changes in the woman's urine through a chemical reaction. Some tests claim they can detect pregnancy as early as one day following the day when the woman's menstrual period would have begun. Positive indications are highly re-

liable. Negative readings are somewhat less reliable, however, and should be followed by a second test a week or so later.

Stages of Prenatal Development

The **gestation period** for different species varies considerably. For bovines, it is similar to humans; elephants require no fewer than 600 days; dogs come to term in approximately 63 days, rabbits in 31, chickens in 21.

Fertilization in the woman usually occurs in the **fallopian tubes**, which link the **ovaries** to the **uterus** (see Figure 4.1). It results from the invasion of the tubes by sperm cells, one of which successfully penetrates the outer covering of the ovum and unites with it. From that moment, a human child begins to form, but it will be approximately 266 days before this individual is born.

The gestation period is usually calculated in lunar months, each month consisting of 28 days — hence 10

TABLE 4.1

Stages of Gestation (Prenatal Development)

The Fertilized Ovum	Also termed the *germinal stage* or the period of the *zygote*. Begins at fertilization and ends with implantation of the zygote (fertilized egg) in the uterine wall about one week later. Still microscopic.
Embryonic Stage	From implantation to the end of the eighth week following last menses. The embryonic stage therefore lasts about five weeks. It is during this stage that most of the important morphological (pertaining to form) changes occur. Accordingly, teratogens (influences that cause malformations and defects) are most influential during this period. At the end of this period, the embryo is close to 2 inches (4.5 cm) long and weighs about two thirds of an ounce (20 grams).
Period of the Fetus	From the end of the second lunar month until birth—usually eight lunar months (224) days later. Accelerating growth curves toward the end of this period.

lunar months, or 280 days, for pregnancy when these days are counted from the *beginning* of the last menstrual period. The true gestation period is nevertheless approximately 266 days because fertilization usually cannot occur until approximately 12 to 14 days later, when ovulation takes place (Pritchard & Mac-Donald, 1984).

The American College of Obstetricians and Gynecologists describes three prenatal developmental stages with clear time boundaries. The stage of the **fertilized ovum** (also called the germinal stage) begins at fertilization and ends with implantation at approximately the end of the first week. The **embryo** stage follows and terminates at the end of the eighth week (calculated from the onset of the last menses rather than from fertilization). The final stage, the **fetus**, lasts from the end of the second lunar month until the birth of the baby. (See Table 4.1 for a summary of the three stages.)

The Fertilized Ovum

After fertilization, the ovum is carried toward the uterus by currents in the fallopian tubes, a procedure requiring between five and nine days. Cell divisions occur during this time, so that the fertilized ovum, which initially consisted of a single egg cell and a single sperm cell, now contains many more cells. It is still no

larger at the end of the first week than it was at the time of fertilization, mainly because its multiplying cells are considerably smaller than the unfertilized ovum. This lack of growth is not surprising, because the ovum has received no nourishment from any source other than itself. At the end of the first week, this pinhead-sized ovum is ready to implant itself in the uterine wall.

The Embryo

The embryo stage begins with the implantation of the fertilized ovum in the wall of the uterus. The ovum facilitates this process by secreting certain enzymes and producing tiny, tentaclelike growths, called *villi*, that attach themselves to the lining of the uterus to obtain nutrients from blood vessels. This is the beginning of the **placenta**, the organ that, while keeping the blood of the mother and of the fetus separate, allows nutrients to pass to the fetus (or embryo) and waste materials to be removed. In time, the placenta and the fetus are connected by the **umbilical cord**, a long, thick cord that is attached, at one end, to the placenta and, at the other, to what will be the child's navel. The umbilical cord consists of two arteries and one large vein and is approximately 20 inches long. It contains no nerve cells, so there is no connection between the mother's

Growth in fetal weight and size becomes more dramatic in the final few months of gestation.

nervous system and that of the child **in utero** (a common medical term meaning "in the uterus"). Note that the placenta serves as a link between mother and fetus, while the umbilical cord links the fetus to the placenta.

The normal course of prenatal physiological development is highly predictable. By the end of the first lunar month (very early in the embryonic stage), the fetus is still only about one quarter of an inch long and weighs much less than an ounce. Despite the size, not only has there been cell differentiation into future skin cells, nerves, bones, and other body tissue, but the rudiments of eyes, ears, and nose have begun to appear. In addition, some of the internal organs are beginning to develop. In fact, by the end of the first month, a primitive, U-shaped heart-to-be is already beating! By

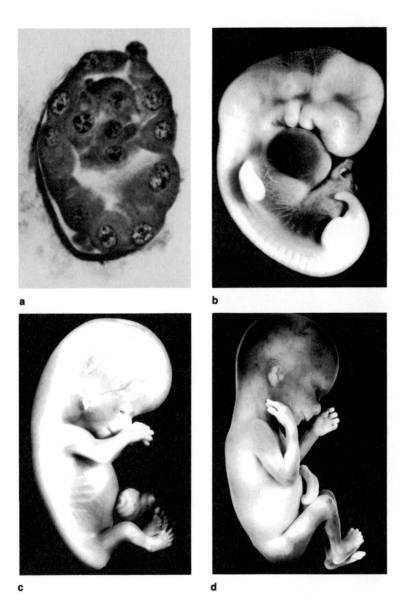

a

b

c

d

Figure 4.2 Development of the embryo at (a) approximately 4 days after conception, (b) 32 days, (c) 8½ weeks, and (d) 15 weeks.

the end of the second lunar month (the end of the period of embryonic development), the embryo is between 1½ and 2 inches long, and weighs close to two thirds of an ounce. All the organs are now present, the whole mass has assumed the curled shape characteristic of the fetus, and the embryo is clearly recognizable as human. Arm and leg buds have appeared and begun to grow, resembling short, awkward paddles. External **genitalia** (sex organs) have also appeared.

The Fetus

It is now the end of the second lunar month. Although the woman is six weeks pregnant, the absolute mass of the organism she carries inside her is quite unimpressive. By the end of the third month, it may reach a length of 3 inches but will still weigh less than an ounce. The head of the fetus is one third of its entire length and will have changed to one fourth by the end

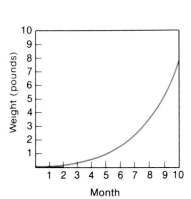

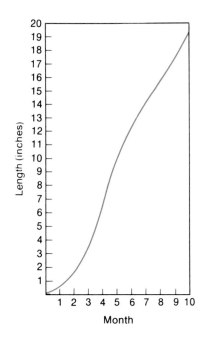

Figure 4.3 Approximate weight and length of the fetus at the end of each lunar month of prenatal development.

of the sixth lunar month and slightly less than that at birth (see Figure 4.2).

During the third month of pregnancy, the fetus is sufficiently developed that if it is aborted it will make breathing movements and will give evidence of a primitive **sucking reflex** and of the **Babinski reflex** (the infant's tendency to fan its toes when tickled on the soles of its feet) if stimulated appropriately. However, such a fetus will have no chance of survival if born now.

During the fourth lunar month of pregnancy, the fetus grows to 6 inches and weighs about 4 ounces. The bones have begun to form, all organs are clearly differentiated, and there may even be evidence of some intrauterine movement. During the fifth month, a downy covering, called **lanugo**, begins to grow over most of the child's body. This covering is usually shed during the seventh month but is occasionally still present at birth. The fetus weighs approximately 11 ounces and may have reached 10 inches by the end of the fifth lunar month.

Toward the end of the sixth month, an obstetrician can feel the baby through the mother's abdomen. The heartbeat, faintly discernible in the fifth month, can now be heard clearly with a stethoscope. The eyelids have separated so that the fetus can open and close its eyes. It is about one foot long and weighs close to 20 ounces. It would have some chance of surviving in a modern hospital if born at this time, despite the immaturity of its digestive and respiratory systems.

The fetus's growth in size and weight becomes more dramatic in the last few months of the final stage (see Figure 4.3). Brain development is also particularly crucial during the last three months of pregnancy, as it will continue to be after birth, especially for the first two years of life. The unborn child's sensitivity to malnutrition is assumed to be related to neurological growth during the latter stages of fetal development. This sensitivity is sometimes evident in lower developmental scores during infancy and impaired mental functioning among children born to malnourished mothers (Lewin, 1975).

Most of the physical changes that occur after the seventh month are a matter of sheer physical growth: from 15 inches (38 cm) and 2.6 pounds (1.2 kg) in the seventh month to 16 inches (41 cm) and 4 pounds (1.8 kg) in the eighth, 17.5 inches (45 cm) and 4.7 pounds (2.1 kg) in the ninth, and 19.6 inches (50 cm) and 7 pounds (3.2 kg) at the end of the tenth (see Table 4.2).

Two terms are sometimes used to describe the general pattern of fetal development: **proximodistal** and **cephalocaudal**. Literally, these terms mean *from*

TABLE 4.2

Prenatal Development According to Lunar Months

Age	Weight	Length	Characteristics
1st month	Negligible	¼ inch	Cell differentiation into those that will become bones, nerves, or other tissues.
2nd month	⅔ ounce	1½–2 inches	All organs present; leg buds and external genitalia just appearing.
3rd month	⅞ ounce	3 inches	If aborted, will make primitive breathing movements and suck; bones forming, organs differentiated.
4th month	4 ounces	6 inches	
5th month	11 ounces	10 inches	Fetal movement (quickening); lanugo appears.
6th month	20 ounces	12 inches	Heartbeat clearly discernible; eyelids present.
7th month	2.6 pounds	15 inches	
8th month	4 pounds	16 inches	All major changes have now occurred; development is largely a matter of increasing weight and length.
9th month	4.7 pounds	17.5 inches	
10th month	7 pounds	19.6 inches	

near to far (proximodistal) and *from the head to the tail* (cephalocaudal). They refer to the fact that among the first aspects of the fetus to develop are the head and internal organs; the last are the limbs and digits.

After 266 days of intrauterine development, the fetus is ready to be born—although some appear to be ready earlier and some later. But before we look at birth, we turn to a discussion of the factors that may be important to the normal or abnormal development of the fetus.

Factors Affecting Prenatal Development

External influences that cause malformations and physical defects in the fetus are called **teratogens** (from *teras*, the Greek word for "monster," so called because such substances were thought to be capable of producing monsters). Accordingly the study of birth defects is called **teratology**.

Among the most commonly recognized teratogens are various maternal illnesses, drugs, chemicals and minerals, and radiation. However, it is difficult to provide a complete listing and description of factors that affect prenatal development because of the highly circumstantial nature of much of the evidence. There is a lot of confusion about such factors, not only because they are very complex but also because many potentially helpful experiments cannot be performed for ethical or moral reasons. Consider, for example, the apparently simple problem of determining whether a particular drug affects the fetus. Seemingly, all that is required is to obtain a group of women to whom the drug has been administered and observe their offspring for any signs of possible effects of the drug. However, the women have usually been given the drug for a particular reason. As a result, the investigator is often unable to determine whether apparent effects on children are caused by the ailment for which the drug was taken or by the drug itself. For ethical reasons, it is not usually possible to administer the drug simply to observe its effect. Furthermore, the effects of prenatal environments are sometimes so subtle that they are not easily detected. Despite difficulties such as these, however, considerable information about the various effects of prenatal conditions on the development of the fetus is now available.

Note that the effects of many teratogens often depend on a variety of factors, both environmental and genetic. That is, the occurrence and the severity of a defect associated with a particular teratogen are often determined by the fetus's genetic background as well as by stresses that might result from the combined presence of other teratogens. Accordingly, the effects of the same teratogen can vary widely from one fetus to another.

Not all external factors that affect the fetus are teratogens (produce defects). There are many positive influences on the developing fetus. Reassuringly, approximately 97 out of every 100 infants born in North America are normal and healthy. In the following sections, however, we look more at teratogens than at positive influences.

Maternal Emotions and Stress

A common folk belief is that the mother's emotional states can be communicated directly to the child. If the pregnant woman worries too much, her child will be born with a frown; if she has a particularly traumatic experience, it will mark the infant, perhaps for life. She must try to be happy and have pleasant experiences so that the child can be born free of negative influences.

Most of these beliefs about pregnancy are simply tales. Because there is no direct link between the mother's nervous system and the child's, the mother's emotional states or disorders are not likely to be communicated *directly* to the unborn child. But because of the intimate relationship between the mother and the child, it is logical to suppose that many of the stimuli that affect her will also have some effect on the child, however indirect.

Some evidence indicates that maternal emotions do affect the child. Increases in fetal activity have been observed following emotional tension in the mother. In addition, mothers who are anxious during much of their pregnancy often have infants who are more irritable and more hyperactive and have more feeding problems (Copans, 1974). One prevalent theory is that an anxious mother produces stress-related hormones that affect the child physiologically and therefore, indirectly, psychologically (Willemsen, 1979).

These findings must be viewed as highly tentative. Not only is it extremely difficult to arrive at valid and useful measures of emotional states in mother and infant, but it is often impossible to control a variety of other factors that might also be related. For example, some of the factors sometimes associated with high maternal stress (poverty, inadequate diet, medical problems) might also be associated with fetal problems. Hence, conclusive statements concerning the influence of maternal emotional states on the unborn are not warranted.

Prescription Drugs

Investigating the effects of drugs on the fetus presents many scientific, ethical, and moral problems. It is clearly impossible to use human subjects in controlled investigations with drugs whose effects will probably be harmful to the fetus. The information is therefore based on studies of animals or on observations of human infants in poorly controlled situations. Generalizing from studies of animals to humans in the case of drugs presents an additional problem because certain drugs may have dramatically different effects on members of different animal species, as well as on children relative to adults (Bowes et al., 1970). Also, keep in mind that normal adult doses of a drug might well represent huge doses for a fetus weighing only ounces, particularly if the drug crosses the placental barrier easily.

Among the better-known prescription drugs that have marked effects on the unborn child are thalidomide, which causes severe morphological (structural or form) changes in the embryo (Lenz, 1966); quinine, which is associated with congenital deafness; barbiturates and other painkillers that reduce the body's oxygen supply, resulting in varying degrees of brain damage; and various anesthetics that appear to cross the placental barrier easily and rapidly, and cause depression of fetal respiration and decreased responsiveness in the infant. Note that the most serious structural changes (physical deformities and abnormalities) that are sometimes associated with drug intake, as well as with other factors such as maternal malnutrition, occur primarily during the embryonic stage of development. After this stage, the fetus's basic structure has already been determined and formed, and is not as vulnerable to external influences (see Figure 4.4).

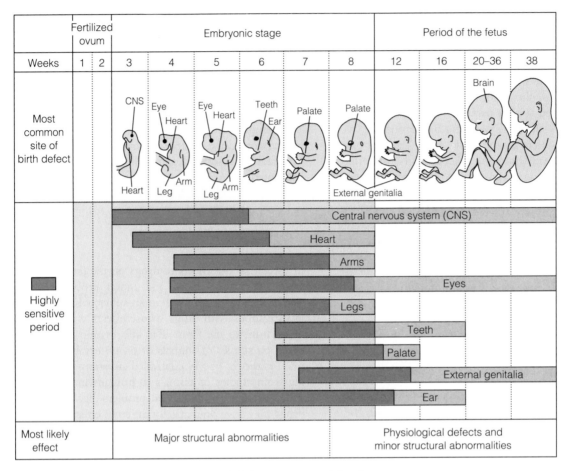

Figure 4.4 The most serious structural defects in prenatal development are most likely to occur in the first eight weeks, although teratogens can have serious consequences throughout gestation.

Among nonprescription drugs that may also have negative effects on the fetus is aspirin, which can increase the tendency to bleed in both mother and fetus (Stockman, 1990), and which is clearly linked with physical deformities among experimental animals (Vorhees & Mollnow, 1987). Also, megadoses of vitamins C, D, A, K, and B₆ have been linked with birth defects (Scher & Dix, 1983).

The prescription drugs mentioned in this section are only a few of the many drugs that are known to be harmful to the fetus. There are many others that do not seem to have any immediate negative effects but whose long-term effects are still unclear. Diethylstilbestrol (DES), for example, is a drug that was heavily prescribed through the 1940s and 1950s for women who were at risk for spontaneous abortions. It wasn't until several decades later that medical researchers discovered a link between DES use by pregnant women and vaginal cancer among girls subsequently born to these women. Because the effect occurs so long after taking the drug, and because it is manifested in only a small percentage of the offspring, it is extremely difficult to detect. For this reason, many medical practitioners discourage the use of prescription drugs by pregnant women unless absolutely necessary.

Chemicals

The effects of chemicals on mother and fetus are also very difficult to determine, partly because the effects of many chemicals are sometimes too subtle and not sufficiently widespread to be easily noticed; and partly because there are so many chemicals in our environments that it is almost impossible to separate their individual effects from one another. There are some 60,000 chemicals currently in use in North America, and several thousand new ones are introduced each year (Sloan, Shapiro, & Mitchell, 1980). Although the majority of these are "contained" in one way or another—that is, they don't find their way into our air, water, or food—and are essentially harmless, others are part of our daily environments in the form of water, air, or food pollutants, or as toxic wastes of various kinds. Unfortunately, their ultimate effects on our lives, and on the lives of those not yet born, are not always known before the fact.

We do know, however, that the ingestion of mercury by expectant mothers may result in severe retardation and physical deformities in their children. Interestingly, mothers (and other adults) may suffer only mild and reversible symptoms, whereas the fetus and young children are likely to suffer severe retardation and other nonreversible neurological damage (Vorhees & Mollnow, 1987). Although mercury occurs naturally in some areas, it is most often a problem where it is an industrial waste. It's also sometimes used to treat seed grains. Its effects received worldwide attention following the births of a large number of severely deformed and retarded infants in Minimata Bay, Japan. The deformities were traced to the presence of high levels of mercury in the fish that inhabitants of this community consumed in great quantities; in this case, the mercury was an industrial waste. The effects of mercury are now known as *Minimata disease*.

Other chemicals that are known to be harmful include a range of hydrocarbons that are used as herbicides and insecticides. These include dioxin and PCBs, both of which appear to be associated with higher incidences of miscarriages and physical deformities. Agent Orange, a chemical widely used to defoliate jungles during the war in Vietnam, is a dioxinlike chemical. It, too, has been linked with fetal abnormalities and death.

In addition to the chemicals that are known to be harmful to the fetus, there are many toxic chemicals whose effects on children and adults are well known but whose effects on fetal development are still unclear. Lead is one example. It is present in the emissions that result from the combustion of certain fuels, in some paints, in certain metal products, and elsewhere. It accumulates slowly in the body, and when it reaches sufficiently high concentrations, it can lead to serious physical and mental problems in children and adults (Weisskopf, 1987).

But these terrible things always happen to other people, strangers, who live in faraway places, don't they?

Nope. They happen where I am and where you are. When the nuclear reactor in Chernobyl spewed radioactive particles into the air in the spring of 1986, their presence could be felt and measured in Norway, Poland, France, and, yes, even in North America. And we do know that radiation is an extremely powerful teratogen that can lead to abortion, stillbirths, and physical abnormalities.

Even here in the Northern wilderness, it seems I have not escaped. My government informs me that certain species of fish in a lake on the shores of which I have a small shelter have unusually high levels of mercury. It cautions me that I should not eat of these fish more than once a week and that they should be avoided altogether by pregnant women.

Nicotine

The harmful effects of smoking on the smoker, as well as the effects of "sidestream," or secondhand, smoke on the nonsmoker, have been well documented. Some of the effects of nicotine and smoking on the fetus also seem clear.

The U.S. surgeon general, following an extensive review of the literature on cigarette smoking during pregnancy, summarizes some of its most important and consistent effects (U.S. Department of Health and Human Services, 1981). Cigarette smoking, the surgeon general concludes, is linked with a higher probability of placental problems in which the placenta becomes detached from the uterine wall, often leading to fetal death or stillbirths; it is associated with significantly lower birthweight, which, in turn, is associated with a higher probability of subsequent complications; it is linked with a higher risk of miscarriages and fetal death; and it is related to a higher incidence of early childhood respiratory infections and diseases. In brief, cigarette smoking is clearly harmful not only to the mother but also to the fetus, the placenta, the infant, and the child.

Caffeine

The effects of caffeine on the fetus remain somewhat unclear. This may be because these effects are different for different individuals and because they do not appear

Many widely used drugs have harmful effects on the unborn fetus. The nicotine ingested during smoking, for instance, has been linked to increases in fetal heart rate, fetal hyperactivity, retardation of growth in utero, and a higher incidence of premature births.

to be very dramatic. Nevertheless, large doses of caffeine given to pregnant rats have been associated with birth defects in their offspring. And some research indicates that the probability of premature delivery is somewhat higher among mothers who consume higher levels of caffeine (Jacobson et al., 1985). However, current evidence suggests that caffeine is not a teratogen, although extremely high consumption might be harmful to the fetus (Brendt & Beckman, 1990).

Alcohol

Alcohol consumption by pregnant women may be associated with various defects in their offspring, collectively labeled **fetal alcohol syndrome (FAS)** (Barr et al., 1990). The major features of this syndrome are problems with the central nervous system that are sometimes manifested in mental retardation, retarded physical growth, and cranial and facial malformations. These malformations typically include a low forehead, widely spaced eyes, a short nose and long upper lip, and absence of a marked "infranasal" depression (the typical depression above the center of the upper lip, going up toward the nose) (Abel, 1984).

With humans, it is difficult to conduct the types of experiments that would allow researchers to deter-

mine precisely what amounts of alcohol, and at what stage of development, will have these effects. Nor is it possible to separate completely the effects of alcohol from those of other drugs that might accompany alcohol use, or from the effects of malnutrition, also a possible corollary of alcohol use. However, a number of studies have looked at FAS among animals and have found, to no one's great surprise, that injections of ethanol (the type of alcohol that is drunk as opposed to the type that might be rubbed on a horse's sore muscles or that might be burned in an engine) in pregnant mice quite readily produce what appears to be FAS in their offspring. Not only are these offspring more likely to be born dead, but many of them will display facial and skull deformations highly reminiscent of those characteristic of FAS children (Rosett & Sander, 1979).

The current consensus is that even in small amounts, alcohol may be harmful to the fetus although it may not necessarily lead to FAS. Accordingly, some researchers speak of "fetal alcohol effects" rather than of FAS. For example, one study compared the effects of heavy drinking (four or more drinks a day) with the effects of more moderate drinking (two or three drinks a day) and those of lighter drinking (fewer than two drinks a day) (Streissguth et al., 1980). Some of the symptoms associated with FAS were found in 19 percent of the children born to mothers in the first group, 11 percent of those in the second, and only 2 percent of those in the third.

How much can a pregnant woman drink, and when? The evidence is not all in, and the conclusions are still tentative. In summarizing the effects of alcohol on the developing fetus, Brendt and Beckman (1990) conclude that consuming six drinks or more of alcohol per day constitutes a high risk, but that fewer than two drinks per day is not likely to lead to FAS. However, a longitudinal study of 449 children found a relationship between even *moderate* consumption of alcohol by pregnant mothers and children's motor performance on tests given at age 4. Children of these moderate drinkers made more errors on fine and gross motor tasks, responded more slowly, and had poorer balance (Barr et al., 1990). Note, too, that binge drinking may be especially harmful to the fetus in the early stages of pregnancy, and that it might be associated with neural tube defects (Graham, 1985).

Given these findings, corroborated by a large number of other investigations, it should come as no surprise that an increasing number of medical practitioners recommend that pregnant women refrain completely from alcohol use.

Substance Abuse

A large number of abused substances can have serious effects on prenatal development.

Narcotics.   Babies born to narcotics addicts are themselves addicted. These infants suffer a clearly recognizable withdrawal syndrome labeled the **neonatal abstinence syndrome**. Its symptoms may include tremors, restlessness, hyperactive reflexes, high-pitched cries, vomiting, fevers, sweating, rapid respiration, seizures, and sometimes death (Chasnoff, 1986). Often, these symptoms don't reach a peak until the infant is 3 or 4 days old. Some physicians recommend methadone maintenance in low doses for the mother during the later stages of pregnancy, and gradual weaning of the infant from methadone after birth (Iennarella, Chisum, & Bianchi, 1986).

In addition to their addictive effects, evident in the neonatal abstinence syndrome, narcotics have also been linked with prematurity and low birth weight, and with behavior problems such as hyperactivity (Kolata, 1978).

LSD and Marijuana.   The effects of substances such as LSD and marijuana remain somewhat uncertain. Although research with pregnant monkeys who were given LSD found chromosomal damage in the mothers and a high rate of stillbirths and early deaths among infants (Kato, 1970), these findings cannot easily be corroborated with humans. As Bolton (1983) points out, mothers who use one or both of these drugs typically drink alcohol as well, and may also use other drugs. In addition, many of them receive little prenatal medical care, some suffer from drug-related illnesses, and many have severely deficient diets. The causes of fetal and birth problems among this group cannot easily be identified.

One attempt to look at the effects of marijuana use on the human fetus and infant was a longitudinal investigation of 700 pregnant women (Fried, 1986). Each woman was interviewed three times during her pregnancy, once in each trimester. Detailed questioning touched on past and present alcohol, caffeine, and nicotine use, with particular emphasis on marijuana use. For the study, women were classified as nonusers, irregular users (one or fewer joints per week), moderate users (2–5 joints per week), and heavy users (5 or more joints per week). In this sample, 80 percent of the women were nonusers, 12 percent were irregular users, 1 percent were moderate users, 3 percent were heavy users, and 4 percent remained unclassified.

Fried (1986) reports that for this sample, there were no differences between marijuana users and nonusers with respect to rate of miscarriages, birth complications, or physical anomalies at birth. The study did find, however, that the gestational period was an average of 1.1 weeks shorter for heavy users. In addition, newborns whose mothers were regular heavy marijuana smokers exhibited more tremors and more intense startle reactions; and they were less responsive to a light directed at their eyes. Fried (1986) speculates that this may reflect minor neurological dysfunction and perhaps an immature nervous system. However, tests of motor and cognitive functioning do not ordinarily reveal any differences between infants of marijuana users and nonusers. Fried suggests that this may be because the tests are not sufficiently sensitive to detect differences that might exist. Additional evidence that the nervous systems of infants of heavy marijuana users may mature more slowly is apparent in the somewhat higher rate of visual problems among these children when they are tested between three and six years later.

Cocaine. A more recent and perhaps increasingly common kind of pregnant drug abuser is the cocaine user. Chasnoff, Burns, Schnoll, and Burns (1985) identified 23 pregnant cocaine users who were part of an ongoing study on the effects of drugs. Twelve of these women used only cocaine; the others also used alcohol or other drugs.

Infants born to cocaine users manifested more startle reactions and more tremors, much like children of heavy marijuana users. In addition, many of their reflexes and motor behaviors were significantly different from those of a control group whose mothers were not cocaine users. These differences included common reflexes such as the Moro reaction (startle reflex), age of standing, age of pulling up to a sitting position, and visual and auditory orientation.

Maternal Health

A wide range of diseases and infections affect the fetus. The best known is probably rubella (German measles); others are herpes, syphilis, gonorrhea, poliomyelitis, and diabetes, each of which can cause mental deficiency, microcephaly (abnormally small head), blindness, deafness, or miscarriage. Cretinism (subnormal mental development, underdeveloped bones, a protruding abdomen, and rough, coarse skin) may be related to a thyroid malfunction in the mother or to an iodine deficiency in her diet. If the deficiency is not too extreme, it can sometimes be alleviated in the child through continuous medication after birth. And AIDS is a more recent, and lethal, threat to the fetus.

Diabetes. Diabetes is a maternal condition that can have serious consequences for the fetus (see Hare, 1989). Before the discovery of insulin, rates of fetal and maternal death from diabetes were very high. Now, however, mortality rates among diabetic mothers are about the same as those among nonpregnant diabetic women. And with timely diagnosis and proper medical management, fetal deaths are generally below 5 percent (Coustan, 1990). Management involves careful monitoring of mother and fetus to assess and control sugar levels (glycemic control). Simple, self-monitoring procedures are available for in-home use.

Although fetal death as a complication of maternal diabetes has been greatly reduced, there is still a two to four times higher rate of birth defects among these infants. The most common defects include congenital heart disease, cleft palates, neural tube defects, and other neurological problems (Barss, 1989). Most of these birth defects result from influences that occur early in pregnancy—hence the importance of careful monitoring from the outset (Coustan, 1990).

Herpes. **Herpes** can also have serious effects on the fetus, particularly if the mother's infection is active at the time of delivery. The probability of the infant's contracting the virus during birth is extremely high—40–60 percent (Eden et al., 1990). In addition, evidence suggests that as many as 50 percent of mothers suffering from active herpes infections give birth prematurely (Babson et al., 1980). Because the newborn does not possess many of the immunities that are common among older children and adults, the herpes virus may attack the infant's internal organs, leading to visual or nervous system problems or death in about 50 percent of cases (Eden et al., 1990). As a result, infants born to mothers infected with the herpes virus are often delivered through cesarean section to prevent infection from occurring.

AIDS. **Acquired Immunity Deficiency Syndrome**, or **AIDS**, is another sexually transmitted disease that is of considerable current concern. First reported in the United States in 1981, it remains incurable and fatal. Estimates are that some 60,000 American men and women have now developed the disease (Trofatter, 1990). And the prognosis is that virtually all will eventually die from resulting complications.

AIDS is transmitted through the exchange of body fluids, primarily through blood–blood or semen–blood exchanges. Accordingly, transmission occurs mainly through anal intercourse (because of the thinness of rectal tissues, which frequently tear during intercourse), through blood transfusions involving infected blood, and through the communal use of hypodermic syringes. Not surprisingly, AIDS is most common among homosexual males and among intravenous drug users.

A great majority of infants and children with AIDS acquired it directly from their mothers through blood exchange in the uterus or during birth. The risk of transmission from infected mother to fetus ranges from 35 percent to 60 percent (Trofatter, 1990). Prognosis for an infected newborn is poor, with the survival period typically being considerably shorter than the 11–15 months that is the average survival period for adults (ACOG Technical Bulletin, 1988).

Pediatric AIDS Mortality

AIDS is a fatal disease transmitted through the exchange of body fluids. Most cases of pediatric (childhood) AIDS are transmitted directly from mother to fetus. In later childhood, AIDS is acquired primarily through blood transfusions and is consequently rarer. With increasing sexual activity after adolescence, incidence of AIDS rises dramatically. Male AIDS cases outnumbered female cases by a factor of almost 10 to 1 in 1989.

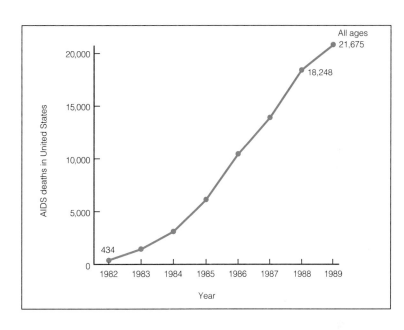

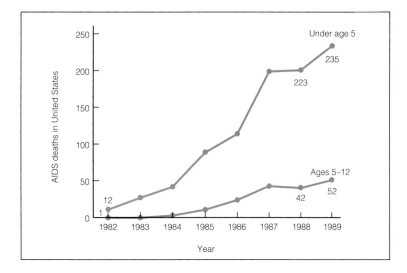

Figure 4.5 Rising number of deaths from AIDS in the United States, 1982–1989. Reported cases of AIDS are much higher. (Adapted from U.S. Bureau of the Census, 1991, p. 83.)

Clearly, high-risk women (current or past intravenous drug users, and those whose sexual partner(s) include bisexual males and/or men who have been or are intravenous drug users) should be tested for the AIDS antibody before considering pregnancy. And if the test is positive, reconsider.

Older Mothers

The mother's age is also related to the well-being of the fetus. We know, as was pointed out in Chapter 3, that the incidence of Trisomy 21 (Down syndrome) is approximately 1 in 1,500 live births for mothers ages 15–24 but increases to 1 in 38 for mothers over 45 (Brock, 1982). We know, as well, that the probability of fathering a child with Down syndrome is 20–30 percent higher for fathers over the age of 55. Nor is Trisomy 21 the only chromosomal disorder related to age. For example, rates of Klinefelter's syndrome as well as Trisomies 18 and 21 increase dramatically with the mother's age (Hsu, 1986). Both Trisomies 18 and 21 may be associated with neural tube defects, congenital heart disease, growth retardation, and other problems.

Another chromosomal abnormality that increases with the mother's age is fragile X syndrome, which is second only to Trisomy 21 as a cause of mental retardation, occurring in approximately 1 out of every 1,000 live births (Herbst & Miller, 1980). It is a sex-linked, primarily male disorder that often underlies a history of retardation among male children in some families (Silverstein & Johnston, 1990).

However, given the availability of prenatal procedures such as chorion biopsy or amniocentesis that now make it possible to determine the presence of a number of chromosomal abnormalities and other defects or diseases, increasing numbers of women, and men, are postponing starting a family. Kopp and Kaler (1989) point out that the greatest increase in fertility rates in recent years has been among women in their early thirties. However, fewer than 7 percent of all births occur to women over the age of 35 (Drugan, Johnson, & Evans, 1990).

In spite of the association between the mother's age and some chromosomal abnormalities, modern health care makes it possible for many women to deliver healthy, full-term babies at ages that would have entailed much higher risk a few decades ago. In fact, when Spellacy, Miller, and Winegar (1986) compared outcomes for 511 pregnancies of women over 40 with more than 26,000 pregnancies of women ages 20–30, they found that age posed little risk when factors such as cigarette smoking and maternal weight were taken into account.

Teenage Mothers

The number of births to teenage girls in North America remains very high relative to the rest of the population. In fact, 14 percent of all births are to girls ages 15–19 (U.S. Bureau of the Census, 1988). And more than half these births are to unmarried teenage parents (National Center for Health Statistics, 1985). The teenage birthrate in the United States is among the highest in the world—approximately 17 times higher than in Japan and 3 times higher than in the former Soviet Union (Davis & Harris, 1982).

Children born to younger teenage mothers are often at a physical, emotional, and intellectual disadvantage relative to children born to older mothers. There are more miscarriages, premature births, and stillbirths among teenage mothers, and surviving infants are more often the targets of abuse and neglect. The developmental scores of these children on various measures are often retarded (Smith, Weinman, & Malinak, 1984). And incidence of low birth weight is as much as three times that for women over 20 (National Center for Health Statistics, 1987).

As Lamb and Elster (1985) point out, however, much of the research fails to take into account the social circumstances of teenage parenthood—the poverty and the lack of social, educational, and medical assistance. In retrospect, it isn't the age of the teenage parent that is the important factor, but the health care available to the expectant mother both before and after the birth of her child. All other things being equal, unless she is very young (less than age 15), if a teenage mother and her infant receive the same medical attention as an older mother, the health and developmental status of her infant will be normal (McCormick, Shapiro, & Starfield, 1984).

But all other things are not often equal for teenage mothers, argues Grow (1979). And they will not be equal unless various agencies provide comprehensive services for teenage parents who keep their children. In the absence of such services, the economic and social conditions under which the majority of teenage mothers are forced to live, and the emotional stresses that accompany these conditions—as well as the demands

Parenthood in Later Life

Women (and men) are now marrying later. In addition, many are postponing having children or deciding not to have any. The percentage of childless women (among those ever married) rose from 16.4 in 1970 to 19.2 in 1986. Accordingly, since 1975 birthrates have dropped at all age levels *except* for older age groups. The greatest increase in birthrate is for women ages 35–39.

Birthrate per 1,000 Women	1960	1965	1970	1975	1978
White	113.2	91.4	84.1	62.5	61.7
Black	153.5	133.2	115.4	87.9	86.7
All women	118.0	96.6	87.9	66.0	65.5
Age of mother:					
10–14	0.8	0.8	1.2	1.3	1.2
15–19	89.1	70.5	68.3	55.6	51.5
20–24	258.1	195.3	167.8	113.0	109.9
25–29	197.4	161.6	145.1	108.2	108.5
30–34	112.7	94.4	73.3	52.3	57.8
35–39	56.2	46.2	31.7	19.5	19.0
40–44	15.5	12.8	8.1	4.6	3.9
45–49	0.9	0.8	0.5	0.3	0.2

	1979	1980	1981	1982	1983
White	63.4	64.7	63.9	63.9	62.4
Black	88.3	88.1	85.4	84.1	81.7
All women	67.2	68.4	67.4	67.3	65.8
Age of mother:					
10–14	1.2	1.1	1.1	1.1	1.1
15–19	52.3	53.0	52.7	52.9	51.7
20–24	112.8	115.1	111.8	111.3	108.3
25–29	111.4	112.9	112.0	111.0	108.7
30–34	60.3	61.9	61.4	64.2	64.6
35–39	19.5	19.8	20.0	21.1	22.1
40–44	3.9	3.9	3.8	3.9	3.8
45–49	0.2	0.2	0.2	0.2	0.2

	1984	1985	1986	1987	1988
White	62.2	63.0	61.9	62.0	63.0
Black	81.4	82.2	82.4	83.8	86.6
All women	65.4	66.2	65.4	65.7	67.2
Age of mother:					
10–14	1.2	1.2	1.3	1.3	1.3
15–19	50.9	51.3	50.6	51.1	53.6
20–24	107.3	108.9	108.2	108.9	111.5
25–29	108.3	110.5	109.2	110.8	113.4
30–34	66.5	68.5	69.3	71.3	73.7
35–39	22.8	23.9	24.3	26.2	27.9
40–44	3.9	4.0	4.1	4.4	4.8
45–49	0.2	0.2	0.2	0.2	0.2

Table 4.3 U.S. birthrates by age, per 1,000 women, 1960–1988.

Source: U.S. Bureau of the Census, 1991, p. 63.

of pregnancy and of childrearing—present many with serious disadvantages. (See Chapter 12 for a further discussion of teenage pregnancy.)

Maternal Nutrition

Starvation and extreme malnutrition can have serious negative consequences for the fetus. During the great Dutch famine (1944–1945), birthrates declined dramatically, more than 50 percent of childbearing women became amenorrheic (stopped menstruating), neonates (newborns) were smaller, and rates of infant mortality and malformations increased (Smith, 1947). For our purposes, however, a more important question concerns the effects of less obvious forms of malnutrition. Unfortunately, it is extremely difficult to separate the sometimes subtle effects of malnutrition from the effects of other variables that often accompany malnutrition (poor medical attention, poor sanitation, drug use, and so on).

Effects sometimes attributed to malnutrition might also be related to these other factors. In addition, malnutrition is seldom limited to the period of prenatal development but usually continues into infancy and even childhood. As Stein and associates (1975) note, perhaps the most plausible (although tentative) conclusions are that the effects of malnutrition are a complex interaction of the severity and the nature of deprivation. Lewin (1975) suggests that intellectual deficits may result from malnutrition that begins before birth and continues for some time afterward; and some of the short-term effects associated with prenatal malnutrition may be reversible given adequate nourishment after birth.

During pregnancy, the mother's energy requirements and her metabolism change. The presence of a growing fetus means that the mother requires somewhere between 10 and 15 percent more calories. And metabolic changes include an increased synthesis of protein, which is important for the formation of the placenta and enlargement of the uterus; a reduction in carbohydrate consumption, the effect of which is to provide sufficient glucose for the fetus; and increased storage of fat to satisfy the mother's energy requirements (Chez & Chervenak, 1990).

Not only must the pregnant woman increase her protein intake, but there is also an increased need for important minerals (for example, calcium, magnesium, iron, iodine, phosphorus) and vitamins (such as A, D, E, C, and some of the B's). Recommended dietary allowances for pregnant women range from 25 to 50 percent above those for nonpregnant women (*Recommended Dietary Allowances*, 1980).

Current medical advice emphasizes that *how much* the woman eats is less important than *what*. With respect to the development of the brain, protein appears to be among the most important ingredients of a good diet. In studies of both humans and rats where expectant mothers had protein-deficient diets, the offspring developed fewer brain cells or performed more poorly on tests of intellectual performance (McKay et al., 1978).

A second relevant aspect of current medical advice contradicts the long-held belief that the woman should be careful to minimize her weight gain during pregnancy. Infant mortality is often lower in countries where pregnant women gain significantly more weight than do pregnant women in the United States or Canada. Maternal weight gain leads to higher fetal weight and reduces the risk of illness and infection. Accordingly, doctors who once cautioned women to limit their weight gain to about 10 pounds now suggest that the optimal weight gain for a woman who begins pregnancy at an average weight is somewhere between 22 and 28 pounds (Chez & Chervenak, 1990); it is even higher for women who are initially underweight. For women who are initially overweight, recommended gains are correspondingly lower.

Unfortunately, this medical advice is more likely to be pertinent to people who will not be exposed to it and who could not take advantage of it in any case. Malnutrition and starvation are seldom a deliberate choice. (See Table 4.4 for a description of influences on the fetus, and Figure 4.4 for a timetable of the most susceptible periods.)

Social Class

The greatest single cause of infant death is premature birth. Furthermore, prematurity is among the most direct causes of cerebral palsy and various forms of mental handicaps. And the factor most closely related to premature births is social rather than medical.

These facts are significant and well documented. Although social class does not explain anything by

TABLE 4.4

Influences on the Fetus

Agent	Some Reported Effects or Associations
Alcohol	Fetal alcohol syndrome; intrauterine growth retardation; microcephaly; mental retardation
Diethylstilbestrol (DES)	Anomalies of cervix and uterus; higher risk of cervical cancer
Lithium carbonate	Heart and blood vessel defects; neural tube defects
Methylmercury	Minamata disease; cerebral palsy; microcephaly; mental retardation; blindness; death
Polychlorinated biphenyls	Cola-colored children; gum, nail, and groin pigmentation; can affect offspring for up to four years after maternal exposure
Radiation	Microcephaly; mental retardation; eye anomalies; visceral malformations
Street drugs	Fetal and pregnancy complications sometimes leading to death; no reported association with malformations
Tetracycline	Tooth and bone staining if exposed during last two thirds of pregnancy
Thalidomide	Limb reduction defects; anomalies of external ears, kidneys, and heart
Iodine deficiency	Hypothyroidism or goiter; neurological damage
Mechanical (constraint in womb)	Defects involving limb development and position; neural tube, lip, palate, or abdominal defects
Maternal starvation	Intrauterine growth retardation; central nervous system anomalies; fetal death
Diabetes	Malformations involving internal organs; caudal dysplasia
Rubella	Mental retardation; deafness; cardiovascular malformations; cataracts
Herpes simplex	Microcephaly; eye defects
Aspirin	Heavy use associated with lowered birthrate; no increase in malformation
Caffeine	Not likely to be a teratogen, although excess consumption may be toxic
Nicotine	Placental lesions; intrauterine growth retardation; increased mortality
Vitamin A	Urogenital anomalies associated with massive doses; ear malformations; neural tube defects; cleft palate; facial abnormalities
Vitamin D	Heart defects; facial malformations; mental retardation

Source: Based on R. L. Brendt & D. A. Beckman. (1990). Teratology. In R. D. Eden, F. H. Boehm, & M. Haire (Eds.), *Assessment and care of the fetus: Physiological, clinical, and medicolegal principles* (Table 17-4, pp. 227–28). Norwalk, Conn.: Appleton & Lange. Reprinted by permission of the publisher.

itself, the high correlation between low social class and higher incidence of premature birth suggests that the living conditions and associated emotional and health consequences attributed to poverty are not conducive to the production of healthy full-term babies (Baker & Mednick, 1984). Research relating to the effects of maternal malnutrition on the fetus, and subsequently on the infant, is directly relevant here. There is little doubt that prenatal and postnatal health care of mothers who live in poverty is rarely comparable to that of middle-class mothers. General diet and protein, mineral, and vitamin intake are often significantly inferior, and the

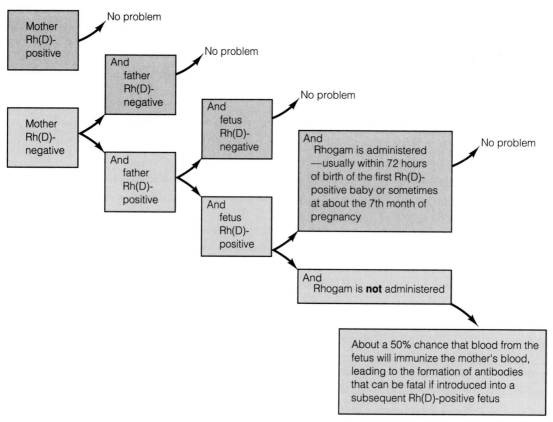

Figure 4.6 Rh(D) immunization flowchart. Immunization occurs when the Rh(D) factor is introduced in the Rh(D)-negative mother's blood, leading to the formation of antibodies that, if they are later introduced into the blood-stream of an Rh(D)-positive fetus, attack the fetus's blood cells in a potentially fatal condition termed *fetal erythroblastosis.* An injection of the drug Rhogam can prevent this from occurring.

effects of these factors are often the consequences of an infant being born poor. Social and moral implications are clear.

Rh(D) Immunization

There is a particular quality of blood in Rhesus monkeys that is often, but not always, present in human blood. Because this factor was first discovered in the Rhesus monkey, it is called the *Rh factor.* Individuals who are lacking this factor are Rh-negative; those whose blood contains the factor are Rh-positive. More precisely, however, it is a specific component of the Rh

blood group, labeled D, that is important for the pregnant mother and her fetus. Introduction of Rh(D)-positive blood into an individual who is Rh-negative leads to the formation of antibodies to counteract the D factor—a process termed *immunization* (Bowman, 1990). If these antibodies are then introduced into an individual with Rh(D)-positive blood, they attack that person's blood cells, causing a depletion of oxygen and, in the absence of medical intervention, death.

Unfortunately, this situation can occur in the fetus (termed *fetal erythroblastosis*) when the fetus has Rh(D)-positive blood and the mother is Rh-negative. Because the Rh factor is a dominant genetic trait, this situation will occur only when the father is Rh(D)-positive (and the mother Rh-negative). If blood from the fetus gets into the mother's bloodstream (*transplacental hemorrhage*), the mother's blood will begin to produce antibodies. These are usually not produced early enough or in sufficient quantities to affect the first child. Subsequent fetuses may be affected, however.

Transplacental hemorrhage occurs in approximately 50 percent of all pregnant women, either during pregnancy or immediately after birth (Knuppel & Angel, 1990). Hence, the chances of Rh(D) immunization are very high—if, of course, the mother is Rh-negative and the father Rh(D)-positive. At one time, this condition was always fatal. Now, however, it is possible for the physician to monitor antibody levels in the mother's blood, determining when levels are high enough to endanger the fetus. At this point, there are several alternatives. If the fetus is sufficiently advanced (32 or 33 weeks, for example), labor might be induced or a cesarean delivery performed and the infant given a complete blood transfusion immediately (Bowman, 1990). If the fetus is not sufficiently advanced, a blood transfusion may be performed in utero.

Fortunately, this type of medical intervention is now seldom necessary because of the development of the drug *Rhogam* (*Rh Immune Globulin* or *RhIG*) in 1968. Rhogam is blood that already contains *passive* antibodies, which prevent the formation of additional antibodies.

It has become routine, even mandatory, for all physicians to ascertain whether a pregnant woman is Rh-negative and whether she is at risk of immunization. This should be done at the time of the first prenatal visit. Bowman (1990) suggests that husbands or partners of Rh-negative women should then be screened. If they too are Rh-negative, there is little chance of fetal erythroblastosis. However, because of the possibility of an extramarital conception, mothers who are Rh-negative and their fetuses should be monitored closely throughout pregnancy.

When an expecting mother is at risk of immunization (that is, she is Rh-negative and the father is Rh(D)-positive), Rhogam is sometimes administered during the seventh month of gestation—even though the incidence of immunization before delivery is low (approximately 2 percent). Current medical guidelines are that all such women be administered Rhogam within no more than 72 hours of delivery, as soon as it has been determined that the fetus is Rh-positive and is therefore at risk of Rh(D) immunization. Similarly,

Rhogam should be administered in the event of the abortion or miscarriage of an Rh(D)-positive fetus if the mother is Rh-negative. The drug needs to be administered at the termination of every Rh(D)-positive pregnancy. (See Figure 4.6 for an Rh(D) immunization flowchart.)

Childbirth

Childbirth is something that happens almost 4 million times a year in the United States—although fertility rates (numbers of women having children) have declined (U.S. Bureau of the Census, 1988). (See Table 4.5.)

Birth in today's industrialized nations is largely a medical procedure. Doctors and other medical personnel work to ensure the safety of the newborn as well as the safety and comfort of the mother. They have at their command techniques and procedures to induce labor, to accelerate it, and even to stop it if necessary. They can administer drugs to lessen the mother's pain, perform blood transfusions on the infant, and deliver through cesarean section.

Elsewhere and in earlier times, birth was a more natural process. It occurred in birthing huts, fields, and forests. Sometimes it was a solitary experience; sometimes there were midwives, healers, or other attendants. We know, too, that it was often a tragic experience—infant mortality was high, and the death of a mother was not uncommon. A century ago, more than 100 of every 1,000 infants died; that number has now been reduced by almost 90 percent (U.S. Dept. of Health and Human Services, 1989). The decline in infant mortality rates is due not only to medical advances but also to improved sanitation and a consequent reduction in maternal and infant infections (see Figure 4.7).

The history of **obstetrics** is a long struggle between the traditions and beliefs of generations of midwives and the inevitable progress of science. It begins with Hippocrates' effort to separate labor from religious rites; progresses through the desperate attempts of men such as Semmelweis to promote cleanliness in hospitals to combat the dreaded killer of women after childbirth, puerperal fever (dramatized in the novel *The Cry and the Covenant*); and ends with current hospital techniques and procedures. Through the 1970s, however, North

Natural Population Increase in the United States

In 1960, when the baby boom was nearing its peak, more than 4.2 million babies were born in the United States. Since then, numbers have remained relatively constant at a figure somewhere between 3.0 and 3.8 million, in spite of substantial increases in population. In 1987, approximately 3.8 million infants were born; and in 1989, over 4 million. Fertility rate (numbers of live births per 1,000 population) has declined, partly as a result of more

	1987	1988	1989
Live Births	3,809,000	3,910,000	4,021,000
Deaths	2,123,000	2,168,000	2,155,000
Natural Increase	1,686,000	1,742,000	1,866,000

Source: Based on U.S. Bureau of the Census, 1991, p. 62.

Table 4.5 Births and deaths in the United States, 1987–1989.

effective contraception, and partly as a result of changed attitudes toward conception and childbearing. In 1988, the fertility rate in the United States for women ages 15–44 was approximately 67.4 per 1,000.

America saw a return to more "natural" forms of childbirth and a corresponding increase in midwifery and "birthing stations." There are indications that this trend has now reversed again—due in part to a tremendous increase in malpractice suits (and corresponding increases in insurance premiums). (See Table 4.6 for a brief sketch of the history of obstetrics.)

Surprisingly, the causes of birth remain almost as much of a mystery today as they have always been. Hippocrates, writing before 400 B.C., thought he knew. The child starts the whole process, he informed his readers. When the fetus has grown too big, there simply isn't enough nourishment available, so it becomes agitated, kicks its feet and flails its arms, and ruptures the membranes that hold it in. And then it forces its way out, headfirst because, measured from the umbilicus, the head part is heavier than the bottom part (see Liggins, 1988).

Hippocrates was wrong, although many believed his speculation right into the 18th century. We now know that fetuses that are dead may go through the process of labor—which would not be possible if they were responsible for initiating it.

Many other theories have been advanced over the years but, as Liggins (1988) concludes, we still don't have "the final chapter of the 2000-year-old search for the cause of labor" (p. 387). But although we don't know its cause, we do understand a lot about the process.

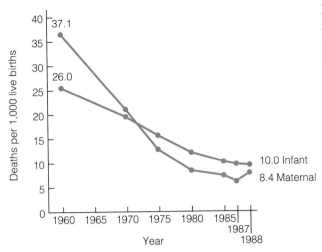

Figure 4.7 Declining maternal and infant mortality rates from delivery and complications of pregnancy and childbirth, 1960–1988. (Based on U.S. Bureau of the Census, 1991, p. 77.)

A Clinical View

Labor is the process whereby the fetus, the placenta, and other membranes are separated from the woman's body and expelled; it ordinarily occurs approximately 266 days after conception, although it can also occur earlier or later than this.

Classifications of Birth.   The physical status of the child is classified according to the length of time spent in gestation and by weight. A fetus born before the 20th week and weighing less than 500 grams (about 1 pound) is termed an **abortion**. A fetus delivered between the 20th and 28th weeks and weighing between 500 and 999 grams (between 1 and 2 pounds) is an **immature birth**. At one time, immature births invariably died; the majority still do, most of them from respiratory failure. But with modern medical procedures, an increasing number survive, some born as much as four months prematurely and weighing as little as 750 grams or less.

The birth of a baby between the 29th and 36th weeks is called a **premature birth**, provided the child weighs between 1,000 and 2,499 grams (between 2 and 5½ pounds). Complications are expected if the child weighs less than 1,500 grams. A few decades ago, only 20 percent of premature infants in the 1,000–1,500 gram range survived. Now between 90 and 95 percent do (*Preemies' diet seen key*, 1988). Low birth weight is associated with social and economic conditions as well as with maternal health, smoking, and other factors (Kopp & Kaler, 1989). In the absence of any detectable causes, the incidence of births under 5 pounds (2.2 kg) is about 3 percent (National Center for Health Statistics, 1987). (Prematurity is discussed in detail later in the chapter.)

A **mature birth** occurs between the 37th and 42nd weeks and results in an infant weighing at least 2,500 grams (5½ pounds). A late delivery is called a **postmature birth**. Both prematurity and postmaturity are associated with higher risk of postnatal death. All newborns, regardless of whether they are premature, are also classified as *small-for-date* (SFD) when they weigh 10 percent less than average newborns of the same gestational age, as *large-for-date* (LFD) when they weigh 10 percent more, or as *average-for-date* (AFD) (see Table 4.7).

The onset of labor is usually gradual and may be described in three stages. That there are exceptions to the normal process is substantiated by numerous fathers who were caught unawares, taxi drivers who drove too slowly, pilots who almost made it, and many others for whom nature would not wait. Although physicians can induce labor, as we saw, the precise cause of the natural beginning of labor remains unknown. Yet more often than not, labor begins at the prescribed time.

Stage 1.   The first stage of labor is the longest, lasting an average of 12 hours for the first baby and varying greatly in length, depending as much on unknown

TABLE 4.6

A Résumé of the History of the Development of Obstetrics

400 B.C.	Hippocrates attempts to separate labor from religious rites.
A.D. 200	Soranus teaches obstetrics to Roman midwives.
1513	The printing press is invented; the first book on obstetrics is published (Roesslin).
1560	Pare rediscovers and describes version and breech extraction.
1647	Chamberlen invents obstetric forceps.
1739	Smellie improves the teaching of obstetrics.
1807	Ergot is introduced in obstetrics.
1847	Holmes and Semmelweis fight puerperal fever.
1860	Pasteur discovers steptococci in puerperal fever.
1867	Lister describes asepsis (sterile procedures).
1900	The development of prenatal care and obstetrics in nursing institutions and in schools of medicine advances rapidly.
1950	The use of drugs in "assisted" childbirth becomes widespread.
1970	"Natural" childbirth is newly popular. Midwifery flourishes and birthing stations spring up.
1980s	The pendulum swings again toward hospital births.

Source: Adapted in part from *Textbook of Obstetrics and Obstetric Nursing* (5th ed.) (pp. 17–18) by M. M. Bookmiller and G. L. Bowen, 1967, Philadelphia: W. B. Saunders.

individual factors as on whether the woman has given birth previously. Generally, labor is longest and most difficult for the first delivery. The first stage consists of contractions of relatively low intensity that are usually spaced far apart at the beginning and eventually occur at shorter intervals. The initial contractions are described as similar to having "butterflies" in one's stomach; they last only a few seconds and are relatively painless. The "butterflies" become more painful and last considerably longer toward the end of the first stage of labor. In this first stage, the **cervix** (the opening to the uterus) dilates to allow passage of the baby from the uterus, down through the birth canal, and eventually into the world. Contractions are involuntary and exert a downward pressure on the fetus as well as a distending force on the cervix. If the **amniotic sac** (the sac filled with amniotic fluid in which the fetus develops) is still intact, it absorbs much of the pressure in the early stages and transmits some of the force of the contractions to the neck of the cervix. If the amniotic

sac has ruptured or bursts in the early stages of labor, then the baby's head will rest directly on the pelvic structure and cervix, thus serving as a sort of wedge.

Stage 2. When the cervix is sufficiently dilated, the second stage of labor, *delivery*, begins. It starts with the baby's head (in a normal delivery) at the cervical opening, face to mother's back, and ends with the birth of the child (see Figure 4.8). The second stage usually lasts no more than an hour and frequently ends in a few minutes.

The fetus ordinarily presents itself head first and can usually be born without the intervention of a physician. On occasion, however, complications arise that require intervention. For example, the head of the fetus is sometimes too large for the opening provided by the mother. In such a case, the physician may make a small incision in the vaginal outlet (an **episiotomy**), which is sutured after the baby is born. Complications can also arise from abnormal presentations of the fetus:

TABLE 4.7

Physical Status of Child at Birth

Classification by Gestation	Time	Average Weight
Abortion	Before 20th week	Less than 500 grams
Immature birth	20th–28th weeks	500–999 grams
Premature birth	29th–36th weeks	1,000–2,499 grams
Mature birth	37th–42nd weeks	At least 2,500 grams
Postmature birth	After 42 weeks	—

Classification by Weight and Gestation

SFD (small-for-date)	10 percent less than average infants of same gestational age
AFD (average-for-date)	Within 10 percent of average weight for gestational age
LFD (large-for-date)	10 percent more than average infants of same gestational age

breech (buttocks first), **transverse** (crosswise), or a variety of other possible positions. Some of these can be corrected prior to birth by turning the fetus manually in the uterus (**version**). Sometimes, the fetus is delivered just as it presents itself.

Stage 3. At the end of the delivery stage, the attending physician or nurse severs the neonate's umbilical cord, places silver nitrate or penicillin drops in its eyes to guard against gonococcal infection, and ensures that its breathing, muscle tone, coloration, and reflexive activity are normal. Following this, the physician assists in the third and final stage of labor and evaluates the condition of the **neonate**, perhaps by means of the Apgar Scale (discussed later in this chapter).

In this third stage, the **afterbirth**—the placenta and other membranes—is expelled. This process usually takes less than 5 minutes and seldom more than 15. The physician examines the afterbirth carefully to ensure that all of it has been expelled. If it is incomplete,

surgical procedures may be employed (frequently **dilation and curettage**, usually referred to as a **D & C**—a scraping of the inside of the uterus).

At the end of the third stage of labor, the uterus should contract and remain contracted. It may be necessary to massage the abdominal area or to administer various drugs to stimulate contraction and to guard against the danger of postpartum (afterbirth) hemorrhage.

Cesarean Delivery. In an increasing number of instances, medical intervention bypasses these three stages of birth through a **cesarean delivery** (almost one quarter of all births in the United States (Placek, 1986). In such cases, birth is accomplished by means of a surgical procedure—an incision in the mother's abdomen and uterus. Lieberman (1987) suggests that cesareans are most often indicated when the mother's labor fails to progress, when previous cesareans have been performed, when the fetus is in a breech presentation, or when the physician detects signs of fetal distress. Cesarean deliveries are ordinarily undertaken before the onset of labor, but can also be performed after labor has begun.

Although cesarean deliveries have clearly saved the lives of many mothers and infants, and alleviated much pain and suffering, the rapid increase in the proportion of cesarean births relative to nonsurgical births has been a source of some concern (deRegt et al., 1986). Although much of this increase clearly results from dramatic improvements in the physician's ability to monitor the fetus prior to birth and during labor, critics charge that not all cesarean deliveries are necessary. When unnecessary, they present potential disadvantages and dangers not inherent in a routine delivery, including greater medical risk to the mother, a longer recovery period, higher risk of infection, and greater costs. In addition, the use of anesthetics during surgery may depress neonatal responsiveness and may be related to the occasional respiratory problems of the infant delivered by cesarean. This problem may be compounded by the fact that infants delivered surgically do not normally experience the same surge of adrenaline-related hormones that is common among infants during normal labor. Among other things, these hormones stimulate respiratory and cardiac activity (Lagercrantz & Slotkin, 1986).

Lieberman (1987) reports that a number of hospitals have succeeded in dramatically reducing rates of

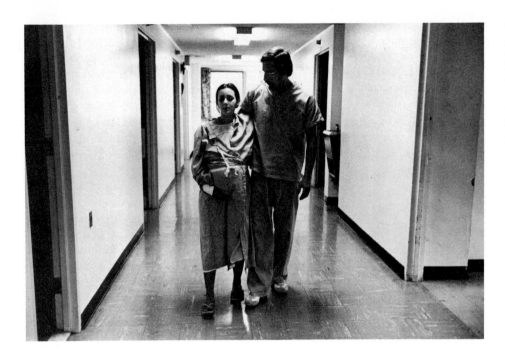

The first stage of labor is usually the longest. It lasts an average of 12 hours for the first infant—less for subsequent births—but varies a great deal for individual women.

cesarean deliveries without any increase in fetal or maternal problems. This is accomplished largely by reviewing the need for a cesarean delivery in cases where the delivery might simply have been done routinely, as sometimes happens for breech births, twins, or patients who have had previous cesareans.

Neonatal Scales

In almost all North American hospitals, newborns are routinely evaluated with the *APGAR Scale*. The scale, shown in Interactive Table 4.8, is almost self-explanatory. Infants receive a score of 0, 1, or 2 for each of five appropriate signs. The maximum score is 10; an average score is usually 7 or better; a score of 4 or less indicates that the neonate must be given special care immediately. The APGAR evaluation occurs 1 minute after birth and 5 minutes after birth, and sometimes at 10 minutes. Five- and 10-minute scores are often higher than 1-minute scores.

A second important scale for assessing the condition of a newborn infant is the *Brazelton Neonatal Behavior Assessment Scale* (NBAS) (Brazelton, 1973). Like the APGAR Scale, it may be used to detect problems immediately after birth. In addition, it provides useful indicators of central nervous system maturity as well as of social behavior. The NBAS looks at 26 specific behaviors, including reaction to light, cuddling, voices, and a pinprick; it also looks at the strength of various reflexes. The scale is particularly useful in identifying infants who might be prone to later psychological problems (Als et al., 1979). For example, parents of infants who are less responsive to cuddling and other social stimulation might be alerted to this from the very beginning and might be able to compensate by providing the infant with more loving contact than might otherwise have been the case.

The Mother's Experience: Prepared Childbirth

The preceding discussion of the delivery of a human child is admittedly clinical and perhaps somewhat like the cold, antiseptic hospitals in which most North American babies are born; it fails to uncover and transmit the magic of the process. We can recapture some of the mystery, however, by looking at the process

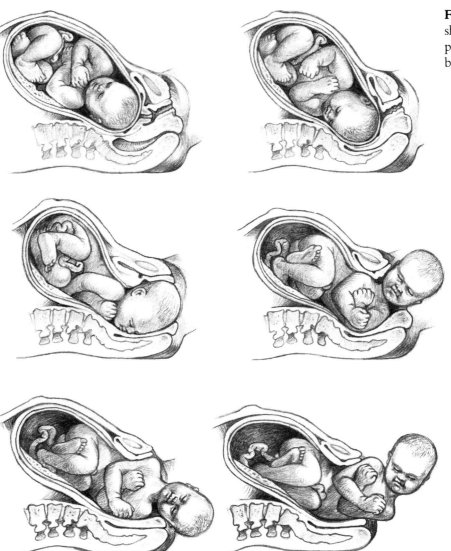

Figure 4.8 This cross section shows the normal, headfirst presentation and delivery of a baby.

from the mother's point of view. In preparation for this discussion, I spoke with several women whose experience qualified them to make subjective comments more valid than those my imagination might supply.

"What's it like, having a baby?" I asked.

"It's a piece of cake," my first interviewee assured me in her characteristic, clichéd way. "It's as easy as rolling off a log."

"It hurts like #@★!!" my second interviewee insisted in her usual profane manner. "It's a hell of a big log!"

Combining these impressions, an absolutely clear picture of the situation emerges.

The inexperienced mother sometimes approaches the event with some degree of apprehension; there is often some pain associated with childbirth. However, advocates of natural childbirth (also called *prepared* childbirth) claim that through a regimen of prenatal exercises and adequate psychological preparations, many women experience relatively painless childbirths.

Natural childbirth, a phrase coined by a British physician, Grantly Dick-Read (1972), refers to the

U.S. Cesarean Deliveries

Cesarean section deliveries have quadrupled in frequency since 1970. Not surprisingly, the highest rates are for older age groups. Although cesarean deliveries have clearly saved the lives of many mothers and infants, some critics argue that they are used too frequently. Although the procedure is routine and low risk, it entails a somewhat higher risk of infection, medical problems for the mother, and respiratory problems among infants (perhaps because infants delivered by cesarean do not experience the same surge of adrenaline-related hormones as infants born naturally).

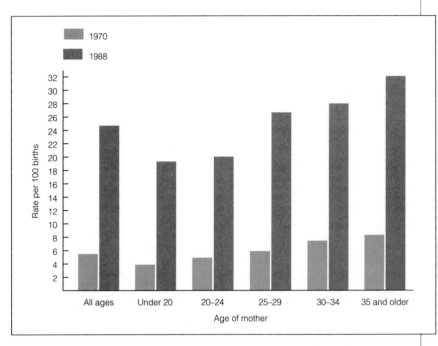

Figure 4.9 Changes in rate of cesareans by age, 1970–1988 (per 100 births). (From U.S. Bureau of the Census, 1991, p. 66.)

process of having a chid without anesthetics. The Dick-Read process recommends relaxing exercises and psychological preparation for the arrival of the child, all directed toward delivery in which painkillers are unnecessary. Natural childbirth is based on the assumption that alleviating the fear of pain, together with training in relaxation, will result in less pain. Dick-Read's hypothesis has proved sound.

Lamaze and Leboyer Methods. Two popular methods of prepared childbirth are the Lamaze and the Leboyer techniques. The Lamaze method teaches expectant mothers a variety of breathing and relaxation exercises. These are practiced repeatedly, often with the assistance of the father or birth partner, until they become so habitual that they will be used almost "naturally" during the actual process of birth. The use of anesthetics during labor is less common among women who are thus prepared. However, the goal of the Lamaze method is not so much to avoid the use of anesthetics as to prepare both father and mother, physically and psychologically, for the birth.

The APGAR Scale

▶ *When she was born, Carla Snipe snorted once, recalls her mother, then yelled about as loudly as anyone in the county ever had. Her color was as much red as pink, claims her mother, and she kicked out strongly enough that the nurse was hard-pressed to hang on to the still-slick infant. What would you guess Carla's Apgar score might have been?*

Score	Heart Rate	Respiratory Effort	Muscle Tone	Color	Reflex Irritability
0	Absent	Absent	Flaccid, limp	Blue, pale	No response
1	Slow (less than 100)	Irregular, slow	Weak, inactive	Body pink, extremities blue	Grimace
2	Rapid (over 100)	Good, crying	Strong, active	Entirely pink	Coughing, sneezing, crying

The Leboyer method is concerned more with the delivery of the infant than with advance preparation of the mother. Leboyer's (1975) technique involves delivering the baby in a softly lit room, immersing the infant almost immediately in a lukewarm bath, and then placing the baby directly on the mother's abdomen. These procedures are designed to ease the infant's transition from the womb to the world; thus the need for soft lights, which do not contrast as harshly with the darkness of the womb as does conventional delivery room lighting, and for a lukewarm bath, which might feel something like amniotic fluid. Leboyer claims that his procedures eliminate much of the shock of birth and result in better-adjusted individuals. Critics suggest that birth in dimly lit surroundings might contribute to the physician's failing to notice important signs of distress or injury and that the dangers of infection are greater under these circumstances than they are when more conventional hospital practices are employed.

Hospitals, Homes, and Midwives. Not only are many mothers choosing to have their babies by natural means, but many are deciding where birth will occur. For some, home is that choice; others choose hospital *birthing rooms*—a homier and more comfortable alternative than a conventional operating or delivery room—or hospital family suites where the father and other siblings can actually stay. Midwives also are sometimes used in North America, though the practice is more common in most European countries. Traditionally, in countries such as Britain, the majority of births were attended to by midwives rather than by physicians. However, with the medicalization of birth, the use of midwives has declined and their role has changed. An increasing number of births are attended to by physicians, and where midwives are used, they are often part of a medical team. Their role on that team has also declined dramatically in importance (Robinson, 1989). In many cases, midwives are used primarily as receptionists or to perform routine tasks like weighing pregnant women and taking urine samples. Although most North American births still occur in hospitals, length of hospitalization is considerably shorter than it once was (often only a matter of hours).

Sedatives in Childbirth. For one mother, childbirth may be quite painful; for another, it may be a slightly painful but intensely rewarding and satisfying experience. Although the amount of pain can be controlled to some extent with anesthetics, the intensity of the immediate emotional reward will also be dulled by the drugs. In addition, sedatives employed may affect the infant. Children delivered without general anesthetics or sedatives are often more alert, more

▶ Subject   Female; age 62; married; three children; four grandchildren; not working outside home; husband recently retired.
(on childbirth)

" *I wouldn't say I wasn't a bit scared the first time. And every time after that too for that matter. I mean, I looked forward to it, to having the babies because that's what we wanted. Everybody wanted kids in those days. But it wasn't an experience that I could honestly say I looked forward to. It might be different now, I think, with classes and everything. I know when my daughter had her last one she went to classes, every week I think, and he did too, her husband. And they both said it was such a nice birth. Maybe there's something to it, the classes. We didn't have that when I had my kids. We just saw the doctor maybe once or twice, unless there was problems, and when the time came, we just went ahead and had the baby. But I guess I'd just as soon not have to go through it again.* "

responsive to the environment, and better able to cope with immediate environmental demands (Brazelton, Nugent, & Lester, 1987). In short, they may have a slight initial advantage, the long-range implications of which are unclear. Local anesthetics do not appear to have the same effects.

Postpartum Depression.   As many as 10 percent of all women suffer from depression after delivery (*postpartum* depression) (Campbell & Cohn, 1991). It isn't clear whether this is due to hormonal changes, to sedating drugs some mothers are given, to disruptions in life-style, or to other factors (Dalton, 1980). Unfortunately, depressed mothers may be a risk factor for newborns, especially if their depression leads them to neglect or reject the infant (Campbell & Cohn, 1991). With support — and time — postpartum depression usually disappears.

The Child's Experience

How do children, the heroes of the early part of this text, react to the process of birth? Their story begins now, for although life begins at conception, legal existence dates from birth. (In some Asian countries, the child is considered to be a year old when born, although even there the making of a child does not require more than 266 days.)

Consider the dramatic difference that birth makes. Prior to this moment the child has been living in a completely friendly and supportive environment. The provision of nourishment and oxygen and the elimination of waste products have been accomplished without effort. The uterus has been kept at exactly the right temperature, and the danger of bacterial infection has been relatively insignificant. In addition to the complete biological support provided by the intrauterine environment, there have been no psychological threats. Now, at birth, the child is suddenly exposed to new physiological and, perhaps, psychological dangers. Once mucus is cleared from the mouth and throat, the newborn must breathe for the first time. As soon as the umbilical cord ceases to pulsate, it is clipped an inch or two above the abdomen and tied off with a clamp. The child is now completely alone — singularly dependent and helpless, to be sure, but no longer a parasite (biologically) on the mother.

Birth itself is not without danger for the newborn. Tremendous pressures are exerted upon the head during birth, particularly if the first stage of labor has been long, and brain damage sometimes occurs. In addition, the infant passes through an opening so small that deformation of the head often results. (For most infants, the head usually assumes a more normal appearance within a few days.) An additional source of pressure on the child's head may be **forceps**, clamplike instruments sometimes used during delivery. Although the fetus can withstand considerable pressure on the head, blood vessels may rupture and cause hemorrhaging. In severe cases, death may result; otherwise, brain damage

Having a baby is as
easy as falling off a log.

is possible due to **anoxia**, in which cranial hemorrhage restricts the supply of oxygen to the brain. Anoxia can also result if the infant's umbilical cord becomes lodged between the body and the birth canal. If this happens, the flow of oxygen through the cord may be stopped (referred to as **prolapsed cord**), also causing brain damage. Symptoms of brain damage often include various motor defects loosely defined as cerebral palsy. Even in cases where there are no overt symptoms of brain damage, there may be minimal damage sometimes linked with impaired neurological, psychological, or motor functioning (Campbell, 1974).

In addition to the physiological **trauma** that accompanies birth, there is a remote possibility of psychological trauma. Rank's (1929) theory of the trauma of birth maintains that the sudden change from a comfortable, parasitic existence to the cold and demanding world creates great anxiety for the newborn child, who is plagued forever after by a desire to return to the womb. Alleged evidence of this unconscious desire is found in the position assumed by many children and adults while sleeping or in times of stress—the characteristic curl of the fetus. However, no substantial evidence supports the theory of birth trauma.

From the child's point of view, then, birth is an indifferent process: The infant cannot reason about it, cannot compare it with other more or less pleasant states, can do nothing deliberately to alter it, and will not even remember it.

Prematurity

Prematurity is defined by a short gestation period (36 weeks or less) and low birth weight (less than 90 percent of average weight for term, usually less than 5½ pounds, or 2,500 grams). It is one of the more serious possible complications of birth, affecting approximately 10 percent of all infants born in the United States. Incidence of prematurity is considerably higher in some countries (Crowley, 1983).

Causes

We do not know the precise causes of premature delivery (Creasy, 1990). However, a number of factors are related to its occurrence. As we saw, these include malnutrition, age, drugs, and nicotine. In addition, infants from multiple births are much more frequently premature than are infants from single births, probably because of space and nutrition limitations within the uterus (see Figure 4.10 and Table 4.9).

Effects

One of the most obvious possible effects of prematurity is death. Only a few decades ago, the chances of death for a premature infant weighing 4½–5½ pounds were

Birth Weight and Prenatal Influences

Prematurity and low birth weight are among the most serious complications of birth. Low birth weight may contribute to infant death or general developmental retardation, including lower intelligence. Factors implicated in low birth weight include smoking and use of other drugs, malnutrition, maternal age, socioeconomic status, and race. The relationship of age, social class, and race to low birth weight and prematurity is probably due primarily to other associated factors such as poorer nutrition and medical attention.

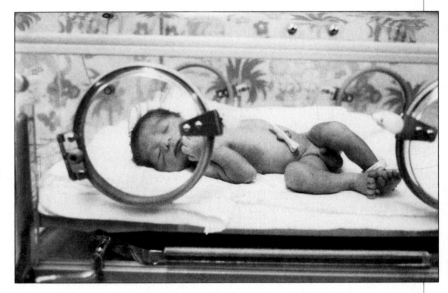

Figure 4.10 The relationship of race to low birth weight (less than or equal to 5 pounds, 8 ounces for 1960 and 1970; less than 5 pounds, 8 ounces for 1980, 1985, and 1988). (From U.S. Bureau of the Census, 1988, p. 13, and U.S. Bureau of the Census, 1991, p. 66.)

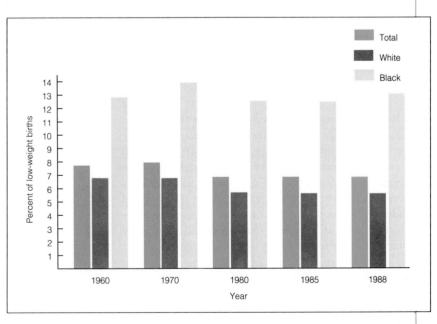

TABLE 4.9

Factors Associated with Higher Risk of Preterm Labor

Major Factors

Multiple gestation

DES exposure

Uterine anomaly

Cervix dilated more than 1 cm at 32 weeks

Two previous second-trimester abortions

Previous preterm delivery

Previous labor during preterm, with term delivery

Abdominal surgery during pregnancy

Uterine irritability

Minor Factors

Febrile (fever) illness

Bleeding after 12 weeks

More than 10 cigarettes per day

One previous second-trimester abortion

More than two previous first-trimester abortions

Source: Based on R. H. Holbrook, Jr., R. K. Laros, Jr., & R. K. Creasy (1988). Evaluation of a risk-scoring system for prediction of preterm labor. *American Journal of Perinatology, 6,* 62. Reprinted with permission of Thieme Medical Publishers, Inc.

approximately six times greater than for an infant weighing 6 pounds, 10 ounces or more. Now, however, the majority of premature infants weighing 4½ pounds or more (approximately 2,000 grams) survive. In fact, as we saw earlier, more than 90 percent of infants who weigh as little as 1,000–1,500 grams survive. Chances of survival decrease 10–15 percent for each 100 grams below 1,000 (Goldsmith, 1990). And half or more of those weighing less than 1,250 grams suffer adverse consequences; one third or more have *severe* physical or mental handicaps (Allen & Jones, 1986).

In view of these rather alarming findings, and given the close relationship between nutrition and prematurity, probably a great deal can be done for unborn children and their mothers through programs of education, nutrition, and housing. Note, too, that not all premature infants suffer noticeable disadvantages relative to their mature peers. Rawlings and associates (1971) examined 68 infants who had weighed less than 4 pounds at birth and found that 87 percent of them were apparently normal. A more pessimistic review of these findings would point out that 13 percent of them were not fully normal (in the sense that averages are considered normal) and that this number far exceeds the incidence of abnormality in the general population.

Prevention

Attempts to prevent the occurrence of preterm labor require being able to identify women who are at greater risk. This cannot be done with certainty since the precise causes of premature delivery are not usually known. However, it is possible to estimate degree of risk given knowledge of the mother's status with respect to the factors most often associated with prematurity—for example, previous preterm delivery, exposure to diethylstilbestrol (DES), the presence of more than one fetus, smoking, and uterine anomalies (see Table 4.9). It is also possible to monitor uterine activity in the home, and sometimes to detect an increase in activity prior to the onset of preterm labor.

There are a number of different approaches to preventing preterm labor, including bed rest, avoiding sexual intercourse, using antibiotics and other drugs, and suturing the cervix. None of these has been clearly proven to be effective, although some evidence suggests that each might sometimes be helpful (Goldsmith, 1990).

Care of Premature Infants

Prematurity is not inevitably linked with physical, psychological, or neurological inferiority. With adequate care, many premature infants fare as well as full-term infants. What are the dimensions of that care? First, they include advances in medical knowledge and technology. Ventilators, for example, make possible the survival of infants whose hearts and lungs are not sufficiently developed to work on their own; so does intravenous feeding with what is termed Total Parenteral Nutrition (TPN). The contents of this nutrition are especially important because they substitute for nutrients that the infant would ordinarily have received as a fetus. Certain fatty acids appear to be importantly involved in brain growth and neuron development during the last trimester of pregnancy (roughly the period of intrauterine growth that a 27-week preterm infant would miss) (*Preemies, diet seen key*, 1988). Accordingly, the premature infant's nutrition has to include these nutrients at the appropriate time and in the appropriate form.

In addition to important medical advances in the care of premature infants, research has looked at the possibility that at least some of the adverse psychological consequences of prematurity might be due to the lack of stimulation the preterm infant receives in an intensive care nursery—or, perhaps more accurately, the inappropriateness of the stimulation.

Scarr-Salapatek and Williams (1973) compared two groups of premature infants. The first of these was treated in the conventional manner. That is, the infants were kept in incubators with a minimum of human contact, a practice that is premised on the belief that premature infants are particularly susceptible to infection and highly vulnerable once infected. The second group was also kept in incubators, but these infants were taken from the incubators for feeding and were talked to and cuddled by their nurses. In addition, their incubators were decorated with mobiles, and after they had left the hospital, they were provided with numerous toys at home. It is highly significant that by the age of 1, these infants were heavier than infants in the control group and scored higher on developmental scales.

Harrison (1985) summarizes 24 studies that have looked at various forms of "supplemental" stimulation for preterm infants. Some studies investigated the effects of tactile stimulation (stroking, holding), while others looked at auditory stimulation (taped recordings of a mother's voice, for example), vestibulary stimulation (oscillating hammock or waterbed), gustatory stimulation (pacifier), or, as in the Scarr-Salapatek and Williams (1973) study, multimodal stimulation. The studies support the conclusion that additional stimulation of preterm infants is beneficial to their development. Positive effects include greater gains in weight, shorter hospital stays, greater responsiveness, and higher development scores on various measures.

The evidence is clear that the traditional "hands-off" treatment once given most premature infants is not the best of all possible worlds for them.

A Reassuring Note

It is often disturbing for nonmedical people to consult medical journals and textbooks in search of explanations for their various complaints. Inevitably, they discover that they have all the symptoms for some vicious infection or exotic disease. So, if you happen to be pregnant at this moment or are contemplating pregnancy, or are otherwise involved in the business, you might find yourself a little apprehensive. I draw this to your attention only to emphasize that there is usually little reason for concern. The intrauterine world of the unborn infant is less threatening and less dangerous than our external world. And it is perhaps reassuring that nature often provides for spontaneous abortions when the embryo or the fetus would have been grossly abnormal. In most cases, the fetus comes to term; when it reaches this stage, the probability that the child will be normal and healthy far outweighs the likelihood that it will suffer any of the defects or abnormalities described in this chapter.

Main Points

1. Early symptoms of pregnancy are uncertain, but simple chemical tests may be performed to detect human chorionic gonadotropin (HCG) in the woman's urine within a few weeks of conception. The gestation period for humans is 10 lunar months (40 weeks or 280 days), beginning from the onset of the last menses (266 days from conception).

2. Prenatal physiological development occurs in three stages: During week 1, the *fertilized ovum* moves down the fallopian tubes and embeds itself in the

uterine wall; from week 1 to week 8, the *embryo* develops so that by the end of the eighth week, all the organs of the infant are present; from week 9 until birth, the *fetus* grows mainly in size and weight and neurologically.

3. External influences that cause malformations and physical defects are labeled *teratogens*. Effects of a single teratogen can vary widely from one fetus to another depending on genetic factors, the presence of other negative or positive influences, and their timing.

4. Very tentative evidence suggests that maternal emotions increase fetal activity, and that maternal anxiety is sometimes reflected in more irritable infants.

5. A wide range of prescription drugs can act as teratogens—for example, thalidomide, which is associated with underdeveloped or absent limbs, and deithylstilbestrol (DES), which appears to be linked with higher incidence of cervical cancer among female offspring. Nonprescription drugs such as acetylsalicylic acid (aspirin) may also be harmful.

6. Among chemicals that can have detrimental effects on the fetus are mercury (Minimata disease), a range of hydrocarbon compounds including dioxins and PCBs (higher incidence of spontaneous abortions and physical deformities), and lead (serious physical and mental problems in children and adults). Radiation can lead to spontaneous abortions and physical abnormalities.

7. Smoking cigarettes increases fetal heart rate and activity, and is associated with significant retardation of fetal growth, higher incidence of premature births, smaller birth weights, higher probability of placental problems, higher risk of miscarriages and fetal death, and higher incidence of childhood respiratory diseases.

8. Tentative evidence indicates that caffeine may increase the probability of premature delivery. Alcohol consumption may lead to fetal alcohol syndrome (FAS), symptoms of which include mental retardation, retarded physical growth, and characteristic cranial and facial malformations (low forehead, widely spaced eyes, short nose, long upper lip, and absence of a marked infranasal depression).

9. Infants born to narcotic addicts are themselves usually addicted at birth; in severe cases, they may die. In addition, narcotics such as heroin and opium are associated with prematurity. Stimulants such as cocaine may also be associated with prematurity.

10. Various maternal diseases and infections such as rubella, syphilis, gonorrhea, and diabetes can lead to mental deficiency, blindness, deafness, or fetal death. Herpes can be transmitted to the fetus during birth and can lead to serious complications including death. AIDS can also be transmitted from mother to fetus (35–60 percent probability) and is fatal.

11. There is a higher probability of some chromosomal defects such as Down syndrome and fragile X syndrome for older parents. Infants born to teenage mothers are at higher risk of physical, emotional, and intellectual disadvantage (more miscarriages, premature births, and stillbirths, and more emotional and physical abuse among those who survive—outcomes associated more with the social and medical circumstances of teenage parenthood than with the mother's age).

12. Famine and malnutrition may lead to lower fertility rates and higher fetal mortality. Social class, because of related medical, nutritional, and drug use factors, is associated with a higher incidence of prematurity and other complications.

13. In the absence of medical intervention, mothers who are negative for the Rh blood factor, where the father is Rh-positive, would be at risk of giving birth to infants suffering from fetal erythroblastosis. This condition is routinely avoided in modern hospitals through use of the drug Rhogam.

14. Birth ordinarily occurs 266 days after conception. Early deliveries are classified as premature (before the 37th week). Newborns are also classified as small-for-date (SFD) if they weigh 10 percent less than average newborns of the same gestational age. Birth occurs in three stages: *labor* (dilation of the cervix, about 9–12 hours), the actual *delivery* (about 1 hour), and the *afterbirth* (the expulsion of the placenta and other membranes, several minutes).

15. The number of cesarean deliveries has increased dramatically in recent years largely as a result of improved technology for fetal monitoring. Critics believe that some cesarean deliveries are unnecessary and should be avoided given the greater stress

and risk for the mother and perhaps the infant as well.

16. Newborns are routinely evaluated within 60 seconds of birth, as well as at 5 minutes and occasionally 10 minutes, by means of the APGAR Scale—a scale that looks at their Appearance (color), Pulse (heart rate), Grimace (reflex irritability), Activity (muscle tone), and Respiration (respiratory effort) (note the mnemonic, or memory, device).

17. Natural, or prepared, childbirth, pioneered by Dick-Read, refers to the preparation for and process of having a child without anesthetics. Two popular methods are the Lamaze and the Leboyer techniques. Birth poses two great dangers for the neonate: The first is cerebral hemorrhage, resulting from extreme pressures in the uterus, in the birth canal, or from the forceps wielded by the obstetrician; the second is prolapse of the umbilical cord and shortage of oxygen.

18. Prematurity appears to be linked to social-class variables such as diet and poor medical attention, to the age of the mother, and to smoking. Its most apparent effects are the greater possibility of death, physical defects, hyperkinesis, and impaired mental functioning.

19. Only a few decades ago, many premature infants weighing less than 2,500 grams died. Now more than 90 percent of premature infants weighing as little as 1,000–1,500 grams (½–⅔ pound) survive. The severity of possible medical consequences of prematurity has been significantly ameliorated by medical advances. In addition, the psychological consequences of prematurity can be offset through increased tactile (stroking, cuddling), auditory, vestibulatory (rocking), gustatory (pacifier), or multimodal stimulation. Still, many premature infants suffer physical or mental handicaps.

Further Readings

The effects of maternal addiction on the fetus are explored in the following collection of articles:

Chasnoff, I. J. (Ed.). (1986). *Drug use in pregnancy: Mother and child.* Boston: MTP Press.

The clinical effects of alcohol on the fetus are examined in detail in:

Abel, E. L. (1984). *Fetal alcohol syndrome and fetal alcohol effects.* New York: Plenum.

The following is a massive collection of detailed medical information on the factors that influence prenatal development (including drugs, diseases, and genes) and on the various medical interventions that are possible:

Eden, R. D., Boehm, F. H., & Haire, M. (Eds.). (1990). *Assessment and care of the fetus: Physiological, clinical, and medicolegal principles.* Norwalk, CT: Appleton & Lange.

AIDS is a topic of considerable current interest—and misinformation. Long's book provides clear answers for 100 of the most common questions asked about AIDS. Anderson's little booklet deals more specifically with AIDS among children:

Anderson, G. R. (1986). *Children and AIDS: The challenge for child welfare.* Washington, DC: Child Welfare League of America.

Long, R. E. (1987). *AIDS.* (The Reference Shelf, Vol. 59, No. 3). New York: H. W. Wilson.

Bellow's novel is an interesting change of pace from the usual fare of academic references: True, it's fiction, but it's also a chilling account of the potential dangers of lead in our environment. Schwarz and Yaffe's collection looks at the effects of other chemicals and drugs on fetal development and on infants:

Bellow, S. (1982). *The dean's December.* New York: Harper & Row.

Schwarz, R. H., & Yaffe, S. J. (Eds.). (1980). *Drug and chemical risks to the fetus and newborn.* New York: Alan R. Liss.

Those interested in alternative approaches to childbirth are referred to the original authors of some of the more popular approaches:

Dick-Read, G. (1972). *Childbirth without fear: The original approach to natural childbirth* (4th ed). (H. Wessell & H. F. Ellis, Eds.). New York: Harper & Row.

Lamaze, F. (1972). *Painless childbirth: The Lamaze method.* New York: Pocket Books.

Leboyer, F. (1975). *Birth without violence.* New York: Random House.

The following is a highly practical and very informative book for prospective parents that not only describes what to expect in normal and higher-risk pregnancies, but also explores the various choices available to parents:

Lieberman, A. B. (1987). *Giving birth.* New York: St. Martin's Press.

Artist unknown: *Baby in Red Chair*, 1800–1825. Abby Aldrich Rockefeller Folk Art Center, Williamsburg, Virginia.

"When *I* use a word," Humpty Dumpty said in a rather scornful tone, "it means just what I choose it to mean—neither more nor less."

Lewis Carroll, *Alice Through the Looking-Glass*

PART

II

Infancy

Chapter 5 Physical and cognitive development: Infancy
Chapter 6 Social development: Infancy

Infans means "without speech." Young infants are *infans*: They have no words upon which to hang meanings. Their meanings, Piaget tells us, are wrapped in sensation and perception. As we see in Chapters 5 and 6, they are meanings of the here and now. If the infant sees a bright red ball, the meaning of the ball is a circular redness—a sort of image on the mind's mirror. Or perhaps the ball's meaning is the peculiar, synthetic, rubbery taste of well-chewed balls; or the magic-aliveness of its skin against the palms or the cheeks; or the trajectory of its mysterious bouncing course down the stairs; or even all these sensations and actions put together in a shapeless, happy kind of meaningfulness.

That's what *ball* means to the prelinguistic infant.

Later, the infant will discover—or perhaps invent—the actual word *ball*. And with experience and increasing sophistication, *ball* will come to mean much more than the "spherical or nearly spherical object" that a dictionary might list as its first definition. It will also come to mean any number of games played with such objects; the roundish part of something; a poorly thrown, off-base, spherical thing; a dance; a good time; to be especially "with it" as in "on the ball," and on and on.

But when *ball* is a fresh, young word, newly invented by the infant, it means, as Humpty Dumpty insists so scornfully, just what the infant chooses it to mean: a specific round object; the act of throwing anything; a request for mom or dad to do something amusing; a means of eliciting approval from some adult; and so on.

Ball is seldom just another four-letter word.

CHAPTER 5

Physical and Cognitive Development: Infancy

And with no language but a cry.

Alfred, Lord Tennyson, *In Memoriam*

In the beginning, the infant has no words — only cries. Words have no meaning for the newborn. They are simply more noises added to the "blooming, buzzing mass of confusion" William James (the 19th-century philosopher and psychologist) imagined the infant's world to be.

But for the 3-year-old, words are like magic spells that can transform the world. Words can make things appear and disappear; they can change tears into laughter; they have an almost palpable reality like cats and colors.

And for teenagers and grown-ups, words have still other meanings and other functions. Among other things, words communicate feelings, ask and answer questions, affirm our meaningfulness to others, and theirs to us.

We are, Kegan (1982) insists, *meaning-making* organisms. From birth until death, we struggle to give the world meaning. And equally important, we struggle to *mean* something to others. Helpless though neonates may be, they are the center of their little worlds, surrounded by people for whom they have very special meaning. As they grow and develop, their worlds expand, and for most, there will seldom again be periods where so many are concerned with their welfare — so many to whom they mean so much. Not surprisingly, much of social development throughout life is directed toward being meaningful — toward meaning something to others.

Do others also *mean* something to the neonate? Does the world have meaning? Does the newborn have primitive ideas, budding little concepts, some sort of pattern or blueprint that will govern its intellectual growth? What does it feel? Is there joy in the beating of its little heart? Is it capable of ecstasy? Does sadness drive its cries? Is there purpose in its movements?

This Chapter

What kind of creature is this little organism? This is not an easy question to answer. In fact, it will take us the remainder of this chapter and most of the next to describe the answers that science — and sometimes good sense — have begun to provide.

But let us start first with the bare bones of an answer; how the flesh hangs may make more sense if we see the skeleton first.

Imagine for a moment that you have been asked to design an organism that begins life in as primitive a condition as a neonate — that is, with as little physical and motor control as the infant has, and with as unsophisticated an understanding of self and world. But you must design this organism in such a way that within two years it can walk, talk, recognize its grandmother, ride a tricycle, laugh, cry . . .

So what do you do? You program it for change. Since you're clever, you pay particular attention to change in three areas: biological, intellectual, and social. Biologically, you design a creature that is capable of converting foodstuffs into nutrients, and you program the effects of these nutrients into a sequence of biological growth and maturation that will, among other things, eventually lead to the organism's control of its movements.

Intellectually, you program your little organism to process an enormous amount of information (see Flavell, 1985). You program it in such a way that it will process this information even in the absence of any immediate and tangible reward (such as a cookie or a kiss) for doing so. You provide it with an information-processing system that is automatically geared to focus on the most informative aspects of the environment. Accordingly, your little organism reacts strongly to surprise and novelty; it searches out the unexpected; it develops ways of organizing the information it gathers; it is programmed to invent concepts and ideas.

Socially, you program into the organism a wide range of emotions to serve as motives for action. They drive the organism to seek relationships with other organisms of the same species, to be gregarious, to love, to strive to *mean* something to others and contribute to the survival of its species.

And one of the crowning achievements in your design of this creature is that you pretune it to attend to speech; you wire it so that it is capable of inventing language.

The infant is just such a creature. To summarize: *A newborn is a primitive, self-driven little sensing machine designed to mature and grow physically in a predetermined way, programmed as an extraordinarily capable information-processing system, endowed with powerful emotions and gregarious tendencies, and pretuned to speech and to the development of language.*

In this chapter, we look at the newborn's growth and behavior, at motor and perceptual development, and at the infant's mind; in the next chapter, we look at social relationships and attachments during infancy, and at infant personality. These two chapters cover infancy, a period that lasts from the first few weeks of life to age 2.

Health and Physical Growth

Newborns are almost completely helpless physically. They cannot ensure that their environments are neither too cold nor too warm; they cannot clean themselves; they have no protection against rain or fire or wild dogs. They can't even find food unless it is put under their very noses.

And then they suck. Sucking is one of those primitive reflexes present at birth in virtually all mammals.

Breast Versus Bottle

The sucking reflex is what ensures the infant's survival. It may seem strange, then, that, in Kessen's (1965) words, "the most persistent single note in the history of the child is the reluctance of mothers to suckle their babies" (p. 1).

For many years a battle was waged on this issue. On one side were the many physicians and philosophers who insisted that mothers should breast-feed their own infants. Their arguments were varied. Some invoked nature. Breast-feeding is natural, they reasoned: All animals do it; therefore human mothers should too. Others argued that breast milk is best for the child simply because "it became accustomed to it in the mother's womb" (S. de St. Marthe, 1797, quoted in Kessen, 1965, p. 2). Others appealed to religion and duty: "The mother's breast is an infant's birthright and suckling a sacred duty, to neglect which is prejudicial

to the mother and fatal to the child" (Davis, 1817, quoted in Kessen, 1965, p. 3). There were some, too, who reasoned that maternal qualities might somehow be transmitted through breast milk. Especially to be guarded against was the milk of foster mothers of dubious virtue and morality, for "Who then, unless he be blind, does not see that babies imbibe, along with the alien milk of the foster mother, morals different from those of their parents?" (Comenius, 1633, quoted in Kessen, 1965, p. 3). (What sort of morals do cows have?)

On the other side of this apparent battle were mothers who, for one reason or another, were reluctant to breast-feed their infants. Their arguments were generally more personal and more private, and their numbers varied through history, growing through certain decades, and lessening again through others.

Is there still a conflict—a breast-versus-bottle controversy? There probably is, although most mothers see the issue as largely a matter of personal choice. The choice is sometimes made on the basis of convenience. It is simply not convenient for many working mothers to breast-feed their infants. Or, it is not convenient for women who carry their infants on their backs, or take them to the fields, to also carry bottles with them—or to lead cows or goats around behind them.

At other times, the choice is made on the basis of current fashion. For example, through much of the early part of this century, breast-feeding declined in popularity in North America so that by the early 1970s, fewer than one in four mothers breast-fed their infants. But in the past several decades, breast-feeding has again increased in popularity (Eiger & Olds, 1987).

What do physicians (and philosophers?) now recommend? Pretty well what they have recommended all along: When possible, mothers should breast-feed their infants (Lieberman, 1987). But their reasons have changed over the years. They no longer appeal to notions of maternal duty or sacred infant rights; nor do they argue that morals are transmitted along with the mother's milk. Science provides these crusty battlers with new ammunition. Mother's milk, science tells us, *is* the best of foods for most newborns. As Lieberman (1987) puts it, it is "species specific" and even infant specific. It contains just about the right combination of nutrients, the right proportion of fats and calories, the almost-perfect assortment of minerals and vitamins. Furthermore, it is easier to digest than cow's milk, and less likely to lead to allergic reactions. And one additional benefit is that it provides infants with a measure

Breast-Feeding in the United States

Through much of history, there appears to have been a controversy about whether to breast-feed. Philosophers, psychologists, religious leaders, physicians, and nurses have typically been in favor of breast-feeding; a number of mothers have not. Ultimately, the choice is a personal one. At present, physicians recommend breast-feeding when possible, especially in nonindustrialized countries where the wholesale abandonment of breast-feeding is related to infant death, most often from diarrheal dehydration (the diarrhea is often associated with the contaminated water used to make infant formula), to the infant's lack of immunity to infections and disease (some immunity is transmitted to the infant through the mother's milk), or to general undernutrition (for most infants, mother's milk is among the most nutritious of early foods). There has been a dramatic increase in breast-feeding in the United States in recent years, especially among more highly educated mothers.

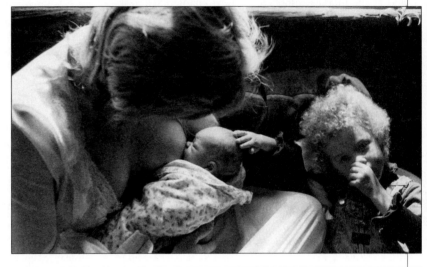

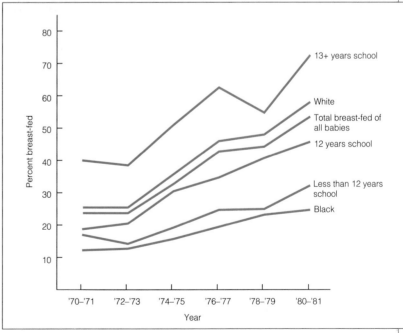

Figure 5.1 Changes in breast-feeding patterns for U.S. women by race and education, 1970–1981. (From U.S. Bureau of the Census, 1988, p. 64.)

enting response. Defined simply, the orienting response is our tendency (and that of other animals and birds) to respond to new stimulation by becoming more alert—that is, by attending or *orienting* to it. It is, as Berg and Berg (1987) put it, a "mechanism that enhances the processing of information in all sensory systems" (p. 268).

In animals such as dogs and cats, the orienting response is clear. On hearing a new sound, for example, a dog will pause, its ears may perk up and turn slightly toward the sound, and its whole attitude says, in effect, "What the *!$! was that?" The human infant may not respond so obviously, but distinct and measurable changes take place, and these in combination define the human orienting response. This reaction includes changes in pupil size, heart rate, conductivity of the skin to electricity (**galvanic skin response**, or **GSR**, also termed *electrodermal response*), and other physiological changes that are observable by using sensitive instruments.

The value of the orienting response to the child psychologist is that it can be used as an indication of attention, because it occurs only in response to novel stimulation to which the individual is then attending. It can also be used as an indication of learning, because it stops when the stimulation is no longer novel. In other words, when an infant has learned a stimulus (it has become familiar), the orienting reaction will no longer take place. In the same way, a dog might *orient* visibly when it first hears a cow in the distance, but will cease to do so when the sound has been identified. Such a decrease in the orienting reaction is termed *habituation*.

An illustration of the use of the orienting reaction in infant research is provided by Moffitt (1971). In this study, heart rates of infants aged 5–6 months were monitored while the infants heard taped repetitions of "gah." When infants first heard the word, their heart rates slowed dramatically—clear indication of an orienting response (Berg & Berg, 1987). With continued repetition of the same word (same voice, same tone, same volume), infants quickly became accustomed to the stimulus, and their heart rates rapidly returned to normal. Suddenly, with no break in inflection, tone, or volume, the tape recording changed: It said "bah" instead of "gah." Heart rate decelerated dramatically and immediately, an observation that leads clearly to the conclusion that 5- to 6-month-old infants are able to tell the difference between sounds as similar as "bah" and "gah." Thus, even though infants cannot tell us whether "mother" sounds the same as "father," whether the color blue looks like red, or whether salt tastes like sugar, we can turn to the orienting response and to other subtle behaviors for answers to some of our questions.

Reflexes

Most of the behaviors in which the newborn engages are reflexive—that is, they do not require learning and can easily be elicited by presenting the appropriate stimulus. Although neonates may engage in some activity that is not reflexive, they probably do not engage in any deliberate activity. Generalized behaviors, such as squirming, waving the arms, and kicking, are sometimes too complex and too spontaneous to be classified as reflexes, but they do not appear to be intentional in the newborn (White, 1985).

Interactive Table 5.1 lists some of the newborn's common reflexes. Probably the best known of these is the sucking reflex, which is easily produced by placing an object in the child's mouth. Reflexive behavior related to sucking is the **head turning reflex**, also called the **rooting reflex**, which can be elicited by stroking the baby's cheek or the corner of the mouth. The infant will turn toward the side that is being stimulated. This reflex is readily apparent in breast-fed babies, who need to turn in the direction of stimulation if they are to reach the nipple. It is less important to the child who is presented with a bottle.

Swallowing, hiccoughing, sneezing, and vomiting can all be elicited by the appropriate nourishment-related stimulation. They are therefore referred to as the **vegetative reflexes**.

A number of common motor reflexes in the newborn have no particular survival value now, but they might have been useful in some less "civilized" time. These include the startle reaction—or **Moro reflex**—which involves throwing out the arms and feet symmetrically and then pulling them back toward the center of the body. There is speculation that the Moro reflex might be important for infants whose mothers live or sleep in trees. If they suddenly fall but react by throwing out arms and legs, they might with luck catch a branch and save themselves. The Moro reflex is sometimes useful in diagnosing brain damage because in normal infants, these reflexes disappear with the development of the brain. As the infant develops control over motor actions, reflexes are inhibited (Hall &

INTERACTIVE TABLE 5.1

Some Reflexive Behaviors in the Newborn

▶ *If you have access to a newborn or young infant, it might be useful for you to provide appropriate stimulation to observe each of these reflexes. With older infants, you might carry out observations of gross and fine motor developments described in Table 5.2.*

Reflex	Stimulus	Approximate Age of Appearance	Approximate Age of Disappearance
Sucking	Object in mouth	2–3 months (in fetus)	Becomes voluntary during first year
Moro	Sudden loud noise	Neonate	3–4 months
Babinski	Tickling the middle of the soles	Neonate	Diminishes by 1 month, disappears by 3–4 months
Palmar grasp	Placing objects in hands	4–6 months (in fetus)	Weak by 8 weeks; gone by 2–3 months
Stepping	Infant vertical; feet lightly touching surface	8–9 months (in fetus)	Gone by 5–8 weeks

Oppenheim, 1987) (see Interactive Table 5.1). However, the Moro reflex is often present later in life in people with impaired motor function.

Other reflexes that disappear in early infancy are the *Babinski reflex* — the typical fanning of the toes when tickled in the middle of the soles of the feet; the **palmar reflex** (grasping — also called the *Darwinian reflex*), which is sometimes sufficiently pronounced that the neonate can be raised completely off a bed when grasping an adult's finger in each hand; and the *swimming* and *stepping reflexes*, which occur when one holds the baby balanced on the stomach, or upright with the feet just touching a surface.

The infant's reflexive behaviors are not always entirely rigid, unmodifiable reactions to external conditions. True, by definition, a reflex is a simple, unlearned, and largely uncontrollable response to a specific set of circumstances. When the nipple is in the mouth, the infant sucks. But two things are noteworthy here. First, very early the infant begins to exercise a degree of control over some of the circumstances that lead to reflexive behaviors. When the stomach is full, the infant may avert its head or purse its lips tightly,

thus avoiding the stimulation that might lead to the sucking response.

Second, beginning very early in life, the infant is capable of modifying some reflexive responses, including sucking. Sucking, Sameroff (1968) informs us, consists of at least two components: the squeezing pressure applied along the sides of the nipple, and the negative pressure (vacuum suction) applied to the tip of the nipple.

In an intriguing study, Sameroff designed a nipple that would record the different pressures applied to the nipple (squeezing pressure and negative pressure at the tip), and that could also be controlled so that it would deliver nutrients under specific conditions. For example, nutrients might be delivered to the infant only as a function of negative pressure at the tip (suction), or as a function of squeezing pressure. When Sameroff used his apparatus with 30 infants as young as 2 days, he discovered that even at this early date, infants were already able to adapt their sucking behavior in response to consequences. When nutrients resulted from squeezing the nipple hard between the tongue and the palate, that's exactly what the infants did; and when nutrients

Although maturation of muscular and neural systems is essential for complex motor activities, experience has a great deal to do with learning to creep and crawl, to walk and run, to jump, and perhaps to fly.

resulted from suction created by negative pressure in the mouth, infants sucked rather than squeezed.

The human organism—programmed to process information, to learn, to change—begins to change very early.

Motor Development

During the first two years of life, infants go through changes that are more profound, say Hazen and Lockman (1989), than any that will occur during the remainder of their lives. Consider that within this period, an initially helpless and totally dependent infant learns to move, to explore, to manipulate objects, to solve practical problems—and also learns to represent symbolically and to communicate.

There is a close link between motor development (the development of control over physical actions) and intellectual development. The infant's ability to manipulate and explore underlies discovery of the properties of physical objects; hence Piaget's label, *sensorimotor*, to describe development in the first two years of life.

The order in which children acquire motor skills is highly predictable, although the ages at which these skills appear can vary considerably. Tables of develop-

mental **norms**, such as that represented by the Denver Developmental Screening Test (see Table 5.2), are sometimes useful for assessing a child's progress. However, here as elsewhere, there is no *average* child.

The sequence of motor development illustrates two developmental principles mentioned briefly in Chapter 4. The first maintains that development is *cephalocaudal*—it proceeds from the head toward the feet. Thus infants can raise the head before acquiring control over their fingers to grasp objects. Fetal development proceeds in the same manner: The head, eyes, and internal organs develop in the embryo prior to the appearance of the limbs.

The second principle is that development proceeds in an inward-outward direction, referred to as *proximodistal*. Development is said to be proximodistal because children acquire control over parts of the body closest to the center before they can control the extremities. Thus children are capable of gross motor movements before they can control hand or finger movement.

Although the sequence in which motor abilities appear probably reflects genetic programming, experience not only drastically affects the age at which various motor capabilities are attained but also can affect their quality. Gerber (1958) reports an investigation of 300 Ugandan infants who, a mere two days after

TABLE 5.2

Age (months) at Which 90 Percent of Norming Sample of Infants Accomplishes Described Task*

Motor Task	Months	Motor Task	Months
Gross		**Fine**	
Prone, head up 90°	3.2	Hands together	3.7
Sits — head steady	4.2	Grasps rattle	4.2
Rolls over	4.7	Reaches for object	5.0
Sits without support	7.8	Sits, takes 2 cubes	7.5
Pulls self to stand	10.0	Transfers cube hand to	
Walks, holding onto furniture	12.7	hand	7.5
Stands alone well	13.7	Thumb–finger grasp	10.6
Stoops and recovers	14.3	Neat pincer grasp of	
Walks well	14.3	raisin	14.7
Walks up steps	22.0	Scribbles spontaneously	25.0
Kicks ball forward	24.0		

* Based on norms from Denver Developmental Screening Test.

Source: From *Denver Developmental Screening Test Reference Manual: Revised 1975 Edition* by W. K. Frankenburg, J. B. Dodds, A. W. Fandal, E. Kazuk, and M. Cohrs, 1975, Denver, CO: University of Colorado Medical Center. Reprinted by permission of the publisher.

birth (all home deliveries without anesthetics), could sit upright, heads held high, with only slight support of the elbows — a feat that most American children cannot accomplish until close to the age of 2 months (Frankenburg et al., 1981). All 300 of these children were expert crawlers before they were 2 months old! As Užgiris and associates (1989) point out, even motor development is influenced by context. One of the purposes of motor action is the development of competence; and competence is always relative to the infant's immediate context.

Perceptual Development

Our existence as human beings depends largely on our ability to make sense of the world and of ourselves. In Kegan's (1982) words, we struggle to discover meaning.

The infant's efforts to understand what things are and what they mean depend on three closely related processes: sensation, perception, and conceptualization. These are the topics discussed in the remainder of this chapter.

Sensation is what happens when physical stimuli are translated into neural impulses that can then be transmitted to the brain and interpreted. Thus sensation depends on the activity of one or more of our specialized sense organs — eyes, ears, and taste buds, for example.

Perception is the brain's interpretation of physical sensation. Wavelengths corresponding, for example, to the color fuscia affect our retinas in specific ways causing electrical activity in our optic nerve. When this activity reaches the part of our brain that deals with vision, we *perceive* the color in question. That we can now conclude that this is the color fuscia and not avocado is a function of the third process, **conceptualization**.

To summarize, sensation is primarily a physiological process dependent on the senses and on neural transmission; conceptualization is a more cognitive (intellectual) process; and perception may be viewed as a bridge between the two.

Infants as Subjects

Young infants, and especially newborns, are not always very good experimental subjects. When Fantz (1963) wanted to see how newborns react to visual stimulation, one of the most important conditions for selecting subjects was whether they kept their eyes open long enough to be shown the stimuli. And when Meltzoff and Moore (1989) investigated the newborn's ability to imitate, even though they choose 93 well-fed infants who showed no signs of hunger and who remained wide-eyed and alert for at least five minutes before the testing, only 40 completed the brief test session. The remainder fell asleep, cried, had spitting or choking fits, or, of all things, had a bowel movement!

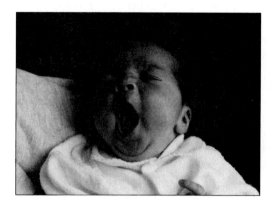

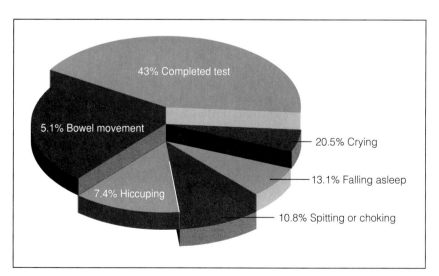

Figure 5.5 Difficulties in testing infants. Only 40 of 93 infants, ages 13.37–67.33 hours, completed an 8-minute test session. Testing had to be abandoned for the remaining 53 for the reasons shown. (Textual data from Meltzoff and Moore, 1989, pp. 954–962.)

Vision

For years, newborns were assumed to have poorly developed vision, with little ability to discern color, patterns, form, or movement. More recent evidence has contradicted many of those early beliefs.

Visual Acuity in the Newborn.

How well can an infant see? Is the world fuzzy and blurred, or is it crisp and clear? Is it 20/20 or better—or worse? How can we possibly find out?

Researchers sometimes report very different estimates of infant visual acuity, depending on the methods used to assess the infant's vision. As a result, a small controversy clouds the field (see Norcia & Tyler, 1985). However, three important facts are clear. First, infants are far from blind at birth, although some of their visual world may be somewhat fuzzy and blurred.

Second, there is a three- to four-fold improvement in the infant's visual acuity between birth and 1 year (Aslin & Smith, 1988). In fact, by the age of 6 months, the infant's visual acuity may be close to that of a normal adult.

And third, the newborn's visual accommodation is more limited than that of adults. It appears that newborns focus most accurately at a distance of approximately 12 inches (30 cm) (Banks, 1980). Significantly, that is approximately the distance of the mother's face when she is feeding the infant. This is one of the ways in which the neonate appears to be programmed to perceive important aspects of its environment.

Color Vision, Depth, and Movement.

Although no one has yet determined exactly when color vision is first present in the infant, we do know that it is well developed by the age of 2–4 months (Bornstein, 1984). By the age of 4 months, infants even show a *preference* for certain colors; they spend more time looking at pure reds and blues than at other hues (Bornstein & Marks, 1982). **Pupillary reflexes** (changes in the size of the pupil caused by changes in the brightness of visual stimulation) and eye movements demonstrate that the neonate is sensitive to light intensity, is capable of visually following a slowly moving object within a few days of birth, and is sensitive to patterns and contours as early as two days after birth (Bornstein, 1988). There is evidence as well that infants younger than 6–8 weeks can perceive contours (or edges) with sufficient contrast but that they cannot yet perceive relationships among different contours or forms (Pipp & Haith, 1984).

In addition to perceiving color, movement, and form, and demonstrating preferences among them, young infants also perceive depth. In Gibson and Walk's (1960) "visual cliff" studies, a heavy sheet of glass is laid over a patterned surface. Half of this surface is flush with the glass and half is three feet lower. Thus an adult standing or sitting on the glass can plainly see a drop where the patterned material falls away from the glass. So can goats that, at the age of a mere day, avoid the deep side, either going around or jumping over it. And so can infants, who, when they are old enough to crawl, typically refuse to cross the deep part, even when their mothers call them from the other side. Thus perception of depth is present at least from the time that the infant can crawl (see Figure 5.6).

For years, a test for depth perception before the infant could crawl seemed impossible. With the refinement of physiological measures, however, it became possible to look at changes in heart rate when infants who could not crawl were simply moved from the shallow to the deep side of the visual cliff apparatus. Doing this, Campos, Langer, and Krowitz (1970) found heart-rate deceleration in infants who were only 1½ months old. This might not mean that they actually perceive depth, but it does indicate that they are perceiving something new or unusual.

Visual Preferences

As we noted, very young infants prefer reds and blues, if looking at these colors longer is an indication of preference. It is possible, although perhaps not likely, that they really don't prefer these colors at all, but are simply puzzled or intrigued by them.

In another study of infant visual preference, 18 infants, ranging in age from 10 hours to 5 days, were shown six circular stimulus patterns of varying complexity, the most complex being a human face (Fantz, 1963). In diminishing order of complexity, the other stimuli included concentric circles, newspaper print, and three unpatterned disks of different colors. Figure 5.7 shows the relative percentage of the total time spent by subjects looking at each of the stimulus figures. The face stimulus was looked at for significantly longer periods of time than the others, indicating not only that infants can discriminate among the various figures but also that they prefer faces—or perhaps that they prefer

a   b

Figure 5.6 Use of the glass-floored visual cliff indicates that depth perception is developed at a very young age in human and other animal babies. In (a), an infant refuses to cross over even after receiving tactile assurance that the "cliff" is in fact a solid surface. In (b), the goat exhibits a similar reaction—although, unlike the human, it can jump to the other side. Goats show this response at the tender age of 1 day. Courtesy William Vandivert, *Scientific American*, April 1960.

complexity. Morton and Johnson (1991) also suggest that infants are born with some innate knowledge about faces that allows them to recognize and be attracted to them. That might clearly have some adaptive function.

Infants not only recognize faces, but seem to prefer certain kinds of faces over others—and that may be very important. Langlois, Roggman, and Rieser-Danner (1990) exposed 60 one-year-old infants to an experimenter wearing either of two professionally constructed, highly realistic masks—one attractive and one unattractive. Their responses to each were markedly different. They withdrew from the attractively masked person far less, played more, and generally showed more signs of positive emotions. Even at age 1, infants seem to prefer attractive people and to react more positively to them.

In a related study, Langlois and associates (1990) presented 1-year-old infants with attractive or unattractive dolls. Again, infants preferred the attractive dolls, playing with them significantly longer than with the unattractive dolls. And, in further studies, infants as young as 6 months seemed to prefer faces judged attractive, whether the faces were male or female, younger or older, black or white (Langlois et al., 1991).

Why? Perhaps, suggest Langlois and associates (1991), because attractiveness is a sort of facial "averageness." Faces created by averaging and digitizing facial features are judged highly attractive (Langlois & Roggman, 1990). Faces that are unusual may be interesting, but "average" faces are more clearly representative of the ideal human gene pool. Average, and therefore attractive, faces are less likely to carry genes that might be harmful.

The significance of these findings is twofold. First, it had long been thought that attractiveness is a learned and culturally determined quality, and that young infants would not likely have been exposed to enough models or to enough value judgments to have developed preferences. But this does not appear to be the case. Second, if infants *prefer* attractive faces, where does that leave ugly parents or grandparents—or brothers and sisters? Or even strangers? Recall the Elder,

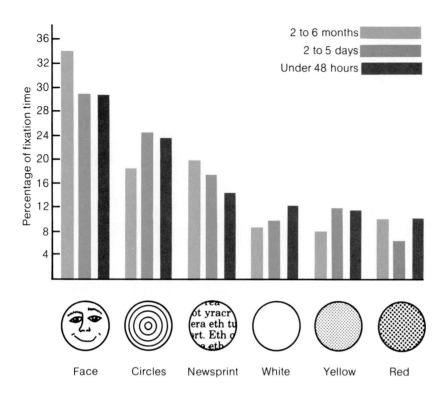

Figure 5.7 Relative duration (percentage of fixation time) of initial gaze of infants in successive and repeated presentations of six circular visual stimuli. The graph depicts infants' preference for the human face and the more complex stimuli. (Based on data in Fantz, 1963, pp. 296–297.)

Nguyen, and Caspi (1985) finding that attractive daughters were treated better by their fathers during the 1930s depression (see Chapter 3). Are attractive fathers and mothers treated differently by their infants? Their children? If so, what might the implications be for the ecological systems defined by the family?

Rules of Visual Perception

The infant, Haith (1980) informs us, does not respond to the visual world in a simple, reflexive manner, response following stimulus in predictable mechanical fashion. Instead, infants behave as though preprogrammed to follow specific rules that seem to be geared to maximizing information. After all, acquiring information is the purpose of perception.

So how do infants look? According to Haith's research, using infrared lights bounced off infants' corneas to reveal eye movements, these are some of the important facts and what they mean:

First, contrary to what we might have expected, infants move their eyes in the absence of light. They scan the darkness in a highly controlled manner, using small movements appropriate for finding shadows, edges, and spots. When viewing a uniformly lit but unpatterned field, their eye movements are broader, sweeping movements that are suitable for discovering bolder contours.

Second, newborns actually *look at* stimuli, positioning their eyeballs so that a maximum amount of visual information falls on the fovea, that part of the retina that has the greatest concentration of visual cells. It is as if the infant's scanning rules are designed to maximize stimulation—and, consequently, to maximize information.

Third, when the newborn looks at a simple stimulus (such as a vertical or a horizontal line), the eyes cross back and forth repeatedly over the edges of the stimulus. The effect of these eye movements is to maintain a high level of firing in the retinal cells affected—and in corresponding areas of the visual cortex.

Haith concludes that, apparently, a single important principle governs the newborn's visual activity: maximize neural firing. It is a built-in principle that ensures that the newborn's visual activity will lead to the greatest possible amount of information. It's a useful principle for an organism that has to be an outstanding information-processing system.

This principle—maximize neural firing—is manifested in four rules that govern how babies look at the world (Haith, 1980, p. 96):

- *Rule 1.* If awake and alert, and the light is not too bright, open eyes.

- *Rule 2.* If in darkness, maintain a controlled, detailed search.

- *Rule 3.* If in light with no form, search for edges by relatively broad sweeps of the field.

- *Rule 4.* If an edge is found, terminate the broad scan and stay in the general vicinity of that edge. Attempt to implement eye movements that cross the edge. If such eye movements are not possible in the region of the edge (as is the case for edges too distant from the center of the field), scan for other edges.

This view of the infant's visual perception as rule-governed and information-oriented rather than stimulus-bound presents a dramatic departure from psychology's traditional approach to these matters, a departure that is evident in many other areas of child study as well. This decade's infant — and child — is no longer merely a passive recipient of external influences, but an active, exploring, information-seeking participant in the world.

Happily, vision is not the infant's only source of information.

Hearing

Unlike the young of many nonhuman species (dogs, bears, and cats, for example), the neonate is not deaf at birth. In fact, physically, the ear is fully grown and potentially functional a few months before birth. But just how sensitive the newborn is to auditory stimulation is still uncertain. Not only are there marked individual variations in responsiveness to sounds, but a variety of indicators of sensitivity — changes in heart rate, respiration rate, EEG activity, electrical conductivity of the skin, as well as the more obvious indicators of attention such as blinking, turning, or starting — have been used in different studies and have sometimes led to contradictory conclusions.

Most investigations indicate that neonates are only slightly less sensitive than adults to sound intensity (loudness, measured in decibels). Their hearing threshold averages somewhere between 20 and 30 decibels, or perhaps a little higher, depending on the types of measures used (Acredolo & Hake, 1982); that of a normal adult is at 0 decibels (the equivalent of a whisper from five feet away). The difference is not significant,

particularly because the intensity level for a quiet conversation is usually above these thresholds (60 or more decibels).

Investigations of infant responsiveness to frequency (high or low pitch) have yielded somewhat inconsistent results, partly because of the criteria employed and the use of subjects of different ages (Aslin, 1987). Studies of older infants have typically shown that sensitivity to higher-frequency sounds increases with age (Trehub et al., 1991), and the general conclusion that infants are more sensitive to higher than to lower frequencies is widely accepted. Some researchers suggest that the common tendency of adults to raise the pitch of their voices when speaking to infants or young children is the result of an unconscious recognition of their greater sensitivity to higher frequencies (Fogel, 1984).

In addition to studies of newborns' sensitivity to loudness and frequency, there have been several investigations of their ability to recognize voices. Amazingly, it appears that an infant as young as 3 days is able to discriminate among different voices and seems to prefer the sound of its mother's voice. In a study in which systematic changes in an infant's sucking were reinforced with the sound of a woman reading a book, the infant responded to the sound of its mother but not to that of other women (DeCasper & Fifer, 1980). Have newborns, in the mere space of 3 days, learned to tell the difference between their mothers' voices and the voices of others? And have they developed a preference for their mothers' voices so soon? DeCasper and Fifer think this unlikely. They suggest that these findings are evidence that the fetus can hear sounds while in the uterus and can distinguish among them. Moreover, if these findings and this interpretation are correct, they provide evidence of learning in utero (Aslin, Pisoni, & Jusczyk, 1983).

In summary, newborns are sensitive to a wide range of sound and seem particularly sensitive to sounds that fall within the range of the human voice, almost as though their systems are pretuned to normal speech frequencies.

Smell, Taste, and Touch

Strong evidence indicates that neonates are sensitive to odors, tastes, and touch. Within hours of birth, they will attempt to avert their faces when exposed to a powerful and unpleasant smell such as ammonia (Lipsitt, Engen, & Kaye, 1963). And their facial expressions are distinctly different when they are exposed to the smell of vanilla versus raw fish (Steiner, 1979). Similarly, they react predictably when sweet, sour, or bitter substances are placed on their tongues, smacking their lips and sometimes protruding their tongues in response to sweet things, puckering their mouths in response to sour tastes, and opening them for bitter tastes (Steiner, 1979). It seems that taste and olfactory (smell) sensitivity is present at birth and does not depend on experience. At the age of a single day, infants can differentiate among solutions varying in type and concentration of sweetener. Almost invariably, they prefer any of these sweeteners to plain water. And, contrary to what we might have been led to believe about the natural wisdom of the body, they prefer sweetened water to milk (Desor, Maller, & Greene, 1978).

Early investigations of the infant's sensitivity to pain had concluded that the neonate is remarkably insensitive to much of the stimulation that children and adults would find quite painful (McGraw, 1943). However, more recent research has not established that the neonate is initially insensitive to pain, although there is some indication that pain sensitivity increases over the first few days of life (Haith, 1986). Studies that have used items from the Brazelton Neonatal Behavioral Assessment Scale (NBAS) have found strong evidence of touch sensitivity in neonates, with no discernible difference between the sexes. The relevant NBAS item involves placing a cloth over the infant's face. Even at the age of 2 hours, the newborn usually responds with strong and abrupt movements that would ordinarily remove the cloth.

Neonates are remarkably alert and well suited to their environment. They can hear, see, and smell; they can turn in the direction of food, suck, swallow, digest, and eliminate; they can respond physically to some stimuli; and they can cry and vomit. They are also singularly helpless creatures, who would surely die if the environment did not include an adult intimately concerned with their survival.

Cognitive Development

Throughout this text, we occasionally pause to reemphasize that the person is really not composed of all the separate layers we have invented to simplify our study. We divide our subject to make it manageable, but we need to remember constantly that we are much more than the sum of these layers.

So far in this chapter, we have looked at the simple, unlearned behaviors of newborns and at their motor and perceptual capabilities, as well as the early development of these capabilities. One layer of paramount importance remains; it is inextricably involved with all other aspects of development, but we shall consider it in isolation: the intellectual development of the infant.

Maya Pines (1966) observed that for a long time, psychology neglected the infant's mind, as if tacitly admitting that babies did not really have minds or that whatever minds they possessed were relatively unimportant at this stage of development. Our views have changed. "Babies are very competent," says Bower (1989). "They are set to use whatever information we give them" (p. ix).

As far back as 1920, Jean Piaget began to map the course of the child's cognitive development. Piaget's story of the growth of children's minds deals with their expanding awareness of the world in which they live and their discovery or invention of ways of interacting with this world. It is a complex and fascinating story, but it is not the whole story; there are other theories of cognitive development, other explanations of how we come to *know*. Some of these are labeled *information-processing* approaches. They look at what is involved in memory: deriving information, abstracting, sorting, organizing, analyzing, and retrieving, for example. We look at memory processes in infancy before turning to Piaget's theory of cognitive development.

Infant Memory

If neonates, ignorant and helpless as they are at birth, are ever to reach the level of competence of the 2-year-old, there is a great deal that they must learn and remember: what is edible and what isn't; how to unwrap bananas and bonbons; how to get from here to there, or somewhere else; how to ask for things; how to get people's attention and spark their interest; and much, much more.

The neonate's memory is not nearly as efficient and as powerful as yours or mine. In fact, a number of researchers have concluded that infant memory is very weak, and that it is more often measured in terms of minutes or hours than days or months (Lipsitt, 1982). Clearly, however, from the very beginning, some basic ability to learn and remember must be present. This primitive ability must then eventually develop into the type of memory that is characteristic of the 2-year-old, the 40-year-old, the 90-year-old.

Investigating Infant Memory.

There are several ways of investigating infant memory, some of which use components of the orienting response described earlier. For example, researchers might look at the infant's response to the same photograph, or to some other stimulus, presented on two different occasions. If the infant remembers something about the photograph, heart rate would not be expected to change in the same way as it might when the infant is presented with a completely new photograph.

A second approach is to look at how long it takes for the infant to *habituate* (become accustomed) to a stimulus. Habituation might be revealed in patterns of eye movements (the infant stops looking at the stimulus) or, again, in changes in components of the orienting response such as respiration or heart rate.

A third measure of infant memory involves the infant's behavior. For example, Rovee-Collier and associates (1980) taught 3-month-old infants how to make a mobile turn by moving their feet (the infant's foot was fastened to a lever that, when moved, caused the mobile to move). Infants remembered the procedure several weeks later.

Characteristics and Development of Infant Memory.

Using measures such as these, investigators have found that even newborns have memories. True, they are not very elaborate memories, but they are a beginning. Within days of birth, for example, newborns are able to recognize their mothers' smell (Macfarlane, 1975) and to discriminate among different speech sounds (Rovee-Collier, 1987) — clearly evidence of memory. But the infant's memory for most things appears to be of relatively short duration. For example, young infants who are conditioned to associate a puff of air with a tone, or a feeding schedule with a bell, may remember from one day to the next, or perhaps for 6 or 10 days. But without any reminders in the interim, all evidence of memory is likely to disappear within a few days (Rovee-Collier, 1987).

Perlmutter (1980) describes three sequential phases in the development of infant memory. In the first, the infant's memory appears to be largely a matter of neurons firing when a new stimulus is presented, and the firing stopping with habituation. As the infant becomes more familiar with the stimulus (that is, learns and remembers), the period before habituation becomes shorter.

The second phase, which begins at around 3 months, is related to the infant's growing ability to accomplish *intended* actions. Infants now actively look and search; they begin to reach, even to grasp; they explore. Also, they show clear signs of *recognizing*; recognition is a sure sign of memory.

And in the third phase, by the age of 8 or so months, infant memories have become much more like our own in that they are more abstract and more symbolic. They remember *classes* of things like fuzzy objects and big people and pets and building blocks and beets.

Memory in adults and in older children is greatly facilitated by certain strategies, the most important of which are *organization, grouping,* and *elaboration.* Infants do not systematically use any of these strategies. But if they are asked to remember something, they try to remember, and they pay attention. These, says Wellman (1988), are *primitive* memory strategies. Wellman notes, as well, that the 2-year-old infant already has some notions about what memory is, and understands such mental event terms as *remember, think, know,* and *pretend.*

There is a great distance between the immature memory of the week-old child who can, with appropriate instrumentation, demonstrate a vague recollection of a familiar smell or sound, and the 1-year-old who mistakenly yells "Dada" when he sees a stranger's familiar-looking back in the supermarket. There is also a vast distance between this 1-year-old's memory and that of the 12-year-old whose cognitive (intellectual) strategies permit mental feats of which the 1-year-old cannot yet even dream. More about memory in Chapter 7; but first we look in more detail at Piaget's view of the development of the infant's mind.

Basic Piagetian Ideas

The infant's world, says Piaget, is a world of the *here and now.* It exists and has meaning when the infant looks at it, smells it, or hears, touches, or tastes it. The infant does not have concepts in the sense that we think of them — no store of memories or hopes or dreams, no fund of information with which to think.

But what the neonate has are the sensory systems and the inclinations that make it into a self-reinforcing information-processing system. That is basically the kind of system described by Piaget — a system that continually seeks out and responds to stimulation and, by so doing, gradually builds up a repertoire of behaviors and capabilities.

Assimilation and Accommodation.

At first, infants' behaviors are largely limited to the simple reflexes with which they are born. In time, these behaviors become more elaborate and more coordinated with one another. The process by which this occurs is one of adaptation, which is made possible through *assimilation* and *accommodation* (described in Chapter 2).

To review briefly, assimilation and accommodation are highly active processes whereby the individual searches out, selects, and responds to information, the result of which is the actual *construction* of knowledge. Imagine, for example, a young child walking on a windblown beach, stooping now and again to pick up pebbles and toss them onto the water. In Piaget's view, there is a *schema* involved here—a sort of mental (or cognitive) representation—that corresponds to the child's knowledge of the suitability of pebbles as objects to be thrown upon the waves, as well as other schemata that have to do with the activities involved in bending, retrieving, and throwing. The pebbles are, in a sense, being assimilated to appropriate schemata; they are understood and used in terms of the child's previous knowledge.

Imagine, now, that the child bends to retrieve another pebble but finds, instead, that she has picked up a wallet. The wallet is clearly not a pebble, and perhaps should not be responded to in the same way. But still, why not? The "throwing things on the big waves" schema is readily available, momentarily preferred. And so the wallet, too, is assimilated to the throwing schema, and the child tries to hurl it toward the water. But the new object's heaviness is sudden and surprising, the child's throwing motion is inadequate, and the wallet falls again upon the sand. Now, when she picks it up again, she doesn't hurl it in quite the same way. She holds it in two hands, grasps it tightly with her pudgy little fingers, and pushes hard with her little legs as she throws. In Piaget's terms, she is accommodating to the characteristics of this object that make it different from the pebbles she has been throwing.

To simplify these sometimes difficult concepts, to assimilate is to respond in terms of preexisting information. It often involves ignoring some aspects of the situation to make it conform to aspects of the mental system. In contrast, to accommodate is to respond to external characteristics and to make changes in the mental system as a result.

Assimilation and accommodation are not separate and independent. They are, as Flavell (1985) put it, two sides of the same cognitive coin. According to Piaget, all activity involves both assimilation and accommodation. It is impossible to react to or understand something entirely new; everything is always understood, at least to some extent, in terms of existing information (assimilation). At the same time, everything to which the infant (or the adult) reacts presents something new and different, and involves some change in information or structure (accommodation).

Equilibration.

The balance between accommodation and assimilation is labeled equilibrium. **Equilibration** is the process by which equilibrium is maintained. At one extreme, if an infant always assimilated and never accommodated, there would be no change in schemata (mental structure), no change in behavior. Everything would be assimilated to the sucking schema, the grasping schema, the looking schema (that is, everything would be sucked, or grasped, or simply looked at). Such a state of disequilibrium would result in little adaptation and little cognitive growth.

At the other extreme, if everything were accommodated to and not assimilated, schemata—and behavior—would be in a constant state of flux. Now the nipple would be sucked, now it would be chewed, now pinched, now swatted—again, an extreme state of disequilibrium resulting in little adaptation.

Equilibration, says Piaget, is an internal tendency that governs the balance between assimilation and accommodation, and that accounts for the *construction* of knowledge—that is, that accounts for adaptation and cognitive growth—throughout development.

Other Factors.

Piaget (1961) describes several other factors that are important in shaping development. One is *maturation*, which refers to a sort of biologically determined unfolding of potential. Maturation—or biology—does not determine cognitive growth but is related to the unfolding of potential. Another factor essential to the child's adaptation and development is *active experience*—the child's interaction with the physical world. A third important factor is *social interaction*—interaction with others—which helps the child develop ideas about things and about people as well as about the self.

These four factors—active experience, maturation, equilibration, and social interaction—are the cornerstones of Piaget's basic theory. To summarize in one sentence: Cognitive growth results from assimilation and accommodation, governed by a need to achieve and maintain equilibrium, and occurring through active experience and social interaction broadly related to unfolding maturation.

It is a large mouthful conceptually.

The Object Concept

Perhaps we can chew its gristle a little more in this section.

The infant's world begins as a world that, although not necessarily William James's "blooming, buzzing mass of confusion," exists only when it is being reacted to, and is understood only in terms of those actions. A nipple exists for infants when they look at it, touch it, suck it, or otherwise respond to it; when it is removed from their immediate perception, it ceases to exist. In Piaget's terms, the infant at this stage has not yet achieved the *object concept*—the realization that objects continue to exist even when they are not being sensed. It is a concept that is so simple, so clear, so *inevitable* for us as adults, that we take it completely for granted. Yet it is absolutely fundamental to our reasoning about the world; our conception of the world demands that objects be real, out there, substantive, and independent of us. There is no "out there" for infants; they must discover the permanence and *objectivity* of objects for themselves. This discovery is one of the truly great achievements of infancy.

How do children discover the reality and the properties of objects? The processes are not clearly understood, but evidently, experience with and exploration of the real world are intimately involved. In a series of investigations, Stambak and associates (1989) videotaped young infants' responses to a variety of objects such as nesting cups or hollow cubes or rods. Analysis of these videotapes reveals that even very young infants organize their behaviors in systematic ways, that their exploration is not simply the random exercising of behaviors. Some subjects typically bang different objects with the rod; some explore the insides of the hollow cubes with their fingers, or their hands if the cubes are large enough. In a sense, they have already begun to invent questions and problems, and to devise little experiments to find answers. In a series of naturalistic observations reported by Sinclair and associates (1989),

infants often spent the entire 20-minute observation session coming back to the same *idea*.

Not only does the exploration of objects by young infants become increasingly systematic with advancing age, it also involves more different activities. As Rochat (1989) puts it, exploration becomes increasingly multimodal between the ages of 2 and 5 months. At first, exploration is mainly visual or oral; later, it also becomes manual. By the age of 3 or 4 months, most infants use both their hands and their mouths to explore. Significantly, the type of manipulation in which the infant engages becomes increasingly dependent on the objects being explored. Some things are more easily understood, more meaningful, when held in both hands, licked and drooled on, and gummed emphatically.

To investigate the infant's understanding of objects, Piaget (1954) devised an experiment in which the investigator shows the child an attractive object and then hides it from view. Piaget argues that if the object exists only when infants are perceiving it, they will make no effort to look for it, even when they have seen it being hidden from view. When children begin to look for an object they can no longer see, this is definite evidence that they can imagine it—that the object continues to exist for them, even when it is unseen.

Piaget found that in the earliest stages, children do not respond to the object once it is removed; next, they progress through a stage during which they search for the object, but only in the place where they last saw it. Finally, they achieve a complete realization of object permanence and can look for objects in a variety of places. The final stage occurs near the middle of the second year of life.

A number of later investigations of the development of the object concept demonstrate that the age of acquisition is probably younger than Piaget suggests (see Wellman & Gelman, 1992). For example, Bower (1989) used the orienting response of very young infants to determine whether an object ceases to exist when it is removed from sight. In one study, the infant is shown a ball, and then a screen is moved between the infant and the ball. A few seconds later, the screen is removed. On some trials, the ball is still there; on others, the ball has been taken away. When infants do not understand object permanence, they should not be surprised if the ball is gone. But they would be surprised to see it gone if they expected it to be there. Bower measured surprise by looking at changes in heart rate. His primary finding is that infants as young as 3 weeks of age appear

TABLE 5.3

Sensorimotor Period: The Six Substages

Substage and Approximate Age (months)	Principal Characteristics
1. Exercising reflexes (0–1)	Simple, unlearned behaviors (schemes) such as sucking and looking are practiced and become more deliberate.
2. Primary circular reactions (1–4)	Activities that center on the infant's body and that give rise to pleasant sensations are repeated (thumb-sucking, for example).
3. Secondary circular reactions (4–8)	Activities that do not center on the child's body but that lead to *interesting* sights or sounds are repeated (repeatedly moving a mobile, for example).
4. Purposeful coordinations (8–12)	Separate schemes becoming coordinated (ability to look at an object *and* reach for it); recognition of familiar people and objects; primitive beginnings of the understanding of causality implicit in the use of signs to anticipate events.
5. Tertiary circular reactions (12–18)	Repetition with variation (repeating a sound with a number of deliberate changes, for example) is experimented with.
6. Mental representation (18–24)	Transition between *sensorimotor* intelligence and a more *cognitive* intelligence; the internalization of activity so that its consequences can be anticipated prior to its actual performance; increasing importance of language in cognitive development.

to have some notion of object permanence, providing the object is hidden from view for only a few seconds. When the object is hidden for a longer time (15 seconds as opposed to 1½), infants at this age all show surprise when the ball is still present after the screen is removed.

In a related study, Baillargeon (1987) found that infants as young as 3½ months seemed to have some primitive notions about the solidity of objects. When one object moved through a space that should have been occupied by another object, they seemed surprised—that is, if the fact that they looked longer at that impossible situation than at another comparable but possible situation can be interpreted as surprise.

Do such findings mean that Piaget was wrong—that infants *do* have a notion of the permanence and independent identity of objects long before the age of 18 months? No. What the studies indicate is that under the proper circumstances, infants appear to have a rudimentary and short-lived recollection of absent objects. However, it will still be a long time before the infant deliberately searches for an object that has not been present just recently (Bower, 1989).

Sensorimotor Development

Piaget believed that children's understanding of the world throughout most of infancy is restricted to their perception of it and the activities that they can perform on it—hence the label *sensorimotor development*. Piaget simplifies the infant's development during this period by dividing it into the six substages summarized in Table 5.3. The most important developments of the sensorimotor period are described on the following pages (see also Table 5.4).

Exercising Reflexes. Little new learning takes place in the first month of life. Infants spend most of their waking hours exercising the reflexes with which they are born—they suck whatever comes in contact with their lips, look at whatever falls into their field of vision, and grasp whatever touches their palm. In addition to the survival functions of some of these activities, they also have important cognitive functions. Through repeatedly exercising these reflexes, the infant eventually gains control over small aspects of the en-

TABLE 5.4

Piaget's Stages of Cognitive Development

Stage	Approximate Age	Some Major Characteristics
Sensorimotor	0–2 years	Motoric intelligence World of the here and now No language, no thought in early stages No notion of objective reality

Preoperational*
  Preconceptual
  Intuitive
	2–7 years
	2–4 years
	4–7 years
		Egocentric thought
		Reason dominated by perception
		Intuitive rather than logical solutions
		Inability to conserve

Concrete operations[†]	7 to 11–12 years	Ability to conserve Logic of classes and relations Understanding of number Thinking bound to concrete Development of reversibility in thought
Formal operations[‡]	11–12 to 14–15 years	Complete generality of thought Propositional thinking Ability to deal with the hypothetical Development of strong idealism

* Discussed in Chapter 7.
† Discussed in Chapter 9.
‡ Discussed in Chapter 11.

vironment (as well as over the activities themselves). By the end of the first month, infants have become relatively proficient at each of these activities, although they still cannot execute more than one action to obtain a single goal. Young infants presented with a visually appealing object can look at it but cannot reach toward it. Deliberately reaching and grasping is a complex activity, depending on the coordination of looking schemes, reaching schemes, and grasping schemes. This coordination is not usually apparent until after the age of 3–5 months (von Hofsten & Lindhagen, 1979).

Primary Circular Reactions.   Early in infancy, children engage in many repetitive behaviors (thumb-sucking, for example) called **primary circular reactions** (1–4 months). These are reflexive responses that serve as stimuli for their own repetition. For example, the child accidentally gets a hand or a finger into the mouth; this triggers the sucking response, which results

in the sensation of the hand in the mouth. That sensation leads to the repetition of the response, which leads to a repetition of the sensation, which leads to a repetition of the response. This circle of action is called a *primary* circular reaction because it involves the child's own body.

Despite the infant's ability at this substage to acquire new behaviors (new adaptations through accommodation to different stimulation), these new behaviors come about accidentally and always involve the child's body. Interaction with the world is still highly one-sided; it is still a world of the here and now—a world that exists and has meaning when it is doing something to the child or when the child is doing something to it.

Secondary Circular Reactions.   Another circular reaction appears during the third substage: the **secondary circular reaction** (4–8 months). Like the primary

According to Piaget, learning about the world requires actual activities such as looking, reaching, tasting, smelling—and sometimes grasping and pulling with single-minded determination.

circular reaction, it is circular because the response stimulates its own repetition, but because it deals with objects in the environment rather than only with the child's body, it is called *secondary*. Six-month-old infants engage in many secondary circular reactions. They accidentally do something that is interesting or amusing and repeat it again and again. By kicking, Piaget's young son caused a row of dolls dangling above his bassinet to dance. The boy stopped to observe the dolls. Eventually, he repeated the kicking, not intentionally to make the dolls move, but more likely because they had ceased moving and no longer attracted his attention. The act of kicking had the same effect again, and again the boy paused to look at the row of dancing dolls. Soon he was repeating the behavior over and over—hence a circular reaction. This is an easily repeated illustration that Piaget labels *behavior designed to make interesting sights and sounds last.*

Purposeful Coordinations. One major achievement of the fourth substage (8–12 months) is the development of the ability to coordinate previously unrelated behaviors to achieve some goal. Infants can now look at an object, reach for it, grasp it, and bring it to

the mouth specifically to suck it. Throughout this sequence, there is clear evidence of intention.

Also during the fourth substage, infants begin to *recognize* familiar objects and people. Because of this, they can now become distressed when mother or father leaves, or when a stranger appears (see Chapter 6).

At this time, too, the infant begins to use signs to anticipate events: Daddy putting on his jacket is a sign that he is leaving; mother putting on her nightgown is a sign that she is not. Understanding that certain events are *signs* that some other event is likely to occur is closely related to the ability to understand causality. For the young infant, whose logic is not always as perfect as yours or mine, the sign itself is often interpreted as the cause. A child who realizes that daddy will be leaving when he puts on his jacket *knows* that the cause of leaving is putting on the jacket—just as the *cause* of going to bed is taking a bath or putting on pajamas.

Tertiary Circular Reactions. In the fifth substage (12–18 months), infants begin to modify their repetitive behaviors *deliberately* to see what the effects will be. Rayna, Sinclair, and Stambak (1989) observed a 15-

This 5-month-old wraps his fist in Lassie's hair and pulls. The hair feels nice and soft, and the dog shakes her head. The infant pulls again . . . and again. Piaget labels this behavior a secondary circular reaction—a behavior designed to make interesting sensations last.

month-old girl whose current preoccupation was with fragmenting or breaking objects. Breaking something often seemed to lead to a repetition of the behavior (hence a circular response), but with deliberate variation (hence tertiary; recall that secondary circular reactions are repetitive with occasional *unintended* variations). For example, in one session, she picked up a ball of clay, scratched at it until a piece had come off, examined the piece, and then repeated the procedure several times, each time examining the clay on her finger. Next, she noticed a ball of cotton, picked it up, and pulled it into two halves; then she pulled one of the halves into two more pieces; and so on. Similarly, in another session, a 15-month-old boy who had been tearing apart bits of clay happened across a piece of spaghetti, pressed it to the floor, broke it, picked up the largest piece, broke it again, and repeated the process a number of times. Once finished, he attempted to break a short plastic stick, and then a pipe cleaner; finally, he tore a sheet of paper into tiny bits.

The most important feature of **tertiary circular reactions** is that they are repetitive behaviors deliberately undertaken to see what their effects will be—that is, to explore.

Mental Representations.   Toward the end of the sensorimotor period, children begin a transition from the sensorimotor intelligence of infancy to the progressively *cognitive* intelligence of childhood. They now begin to represent objects and events mentally, and to arrive at *mental* solutions for problems. Also, they can now anticipate the consequences of some of their activities without having to rely solely on trial and error. In Piaget's terms, they have begun to internalize (represent mentally) actions and their consequences, without having to actually carry them out.

An illustration of this growing ability to internalize action is provided by Piaget's description of his daughter's response to a matchbox problem. She had been given a partly open matchbox containing a small thimble. Because the opening was too small for the thimble to be withdrawn she had to open the box first. A younger infant would simply grope at the box in an attempt to remove the thimble. But Piaget's daughter, then 22 months, appeared instead to consider the problem, opening and closing her mouth and hands very much as though providing external manifestations of internal thought processes. Finally, she placed a thumb or finger directly into the box's partial opening, opened it, and removed the thimble.

The ability to conceptualize the environment is also reflected in infants' mushrooming language development, which, according to Piaget, is greatly facilitated by their growing ability to imitate.

Imitation in Infancy

In the earliest stages of imitation, infants are able to imitate objects, activities, or people that are immediately present. Stick your tongue out in front of a 3-month-old, and a tongue is likely to be stuck right back out at you; wink and the infant might well wink right back — but with both eyes, never just one.

Exactly when the ability to imitate first appears is a matter of some controversy. Some researchers report that at a mere 2 weeks of age, infants already are able to imitate simple actions like sticking out the tongue or opening the mouth wide (Meltzoff & Moore, 1977, 1979, 1983, 1989). Others claim to have found even earlier instances of imitation. For example, Reissland (1988) looked at imitation among 12 neonates in the first *hour* after birth. All these infants had been delivered without complications and without drugs, and all were awake and alert. Models bent over the infants and either widened their lips or pursed them. The results? Infants moved their lips in accordance with lip movements of the models significantly more often than at variance with them. Reissland concludes that the ability to imitate is already present at birth.

Some researchers do not agree that neonates are actually imitating when they stick out their tongue or purse their lips in apparent response to a model doing the same thing (for example, Masters, 1979, and Jacobson & Kagan, 1979). Perhaps infants do not truly imitate these facial gestures, but instead simply manifest a generalized, almost reflexive response related mainly to feeding, and simply *released* by the nearness of the model (Kaitz et al., 1988). It is possible, says Anisfeld (1991), that increased tongue protrusion *following* modeling occurs because tongue protrusion has been inhibited *during* modeling.

Meltzoff and Moore (1989) disagree. They exposed 40 infants, ages 16–67 hours, to models who either protruded their tongues or shook their heads. Infants were equally able to imitate head-shaking — a nonvegetative behavior — and tongue protrusion. Meltzoff and Moore argue that the evidence supports the conclusion that infants have a general ability to match certain adult behaviors. However, they note that imitative behavior in the newborn is not completely automatic and easily triggered, and that it is more easily brought about for certain behaviors than for others. They suggest, too, that the inborn capacity to match the behaviors of others may be very important for social and cognitive development.

Deferred Imitation

Many of the imitative behaviors of the very young infant do not continue when the model is no longer present. The infant is initially capable of imitating only when the model is there, or within a very short period of time thereafter. This may be related to the difficulty infants experience in separating the objects they perceive from their perception of them, and their consequent failure to realize that objects continue to exist independently of them. Largely for this reason, Piaget (1951) suggested that imitation is not likely to occur before the age of 9–12 months.

There is, in fact, no important contradiction here. Piaget was referring not to the simple imitation of a gesture or movement in the presence of a model, but to what is labeled **deferred imitation** — the ability to imitate something or someone no longer present. When 2-year-old Amanda dresses up in her mother's shoes and struts in front of a mirror in the absence of her mother, she is practicing deferred imitation.

A study by Meltzoff (1988) provides evidence of the kind of deferred imitation of which Piaget spoke. In this study, a group of 14-month-old infants was allowed to observe a model performing six different actions with six different objects. Some of these actions were clearly novel for the infants, never occurring in the course of their daily activities.

Following these training sessions, the objects were removed immediately, without the infants having been given an opportunity to interact with them. When subjects were presented with the same six objects a full week later, they showed considerable evidence of precise imitative behavior.

The significance of deferred imitation is considerable for the cognitive development of the infant, depending, as it does, on the infant's ability to represent mentally and to remember. And, according to Piaget, it is one of the achievements that underlies the development of language.

Language and Communication

Despite its tremendous power, language is not essential for **communication**. Much of our communication involves actions and gestures, for example. And animals that do not have language can nevertheless communicate danger: Whitetail deer wave their tails; pronghorn antelope bristle their rump patches; ground squirrels whistle. Some insects, such as bees or ants, can also communicate the location of food sources (Gallistel, 1989).

Communication between humans and other animals also occurs. An animal trainer who instructs his dog to roll over is communicating with the animal (at least when the dog obeys—and perhaps even when the dog does not obey). The animal can also communicate with its master, as dogs frequently do when they are displeased, hungry, or otherwise agitated. This communication, however, is a far cry from that made possible by language. The parrot who can say "Polly wants a cracker" is not only boringly conventional but also probably incapable of saying "Polly does not want a cracker, heh, heh," with the intention of conveying a different meaning.

A Definition of Language

The parrot merely mimics; it does not communicate. It is incapable of deliberately rearranging sounds according to established rules with the intention of conveying meaning. It does not know language.

Language may be defined as the use of arbitrary sounds with established and accepted referents, either real or abstract, that can be arranged in sequence to convey different meanings. This definition includes what Brown (1973) describes as the three essential characteristics of language: displacement, meaning, and productiveness.

Language involves *displacement* by making it possible to represent objects and events that need not be immediate—that are displaced in both time and space. One of its primary functions is the communication of *meaning* (semanticity).

Although **psycholinguists** (those who study the relationship between language and human functioning) don't always concur as to the best definition for *meaning*, we, in our ordinary conversations, tend to agree much more than disagree. Indeed, it is because you and I have similar meanings for words and sentences that we can communicate as we are now doing.

The third characteristic of language, *productiveness*, means that—given a handful of words, a set of mutually accepted rules about the manner in which they can be combined, and agreement about the significance

of the various pauses, intonations, and other characteristics of speech—we can, in a sense, produce meaningful language almost forever. Language presents so many possibilities for meaningful combinations that almost every day of your life you will say something that no one else has ever said in exactly the same way. Language makes you creative.

Elements of Language

There are four basic components of language: Phonology, semantics, syntax, and pragmatics. Each is essential for effective communication with language.

Phonology refers to the **phonemes**, or sounds, of a language. A phoneme is the simplest unit of language and is nothing more complex than a single sound, such as is represented by a consonant or a vowel. There are 45 phonemes in the English language.

Phonemes can be combined to form **morphemes**, which are the units of meaning in language and, therefore, the building blocks of **semanticity** (meaning). Morphemes may be made up of sounds, such as *ing* or *ed*—word endings that affect the meanings of words—or of whole words. Children cannot produce morphemes until they can first pronounce the phonemes.

Organizing words into meaningful sentence units requires an intuitive knowledge of **syntax**, or grammar—the rules governing correct word combinations.

As children practice and master sounds (phonemes), meanings (semanticity), and grammatical rules (syntax), they must also learn a large number of unspoken rules and conventions governing conversation; these are the **pragmatics** of language (Bates, 1976). An implicit knowledge of pragmatics is what tells children when and how they should speak. It includes all the rules and conventions governing manners of expression, intonation, accents, and all the other subtle variations that give different meanings to the same morphemes and that might vary from one context to another. For example, that parents use shorter sentences, speak in higher-pitched voices, and use more concrete names and fewer abstractions when speaking with infants than with other adults is a function of their knowledge of pragmatics.

Phonology, semantics, syntax, and pragmatics are the elements of language. Most of us acquired these elements in a painless, effective, and efficient way without really being conscious of what we were doing.

Language consists of sounds (phonology) that have meaning (semantics) when used according to certain grammatical rules (syntax) as well as practical rules (pragmatics). But communication involves far more than simply language. This toddler already possesses a wealth of nonverbal gestures that makes it far easier to say, "Mom, the cat's digging up your hibiscus again."

Language Development in Infants

Early studies of how children acquire language concentrated on counting the number of words children had in their vocabularies at a given age. These studies revealed that passive vocabularies of infants and young children far exceed their active vocabularies; that is, in the early stages of language learning, they can invariably understand many more words than they can use in their own speech. And before using words in speech, most also develop a range of communicative gestures (Bates et al., 1989).

Another way of approaching early language development is by examining the *quality* of the language acquired, rather than by estimating vocabulary size at different ages. Contemporary linguists treat the developing child as a fellow linguist; they examine the progression of children's knowledge of each of the elements of language, not only to learn how the child acquires the ability to use language but also to learn more about language itself.

For convenience, language learning frequently is divided into two major stages: the prespeech stage followed by the speech stage. The prespeech stage involves the gradual development of meaningful speech sounds; the speech stage is best described in terms of a progression from sounds to words to grammar and pragmatics (see Table 5.5). The prespeech stage lasts from birth to about the end of the first year or the early part of the second and terminates with the utterance of single words. During this first stage, infants engage in

TABLE 5.5

Age at Which 50 Percent and 90 Percent of Infants Demonstrate a Given Language Capability*

	Age (months)	
Language Capability	50 Percent	90 Percent
Responds to bell		1.6
Laughs	2.0	3.3
Squeals	2.2	4.5
Says "dada" or "mama," nonspecific	6.9	10.0
Imitates speech sounds	7.0	11.2
Says 3 words other than "mama," "dada"	12.8	20.5
Points to 1 named body part	17.0	23.0
Combines 2 different words	19.6	24.3

* Based on norms from Denver Developmental Screening Test.

Source: From *Denver Developmental Screening Test Reference Manual: Revised 1975 edition* by W. K. Frankenburg, J. B. Dodds, A. W. Fandal, E. Kazuk, and M. Cohrs, 1975, Denver, CO: University of Colorado Medical Center. Reprinted by permission of the publisher.

three different speech-related behaviors: They cry; they develop a repertoire of gestures, many of which are intended to communicate desires; and they practice babbling.

Early Achievements

Bates (1976) summarizes the language-related achievements of the infant prespeech period in terms of two critical achievements that generally occur between the ages of 9 and 13 months. The first is marked by the appearance of the intention to communicate and can be seen in the conventional signals and gestures that clearly have meaning for both infant and caregiver. Squirming and gazing intently at the milk bottle are pragmatic (effective) ways of saying to mama, "If I don't get that bottle soon, I'm gonna yell!" The development of gestural communication, says Bijou (1989), is an important step toward communicating vocally.

The second critical achievement is the discovery of symbols—the discovery that things have names (Bates, 1976). This should not be confused with the simple ability to represent. As Mandler (1984) makes clear, there are two kinds of representation. *Simple* representation involves nothing more complex than memory. All that is in memory is represented. In this sense, the newborn's ability to suck involves representation. But this type of representation is a far cry from *symbolic* representation—the type of representation that defines semanticity (meaning) and that is essential for language. Symbolic representation begins with the infant's discovery that things can be named, that they can be symbolized with sounds. Ultimately, children learn to speak so that they can communicate, Rice (1989) tells us. Thus they can achieve important social goals.

Language Origins

Research dealing with the origins of language has been particularly interested in the pragmatics and semantics of the infant's first gesture and sounds (Bates et al., 1981; Terrace, 1985). Researchers believe that the ability to use and to understand words grows out of a complex series of interactions between infant and parents. These interactions, referred to collectively as the *Language Acquisition Support System (LASS)* by Bruner (1983), involve such things as learning how to make eye contact, how to direct attention through eye movements and gestures, and how to take turns.

Knowing when and how to take turns is basic to adult conversation. When we have conversations, we wait for the signals that tell us it's our turn; and we give others their signals (well, most of us do; there are some who simply shout a little louder). Most of us have learned the rules that govern turn-taking without really knowing that we've learned them, and without, in most cases, being able to verbalize them. Investigators such as Duncan and Fiske (1977) inform us there are a handful of signals that tell us when we may speak, and by which we tell others that it is their turn. These include an upward or downward change of pitch at the end of an utterance, the completion of a grammatical clause, a drawl on the last syllable, or the termination of gesture. These are among the signals that infants have to know if they are eventually to converse in socially acceptable ways. And amazingly, they seem to have a relatively sophisticated awareness of turn-taking signals at very young ages.

In one investigation, Mayer and Tronick (1985) found that even at 2 months, infants and their mothers are already taking turns in their verbal interactions. Mayer and Tronick videotaped 10 mothers and their infants in face-to-face interaction for 3-minute periods when the infants were 2, 3, and 5 months of age. Analysis of the videotapes revealed that not only did infants rarely vocalize (other than for occasional "fussy" vocalizations) when their mothers were speaking but also they seemed to understand their mothers' turn-giving signals. They responded to head and hand movements as well as to changes in intonation at the ends of utterances, to terminal drawls, and to the completion of grammatical clauses. Accordingly, they cooed and smiled primarily during their mothers' pauses. Mothers, for their part, modified the number of turn-giving signals given depending on their children's responsiveness. This is very much what adults do. As Duncan and Fiske (1977) note, although a single turn-taking cue is often sufficient for smooth transitions in adult conversations, quite often more than one cue is given. The more cues given, the more likely it is that the listener will take a turn.

So, even here in the early months of the prespeech stage, the infant shows a readiness for language—even for conversation—that is little short of astounding. As Mayer and Tronick (1985) observe, it is as if the infant were "preadapted for social engagement," and as if the mother has an implicit knowledge of this fact. Also, even in the nursing behavior of mother and infant, Kaye (1977) found turn-taking behavior very similar to that which might occur during a dialogue.

First Sounds

Verbal communication depends upon sounds—the ability of the infant to discriminate among them, and the ability to produce them.

Sound Discrimination. Some evidence suggests that infants have a built-in capacity to discriminate sounds. Recall, for example, the Moffitt (1971) experi-

ment described earlier in this chapter in which the heart rates of 5- and 6-month-old infants were monitored while they were exposed to taped recordings of the sounds "bah" and "gah." Changes in heart rate whenever the sound changed indicated that these infants could quite easily tell the difference between them.

Some sounds may be more difficult to tell apart than others. For example, infants sometimes have difficulty discriminating "sa" from "za," but they can much more easily tell the difference between "sa" and "fa" or "va" and "sa" (Eilers & Minifie, 1975). With increasing language experience, however, they eventually are able to discriminate reliably among these sounds. But if the sounds are not part of their language, even as adults they may experience difficulty discriminating among them (the sounds "la" and "ra" for a native Japanese speaker, for example) (Miyawaki et al., 1975).

Sound Production. Discriminating among sounds is one aspect of early language learning; producing intended sounds is the other. It starts with the crying, the cooing, and the eventual babbling of the infant. Eventually, it progresses to the word. And beyond.

Infants as young as 3 weeks produce three kinds of sounds, reports Legerstee (1991): the longer, *melodic* sounds characterized by variable pitch; *vocalic* sounds, which are short, more nasal bursts characterized by relatively uniform pitch; and *emotional* sounds such as laughing, crying, and fussing. The remarkable thing about these sounds is that even in early infancy, their emission is context-dependent. In a longitudinal investigation of eight infants ages 3–25 weeks, Legerstee (1991) found that melodic sounds typically occur when mothers are conversing with their infants; that vocalic sounds are more common with unresponsive adults; and that emotional sounds occur far more often in contexts involving other people than in situations where the infant is interacting with an inanimate object such as a doll.

It was long believed that all the sounds of every language in the world are uttered in the **babbling** of an infant—even in the babbling of deaf infants. This belief leads directly to the conclusion that the ability to produce speech sounds is innate, a conclusion that does no appear to be entirely true. For example, although the first sounds uttered by deaf infants are very similar to those of hearing children, their later vocalizations are typically quite different. These first sounds, say

Eilers and Oller (1988), are precursors to the form of babbling in which infants finally utter well-formed syllables with clearly articulated consonants and vowels—a stage that does not occur until some time between 7 and 10 months. Before then, infants make unarticulated noises—they goo, squeal, growl, whisper, and yell. And although it might be possible to discern many sounds that resemble those found in the world's 5,000 or so languages in these early infant sounds, their utterances remain unsystematic and do not obey the laws of syllables (requiring clarity and a complete vowel of adequate duration).

Infants' first sounds are "soft sounds," notes Bijou (1989), but eventually they gain control over their sound-producing apparatus. Also, they discover that producing sounds is "fun," as evidenced by the many hours contented infants may spend in solitary babbling without any prompting. As a result, by the age of 10 months, most hearing children babble clearly, systematically, and repetitively. Deaf children do not reach this stage until later. "It cannot be maintained," say Eilers and Oller (1988), "that babbling is independent of hearing" (p. 23).

While certain sounds appear in the babbling of almost all infants, many other sounds are almost never heard even though they are an important part of some languages. The most common sounds that infants babble are the ones that are easiest to produce given the anatomical structure of their vocal apparatus. Most common among these are certain consonants such as *b, d, w,* and *m* (described by linguists as *stop, glide,* or *nasal* consonants). Thus words like *mama, papa,* and *dada* are among the simplest for virtually all infants. In fact, some researchers believe that "mama" and "papa" are common to an astounding number of the world's languages precisely because they are among the first systematic sounds infants babble. In many of these languages, says Ingram (1991), "'Mama' emerges as a general request for the fulfillment of some need, while 'papa' is a more descriptive term for parents" (p.711).

The First Word. Not surprisingly, "mama" or "papa" is the first clearly recognizable word spoken by many infants. However, it is seldom easy to determine when infants say their first word.

Most infants repeat a sound such as "bah" many times before it becomes associated with an object. The point at which the sound "bah" ceases to be babble and

becomes a *word* (*ball,* for example) is nearly impossible to determine but has usually occurred by age 1. The appearance of the first word is rapidly followed by new words that the child practices incessantly. But even before learning words, infants have begun to show signs that they understand much more than they can say—words that will not be part of their active vocabulary for some time, as well as entire sentences. "Stick out your tongue," a child is told by a proud parent, and out comes the tongue. "Show daddy your hand," and the hand appears. "Can you wink?" Sure can. Two eyes, though.

Most of an English-speaking child's first words are nouns—simple names for simple things that are part of the here and now: "banket" (blanket), "dog," "mama," "milk." Verbs, adjectives, adverbs, and prepositions are acquired primarily in the order listed, with the greatest difficulty usually having to do with pronouns, especially the pronoun *I* (Boyd, 1976).

For convenience, the acquisition of language is described here in six sequential stages (Wood, 1981). The first, a prespeech stage, lasts until about age 1, and consists of the crying, the cooing, the babbling, and the communicative gestures just described. The following two stages—the *sentencelike word* and *two-word sentences*—are described next. The final three stages are discussed in Chapter 7. (See Table 5.6 for a summary of the six stages.)

The Sentencelike Word (Holophrase)

Some time after the sixth month (usually around age 1), children utter their first meaningful word. This word's meaning is not limited to one event, action, or person, but is interpreted as meaning something that an adult would require an entire sentence to communicate; hence the term *holophrase.* McNeill (1970) suggests that children's knowledge of grammar is innate, that they have notions of grammar long before they arrive at an understanding of how to express different grammatical forms in adultlike ways. Thus, although most holophrases refer to nouns, they are not used simply for naming. When a chid says "milk," she might mean, "There is the milk." She might also mean,

TABLE 5.6

Stages in Children's Development of Grammar

Stage of Development	Nature of Development	Sample Utterances
1. Prespeech (before age 1)	Crying, cooing, babbling.	"Waaah," "dadadada."
2. Sentencelike word (holophrase) (by 1 year)	The word is combined with nonverbal cues (gestures and inflections).	"Mommy." (meaning: "Would you please come here, mother.")
3. Two-word sentences (duos) (by 1½ years)	Modifiers are joined to topic words to form declarative, question, negative, and imperative structures.	"Pretty baby." (declarative) "Where Daddy?" (question) "No play." (negative) "More milk!" (imperative)
4. Multiple-word sentences (by 2 to 2½ years)	Both a subject and predicate are included in the sentence types. Grammatical morphemes are used to change meanings (*ing* or *ed*, for example).	"She's a pretty baby." (declarative) "Where Daddy is?" (question) "I no can play." (negative) "I want more milk!" (imperative) "I running." "I runned."
5. More complex grammatical changes and word categories (between 2½ and 4 years)	Elements are added, embedded, and permuted within sentences. Word classes (nouns, verbs, and prepositions) are subdivided. Clauses are put together.	"Read it, my book." (conjunction) "Where is Daddy?" (embedding) "I can't play." (permutation) "I would like *some* milk." (use of "some" with mass noun) "Take me *to* the store." (use of preposition of place)
6. Adultlike structures (after 4 years)	Complex structural distinctions made, as with "ask-tell" and "promise."	"Ask what time it is." "He promised to help her."

Source: Based in part on Barbara S. Wood, *Children and communication: Verbal and nonverbal language development* (2nd ed.), © 1981, p. 142. Reprinted by permission of Prentice-Hall, Inc., Englewood Cliffs, New Jersey.

"Give me some milk," "I'm thirsty," "Are you finally going out to buy some milk?" or "Do it to the cow again."

Two-Word Sentences

Not surprisingly, the progression of speech development is from one word to two (by about 18 months) — and later to more than two. There does not appear to be a three-word stage following this two-word stage, but rather a *multiword* stage, where sentences range in length from two to perhaps five or more words (Brown, 1973).

Children continue to acquire words during the second year, but the range of syllables available to them is limited. Many of their words are one- or two-syllable words, which often repeat the same syllable in different combinations. For example, the child says "mommy," "daddy," "baby," "seepy" (sleepy), "horsy," and "doggy." Even when it is incorrect to do so, the child may frequently repeat the syllable in a one-syllable word, as in "car car" or "kiss kiss." In an attempt to communicate with children on their level, parents sometimes exaggerate the trivial errors committed by their infants in the course of learning to speak. The result is occasionally something like, "Wou my itsy bitsy witta baby come to momsy womsy?" But there is no evidence that parental models of this type hinder the acquisition of language. In the early stages, the warmth of the interaction may be more important than the nature of the language employed. And, in fact, some evidence suggests that parents unconsciously fine-tune their speech to their children's level of understanding (see Chapter 7), and even modify pitch when speaking to infants. When Fernald and Mazzie (1991) had mothers reading a story to 14-month-olds, and the same story to adults, differences were striking and consistent. Mothers regularly use higher pitch with infants, especially to emphasize words.

The transition from holophrases to two-word sentences (duos) generally occurs around the age of 18 months. Bates, O'Connell, and Shore (1987) point out that this process begins slowly, with the relatively hesitant combining of familiar words, but that their use increases very rapidly once the infant begins to understand the number of meanings that can be conveyed with two-word sentences. Speech at this stage is telegraphic in that it eliminates many parts of speech while still managing to convey meanings. "Dog allgone" is a two-word utterance "telegraphed" from the lengthier adult equivalent, "The dog is not in this location at this particular time."

Whether precise grammatical functions can be accurately assigned to these two-word utterances is uncertain. The functions of the words *fish* and *eat* in the two-word utterance "fish eat" are, in fact, dependent upon the intended meaning. But because the child does not employ number agreement (for example, "fish eats" to mean "the fish eats," and "fish eat" to mean "I eat fish"), or order ("eat fish" versus "fish eat") to signal meaning, the psycholinguist can never be certain that children at this stage are aware of grammatical functions (Clark & Clark, 1977).

By the age of 2, infants have reached the point where they can name all the familiar objects and people in their environment and combine words in meaningful sentencelike units. They can also use adjectives and adverbs, questions, and simple negatives and affirmatives; and they have begun to learn a variety of subtle and implicit rules governing intonation, inflection, and the rules that guide conversations.

But there is much more to be learned; there are three stages remaining in our six-stage description of

the sequence of language acquisition. The story of that sequence continues in Chapter 7.

From Sensation to Representation

As we noted at the beginning of Part II, the word *infant* derives from the Latin word *infans*—literally, "without speech." And, indeed, throughout much of the period that we arbitrarily label *infancy*, the child is without speech. But, as we have seen, one of the major accomplishments of this period is the beginning of the acquisition of language.

The world of infants is initially a world of the here and now, a world populated only by those objects and feelings that are immediately perceived, a world that cannot be represented symbolically but can only be acted upon and felt. But the infant's capacities to act and feel are far more impressive than we have long believed—perhaps even more impressive than most of us still believe.

Although the term *sensorimotor* describes well the predominant relationship between the infant and the world, it does not describe the most important cognitive achievements of the first two years of life. Some of these achievements are apparent in Table 5.7, which depicts important events in mental development during infancy.

By the time the child is 2, the world no longer exists only in the immediate *sensible* present. Objects have achieved a permanence and an identity that no longer depend solely on the child's activities; there is a dawning understanding of cause-and-effect relationships; language is rapidly exercising a profound effect on cognitive development. These achievements, together with children's recognition of their own identities—their selves—represent a dramatic transition from a quasi-animalistic existence to the world of thought and emotions as we know it. But even though it is a dramatic transition, at least in its import, it is neither sudden nor startling. Those who follow the lives of individual children closely (and daily) would never see the transition from sensorimotor intelligence to preoperational thought. It happens suddenly and irrevocably on the second birthday only in textbooks. Real life is less well organized.

TABLE 5.7

Average Ages for Mental Development in Infants

Age (months)	Mental Behavior Anticipated
0.2	Regards person momentarily, responding either to speech or to movements.
0.7	Eyes follow moving person.
0.7	Makes definite response to speaking voice.
1.5	Smiles or laughs in response to another person's speaking to and smiling at him or her.
2.0	Visually recognizes mother; expression changes when infant sees mother bending over to talk to him or her.
2.6	Manipulates red ring placed in child's hand or grasped by child.
3.8	Carries red ring to mouth during free play.
3.8	Inspects own hands.
4.1	Reaches for cube, even if not actually touching it.
5.1	Laughs or shows pleasure when held and played with.
5.8	Lifts cup with handle.
6.0	Looks for spoon that has fallen.
9.1	Responds to verbal request *not* accompanied by gesture.
12.0	Turns pages of book, even if effort is clumsy.
14.2	Says two words meaningfully (approximations all right if clear).
20.6	Puts two or more words denoting two concepts into one sentence or phrase.

Source: Adapted from *Bayley Scales of Infant Development* by N. Bayley, 1969. Reproduced by permission. Copyright © 1969 by The Psychological Corporation, New York, N.Y. All rights reserved.

Main Points

1. A newborn is a primitive, self-driven little sensing machine designed to mature and grow physically in a predetermined sequence and at a relatively predictable pace, programmed as an extraordinarily capable information-processing system, endowed with powerful gregarious tendencies and strong emotions, and pretuned to the development of language.

2. Breast milk is among the most easily digested sources of nourishment for infants. In developing countries, breast-feeding is especially useful in guarding against the possibility of diarrhea and other infant illnesses against which the mother's milk sometimes provides a degree of immunity.

3. Optimal brain development in early infancy is profoundly influenced by nutrition (especially protein) and stimulation.

4. Sudden infant death syndrome (SIDS) accounts for the unexpected and largely inexplicable deaths of approximately 2 of every 1,000 apparently healthy

infants. It is more common among males, rarely occurs after the age of 6 months, and is sometimes associated with a mild upper-respiratory infection, with apnea, with lower APGAR scores, or with other factors, none of which have been shown to cause it.

5. The orienting response, a useful measure of interest, attention, and learning in infants, is our tendency to respond to new stimulation by becoming more alert. It is revealed in changes in heart rate, respiration rate, electrical activity of the brain, and conductivity of the skin to electricity.

6. The behavioral repertoire of the neonate consists largely of reflexes: the sucking, Moro, Babinski, palmar (grasping), and the swimming, stepping, swallowing, and sneezing reflexes. Many of these disappear with the development of the brain and the achievement of voluntary control over movements.

7. Motor capacities develop sequentially but at varying ages, and seem to be governed by two principles: *cephalocaudal* (head to tail) and *proximodistal* (near to far).

8. Sensation is primarily a physiological process involving the senses and neural transmission; conceptualization is an intellectual activity involving processes such as thinking and understanding; and perception, our interpretation of sensation, is a sort of bridge between sensation and conceptualization.

9. Visual capacities are well developed in the newborn. The infant's looking seems to be directed toward maximizing information (by maximizing neural firing using systematic visual scanning). The rules that govern looking behavior (according to Haith) are: (1) If awake and alert, open eyes; (2) even in darkness, search with controlled eye movements; (3) in unpatterned light, search for edges and patterns; (4) if an edge is found, examine it more closely (short eye movements back and forth across the edge, maximizing stimulation in the foveal area).

10. Neonates are slightly less sensitive than adults to sound intensity (loudness). Sensitivity to higher frequencies increases with age. Infants appear to recognize and prefer their mothers' voices at ages as young as 3 days. They prefer pleasant odors (such as vanilla) to those less pleasant (ammonia or raw fish) almost from birth. Similarly, they prefer the sweet to the bland, they distinguish easily between sour and bitter tastes, and they appear to be sensitive to touch (and to pain), at least within a few hours of birth.

11. Information-processing explanations of cognition look at the processes involved in memory: deriving information, abstracting, sorting, organizing, analyzing, and developing strategies for learning and remembering. The neonate's memory is not as efficient, as powerful, or as long-term as that of older children or adults, but there is memory for smells and sights within days of birth. By the age of 3 months, infants actively search and show signs of recognition.

12. In Piaget's theory, adaptation (cognitive growth) results from the interplay of assimilation (responding in a habitual and preferred way based primarily on preexisting information and well-practiced capabilities) and accommodation (adapting behavior to some external characteristic or quality). Equilibration is the tendency to balance assimilation and accommodation. Other important factors in cognitive development are maturation, social interaction, and active experience.

13. Piaget's six substages of the sensorimotor period are as follows: (1) exercising reflexes (0–1 month — little new learning, repeated practice of simple reflexes); (2) primary circular reactions (1–4 months — repetitive behaviors centering on the infant's body); (3) secondary circular reactions (4–8 months — new repetitive behaviors centering on the environment); (4) purposeful coordinations (8–12 months — coordination of activities in goal-oriented behaviors); (5) tertiary circular reactions (12–18 months — exploration of the environment by deliberately modifying repetitive behaviors); and (6) mental representation (18–24 months — gradual transition to a more symbolic, more conceptual intelligence).

14. There is increased frequency of simple infant behaviors like tongue protrusion following exposure to a model, even in very young infants. It is not entirely clear that these are always imitative behaviors. Evidence of *deferred imitation* (the ability to imitate a model that is no longer present) is seen by the age of 9–12 months, depends on the ability to represent mentally and to remember, and is therefore of considerable importance in cognitive development.

15. Language involves the use of arbitrary speech sounds that have accepted meanings. It is characterized by *displacement* (allowing the representation of objects and events not now present); *meaningfulness* (also termed *semanticity*, a term that refers to the significance of words and expressions); and *productiveness* (allowing the generation of an unlimited number of novel but meaningful combinations, given an appropriate vocabulary and knowledge of relevant grammatical rules).

16. Infants may have a built-in capacity to discriminate certain sounds; also, they are able to produce many sounds in their babbling, but some sounds are more common than others, and some rarely appear. Babbling, involving well-formed syllables—as opposed to coos, squeals, and cries—becomes systematic by the age of 7–10 months. Linguistic experience eventually modifies the infant's ability to discriminate and to produce sounds.

17. The four basic elements of language are *phonology* (sounds, *phonemes* being the simplest sounds of a language), *semantics* (the meanings of words), *syntax* (grammar or rules that govern relationships among parts of speech), and *pragmatics* (rules and conventions concerning how and when to speak).

18. The ability to use and understand words grows out of a complex series of interactions between parents and young infants. Infants as young as 2 months have a relatively sophisticated awareness of the turn-taking signals used in conversation.

19. In the prespeech stage of language development (first year of life), the infant coos, gurgles, cries, and babbles. These are the early roots of language. Two important achievements of this stage are the development of the intention to communicate and the discovery that things have names.

20. The normal course of language acquisition begins with the appearance of the first meaningful word around age 1. The first word, often used in combination with a variety of nonverbal cues and gestures, is often sentencelike in nature (a *holophrase*). Two-word sentences appear around the age of 18 months. These are telegraphic, condensing considerable information into two words.

Further Readings

The following is a simple, nontechnical description of development during the first three years of life; it offers many practical suggestions that might be useful for parents interested in understanding and promoting the intellectual development of their infants:

White, B. L. (1985). *The first three years of life* (rev. ed.). Englewood Cliffs, NJ: Prentice-Hall.

A clear and useful account of Piaget's theory is:

Wadsworth, B. J. (1989). *Piaget's theory of cognitive and affective development* (4th ed.). New York: Longman.

Bower's book is a stimulating explanation of how experience makes the rational infant even more competent:

Bower, T. G. R. (1989). *The rational infant: Learning in infancy*. New York: W. H. Freeman.

Those interested in the details of Piaget-type investigations with infants might consult the following translation:

Sinclair, H., Stambak, M., Lézine, I., Rayna, S., & Verba, M. (Eds.). (1989). *Infants and objects: The creativity of cognitive development*. New York: Academic Press.

An outstandingly clear and well-written account of cognitive development that examines Piaget's theories in considerable detail is:

Flavell, J. H. (1985). *Cognitive development* (2nd ed.). Englewood Cliffs, NJ: Prentice-Hall.

The major premise of this captivating and sometimes disturbing book is that we have grossly underestimated the infant's intellectual capacities and that, worse still, we damage and even destroy much of that capacity:

Pearce, J. C. (1977). *Magical child: Rediscovering nature's plan for your children*. New York: Bantam Books.

This short book by Haith presents an intriguing account of how the newborn uses vision as an information-gathering system:

Haith, M. M. (1980). *Rules that babies look by: The organization of newborn visual activity*. Hillsdale, NJ: Erlbaum.

The early development of language in infants is described in more detail in:

Carroll, D. W. (1986). *Psychology of language*. Monterey, CA: Brooks/Cole.

Wood, B. S. (1981). *Children and communication: Verbal and nonverbal language development* (2nd ed.). Englewood Cliffs, NJ: Prentice-Hall.

port that most mothers respond quickly to hunger cries or to cries of pain, and that they readily discriminate between the two—although most mothers seem to be more sensitive to the general distress level of the infant than to the cause of the distress. Interestingly, first-time parents tend to respond to infant crying sooner than parents of more than one child. And mothers are more attentive than are fathers (Donate-Bartfield & Passman, 1985).

The meanings of an infant's cries are apparently not universal, however. Isabell and McKee (1980) observe that in many primitive cultures where the child is carried about constantly by the mother, mother–infant communication can occur through physical contact. In these cultures, there appears to be little need for the vocal signals of distress that we have come to expect from our infants. For instance, among South American Indian tribes in the northern Andes, infant crying is extremely rare and is invariably interpreted as a sign of illness. Why else would a warm, well-fed, and constantly embraced infant cry?

Smiling and Laughing

Smiling, a universal phenomenon among human cultures, is a fleeting response in the warm, well-fed infant and appears to occur as early as 2–12 hours after delivery (Wolff, 1963). This early smile involves the lower part of the face, not the upper cheeks and eyes, and is described as a reflex smile rather than as a true social smile.

In the weeks and months following birth, infants smile in response to an ever-widening range of sights and sounds. The social smile occurs first in response to a human voice (by the third week). By the age of 3½ months, infants smile more in response to familiar than unfamiliar faces (Gewirtz, 1965). Accordingly, Gewirtz has identified three stages in the development of smiling behavior. The first phase, spontaneous or reflex smiling, occurs in the absence of readily identifiable stimuli and is often, although perhaps incorrectly, attributed to gas pains. Social smiling, the second phase, occurs initially in response to auditory and visual stimuli that are social in nature—that is, they are related to other humans. Finally, the child manifests the selective social smile, common among children and adults, which occurs in response to social stimuli that the child can presumably identify as familiar. With the appearance of the selective social smile, children smile less often in response to an unfamiliar voice or face and display more withdrawal behavior and other signs of anxiety in the presence of strangers. (More about stranger anxiety later in this chapter.)

Hodapp and Mueller (1982) note that the development of smiling in infants follows the same general pattern as the development of crying. Initially, infants smile and cry in response to internal states—primarily gastric disturbances. Hodapp and Mueller use the term *endogenous* (related to internal states) to describe these smiles and cries. With the passage of time, however, both crying and smiling become more *exogenous* (responsive to external stimuli). By the age of 4 or 5 weeks, many infants will interrupt their feeding to smile when they hear their mother's voice. Similarly, crying now occurs in response to external sources of frustration such as having a pacifier presented and then taken away. In brief, the early development of these behaviors follows an internal-to-external progression. Whereas the first instances of smiling and crying are mainly physiological, within a short period of time, cognitive elements (such as those involved in recognizing a voice, a face, or an object) are clearly involved.

At about 4 months, infants begin to laugh in addition to smiling. Initially, laughter is most likely to occur in response to physical stimulation such as tickling; later, infants laugh in response to more social and eventually more cognitive situations (for example, seeing other children laughing) (Sroufe & Wunsch, 1972). Although the function of laughter in infants has never been very clear, perhaps because it has not been investigated much, Sroufe and Waters (1976) suggest that it probably serves to release tension. Fear, by contrast, signifies a continued building up of tension.

Smiling and laughing are undoubtedly of crucial importance in parent–child interaction. Both research evidence and common sense suggest that parents look for smiles and other nonverbal gestures in their infants as evidence that they are themselves worthwhile and loved—even as infants look to parents for signs of approval and affection.

The bidirectionality of mother–child influence is evident in a variety of situations. Fretting and crying on the part of an infant trigger soothing behavior in the mother: rocking, singing, talking quietly, and so on. In turn, the mother's soothing behavior quiets the infant. Perhaps the infant's quiet behavior now leads to a mutual gaze. Has the infant learned to be quiet and loving in response to the mother's soothing behavior? Or has the mother learned to be soothing in response

Infants smile spontaneously shortly after birth. Thereafter, they smile in response to sights and sounds and eventually in response to a human voice.

to the infant's crying? Probably both, given the bidirectionality of influence.

And what about fear? Does it, like smiling and crying, stem initially from internal conditions? Or is it always a response to the environment?

Wariness and Fear

Fear, argued Watson and Rayner (1920), is the infant's unlearned response to loud noises and sudden loss of support. Later, some infants learn to fear a wide range of stimuli; others remain relatively unperturbed in the face of environmental changes. Fear of heights appears to be almost universal in infants by the age of 13–18 months and is present in more than 20 percent of all children by the age of 7 months (Scarr & Salapatek, 1970). Fear of strangers is not ordinarily seen until after 6 months and becomes most common by the age of 2 years. Other situations that may evoke fear in an infant typically involve some unexpected change. For example, a jack-in-the-box may be frightening; so might an experimenter or a parent wearing a mask. In addition, separation from the mother is frightening for some

Infant Temperaments*

▶ *What sort of infant were you? Ask your mother, your father, a sibling, or someone else who can tell you. Do you see any relationship between who you are now and what you were like as an infant?*

Temperament	Description	Approximate Percentage
Easy	Regularity in eating and sleeping (high rhythmicity); high approach tendencies in novel situations; high adaptability to change; preponderance of positive moods; low or moderate intensity of responses	40
Difficult	Irregularity in eating and sleeping (low rhythmicity); withdrawal in novel situations; slow adaptation to change; preponderance of negative moods; high intensity of reactions to stimulation	15
Slow to warm up	Low activity level; high initial withdrawal from unfamiliar; slow adaptation to change; somewhat negative mood; moderate or low intensity of reaction to stimulation	10
Varying mixtures	Unclassified	35

* Thomas and Chess (1981) caution that these temperaments do not exhaust all possibilities. In addition, although it is sometimes convenient, as well as apparently logical, to classify infants in these ways, there are wide ranges of behaviors within each category. "Easy" children don't all react the same way to the same situations; nor do all "difficult" children. Furthermore, some 35 percent of all infants appear not to fit any of these categories.

Source: Based on classifications used by Thomas, Chess, and Birch (1968, 1970, 1981) in the New York Longitudinal Study (NYLS).

not be confused with shyness. Shyness is a discomfort or fear in social situations; low sociability refers to a low need (or desire) to interact. Accordingly, a person might be very low in sociability, yet not the least bit shy.

Another approach to understanding temperament is physiological (Strelau, 1989). It relates to Pavlov's observation that some individuals have more excited nervous systems than others — that their physiological reactions to stimulation are different. Differences in physiological reactions such as brain wave activity, heart rate, or motor responses may underlie specific temperament characteristics. For example, Stifter and Fox (1990) showed that measures of heart-rate variability are closely related to infant reactivity in the first year of life. Similarly, Kagan and Snidman (1991) classified infants into two broad groups: those who have

a tendency to approach unfamiliar events, and those who have a tendency to avoid such events. They found that the *avoidance-prone* (or *inhibited*) infants were also those who cried more easily and who displayed lower levels of motor activity. "This implies but does not prove," say Kagan and Snidman, "that variation in the excitability of brain areas that mediate motor activity and crying participates in the actualization of the temperamental categories" (p. 856).

The Implications of Infant Temperament

"An infant's temperament," say Kagan and Snidman (1991), "renders some outcomes very likely, some moderately likely, and some unlikely — although not

► Subject   Female; age 48; widowed;
two children, both
independent; manager of a
cleaning business.
(concerning her children)

....

66 *They were real different when they were
babies, you know. I mean Luke was a holy
terror. Just about drove me crazy, always
hollering for something or needing a change or
falling out of his crib. He did that more than
once. Wonder he didn't scramble his brains.
And Chris, he was just about the opposite.
Never cried or nothing unless he was real sick
or hurt. Right through school, too, Chris he
never complained. Just done his work, but
his brother, he was two years younger, Luke
was. Well Luke, he complained, all right,
and he got himself into trouble more times!
Nothing serious, mind you. Just kid stuff.
Never got kicked out of school or anything
like that. . . .*

*Now? Well, I don't know. They're grown
up. They're different all right. I mean Chris
is more quiet and all, but Luke settled down
a lot when he grew up. Marriage is what did
it.* 99

impossible—depending on experience" (p. 856). Specifically, the temperament they label *uninhibited to the
unfamiliar*, characterized by a tendency to approach in
strange situations, is likely to lead to spontaneous, fear-
less, outgoing youngsters. In contrast, infants who are
markedly inhibited in the face of the strange or novel
are likely to continue to manifest timidity and shyness
at the age of 8 years.

Thomas and Chess (1981) also found some long-
term consequences of temperament. Specifically, infants of difficult temperament were more likely to manifest problems requiring psychiatric attention. Of the

42 children (out of a sample of 141) who had such
problems, 70 percent had been classified as difficult
infants and only 18 percent as "easy" children.

To the extent that infant characteristics are related
to later behaviors, early identification of these characteristics might be of tremendous value for parents,
educators, and others concerned with the welfare of
children. Thus the NYLS has led to attempts to identify "high-risk" infants, as well as to various suggestions relating to the best way of reacting to this risk.
However, there are some potential dangers in these
attempts. As Rothbart (1982) notes, labeling infants as
difficult, particularly when parents have not thought of
them in that way, may lead parents to expect problems,
might change their reactions to their infants, and
might, indirectly, be related to the appearance of the
problems.

Kagan and Snidman's follow-up of infants through
the first two years of life found remarkable consistency
in their temperaments—a finding they attribute to the
biological basis of temperament. But this does not
mean, they caution, that genetically influenced aspects
of temperament inevitably determine our personalities—that our contexts are of no importance. In fact,
knowing something of an infant's temperament may
be very useful in allowing us to alter contexts in beneficial ways. Thomas, Chess, and Korn (1982) suggest,
for example, that "easy" children, because of their high
adaptability, will respond well to a variety of parenting
styles (such as permissive or authoritarian). In contrast,
a more difficult infant may require more careful parenting. Because these children adapt more slowly and
respond less well to novelty and change, they require
consistent and patient parents. Also, given their more
intense and more negative moods, they are not likely
to react well to highly authoritarian or highly punitive
parents.

The contribution of temperament to the infant's
development, and its relationship to the behavior of
parents, presents yet another example of the extent to
which parent–infant influences are bidirectional. Consider, as an illustration, the case of the *easy* child. Such
an infant adapts readily to changes, establishes predictable feeding and sleeping routines, is highly responsive
to parents but not easily alarmed by change, and, perhaps most important, appears to be happy most of the
time. As Thomas and Chess (1981) note, parents react
with pleasure to such a child. They feel somehow responsible for what the child is; they think of themselves
as wonderful parents. They smile and laugh as they
tend their *easy* little infant, and the infant smiles back.

They gaze at each other, and everything they say and do tells the other how wonderful he or she is.

But the difficult child does not smile as much, cries more, is not so regular about eating and sleeping, fusses and whines and complains, and does not adapt as quickly to changes. Hence, social progress seems slower, and the message the parent receives does not say, "You're wonderful, dear wonderful parent," quite so loudly. Instead, it might say, "As a parent, you're just so-so," or, worse yet, "As a parent, you ain't worth *#$%!" Not all parents will read the same message, of course. Nor will all react in the same way. But there are some who will feel anxious and guilty about their *difficult* or *slow-to-warm* infant—some who will try too hard to change the infant, or who will silently give up and perhaps, without even knowing it, begin an insidious process of rejection.

Temperament in Context

Chess and Thomas (1989b) make the important point that although temperament has a biological basis, it is constantly evolving as a result of child–context interaction. Consequently, developmental outcomes are not always easy to predict. The infant who is initially difficult may become an adolescent whose charm, grace, and other good qualities make a mother blush with pride; and the one who is initially easy may, it's true, become a thoroughly reprehensible, no-good #@%&*. Or worse.

A Cross-Cultural Illustration. DeVries and Sameroff (1984) studied infant temperament among three African tribes: the Kikuyu, Digo, and Masai. The Kikuyu are a relatively modern, wage-earning or farming society. They view infants as vulnerable, toilet train them later than other tribes, and allow them to develop motor skills at somewhat later ages. Among the Kikuyu, a number of individuals and groups other than the mother are involved in child care.

The Digo are a Bantu tribe who farm and fish, and who have a much more leisurely life-style than the Kikuyu. They live in clusters of extended families in large dirt houses with grass roofs. Digo mothers monitor their infants closely, and respond quickly to their cries. They expect a high level of motor and social development by the age of 3–5 months.

The Masai are a pastoral tribe; they live mostly on milk and meat from the herds they tend. Accordingly, their life centers around their cattle and, to some extent, around the corn crops they cultivate. They live in small mud huts in the center of their cattle corrals. Tuberculosis, trachoma, and other parasitic diseases are common among Masai children. Mothers spend most of their day with their children, breast-feeding them until the age of 2–3 years, and carrying them around on their backs during the day until the child is old enough that others can care for it.

When deVries and Sameroff observed Masai, Kikuyu, and Digo infants, they found a high relationship between temperament and cultural factors such as maternal orientation, child-rearing customs, degree of modernization, and important events early in the child's life. Classifications for Masai and Digo infants were, on the whole, more positive, with significantly more infants being classed *easy* rather than *difficult*. It is no surprise that Digo infants, reared in an easy-going, leisurely environment, were marked by less "rhythmicity." The Digo, deVries and Sameroff inform us, are concerned with the "here and now" needs of the infants, and far less with regularity in their patterns of feeding and sleeping. However, that the Kikuyu infants should be less adaptable, less approaching, more intensely reactive, and more negative than the Digo and the Masai is not as easily explained. What deVries and Sameroff (1984) conclude is that the data strongly support the hypothesis that "temperament is influenced by infant experiential factors" (p. 94).

Goodness-of-Fit: Context and Temperament. Within an ecological model of child development, interactions and mutual accommodations are all-important. Understanding the relationship between temperament and developmental outcomes requires taking into account accommodations that occur in the face-to-face interactions of infant and important others (*microsystem*). In Lerner and associates' (1986) terms, the most optimal situation is one in which high *goodness-of-fit* exists between infant and context. This situation occurs when external demands and expectations are compatible with the infant's basic temperament—that is, with the infant's inclinations and customary ways of doing things. Conversely, a poor fit exists when the infant's temperament is not in accord with environmental demands.

For example, Marlis (who, you may recall, is a difficult infant) reacts loudly and impatiently to frustration. Her father is distressed and annoyed at this behavior because he expects and wants Marlis to be more like Brad. There is a poor fit here, and the result is conflict and strain in the relationship between Marlis and her father.

A cross-cultural illustration makes the point well. In the deVries and Sameroff (1984) study of temperament among three African tribes, the researchers assumed that difficult infants would be at higher risk of later problems than easy infants. This was the case in two of the tribes; but it was not true for the Masai. DeVries (1989) reports that when the tribe was revisited between four and six months later, things were far better for the difficult infants. In fact, mortality was much higher among the easy infants. Why? There had been a serious drought in the region, and many infants had died or suffered malnutrition and disease. But the difficult infants had fared best. DeVries speculates that these infants probably yelled and hollered more when they were frustrated and hungry—and succeeded more often in being fed. Thus a particular environmental characteristic "fit" better with the difficult temperament—a temperament that, under most circumstances in our culture, seldom "fits" as well as the easy temperament.

Difficult temperaments do not always lead to poor fit; nor do easy temperaments always result in high goodness-of-fit. Goodness-of-fit would be higher than expected, for example, if Marlis's father takes pride in his daughter's lustiness, her independence, her aggressiveness. And if Brad's parents were uneasy at how "easy" he is, afraid that he might not cope well in what they think is a dog-eat-dog world, goodness-of-fit between his temperament and his context might be unexpectedly poor. Here, as elsewhere, we need to consider the characteristics of the person, *in interaction with* characteristics of the context.

Early Attachment

Among the most important interactions in the early life of the infant are those having to do with parent–infant attachment.

The infant has two principal tasks, say Greenspan and Lieberman (1989). The first involves achieving a balance between what the organism needs and what it assimilates—a balance termed *homeostasis*. At a biological level, homeostasis is maintained when the infant is not too hungry, thirsty, cold, or hot. Maintaining homeostasis is greatly facilitated by infants' increasing

ability to regulate or control their behavior as they interact with the environment.

The second task, very closely related to maintaining homeostasis, is that of forming an attachment—generally with a principal caregiver to begin with, later with other individuals in the immediate environment (the microsystem). Within these attachments, developing infants learn to communicate, both through gestures and language; and they begin their exposure to culture. Language and culture, Vygotsky insists, are what make all higher mental functions possible.

Studying Attachment

Attachment is a powerful emotional bond, impossible for an infant to describe for us, and not easy to study. Measurements of infant attachment are always indirect. Investigators look at behaviors that are directed toward the object of attachment (crying, smiling, vocalizing, following, clinging, holding, and so on); they focus on the infant's reaction to strange situations and on physical contact between parents and infant; or they look at the infant's reaction to being separated from a parent (Ainsworth et al., 1978).

One of the problems that affects infant attachment research is the difficulty of conducting the types of controlled experiments required. Infants cannot be deliberately separated from their mothers at different times in their lives, and for different periods of time, to determine the effects of separation; nor can they be brought up in complete social isolation. Considerations such as these have led to a series of studies in which infant monkeys were taken from their mothers at birth and raised in isolation or with wire models vaguely resembling monkey mothers (Harlow, 1958, 1959) (see Figure 6.1). These studies seem to indicate that depriving infant monkeys of their mothers has serious negative consequences for their later adjustment. Unfortunately, however, they do not tell us very much about human infants—and perhaps not very much about infant monkeys, either, according to Ainsworth (1984).

Mother–Infant Bonding

Mother–infant bonding describes the formation of an emotional or attachment bond between mother and infant. Although *bond* is often used as though it were synonymous with *attachment*, mother–infant bonding

Mother-Deprived Monkeys

Infant monkeys who are raised in isolation later experience serious developmental problems often manifested in an inability to achieve sexual relations. Female monkeys raised under such conditions who then have infants of their own will often reject them. But when the mothers of infant monkeys are replaced by a substitute, infants typically form a strong attachment to the substitute. Research that has compared infant monkeys' attachment to cloth-covered and wire mother-substitutes indicates that quality of physical contact is especially important for monkeys.

The infant monkey remains on the terry cloth mother even though he must stretch to the wire model in order to feed.

Figure 6.1 Amount of time spent by infant monkeys on cloth and wire surrogate mothers. The results show a strong preference for the cloth mother regardless of whether the infant was fed on the wire model (broken line) or on the cloth model (solid line). (From Harry F. Harlow, Love in infant monkeys, *Scientific American*, 1959, 200, 68–74. Copyright 1959 by Scientific American, Inc. All rights reserved. Used by permission.)

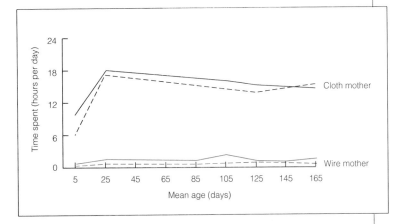

Some theorists argue that infants have built-in biological preadaptations that facilitate mother–infant attachment—for example, the infant's built-in visual accommodation for approximately the distance of the mother's face during feeding, and the infant's sensitivity to the human voice.

refers primarily to the very early, biologically based attachment that the mother develops for her infant. *Attachment* is a more general term that includes the host of *positive* emotions that link parents, children, and other people as well.

The term *bond*, in this context, is defined in much the same way as it is by ethologists (those who study animal behavior in natural settings)—that is, as a biologically based link that forms between a mother and her offspring under appropriate circumstances. Among nonhuman species, these appropriate circumstances generally involve nothing more complicated than the mother being exposed to her infant during some *critical period* that generally begins at birth and lasts for a short period of time thereafter. In the absence of appropriate experiences during this critical period, bonding failure typically occurs. Theorists such as Bowlby (1958) and Klaus and Kennell (1983) argue that infants kept from their mothers at birth may fail to bond with them. They suggest, as well, that failure to establish a strong mother–infant bond is detrimental to the future adjustment and emotional health of the child, and may be related to such things as child abuse or "growth failure."

Growth failure, or *failure to thrive (FTT)*, is a condition in which an apparently normal infant fails to gain weight, falling to the bottom 3 percent of normal standards. Abramson (1991) reports significantly more expressions of negative emotion among these infants. In addition, the condition is marked by listlessness, loss of appetite, illness, and, in its more extreme manifestations, even death. Researchers such as Bowlby (1940) and Spitz (1945) first noticed this condition among institutionalized infants, and attributed it to lack of mothering. Because of this, FTT is also called *maternal deprivation syndrome*.

Bonding Mechanisms

Theorists such as Bowlby argue that because of the importance of the mother–infant bond, there must be powerful genetic predispositions that ensure its formation. Clearly, no emotional bond links the infant to its mother immediately at birth. A neonate taken from its mother and given to another will surely never know the difference unless, of course, the facts are disclosed later.

But that a bond does form with the primary caregiver(s) is also clear. Wellman and Gelman (1992) point out that the infant has certain biological *preadaptations* that facilitate the development of this bond. These include perceptual biases such as the infant's built-in visual accommodation for a distance of approximately 8–10 inches (about the distance to the caregiver's face during feeding), the young infant's apparent preference for the human face, and a sensitivity and responsiveness to the human voice. They also include some reflexive response tendencies that seem especially designed for social interaction. Like the young of most mammals, for example, the human infant clings and turns and roots and sucks. One of the functions of these vegetative reflexes is surely to ensure that the infant obtains nourishment and survives. But more than this, feeding is among the first important social interactions between caregiver and infant. Almost invariably, feeding leads to the mutual gaze that is highly significant in the development of attachment, and that appears to be universal between mothers and infants in different cultures (Fogel, Toda, & Kawai, 1988).

Schaffer (1984) also suggests that certain biological rhythms are geared to social interaction. Some, like those expressed in the infant states of waking and sleeping, are modifiable and eventually become attuned to the mother's cycles of waking and sleeping. Others, like the rhythms apparent in sucking behavior, seem to contain many of the elements of a dialogue and may underly the learning of the turn-taking rules that are a fundamental part of conversations with language. Apparently, the infant sucks in organized and relatively predictable patterns — short bursts of activity followed by pauses (Kaye, 1977) — and the mother is unconsciously attuned to these rhythms, adjusting her behaviors to those of the infant. During the sucking bursts, she is typically quiet; but during the pauses, she jiggles or strokes the infant, or talks to it.

The existence of biological preadaptations that facilitate the formation of bonds between caregiver and infant are evidence, says Bowlby (1958), that powerful biological forces are directing both mother and infant toward mutual attachment. Attachment had important survival value at a time when physical survival was threatened by the "hissing serpents and dragons of Eden" (Sagan, 1977).

The Importance of Bonding

Dragons and serpents no longer lurk so blatantly in our forests — or parking lots. But, say Klaus and associates (1972), there is a critical period very early in our lives during which we *must* have contact with our mothers so that a bond may form. Bonding failure, they claim, can have serious negative consequences later.

The evidence? Klaus and associates (1972) randomly selected a group of 28 low-income mothers and allowed half of them extended contact with their infants immediately after birth (1 hour of the first 2 hours following birth), as well as 5 additional hours of contact with their infants on each of the first 3 days following birth. The remaining 14 mothers, serving as a control group, saw their infants regularly at feeding time in conformity with hospital routine.

Interviews and observations one month later indicated that mothers in the extended-contact group were significantly more bonded to their infants, showed more concern for them, and expressed considerably more interest in them. These mothers tended to cuddle their babies more, to engage in more verbal interaction with them, and to spend more time in mutual gazing. And follow-up studies, undertaken when the infants were ages 1 and 2, still revealed significant differences between extended-contact and control-group mothers, not only in terms of attachment but also in terms of verbal interaction as well (Ringler et al., 1975). Other research indicates that extended contact between mother and infant immediately following birth may be manifested in closer infant–mother attachment and in physical development (greater weight gains) as well as in measured intelligence (see, for example, Kennell, Trause, & Klaus, 1975).

Looking only at these studies, it would be tempting to conclude that there is a critical period early in the lives of neonates during which contact with the mother (or perhaps some other important caregiver) is of absolutely fundamental importance. However, a raft of subsequent studies has failed to replicate the most important of the Klaus and Kennell findings (see, for example, Schaffer, 1984). Goldberg (1983), for one, concludes that the evidence of a critical period and of lasting harmful effects of "bonding failure" is totally unconvincing.

It seems plausible, as Wasserman (1980) argues, that the formation of attachments is sufficiently important to human development that the infant and mother likely can take advantage of other opportunities for bonding without harmful consequences. In a careful investigation, Egeland and Vaughn (1981) found no greater incidence of abuse, neglect, illness, or adjustment problems among children who had been separated from their mothers for a period of time immediately after birth. This does not mean, of course, that maternal deprivation or rejection are irrelevant. As we saw, they can lead to serious conditions like *growth failure*. However, the importance of a crucial few hours immediately after birth has not been clearly established.

Stages of Attachment

According to ethologists such as Bowlby (1969), the why of infant attachment is clear. After all, the infant's very survival demands a solicitous caregiver. What better way to assure that the caregiver will be there when needed than to program into the human gene pool powerful parent–infant attachment tendencies? However, nature does not program the attachment itself; it develops later. Nor do genes limit attachment to the biological mother or father.

Bowlby describes four phases in the infant's development of attachment. Through each phase, the infant's behavior seems to be guided by a single overriding principle: *keep the attachment object close*. And in most cases, that attachment object is the mother.

Preattachment. The first phase, *preattachment*, spans the first few weeks of life. From the very beginning, the infant seems predisposed to identify and respond to social stimulation—especially from mothers (Wellman & Gelman, 1992). From very shortly after birth, infants will often move their bodies in synchrony with adult human speech, but not in synchrony with disconnected vowel sounds, or even rhythmic tapping sounds (Condon & Sander, 1974); and within the first month of life, they are able to discriminate their mother's voice from that of other women, and show marked preference for it (DeCasper & Fifer, 1980).

Attachment in the Making. During the second phase, *attachment in the making*, there is marked emphasis on behaviors that promote contact with important adults—for example, crying and smiling as well as sucking, rooting, clinging, looking at, and following with the eyes. The second phase culminates in clearly identifiable attachment during the second half of the first year of life. At this time, the infant manifests the "selective social smile"—the smile that occurs in recognition of familiar faces. At the same time, smiling in response to unfamiliar faces becomes less common.

Clear-Cut Attachment. The third phase, *clear-cut attachment*, becomes evident with the infant's development of locomotor abilities. Now infants are able to attract the mother or father's attention not only by smiling, crying, reaching, and so on; they can also crawl over and grab a leg; they can climb up and wrap themselves around a neck; they can cling to the strings that hang from the rear of old-fashioned, pre-Velcro aprons.

Goal-Corrected Attachment. Some time in the second year, Bowlby informs us, the infant enters a phase of *goal-corrected attachment*. The infant has now developed notions of self and has begun to understand something of the point of view of others. Gradually, infants learn to make inferences about the effects of their behaviors, as well as about their parents' behavior; and they learn to affect the behavior of parents in ways more subtle that crying, smiling, yelling, or toddling

TABLE 6.5

Sequential Phases in the Development of Infant Attachment

Phase	Approximate Age	Important Behaviors
Preattachment	First month	Crying, smiling, rooting, clinging, sucking, looking at; movements synchronized with adult speech; discrimination of mother's voice
Attachment-in-the-making	Into second half of first year	Singling out objects of primary attachment; selective social smile — directed more toward attachment objects or persons than toward the unfamiliar
Clear-cut attachment	Second half of first year	Continued use of behaviors designed to draw attention — smiling, crying, squirming; use of newly developing locomotor skills to approach attachment object or person
Goal-corrected attachment	Second year	Begins to adopt mother's point of view and to make inferences about mother's behavior; manipulation of mother's behavior in more subtle ways following gradual recognition of cause-and-effect relationships

Source: Based on Bowlby, 1969.

over and grabbing hold. (See Table 6.5 for a summary of Bowlby's sequential phases.)

Ainsworth (1973) makes the important point that one of the major functions of the infant's early behavior is not only to foster and maintain a high degree of attachment, but also to permit exploration of the environment. For this reason, the infant has to strike a balance between proximity-seeking behavior and exploratory behavior. At the same time, it's important to maintain a sense of security about the environment and about the attachment. Thus Ainsworth speaks of two related concepts that motivate much of what the infant does: the *attachment–exploration balance* and the *secure-base phenomenon*. It is noteworthy that when the mother (or some other important attachment object/person) is absent, many infants will cease exploratory behavior.

Others are less likely to do so; their attachments seem to be different.

Types of Attachment

How do you determine whether, to whom, and how strongly an infant is attached? One way is Ainsworth and associates' (1978) *Strange Situation* procedure, a pro-

cedure sequenced as follows (each event lasts approximately 3 minutes):

1. Mother and baby enter a room.
2. Mother puts baby down; stranger enters; speaks with mother; shows baby a toy; mother leaves.
3. If baby cries, stranger attempts to comfort; if baby is passive, stranger attempts to interest it in a toy.
4. Mother returns, pauses in doorway; stranger leaves; mother leaves.
5. Baby is alone.
6. Stranger comes back.
7. Mother returns; stranger leaves.

What the Strange Situation provides is a way of assessing attachment under stress. It permits researchers to determine the infant's anxiety or security in these circumstances. When Ainsworth and associates placed 1-year-old infants in the Strange Situation, they discovered attachment behaviors that sorted themselves into three categories.

Securely attached infants are those who use the mother as a base for exploration — who go out freely and play in the room, but who often reestablish contact, either by looking at the mother, interacting verbally,

INTERACTIVE TABLE 6.6

Types of Infant Attachment

▶ *In first grade, George Leroy used to get such severe stomachaches that he often had to be taken home to his mother. "He's always been like that," claimed his mother. "Why, when he was little, he used to raise a stink every time I had to leave him. And one time, when I come back from bowling or something, he up and heaved his potty at me, he was still so mad, and the dang thing was about . . . as heavy as a brick." According to Ainsworth's classification, what sort of attachment did George display toward his mother?*

Attachment Classification	Common Behavior When Mother Leaves or Returns	Approximate Percentage of Population
Secure	Uses mother as base from which to explore; upset when she leaves; greets her return positively and reestablishes physical contact	68
Anxious		
Avoidant	Rarely cries when mother leaves; ignores mother when she returns or actively avoids her, sometimes pushing her away or pointedly not looking at her	20
Ambivalent	Very upset when mother leaves; often angry when she returns; may push her away while seeking proximity (hence, ambivalence)	12

Source: Based on *Patterns of Attachment* by Ainsworth et al., 1978, Hillsdale, NJ: Erlbaum.

or returning to her physically. When the mother leaves, these infants are upset and often stop their exploration. During the reunion episodes, they greet the mother warmly and try to reestablish physical contact or some sort of interaction with her. Securely attached infants manifest few, if any, negative reactions toward their mothers during reunion.

In contrast, anxious infants are those who display significant negative behavior toward the mother during reunion events. Some of these infants, the **avoidant**, either ignore the mother's reentrance or actively avoid contact with her—sometimes by looking away, sometimes by pushing her away physically. Interestingly, they rarely cry when the mother leaves.

A second group of anxious infants, the **ambivalent**, are very upset when the mother leaves. Their behavior is apparent evidence of strong attachment. Strangely, however, they often display anger when

the mother returns. The anger is sometimes very subtle; for example, they might push the mother away even when they appear to want to be held (hence the ambivalence).

The majority of infants in Ainsworth's research—approximately two thirds of them—can be classified as securely attached; approximately one fifth are avoidant, and the remainder are ambivalent (see Interactive Table 6.6).

The Implications of Attachment

Patterns of attachment appear to reflect relatively stable qualities. Waters (1980) reports, for example, that there is little change in classification between the ages of 12 and 18 months. However, this is not the case when major changes occur in the infant's context such as somebody leaving or dying (Waters, Hay, & Richters, 1986). Similarly, infants who are maltreated often display marked instability of attachment, and are also more likely to be insecurely attached (Schneider-Rosen et al., 1985).

There is mounting evidence that securely attached infants — who, as we noted are in the majority in North American cultures — fare better in the long run (in these cultures). These infants are often more competent, better problem solvers, more independent, more curious, and perhaps more resilient. In contrast, insecurely attached infants are somewhat more likely to be overly dependent and to experience problems in school (see Collins & Gunnar, 1990).

Clearly, attachments are a function of interactions. Furthermore, the nature of these interactions, and their outcomes, will be influenced by the characteristics of both infant and caregiver (or other significant people in the child's context). Hence the importance of the family — and of the culture in which the family is embedded, because it, too, influences child-rearing practices and attitudes toward children. Our North American macrosystem is relatively child-centered: It emphasizes the rights of children, and it encourages parents to provide physically and psychologically safe environments. Not surprisingly, then, more than two thirds of infants appear to be securely attached (perhaps it should be surprising that as many as one third are not!).

Elsewhere in the world, cultures reflect different values, and sometimes child-rearing practices and attitudes toward children are quite different. In some of these cultures, insecurely attached infants are far more common than in North America (for example, West Germany, Japan, and Israel; see Sagi, Ijzendoorn, & Koren-Karie, 1991).

Whether parents should attempt to change their infants' predominant patterns of attachment — and indeed, whether they would be very effective in doing so — are important issues. Unfortunately, they are also very complex issues. What does seem clear is that all infants must be provided with an opportunity to develop attachments that will provide them with the security they need to engage in the exploration of a bewildering, exciting, and sometimes frightening world. Those opportunities are not always related solely to the presence of the mother. Grandparents, siblings, uncles, and aunts can also be important.

So can fathers.

Fathers and Infant Attachment

Our traditional views of the family and of mother–father roles have typically focused on the importance of the mother in the early social development of the infant — and on the father's relative unimportance. Most of our developmental theorists (Freud, for example) argue that the father becomes important after the age of 2 or 3. Furthermore, many of these theorists have viewed the infant as largely incompetent — as passive and reflexive, as being moved by primitive physiological needs but seldom by a need to discover and to know. Little wonder that the father has not been seen as playing an important role.

Some of these traditional values are still the norm in many of the world's cultures. For example, Ho (1987) reports that in China, looking after the young is still largely a female function; the father's role is more that of a disciplinarian. There, traditional values stress filial devotion and respect — that is, children, and especially sons, are taught to respect and obey their fathers (and grandfathers). Recently, however, there appears to have been a dramatic decline in some of these filial values. At the same time, fathers have begun to involve themselves more in child rearing.

In North America, too, important changes are rapidly altering our conception of the father's role. These include an increasing number of "father-assisted" childbirths, in which the father has an opportunity to interact with the infant as early as does the mother. In addition, changing work patterns and changing male-female responsibilities in the home have done a great deal to change the role of the father with his infant. As Lamb (1987) notes, mothers continue to be extremely important to the infant, but they are not unique. Fathers and other caregivers are also tremendously important. In fact, considerable research indicates that newborns and young infants may form attachments almost as strong with fathers as with mothers (Collins & Gunnar, 1990).

In summarizing the research on father–infant attachment, Collins and Gunnar (1990) conclude that fathers are as competent and as important as mothers in a caregiving role. But there are some systematic differences between mother–infant and father–infant interactions. Fathers spend more time in play interactions with their infants; mothers spend more time in nurturant roles (feeding, bathing, changing). As a result, some infants — especially males — display more *affiliative* behaviors toward fathers than toward mothers

Traditional psychological theories have tended to ignore the father's role in the infant's development. Today, however, as fathers take a more active role in child care, we're learning that infants can form strong attachments with their fathers.

(Lamb, 1980). Affiliative behaviors are defined as behaviors that demonstrate a social relationship that stops short of being attachment. Evidence of **affiliation** includes smiling, looking at, laughing, and giving; evidence of attachment might include seeking to be close, clinging, wanting to be picked up, putting the head in the lap, snuggling, and so on.

In a study of 20 infants, Lamb (1980) found that fathers fared extremely well in the attachment (seeking proximity, touching, approaching, wanting to be held) and affiliation (smiling, looking at, vocalizing, laughing, and giving) their infants displayed toward them. There was little difference in the amount of attachment behavior directed toward mother or father, although both received far more attachment behavior than did a stranger. However, fathers were recipients of more affiliative behaviors than were mothers.

It appears that infants (especially males) begin to affiliate with their fathers at a very young age when they are given the opportunity to do so (Lamb et al., 1983). Lamb suggests that here, at the age of 2, is evidence of the beginning of same-sex modeling. Although fathers seem to interact more (touching and talking) with sons than with daughters, and with firstborns more than with later children, they appear to be as competent as mothers in caregiving roles (feeding, changing, bathing) (Lamb, 1976a, 1976b). In an unfamiliar situation, the departure of both the father and the mother is followed by signs of distress, whereas

the departure of a stranger leads to an increase in play behavior (Bridges, Connell, & Belsky, 1988).

What such studies have established is that the father is far from irrelevant in the early development of the infant. However, the mother typically has considerably more contact with young infants than does the father.

Strangers and Separation

Investigations of parent–child attachment often look at the effects of maternal deprivation and separation. Clearly, one indication of an infant's attachment to parents and of their importance is the infant's reactions when the parents are gone.

There are two broad groupings of studies of infant–parent separation. One deals with the effects of short-term separations, and looks at *separation protest*. Ainsworth's Strange Situation, described earlier, is a good example of this type of study. The second type of study looks at the consequences of long-term separation from the principal caregiver. Studies of the effects of divorce on infants exemplify this approach. Also, there are studies that examine parent–child attachment by studying the reactions of infants to strangers. If, for example, Susie's behavior is identical for all adults, it's unlikely she has formed a strong attachment to her mother or father. But if she reacts with fear and anxiety in the presence of strangers, she has at least learned to equate her parents with comfort and security.

Stranger Anxiety

Fear of strangers occurs in many infants, but not usually before the age of 9 months (Eckerman & Whatley, 1975). As we saw, lack of fear in the first few months indicates that children have not yet formed strong attachments to any particular person. That fear develops at all may be because once children have become familiar with their environment, they develop certain expectations. The appearance of unexpected events is incongruous with the infant's expectations and leads to anxiety — the "incongruity hypothesis" (Hunt, 1964).

The Incongruity Hypothesis.

An indirect test of the incongruity hypothesis is provided by Schaffer's (1966) investigation of the onset of fear in children. Schaffer looked at the relationship between social variables (maternal availability, number of siblings, exposure to strangers) and infant responses when confronted with strangers. He found only two variables related to stranger anxiety: number of siblings and exposure to strangers. Infants who are in contact with the largest number of people (strangers and siblings) are less likely to manifest fear, react with the least amount of fear, and cease to be afraid of strangers at an earlier age than infants with fewer contacts. This finding is consistent with the incongruity hypothesis, because early exposure to a wide variety of strangers would eliminate or at least reduce the incongruity associated with the presence of a stranger.

Not all infants react the same way to the departure of a parent. In one study, Jacobson and Wille (1984) studied the reactions of 93 children, ages 15–18 months, to brief periods of separation from their mothers. They found that previous separation experience was closely related to the amount of distress the children manifested, although the relationship was curvilinear. Specifically, children who had experienced moderate amounts of maternal separation were best able to cope with the absence of their mothers; it was as if they had learned that the separation would be only temporary. Those who had experienced either very little or a great deal of separation were the most distressed, perhaps because they had had too little opportunity to learn about separation or because they had learned that separation would be frequent or prolonged.

Preparing Infants for Separation.

Contrary to what we might expect, trying to prepare young preschoolers in advance for an upcoming separation from the mother does not always work as intended. Adams and Passman (1983) had one group of mothers of 2 to 2½-year-old children discuss their upcoming departure for 3 days preceding the event; a second group did not prepare their children in advance. At the time of departure, some of the mothers in both groups provided a brief explanation of their departure and then either left immediately or lingered for 1 minute; others left in their "natural" way. Interestingly, children who had not been prepared in advance showed less distress after the mothers' departure than children whose mothers had discussed their departure during the previous 3 days. And those whose mothers did not linger after explaining they were leaving also showed less distress than those whose mothers lingered for 60 seconds. One possibility, argue Adams and Passman, is that the lengthy preparation actually teaches children to become alarmed. In the same way, lingering just prior to departure may teach the child that displaying anxiety might delay the departure.

It follows from these studies that the child who is most likely to be free of strong anxiety at the mother's absence (or that of the father or other caregiver) or in the presence of strangers is one who has many siblings, who has frequently been exposed to strangers, whose mother leaves "naturally" without lingering, and who has been separated from the mother moderately often. There is evidence, too, that mothers whose parenting is *secure* (rather than dismissing or preoccupied) have infants who are more comfortable with separation (Crowell & Feldman, 1991).

Security Blankets

A series of intriguing studies has examined the role of the blanket in the life of the American child. No less than one half of all middle-class American children exhibit strong attachments to inanimate objects, the two most common of which are, not surprisingly, the blanket (60 percent of children) and the pacifier (66 percent; Passman and Halonen, 1979). Attachment to pacifiers lessens by age 2 but remains high for blankets through most of the preschool period. In one study, Passman and Weisberg (1975) compared the effectiveness of mothers and blankets in reducing a child's anxiety in a strange situation. They found that children

Charles Schulz © 1956 United Feature Syndicate, Inc.

The Immediate Impact of Mother–Child Separation on Infants Ages 3–16 Months

Impact	Percentage
No disturbances	15
Mild disturbances	36
Moderate disturbances	23
Severe disturbances	20
Extreme disturbances	6

Source: Based on data provided by L. J. Yarrow and M. S. Goodwin, 1973, "The Immediate Impact of Separation: Reactions of Infants to Change in Mother Figures." In L. J. Stone, H. T. Smith, and L. B. Murphy (Eds.), (1973), *The Competent Infant: Research and Commentary.* New York: Basic Books.

who were attached to their blankets displayed no more anxiety than children who were not attached to blankets but whose mothers were present—as long as these children had their blankets close by. In fact, they played and explored more than children who had no mother, favorite toy, or blanket present. Related studies (Passman, 1974, 1977) also found that a blanket was as effective as the mother in a school-like situation for children who were attached to their blankets. Other research has shown, however, that in situations of higher stress or arousal, the mother becomes more effective than a blanket or other inanimate attachment object in reducing anxiety (Passman, 1976; Passman & Adams, 1982). In play situations, pacifiers (Halonen & Passman, 1978), color photos of mothers (Passman & Erck, 1978; Passman & Longeway, 1982), and even

videotapes of mothers (Adams & Passman, 1979) are sometimes as effective as the actual presence of mothers.

Winnicott (1971) refers to objects like teddy bears and blankets as **transitional objects** because they become the focus of children's affection and attention while they are in transition between a state of high dependence on the parent and the development of a more independent *self*. According to this view, the development of self requires *separation* from the parent and *individuation*—the recognition of one's own individuality (Harter, 1983). The process of separating and becoming independent gives rise to anxiety; the blanket or the teddy bear serves to comfort the child.

To summarize, in North American cultures, attachment to blankets, teddy bears, pacifiers, and other inanimate objects is highly common. These objects are sometimes useful in reducing a child's anxiety in strange situations; and perhaps they bring comfort and joy to young hearts in less stressful situations. But, some parents worry, is the child who is attached to these inanimate, nonsocial objects perhaps more insecure and less well adjusted than the child whose attachments are more social?

Not likely, says Passman (1987). In a study of 108 preschoolers, he found little relationship between at-

TABLE 6.8

Severity of Reaction to Maternal Separation, According to Age (Percentage of Infants)

Severity of Reaction	Under 3 Months	3–4 Months	4–5 Months	6 Months	9 Months
Slight or no reaction	100	60	28	9	0
Moderately severe to very severe	0	40	72	91	100

Source: Based on data provided by L. J. Yarrow and M. S. Goodwin, 1973, "The Immediate Impact of Separation: Reactions of Infants to Change in Mother Figures." In L. J. Stone, H. T. Smith, and L. B. Murphy (Eds.), (1973), *The Competent Infant: Research and Commentary.* New York: Basic Books.

tachment to blankets and general fearfulness. "Blanket-attached children," he concludes, "are thus neither more insecure nor more secure than are others."

Long-Term Separation and Deprivation

Spitz (1945, 1954) and Bowlby (1940, 1953) were among the first to describe the harmful effects of parent–child separation. Spitz (1945), reporting on the fate of institutionalized children, claimed that they had significantly higher mortality rates, that they were retarded in physical development, and that their emotional development was so severely thwarted by lack of *mothering* that they frequently withdrew, became depressed, and sometimes died as a result. In effect, what he described is FTT, or failure to thrive, (described earlier). As we saw, there is evidence that if children are prevented from forming a bond with a primary caregiver for a prolonged time, they may suffer emotional disturbances or even FTT.

The effects of separation from a caregiver are highly dependent upon the infant's age. In general, maternal (or parental) separation prior to the age of 6 months does not have the same consequences as separation that occurs later (Collins & Gunnar, 1990). Children separated from their parents after the age of 6 months are likely already to have formed a strong attachment to them. Any unhappy effects of separation may be due to the rupturing of this affectional bond, rather than to the child's being deprived of a mother or father. That is, if children are separated from their mothers before becoming strongly attached to them, we might expect that separation will not be especially traumatic.

Yarrow and Goodwin (1973) studied 70 adopted children between birth and 16 months of age. All of these children were in foster homes prior to adoption, and all were assumed to have had normal environments both before and after adoption. The aim of the study was to discover the effects on the infant of separation from a parent figure. Because children were adopted at various ages, it was also possible to examine differences in their reactions as a function of age.

Not surprisingly, reactions were least severe for children under 3 months of age, but only 15 percent of all the children were completely free of all disturbances. The remainder manifested disturbances of varying severity (see Tables 6.7 and 6.8). These disturbances were most obvious in the infant's sleeping schedule and feeding behaviors, in social reactions (withdrawal, for example), and in emotional behavior (crying). Disruptions in social reactions included decreased social responsiveness; increased stranger anxiety; and specific disturbances in interactions with the new mother figure, expressed in feeding difficulties, colic, digestive upsets, and, most strikingly, physical rejection of the new mother or excessive clinging to her. In addition, developmental scores were lower in 56 percent of the cases following adoption. Separation from the mother or mother figure apparently has an adverse effect on most significant aspects of the infant's development.

In conclusion, it is clear that permanent loss of a parent, as happens through death or sometimes through divorce, can have serious negative consequences for the infant—and for the older child as well (see Chapter 8). What about regular but temporary loss of parental contact, as happens in many forms of child care?

Infant Day Care

As many as one out of every two North American preschool children is now in day care (Phillips, McCartney, & Scarr, 1987). And, with increasing numbers of mothers going back to work within weeks of childbirth, the fastest-growing type of day-care facility is *infant* day care. Given what we know about the importance of caregiver–infant interaction and attachment, questions relating to the effects of day care on the social, emotional, and intellectual development of infants become critically important. (See Chapter 8 for a discussion of the effects of day care on older children.)

Gamble and Zigler (1986) summarize a large body of research that has looked at the effects of day care on the infant's attachment to parents and on different aspects of social behavior. An important concern of this research has been to determine whether day care either can prevent the formation of parent–infant attachments or can serve to redirect that attachment toward a different caregiver. Reassuringly, all available evidence suggests not. Apparently, the infant's primary attachment to parents can be established in a wide variety of circumstances and is highly resistant to disruption. Konner (1982) reports that it occurs in societies as disparate as the !Kung, where infants are in immediate contact with their mothers 24 hours a day, and in the Israeli *kibbutzim*, where infants have contact with their mothers only for a short period each afternoon and on weekends.

Still, even though day care does not, *in general*, appear to disrupt parent–infant attachment bonds, some evidence suggests that the stress involved in repeated short-term separation from the mother might lead to the development of what Ainsworth labeled *anxious* or *insecure* rather than *secure* attachment (Belsky & Rovine, 1988). We should hasten to point out, however, that some infants seem far less vulnerable than others to the stresses of separation from their mothers (Egeland & Sroufe, 1981). By the same token, some may be more vulnerable. Studies reviewed by Gamble

and Zigler (1986) suggest that boys are more often in the vulnerable group than are girls.

In summarizing a number of studies on infant day care, Clarke-Stewart (1989) draws two principal conclusions. First, the evidence suggests a somewhat higher probability that day-care infants will avoid their mothers after separation—that they will be insecurely attached. Second, these children are sometimes less obedient later and may be more aggressive with their peers.

Clarke-Stewart cautions that the meaning of these findings is still unclear. We do not know whether slightly higher aggressiveness and independence are negative or whether they might even be marks of more rapid maturation—perhaps even an advantage. Here, as elsewhere, it is likely to depend on the individual child and the context in which the child interacts.

Where day care does have apparently detrimental effects on infants, these effects are often associated with *poorer*-quality day care. In contrast, high-quality day care is likely to have beneficial effects on most infants and older children. (See Chapter 8 for a discussion of the characteristics of high-quality day care.)

It is worth noting that most of the research in this area has focused on discovering the possible *negative* consequences of alternate forms of care for children—and has been largely unsuccessful in doing so. The focus must now change, says Silverstein (1991). Instead of continuing to search for the negative consequences of mothers' working and of alternate child care, research should focus on documenting "the negative consequences of not providing high-quality, affordable day care" (p. 1025).

Parenting in Infancy

Belsky, Lerner, and Spanier (1984) summarize a vast body of research that has looked at the effects of parents on infants. They describe six dimensions of mothering (or parenting, or simply caregiving) that their research has shown to be most closely related to the infant's social, emotional, and intellectual well-being: *attentiveness, physical contact, verbal stimulation, material stimulation, responsive care,* and *restrictiveness.* The first five of these have positive effects; the last is more negative. Parents who are attentive to their children (for example, look at them more); who touch them, play with them, cradle and rock them; who speak to them and provide them with objects to look at, to touch, to taste, to smell;

Mothers in the Work Force

In 1976, fewer than one third of all mothers were in the work force within 1 year of giving birth. Over the next 10 years, that number increased by more than 50 percent. Interestingly, in 1976, younger mothers (ages 18–29) were more likely than older women to go back to work while their children were still infants; in 1986, older mothers (ages 30–44) were more likely than younger women to return to work. More infants than ever before are in some type of day care. By 1989, more than half of women with children under 1 *and husbands at home* worked; about 75 percent of those with teenagers were in the work force (U.S. Bureau of the Census, 1991).

Figure 6.2 Changes in percentages of women who enter the work force within 1 year of giving birth (1977–1979 data extrapolated). (From U.S. Bureau of the Census, 1988, p. 65.)

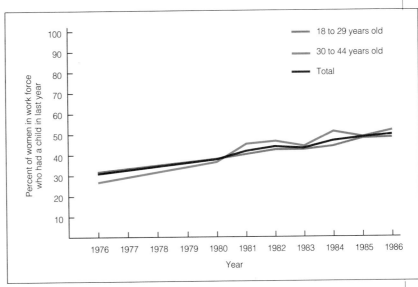

and who are responsive to their cries and to their other signals of distress, amusement, interest, or amazement are more likely to have intellectually advanced and emotionally well-adjusted infants. Those who are restrictive in the sense that they verbally and physically limit the infant's freedom to explore may, to some extent, influence their intellectual development negatively.

In summarizing this summary, Belsky, Lerner, and Spanier (1984) point out that those parents who are most likely to promote the most optimal cognitive development during infancy are those who serve as, or give the child access to, the greatest sources of stimulation (speaking, holding, touching, responding to, providing toys, and so on). Those who are restrictive—that is, those who limit the amount of stimulation to which the infant is exposed—are likely to have an opposite effect. (See Chapter 8 for a discussion of parenting styles, specifically as they relate to early childhood.)

Early Gender-Role Influences

Gender roles (or **sex roles**) are defined by the particular combination of attitudes, behaviors, and personality characteristics that a culture considers appropriate for the individual's anatomical sex—in other words, that is considered *masculine* or *feminine*. Sex-typing, or gender-typing, is the psychological expression used to describe the process whereby boys and girls learn masculine and feminine roles.

Although it might be tempting to think that masculinity and femininity are primarily the products of genetically ordained physiological and hormonal differences between males and females, there is considerable evidence that this is only partly the case. In some cultures, behaviors that we might consider feminine are expected of men and are therefore masculine; at the same time, the aggressiveness and dominance that we think of as masculine characterize women (see Chapter 12 for more details). Clearly, cultures and families have a great deal to do with the eventual gender roles of their children.

When does sex-typing begin? At the very beginning. When an infant is born, the attending physician or midwife doesn't say, "Holy Jeepers, lady, it's a *baby*!"

No. The key word is not *baby*—it's "boy" or "girl." The simple anatomical fact of being boy or girl

tells mother and father and all the significant others what to think and how to react. The knowledge that it's a "boy" or "girl" even colors the parents' perceptions. When Rubin, Provenzano, and Luria (1974) asked 30 parents to describe their day-old infants as they would to a relative or a close friend, without any hesitation they spoke of their alert, strong, well-coordinated, firm, and hardy sons. In contrast, they described their daughters as weaker, finer-featured, softer, less attentive, and more delicate. Yet these parents, especially the fathers (who were most guilty of exaggerating the sex-appropriate characteristics of their sons), had scarcely had any opportunity to interact with their infants. And hospital records indicated clearly that these male and female infants were *indistinguishable* from one another in terms of weight, muscle tone, activity, responsiveness, and so on.

Pogrebin (1980), in a provocative consideration of these issues, suggests that we are a little like the Mundugumor of New Guinea. The Mundugumor believed that a variety of signs could be used at birth to predict what the individual would become. For example, they were convinced that only those infants whose umbilical cords were wound around their necks at birth stood any chance of becoming great artists. Amazingly, they were right! All Mundugumor artists whose talents were accepted as outstanding had, in fact, been born with their umbilical cords twisted around their necks!

Our fortune-telling is not so primitive, is it? We know it's ridiculous to think that the position of the umbilical cord is of any consequence. Instead, we look for appendages between the legs of our infants. To a considerable extent, these tell us how to interact with our infants, what to expect of them, what sorts of toys they are most likely to enjoy, what their personalities should be. Their presence or absence also allows us to predict whether the infant will grow up to be strong, alert, and aggressive—or weaker, more delicate, more sensitive, and more emotional. And, amazingly often, our predictions are every bit as accurate as those of the Mundugumor. (More about the development of gender-role differences in Chapters 8 and 12.)

Exceptionality

This text deals primarily with the physical, intellectual, and social development of the average person from conception until death. It is worth repeating, however, that there is no average person, that the *average* is simply

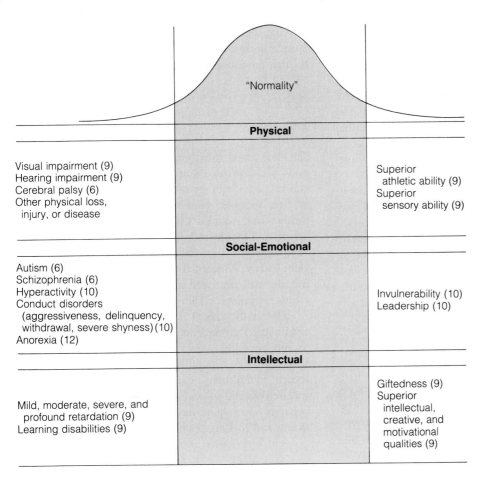

Figure 6.3 The physical, social-emotional, and intellectual dimensions of exceptionality. (Numbers in parentheses indicate chapters where specific exceptionalities are discussed.)

"Normality"

Physical

Visual impairment (9)
Hearing impairment (9)
Cerebral palsy (6)
Other physical loss,
   injury, or disease

Superior
   athletic ability (9)
Superior
   sensory ability (9)

Social-Emotional

Autism (6)
Schizophrenia (6)
Hyperactivity (10)
Conduct disorders
   (aggressiveness, delinquency,
   withdrawal, severe shyness) (10)
Anorexia (12)

Invulnerability (10)
Leadership (10)

Intellectual

Mild, moderate, severe, and
   profound retardation (9)
Learning disabilities (9)

Giftedness (9)
Superior
   intellectual,
   creative, and
   motivational
   qualities (9)

a mathematical invention, although a very useful one. If we had no average person about whom to speak, we would have to speak instead of individuals. And there are so many different ones — more than 5 billion now — that the task would be absolutely overwhelming.

Still, we need to keep in mind that our average is a fiction, and that the individual — Robert, Shannon, Jennifer, David — is our reality and our main concern. We need to keep in mind, too, that some individuals depart so dramatically from our average that they are worthy of study in their own right. These individuals are *exceptional*. **Exceptionality** is a two-sided concept: On the one hand, there are those who are exceptionally gifted; on the other, there are those who lack normal abilities and competence. Furthermore, exceptionality is found in each of the three major areas of human development: social, physical, and intellectual (see Figure 6.3).

In this section, we deal briefly with some of the most common manifestations of physical and social-emotional exceptionality in infancy. In Chapter 9, we

look at physical and intellectual exceptionality in childhood; and in Chapter 10, we look at social-emotional exceptionality.

Cerebral Palsy

The condition labeled *cerebral palsy* is not a disease but a collection of symptoms (a *syndrome*) that includes motor problems, and may also include psychological problems, convulsions, or behavior disorders. An alternate label for this condition is *significant developmental motor disability* (Abroms & Panagakos, 1980); also, it was originally known as *Little's disease* after the surgeon who first described it. It is associated with brain damage and varies in severity from being so mild that it is virtually undetectable to being sufficiently serious that it is manifested in paralysis.

Cerebral palsy is most often a congenital disease; that is, it is present at birth in more than two thirds of all cases (Verhaaren & Connor, 1981). It is often associated with anoxia (lack of oxygen before, during, or after birth). It can also result from maternal infection and disease, as well as from postnatal brain injury that sometimes results from diseases such as meningitis or encephalitis.

Estimates of the prevalence of cerebral palsy are uncertain because many of the milder cases are not reported, particularly because there is no "cure" for the condition. Estimates cited by Abroms and Panagakos (1980) vary from 1.63 to 7.5 cases for every 1,000 live births.

One of the most common symptoms of cerebral palsy is spasticity (inability to move voluntarily) in one or more limbs, or dyskinesia (abnormal movements). These motor impairments are sometimes sufficiently severe that it is difficult to assess the child's intellectual ability. As a result, it was often assumed that intellectual deficits were common among those suffering from cerebral palsy, but we now know that fewer than half are mentally retarded (Erickson, 1987).

Epilepsy

Also a neurological impairment, *epilepsy* is a seizure disorder whose causes are unknown. Seizures involve abnormal electrical activity of the brain. The more serious forms of epilepsy (sometimes termed *grand mal*, as opposed to *petit mal*) can often be controlled with drugs. Petit mal seizures, which last 1–30 seconds, are manifested in a momentary "absentness" of the child and are sometimes accompanied by rhythmic, fluttering movements of both eyelids (Abroms & Panagakos, 1980). Seizures may occur frequently and are sometimes interpreted by parents or teachers as a sign that the child is deliberately not paying attention. In more than 70 percent of all cases, petit mal seizures cease altogether by the age of 18 (Nealis, 1983).

Other Physical Problems

A large number of other physical problems sometimes require special educational or health services. These include diseases and conditions such as muscular dystrophy, cancer, asthma, diabetes, and the absence of one or more limbs, as well as paralysis. Some are congenital, some result from infections and diseases after birth, and others result from accidents of various kinds. Many cases are associated with serious emotional and social problems, which are often related to difficulties the child experiences in being accepted by others and in developing a positive self-concept. Hence, a great deal

of what special education programs, parents, and therapists can do for physically exceptional children relates to their emotional and social well-being.

Pervasive Developmental Disorders

Tim was an apparently normal, healthy child, the second child born to a couple in their early twenties. He was an "easy" infant who cried very little, and who, in fact, appeared most content when left alone. The mother later recalled that he didn't smile as a young infant, and that he didn't appear to recognize her. Still, he progressed apparently normally through his first year; in fact, he learned to walk at the young age of 9 months and displayed advanced motor development, seldom tripping or falling, as most toddlers do.

But at the age of 2, he still could not speak. An examination showed his hearing to be normal, and his parents hoped he would be a "late bloomer." But even at the age of 3, Tim still did not respond to his parents' speech. In addition, he had developed few social skills, and he engaged in unusual and repetitive behaviors—behaviors like spinning the wheels of his toy car or sitting and rocking his body endlessly.

Tim's condition is rare—probably far less than 1 case in 100,000 (Werry, 1972). It is among what are now labeled *childhood-onset pervasive developmental disorders* (formerly labeled *childhood psychoses*). Pervasive developmental disorders are defined by the American Psychiatric Association (1980) as "disorders . . . characterized by distortions in the development of multiple basic psychological functions that are involved in the development of social skills and language, such as attention, perception, reality testing, and motor movement" (p. 86). The child's symptoms must meet the following criteria for diagnosis as childhood-onset pervasive developmental disorder:

- Severe and consistent impairment in social relationships (for example, inappropriate emotional responses, lack of empathy, inappropriate clinging, asocial behavior)
- At least three of the following:
  1. sudden episodes of "free-floating" anxiety; panic attacks; extreme reactions to ordinary occurrences
  2. inappropriate emotional reaction; lack of fear; excessive rage
  3. resistance to change

4. bizarre motor movements such as posturing, walking on tiptoes, or finger or hand movements

5. speech abnormalities such as monotonous or "singing" voice

6. extreme sensitivity or insensitivity to external stimuli

7. self-mutilation such as pulling out hair, head banging, biting or hitting self

■ Onset between 30 months and 12 years

■ Absence of delusions; hallucinations; incoherence; or bizarre associations

Clinicians sometimes differentiate between two types of childhood-onset pervasive developmental disorder: childhood **schizophrenia** and **autism**. One of the main differences between the two is that autism manifests itself much earlier (before the age of 30 months). In addition, autism is characterized by extreme isolation or *aloneness*, manifested in a lack of verbal and physical contact, as well as by an apparently strong need to have everything remain the same. Also, the autistic child typically has grossly impaired or completely absent language development.

It's not very important to differentiate between autism and childhood schizophrenia, since treatments are virtually identical, the more common being tranquilizers and antipsychotic drugs. Although there is little evidence that they alleviate the condition, they are useful in making patients more manageable. The use of psychotherapy—psychoanalysis, for example—also has not been demonstrated to be particularly useful. However, behavior therapies beginning early in the child's life and sustained over a long time are sometimes beneficial. None, including the behavior therapies, is likely to make an autistic child act normally (Erickson, 1987).

Follow-up studies of children diagnosed as having pervasive developmental disorders have not provided much reason for optimism. Combining several long-term studies that looked at these children between 5 and 10 years after initial diagnosis, DeMyer and associates (1973) found that only 1–2 percent recovered sufficiently to later be classified as normal. Another 5–15 percent were almost normal, and 16–25 percent were in poor condition. Not surprisingly, the prognosis is best for those who develop language skills.

The Whole Infant

There is something frustrating about fragmenting the developing infant into such psychologically convenient categories as description of capabilities, physical development, motor development, social-emotional development, intellectual development, and so on. We lose the individual in the interminable and sometimes confused array of beliefs, findings, tentative conclusions, convincing arguments, and suggestions. The theoretical infant is a hypothetical average. And although many infants are very close to the hypothetical average child when they are 1 month old, fewer are still average at the age of 2 months, even fewer at the age of 6 months, and almost none by the age of 1 year. By the time the child becomes as old as you or I, the average individual will no longer exist but will appear only in the oversimplified theories of the social scientist or in the files of the market researcher who wants to know what the "average" person is wearing this spring.

Each person is an integrated whole, whose intellect, emotions, and physical being all interact; each part is inextricably linked with and dependent upon every other part of the living organism. However, if we attempt to describe a person in that way, the sheer complexity of the task might overwhelm us. And so we continue to speak of the isolated forces that affect human development as though they exist apart from the integrated, whole person. But it bears repeating that our divisions, although necessary, are artificial and sometimes misleading.

Main Points

1. Influence in infant–parent interactions is bidirectional and strongly influenced by the characteristics of both parent and infant (the microsystem) as well as by the larger context. Furthermore, relationships within the family are not simply *dyadic* (involving two people) but *triadic* (involving three units, one of which is often the family as a *system*) or even more complex.

2. Infant states reflect basic individual differences very early in life. Common infant states include *regular sleep, irregular sleep, sleep, drowsiness, alert inactivity,* and *focused activity*. Average newborns sleep approximately 75–80 percent of the time.

3. Izard and others suggest that infants' facial expressions and other behaviors reveal that they may be capable of feeling as many as 10 distinct emotions. Infants' cries may be expressions of different underlying emotions that mothers can differentiate. Wolff identifies four infant cries: *rhythmical* (most frequent), *hunger, anger,* and *pain.*

4. The reflexive smile is often present only hours after birth, although the social smile, which usually occurs first in response to a human voice, is uncommon before the age of 3 weeks. By the age of 4 months, infants often laugh in addition to smiling. Both crying and smiling progress from an initial phase in which the response seems to be related to internal states such as gastric disturbances and hunger (*endogenous*) to a later phase in which the response is more under the control of external stimulation such as the appearance of a familiar face (*exogenous*). Smiling and crying are important in the development of parent–infant attachment.

5. Among newborn infants, fear responses may be brought about by loud noises or sudden loss of support; among older infants, by the presentation of the unexpected. Fear of strangers is not common before the age of 6 months and appears to be related to the infant's ability to distinguish between the familiar and the unfamiliar.

6. Infants exercise some control over their emotions through *other-directed regulatory behaviors* (smiling, looking interested, for example, in order to make a caregiver do something) and *self-directed regulatory behaviors* (turning away, sucking the thumb, or engaging in other self-distractive behaviors).

7. Individual differences among adults are often referred to as *personality* differences; those among infants, as differences in *temperament*. Temperament characteristics are assumed to have a strong genetic basis and to be present very early in life. Thomas, Chess, and Birch's New York Longitudinal Study (NYLS) identified nine characteristics of infant temperament, particular combinations of which are associated with three types of children: difficult, easy, and "slow to warm up." Some evidence suggests that "difficult" infants (lack of rhythmic-

ity, withdrawal from the unfamiliar, slow adaptation to change, intense negative moods) run a higher risk of behavior and emotional problems than do "easy" children.

8. Although temperament appears to have a strong genetic basis, experiences are also important, as is evidenced in different cultures where infants manifest culture-related temperaments. The infant's temperament may contribute to developmental outcomes by affecting how parents interact with them and how they feel about themselves as parents.

9. An ecological model of human development suggests that the "goodness-of-fit" between the infant's temperament and environmental demands may affect developmental outcome. Knowledge of goodness-of-fit might be important in identifying infants who are vulnerable or whose contexts place them at risk. In our culture, "easy" infants usually fit better.

10. Forming an attachment, (a strong, positive emotional relationship), usually with a primary caregiver (later with others), is one of the most important tasks of early infancy. *Bonding* refers to the biologically based processes by which parents and infants form attachment links.

11. Ethologists such as Bowlby argue that given the importance of attachment for survival, there are powerful genetic tendencies toward the formation of caregiver–infant bonds. These tendencies are apparent in genetic preadaptations that facilitate infant–caregiver interaction (for example, perceptual biases that sensitize the infant to the human voice and that are evident in a preference for the human face, as well as response tendencies evident in rooting and sucking reflexes) as well as in certain biological rhythms.

12. Mother–infant bonding and infant attachment to the mother appear to be important to the healthy development and adjustment of the infant. It has not been established, however, that there is a critical period during which this bonding must occur or that it can occur only with the mother.

13. Bowlby identifies four sequential phases in the development of infant attachment: *preattachment* (first month: crying, smiling, clinging, sucking, responding to caregiver voice); *attachment-in-the-making* (into second half of first year: selective social smile); *clear-cut attachment* (after 6 months: use

of motor skills to approach attachment object); and *goal-corrected attachment* (second year: more subtle manipulation of attachment person's behavior).

14. Ainsworth's Strange Situation studies reveal two major types of infant–parent attachment. *Securely* attached infants (use mother as base from which to explore; upset when she leaves; react positively and attempt to reestablish contact when she returns); and *anxiously* attached, who may be *avoidant* (rarely cry when mother leaves; ignore or avoid her when she returns) or *ambivalent* (very upset when mother leaves; often angry when she returns).

15. Infants appear to become equally attached to their mothers and fathers when given the opportunity to do so, but they display more affiliative ("let's be friends") behavior toward their fathers. This is especially true of boys.

16. *Transitional objects* such as blankets and teddy bears are sometimes as effective as a parent in reducing anxiety in some stressful situations.

17. High-quality infant day care does not appear to disrupt parent–infant bonds or to prevent their formation and has no consistent negative effects.

18. Among important dimensions of parenting in infancy are attentiveness, physical contact, verbal stimulation, material stimulation, and responsive care—each of which has positive effects on the infant's social and intellectual development—and restrictiveness, the effects of which are more negative.

19. From the moment of birth, a subtle process of gender-typing begins. Many mothers and fathers react differently to male and female children, interact with them differently, have different expectations of them, and perceive them differently.

20. Exceptionality has both positive and negative dimensions. Exceptional children are those who require special education and related services to realize their full human potential. Physical exceptionality may be evident in cerebral palsy, epilepsy, a variety of diseases, congenital physical problems, or physical problems resulting from accidents. Emotional exceptionality may be apparent in childhood-onset pervasive developmental disorders, which are rare but very serious early forms of emotional disorders.

21. Although relatively fragmented aspects of the child have been discussed in this chapter, it is the whole person—the *individual*–with whom we are concerned.

Further Readings

Valsiner's collection of articles is an excellent illustration of how contemporary developmental psychologists are taking into account the influence of cultural, historical, and family systems on developmental outcomes:

Valsiner, J. (Ed.). (1989). *Child development in cultural context.* Lewiston, NY: Hogrefe & Huber.

A good summary of research and applications in temperament research is contained in:

Carey, W. B., & McDevitt, S. C. (Eds.). (1989). *Clinical and educational applications of temperament research.* Berwyn, PA: Swets North America.

There is not enough child care in North America; nor is there enough *quality* child care, says Angela Browne Miller in this provocative book:

Browne Miller, A. (1990). *The day care dilemma.* New York: Plenum.

In the following book, Bowlby examines mother–infant interaction, with special emphasis on the development of attachment:

Bowlby, J. (1982). *Attachment and loss* (Vol. 1): *Attachment* (2nd ed.). New York: Basic Books.

The following collection of readings provides a detailed examination of many of the topics covered in this chapter:

Field, T. M., & Fox, N. A. (Eds.). (1985). *Social perception in infants.* Norwood, NJ: Ablex.

Pogrebin's book is a provocative analysis of the role parents play in gender-typing their infants:

Pogrebin, L. C. (1980). *Growing up free: Raising your child in the 80's.* New York: McGraw-Hill.

Mary Cassatt: *The Boating Party*, 1893–1894. National Gallery of Art, Washington, DC,
Chester Dale Collection.

When you think that the eyes of
your childhood dried at the sight
of a piece of gingerbread and that a
plum-cake was a compensation for
the agony of parting with your
mamma and sisters; O my friend
and brother, you need not be too
confident of your own fine feelings.

William Makepeace Thackeray,
Vanity Fair

PART

III

Early Childhood

Chapter 7 Physical and cognitive development: Early childhood
Chapter 8 Social development: Early childhood

With the proliferation of day care, perhaps preschoolers no longer sense so profound an agony at parting from mama. Perhaps, too, with the reduction in the size of the family, there are no sisters to bring to the eyes tears of sadness—or of joy.

Still, it's true: Preschoolers often don't need more than a piece of gingerbread or a plum-cake to dry their tears. At the same time, they don't need a very serious personal crisis to make them cry.

As we see in the next two chapters, their understanding of the world is different from ours. So, too, are their emotional responses. It is as though the line between joy and sorrow has not yet been firmly drawn; it is easily crossed. Tears and laughter come more easily. I can move Jennie from gladness to tears if I take her stuffed toy from her. But now, if I give her a cookie (or a plum-cake), she smiles.

We, too, can still cry when someone takes our stuffed toys. But what will dry our grown-up tears? Where are our gingerbreads and our plum-cakes?

CHAPTER 7

Physical and Cognitive Development: Early Childhood

Life is good only when it is magical and musical.

Ralph Waldo Emerson,
Society and Solitude:
Works and Days

Early childhood is like that, magical and musical. For the first seven or eight years of life, Pearce (1977) informs us, the child often does not bother to check thinking against reality. Thinking is wishful, fantastic. It somehow assumes that reality can be changed or controlled by thoughts, that thoughts enter the real world and make of it what we wish. Thus it is that a magic spell can produce a witch or a princess, a silver thread or a pot of gold. Thus it is, too, that a kiss can cure a *booboo*, a pat can dispel a tummyache, and a mother can make a dragon smile.

Of course, we adults don't believe such things. We know that princesses, like peasants, are born; that pots of gold are mostly imaginary; that kisses can hurt too; and that a pat cannot really touch a tummyache.

Those are facts.

And our dragons never smile.

This Chapter

We do not gladly accept, or perhaps even understand, the magical child, says Pearce (1977). Our psychologies and our research ask instead: "How can the child be made to attend to reality? Or how can we make the child abandon magical thinking?" (p. xv).

In this chapter, we examine the early development of thinking in the child, and the development of language. But first, we look at physical growth and motor development in children ages 2–6.

Physical Growth

A comparison of the 6-year-old with the 2-year-old provides some idea of developmental changes during the preschool years. The difference between the two

is phenomenal, despite the fact that physical development during childhood is generally characterized by a marked slowdown compared with infancy. Figures 7.1 and 7.2 trace the physical development of boys and girls from the age of 2 to the age of 6. Comparing these data with Figures 5.2 and 5.3 reveals a dramatic deceleration in growth rates after the period of infancy, particularly in height.

Different growth rates for different parts of the body help explain some of the changes that occur between the ages of 2 and 6. The thick layers of fat that give 1-year-old children their babyish appearance begin to disappear slowly during the second year of life and continue to recede gradually. In effect, these tissues grow much more slowly than other tissues, so that by the time children have reached the age of 6, their layers of fat are less than half as thick as they were at the age of 1. Partly because of this change, they begin to look more like adults.

Other changes as well account for the gradual transition from the appearance of infancy to the appearance of young boyhood or girlhood. Not only does the relative amount of fatty tissue change during the preschool years, but its distribution changes as a result of the more rapid growth of bone and muscle. The squat appearance of infants is explained by the fact that their waists are about as large as their hips or chests. Six-year-old children, by contrast, have begun to develop waists that are smaller in girth than their shoulders and hips. This becomes even more evident in early adolescence than at the end of the preschool period.

The larger waists of infants are also due in part to the relative size of the internal organs, many of which grow much more rapidly than other parts of the body. Given space limitations between the child's pelvis and diaphragm, their abdomens protrude. This condition changes as they grow in height during the preschool years.

Figure 7.4 on page 229 portrays other changes in body proportions that account for the different appearance of the 6-year-old. The head of a 2-month fetus is approximately half the length of the entire body. At birth the head is closer to one fourth the size of the rest of the body. By the age of 6, it is close to one eighth the size, which is a short step removed from the head-to-body relationship typical of the normal adult with a normal-sized head: one tenth. Between the ages of 2 and 6, the head changes from approximately one fifth to one eighth of total body size—a noticeable change. Because of this change, and because of changes in the distribution

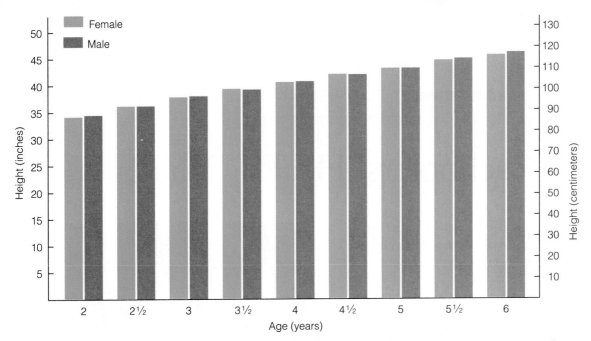

Figure 7.1 Height at 50th percentile for U.S. children ages 2–6. (Adapted from the Health Department, Milwaukee, Wisconsin; based on data by H. C. Stuart and H. V. Meredith, prepared for use in Children's Medical Center, Boston. Used by permission of the Milwaukee Health Department.)

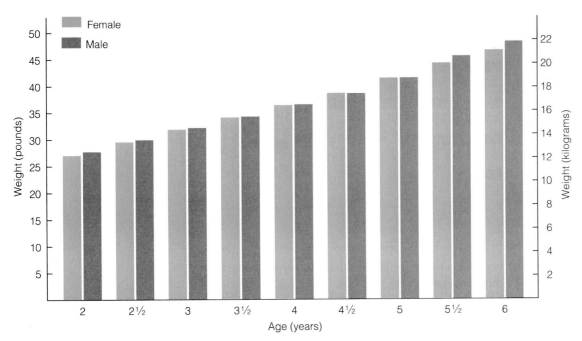

Figure 7.2 Weight at 50th percentile for U.S. children ages 2–6. (Adapted from the Health Department, Milwaukee, Wisconsin; based on data by H. C. Stuart and H. V. Meredith, prepared for use in Children's Medical Center, Boston. Used by permission of the Milwaukee Health Department.)

Preschoolers' Health Problems

Most preschoolers occasionally suffer from illness or injury serious enough to require medical attention or to keep them home at least one day. In fact, only 2 or 3 of every 100 preschoolers will *not* have an upper-respiratory infection at least once (a cold, for example), and almost one third will suffer some physical injury. Between ages 5 and 17, the rates for all common health problems decline — except for injuries. At all ages except after 65, rate of injuries is higher for males than females.

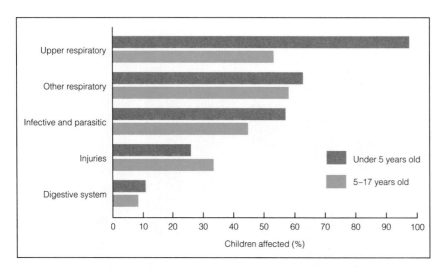

Figure 7.3 Preschoolers' and older children's susceptibility to injury and illness. The graph shows the percentage of children who will be affected at least once by the indicated condition. (Adapted from U.S. Bureau of the Census, 1990, p. 118.)

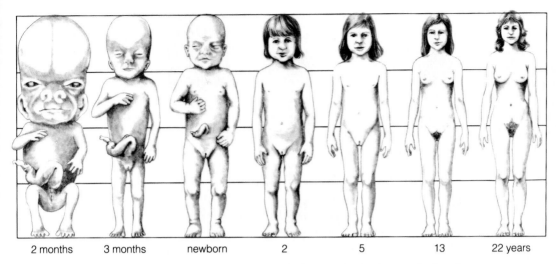

2 months   3 months   newborn   2   5   13   22 years

Figure 7.4 Changes in form and proportion of the human body during fetal and postnatal life. (From Jensen et al., *Biology*, 1979, p. 233. Used with permission of Wadsworth Publishing Company.)

of fat and in the space that the child now has for internal organs, the 6-year-old looks remarkably like an adult; the 2-year-old looks more like a typical baby.

Motor Development

Infants' most significant motor achievement is learning to walk. At the same time that they learn to walk, they also learn to coordinate other motor activities that they have been practicing. so that by the age of 2 they are remarkably adept at picking up objects, stacking blocks, unlacing shoes, and performing a host of other motor activities. It is through actual activity and experience with objects that children learn about their properties—and about sorting, classifying, and counting, says Piaget. Hence, the close alliance between activity and early intellectual development.

In infancy, infants acquire abilities such as those involved in both locomotion and grasping. In early childhood, children continue to make progress in motor development, and their locomotion becomes more certain as they lose the characteristic wide-footed stance of the toddler (from 18 months to 2½ years). As their equilibrium stabilizes and their feet move closer together, their arms and hands also move closer to their bodies. Thus they lose both the wide stance and the appearance of a tightrope walker as they no longer need to maintain balance with both arms and feet. As their walking improves, they acquire the ability to climb stairs standing upright and completely unassisted, and eventually to hop with two feet and to skip.

Tracing and Copying Geometric Shapes

Preschoolers also develop a variety of other motor skills that are closely related to increasing control and coordination of fine muscle movements. Among these are the skills involved in tracing geometric figures or in copying them freehand. Gesell (1925), whose work maps out in detail the sequential progression of children's motor development, reports that before age 2, the child is usually incapable of copying a circle or a horizontal line although the 2- to 3-year-old can do so quite easily. By age 4, children can also copy a square and a rectangle, but not a diamond (see Figure 7.5).

As Broderick (1986) points out, successfully copying geometric figures is more than just a fine motor task; it also requires important perceptual, cognitive, and motor abilities. Visual abilities are involved when

Tying shoelaces is a complex cognitive and motor task usually acquired in the preschool period. It requires not only that children understand the particular twists, loops, and insertions that form knots and bows, but also that they have developed the motor coordination to manipulate laces in appropriate ways. The entire procedure demands great concentration and skill, not to mention a little luck.

children perceive a shape and compare it with their own copy; cognitive abilities are at play when children successfully interpret the requirements of the task, plan an approach, and evaluate its execution, sometimes modifying and correcting; and, of course, fine motor abilities are involved in carrying out the task.

Children as young as 1 or 2 can easily discriminate among different geometric forms, says Broderick (1986); but they cannot copy them. In an investigation of the drawing skills of 80 children, she found that although 5- and 6-year-olds can draw quite recognizable squares, they cannot draw diamonds. Strangely, many 12-year-olds and adults experience difficulty with diamonds. Although what they draw is usually clearly recognizable as a diamond, the figures are often oriented many degrees to one side. And even adults often make highly noticeable errors in angularity—that is, opposing angles of the diamonds are sometimes quite different from each other, although not nearly as much as is the case for younger children.

Given the close relationship between motor and cognitive development in early childhood and the highly predictable sequence for learning to copy geometric figures, it is not surprising that a large number of intelligence tests include such items (for example, the Revised Stanford-Binet and the Wechsler).

Assessing Motor Development

All parents are concerned about the developmental progress of their infants and children. They feel proud of their offsprings' accomplishments, and are sometimes distressed and worried when their children do not develop as rapidly as they expect—or as rapidly as someone else's children.

Here, as in all areas of human development, there are no absolute norms, no definite, preestablished levels of performance that must be reached by certain ages. Our definitions of what is normal are vague and inexact. Still, psychology and medicine provide us with indications of what we might expect; and this information provides benchmarks against which to evaluate our children—if we must.

A variety of different scales of infant and child development can be used for these purposes. As we

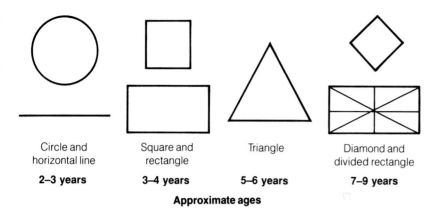

Circle and horizontal line	Square and rectangle	Triangle	Diamond and divided rectangle
2–3 years	**3–4 years**	**5–6 years**	**7–9 years**

Approximate ages

Figure 7.5 Usual order of difficulty for copying simple geometric designs reasonably well. Because of the close relationship between motor and intellectual development in early childhood, some intelligence tests for young children include items such as these.

saw, there are neonatal scales with which to assess the physiological and neurological condition of the newborn (for example, the Brazelton Neonatal Behavioral Assessment Scale and the APGAR). There are also scales to assess motor and mental development in infancy (for example, the Bayley Scales of Infant Development). And there are developmental scales that span infancy and childhood (for example, the Denver Developmental Screening Test and the Gesell Developmental Schedules). Each of these instruments provides simple tasks that can be presented to the infant or child, or describes observations that can be made. More importantly, each also provides tables of norms describing what sorts of infant or child behaviors can be expected at different ages.

The Denver Developmental Screening Test, for example, was initially designed primarily to permit identification of infants and children suffering from developmental delays (Frankenberg et al., 1981). Accordingly, age norms are provided corresponding to the levels at which 25, 50, 75, and 90 percent of children are expected to demonstrate a given capability. Four different areas are examined by the test: language, personal-social, fine-motor, and gross-motor. (See Interactive Table 7.1 for examples of fine-motor and gross-motor tasks pertinent to early childhood.) A child is considered to be developmentally delayed when incapable of a task of which 90 percent of children of the same age are capable. Isolated developmental delays are not considered serious. But when a child is delayed on two or more tasks *and* in more than one area, further assessment may be required.

Like most other instruments that try to measure psychological and motor functioning in the early years, the Denver Developmental Screening Test does not provide highly precise and completely reliable measurements. Research suggests that when used with infants and young children, it leads to a relatively high proportion of underreferrals — that is, it fails to identify a number of children with developmental problems (Francis, Self, & Horowitz, 1987).

Motor and Cognitive Development

The child's physical development and the development of motor skills are closely related; the acquisition of many skills depends on development of the required musculature and on control of these muscles. The relationship of physical development to the other areas of development is perhaps not so obvious, although no less real. For example, a child's play, particularly when it involves peers, is often influenced by motor skills because various aptitudes are called for in different games. A child who is still incapable of jumping with both feet is not likely to be invited by older children to join in a game of jump rope; a child who cannot grasp marbles skillfully enough may be left out of the traditional spring marble games. Conversely, the child who is precocious in physical and motor development is likely to be the first one asked to participate in games — indeed, may be the one to initiate them.

INTERACTIVE TABLE 7.1

Age at Which 50 Percent and 90 Percent of Norming Sample of Children Accomplish Described Task★

▶ *As a course project, you might conduct an in-depth single-case study of motor development in a preschooler, or compare two or more preschoolers, using some of the tasks described here.*

Motor Task	Approximate Ages (years)	
	50 Percent	90 Percent
Gross		
Kicks ball forward	1.7	2.0
Throws ball overhand	1.6	2.6
Balance on 1 foot 1 second	2.5	3.2
Pedals tricycle	2.0	3.0
Broad jump	2.8	3.2
Balance on 1 foot 5 seconds	3.2	4.3
Catches bounced ball	3.9	5.5
Walks backward heel to toe	4.7	6.3
Fine		
Scribbles spontaneously	1.1	2.1
Tower of 4 cubes	1.5	2.2
Imitates vertical line within 30°	1.8	3.0
Tower of 8 cubes	2.0	3.4
Picks longer line 3 of 3	2.9	4.4
Draws man, 3 parts	4.0	5.2
Draws man, 6 parts	4.8	6.0

★ Based on norms from Denver Developmental Screening Test.

Source: From *Denver Developmental Screening Test Reference Manual: Revised 1975 Edition* by W. K. Frankenburg, J. B. Dodds, A. W. Fandal, E. Kazuk, and M. Cohrs, 1975, Denver, CO: University of Colorado Medical Center. Used with permission.

Clearly, then, physical and motor development may have an influence on the general social development of the child; game playing is one important means of socialization. (More about this in Chapter 8.)

As we have seen, the relationship between motor and intellectual development in the early years is an important aspect of Piaget's theory. When the infant's world is a world of the "here and now," it is a world that has meaning only in action. The object exists only when the infant looks at it; its meaning is what can be done with it *now*.

But as the infant gains control over fine- and gross-motor movements, it eventually becomes possible to go to an object, to look behind it, to pick it up—to *explore* it. These seemingly simple but initially impossible acts open up an entirely new world of cognitions.

So it continues throughout early childhood. The child's increasing refinement of control over motor movements, and an ever-growing store of experiences with real objects, leads gradually to an intellectual (cognitive) understanding of some of the properties of things—and eventually to an understanding of abstractions such as the principles that govern the use of numbers, or the formation of classes. These are some of the subjects to which we turn next. (See Table 7.2 for a summary of some physical and motor achievements between ages 2 and 5.)

Cognitive Development

We do not expect our preschool children, much less our infants, to be completely logical. We are seldom surprised when our 3-year-old insists loudly that a small cat, identical to her small cat, must surely be hers; we are not shocked by the 4-year-old's apparent failure to realize that there really are not more candies in his sister's dish when they are all spread out; we express little dismay when our 2½-year-old calls a duck a chicken. These instances of *egocentric, perception-dominated*, and *illogical* thinking simply amuse us; that is what we expect of young children.

But we would be surprised if our 7-year-olds continued to insist on calling all reasonably shaggy-looking pigs "doggy," if they refused to believe that six ounces of soft drink in a glass is the same amount as six ounces in a bottle, or if they thought that they could decrease the mass of a wad of gum simply by stringing it out

T A B L E 7 . 2

Physical Characteristics of the Child from 2 to 5 Years Old

At Two Years Begins to	At Three Years Begins to	At Four Years Begins to	At Five Years Begins to
Walk	Jump and hop on one foot	Run, jump, and climb with close adult supervision	Gain good body control
Run	Climb stairs by alternating feet on each stair	Dress self using buttons, zippers, laces, and so on	Throw and catch a ball, climb, jump, skip with good coordination
Actively explore environment	Dress and undress self somewhat	Use more sophisticated eating utensils such as knives to cut meat or spread butter	Coordinate movements to music
Sit in a chair without support	Walk a reasonably straight path on floor		Put on snowpants, boots, and tie shoes
Climb stairs with help (two feet on each stair)	Walk on balance beam	Walk balance beam with ease	Skip
Build block towers	Ride a tricycle	Walk down stairs alone	Jump rope, walk in a straight line
Feed self with fork and spoon	Stand on one foot for a short time	Bounce and catch ball	Ride a two-wheel bike
Stand on balance beam	Catch large balls	Push/pull wagon	Roller skate
Throw ball	Hop	Cut, following lines	Fold paper
Catch	Gallop	Copy figure **X**	Reproduce alphabet and numbers
Jump	Kick ball	Print first name	Trace
Push and pull	Hit ball		
Hang on bar	Paste		
Slide	String beads		
	Cut paper with scissors		
	Copy figures ○ and +		

Source: From G. W. Maxim (1989). *The Very Young* (3rd ed.). Columbus, Ohio: Merrill. p. 399. Copyright © 1989 by Macmillan Publishing Company. Reprinted with permission of Merrill, an imprint of Macmillan Publishing Company.

and wrapping it around their ears! These illustrate some of the intellectual (or cognitive) differences that we expect between preschoolers and older children.

The Preschooler's Memory

Between birth and the end of the early childhood period (around age 6), children are exposed to, learn, and remember an overwhelming assortment of things: the identities of people and animals; the locations of things; numbers, letters, and songs; thousands of words, and all sorts of complex rules for putting them together.

From the very beginning, we clearly have some ability to learn and to remember. But, as we saw in Chapter 5, the neonate's memory is very brief. The effects of simple conditioning procedures sometimes last only hours, or perhaps a day. Still, the infant is not long confused about whether this is his mother's voice, or her face. Recognition of things like voices and faces is a certain sign of memory. But there are some important differences between the memories of infants and those of adults. Chief among them is that the infant does not deliberately and systematically organize, group, or elaborate material to remember it—and these three activities are the most important memory strategies of adults and older children.

By the age of 5, many children can copy a cross, a diamond, a circle, or a square reasonably well; most, like this bespectacled tyke, can also scribble and scratch.

Incidental Mnemonics.   A number of researchers argue that the preschooler rarely uses systematic strategies for remembering. Most of what the preschooler remembers is the result of what Wellman (1988) calls *incidental mnemonics*. Incidental mnemonics are not deliberate; hence they are not really strategies. They are what happens when someone pays attention, for whatever reason, and later remembers, or when someone is exposed to the same thing often enough that it becomes familiar and known. Remembering, in these cases, is not the result of a deliberate and systematic attempt to elaborate or to rehearse, but is, in a sense, involuntary.

We know that incidental mnemonics underlie much of the preschooler's learning. Because these are incidental and involuntary processes, and because there is little evidence of adultlike strategies such as deliberately rehearsing or organizing, researchers have assumed that memory strategies develop only in later childhood. The evidence suggests that this is wrong, says Wellman (1988). Preschoolers do use deliberate strategies to help them remember. But two things are noteworthy about these strategies: First, they seldom involve deliberate reorganization or elaboration, or even rehearsal; second, many of the preschooler's mnemonic strategies are faulty in the sense that they are misused and often do not lead to an improvement in memory.

Preschoolers' Strategies.   That preschoolers deliberately use memory strategies seems clear from a number of different studies. For example, Wellman (1988) asked 3-year-olds to bury a toy in a sandbox before leaving the room with the experimenter. Some of the children were asked to remember where they had buried the toy; others were asked if there was anything they would like to do before leaving, but were given no instructions about remembering. Strikingly, half the children who had been instructed to remember the toy's location *marked* it by placing a mound over the object, by marking the sand, or sometimes by placing another toy on top of it; only 20 percent of the no-instruction group did likewise (see Figure 7.6).

Marking the toy's location is an intelligent and effective strategy. As we noted, however, many of the preschooler's memory strategies are not so effective. Heisel and Ritter (1981) asked 3- and 5-year-olds to hide an object in one of 196 separate containers arranged in a 14-foot-square matrix and instructed some of them to remember where they had hidden the object. Significantly, many of the children in both age groups used memory strategies when they had been instructed to remember. The strategies used by the 5-year-olds were often very effective — namely, hiding the object in one of the corner locations, since these could be

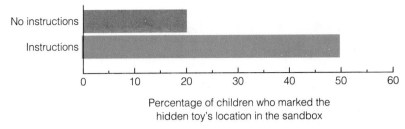

Figure 7.6 Three-year-olds were asked to hide a toy in a sandbox. Half of those (the instructions group) who were asked to try to remember where the toy was hidden marked its location; only 20 percent of the no-instructions group did likewise. Young children may be capable of using simple memory strategies, but often do not do so spontaneously.

remembered and relocated very easily. But what is perhaps most striking is that the 3-year-olds' strategies, while every bit as consistent as those of the older children, were often very ineffective. Almost half these 3-year-olds tried to hide the object in the same location on every trial, thus demonstrating that they were using a systematic strategy; but the location was typically somewhere near the center of the array. As a result, when they were later asked to find the object, these children fared almost as poorly as those who had not used strategies.

The overuse of an inappropriate memory strategy is one of the most common mistakes made by young children trying to remember, says Wellman (1988). An important developmental change in memory strategies is a gradual reduction in the use of faulty strategies and an increase in more effective strategies. Effective strategies increase dramatically in elementary school.

Development of Strategies. Ornstein, Baker-Ward, and Naus (1988) summarize the progression of children's development of memory strategies in five stages:

- *Stage 1.* In the beginning, the young child doesn't deliberately use strategies to remember.

- *Stage 2.* The preschooler may occasionally use strategies, but these don't always result in memory improvement.

- *Stage 3.* In the early elementary school years, children use somewhat more effective strategies, but are often distracted by irrelevant information.

- *Stage 4.* Later, strategies become increasingly effective and are applied in a variety of settings.

- *Stage 5.* Finally, as a result of repeated practice with memory strategies, their use becomes habitual and automatic.

In summary, preschoolers are clearly able to remember. But in most cases, memory results not from the deliberate use of memory strategies, but from incidental mnemonics—for example, paying attention to something or being exposed to it more than once. In contrast, the elementary school child often deliberately uses memory strategies.

One of the important differences between the older memorizer and the preschooler is that older children have acquired some understanding of the processes involved in learning and remembering. They have developed intuitive notions of themselves as information processors, capable of applying strategies and of monitoring and changing them as required. In the current jargon, they have developed some of the skills involved in **metamemory** (defined as the knowledge that children have about the processes involved in remembering) (Borkowski, Milstead, & Hale, 1988). (More about the memories of older children in Chapter 9.)

Piaget's View

In Chapter 5, we looked at the *sensorimotor* intelligence of the infant—Piaget's label for his first major stage of intellectual development, so called because the infant's

TABLE 7.3

Piaget's Stages of Cognitive Development

Stage	Approximate Age	Some Major Characteristics
Sensorimotor	0–2 years	Motoric intelligence World of the here and now No language, no thought in early stages No notion of objective reality
Preoperational Preconceptual Intuitive	2–7 years 2–4 years 4–7 years	Egocentric thought Reason dominated by perception Intuitive, rather than logical, solutions Inability to conserve
Concrete operations	7 to 11–12 years	Ability to conserve Logic of classes and relations Understanding of number Thinking bound to concrete Development of reversibility in thought
Formal operations	11–12 to 14–15 years	Complete generality of thought Propositional thinking Ability to deal with the hypothetical Development of strong idealism

intelligence involves immediate sensation and perception. The next major Piagetian stage is labeled *preoperational*—so called because children do not yet think operationally.

In Piaget's theory, an operation is a thought characterized by specific logical properties—a logical thought. The child who believes that he has more gum when he rolls it into a fat ball and less when he spreads it out like a thin pancake on his sister's pillow is demonstrating *pre*operational thinking.

Piaget divides the preoperational period (ages 2 to approximately 7) into two subperiods: The first, lasting from ages 2 to 4, is termed *preconceptual*; the second, from ages 4 to 7, is called *intuitive* (see Table 7.3).

Preconceptual Thinking

The major intellectual difference between the sensorimotor child and the preschooler is in the means each has of representing the world and reasoning about it.

The young infant's intelligence is initially rooted in sensation and action, but toward the end of the second year, and especially with the advent of language, infants begin to symbolize. They begin to represent actions mentally and to anticipate their consequences, and they begin to develop some notion of causes—of actions as means to ends.

Preconcepts. As children begin to symbolize, they develop the ability to represent mentally (internalize) objects and events in the environment and to relate them in terms of common properties. Thus they develop **concepts**. But these concepts are not as complete and logical as an adult's, and are referred to as **preconcepts**.

Despite their incompleteness, preconcepts are nevertheless sufficient to permit the child to make simple classifications necessary for identifying objects. Thus children recognize a man because they have a budding concept that tells them that a *man* is whatever walks on two legs, has hair, wears pants, and speaks in a gruff voice. By noting their characteristics, children can identify dogs, birds, elephants, and houses. What they frequently cannot do, however, is distinguish among different individuals belonging to the same species. Piaget illustrates this with his son, Laurent, who pointed out a snail to his father as they were walking. Several minutes later they came upon another snail, and the child exclaimed that here again was the snail. The child's apparent failure to recognize that similar objects can belong to the same class and still be different objects — that is, can retain an identity of their own — is an example of a preconcept.

There are two other striking features of the child's reasoning processes during the preconceptual period. These are given the imposing labels *transductive reasoning* and *syncretic reasoning*.

Transductive Reasoning.
Transduction can be contrasted with the two broad types of *logical* reasoning: *deductive* and *inductive*. To deduce is to go from the general to the particular. For example, from my knowledge that mammals give birth to live young, I might deduce that a three-toed sloth (a specific mammal) gives birth to tiny sloths. In contrast, to induce is to go from a number of specific examples to a broader generalization. Thus, after observing several barn swallows build nests of mud and a cementlike type of saliva, I might generalize that all (or most) barn swallows build similar nests.

Transductive reasoning makes inferences from one particular to another — that is, from one instance to another. Thus, if I find that one red-headed person has a particularly charming personality, I might *transduce* that a second red-headed person will also be charming. Transductive reasoning can occasionally — and somewhat accidentally — lead to a correct inference; it can also lead to totally incorrect conclusions. Consider the following as a second example:

A flies; B flies; therefore, B is A.

Clearly, if A is a bird and B is also a bird, then A is a B and vice versa. If A is a plane and B is a bird, the same reasoning process leads to an incorrect conclusion. Thus a preschooler can unashamedly insist that cats are dogs and chickens are turkeys.

Syncretic Reasoning.
The preschooler's classification behavior is also marked by the use of **syncretic reasoning**, in which different objects are grouped according to the child's limited and frequently changing rules. For example, a 2-year-old child who is placed in front of a table bearing a number of objects of different kinds and colors and who is asked to group those objects that go together might proceed something like this: The blue truck goes with the red truck because they both are trucks, and this thing goes with them because it is blue and that truck is blue. Similarly, here is a ball and here is a marble and they go together, and here is a crayon that is yellow like the ball so it goes with them too. The point is that the preschooler's rules change; young children see no reason to use the same rule every time. We adults, whose thinking is not so magical, don't have the same luxury.

Intuitive Thinking

The period of *intuitive thinking* begins about age 4 and ends about age 7. It is labeled *intuitive* because much of the child's thought is based on immediate comprehension rather than on logical processes. Children solve many problems correctly, but they do not always do so using logic. Piaget refers to a problem in which a child is shown three balls that are then inserted into a hollow tube so that the child can no longer see them. The balls are blue, red, and yellow. At first, when the tube is held vertically, the child knows clearly which ball is on top. Then, the tube is turned a half rotation (180°), and the subject is asked which ball is now at the top. Alternatively, it may be turned a full rotation, one and a half turns, two turns, and so on. Piaget found that as long as children could continue to *imagine* the position of the balls inside the tube, they could answer correctly, but they could not arrive at a rule concerning the relationship between odd and even numbers of turns or half turns and the location of the balls. In other words, the solution to the problem was achieved through intuitive mental images rather than through logical reasoning.

Intuitive thinking is also characterized by difficulties in deciding what should be included in a class or category; egocentricity (inability to adopt another's point of view); and a marked reliance on perception. Each of these qualities is illustrated next.

Classification.
The preschooler's difficulties with class inclusion are easily demonstrated in studies that present the child with a collection of objects made of

Figure 7.7 Experiments concerned with preoperational thought.

Preconceptual period: 2–4 years

Preconceptual — Similar objects are assumed to be identical.

Transductive — Reasoning from particular to particular.

a dog
(is furry, likes balls)

(is furry, likes balls, must also be a dog)

Syncretic — Groupings according to idiosyncratic and changing criteria.

"Put those that go together on the table."

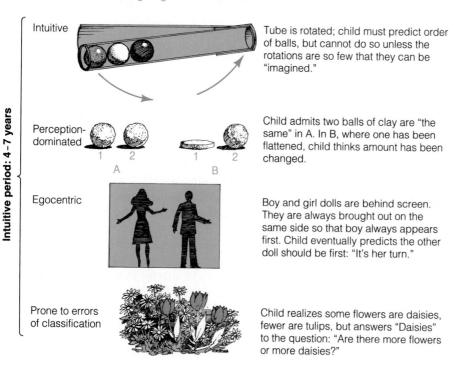

Intuitive period: 4–7 years

Intuitive — Tube is rotated; child must predict order of balls, but cannot do so unless the rotations are so few that they can be "imagined."

Perception-dominated — Child admits two balls of clay are "the same" in A. In B, where one has been flattened, child thinks amount has been changed.

A   B

Egocentric — Boy and girl dolls are behind screen. They are always brought out on the same side so that boy always appears first. Child eventually predicts the other doll should be first: "It's her turn."

Prone to errors of classification — Child realizes some flowers are daisies, fewer are tulips, but answers "Daisies" to the question: "Are there more flowers or more daisies?"

two subclasses—for example, 20 wooden beads, 15 of which are brown and 5 of which are blue. The subject is asked what the objects are. "They are wooden beads," the child answers. The experimenter then divides them into the two subclasses, brown beads and blue beads, and asks whether there are more brown beads or more wooden beads. The answer is obvious, you say? Not to the child at this stage of development. The most common reply is, "There are more brown beads." It is as if breaking down a class into its subparts destroys the parent class.

Egocentricity. A study in which a girl doll and a boy doll are placed side by side on a piece of string illustrates the egocentric nature of the preschooler's thought. The experimenter holds the ends of the string in both hands and stands behind a screen that hides the dolls from the child's view. The child is asked to predict which of the dolls will appear first if the experimenter moves the string toward the right. Let us assume that the boy doll appears first. The experimenter then returns the dolls to their original position and repeats the same question, "Which of the dolls will now appear

Head Start in action.

program ("Bush Calls for Unprecedented Increase," 1992).

Because of the variety of approaches used in these projects, it has been difficult to assess their effectiveness. Many early studies indicated that children enrolled in Head Start programs continued to be inferior to more advantaged children who had not been exposed to such programs, and critics were quick to conclude that huge amounts of money had been squandered in poorly planned, poorly executed, and basically ineffec-

tive programs (Bronfenbrenner, 1977b). However, subsequent research has sometimes found quite dramatic improvements resulting from Head Start programs. Previous researchers, say Lee, Brooks-Gunn, and Schnur (1988), often failed to look at initial differences between groups exposed to Head Start and comparison groups. When they found that disadvantaged groups were still disadvantaged *after* the programs, they concluded that the programs had not worked. A study of 969 subjects conducted by Lee and associates found that although Head Start programs did not eliminate the difference between Head Start children and comparison groups, they did reduce it.

Following a review of various studies of Head Start programs, Haskins (1989) concludes that such programs have an immediate, positive impact on children, although the long-term effects are not as pronounced or as clear. However, the *best* forms of preschool education may produce detectable long-term benefits in "life success measures"—such as, for example, reductions in teenage pregnancy, delinquency, unemployment, and reliance on welfare assistance.

Types of Compensatory Programs.

What are these *best* forms of preschool intervention? It depends, of course, on what the goals are. If we measure success in terms of preparation for academic tasks, the most effective forms of intervention are typically highly specific, "model" approaches (Haskins, 1989). These are usually based on identifiable theories and characterized by well-formulated approaches and carefully developed materials.

Among the better-known model approaches that have sometimes been used as Head Start programs (or in other nursery school or kindergarten programs) are the *Direct Instruction approach*, and the *Montessori method*. The Direct Instruction approach, initiated by Bereiter and Engelmann (1966), presented a sharp contrast to the traditional approach of most kindergartens and nursery schools. Instead of being primarily child-centered and emphasizing social and emotional development, it is instructor-centered, and emphasizes the teaching of skills and concepts. Instructional methods are highly structured, and involve *telling* the children and *asking* them to repeat, alone or in unison. It teaches reading, language, and arithmetic. Not surprisingly, it has shown some marked positive results in these areas (see Figure 7.9).

Direct Instruction has its critics, however. Some fear that such approaches place too much emphasis on learning basics, on repetition, on drill, on success. They argue that the high-pressure, achievement-oriented principles that underlie Direct Instruction violate our fundamental belief in the rights of children to play, to enjoy, to dream, to make magical, nonrealistic things.

The Montessori method, which dates back to the turn of the century (Montessori, 1912), is another very structured approach to preschool education. It was initially developed for use with mentally retarded children, but has proven highly effective and popular as

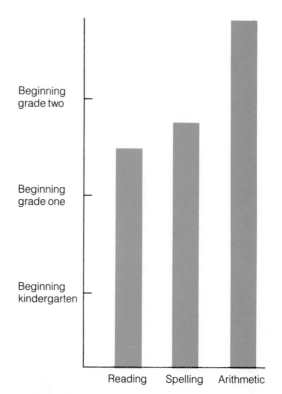

Figure 7.9 Mean achievement scores in three areas for 15 subjects in the Bereiter–Engelmann direct instruction program. At the time of testing, the children had completed their kindergarten year. (Based on data reported by Bereiter & Engelmann, 1966, p. 28.)

a general program. Unlike most preschool programs, it is designed for use in elementary and high school as well.

One of the distinctive features of the Montessori approach is the use of specially developed materials for teaching sense discriminations. Montessori believed that all learning stems from sense perception and can therefore be improved by training the senses. Perhaps the best known of her materials are large letters of the alphabet covered with sandpaper, which are used to teach the child to read. The prescribed teaching method requires not only that children look at the letters, but also that they trace their shapes with their fingertips, saying the sound of the letter and getting a tactile sensation of it at the same time. (See Figure 7.10 for examples of some Montessori materials.)

Evaluations of Montessori programs have generally been quite positive, in spite of the criticism that

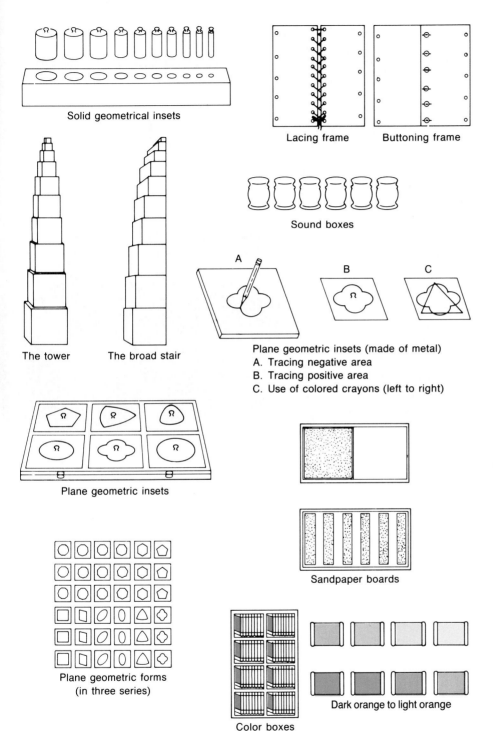

Solid geometrical insets

Lacing frame Buttoning frame

Sound boxes

The tower The broad stair

Plane geometric insets (made of metal)
A. Tracing negative area
B. Tracing positive area
C. Use of colored crayons (left to right)

Plane geometric insets

Sandpaper boards

Plane geometric forms
(in three series)

Color boxes

Dark orange to light orange

Figure 7.10 Some traditional Montessori materials.

Working Mothers and Preschool Children

In 1989, 51 percent of U.S. children between the ages of 3 and 5 (a total of 5.6 million children) had mothers who were employed. Of these, 3.9 million had mothers employed full-time and 1.7 million had mothers employed part-time. Another half million had unemployed mothers, and 4.25 million had mothers who were not in the labor force. Of the more than 11 million U.S. children ages 3–5 in 1989, about 6 million were in nursery schools and kindergartens. Only 14 percent of the 5-year-olds were not enrolled in preprimary schools.

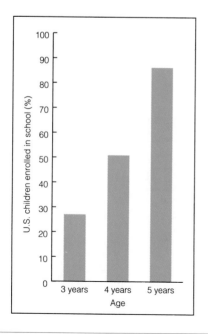

Figure 7.11 Preprimary school enrollment, 1989, for U.S. children ages 3–5. (Adapted from U.S. Bureau of the Census, 1991, p. 41.)

dard dialect. Others argue, however, that since most commerce outside school takes place in the majority language, those who only know other dialects of that language will be at the same disadvantage outside school as they are in it.

So the questions remain unanswered.

Speech and Language Problems

We assume that by the time children reach school age, their language skills will be sufficiently developed for them to understand and follow instructions, express interests and wants, tell stories, ask questions, carry on conversations—in short, communicate. Sadly, that is not always the case.

There are a number of different language and speech problems, each of which can vary tremendously in seriousness (see, for example, Schiefelbusch & McCormick, 1981). At one extreme are children who, because of severe mental retardation, neurological damage or disease, mental disorders such as autism or childhood schizophrenia, or deafness, are essentially nonverbal. Their communication might consist of a few gestures or signs.

There are others whose speech is largely incomprehensible, sometimes because of poor conceptual development, so that thought sequences seem illogical and speech becomes largely nonsensical, and sometimes because of speech production problems such as are reflected in poor articulation, voice control problems, and stuttering.

And there are those whose language development is less advanced than normal, perhaps because of mild mental retardation or a learning disability. One view is that these children don't learn different language forms or acquire language differently; their skills simply develop more slowly. Some of these children are of normal or above-normal intelligence and have no deficiencies other than their problems with language. However, because of our schools' predominantly verbal teaching and testing methods, many of these children are viewed as intellectually handicapped, and their language problems may be interpreted as the result of inferior ability rather than as the cause of poor achievement.

It is not clear what causes language problems in the absence of other handicaps. Although an impoverished and unstimulating home context may sometimes be implicated, in some cases children of apparently normal intelligence from advantaged backgrounds experience significant developmental delays or language impairments (Rice, 1989).

Speech problems and delayed language development are most common among children who have some other handicap—that is, retarded children and others suffering from motor, neurological, or mental disorders. They are relatively uncommon among the majority of children.

Language and Thought

The significance of language acquisition for children is obvious in many respects. Not only does language allow children to direct the behavior of others in accordance with their wishes (as when children ask for something) but also it provides a means for acquiring information that would otherwise be inaccessible (as when children ask questions, listen to stories, or watch television). In addition, language is closely involved in logical thought processes, although the exact relationship between thinking and language remains uncertain.

One extreme position, the Whorfian, maintains that language is necessary for thought (Whorf, 1941, 1956). In contrast, Piaget and Vygotsky argue that thought often precedes language. Piaget points out, for example, that the development of certain logical concepts often precedes the learning of words and phrases corresponding to those concepts. Words such as *bigger, smaller, farther*, and so on do not appear to be understood until the concepts they represent are themselves understood.

Both Vygotsky and Piaget argue that language and thought first develop independently. Thus there is considerable evidence of what we consider to be thought among preverbal children and nonhuman animals. But after the age of 2, language and thought become more closely related. After that age, thought becomes increasingly verbal, and language acquires the capacity to control behavior.

The Vygotsky view, described in Chapter 2, holds that speech has three separate forms, each with different

TABLE 7.6

The Role of Language: Vygotsky's Theory

Stage	Age (years)	Function
Social (external)	to 3	Controls the behavior of others; expresses simple thoughts and emotions
Egocentric	3–7	Bridge between external and inner speech; serves to control own behavior, but spoken out loud
Inner	7+	Self-talk; makes possible the direction of our thinking and our behavior; involved in all higher mental functioning

functions. *Social speech* is directed toward others to control their behavior or to express simple thoughts and emotions. *Egocentric speech* (common between 3 and 7) is a form of self-talk spoken out loud that serves to control the child's own behavior. And *inner speech* is inner self-talk that provides a means for directing our thinking and our behavior. Language, says Vygotsky, allows us to participate fully in culture. It is the source of all our higher mental functioning (Confrey, 1991). (See Table 7.6.)

A Conclusion

There are two forms of the Whorfian hypothesis. The strongest form argues that thought depends on language, and that it will not occur in its absence. The weaker version maintains that language *influences* thinking.

To accept the more extreme position would be to deny that those who are prelinguistically deaf and who have not learned an alternate communication system can think. We would also have to believe that our prelinguistic infants cannot think, and that among those who have begun to develop language, thought is restricted to that for which the thinker has pertinent language symbols. And we would have to believe that cows cannot think.

We don't believe all these things (though not everyone knows that cows can think). So we accept that thought can occur in the absence of language. At the same time, however, research and common sense inform us that our sophisticated thought processes are inextricably bound with language—as are our belief systems, our values, our worldviews (Hunt & Agnoli, 1991). So convinced are we of this that attempts to bring about difficult social changes often begin with attempts to change language. Antiracist and antisexist movements are a case in point. In the first edition of this text, it was acceptable to use masculine pronouns as though all children, all psychologists, and, indeed, all significant people, were male. Speaking of one of 17th-century scientist, mathematician, inventor, philosopher, and writer Blaise Pascal's *Pensées*, for example, I wrote: "One of the paradoxes of human existence is that despite man's great intelligence it is impossible for him to know where he came from or where he is going" (Lefrançois, 1973, p. 351).

That this type of chauvinistic sexism is no longer acceptable in our language may eventually be reflected in its eradication from our thoughts and those of our children.

Communicating and Conversing

Language is more than a collection of sounds, combinations of which refer to objects and actions, and the expression of which conveys our meanings; and it is more than a means by which we think and express our thoughts. Language is the means by which we draw information from past generations, record our own small contributions, and pass them on to generations that will come later. It is the great binding force of all cultures.

But infants, newly learning language, are not concerned with its great cultural contributions. Their first concern is with communicating, and their first communications are simple assertions ("that dog," "see daddy," "my ball") or requests ("milk!" "more candy"). Their second concern is with conversation.

A conversation is an exchange typically involving two or more people, although some people do talk to themselves. It is generally verbal, although it can consist of a combination of gestures and verbalization, or it can consist entirely of gestures, as in the case of American Sign Language (ASL). Genuine conversational exchanges begin about the age of 2. Initially, they are highly telegraphic, as is the child's speech; there are not a great many variations possible when one's sentences are limited to a single word. A short excerpt from an intelligent conversation with one of my own children illustrates this:

Him: *Fish*

Me: *Fish?*

Him: *Fish!*

Me: *Fish? Fish swim.*

Him: *Fish! Fish! (The conversation becomes more complex.)*

Me: *There are fish in the lake. (An original thought, meant to stimulate creativity.)*

Him: *Fish (Pointing, this time, in the general direction of the lake—I think.)*

From this primitive, repetitive conversation, children progress to more complex expressions and begin to learn the importance of subtle cues involving intonation, accentuation of words, rhythm of sentences, tone, and accompanying gestures. They learn, as well, about the implicit agreements that govern our conversations—the well-accepted rules that determine who shall speak and when, whether interruptions are permissible and how they should occur, what information must be included in our conversations if we are to be understood, and what we can assume is already known. In other words, they learn, as Krauss and Glucksberg (1977) put it, the rudiments of *social* as opposed to *nonsocial* or egocentric speech—they learn pragmatics.

Thus, more or less, does the infant progress from a sound to a word, from one word to two, from an expression to a conversation, from a conversation to a book. . . .

Main Points

1. There is a gradual slowing of sheer physical growth after infancy. In addition, different parts of the body grow at different rates (the head grows more slowly, for example) so that a typical 6-year-old looks more like an adult (and less like an infant) than a 2-year-old does.

2. Among significant motor achievements of infancy are learning how to walk and to coordinate other motor activities, including those involved in copying and tracing geometric designs—a task that involves perceptual, cognitive, and fine-motor skills. At birth, motor functioning may be assessed with scales such as the APGAR; later assessments use scales such as the Denver Developmental Screening Test.

3. Preschoolers' memories result largely from *incidental* mnemonics (paying attention, repeated exposure) rather than from the deliberate use of strategies (such as organizing or rehearsing). However, older preschoolers may deliberately use strategies when instructed to remember something, although these are sometimes inappropriate.

4. Piaget's preoperational period has two substages. Preconceptual thinking (2–4) is marked by errors of classification (*preconcepts*, where similar objects are reacted to as though they were *identical*), by transductive reasoning (conclusions based on superficial particulars), and by syncretic reasoning (objects are grouped on the basis of personal and changing criteria). Intuitive thinking (4–7) is

characterized by egocentricity (difficulty adopting another's point of view), by errors of class inclusion (believing, for example, that a bouquet of 10 roses and 2 daffodils contains more roses than flowers), and by a marked reliance on perception.

5. Replications of many of Piaget's experiments have typically found a developmental sequence very similar to that which he described, although some of the capabilities he describes are sometimes acquired at ages younger than those he reported for his subjects. The neo-Piagetians present a somewhat more optimistic view of the preschool child, emphasizing that one of the major achievements of this period is the ability to relate one or more ideas or concepts.

6. As a result of their ability to relate concepts, preschoolers can classify and solve simple class-inclusion problems. In addition, they have a remarkable understanding of number that reflects both number abstraction skills (understanding of numerosity, based on universal counting principles) and numerical reasoning (understanding of some of the effects of transformations).

7. Another major achievement of the preschooler is the rapid development of language capabilities — capabilities that have their roots in the sensorimotor period.

8. Preschool education programs include nursery schools, day-care centers, and a variety of other facilities. Children who attend nursery schools are sometimes more confident, more outgoing, and more self-reliant than children who don't. In general, compensatory preschool programs (Head Start, for example) have measurably positive effects on cognitive and social development.

9. The Direct Instruction approach (Bereiter and Engelmann) stress the three r's and uses drill and repetition with reinforcement. Montessori's approach emphasizes sense training and makes use of specially designed materials. Kindergartens, which are now typically part of the regular school program, may use either of these approaches or any of a variety of others, although most are simply eclectic.

10. Some fear that emphasis on formal instruction at the preschool level hurries children unnecessarily and robs them of their childhood.

11. Language — the use of arbitrary sounds with established and accepted referents, either real or abstract, that can be arranged in sequence to convey meaning — appears to be unique to humans.

12. The child goes from one-word sentences (holophrases) to two-word sentences (duos) and then to multiple-word sentences (rather than simply to three-word sentences). Multiple-word sentences appear by age 2–2½ and make extensive use of grammatical morphemes such as *ing* and *ed* to convey meaning. More complex sentences and adult-like grammatical structures are typically present by age 4.

13. Experience clearly affects language learning. The mother (and other caregivers) plays an important role as language teacher, her speech patterns being strongly influenced, sometimes in subtle ways, by the presence of an infant. *Motherese* is characterized by shorter sentences, more repetition, simpler and more concrete concepts, and exaggerated intonation. In a sense, it is *fine-tuned* to a level approximately six months in advance of the child's current language development.

14. Imitation and reinforcement are not completely adequate explanations for the observation that the earliest speech sounds of all infants are very similar and for the fact that infants make few directly imitative mistakes as they learn language. Chomsky describes the role of biology in language learning in terms of a metaphor of a *language acquisition device (LAD)*. This metaphor suggests that children learn language as if they were neurologically predisposed to do so. The metaphor is useful in explaining the ease and rapidity with which children learn overwhelmingly complex grammars.

15. Learning two languages is not a particularly difficult task for children who are exposed to both languages from infancy. Learning a second language later is often much more difficult and may sometimes be a *subtractive* experience (that is, learning the second language has a negative influence on the first; sometimes this is found where minority language speakers are schooled exclusively in a majority language), or an *additive* experience (that is, learning the second language has positive effects on the first; often this is the case where a minority language is learned as a second language in a school immersion setting).

16. The *standard* language (majority dialect) is the language form that is viewed as grammatically correct and acceptable, and against which other forms of the language (*nonstandard*) are judged. Children who speak nonstandard dialects are often at a disadvantage in school—not so much because their language is less sophisticated but because it is different.

17. The language sophistication of most school-age children is sufficient for them to ask and answer questions, tell stories, follow instructions, engage in conversations, and so on. However, some children experience language and speech problems ranging from complete absence of speech and comprehension to minor articulation and voice problems. These problems are often related to mental retardation, neurological damage or disease, mental disorders such as autism, or deafness.

18. Vygotsky describes three stages in the development of speech: *social* (*external*) speech, which is used to control others and to express simple thoughts (to age 3); *egocentric* speech, which is used to control one's own behavior but is spoken out loud (3–7); and *inner* speech, which involves silent self-verbalizations to direct one's own thought and behavior (7 through adulthood).

19. Evidence suggests that language sophistication can contribute significantly to higher mental thought processes. The strong version of the Whorfian hypothesis maintains that language precedes and is necessary for thought. A weaker version is that language *influences* thought. Piaget notes evidence of thought prior to language (and in nonhuman animals). Vygotsky suggests that language and thought initially develop independently but become more closely linked after the age of 2.

Further Readings

The following are good sources of information about cognitive developmental research. They are highly representative of the neo-Piagetians:

Flavell, J H. (1985). *Cognitive development* (2nd ed.). Englewood Cliffs, NJ: Prentice-Hall.

Shulman, V. L., Restaino-Baumann, L. C. R., & Butler, L. (Eds.). (1985). *The future of Piagetian theory: The neo-Piagetians*. New York: Plenum.

A clear and readable summary of Piaget's theory is provided by:

Wadsworth, B. J. (1989). *Piaget's theory of cognitive and affective development* (4th ed.). New York: Longman.

Language development is described in more detail in:

Carroll, D. W. (1986). *Psychology of language* (2nd ed.). Pacific Grove, CA: Brooks/Cole.

Wood, B. S. (1981). *Children and communication: Verbal and nonverbal language development* (2nd ed.). Englewood Cliffs, NJ: Prentice-Hall.

A highly readable paper that summarizes and analyzes research on ape-language studies and that also provides a useful account of current knowledge and beliefs about human language learning is:

Terrace, H. S. (1985). "In the beginning was the 'Name.'" *American Psychologist 40*, 1011–1028.

The Greenberg and Tobach book is a fascinating collection of papers dealing with language and thinking in both animals and humans:

Greenberg, G., & Tobach, E. (1987). *Cognition, language and consciousness: Integrative levels*. Hillsdale, NJ: Erlbaum.

The book by Cummins and Swain provides an account of bilingual education programs and their effects:

Cummins, J., & Swain, M. (1986). *Bilingualism in education: Aspects of theory, research and practice*. London: Taylor & Fry.

CHAPTER 8

Social Development: Early Childhood

Sweet childish days, that were as long
As twenty days are now.

William Wordsworth, *To a Butterfly*

Most of us are victims of a curious phenomenon called *infant amnesia*: We remember virtually nothing about our infancies. No one knows for certain why we experience infant amnesia. It isn't simply because our infancies are so far behind us, because a 50-year-old remembers things that happened 30 years earlier but a 15-year-old remembers little of what happened only 13 years before. One theory is that parts of the infant's brain associated with memory are insufficiently mature to permit long-term remembering; another is that the infant's memory strategies are too primitive to allow the organization and associations required.

Our memories of early childhood are usually not much better than those of our infancies. What we retain are often global sorts of impressions, vague feelings, jumbles of emotions and events.

Time robs even our adult memories of crispness and clarity.

Yet most of us agree, when we analyze our childhood recollections, that the days of our early childhood were unbelievably long. We remember how it was possible to do a million things every day and still have time left over, how vacations stretched forever. But the days were never too long. There was so much playing to do that even days 20 times longer than they are now could never be too long.

Were the days of childhood long because they were filled with play? Are our adult days so desperately short because we have forgotten how to play?

This Chapter

Play is one of the topics of this chapter on social development in early childhood (ages 2–7). Play is important to the child's social, physical, and intellectual development; it can also be fun.

We also look at Erikson's description of the social competencies of early childhood, and at Bandura's account of the role of imitation (observational learning) in the process of socialization. We discuss the development and the implications of gender roles, which, even in the preschool period, are enormously significant. We examine the role of the family in the early socialization of the child, focusing on current issues such as separation and divorce, single-parent families, and remarriage. And we evaluate alternate forms of child care, paying attention to the general effects of day care and to the characteristics of high-quality care.

Socializing Emotions

Preschoolers do not have as fine a control as we do over the emotions they feel—or over their expression. They control their emotions more through behavior than through cognition; and they are more easily moved to tears and to laughter. Put another way, their emotions are not completely socialized.

The socialization of emotions involves at least three things: learning to interpret emotions, achieving some control over them, and learning when, where, and how displaying them is appropriate and expected.

Interpreting Emotions

One of the important developments in infancy is the gradual discovery by children that they are *selves*—that they are separate and individual, and that they are capable of feelings (Kopp & Brownell, 1991). Along with the recognition of the self as separate comes the realization that others, too, are separate and permanent and also capable of feelings.

Initially, the infant does not know how to interpret the feelings of others. Facial expressions of joy or sadness, for example, are meaningless for the 1-month-old infant. But sometime between the ages of 3 and 6 months, there appears a growing recognition not only that others are capable of emotional reactions, but that these can be inferred from expressions and from behavior (Oster, Daily, & Goldenthal, 1989). By the age of 9 months to 1 year, infants in ambiguous situations actively search other people's faces as though looking for a clue that might guide their own behavior. When they see others crying, they are likely to feel sad—perhaps even to cry. And if others laugh and are happy, they, too, are more likely to be joyful (Termine & Izard, 1988).

During the preschool years, children's ability to make inferences about other people's emotions, and to interpret their own emotions, appears to be relatively imprecise. When Brown, Covell, and Abramovitch (1991) asked preschoolers how they would feel following a story event associated with happiness, sadness, or anger, they typically responded in terms of an intense emotion. And when, later in the story, an event occurred that would lead to a lessening of the emotion, preschoolers often thought they would feel a *different* emotion. If they had been sad earlier, now they would be happy. Strikingly, it seldom occurred to them that they might be *more* or *less* sad or happy. In contrast, older children in the same study often thought they would feel a different degree of the same emotion.

If specifically asked to describe what they think someone else is feeling, preschoolers might infer that someone feels "good" or "bad" because he or she is crying or laughing. They don't yet look for underlying causes upon which to base inferences. Not until later childhood, or even adolescence, do children spontaneously analyze others' emotions, trying to sort them out and understand their causes (Hughes, Tingle, & Sawin, 1981).

Furthermore, early in the preschool period, children cannot readily tell the difference between emotions that are real and those that are a pretense. Thus, if someone falls but jumps up and "laughs it off" in embarrassment, the 2-year-old is likely to conclude that the person is happy. In contrast, in the same situation, the 5-year-old is likely to interpret the event more accurately, realizing that the person who has fallen is, in fact, pretending. Harris and Gross (1988) speculate that children probably discover that some expressions of emotion are false when they begin to realize that they are themselves able to mislead others about their own emotions. This realization usually appears sometime between the ages of 4 and 6.

Regulating Emotions

We saw in Chapter 6 that even very young infants are capable of simple behaviors whose effect is to control the emotions they feel. For example, a frightened infant might close his eyes, suck his thumb, or snuggle his face in his mother's lap—an example of what Gianino and Tronick (1988) call *self-directed* regulatory behaviors. Alternatively, an infant might push away an object that is frightening her—an example of *other-directed* regulatory behaviors.

Preschoolers, with their ever-expanding mobility and rapidly developing cognitive and social skills, become increasingly adept at avoiding situations that lead to negative emotions, and at seeking out and maintaining those associated with good feelings. But, a little like infants, their control of emotions is *situational* and *behavioral* rather than cognitive. When they hear the ice-cream truck's bell, they run to get mother—or money; and when the frightening part of the story comes, they close their eyes and cover their ears. In the Brown, Covell, and Abramovitch (1991) investigation in which children were questioned following emotion-related events in stories, the younger children saw emotions as being situation specific. Hence, to change a feeling, change the situation. A child who is sad over losing a favorite toy will nevertheless be happy when she goes to bed. Why? "Because I won't have to look for it."

In contrast, the older child's control of emotions is more cognitive. One way of not feeling sad about a lost toy, the older child insists, is not to think about it—or to think a happy thought. Most of us are more like older than younger children.

Emotional Expression

As noted previously, infants are easily moved to tears—or to laughter. It doesn't shame them to cry in front of strangers; nor does it embarrass them to laugh and be foolish. But preschoolers are a little more restrained; they have begun to learn what researchers call *display rules*.

One aspect of display rules has to do with learning when and how it is appropriate to display certain emotions; another deals with understanding the emotional expressions (emotional displays) of others. Part of display rule learning involves discovering that expressed emotion does not always correspond with underlying emotion. Even young children are able to smile when they lie, or pretend it doesn't hurt when it would be embarrassing to cry.

It is not clear how preschoolers learn simple display rules such as, for example, the rule stating that if you are disappointed with a gift, you should not cry in front of the giver. When Cole (1986) filmed 3- to 4-year-old girls opening a disappointing gift either alone or in front of the giver, she found highly noticeable differences between the facial displays in the two situations. Although the girls' disappointment was evident when they opened the gift alone, most of them covered their feelings with smiles when the giver was present. What is interesting, however, is that these girls were unaware of their deception. Apparently, preschoolers learn to control their emotional expression before they realize the effects of their behavior on others.

Lewis, Sullivan, and Vasen (1987) report that although older preschoolers attempt to control their emotional displays, they are successful with only a limited number of emotions. Even we adults are not always able to hide our feelings. If someone gives us a rose when we fully expected a whole garden, we might find it very difficult to smile — even though our socialization is far more advanced than that of children.

Theories of Social Development

Socialization is the process by which children learn behaviors appropriate for people of their sex and age. It is the means by which they acquire the traditions, beliefs, values, and customs of their people; the means by which they learn the rules of membership in a group — rules like how and when to display emotion.

Socialization is clearly a culture-bound process, defined and determined by context. For example, North American audiences clap their hands, cheer, and whistle when they are pleased; European audiences whistle when they are displeased. Thus what is learned might vary a great deal depending on the context — a fact that makes our average child even more of a myth. But the processes by which socialization occurs are highly similar in different cultural contexts.

Erikson's Psychosocial Stages

As we saw in Chapter 2, an important theory of social development is Erik Erikson's. It describes the child's development in terms of a series of stages, each characterized by conflicting tendencies, and each requiring the attainment of some new competence. The theory's emphasis is clearly on *social* development (hence the label *psychosocial* development).

The first three of Erikson's psychosocial stages span the years from birth to around the end of the preschool period. To review briefly, the first, *trust versus mistrust*, lasts through most of infancy. The task here is to develop sufficient trust in the world to be able to go out and explore. Throughout this period, the most important influence in the infant's life is clearly the principal caregiver(s) — often, though by no means always, the mother.

The second stage, *autonomy versus shame and doubt*, spans the first year or so of the preschool period. At this time, children begin to discover that they are authors of their own actions — a discovery that is closely linked with the development of intentionality.

The third stage, *initiative versus guilt*, spans the remaining preschool years. The new sense of competence required of the child involves a sense of initiative — a sense of personal agency. But there still lingers a desire to retain the comfort and security that come from allowing other people — especially parents — to maintain responsibility. (See Table 8.1.)

According to Erikson's theory, then, much of "growing up" during the preschool period involves developing a sense of an autonomous self — a self that is capable of forming intentions and of behaving in effective ways. This task is greatly facilitated by the infant's physical exploration of the environment, as well as by mushrooming language skills that make it possible to explore in other ways — as, for example, when the 4-year-old bombards caregivers with questions. The development of social competence through the preschool period also requires achieving progressive independence from parents. The overprotective parent

TABLE 8.1

Erikson's Psychosocial Stages of Preschool Development

Stage	Approximate Age	Principal Developmental Tasks
Autonomy vs. shame and doubt	18 months to 2–3 years	Developing a sense of control and mastery over actions
		Learning that one is autonomous, that intentions can be realized
		Overcoming the urge to return to the comfort of trusting parents, and especially the mother, to do all important things
Initiative vs. guilt	2–3 to 6 years	Developing a sense of self, largely through identifying with parents
		Developing a greater sense of responsibility for own actions
		Achieving progressive independence from parents

who does not easily permit independence may make the child's progression through Erikson's stages more difficult. (See Chapter 2 for more details.)

Social Imitation

Erikson (1968) believed that one of the important mechanisms by which preschool children become socialized is *imitation*—especially in the first two or three years of life. Later, *identification* (a process whereby children do not merely imitate models, but adopt their values and beliefs, in a sense, becoming *like* them) becomes more important.

As we saw in Chapter 2, an important theory of social learning based on imitation is advanced by Albert Bandura. To summarize briefly: Bandura's theory stems from a behavioristic tradition. It attempts to explain the complex effects of modeling partly in terms of rewards and punishments. But it is also a cognitive theory: It gives a fundamentally important role to the *informative* function of models, and to the observers' understanding and interpretation of that information. It is what the observer imagines and expects that is important in learning through imitation.

Bandura describes three separate effects of imitation: (1) the modeling effect, evident in learning new behavior; (2) the inhibitory and disinhibitory effects, in which the rewards or punishment a model receives serve to bring about (*disinhibit*) some previously suppressed behavior, or, alternately, to *inhibit* current be-

havior; and (3) the eliciting effect, where the model's behavior elicits a related behavior in the observer.

Imitation-based theories of social learning are especially useful for explaining how children in nontechnological societies learn how to do things such as set snares and traps, or wield brooms and corn-grinding stones. But most of us no longer need to learn how to operate a corn-grinding stone or lay out a trap. So what do we learn from social imitation?

Cooperation and Competition. Among other things, perhaps we learn important social tendencies such as cooperation and competition. In fact, considerable research supports the belief that children are *socialized* to be cooperative or competitive by their immediate social environment (Madsen, 1971). Children from different ethnic groups can differ remarkably in terms of cooperation and competition.

Studies of cooperation and competition often use the four-person *cooperation board* (Madsen, 1971). Children sit at each of the four corners of an 18-inch square covered with a piece of paper that may be marked with target circles as shown in Interactive Figure 8.1. Near the center of the paper is a heavy Plexiglas cone that holds a pen, which is moved over the paper by means of four strings that pass through eyelets at each of the four corners of the board. As it moves, the pen traces a line on the paper. In a typical experiment, children are asked to draw a line through each of the targets in numbered sequence, or they may be required to draw a line through *their* assigned circle (the one to the left or right of their particular corner). Note that this can

At a very early age, we begin to learn through imitation. We learn all sorts of things, like how to feed babies or speak a language. We also learn what sorts of behaviors are considered appropriate for our sex. But is it appropriate for a teddy bear to learn to drink milk?

only be accomplished if children *cooperate*. That is, no one child, by pulling his or her string alone, can cause the pen to pass over an assigned circle.

In a variation of this procedure, target circles might be drawn under the strings at each of the four corners. Now it is possible for a child to draw a line through a corner circle simply by pulling harder than anybody else — that is, by *competing* and winning. If one child is strong enough to win by competing, it is also possible for that child to prevent everybody else from drawing lines through their circles.

Madsen and Lancy (1981) used the cooperation board to look at competition and cooperation among two groups of Papua New Guinea children: the Im-

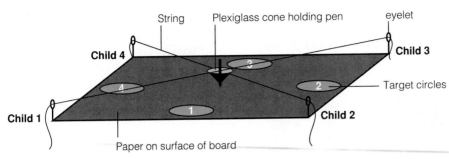

Child 4

Child 3

Child 1

Child 2

String   Plexiglass cone holding pen   eyelet

Target circles

Paper on surface of board

Interactive Figure 8.1   Cooperation board. (Adapted from Madsen & Lancy, 1981, p. 397.) Examine the layout of the board. Imagine that you are the child sitting in position 1; three other children occupy positions 2, 3, and 4. Each of you has grasped the string that runs from the cone at the center. You know that if you pull hard enough, the cone will slide toward you and the pen will draw a line right to your corner. The four of you are asked to draw a line through each of the target circles in order, from 1 to 4. What do you need to do to succeed? Suppose, now, that the target circles are moved so that each is placed directly under the string at the four corners of the board. To win this game, you have to pull the pen so that it traces a line through *your* circle. But there doesn't have to be just one winner; all four can win. Suppose, further, that you know you are the strongest one of the four, and that if you pull hard enough, *no one else can win.* How do you think you would have acted as a child?

bonggu, a highly intact tribal group whose traditional way of life is based on cooperation; and the Kila-Kila, a more heterogeneous group, heavily influenced by rapid modernization and living in an urbanized setting characterized by violence and crime.

First, children were instructed simply to draw a line through the numbered circles, in order, and were rewarded *as a group* for being successful (each child was given a coin). After three 1-minute trials under this group-reward condition, subjects were asked to write their names next to one of the circles (either to their right or left), and were told they would receive a coin each time the line passed through *their* circle. Now, in order to be successful, subjects must cooperate. If they don't, the most competitive and aggressive subject will simply succeed in pulling the pencil over to a corner. Subjects were then given three additional 1-minute trials.

The results of the study are striking. There were no differences between the Imbonggu and the Kila-Kila on the first three trials. Each of the groups improved on every trial, and by the third trial, each succeeded in crossing an average of slightly more than 12 circles. But the results on the fourth, fifth, and sixth trials,

where subjects were being rewarded individually rather than as a group, are striking. Whereas the Imbonggu continued to improve on each of the trials—a clear sign that they continued to cooperate—the performance of the Kila-Kila foursomes deteriorated completely. In fact, two thirds of the Kila Kila groups did not cross a single circle on the fourth trial; in contrast, the Imbonggu group that cooperated the least still managed to cross six circles (see Figure 8.2).

Undoubtedly, competitive and cooperative tendencies are markedly different between these tribal groups. Madsen and Lancy (1981) attribute this difference to their "primary group" affiliations—that is, to the cultural groups in which the children have been socialized. Similar research has found the same sorts of patterns among various other groups where the cultures are different in terms of cooperation and competition. Thus rural Mexican children have been found to be more cooperative and less competitive than urban children—as have *kibbutz* Israeli children compared with urban Israeli children, Blackfoot Indians compared with urban Caucasians in Canada, urban and rural Colombians, urban and rural Maoris in New Zealand, and various other groups (Madsen & Lancy, 1981).

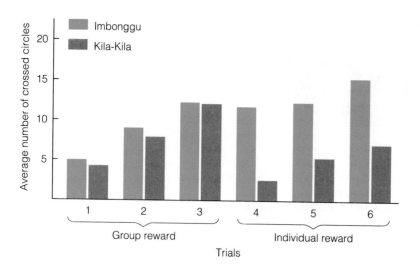

Figure 8.2 Differences in cooperation and competition between Imbonggu and Kila-Kila children. (Adapted from Madsen & Lancy, 1981, p. 399.)

Observational Learning in Complex Societies. It seems reasonable to suppose that observational learning—social imitation—is involved in the acquisition of important cultural values and tendencies (reflected, for example, in competition and cooperation) even in diverse and heterogeneous societies like ours. Most of the Imbonggu are cooperative because their primary groups—their immediate families and friends—are mostly cooperative. And most of the Kila-Kila belong to more competitive primary groups. But we are not so homogeneous. Some of us are gentle and cooperative, and some fiercely competitive. And others, of course, are probably both, depending on the situation.

Still, we too are socialized. Observational learning is also prevalent in our culture. But our models are perhaps not as simple, not as obvious, as they might be in a more homogeneous society. A model need not be a real person whose behavior is copied by another. Anything that serves as a pattern for behavior may be considered a model: literature, movies, television programs, verbal and written instructions, religious beliefs, folk heroes. Frequently, especially in the industrialized world, models are **symbolic** rather than living people.

One of the most powerful of these symbolic models may well be your television set, a piece of equipment whose influence we have had considerable difficulty in clarifying (we look at this topic in detail in Chapter 10).

Another very powerful source of social influence are the young child's playmates, for in play, there is both competition and cooperation.

Play

Play is activity that has no long-range goal—although it might have some immediate objectives (to hop from here to there, to make a sand hill, to fly a kite). Play is what children, and grown-ups, do for the fun of it. But that play has no ultimate purpose does not mean it is unimportant and useless. "Play," says Weininger (1990), "has to do with exploration, curiosity, sensory-motor activity, social activity, verbal imitation" (p. 15). Play is centrally involved in the child's social, physical, and intellectual development (Varga, 1991).

Functions of Play

Ethologists argue that practice play among animals is useful in developing and exercising physical skills that might be important in hunting prey or escaping predators (Aldis, 1975). In addition, play might also serve to establish social position and to teach acceptable behaviors such as in the mock-fighting, rough-and-tumble play of lion cubs or chimpanzees.

Some of the functions of play among children are, in some respects, not very different from those among animals. Certain kinds of **practice** (or **sensorimotor**) play are useful in developing and exercising physical skills, and might also contribute to social adaptation. Other forms of **pretend** (or **imaginative**) play might have quite different functions. Imagining involves important cognitive abilities related to symbolizing, imitating, anticipating, and problem solving. Not surpris-

TABLE 8.2

Types of Play

Play Type	Example
Practice	
Solitary	Bouncing a ball, up, down, up, down . . .
Social	Playing baseball
Pretend	
Solitary	Giving a doll pretend tea
Social	Dramatizing monsters in a group

ingly, research reports positive correlations between play and level of cognitive development (Trawick-Smith, 1989). Erikson believed that play is one of the means by which children learn to master reality (Hrncir, 1989). Similarly, Johnson and Yawkey (1988) argue that one of the most important functions of play is to help the child relate and understand different events. Both practice and pretend play can be solitary (a single player) or social (at least two players). (See Table 8.2.)

Note that these simple categories of play are not mutually exclusive. A single "game" or play session might involve elements of practice and pretend games, and might be solitary in some respects and social in others. And, as we shall see, there are different types of social play.

And quite apart from whatever larger purpose play might serve, much of it is simply fun. Why else play?

Practice Play

Practice play is mainly physical activity. Practice play is evident among the young of many animals (for example, a kitten chasing a ball; Vandenberg, 1987).

Practice play involves the manipulation of objects or the performance of activities simply for the sensations involved. It is the only type of play of which infants are capable during the early stages of development. Practice may consist of motor activities such as creeping, crawling, walking, running, skipping, hopping, waving a hand or a foot or any other part of the anatomy that can be waved. It also includes manipu-

lating objects such as balls, blocks, or bolognas. It is evident in countless solitary games of young children, such as moving the hand along the steep precipice of the table edge and roaring "*rrrrrr*" deep in the throat, in the manner of a well-tuned motorcycle; running around a room with arms spread wide, sputtering like a badly tuned airplane, "*abrabrabrabrabr*"; or jumping up and down on the couch and repeating rhythmically "*upupupupupupup*." But these last activities are not simply practice play; they are also pretend play.

Pretend Play

Pretend play involves imagining that the player, other persons, activities, or objects are something other than they really are.

Fantasy Versus Reality. Little children are sometimes uncertain about the difference between reality and fantasy. Three-year-old Mollie wants to play a pretend game with the other nursery school children, but she knows some *pretend* bad thing is going to happen. The child is scared. "What if the bad thing doesn't know it's pretend?" she asks (Paley, 1986, p. 45).

"Go to sleep, Mollie," Libby orders. "There might be something dangerous. You won't like it."

"I know it," Mollie says. "But I got a bunk bed at home and I sleep there."

"Bunk beds are too scary," Amelia says.

"Why are they?" Mollie looks worried.

"It's a monster, Mollie. Hide!" (Paley, 1986, p. 45).

But Mollie protests that there are no monsters in her house today. Still, she is unwilling to take any chances:

"I'm going to be a statue," Mollie whispers. "So he won't see me." (p. 45).

Now Frederick comes roaring in on all fours. "I'm a lion. I'm roaring," he says.

"Is he scaring you, Mollie?"

"No."

"Is anyone scaring you?"

"The bunk bed," she answers solemnly (p. 45).

Mollie, like many other 3-year-olds, can create her own ghosts and monsters; and she has developed her own ways of dealing with them. If they become too threatening, she can become a statue so they won't see her, or she can hide by the teacher—or she can, ultimately, resort to her knowledge that the monsters are pretend monsters.

But when others create monsters, Mollie can never be quite certain that they are truly *pretend pretend*. Perhaps, just perhaps, one of them might be *real pretend*.

We, of course, do not suffer from the same limitations as does Mollie (nor do most of us enjoy quite as boundless an imagination). We have somehow learned to tell the difference between fantasy and reality; we can dismiss our monsters if they frighten us. Can't we?

DiLalla and Watson (1988) had children play monster and superhero pretend games with an experimenter. They found that at the youngest ages (3 and 4 years in this study), subjects did not readily differentiate between fantasy and reality. If, while playing, they were brought back to *reality* by some interruption, they could not easily return to the fantasy after the interruption. However, older subjects (5- and 6-year-olds) could go in and out of a fantasy character, invent new characters, or transform old ones at will. When younger subjects were asked about the meaning of *pretend*, they could not answer, but typically simply ignored the question. In contrast, older subjects were able to discuss the meanings of *real* and *pretend*.

Types of Pretend Play. The child's pretend play includes a variety of activities. There is play in which children imagine that they are someone or something else: Boys are often superheroes such as Superman (or superantiheroes such as dragons or monsters); girls are often mothers or nurses (Paley, 1984). There are games in which children imagine that the activities they undertake are something other than what they really are or that the objects with which they play are something different.

One type of imaginative play becomes increasingly prevalent as the preschooler ages: daydreaming. Unlike the types of imaginative play in which the child actively engages in fantasy, daydreaming simply involves the imagining without the activity. Greenacre (1959) reports that daydreaming becomes more prevalent when children reach school age. Prior to that time, their activity-oriented behavior does not lend itself to unlimited daydreaming.

Another type of imaginative play involves the imaginary playmate — constant companion and friend to approximately half of all preschool children (Pines, 1978). These imaginary friends, complete with names and relatively stable personality characteristics, are spoken to, played with, loved, and hated by their creators. They are given names, forms, and places, and the young preschooler will seldom admit their imaginary nature.

The Implications of Imagination. In the play behavior of young children we find the first manifestations of imagination — manifestations that occur largely in the fantastic, the unreal. Fantasy has not always been encouraged by students of childhood or by grandparents. In a less enlightened age, daydreaming might have been feared as one possible manifestation of lack of contact with reality. Imaginary playmates would have been feared even more and seldom invited to dinner or even to tea. Wertham (1954) included fairy tales among those aspects of fantasy that would surely be harmful to young children, and Hurlock (1964) cautioned against the possibly harmful effects of daydreaming, claiming that children who daydream too much might suffer physically from inactivity and also psychologically from an eventual overreliance on daydreams.

Research and theory should do a great deal to relieve any leftover fears of imagining and pretending that we might have. Contemporary theorists believe that pretend play has a very constructive role in the development of cognitive and social skills. Piaget (1951), for example, views symbolic (pretend) play as one of the means by which the child progresses to more advanced forms of thought. Pretend play, along with deferred imitation and language, is one of the surest signs of mental representation.

Pretend play, says Leslie (1988), contributes to one of the cognitive capacities that sets us apart from other species: It eventually enables us to think about ourselves and about others as thinkers — as organisms capable of having different states of mind. When mother puts a banana to her ear and says "Hello," 4-year-old Nancy recognizes at once that the banana is a pretend telephone. But there is no confusion here between reality and fantasy; she knows very clearly that this is a banana. What is also clear to Nancy, however, is that mother can have different states of mind — and that she can, too. Nancy has begun to develop a "theory of mind," says Leslie. And one important aspect of this theory is the recognition of others and of self as thinkers capable of deliberately selecting and manipulating ideas — even pretend ideas. Here, in the preschool period, is the dawning of what psychologists label *metacognition* — knowing about knowing.

If pretending, daydreaming, and creating imaginary playmates served as some sort of compensation

TABLE 8.3

Classifications and Examples of Children's Social Play

Classification	Possible Activity
Primitive social	"Peek-a-boo."
Solitary play	Child plays alone with blocks; other children in same room play independently with other toys.
Onlooker play	Child watches others play "tag" but does not join in.
Parallel play	Two children play with trucks in sandbox but do not interact. They play beside each other but not together.
Associative play	Two children play with dolls, talk with each other about their dolls, lend each other diapers and dishes, but play independently, sharing neither purpose nor rules.
Cooperative play	"Let's pretend. You be a monster and I'll be the guy with the magic sword and . . ."

INTERVIEW

▶ Subject   Male; age 7.
▶ Question   "How do you play this game?" (a miniature portable video game)

. . . .

66 *See here. You press this button. This one. And a little guy comes out. You have to jump over the barrels and go up here. This way, then up here. If the barrel hits you, your man is dead. You have to rescue the girl. Darn, he got me!* 99

for an unhappy or disturbed childhood, as Freud believed, then we might expect pretend play to be more common among unhappy, disturbed, and perhaps lonely children. In fact, however, imaginative play is more prevalent among children whose biological and psychological needs are reasonably well satisfied (Freyberg, 1973). In societies where children have to assume work responsibilities at very early ages, there is far less childhood play; the same is also often true of children who are economically and socially disadvantaged (Schwartzman, 1987).

Social Play

Social play is any type of play that involves interaction among two or more children. Either pretend or practice play can be social when it involves more than one child.

Skipping rope alone in the darkness of one's basement is a solitary practice activity; skipping rope out on the playground with others turning the rope—"pepper, pepper, salt and . . ."—is a cooperative or social activity. Similarly, creating elaborate and fantastic daydreams in the solitude of one's bedroom is solitary pretend play; playing *let's pretend*—"you be the veterinaman [*sic*] and I'll be the dog"—is social pretend play.

Early in this century, Parten (1932) observed the play behavior of groups of nursery school children and identified five manifestations of play describable in terms of the type and amount of peer interaction involved. Although these appear sequentially, they also overlap (see Table 8.3).

Solitary Play. In *solitary play*, the child takes little notice of others, preferring instead to play alone with toys or to engage in some solitary motor activity. Much of the child's play before the age of 2 is solitary, although there are examples of primitive forms of cooperative play sometimes even before the age of 6 months (Brenner & Mueller, 1982). *Peek-a-boo* games as well as a variety of games that include tickling, tossing, and related activities are good examples. Although these typically occur with parents or with older children rather than with peers, there are also examples of nonsolitary play among peers prior to the age of 2 (Ross, 1982). Such play typically involves what Brenner and Mueller refer to as *shared meaning* (rather than shared rules) and is illustrated in the "chase" games of toddlers or in the "touch me and I'll touch you" game.

Onlooker Play.

As the label implies, *onlooker play* consists of a child simply watching others play but not participating actively. Onlooker play occurs throughout childhood. Frequently, the onlooker may talk with the players, perhaps even giving them advice or asking questions.

Parallel Play.

In *parallel play*, children play side by side, often with similar toys, but do not interact, do not share the activities involved in the game, and do not use any mutually accepted rules. Parallel play is nevertheless social play of a primitive sort, because it involves two or more children who apparently prefer to play together even if they don't interact. Some research indicates that the presence of toys often detracts from social interaction and leads to parallel or perhaps solitary play, particularly among very young children (Vandell, Wilson, & Buchanan, 1980). Not surprisingly, children are more likely to interact with each other in the absence of toys.

Associative Play.

As children get older, they become more interested in interacting with peers in *associative play*. This type of play is characterized by interaction among children, even though they continue to play separately. In associative play, children sometimes share toys, but each child plays independently without mutually accepted goals or rules.

Cooperative Play.

Children engaged in *cooperative play* help one another in activities that require shared goals and perhaps even a division of roles. Although most research on preschoolers' play behavior indicates that associative and cooperative play are not common before the age of 4 or 5, there is sometimes evidence of cooperation in the play of much younger children. Rubin, Maioni, and Hornung (1976) report that preschoolers who have had considerable experience with similar-aged peers (in day-care facilities, for example) are more likely to play cooperatively whenever they can than are children reared in more solitary circumstances.

One example of cooperative play is found in "play-fighting," or rough-and-tumble play, especially of boys. Play-fighting takes up about 10 percent of free play time on playgrounds. It is more common among schoolchildren than preschoolers (Costabile et al., 1991).

Another example of cooperative social play is found in the dramas that children sometimes enact in their pretend play.

"You be the baby."

"I be the baby."

"I be the mother."

"You be the mother. I be the baby."

"If you're bad . . . if you wee-wee your diaper, well, you know . . ." (making an abrupt spanking gesture, but smiling broadly all the while).

Garvey (1977) found that the most common roles in dramatic play were mother–infant, mother–child, or mother–father. She found, too, that children often reveal their fears and worries, and their hopes and aspirations, in their dramatic play. Social play of this kind is more than just fun; it provides an important opportunity for acquiring and practicing behaviors involved in social interaction, for developing cooperative behaviors, for learning how to resolve conflict, and for fostering imagination and creativity.

Also, as Paley (1984) points out, in the roles that children adopt for their pretend dramas—monster or mother, baby or father, superhero or witch—they reveal much about the gender roles with which they are comfortable. (See Interactive Table 8.4 for information about *where* children play.)

Gender Roles in Early Childhood

In most cultures, including ours, there are, on average, marked differences between the ways in which males and females are expected to think, act, and feel. The range of behaviors that are considered appropriate for males and females—in other words, that are considered masculine or feminine—together with the attitudes and personality characteristics associated with each, define **gender roles**. The learning of sex-appropriate behavior is **gender-typing**.

In Chapter 6, we saw that gender-typing begins from the moment of birth, when the mere fact that the child is male or female *determines* much of what a parent's reactions to the infant will be—as is apparent when parents unabashedly describe their newborn sons

INTERACTIVE TABLE 8.4

Children's Favorite Play Places and Activities

▶ *Can you recall the five favorite play places (activities) of your childhood? Robin Moore (1986) asked 48 boys and 48 girls ages 9–12 to make maps or drawings of their favorite play places and then interviewed each child. He also accompanied 24 of them to their favorite play places and interviewed their parents. How do their favorite play places and activities compare with yours?*

Place	Frequency Cited (%)
Lawns	71
Playgrounds, play equipment, schoolyards	65
Own home	51
Local parks	40
Single trees	36
Through streets	34
Pavements	30
Other dwellings	29
Fences	28
Friends' homes	25
Footpaths	24
Swimming pools	19
Sports fields	18
Flowers, miscellaneous structures	17
Ponds and lakes	16
Shrubs	15
School, friends	13
Traffic, bridges	11
Self-portrait, topography, dirt and sand	10
Tree clusters, yards and gardens	9
Hills, asphalt and concrete	8
Car parks, climbing trees, woodland, abandoned buildings	6
Other	≤5

Source: From *Childhood's Domain: Play and Place in Child Development* by R. C. Moore, 1986, London: Croom Helm. Reprinted by permission of the publisher.

as strong, lusty, vigorous, and alert, and their newborn daughters as fine-featured, delicate, and pretty (Rubin, Provenzano, & Luria, 1974).

Sex Differences in Play

When only 3, boys will gladly pretend to be babies, mothers, fathers, or monsters. Most are as comfortable wearing the discarded apron and the nursery school teacher's high-heeled shoes as the fire fighter's hat or the cowboy boots. They play in the "doll corner" as easily as do the girls.

But when they are 5, Paley (1984) informs us, the atmosphere in the doll corner changes dramatically. Now when there are pretend games, the boys are monsters and superheroes; and in the pretend games of the girls, there are princesses and sisters. But these are not the only changes that come with age. In Paley's (1984) words:

> In the class described in this book, for example [a kindergarten class], you hop to get your milk if you are a boy and skip to the paper shelf if you are a girl. Boys clap out the rhythm of certain songs; girls sing louder. Boys draw furniture inside four-story haunted houses; girls put flowers in the doorways of cottages. Boys get tired of drawing pictures and begin to poke and shove; girls continue to draw. (p. xi)

Several relatively consistent findings have emerged from studies that have looked at sex differences in play behavior. To begin with, there is little evidence of any greater predisposition toward pretend play in either girls or boys (Singer, 1973). But there is repeated evidence of gender-typing with respect to the toys that boys and girls are given and the toys they choose. Rheingold and Cook (1975) looked at the rooms of 96 children and found, not surprisingly, that boys are given what we consider to be male-typed toys: trucks, airplanes, boats, soldiers, and guns. Girls are given dolls, plastic dishes, cooking utensils, and dollhouses.

Additional sex differences with respect to play behavior are that boys employ more physical space in their play, play outdoors more, and engage in more rough-and-tumble and noisy play; girls are more interested in "nurturant" play (helping, caring for). Boys tease, wrestle, push, run, and engage in gender-typed role-playing games, in which they are fire fighters,

Gender-typing in selection of toys and in play activities is often evident at a very early age—not only in the toys and activities children choose but also in those selected for them by parents.

builders, warriors. In contrast, girls often play "house," cooking, cleaning, looking after children, and helping each other with aprons, hats, and other items of clothing (Pitcher & Schultz, 1983).

These sex differences are less apparent among 2-year-olds, where there is a great deal of cross-sex play, than among 5-year-olds, where boys tend to play more often with other boys, and girls with girls. Pitcher and Schultz (1983) note that societies, and consequently parents, have traditionally attempted to maximize sex differences in the play (and other interests) of

young children—sometimes even punishing and ridiculing children whose games seem less appropriate for their sex.

Determinants of Gender Roles

Like most other aspects of human development, gender differences involve the interaction of biological and contextual forces. Contextual forces likely are influential at least partly through imitation and identification.

Boys learn to behave as "boys" and girls as "girls" at least partly through identifying with their parents and with other males and females.

Awareness of Gender Identity.

A more cognitive explanation is that gender-typing results from the child's understanding of the meaning of gender. Kohlberg (1966) describes three stages which reflect the child's increasing awareness of gender.

- *Stage 1. Basic gender identity* describes the initial stage where the infant recognizes simply that he is a boy or she is a girl.
- *Stage 2. Gender stability* refers to the realization that gender is permanent and unchangeable.
- *Stage 3. Gender constancy* reflects the child's eventual understanding that superficial changes (in ways of behaving or dressing, for example) are irrelevant to one's basic gender.

Kohlberg argues that once children become aware of their gender identity and its meaning, they actively participate in organizing their behaviors as well as their environments to conform to sex-appropriate patterns. Having decided that she is female, a girl selects feminine toys and behaviors. And having decided that he is male, the boy leaves the doll corner, returning only to raid it with phasers and missiles, or to haunt it as a pretend monster. Not surprisingly, the most widely used indicators of gender-typing at the preschool level are based on selection of toys and activities. In the elementary school years, more abstract measures of self-perception are possible (Boldizar, 1991).

Genetic Influences.

Genetic influences are an important factor in determining some gender-role differences. Lynn (1974) presents the following argument: If a difference is genetically based, it would (1) be displayed at a very young age, before environmental forces could have influenced it; (2) be evident in a wide variety of cultures; (3) be seen among subhuman primates; and (4) be related to the effect of hormones on masculinity and femininity. All these criteria appear to be satisfied with respect to the greater aggressiveness of males. Males are more aggressive than females at an early age (Maccoby & Jacklin, 1980); differences are consistent in most cultures and also for nonhuman primates (Mitchell, Arling, & Moller, 1967); and the injection of male hormones into pregnant mothers increases the subsequent aggressiveness of female children who are in utero at the time (Money & Ehrhardt, 1968).

Other Influences.

We should not conclude, however, that the greater aggressiveness of males in this culture is inevitable given probable genetic differences related to aggression. The influence of cultural and family-based factors cannot be discounted. Parents treat manifestations of aggression in children differently according to their sex; they are more likely to punish it in girls and reward it in boys (Askew & Ross, 1988). In addition, daughters are less likely to be permitted the kinds of independent explorations that sons are. When mothers are asked at what ages they would allow their children to play alone outside, to cut with scissors, and so on, ages are almost always higher for girls than for boys.

Cultural models provided on television, in books, and throughout most of society tend to reinforce children's developing notions of behaviors, attitudes, and interests that are most clearly appropriate for their sex (Askew & Ross, 1988). Occupations requiring physical aggression and strength have traditionally been restricted to males, whereas those requiring nonaggressive, passive, nurturant behavior have been considered more appropriate for women. As Connell (1985) notes, almost all the soldiers, police officers, prison wardens, bureaucrats, and politicians who control the machinery of collective violence are men—as are most murderers, rapists, and muggers.

Are these sociocultural facts a result of innate biological differences? Or do sociocultural expectations simply exaggerate these differences? In other words, do basic, genetic sex differences cause societies to ascribe different roles to the sexes, or do these different roles cause the sex differences? Is this a chicken-and-egg problem?

The Contemporary Family

"From the beginning of life," writes Stratton (1988), "it is overwhelmingly the family that mediates cultural and social values and presents them to the child" (p. 5). Its importance can hardly be overstated.

The intact **nuclear family** was once North America's most prevalent family; only a few years ago, more than 85 percent of all children lived in families consisting of two parents and approximately half of one sibling, this latter phenomenon made possible solely through those statistical manipulations that revealed the average family size to be around 3.19—and dropping (U.S. Bureau of the Census, 1988). In contrast, a majority of the world's societies have traditionally been characterized by **extended families**—parents, immediate children, grandparents, uncles, aunts, cousins, and various other assorted relatives.

Our vision of the "typical" North American nuclear family—mother, father, and one or two children—has the father as breadwinner, although mother, too, might work. This view is a myth, argue Lamanna and Riedmann (1988). They point out that at present, fewer than 30 percent of all families conform to this stereotype. Of the remainder, a large and growing proportion are single-parent families. Almost 90 percent of one-parent families are headed by a mother (U.S. Bureau of the Census, 1990).

The increase in the proportion of one-parent families is due to several factors. Although the number of unmarried women having babies and keeping them has increased, and the number of widowed parents has also increased, neither of these facts accounts for many one-parent families. The single most important contributing cause is clearly a dramatic rise in divorce rates—a rise of more than 700 percent during this century (see the sections on divorce later in this chapter and Chapters 14 and 16).

Although the family can easily be described in terms of its composition (mother, father, children), it is not at all easily described as a unit of social influence. To begin with, the family is a dynamic, rather than a static, unit: dynamic in the sense that it is a system of changing relationships—an ecology that changes with the addition of new members (and sometimes the loss of old ones), with the aging and changing of its members, and in response to influences from its wider context.

Parenting in Early Childhood

In Chapter 6, we reviewed findings indicating that the most important features of caregiving for the infant are *attentiveness, physical contact, verbal stimulation, material stimulation, responsive care,* and *absence of restrictiveness.*

As infants age and as their verbal, motor, and intellectual abilities blossom, important dimensions of parenting begin to change. But parenting is no less important for children than for preschoolers.

Parenting Styles. Baumrind (1967) looked at the parenting styles associated with three groups of children: the first described as buoyant, friendly, self-controlled, and self-reliant; the second as discontented and withdrawn; and the third as lacking self-reliance and self-control.

There were some striking and consistent differences among parents. Parents of children in the first group were significantly more controlling, demanding, and loving than parents of either of the other groups. Parents of the discontented and withdrawn children were also controlling, but were detached rather than warm and loving. And parents of the children who lacked self-reliance (had low self-esteem) were warm but highly permissive.

On the basis of studies such as these, Baumrind identifies three styles of parenting, each of which is characterized by different types of parental control (Baumrind, 1989): permissive, authoritarian, and authoritative.

Permissive parenting is a nonpunitive, nondirective, and undemanding form of parental control. Permissive parents allow children to make their own decisions and to govern their own activities. They do not try to control through power that comes from authority, physical strength, status, or the ability to grant or withhold rewards but might, on occasion, try to appeal to the child's reason.

Authoritarian parenting is grounded on firm and usually clearly identified standards of conduct. These are often based on religious or political beliefs. The authoritarian parent values obedience above all and exercises whatever power is necessary to make the child conform. Children in authoritarian homes are given no responsibility for personal decisions and are not involved in rational discussion of the family's standards.

Authoritative parenting falls somewhere between permissive and authoritarian control. It uses firm control but allows for rational discussion of standards and expectations; it values obedience but tries to promote independence. Authoritative parents, in contrast with authoritarian parents, are those whose standards derive more from reason than from dogma. (See Interactive Table 8.5.)

Interestingly, the parenting styles of mothers and fathers within families tend to be more alike than different. Bentley and Fox (1991) compared the responses of 52 pairs of mothers and fathers of 1- to 4-year-olds with the Fox Parenting Inventory (Fox, 1990). The scale measures three areas of parenting: (1) *expectations* ("My

Some parents are severe, dogmatic, highly controlling (authoritarian). Others, like the father shown here, are more permissive. Some child-care experts suggest that neither of these parenting styles is as desirable as *authoritative* parenting—parenting that is based on reason and rules but that encourages independence.

child should use the toilet without help"), (2) *discipline* ("I yell at my child for whining"), and (3) *nurturance* ("I read to my child at bedtime"). Although mothers received higher nurturance scores than fathers, mothers and fathers did not differ on expectations or discipline.

Novice and Expert Parents.

Some parents are probably better at parenting than others. In Cooke's (1991) terms, some are *novices*, and some *experts*. How are the two different? Among other things, experts are better at sensing the child's needs and goals, especially in problem-solving situations; they have better general knowledge of child development and child rearing; they have consciously thought about their roles and their

goals; and they foster activity that provides their children with opportunities to be self-directive.

These characteristics of *expert* parents are most evident in *competent* children—that is, in children whose measured achievement compares favorably with that of other children. Other dimensions of effective parenting do not have outcomes as clearly measurable but may be even more important. For example, Dix (1991) suggests that parents' emotions can be used as an indication of the quality of parenting. Parenting is an emotional experience, says Dix, "because children are vital to parents' daily concerns and life goals. Emotions are barometers for relationships because they reflect parents' assessments of how well interactions are proceeding"

Baumrind's Parenting Styles

▶ *Study the characteristics and examples of each of the three styles described by Baumrind. Now try to determine which of these best describes how you were reared, and which describes how you will rear (are rearing/have reared/would rear) your own children. Do you suppose your parents' parenting styles reflect that of their parents? Do yours?*

Style	Characteristics	Examples
Permissive	Laissez-faire Nonpunitive Child responsible for own actions and decisions Autonomy more important than obedience Undemanding	"Okay, I mean sure. Whatever you want. You decide."
Authoritarian	Dogmatic Very controlling Obedience highly valued Self-control and autonomy limited Little recourse to reasoning	"You're going to darn well study for 40 minutes right now. Then you say your prayers and go right to bed. Or else."
Authoritative	Based on reason Permits independence but values obedience Imposes regulations but allows discussion	"Don't you think you should study for a while before you go to bed? We'd like you to get good grades. But you know we can't let you stay up that late. It isn't good for you."

(p. 19). Even competent parents report frustration and occasional anger with their children. But most parents report far more positive than negative emotions—except in dysfunctional families.

Do Parents Make a Measurable Difference?

Which parenting style is best? And will it be best under all circumstances? Or are parents all that important?

The Freudian model says, yes, parents are very important because children are extremely sensitive to the emotional experiences of their early lives, and especially to their relationships with their parents. And the behavioristic model also says yes, because children are highly responsive to the rewards and punishments of their environments.

But the research is not entirely clear. Although retrospective studies with delinquent and troubled adolescents and adults have generally found that their childhoods were marked by a variety of traumas, sometimes associated with "broken" homes, alcoholic or abusive parents, poverty, authoritarianism, rejection, and a variety of other factors, nonretrospective studies have not always corroborated these findings. When researchers attempted to predict which children would later be maladjusted and which would be happy and adjusted on the basis of considerable information concerning their home lives, they were unsuccessful two thirds of the time (Skolnick, 1978). Indeed, some very brilliant, well-adjusted, and successful individuals had childhood environments that might be generously described as poor. It seems that predicting the effects of child-rearing practices is far more difficult than explaining these effects after the fact. And what this indicates

Research has not established that any one child-rearing method is invariably better than all others. In general, parents who love and care for their children are most likely to do the right things. Baumrind advocates that parenting be warm and loving but also firm. In her terms, parents should be authoritative, not authoritarian.

most clearly is that our after-the-fact explanations might have been entirely wrong in the first place.

One of the most painstaking studies of parent–child influences was conducted in the early 1950s by Sears and his associates (Sears, Maccoby, & Levin, 1957). They interviewed 379 mothers of kindergarten children, rated each on more than 100 child-rearing practices, and looked at the relationships between these practices and the personalities of their children.

McClelland and associates (1978) later tracked down 78 subjects from the original Sears study; they were now 31 years of age. They interviewed these subjects in depth, and brought 47 of them into a clinical setting for a series of psychological tests. The conclusion: "Wide variations in the way parents reared their children didn't seem to matter much in the long run. Adult interests and beliefs were by and large not determined by the duration of breast-feeding, the age and severity of toilet-training, strictness about bedtimes, or indeed any of these things" (1978, p. 46).

Following extensive investigations of the relationships between behavior and characteristics of parents and the personalities of their children, Baumrind (1977), like McClelland, concludes that no specific child-rearing practices should be advocated over others (regarding breast-feeding and toilet training, for example). But some general characteristics of parents, reflected in their behaviors and attitudes toward their children, might have highly positive effects — and negative ones, too. Baumrind found, for example, that parents who were firm and directive were more likely to have children who would be responsible (as opposed to socially disruptive and intolerant of others) and active (as opposed to passive). But what she advocates is not *authoritarian* but *authoritative* parenting — parenting that is firm but reasonable, demanding but warm, nurturing, and loving. "The optimal parent–child relationship at any stage of development," says Baumrind (1989), "can be recognized by its balance between parents' acknowledgment of the child's immaturity — shown by providing structure, control, and regimen (demandingness) — and the parents' acknowledgment of the child's emergence as a confident, competent person — shown by providing stimulation, warmth, and respect for individuality (responsiveness)" (pp. 370–371).

Baumrind also argues against the permissiveness that was ushered in and justified by what is sometimes termed the *Spock era* of child rearing. She suggests that the advocacy of permissiveness is based on a number of false assumptions, especially that firm feeding habits, toilet training, spanking, and other forms of punishment are unquestionably bad and that unconditional love is good. She points out that punishment is effective and does not rupture attachment bonds between parents and children, providing it is reasonable punishment by a loving parent; that unconditional love is likely to lead to the development of selfish and "obnoxious" children; and that no good research evidence supports a belief that toilet training or insistence on regular feeding habits is inadvisable.

In interpreting studies such as these, we should keep in mind that our measures of parenting styles and of parental characteristics are crude and inexact. So, too, are most of our measures of child happiness and competence. Science has difficulty understanding and quantifying the warmth that might exist between a loving parent and a child — or, indeed, even between an abusive parent and a child. In the end, the finding

that parenting styles make no difference might well reflect our failure or inability to measure the right things — or to measure them accurately.

Parents do make a difference, but our recommendations concerning the best parenting styles must be tentative. "At the most simple level," says Christopherson (1988), "if the children are basically happy, the parents are probably not doing too much that is wrong" (p. 133). At a more detailed level, he offers seven guidelines for child-rearing practices (pp. 133–136):

- Behavior and relationships with others depend on the extent to which the child's basic needs are met.

- Parents need to recognize each child as a unique individual.

- The faith, honesty, confidence, and affection between the parent and child affects the quality of the parent–child relationship.

- Parents should separate the worth of a child from the behavior.

- The child should be allowed as much freedom as possible to make mistakes and discoveries, but to do so with safety and respect for the rights of others and for the social convention.

- Parents should arrange the environment to encourage prosocial behavior.

- Parents should be ready to lend support directly or indirectly through physical or verbal guidance.

As McCartney and Jordan (1990) note, the conclusions of parenting research have not always been clear because researchers have tended to use simple models that were not adequate for the complexity of the interactions involved. If the conclusions are to be valid and useful, they argue, researchers must adopt ecological systems models such as that proposed by Bronfenbrenner (see Chapter 2). That is, they must look at parenting or child-care effects in light of characteristics of the child's face-to-face interactions (microsystem) as well as other interactions that impinge more indirectly on children (meso-, exo-, and macrosystems). Furthermore, they have to take into consideration the interconnectedness of these systems, and how children's individual characteristics modify, and are modified by, their ecologies.

The equations are more complex than we had thought; parts are still missing. And our new ecological systems models suggest that finding the missing parts will require considering the possibility that parenting styles that are excellent for certain children in given circumstances may be quite disastrous for other children—or under different circumstances.

Parent Training

How do parents learn to care for children? In many close-knit and allegedly *primitive* societies, the old ones show the young ones what must be done.

But it is not so simple in our more complex and more impersonal societies. Many parents have had little exposure to parenting and do not have ready access to the wisdom of the old ones. Who will teach them?

As we saw in the preceding section, child-care advice is sometimes implicit, or even explicit, in the results of developmental research. However, most parents do not have access to this research and might not derive much immediate practical advice from it if they did. Some of these parents will simply rely on their own intuition, common sense, and intelligence. But many others will turn to one or more of three major groups of commercial child-care advisors: (1) the medical profession, whose advice has historically gone far beyond the restoration and maintenance of physical health and has also included psychological health; (2) books, which are the most preferred source of child-care advice for most parents (Abram & Dowling, 1979); and (3) parent-training courses.

There are a handful of well-known and widely established parent-training courses, including Gordon's Parent Effectiveness Training (P.E.T.), Adler's Systematic Training for Effective Parenting (S.T.E.P.), and Berne's Transactional Analysis (TA) (Berne, 1964; Dinkmeyer & McKay, 1976; Gordon, 1975, 1976; Harris, 1973).

Parent-training courses require relatively lengthy training and practice sessions. They are almost invariably based on a recognition of the human rights of children, they take into consideration their needs and desires, and they tend to discourage the more punitive approaches to parental control. Accordingly, shouting, threatening, physical punishment, and anger-based behaviors are strongly discouraged; reasoning and encouragement are encouraged. The ultimate aim is to foster a warm, loving, and nurturant relationship between parent and child. The principal method by which each of the various techniques operates involves communication. Put another way, what most parent-education programs have in common is (1) they en-courage parents to be *authoritative* (firm, democratic, reasonable, respectful) rather than authoritarian (harsh, controlling, demanding, dogmatic, powerful) or permissive (laissez-faire, noncontrolling, weak), and (2) they teach specific techniques to help parents become authoritative.

Their major collective weaknesses include the fact that the solutions they provide are often too simplistic for the complexity of the problems with which parents must occasionally deal; they typically do not take into account important differences among children of different ages and sexes; and they sometimes mislead parents into thinking that all answers are to be found in a single method (Brooks, 1981).

Family Composition

Parenting styles are one feature of the family; there are others. The family, says Hoffman (1991), is a dynamic (changing) and interactive social unit. The experiences that siblings have in the same family can be very different depending not only on characteristics of the child, the parents, and other siblings, but also on factors such as birth order and family size.

Birth Order

Galton (1896) was among the first to note the effects of **birth order** when he observed that there was a preponderance of firstborn children among great British scientists. Since then, research has attributed many advantages to being the first born (or an only child). Among them are more rapid and more articulate language development, higher scores on measures of intellectual performance, higher scores on measures of achievement motivation, better academic performance, more curiosity, and a higher probability of going to college (see Ernst & Angst, 1983; Melican & Feldt, 1980; Page & Grandon, 1979). And, for what it's worth, the probability of a firstborn child going into space seems considerably higher than that of a later-born child (*Newsweek*, 1969).

There are a number of plausible explanations for the observed effects of birth order. Certainly, these effects are not due simply to being a firstborn, a middle, or a lastborn child, but to the fact that the interactions and relationships to which the child is exposed are influenced by position in the family. As Zajonc and Markus (1975) point out, a firstborn child enjoys a close relationship with two adult models. It is hardly surprising that language development should be more accelerated under these conditions than it might be if the child had been born later or had been one member of a multiple birth.

Before we go running off bragging that we're firstborns or only children — or complaining that we're not — we should note that the contribution of birth order to intelligence and academic achievement may, after all, be quite negligible. Following a massive investigation of 9,000 high school students and their brothers and sisters (a total of more than 30,000 subjects), Hauser and Sewell (1985) found that the importance of birth order was quite trivial. What appears to be important is not whether you are firstborn or later-born, but the size of your family.

Family Size

In general, although things may be *cheaper by the dozen*, the larger the family, the more limited the advantages to the children. In the Hauser and Sewell study, family size had a significantly negative impact on schooling. In addition, some investigators report lower intelligence test scores among members of larger families (Grotevant, Scarr, & Weinberg, 1977; Zajonc, 1976). In explaining these findings, Zajonc argues that the *intellectual climate* in homes with large families is, on the average, less conducive to cognitive development than the climate characteristic of homes with smaller families. However, here as elsewhere, we cannot easily separate the effect of family size from the effects of social class, religion, or rural versus urban environment. Unfortunately, as Page and Grandon (1979) observe, much of the research that has been used to support findings related to family size has not taken into consideration the fact that large families are far more common among the poor, the culturally deprived, and certain ethnic minorities. When these factors are taken into account, socioeconomic status emerges as a more important predictor of intelligence and academic achievement that does family size or birth order (Doby, 1980; Page & Grandon, 1979).

In summary, birth order and family size are related to intellectual development. But the relationships are not very strong and seem to be due primarily to socio-economic factors associated with large and small families (larger families are more common among lower socioeconomic groups).

We should always bear in mind that the conclusions of our social sciences are usually based on the average performance of large groups of individuals. Within these groups, there are those whose behavior does not come close to matching the predictions that social science might make based on its conclusions. Thus there are saints and geniuses whose siblings numbered in the tens and twenties, and there are poltroons and oafs who were born first into tiny little families.

Life is not that simple.

One-Parent Families

Close to half of all American children are spending (or will spend) an average of six years in a family with only one parent. The large majority of these one-parent families, most of which are headed by mothers rather than fathers (see Figure 8.3), results from separation or divorce; a smaller proportion results from the death of a parent or from bearing children out of wedlock. In addition, Amato and Keith (1991) cite projections that parents of 38 percent of white children and 75 percent of black children in the United States will divorce before the children are 16.

General Effects of Loss of a Parent

There is considerable evidence that separation and divorce, or the death of one parent, is a difficult — sometimes traumatic — experience for most children. Allison and Furstenberg's (1989) investigation of 1,197 children found that marital breakup had widespread and lasting effects evident in higher incidences of problem behavior, increased psychological distress, and poorer academic performance. Similarly, Amato and Keith's (1991) summary of 92 individual studies (termed a *meta-analysis*) of the impact of divorce found significant negative effects on school achievement, behavior, adjustment, self-concept, and relations with both the remaining and the departed parent. These effects vary considerably depending on such factors as the child's age, the relationship of the child to the departed as well

Changes in the U.S. Family

The average size of the American family has declined in recent decades and is now at about 3.17 persons. As population has increased, the number of married couples has also increased. But whereas families with both spouses present increased by 33 percent between 1960 and 1990, the number of male-headed families increased by a whopping 126 percent in the same period. And yet, there are still about five times more female-headed households — some 10.9 million in the United States in 1990, an increase of 141 percent between 1960 and 1990.

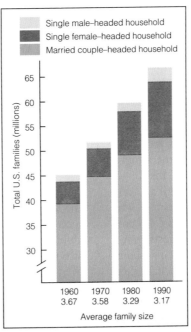

Figure 8.3 Changes in U.S. average family size and increases in single-parent families, 1960–1990. (From data in U.S. Bureau of the Census, 1991, p. 45.)

as to the remaining parent, and parental relationships following breakup of the marriage. We look at each of these factors next.

Age-Related Effects of Divorce

The Amato and Keith (1991) meta-analysis concludes that the negative effects of divorce are related to the ages of the children. In almost all investigations, the most serious effects are on children in the middle age groups—mainly elementary and high school—with college students least affected.

An ongoing investigation of 60 families in which divorce occurred provides more specific information about how children of different ages react to their parents' divorce (Wallerstein & Kelly, 1974, 1975, 1976, 1980).

The early effects of parental separation for the youngest group (2- to 3-year-olds) includes regression manifested in loss of toilet habits, bewilderment, and clinging behavior directed toward strangers. In some cases, development is still retarded one year later.

Three- and 4-year-old preschoolers show loss of confidence and self-esteem, and are quick to blame themselves for the departure of the father. As Neal (1983) observes, preschoolers typically understand divorce as a question of one parent leaving *them*, rather than parents leaving each other. They are likely to think they have done something "bad" to cause the parent to leave.

The next age group (5- and 6-year-olds) is less affected developmentally, although some of the daughters tend to deny the situation and to continue expecting their fathers' return.

The 7- and 8-year-olds are understandably frightened by the divorce and intensely saddened, many of them missing their fathers constantly. Many of these children also live in fear of making their mothers angry, perhaps imagining that she too might leave them.

Nine- and 10-year-olds initially react with apparent acceptance, many of them trying to understand why the divorce has occurred. But their outward calm covers feelings of anger, sometimes intense hostility toward one or the other parent (or both), and shame (Wallerstein & Kelly, 1976). A year later, half these children seem to have adjusted, with resignation and some lingering sadness, to their new situation. However, half suffer from varying degrees of depression, low self-esteem, poorer school performance, and poorer relationships with peers.

Interviews with young adolescents (ages 12-14) reveal a much deeper understanding of their parents' divorce (Springer & Wallerstein, 1983). Many adolescents are keen observers and analyzers of interactions between their parents, and many are able to evaluate the situation objectively. Many arrive at plausible psychological explanations for their parents' divorce. Unlike younger children, they are much less likely to harbor feelings of guilt about the divorce or hostility toward one or both parents. However, some of these children, who initially seem to cope well, later manifest varying degrees of anger, resentment, and maladjustment—an example of what Wallerstein (1989) labeled the "sleeper" effect.

Sex-Related Effects of Divorce

Some researchers have suggested that boys are more adversely affected by divorce than are girls (Guidubaldi & Cleminshaw, 1985; Hetherington, Cox, & Cox, 1979). This is especially true if loss of the father occurs before age 5 (Warshak & Santrock, 1983). However, the Amato and Keith (1991) meta-analysis indicates that sex differences are not very pronounced. Other than for the fact that boys sometimes exhibit more unhappiness or emotional distress following a divorce than do girls, there is no consistent pattern of greater negative effects for boys than girls. In short, there is no greater incidence of behavior problems, of difficulty in school, of lowered self-esteem, or of problems with parent–child relationships.

Contextual Influences of Divorce

One of the remarkable findings of the Amato and Keith (1991) meta-analysis of 92 studies was that the year of the study is related to its outcome. In general, more recent investigations are finding *less negative* effects on children. Apparently, the impact of divorce was far stronger in the 1950s and 1960s than is now the case. Why? Perhaps because divorces were less common, less culturally acceptable, and more difficult to arrange. Consequently, both children and parents would be more likely to have to cope with disapproval, and would be provided with less support. Perhaps for these same reasons, the consequences of divorce are less severe in the United States than they are in many other countries (Amato & Keith, 1991).

Why Divorce Has Negative Effects

There are at least three reasons why divorce might affect children negatively.

Father (or Mother) Absence.   Much of the research in this area has focused on, and has attributed negative consequences to, the father's absence. We might expect that father absence could affect children either because the roles traditionally filled by the father would no longer be filled (or might be filled less adequately by the mother, who must also continue to carry out her own roles) or because the absence of the father has an effect on the mother, who then interacts with her children differently. These traditional father roles are, on the one hand, economic and, on the other, psychological. Freudian theory suggests, for example, that the presence of both parents is especially crucial during the phallic phase of development (ages 4–6), when children resolve their Oedipus or Electra complexes, identify with the like-sexed parent, and begin to develop appropriate gender roles. Accordingly, the presence of a father is especially important for young boys. But it is also crucial for girls, not only because a father's behavior indicates to a daughter what men should be like when she begins to date, but also because of the role a loving and accepting father plays in the development of a daughter's self-esteem. Similarly, the absence of a mother, an increasingly common situation, might be expected to have effects on boys that are different from those on girls.

Economic Impact.   The economic circumstances of the one-parent home are, on average, considerably less advantageous than those of the two-parent family. The average income in mother-headed homes is often less than half that of father-headed homes; many are well below the poverty level (Weitzman, 1985). The change from relative affluence to poverty can be especially difficult for children whose peers are more advantaged. Economic hardship also increases the risk of trouble with the law, and is associated with a higher probability of not finishing school.

Family Conflict.   A third explanation for the negative effects of divorce relates to stresses associated with conflict between parents both before and during the process of separation. One of the most striking findings revealed in the research summarized by Amato and Keith (1991) is that children living in high-conflict but *intact* families fared less well than children whose parents had divorced: They manifested more adjustment difficulties, lower self-esteem, and more behavior problems. This is strong evidence, conclude Amato and Keith, that family conflict is an important explanation for the negative effects of divorce.

Some Conclusions

Marital disruption and its effect on children is a complex subject. There are too many variables involved for us to grab them easily, lay them flat on the tables of our reason, see their interrelatedness, and understand and summarize them. Even our simplest summaries remain in need of further summarizing and simplification.

Peterson, Leigh, and Day (1984) provide a possibility—an approach that separates the variables involved and underlines their relationship. They present what they refer to as a "middle range theory of the potential impact of divorce." It is a theory that deals with two principal variables. The independent variable is the degree of *parental disengagement*. (An *independent variable*, recall, is a variable that, in an experiment, is manipulated by the experimenter; it is the variable that is expected to have an effect on outcomes.) The dependent variable is the child's *social competence*. (A *dependent variable*, remember, is that which is presumably affected by the independent variable.) So, the degree of parental disengagement—which ranges from varying levels of marital discord through temporary separation, long-term separation, divorce, and death—may affect the child's social competence, which is manifested in the child's ability "to engage in social relationships and possess adaptive psychological qualities" (Peterson, Leigh, & Day, 1984, p. 4).

In examining the relationship of these two variables—parental disengagement and the child's social competence — Peterson, Leigh, and Day (1984) take into account much of the wealth of research in this area and reduce it to a handful of conclusions:

- The higher the degree of disengagement, the greater the impact on the child. In other words, divorce would generally be more stressful than temporary separation. By the same token, a situation in which one of the parents breaks all ties with the child would be more stressful than one in which both parents continue to maintain close ties with the child.

- The severity of the *immediate crisis* brought about by the divorce is closely related to the negative impact of divorce. Children who have been abused or neglected by a parent are less likely to view the divorce as a very serious calamity, and are likely to experience a lower degree of stress.

- The more accurate the child's perception of the parents' relationship prior to marital breakup, the less negative the consequences. Those who incorrectly view their parents' relationship as "happy" immediately before separation or divorce suffer the highest stress.

- The more positive and amicable the parents' relationship following marriage breakdown, the less negative the effect on the child.

- The closer the relationship between the leaving parent and the child prior to marital breakup, the more serious the effect on the child.

- Age is related to the severity of consequences in a curvilinear fashion, with the most serious consequences occurring for children between the ages of 3 and 9, and the least severe occurring before and after those ages.

A Final Word

There are several dangers implicit in interpreting studies such as these. One is that we might inadvertently stress either the negative or the positive aspects of divorce. Although divorce is almost invariably a trying time for children, living in conflict (and sometimes with physical and mental abuse) can also be very trying. Lowery and Settle (1985) review several studies suggesting that at a certain point, family conflict in the intact home has negative effects on children greater than the potentially negative effects of divorce — a conclu-

sion supported by the Amato and Keith (1991) meta-analysis. When that point is reached, divorce often *is* the best solution, both for parents and for their children. In addition, we also have to be careful not to mistakenly assume that what might be true *on the average* must also be generally true. We might mistakenly conclude, for example, that divorce is always detrimental to the welfare of children that intact families are always good. This is clearly not the case — especially when the divorced mother is competent, clear about child-rearing goals, and relatively free of psychological symptoms such as depression or anxiety (Barratt, Roach & Colbert, 1991; Machida & Holloway, 1991).

It bears repeating that some loving single parents can effectively overcome whatever trauma might be associated with the loss of one parent, and that there are countless two-parent families in which parenting is inadequate and love is seldom if ever shown.

Children in Stepfamilies

Although about half of all American children will spend at least some time in a one-parent family, many of these also eventually become members of stepfamilies (also called a *blended* or *remarried* family). A *stepfamily* is the family grouping that results from the remarriage of a widowed or divorced parent and in which, consequently, only one of the two married adults in the family is the child's biological parent. Currently, almost one in every five American families with children under 18 is a stepfamily (Glick, 1989); and projections are that the proportion may reach one in two by the year 2000.

Interestingly, stepfamilies are not as enduring as first marriages; they have a 50 percent higher probability of ending within five years (Pill, 1990). In addition, remarriages in which there are stepchildren are more likely to dissolve than if there are no children, especially if the children are older (above 9) (Visher & Visher, 1988).

Research on stepfamilies and stepchildren is still somewhat limited, perhaps not only because stepfamilies are far less common than nuclear or one-parent families, but also because of the number and complexity of relationships that can exist within a stepfamily. For example, the marriage of a man and woman who have both been married previously and who both have children can create an overwhelming number of new relationships involving the biological relatives of each of the stepparents, not to mention previous spouses and their parents, siblings, uncles, aunts, and cousins.

Loss of a parent through separation, divorce, or death is, as we have seen, usually a difficult experience for children. Unfortunately, the remarriage of the parent in a one-parent family does not automatically do away with the difficulties. Indeed, it often brings a whole new set of problems. Hetherington, Stanley-Hagen, and Anderson (1989) report that adjustment to remarriage appears to take longer than adjustment to divorce, especially for older children. The child who has had to cope with the initial disruption of the family must now cope with another reorganization of the family. And whereas remarriage is almost invariably seen as a gain by the child's parent, because it serves to reestablish an important relationship, it is often seen as a loss by the child, implying a change in the relationship between the child and the natural parent. Many children experience feelings of abandonment following the remarriage of a parent, because much of the time and attention that the parent had previously given them is now given to the stepparent (Visher & Visher, 1982).

In addition to the loss, real or imagined, of some of the biological parent's attention and, perhaps, affection, the stepchild must now also establish new relationships with the stepparent, with stepsiblings if there are any, and perhaps with a new set of grandparents and other relatives (Ihinger-Tallman, 1987). Furthermore, the stepchild's role in the family often changes. This can be particularly difficult in the case of adolescent children. Their newly developed adult roles, sometimes accelerated by the absence of the parent (for example, the boy has become "man of the house" following his biological father's departure), can be severely disrupted by the appearance of a new stepparent. Similarly, the creation of a new stepfamily can disrupt established patterns of control and discipline, and can sometimes lead to serious problems ("You're not my dad! I don't have to listen to you!")

Other problems sometimes associated with the stepfamily include sexual fantasies and inclinations between stepsiblings as well as between children and their stepparents (and resulting feelings of guilt and confusion); stepsibling rivalry and competition; ambivalence concerning what the stepchild's role in the family should now be; confusion regarding whether and how the departed parent should continue to fit into the child's life; and the need for the child to abandon the fantasy and the wish that the natural parents might one day be reunited (Chilman, 1983).

Fortunately, the effects of stepfamilies on children are seldom inevitably and entirely negative. The fairy-tale stereotype of the stepfather or stepmother as the wicked wielder of terrible powers is, in fact, a fairy tale. Clearly, most stepparents are kind and considerate people who want to love and be loved by their stepchildren. And when the initial adjustments required by the creation of the stepfamily have been made, the stepchild might, in many cases, be as fortunate as many in intact nuclear families.

Day Care

In the old days, most North American children spent their preschool years in intimate contact with their mothers, a situation that Bowlby (1982), Klaus and Kennell (1983), and others would consider an ideal child-rearing arrangement. Today, an ever-increasing number of children are cared for during the day by others. In fact, day care is now the norm for more than 50 percent of all U.S. preschool children, a percentage that is climbing (Browne Miller, 1990). Almost 75 percent of mothers of preschoolers now work, and it is becoming increasingly common for many mothers to go back to work within weeks of childbirth. Gamble and Zigler (1986) report that *infant* day care is the fastest growing type of supplemental care in the United States. And, in addition to arranged care for children, there are self-supervised or *latchkey* children, so called because their parents sometimes hang keys around their necks so they can let themselves into their homes after school (Long & Long, 1983). Self-supervision is sometimes associated with more behavior problems (Vandell & Ramanan, 1991).

General Effects of Day Care

The growing number of children in day-care facilities is due not only to an increase in the number of one-parent families where the parent must work but also to the large number of families where both parents work—sometimes because of financial need, often for other reasons.

Day care takes a variety of forms, ranging from situations in which families can afford to hire a private caregiver to substitute for the mother during her absence, with the caregiver in the child's home, to institutionalized centers involving large numbers of children and several caregivers. Research and speculation have been less concerned with day care in private homes than with centralized day care. What are the effects of day care on children?

Bronfenbrenner, Belsky, and Steinberg (1977) reviewed several dozen studies, most of which compared day-care and home-care children in terms of social, intellectual, and motor development. Cognitive differences were seldom significant. A number of studies found a slightly greater tendency for day-care children to interact with others (both peers and adults), and several reported somewhat more aggressiveness among day-care children. Kagan, Kearsley, and Zelazo (1977) found few important differences between a group of 33 infants who attended a day-care center and comparable children who were kept at home by their mothers. On a battery of measures administered on eight occasions — and including assessments of attentiveness, language development, self-confidence, memory, and maternal attachment — day-care and home-care infants performed equally well.

Unfortunately, studies such as these do not permit us to make a final evaluation of the social, cognitive, and emotional effects of day care in general. There are several reasons for this. First, much of the research has looked at children from middle- or upper-class backgrounds where day care is often provided by university-affiliated centers. For example, the Kagan, Kearsley, and Zelazo study was conducted in a Harvard University day-care center. Centers such as this are typically more development-oriented, both in cognitive and social areas, than are the larger and often more custodial institutions to which a great many working mothers take their children.

Second, early investigations of the effects of day care were concerned primarily with comparing day care with home care. Accordingly, the questions asked were global questions: Are day-care children as advanced socially? As advanced cognitively? As well adjusted?

In general, the available evidence suggests that day care does not have detrimental effects on young children (Silverstein, 1991). In fact, it is quite possible that competent day care might have noticeable beneficial effects on certain children (those from less advantaged backgrounds, for example).

Quality of Day Care

The quality of care provided in day-care facilities is closely related to children's social development, to the quality of parent–child interactions, and to the child's general cognitive development (Peterson & Peterson, 1986; Phillips, McCartney, & Scarr, 1987). In the Phillips, McCartney, and Scarr study, which involved 166 day-care children, a significant relationship was found between indicators of day-care quality (such as staff–child ratio, caregiver–child interaction, equipment and supplies, and so on) and the child's social development as revealed in measures of intelligence, considerateness, sociability, task orientation, and dependence. In the Peterson and Peterson study, day-care quality was assessed in terms of three components: variety of equipment available, degree of caregiver involvement with children, and evaluation of the setting, activities, curriculum, and teacher behavior. The study looked at the relationship between quality of day care and parent–infant interaction. Children from lower-quality centers had more difficulty following instructions and less sustained dialogues with their mothers; they also tended to use more single-statement utterances. In contrast, children who attended higher-quality centers tended to engage in sustained dialogues and to display more maturity in following instructions. The authors suggest that children learn patterns of adult–infant interaction in day-care facilities. In lower-quality centers, which are characterized by a high ratio of children to caregiver, interactions tend to be briefer and less frequent.

Finding Quality Day Care

Although research indicates that day care in general does not usually have detrimental effects on young children, there is evidence that *good* day care might have decidedly beneficial effects; conversely, *bad* day care might have the opposite effects. How can parents determine what is likely to be good or bad day care?

In a highly practical book, Endsley and Bradbard (1981) present some advice. They suggest that although it is difficult to evaluate different day-care programs, those that are very bad may have a number of characteristics in common, as might those that are excellent. Among characteristics of poor programs are unsanitary physical surroundings, physical hazards, overcrowding, lack of materials and activities, and poorly trained staff (Endsley & Bradbard, 1981). In contrast, high-quality programs have better financial resources and better trained, highly motivated staff (Endsley & Bradbard, 1981, p. 33).

Kagan (1978) stresses that what appears to be important in day care is that the ratio of staff to children be kept low, that staff be reasonably knowledgeable with respect to child development, and that children be given ample opportunity to exercise social, cognitive, and language skills.

How does a parent assess day-care facilities with respect to these characteristics? Not by paying a great deal of attention to the Yellow Pages or to newspaper advertising, but through personal references and, perhaps more important, by visiting the centers, observing them in operation, and talking with the people in charge.

Vertical and Horizontal Relationships

"Whoever is delighted in solitude is either a wilde beast or a God," Francis Bacon informs us. That may not be entirely true, but the point is nevertheless important:

Social interaction and social competence are fundamental to human happiness.

How does the infant become a socially competent child? And eventually a socially competent adolescent and adult? Mainly as a result of experience in close relationships, claims Hartup (1989). Growing children develop two kinds of relationships, the quality of which may affect them for the rest of their lives: *vertical* relationships and *horizontal* relationships.

Vertical relationships exist between two individuals who have different amounts of status or social power. The first of the infant's relationships, that with the mother, is a vertical relationship. Relationships with older relatives, with teachers, perhaps with employers, are also examples of vertical relationships.

The principal function of vertical relationships in childhood is to provide security; in addition, vertical relationships serve an important instructional function. Through relationships such as that between caregiver and infant, basic social skills begin to emerge.

Horizontal relationships are relationships between equals—for example, peer friendships. Horizontal relationships, says Hartup (1989), are the contexts within which the basic skills that emerge in the caregiver–infant relationship are elaborated. The "construction of well-functioning relationships," he asserts, "may be the most significant achievement in the child's socialization" (p. 125).

Main Points

1. Socializing emotions requires learning how to interpret feelings, achieving some control over them, and learning rules of emotional display. During the preschool period, emotional control is more behavioral than cognitive. Children are more easily moved to tears—and laughter—than adults.

2. Erikson's stage theory of social development describes the resolution of psychosocial conflicts through the development of competence. Stage 3, *initiative versus guilt*, spans the preschool period, and involves developing a sense of personal agency and accepting responsibility for one's actions.

3. Bandura's imitation theory of social development asserts that much social learning takes place through observational learning (imitation), including acquiring such socially important characteristics as the tendency to cooperate or to compete, which are highly influenced by the individual's immediate culture.

4. Practice play may be useful for developing and exercising important physical skills, as well as for establishing social position and teaching acceptable forms of behavior. Pretend play is closely related to cognitive development. Social play underlies

personality development and the development of social skills.

5. Infants as young as 1 year of age are often capable of pretend play (for example, pretending to be asleep or pretending to eat). Later, during the preschool period, boys' pretend play often involves monsters or superheroes; girls' pretend play is often more concerned with home-related or nurturant themes. Daydreaming and imaginary playmates are forms of pretend play.

6. Social play, which involves interaction among two or more children, may be *onlooker play* (looking without joining in), *parallel* play (playing independently side by side), *associative play* (playing together without sharing rules), or *cooperative play* (sharing of rules and goals).

7. Gender roles, the range of behaviors that are considered appropriate for males and females, together with the personality characteristics common to what we think of as *masculinity* and *femininity*, appear to result from an interaction of genetic and contextual forces.

8. Sex differences in play are evident in the tendency of boys to play more physically, in the toys they select and are given, and in the roles they assume in their pretend games (boys are monsters, villains, superheroes; girls are cooks, mothers, babies). These differences are more apparent later rather than earlier in the preschool period.

9. A cognitive explanation for gender-typing (the learning of gender roles) describes three stages in the child's understanding of gender: recognizing basic gender identity, that is, maleness or femaleness; realizing that gender is stable, permanent, and unchangeable; and realizing that superficial changes, in dress or behavior, for example, do not alter gender.

10. Genetic influences on gender differences are especially evident in the greater aggressiveness of males. Contextual influences are reflected in the fact that most parents treat boys and girls differently, rewarding aggression, independence, and boisterousness in boys, and nurturant, affective, compliant behavior in girls.

11. A nuclear family consists of mother, father, and children. Extended families include many other blood relatives. The family is a highly dynamic social unit; it changes as a function of external pressures and as a result of internal events. Here, as elsewhere, influence is bidirectional.

12. Baumrind describes parenting styles as permissive (nonpunitive, noncontrolling, nondemanding), authoritarian (dogmatic, controlling, obedience-oriented), or authoritative (firm but based on reason, nondogmatic, geared toward promoting independence but encouraging adherence to standards).

13. Both the psychoanalytic and the behavioristic models probably exaggerate the extent to which the child is susceptible to external influences. It is difficult to predict future adjustment and personality characteristics of children on the basis of what might be known about the child-rearing practices of their parents. However, in North American contexts, an authoritative (or democratic) child-rearing style may be better than a permissive or authoritarian style.

14. Three important sources of child-care advice are the medical profession, books, and parenting courses. Although books and courses sometimes present simplistic solutions for complex problems, they are generally very valuable and widely consulted.

15. Firstborn and only children are more achievement oriented than their siblings, and have a tendency to achieve at a higher level. Children from larger families on the average do less well than children from smaller families on measures of intellectual performance, a fact that might be due as much to any of several social variables as to family size itself.

16. Preschool children often view divorce as a parent leaving *them* (rather than parents leaving each other) and think the divorce has occurred because they have been "bad." Older children often experience considerable anger and hostility, mixed with sadness. Adolescents view the situation more realistically and often become highly analytical about their parents' relationship and the reasons for the divorce.

17. The emotional effects of divorce depend on the age of the child, on sex (perhaps slightly more difficulty for males), and on context (less severe impact now than three decades ago). In general, the effects of divorce on young children are a function of the degree of parental disengagement (divorce is more stressful than temporary separation), the relation-

ship between child and parents (the effect is more severe if the relationship is loving than if it involves maltreatment), the accuracy of the child's perception of parental relations (crisis is more serious if unanticipated), the age of the child (more serious for children between 3 and 9), and the child's sex (when fathers leave, the effect is more serious for boys than for girls).

18. Some of the effects of one-parent families on children may be due to the lack of a father; they may also be due to altered economic conditions or to conflict before and during separation.

19. Stepfamilies result from the remarriage of a widowed or divorced parent. Stepchildren sometimes face problems relating to loss of some of the parent's time and affection, establishing relationships with stepfamily members, and abandoning the fantasy that the biological parents may reunite. In many cases, these potential problems are insignificant or nonexistent.

20. Day care does not generally have negative effects on the social, emotional, or cognitive development of children and can, in fact, have beneficial effects. Important factors to consider when selecting a day-care facility include staff–children ratio, physical environment, equipment and materials provided for children, financial resources, and the qualifications of staff members.

21. The construction of well-functioning relationships may be the child's most significant social achievement.

Further Readings

Paley's books offer a fascinating, often delightful, description of life in the preschool. The first of these short books follows 3-year-old Mollie through a year of nursery school, revealing her excitement and her fears in the little dramas that are an intrinsic part of Paley's classes. The second follows the lives of a kindergarten class, providing fascinating insights into how they struggle to arrive at their own understanding of what it means to be a boy or a girl:

Paley, V. G. (1986). *Millie is three: Growing up in school.* Chicago: University of Chicago Press.

Paley, V. G. (1984). *Boys and girls: Superheroes in the doll corner.* Chicago: University of Chicago Press.

In recent years, the number of one-parent, father-headed homes has increased even more rapidly than single-parent, mother-headed homes — although the latter is still far more common than the former. Greif's book presents a detailed look at the implications of single-fatherhood. Nofsinger's book is an annotated bibliography of books, articles, and video material relating to the impact of divorce on children:

Greif, G. L. (1985). *Single fathers.* Lexington, MA: Heath.

Nofsinger, M. M. (1990). *Children and adjustment to divorce: An annotated bibliography.* New York: Garland.

For an intelligent discussion of sexism in education, as well as in everyday life, and suggestions about measures that can be taken to counter it, see:

Askew, S., & Ross, C. (1988). *Boy's don't cry: Boys and sexism in education.* Milton Keynes and Philadelphia: Open University Press.

The Cataldo book describes and evaluates a great many parent-education programs, and gives numerous sources of child-care information for parents. The Endsley and Bradbard book provides checklists that can be used as a practical guide for evaluating day-care facilities:

Cataldo, C. Z. (1987). *Parent education for early childhood: Child-rearing concepts and program content for the student and practicing professional.* New York: Teachers College Press.

Endsley, R. C., & Bradbard, M. R. (1981). *Quality day care: A handbook of choices for parents and caregivers.* Englewood Cliffs, NJ: Prentice-Hall.

Winslow Homer: *Crack the Whip*, 1872. The Metropolitan Museum of Art, New York, gift of Christian A. Zabriskie, 1950. (50.41)

"Suppose there are two mobs?" suggested Mr. Snodgrass. "Shout with the largest," replied Mr. Pickwick.

Charles Dickens, *Pickwick Papers*

IV

Middle Childhood

As we see in Chapters 9 and 10, there are more than just two mobs in middle childhood. All compete for the child's attention. "This way," the mobs clamor. "Everybody is going this way. You should go where everybody is going."

"Study!" schools say. "It's *important* for your future!"

"Play!" friends and peers urge. "It's just so dang much fun!"

"Watch!" television demands. "Never mind playing and studying. Watch and then run out and buy what I sell you!"

"Read!" the newstands coax. "Look at the pretty pictures. Become a comic-book *collector*!"

"Caution!" parents advise. "Find some balance, my child. Study, play, watch, read. Be cautious. *And* do the dishes!"

Is the child just some piece of clay to be shaped by the strongest or the most determined hands? Or is there a *self* that emerges through childhood and into adulthood—a self that evolves from the budding consciousness of the infant, that learns intention and willfulness and the making of choices, that develops notions of worth and feelings of effectiveness, or sometimes of powerlessness?

Perhaps, Mr. Snodgrass, even if there are two very large and very loud mobs—or even a dozen of them—you should not simply shout with the largest.

If you have a self, you might first want to listen to what each has to say.

CHAPTER 9

Physical and Cognitive Development: Middle Childhood

Je préfère la pensée à l'action, une idée à une affaire, la contemplation au mouvement.
(I prefer thought to action, an idea to an event, reflection to activity.)

Honoré de Balzac, *Louis Lambert*

"Pensée, c'est voir," insists Balzac's Louis Lambert (to think is to see). Little surprise he should prefer thought to action.

But thinking is somewhat less than actually seeing. There are details, colors, textures that are obscured in our mind's eye. When we imagine a rose, what most of us see is a vague composite of the roses we have known — a merging of indistinct petals, a dim suggestion of stems and leaves, a splash of nameless color. Our mental roses are limp; they have no scent; they do not prick.

Still, in other ways thinking can be more than actually seeing. I have never *seen* a teal-blue rose, never smelled a mustard-scented rose, never touched a rose made of stars.

In my imagination, I can create things that I will never see.

This Chapter

The child's imagination is not always so boundless; it is tied more closely to the real, the observable, the touchable and smellable. Ten-year-old Laura scrunches up her face in concentration and nods vigorously when I ask her to imagine what a teal-blue rose would look like. But when I ask her, "What does it smell like, this teal-blue rose?" she answers, with just a hint of scorn, "There's isn't no such thing anyway!"

Her thinking is what Piaget labels *concrete*; it deals less easily with the abstract and hypothetical than does our logic. Still, the logic that governs the schoolchild's thinking is a vast improvement over that of the preschooler.

This chapter traces the continued growth of the child's mind through **middle childhood** (approximately ages 6–12). It looks at how children know and remember, how they solve problems, how they develop notions of themselves as effective processors of information. It deals with the growth of normal intelligence, as well as with exceptionality. But first, it looks at physical development.

Physical Development

The physical development of many of the world's children is far from optimal — sometimes because of inadequate diet, and sometimes simply because of lack of exercise. Estimates are that as many as 30 percent of all North American children may be obese (Cusack, 1984); and as we saw in Chapter 1, vast numbers of the third world's children are undernourished. These observations underline the importance of knowledge about the normal course of physical development and about the contributions of nutrition and exercise to physical and mental well-being.

Growth

Although girls tend to be slightly shorter and slightly lighter than boys from birth to the end of the preschool period, the growth curves for each are almost identical; that is, both gain at approximately the same rate. This pattern changes in middle childhood. As Figures 9.1 and 9.2 show, although the average girl is three fourths of an inch (2 cm) shorter at the age of 6, she has caught up with and surpassed the average boy by the age of 11 and is still slightly taller at the age of 12. With respect to weight, girls are close to 2 pounds (1 kg) lighter at the age of 6 and do not catch up with boys until the age of 11. Between the ages of 11 and 12, however, girls undergo a sudden spurt of weight gain that puts them 3 pounds ahead of boys in a single year. Chapter 11 points out that not until the age of 14½ do boys overtake girls in weight, and at 13½ they exceed girls in height.

Another trend of physical growth that continues throughout middle childhood is a gradual decrease in growth of fatty tissue, coupled with increased bone and muscle development. Muscle development is generally more rapid in boys, whereas girls tend to retain a higher percentage of body fat (Smoll & Schutz, 1990).

The growth spurt in height and weight during this period occurs approximately two years earlier for girls than for boys, *on average*. For some, it occurs months or even years later (or earlier) than for others. As a result, there are sometimes dramatic height differences among children of the same ages. This can be a source of acute embarrassment for children. At a time when peer approval has become among the most important things in life, it may be a great misfortune to be either

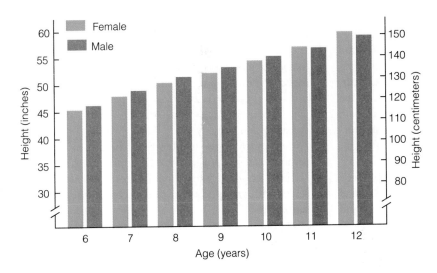

Figure 9.1 Height at 50th percentile for U.S. children. (From the Health Department, Milwaukee, Wisconsin; based on data by H. C. Stuart and H. V. Meredith, prepared for use in Children's Medical Center, Boston. Used by permission of the Milwaukee Health Department.)

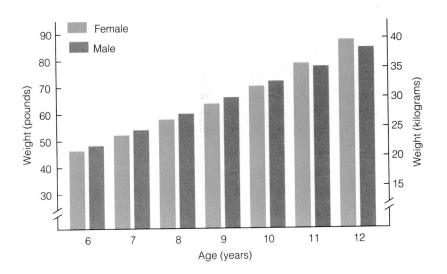

Figure 9.2 Weight at 50th percentile for U.S. children. (From the Health Department, Milwaukee, Wisconsin; based on data by H. C. Stuart and H. V. Meredith, prepared for use in Children's Medical Center, Boston. Used by permission of the Milwaukee Health Department.)

precocious or retarded in physical development. It is humiliating for a boy to suddenly find that his younger sister has become taller than he; the humiliation is often accompanied by the fear that he will continue to be short. It is probably equally uncomfortable to be the tallest boy or the tallest girl in the class and to live with the secret fear of being a tall, skinny freak.

Nature sometimes compensates for initial discrepancies. The tall girl finds that she was an early bloomer; she stops growing at the time when her peers begin their growth spurts, and in a short time she finds herself surrounded by equals. The short boy discovers that he was just a slow starter; when his seemingly more fortunate friends have nearly reached their adult heights, he suddenly stretches skyward.

But nature does not always make up for early differences. The early bloomer does not invariably stop growing while later developers catch up. We are not all destined to reach the same end. Clearly, some end up short and others tall; some are light and others heavy. Unfortunately, our hypothetical average child hides these individual differences. (See Chapter 11 for a discussion of the psychological effects of early and late maturation.)

Nutrition and Health

If they are well nourished, between the ages of 6 and 12 children grow 2–3 inches (4.4–6.6 cm) and gain about 5–7 pounds (approximately 2–2.75 kg) each year. Normal gains in height are a better indicator of the long-term adequacy of the child's nutrition than are weight gains; gains in weight often reflect the shorter-term effects of nutrition (Pipes, Bumbals, & Pritkin, 1985).

During middle childhood, there is a strong need for protein in the child's diet, as well as for vitamins and minerals (especially calcium because of the rapid development of the skeleton). Unfortunately, as we saw in Chapter 1, many of the world's children are not well nourished, and many millions die of starvation each year. Although starvation is uncommon in North America, malnutrition is not. Malnutrition takes one of two forms: overnutrition, often leading to obesity; and undernutrition, often reflected in the intake of foods low in protein and essential vitamins and minerals.

Obesity. The most common nutritional problem among children in North America is obesity, which may affect as many as 30 percent of all children (Cusack, 1984). Obesity is a serious condition that is difficult to rectify. Its relationship to cardiovascular and other health problems is well known; its implications for the child's social and emotional well-being are perhaps less obvious but no less real. Not only does the severely obese child often find it difficult to participate in games and activities that are an important part of the lives of many children, but such a child may be subjected to the ridicule and ostracism that is reflected in the countless derogatory nicknames children invent ("Tubby," "Porky," "Fatso," "Blimp," and others even less kind).

Obesity in children is linked to several factors. Overeating is clearly the most important: Children simply take in more than they expend in growth and activity. This, of course, does not mean that the obese child eats excessively all the time. In fact, many obese children might eat only slightly more than they require each day, but the cumulative long-term effect is obesity.

Also important is the child's genetic background: Some children are clearly more susceptible to obesity than others. Those whose parents are themselves obese are far more likely to also become obese than are children of slim parents (Brownell & Walden, 1984).

A third very important factor in childhood obesity is inactivity. Children who lead sedentary lives, who spend much of their day watching television, are more likely to gain excess weight. Watching television is especially important in contributing to weight gain, not only because it is physically passive but also because it encourages high-calorie snack and drink consumption.

A fourth factor in obesity is the use of food as a reward—or a punishment. Children who are given "treats" for good behavior may learn to *reward* themselves with junk food—or to console themselves in the same way.

Although obesity is difficult to reverse, it can be prevented in most children even where genetic background predisposes the child to gaining excess weight. Two factors need to be controlled: diet and exercise. Children need to be encouraged to develop good eating habits. Care must be taken to ensure that they consume adequate amounts of proteins, vitamins, minerals, and fibers—and also that they resist the ever-present temptation of junk foods. Contrary to popular wisdom, the body does not automatically hunger for specific minerals, vitamins, or other nutrients it might lack. Even animals do not select the most nutritious meal when there are other more appealing alternatives (Galef, 1991).

Diseases and Infections. Although the development of vaccines has drastically reduced the incidence of diseases and infections among children, most nevertheless suffer occasionally from various problems. Most common are respiratory infections such as colds. Less common are communicable diseases such as chicken pox, mumps, mononucleosis, and measles. Very uncommon are vaccine-preventable diseases such as tetanus, poliomyelitis, pertussis (whooping cough), and smallpox. Rabies, too, is uncommon.

Motor Development

Children's muscular control continues to develop during the years from 6 to 12. Early in this period, their control of large muscles is considerably better than their control over smaller muscles (an explanation for the inelegant writing of first- and second-grade children). By the end of middle childhood, control of the large muscles has become nearly perfect and control over the small muscles is much improved.

Participation in activities requiring greater skill becomes possible as children's motor control, strength, agility, and coordination increase. Such activities contribute significantly to social as well as physical development.

Changes in locomotor skills, agility, coordination, and physical strength demonstrate consistent differences between the sexes; they may also be important in explaining the child's interests. For example, throughout middle childhood, the boy's physical strength (measured in terms of grip strength) is superior to the girl's even though the average girl is taller and heavier than the boy (Corbin, 1980). Similarly, boys consistently outjump girls after the age of 7, presumably because boys have greater leg power and arm–leg coordination for jumping than do girls. Johnson (1962) also found that boys did better than girls in tests of kicking, throwing, catching, running, broad jumping, and batting. But girls surpass boys in a number of motor skills during middle childhood, particularly when the skills require muscular flexibility, balance, or rhythmic movements, such as those in hopscotch and rope skipping and some forms of gymnastics (Cratty, 1978).

Not surprisingly, these differences are consistent with the gender-typing of these activities. That is, rope skipping and hopscotch have traditionally been more feminine than masculine; throwing balls, catching, running, and jumping are considered more masculine. In addition, the differences between boys and girls, where there are differences, are seldom very great. There is typically a great deal of overlap so that in activities where boys are better than girls, some girls are better than some boys; conversely, where girls are, on the average, better than boys, some boys are nevertheless better than some girls (Lockhart, 1980).

It is important to note that although sex differences in motor skills are usually very small during middle childhood, after adolescence the disparity increases dramatically (Smoll & Schutz, 1990), generally in favor of the males. As noted, however, this is not the case for some skills such as those requiring balance, where girls perform better than boys (Laszlo, 1986).

What is not clear is the extent to which sex-related differences in motor skills, both in childhood and later in adolescence, result from innate biological differences between the sexes, and the extent to which cultural norms, expectations, and experience are involved. We do know, however, that at least for some activities, proportion of adipose (fatty) tissue is closely related to performance *for both boys and girls*. In a comparison of the motor performance of more than 2,000 children ages 9–17, Smoll and Schutz (1990) found that fatness alone accounted for as much as 50 percent of the variance between males and females. Since females *on average* retain significantly more adipose tissue than boys from early childhood on, some of the observed male–female differences in motor performance are probably related to this biological difference. We should note, however, that in this same investigation, with advancing age, sex differences in motor performance were increasingly influenced by environmental factors.

It bears repeating that sex differences in motor skills are often trivial. And although some of these differences are a function of innate biological differences, social expectations and environmental opportunities also influence the activities in which youngsters become interested and proficient.

Some Physical and Sensory Problems

As we saw in Chapter 6, not all children are born with normal sensory abilities or physical skills; nor do all have the same potential to develop these. Those who differ markedly from the average are termed *exceptional*.

Exceptionality may be seen in all areas of human development: physical and motor, intellectual, and social-emotional. In each of these areas, exceptionality may be positive; that is, it might be manifested in extraordinary talents and skills. Or it may be negative; it might be apparent in deficits and disorders. Later in this chapter, we look at both the positive and negative dimensions of intellectual exceptionality in middle childhood. Here we look briefly at physical and sensory problems.

Visual Impairment.
Those who can see at 20 feet what a "normal" person can see at 20 feet are said to have 20/20 vision (or normal vision); those who can see at 20 feet what normal people see at 200 feet are said to have 20/200 vision and are classified as legally blind if their *corrected* vision in their better eye is no better than 20/200. Accordingly, many individuals who are classified as legally blind do, in fact, *see*; this is one reason why the term *visually impaired* is highly preferable to *blind*. Approximately half of all legally blind children can read large type or print with the help of magnification. For the special education teacher, it is especially important to determine whether a child will be able to learn to read visually or will have to learn to read by touch. For those who can read visually, the "special" qualities of education might not need to go beyond providing magnifying equipment or large type, unless there are other problems involved. Multiple handicaps are not uncommon (Donovan, 1980).

Special classrooms and special teachers for visually impaired children are much less common than they once were; many of these children are now being educated in regular classrooms, a practice termed *mainstreaming* (about which more is said later in this chapter). Those who must learn to read Braille, however, require special equipment and teachers (Nolan, 1978).

Hearing Impairment.
Deafness is the inability to hear sounds clearly enough for the ordinary purposes of life. The *hard of hearing* are described as those who suffer from some hearing loss but who can function with a hearing aid and sometimes without.

A useful way of describing deafness is to distinguish between prelinguistic and postlinguistic deafness — in other words, between loss of hearing that occurs prior to learning a language and that which occurs later. Unfortunately, loss of hearing is most often congenital (present at birth) or occurs within the first two years, often resulting from infections such as *otitis media*, an inflammation of the middle ear (Erickson, 1987). Fewer than 1 child in 10 who is deaf lost hearing after the age of 2.

In terms of cognitive development, deafness generally presents a far more serious handicap than does visual impairment, largely because of the severe difficulties it presents for learning to understand and to speak — hence the historical, but no longer popular, expression "deaf and dumb" or "deaf-mute." There is little evidence that the visually impaired are intellectually handicapped as a result of their blindness, but the same is not true of those who are hearing impaired. Although there is considerable controversy concerning whether deaf children are as intelligent as children with normal hearing (see Berdine & Blackhurst, 1985), their academic achievement often lags behind, a problem that can be attributed largely to language deficiencies. Furth (1973) points out that only a very small percentage of deaf individuals ever progress far enough in their development of language skills that they can read and understand a college-level text. This, of course, applies to the prelinguistically deaf and not to those whose loss of hearing occurred after they had already learned a language.

In addition to the academic problems associated with deafness, there are often emotional and social problems. These problems probably result from lack of social interaction, resulting from impaired ability to communicate through language. Meadow (1975) notes that these emotional problems are frequently mani-

uncertain but that Piagetian rules of logic are more universal. However, the rigged balance scale presents a real-life problem rather than a problem in logic. Specifically, in this situation, children are not deciding whether the logical rule is correct (they know it is) but whether the scale is correct.

Acceleration of Conservation

American researchers and educators were fond of asking Piaget questions such as these: "If we can accurately describe some of the important capabilities that children develop and the sequence in which these appear, might it not also be possible to accelerate their appearance by providing children with appropriate experiences? And could we not, by so doing, speed up the developmental process, increase children's cognitive capabilities, and perhaps even make them more intelligent?"

But Piaget did not have direct answers based on his own research. He had always been more concerned with the description and explanation of cognitive development than with attempts to change its ordinary course. However, an impressive number of other researchers have attempted to answer these questions. Most have looked at the possibility of accelerating the development of concepts of conservation — concepts that are simply defined, easy to measure, and highly significant in general cognitive development. The assumption is that if the acquisition of concepts of conservation is truly important in the child's cognitive development and if it can be accelerated through training, then it might be possible to design school programs that are more beneficial for cognitive growth than those presently in use.

Many of the studies designed to teach conservation to young children before they would be expected to acquire it naturally were not successful or have reported mixed success. Investigators have tried a variety of approaches. Siegler and Liebert (1972) accelerated acquisition of liquid conservation by providing children with rules and with information concerning the accuracy of their responses. Rosenthal and Zimmerman (1972) used a conserving child as a model. Many nonconserving subjects later demonstrated conservation on related but not identical tasks. But when these investigators used instruction in relevant rules rather than models, they were unsuccessful in accelerating conservation. And Kuhn (1972), who also used modeling, failed to increase conservation behavior appreciably in subjects.

In summary, the conclusion that development can be altered easily and significantly through short-term training programs in specific areas is not supported by the available evidence. Conservation can be accelerated, but training programs need to be detailed and systematic, especially if the children are still some distance from acquiring conservation naturally (see Furth, 1980; Gelman & Gallistel, 1978). Whether such efforts, when successful, contribute significantly to intellectual development — or to happiness and self-esteem — remains unclear.

Seriation, Number, and Classes

In addition to acquiring various conservations, children acquire or improve three other abilities.

Classes.   First, during this period, they learn to deal with *classes*, achieving the capacity to understand class inclusion and to reason about the composition and decomposition of classes. An 8-year-old child would be unlikely to make a mistake when asked to decide whether there are more roses or more flowers in a bouquet of 15 roses and 5 tulips. At this level, children understand that roses make up a subclass of the larger class, flowers. Similarly, they have little difficulty multiplying two classes in the problem "If there are blue balls and gray balls, and some are large while others are small, how many different kinds of balls are there?" (The answer is illustrated in Interactive Figure 9.5.)

Recall from Chapter 7 that preschool children, too, have some ability to deal with class inclusion problems. Many have little difficulty with questions of the form "A Siamese is a cat but not an alley cat. Is a Siamese an animal?" However, they typically cannot respond correctly to the flowers problem.

Series.   A second achievement of the period of concrete operations is an understanding of **seriation** (ordering in sequence). One of Piaget's seriation tasks involves presenting the child with a series of objects — for example, a group of dolls, each a different length so that the objects can be arranged from longest to shortest. The bottom row of Figure 9.6 illustrates the arrangement desired, quickly produced by the child in concrete operations even when both series are presented in random order. The preoperational child is ordinarily incapable of responding correctly, even with a single series. A typical response is to place several of the dolls in order while ignoring the fact that others may fit in

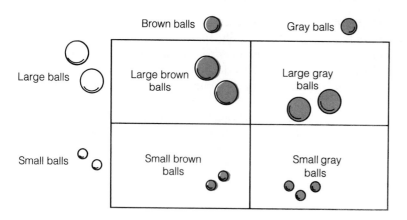

Interactive Figure 9.5 Suppose X comes in exactly two shapes, each of which can be either black or white. How many different X's are there? Right. There are four. The concrete operations child may have some difficulty with this simple classification problem because it's too *abstract*. X is not concrete enough. The problem is simpler if we ask, instead, "How many kinds of balls do we have if we have big and small gray ones, and big and small brown ones?" Such a problem can be used to test a child's ability to classify objects.

between those that have already been positioned. If the next doll the child selects is too short to be placed where the child intended it to be (at the upper end), it is placed without hesitation at the other end, even though it might be taller or shorter than the doll that is already positioned there. The child does not understand that if A is greater than B, and B is greater than C, then A must also be greater than C. Understanding this concept eliminates the necessity of making all the comparisons that would otherwise be necessary.

Number. A third achievement of concrete operations is a better understanding of *number*—an achievement that depends on some of the logical rules involved in classification and seriation. The ordinal properties of number (their ordered sequence—first, second, third, and so on) depend on a knowledge of seriation; and their cardinal properties (their quantitative properties—the fact that they represent collections of different magnitude) depend on a knowledge of classification. As we saw in Chapter 7, many preschool children already have an impressive knowledge of number, a fact Piaget largely overlooked as he searched for the limitations of preoperational versus operational thought.

A Summary of Concrete Operations

An *operation* is a thought that is characterized by rules of logic. Because children acquire conservations early in this period, and because these concepts are manifestations of operational thinking, the period is called *op-*

erational. It is also termed *concrete* because children's thinking deals with real objects or those they can easily imagine. Children in the concrete operations stage are bound to the real world; they don't yet have the freedom made possible by the more advanced logic of the formal operations stage: freedom to contemplate the hypothetical, to compare the ideal with the actual, to be profoundly unhappy and concerned about the discrepancy between this world and that which they imagine possible.

The Child as Information Processor

Piaget's view of the growth of mind is one approach to understanding the intellectual development of children; there are others. Some, as we have seen, are concerned with exploring the accuracy and the usefulness of Piaget's system. These approaches have informed us that Piaget's stages are not entirely universal, that transitions between them are not very abrupt, and that there are sometimes marked variations in the responses of a single child to problems that appear to require the same underlying logic. Still, Piaget's system continues to be the most widely known and widely researched of cognitive developmental theories.

But there is another view of the cognitive development of the child. In many ways, this view complements rather than contradicts Piaget.

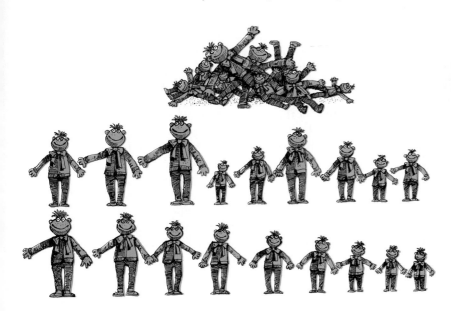

Figure 9.6 A test of a child's understanding of seriation. The elements of the series are presented in random order, and the child is asked to arrange them in sequence of height. The top row was arranged by a 3½-year-old, the bottom by an 8-year-old.

It begins, as all views of the developing person must, with the observation that a newborn infant is very different from an older child—or an adult. Among other things, infants do not know that day follows night, which itself follows day; that butterflies whisper to each other when they perch on buttercups in the sunshine; or that tigers have tails. In fact, they are strangers to their very own hands and feet, strangers to the world. These things are not *familiar* to them. And, as Rheingold (1985) points out, the process of development is a process of becoming familiar with the world.

The difference between the newborn, who is almost totally unfamiliar with everything around, and the older child, who has learned about tigers, tautologies, and tarantulas, can be described in a number of ways. We can say, with Piaget, that the developing child, through the processes of assimilation and accommodation, has *constructed* a sort of reality that conforms, more or less, to certain logical rules, which, in turn, define a sequence of orderly stages.

Or we can say that the developing child begins with no knowledge base, few strategies for dealing with cognitive material, and no awareness of the self as a knower or as a processor of information. This approach permits us to view development as the business of acquiring a knowledge base, developing cognitive strategies, and gradually developing an awareness

of self as a knower. This is an **information-processing approach** to cognitive development.

There are three important things that the information-processing approach looks at: the knowledge base and its creation; the processes and strategies by which information becomes part of the knowledge base or is retrieved from the base; and the emergence of the child's awareness of self as a player of what Flavell (1985) calls the game of cognition. The first two relate to human memory: The individual's knowledge base is made up of what is in memory; and the strategies that enable the child to develop and use a knowledge base are those that permit adding things to or retrieving things from memory. The third component, the recognition of the self as a knower capable of using and evaluating strategies, involves what is termed **metacognition**. Literally, metacognition refers to *knowing about knowing*.

Memory

Our information-processing model views the child as a consumer and processor of information—as a little organism that sheds its ignorance as it builds up a store of memories. The most common description of this model is based on the work of Atkinson and Shiffrin (1971), which describes the human information

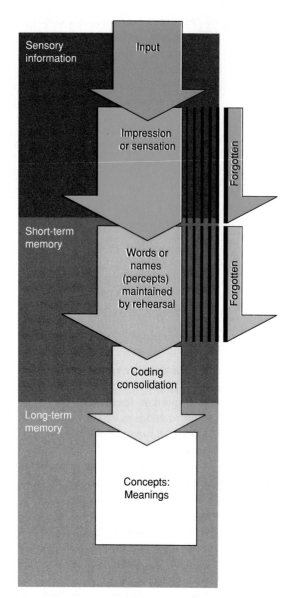

Figure 9.7 The three components of memory. Sensory information first enters sensory memory. From there it may go into short-term memory, where it is available as a name or word, for example, as long as it is rehearsed. Some of the material in short-term memory may then be coded for long-term storage, where it might take the form of meanings and concepts. These three components of memory do not refer to three different locations in the brain or other parts of the nervous system, but to how we remember — or, more precisely, how we study memory. (From Guy R. Lefrançois, *Psychological Theories and Human Learning.* Copyright 1982 by Wadsworth, Inc. Reprinted by permission of Brooks/Cole Publishing Company.)

processor in terms of three types of information storage: sensory memory, short-term memory (also called *working memory*; Dempter, 1985), and long-term memory. Each of these is distinguished primarily by the amount and nature of processing that it involves. The term *processing* refers to mental activities such as sorting, analyzing, rehearsing, and summarizing (see Figure 9.7).

Sensory Memory. **Sensory memory** is nothing more elaborate than the momentary impressions asso-

ciated with sensory stimulation. It requires virtually no cognitive processing. Our sensory systems (vision, hearing, taste, smell, touch) are sensitive to an overwhelming array of stimulation that constantly bombards them. Most of this stimulation is not attended to. You cannot, at every moment, be aware of all the sights, sounds, tastes, smells, and feelings that are immediately possible — that require only that you *pay attention*. Hence, most of the sensory stimulation that surrounds us is not processed at all but has only a fleeting (less than 1 second) and unconscious effect on memory.

Short-Term Memory.

Your ability to recall the beginning of a sentence as you read it illustrates **short-term** (or *working*) **memory**. If you can't remember the beginning of the sentence, it is usually because you aren't paying attention. In a sense, then, short-term memory is equivalent to attention span. As Calfee (1981) puts it, it is sort of a scratch pad for thinking. But this scratch pad has two important limitations: First, its capacity for adults appears to be limited to about seven items (plus or minus two; Miller, 1956); second, it seems to hold material only for seconds rather than minutes.

But these storage limitations are not as serious as they might seem. Although we seem to be able to attend to only about seven items at once, a process called **chunking** can be used to increase memory capacity significantly. Chunking is nothing more complex than grouping into related units. Miller (1956) illustrates the process by reference to a change purse that can hold only seven coins. If you put seven pennies into this purse, its capacity is seven cents. However, if you fill it with seven groupings (chunks) of coins, such as nickels, dimes, or quarters, its capacity increases dramatically.

Some people slip golden coins into the purses of their memories.

One common measure of short-term memory is to have subjects try to repeat a sequence of unrelated numbers they have just heard—a task that is used on a number of intelligence tests. Average adolescents and adults are able to repeat correctly six or seven (or sometimes even nine) digits. In contrast, 6-year-olds will typically succeed in repeating only two or so.

The child's limited *working* memory may be very important in explaining some aspects of cognitive development. Siegler (1989), for example, suggests that children are often unable to solve certain problems simply because they cannot keep in mind all relevant information simultaneously. And Case (in Case et al., 1988) claims that the most important constraint on the child's ability to understand and solve problems is simply a limitation on short-term storage space.

Sensory memory, as we saw, does not involve cognitive processing but is a fleeting impression, almost like an echo. In contrast, short-term memory is highly dependent upon *rehearsal* or repetition. When I look up and dial a new telephone number, by the time I have finished dialing, I will usually no longer remember the number.

Long-Term Memory.

But if I think I might need the number again tomorrow, there are several things I can do. One is to write it down so that I will not have to remember it. That would impose little cognitive strain. I would not have to use any of the strategies required to move material from short-term to long-term storage. Still, it would require the use of long-term memory; tomorrow I would have to remember not only that I made a note of the number but also where the note is. And I would have to remember a tremendous range of other information as well, including how to translate telephone numbers into the orderly and sequential act of dialing, how to speak and listen with a telephone, and so on. Put another way, even as habitual a behavior as using a telephone requires a tremendous knowledge base. And our knowledge base is, in effect, our **long-term memory**. It includes everything we know—about ourselves, about the world, about knowing.

Our contemporary models or metaphors for long-term memory are almost invariably associationistic. They are based on the notion that all items of information in our memories are *associated* (connected) in various ways. It is precisely because of these associations that we are able to remember so impressively.

The associationistic view of human memory has led to a number of abstract models or labels to describe what is stored in long-term memory over periods of minutes, weeks, or years. These cognitive models relate to associations that are based on meaning. They make use of various labels, including *nodes, schemata, scripts, frames, networks, categories, coding systems,* and others. The labels serve as metaphors and not as literal descriptions. They do not say long-term memory *is* such and such. Rather, they say long-term memory is *like* such and such or might be *compared* to such and such (Bransford, 1979).

Schemata and Scripts

Historically, much of the research on memory has dealt with the ability to remember specific items (numbers, words). However, there may not be a very close relationship between the ability to remember a list of 12 items and remembering in real-life situations. It seems intuitively clear that in most real-life situations, we

Complex, strategy-oriented games such as chess make heavy demands on long-term memory processes, and especially on organization. Many chess masters can reproduce the position of the pieces in a half-played chess match after glancing at the board for only a few moments, presumably because of their knowledge of a variety of schemata and scripts relating to the positions of chess pieces. In contrast, novice players might be hard-pressed to remember the positions of only a handful of pieces.

remember *meanings* rather than specific instances. When someone tells you a funny story, you remember its gist and perhaps the wording of its punch line but seldom the exact wording, the pauses, the intonations, and the facial expressions of the speaker. Put another way, what appears to be remembered are the cognitive beasties sometimes called *schemata*. Schemata are like clusters of knowledge that define concepts. They are what we know about this or that. Our schemata relating to aardvarks might include items of knowledge relating to size, color, characteristic sounds, and general reputation. They might also include some affective (emotional) reactions having to do with the taste of these creatures or their smell. If someone tells me a story about aardvarks, what I remember of the story will be profoundly influenced by my aardvark schemata (Smith & Graesser, 1981).

One aspect of schemata that is particularly important in remembering real-life things such as what goes with what, how stories turn out, or even whether desserts come before or after soups and salads, is called a **script**. Scripts are the part of cognitive structure (of knowledge—hence of schemata) that deal with routines and sequences. We all know the script for going into a restaurant, eating, and ordering—which is why the first part of this sentence jars. Our scripts say ordering and *then* eating.

Research on children's memories indicates that their memory for stories, like ours, is highly dependent on their relevant schemata and scripts. For example, when children are told script-based stories, they tend to fill in gaps according to their personal scripts. In one study, Johnson, Bransford, and Solomon (1973) presented subjects with the following short passage:

> John was trying to fix the birdhouse. He was pounding the nail when his father came out to watch him and to help him do the work.

A current account of research and theory on memory development in childhood is presented in:

> Brainerd, C. J., & Pressley, M. (Eds.). (1985). *Basic processes in memory development: Progress in cognitive development research.* New York: Springer-Verlag.

A good description of some common psychological tests, together with several fascinating case studies, is:

> Siegel, M. G. (1987). *Psychological testing from early childhood through adolescence: A developmental and psychodynamic approach.* Madison, CT: International Universities Press.

A provocative and practical book dealing with the development of creativity, critical thinking, and problem-solving skills is:

> Fisher, R. (1990). *Teaching children to think.* Oxford: Basil Blackwell.

Current trends and controversies in special education are discussed in:

> Schmid, R. E., & Nagata, L. M. (1983). *Contemporary issues in special education.* New York: McGraw-Hill.

Renzulli's book describes 15 elementary and secondary school programs for gifted learners:

> Renzulli, J. S. (Ed.). (1986). *Systems and models for developing programs for the gifted and talented.* Mansfield Center, CT: Creative Learning Press.

Aylward presents the basics of psychological testing of children, and provides clear and useful descriptions of major intelligence tests as well as of tests useful for diagnosing specific abilities (or disabilities) in a brief book:

> Aylward, E. H. (1991). *Understanding children's testing: Psychological testing.* Austin, TX: Pro-Ed.

CHAPTER 10

Social Development: Middle Childhood

A manner rude and wild
Is common at your age.

Hillaire Belloc,
Bad Child's Book of Beasts

Eight-year-old Thomas is a case in point. "You know what that little beggar did last night?" his father asked by way of introduction, and the way he said it, you could tell maybe he would brag a little, that he really wasn't all that upset with the little beggar. "Drove across the lake," his father continued.

"Drove across the lake?"

"In the boat."

"What?"

"Yep. Took the key from behind the door, fired her up, and zoomed right over to Billy's place."

"He's only 8," I said. "That's a 90-horse you got there."

"He knows how to run it," his father answered. "Full speed all the way too. Have to hide the key now. Car key too. He's a wild one, that little beggar." It was less complaint than boast.

But surely not all children are rude and wild through middle childhood. Some, of either sex, must also be polite and gentle and well behaved.

Given a thousand 8-year-olds, will they be found to be more rude than polite? More wild than restrained?

This Chapter

This chapter presents the beginning of an answer. It looks at how children are socialized through the middle years, how they become caring and concerned individuals, and how they develop notions of who they are and of their self-worth. It examines the role of parents, peers, and friends in shaping the developmental process. It looks, too, at how important the school and television are in the child's context.

Like little beggar Thomas's pranks, much of the wildness—and the rudeness—of middle childhood is playful. Sadly, some is not. There are dysfunctional families where children are neglected and abused, sometimes in shocking ways. This chapter closes with a look at child maltreatment, followed by a discussion of social-emotional exceptionality.

The Development of Social Cognition

Cognition refers to knowing; *metacognition* is knowing about the self as a knower; and *social cognition* is awareness of self and of others, of people and their behaviors. As Showers and Cantor (1985) note, social cognitions help us make sense of situations.

The development of social cognitions begins in early infancy and is thought to be closely linked with the development of the self-concept. Most developmental psychologists believe that the child is not born with a notion of self—that a newborn cannot differentiate between the self and the nonself (Olson, 1981). One of the important things that happens during infancy is that the child gradually begins to differentiate the self from what is "out there." At the same time, the infant begins to recognize that there are things out there that are persons and other things that are nonpersons. Perhaps even more important, the infant begins to form attachments to one or more of the person-things. Thus begins the process of socialization (Case, 1991).

But the infant's social cognitions unfold slowly and reflect many of the limitations that characterize nonsocial cognitions. Recall how young infants, and even preschoolers, have difficulty adopting another person's point of view, as is illustrated by Piaget's mountain problem (see Chapter 7). They experience a similar difficulty with respect to social cognitions: They cannot easily make inferences about what other people are thinking or feeling. Indeed, to begin with, they are not even aware that other people exist and that they, too, have feelings and motives. The beginnings of the ability to interpret another person's social-emotional point of view—in other words, to empathize—is an essential first step in the development of social cognitions.

Role Taking and Empathy

Altruism and other forms of prosocial behavior imply caring and concern for others. They imply, as well, that those who care must be able to adopt the point of view of others. If not, they would not be able to care. Hence, there are both affective (for example, caring) and cognitive (being able to adopt another's point of view) aspects to empathy (Eisenberg, 1989).

Investigations of cognitive role taking have focused on the extent to which children are able to infer that other people may think differently from the way they do. Shantz (1975, 1983) summarizes this research in terms of four sequential stages that appear to characterize the development of cognitive role-taking skills. At the earliest stage, the child is unaware that another person is capable of having independent thoughts (or awareness). This realization seems to become general by the age of 6 and defines the second stage. During the third stage (about age 8), children realize that their own behavior may lead to inferences by others. The fourth stage, the ability to infer relatively accurately what other people are thinking, develops about the age of 10.

Selman (1980, 1981) has conducted extensive investigations of the development of social cognitions in children and summarizes their results in terms of stages, much as Piaget did. He describes the development of the child's ability to adopt and to understand another person's point of view (*perspective taking*) in terms of five stages, labeled from 0 to 4. In his investigations, he used stories that present a moral dilemma. For example:

> Holly is an 8-year-old girl who likes to climb trees. She is the best tree climber in the neighborhood. One day while climbing down from a tall tree, she falls off the bottom branch but does not hurt herself. Her father sees her fall. He is upset and asks her to promise not to climb trees any more. Holly promises.
>
> Later that day, Holly and her friends meet Shawn. Shawn's kitten is caught up in a tree and can't get down. Something has to be done right away, or the kitten may fall. Holly is the only one who climbs trees well enough to reach the kitten and get it down, but she remembers her promise to her father. (Selman, 1980, p. 36)

The story was read to each child, who was then asked whether Holly knows how Shawn feels about the kitten, what Holly thinks her father will do if she climbs the tree, how Holly's father will feel if he knows she has climbed the tree, and what the child being questioned would do in the same situation.

Selman's role-taking stages, illustrated by reference to the kitten story, are as follows:

- *Stage 0. The egocentric viewpoint.* Until about the age of 6, children are largely unaware of the existence of any perspective, or role, other than their own, very personal view. When asked how someone else is likely to feel, their responses reflect the feelings they would themselves experience: "Her daddy will be happy 'cause he likes the kitten."

- *Stage 1. Social-informational role taking.* Between ages 6 and 8, children become aware that others have different points of view, different perspectives. But they have little understanding of the reasons for these different points of view and are likely to assume that anybody who knew what they know would think and feel as they do: "He'll be mad 'cause he doesn't want her to climb trees!"

- *Stage 2. Self-reflective role taking.* Children ages 8–10 have gradually become aware that the feelings and thoughts of others, as well as their own personal feelings, can be inferred by others. But they respond only in terms of one or the other of the individuals involved: "Her father will understand why she climbed the tree."

- *Stage 3. Mutual role taking.* Between 10 and 12, children can switch effortlessly from one point of view to another and can interpret and respond as an objective onlooker might: "Holly and her father can talk to each other. They will understand each other. They can work it out."

- *Stage 4. Social and conventional system rule taking.* From ages 12 to 15 and beyond, adolescents can use the principles and the ideals of their social systems, political ideologies, or religions to analyze and evaluate their perspectives as well as those of others: "It depends on whether her father thinks the cat's life or Shawn's feelings are more important than obedience. Besides, . . ." (See Table 10.1.)

TABLE 10.1

A Developmental Progression in Social Cognition★

Selman's Perspective-Taking Stages	Examples
0: Egocentric (to 6 years)	"There is no perspective but mine. People feel the way I would in that situation."
1: Social-informational (6–8)	"Okay, so others have a point of view too, but they would feel the way I do if they had the same information."
2: Self-reflective (8–10)	"Actually, we can have different points of view. There's hers and there's mine. I can see mine; she can see hers."
3: Mutual (10–12)	"Well, maybe I can see hers and she can see mine. We can even talk about our different points of view."
4: Social-conventional (12–15 +)	"Actually, within the context of discombobulism, and taking into consideration the teachings of MUMU and the charter of personal delimitations, her point of view is totally absurd."

★ *Social cognition:* Awareness of self; awareness of others as *selves* capable of feelings, motives, intentions; ability to adopt the perspective of others and infer their emotions, motives, intentions; realization that others can infer our intentions and feelings.

Self-Worth

Social cognition involves an awareness of others as distinct selves, and an awareness of the self—a *self-concept*. Concepts such as self-worth, self-esteem, or self-concept are all aspects of what we referred to in Chapter 2 as *self-referent* thought—thought that has to do with our selves. It is in that sense, say Wells and Stryker (1988), that the self is *reflexive* (involves reflection). In addition, a sense of self implies *intention* or willfulness, and is the result of a *social* process (Schneider, 1991).

Some Definitions

In common usage, *self-concept* is an evaluative term that refers primarily to how we view ourselves. People have *positive* self-concepts when they think well of themselves, and *negative* self-concepts when they do not think much of themselves. In fact, however, **self-esteem** and **self-worth** are better terms because they are clearly evaluative.

There are aspects of the self-concept that are not evaluative. They have to do with abstract, cognitive notions of what the self is rather than with whether the self is good or bad, worthwhile or worthless, lovable or detestable, moral or immoral.

Theoretical Approaches to Self-Worth

There are two major, and very old, approaches to explaining self-worth (or self-esteem). The first, William James's *discrepancy theory* (1892), says: My self-worth is a direct function of the difference between what I would like to be and what I think I am. The closer my actual self (as I perceive my *self*) is to my ideal self (the way I would like to be), the more I will like myself, and hence the higher my self-esteem.

The second approach, Cooley's *looking-glass theory* (1902), says: My self-worth is a direct function of what I think others think of me; my worth is reflected in their behavior toward me (hence Cooley's expression *looking-glass self*). If people avoid me, that is evidence

TABLE 10.2

Two Theories of the Basis of Self-Worth

Theory	Example of Reasoning Process
Cooley: Looking-glass self (What I think important others think of me)	"Willie asked me out. Billy asked me out. Sam looks at me as if he wants to ask me out, and he could go out with anybody in the school. I must be pretty attractive."
James: Discrepancy between actual and ideal self (What I would like to be versus what I think I am)	"I'm a blonde, which is what I would want to be if I had a choice. My skin is clear, and I like my eyes—nice blue. Physically, I know I'm well, pretty attractive. But I've just been pulling off C's in school, which is the pits. I want at least B's."

that I am not very worthy; if they appear to seek me out, the evidence is more positive. Those who are most important in serving as mirrors in whose behavior I can view my *self* are people who are important to me (part of the microsystem, in Bronfenbrenner's terms). For the preschooler, the microsystem involves mostly face-to-face interactions with parents and, to some extent, siblings. For the elementary school child, the microsystem will come to include peers and teachers as well—and perhaps coaches, mentors, tutors, religious leaders, and so on. (See Table 10.2.)

Measuring and Investigating Self-Worth

Harter (1985a, 1985b, 1987, 1988) has developed an instrument for measuring self-worth based directly on James's discrepancy theory and Cooley's looking-glass approach: the *Self-Perception Profile for Children*. It asks children how well they think they do in each of the five areas considered important for self-worth: athletic, scholastic, social, physical, and moral. In some studies, children are also asked how *important* they think it is to do well in these areas. This allows investigators to compute the difference between actual performance (competence) and the child's wishes, thus providing a measure relating to James's approach to self-worth.

In some studies, children might also be asked to what extent they feel their importance is recognized by others, how well others treat them, and whether they think they are liked, admired, and respected. This line of questioning provides information relating to the regard in which others hold the child (Cooley's approach).

Finally, children might be asked questions relating to a more global concept of self-worth—to how well they like themselves as people.

Studies such as these permit investigators to answer some important questions. For example: Are competence/aspiration–based estimates of self-worth (James's theory) actually related to global notions of self? Are "looking-glass" estimates (Cooley's theory) related to general concepts of self-worth? Are discrepancies between competence and the ideal more important in one area than another? (For example, are athletics more important than scholastics?) Are there developmental changes in areas of importance? Is source of approval and social regard important?

Harter (1987) provides answers for a number of these questions based on her investigations of third-through eighth-grade children (approximately 8–13 years of age). Prior to the age of 8, children do not seem to have a single, clearly defined, and measurable notion of self-worth; accordingly, younger children are not included in her samples.

Five Findings. First, although children have a general estimate of personal worth, they also make individual estimates of self-worth in at least five separate areas: scholastic competence, athletic competence, social acceptance, physical appearance, and behavioral

INTERACTIVE TABLE 10.3

Areas in Which Children Evaluate Their Self-Worth★

▶ *Think back to when you were in seventh or eighth grade. Were you very concerned with how you looked? With your grades? With your athletic skills? Was having a lot of friends and being well liked important? Was it important to be good? Rank each of the areas described below in terms of their importance to you in seventh or eighth grade. How does your ranking compare with that shown in Table 10.4?*

Area	Description
1. Scholastic competence	How competent or smart the child feels with regard to schoolwork
2. Athletic competence	How competent the child feels at sports and games requiring physical skill or athletic ability
3. Social acceptance	How popular or socially accepted the child feels with peers
4. Behavioral conduct	How adequate the child feels with regard to behaving in the way one is supposed to behave
5. Physical appearance	How good-looking the child feels; how much the child likes such characteristics as height, weight, face, and hair

★ *Note:* Children's estimates of self-worth are based on (1) what significant other people (the microsystem) think of the child's capabilities and worth (Cooley's looking-glass theory) and (2) the extent to which the child lives up to personal ideals and aspirations (James's discrepancy between aspirations and competence theory). Both kinds of evaluations occur in the five areas described here.

Source: Based on Harter, 1987.

conduct (see Interactive Table 10.3). In other words, some children may see themselves as athletically competent (good and worthwhile); but these same children may have decided that they are not "good" in a moral sense, or that they are not as worthwhile scholastically.

Second, the child's judgments of self-worth reflect both major sources described by James and Cooley. That is, the difference between competencies (in each of the five important areas) and the child's aspirations and desires is reflected in estimates of self-worth. At the same time, how others regard the child also influences self-esteem.

Third, not all five areas are equally valued by every child. High or low competence in important areas will exercise a more powerful influence than competence or incompetence in less important areas. If athletics are more highly valued than being good (behavior conduct), not being a good athlete will be more damaging to self-esteem than misbehaving. In Harter's studies,

physical appearance is clearly the most important area in determining self-worth, both for the younger (grades 3–6) and the older (grades 6–8) children. Children who see themselves as attractive are most apt to like themselves. For both these age groups, behavioral conduct (goodness of behavior in a moral sense) was least important. (See Table 10.4.)

Fourth, as we noted, some sources of social regard and support are more important than others. For example, it might not matter very much that some anonymous fan yells disparaging remarks while 10-year-old Willie stands at the plate waiting for the pitch; but it might matter a great deal if his coach later makes the same remarks. In Harter's (1987) studies, the most important sources of support in determining self-worth, for both younger and older children, are parents and classmates, not friends or teachers. It is noteworthy that parents retain their importance through these years, since this contradicts a popular belief that as peers be-

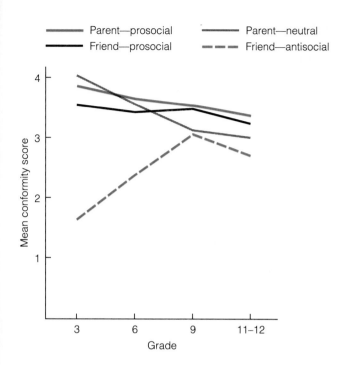

Figure 10.2 Changes in average conformity scores as a function of age and source of pressure. (From T. J. Berndt, "Developmental Changes in Conformity to Peers and Parents," *Developmental Psychology, 15*, p. 613. Copyright 1979 by the American Psychological Association. Reprinted by Permission.)

are important changes in the ways in which children interact with and conform to their parents.

In early childhood, parental authority is largely unquestioned. This does not mean that all children always obey their parents. Sometimes temptation or impulse are just too overwhelming. And sometimes, too, parents overstep the unwritten but clearly understood boundaries of authority. As Braine and associates (1991) note, parental authority does not extend to immoral acts; nor can it be permitted to infringe on important areas of personal jurisdiction such as choice of friends.

In later childhood and adolescence, parental authority is subjected to more constraints, and the child's area of control increases. Berndt (1979) asked 251 children in grades 3, 6, 9, and 11–12 to respond to hypothetical situations in which parents or peers urged them to do something antisocial, prosocial, or neutral.

As might be expected, he found that conformity to parents decreased steadily with age, and conformity to peers increased. Significantly, however, peer conformity does not increase forever, but increases from early childhood until it reaches its peak at around grades 6–9 (roughly ages 11–14); it then begins to decline again.

Unfortunately, the Berndt study does not directly compare the degree of children's conformity to peers with conformity to parents (it included no situations where parents urged children to perform antisocial acts). In addition, because the situations were hypothetical ("What would you do if . . . ?"), there is no way of determining how children would actually behave under similar circumstances in real life. Nevertheless, the results as summarized in Figure 10.2 confirm the observation that parental influence is initially relatively high but declines, whereas peer influence increases at least until the upper end of middle childhood.

Research conducted by Prado (1958) illustrates the shift in allegiance from family to peers during the transition from middle childhood to adolescence. Prado selected two groups of boys; each boy had indicated that his father was his favorite parent. One group consisted of boys ages 8–11; the second group contained boys ages 14–17. For the experiment, a boy and his father were brought to a laboratory, along with the boy's best friend—a boy of similar age who had been selected as the "best friend" on the basis of interviews and questionnaires. The friend and the father were asked to throw darts at a target. The target was arranged so that the boy could not see the exact scores

As children become older, the peer group becomes a more important socializing force. Every boy in this photograph will be influenced by the others. For each, the peer group plays an important role in determining how he dresses, the music he likes, the slang he uses, and his immediate interests. Significantly, however, his long-term goals, his ideals, and his basic values are probably more closely related to the values and goals of his parents than to those of his peers.

made by his father or his friend. His task was to estimate their performance. Strikingly, the younger boys consistently overestimated the scores made by their fathers and underestimated those made by their friends. In contrast, older boys tended to underestimate their fathers' scores and overestimate their friends' scores.

We should be cautious in interpreting studies such as these, however. That children now conform more to peers and somewhat less to parents, or that they overestimate how peers will perform in a trivial task, does not mean that peers are more important than parents in the life of the child. That is clearly not the case, as forcing children to select between parents and peers would quickly prove. Furthermore, as we saw earlier, the approval and regard of parents continues to be as important as that of peers, and more important than that of friends, in influencing feelings of self-worth.

Here, as in other areas of human development, relationships are complex and interactive. It would be misleading and simplistic to consider parent–child relations on the one hand, and child–peer relations on the other, as though they were completely isolated and unrelated. There is evidence, for example, that the kind of relationship a child has with parents is very closely related to later relationships with peers (Elicker & Sroufe, 1989). Securely attached infants are more likely to later have good relationships with peers. Similarly, the most socially competent preschool children are often those who have the most positive and playful relationships with parents (Parke, 1989). And supportive parenting during late childhood and early adolescence is closely related to competence in interaction with peers (East, 1991).

Peer Acceptance and Rejection

Peer acceptance or rejection (**sociometric status**) is typically assessed using one of two methods: *peer ratings* or *peer nominations* (Terry & Coie, 1991). In a peer-rating study, members of a group (for example, a classroom) might be asked to rate all members of the group in terms of how well they like them, whether they would like to play with them, how smart they are, how pop-

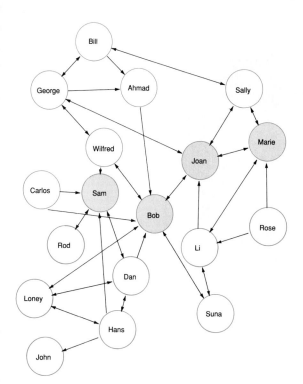

Figure 10.3 A sociogram of friendships in a fourth-grade classroom.

ular, and so on. A study using peer nominations might ask participants to name the three individuals they like best, the three they like least, the three smartest kids, and so on. Data gathered in this way can then be analyzed to provide an index of sociometric acceptance or rejection, and can sometimes be depicted pictorially in a **sociogram** (see Figure 10.3). Information of this kind is sometimes useful in research that looks at the qualities associated with popularity or social isolation.

Qualities Associated with Peer Relationships.

The characteristics of children most likely to be accepted by peers vary, depending on age and sex. In general, children who are friendly and sociable are more easily accepted than those who are hostile, unsociable, withdrawn, or indifferent (Putallaz & Gottman, 1981). Similarly, children who are intelligent and creative are more acceptable than those who are slow learners or retarded (Green et al., 1980). Size, strength, athletic prowess, and daring are particularly important characteristics for membership in boys' peer groups; maturity and social skills are more important for girls,

particularly as they approach adolescence (Langlois & Stephan, 1981). Attractiveness is important for both (Hartup, 1983). In Harter's (1987) study of self-worth, physical appearance was, in fact, what children thought was most important for being liked.

Characteristics that are often associated with peer rejection are those that make the child different or that are perceived as undesirable. In a study of 362 8- to 11-year-olds, Pope, Bierman, and Mumma (1991) found that aggressive, hyperactive, and immature boys were likely to be rejected. Similarly, Juvonen (1991) reports that those who engage in behaviors others consider deviant (rule-breaking, for example), are more likely to be rejected.

Social Competence.

The observation that friendly, socially competent children have more friends (have higher *status*, as sociologists put it) raises an interesting and important question: Are these observed differences between high-status (accepted) and low-status (rejected) children the causes or the results of their status? That is, do friendly children have many friends because they are friendly? Or are they friendly because they have many friends? Similarly, does social rejection lead to socially incompetent behavior, or does socially incompetent behavior lead to social rejection?

Research strongly suggests that popular children are popular because they are more competent socially and that unpopular children lack social skills (Asher & Renshaw, 1981). In other words, how a child interacts with others is a primary cause of social status. This is not to deny that social status also influences how a child interacts.

In support of the view that social competence is an important influence on social status, Asher (1983) reports studies in which children are observed in situations in which they are exposed to unfamiliar peers. Strikingly, after only a handful of play sessions, these children have achieved a status remarkably similar to that which characterizes their interaction with familiar peers. Perhaps even more important, certain characteristics of the interaction styles of the high-status children become readily apparent. According to Asher (1983), these reflect three important qualities of social competence.

First, socially competent children quickly sense what is happening in an unfamiliar social situation and are able to modify their behaviors accordingly. They are less likely to engage in behaviors that are inappropriate or unexpected than are socially incompetent

Research indicates that the most popular children are the most competent socially. Socially competent children sense quickly what is happening in an unfamiliar social situation, are least likely to engage in inappropriate or unexpected behaviors, are patient with relationships, and are able to respond to the leadership of others as well as to initiate activity. Socially competent children usually have many friends as well as one or two best friends. Best friends tend to be similar in important ways — and perhaps in more trivial ways, too, such as loss of front teeth.

children. Second, social competence is evident in an ability to respond to what others initiate, rather than simply to initiate. And third, the socially competent are more patient with social relationships. They realize that relationships develop slowly over time; they do not insist on becoming leaders or best friends immediately. Put another way, their social cognition (awareness of the traits and feelings of others) may be more advanced than that of lower-status children.

Sociometric Status

We are not all equally loved and sought after by our friends. Indeed, not all of us have friends. Some of us are *social isolates.*

Two definitions of social isolation are often used in studies of this phenomenon. The first looks at frequency of interaction: The socially isolated are those

who do not often interact with peers or even with adults. The second looks at the nature and extent of peer acceptance: The socially isolated are those who are seldom selected as "best friend" by anyone, and who might often be chosen as "someone I don't really like very much." These two definitions are different, says Gottman (1977). Some children are liked and accepted but do not interact much with their peers; at the same time, some children are very low on everybody's list of "my best friends" or "who I would most like to be with" or "who I would most like to be like," but they nevertheless interact frequently with peers.

In an attempt to investigate these definitions and to arrive at a clearer description of social isolation, Gottman conducted a study involving 113 children enrolled in Head Start classrooms. Each of these children was observed at length by three observers. Observations were based on a time-sampling procedure and involved detailed recordings of peer–peer and peer–

INTERACTIVE TABLE 10.5

Five Categories of Social Status

▶ *Almost every class has a sociometric star—an intelligent, socially skilled, athletic, attractive, well-liked, and well-rounded person. In my sixth-grade class, we also had heavy-limbed, round-shouldered, slow-moving John-George, who was the butt of all our cruel jokes, and who was never invited to join in any of our out-of-school activities. Can you think of at least one individual you have known who fits each of the five categories described here?*

Category	Characteristics
Sociometric stars	Especially well liked by most peers.
Mixers	High peer interaction. Some well liked; others not.
Teacher negatives	Typically in conflict with teachers. Some are liked; others not.
Tuned out	Not involved; are ignored rather than rejected.
Sociometric rejectees	Not liked very much. Rejected rather than simply ignored.

Source: Based on Gottman, 1977, 513–517.

teacher interaction, as well as observations when the child was alone. In addition, a "picture" sociometric technique was employed. It involved presenting each child with a random arrangement of classmate photographs, making sure the child recognized each of the photographs, and asking for three positive choices (someone they especially liked at school) and three negative choices (someone they did not like as much).

Gottman's data suggest five distinct categories of children (see Interactive Table 10.5). *Sociometric stars* include those who are consistently "especially liked." *Teacher negatives* are typically in conflict with teachers. These students might or might not be low on measures of peer acceptance. *Mixers* are those who interact most with peers. These, too, might be high or low on measures of acceptance. The *tuned out* are those who are frequently not involved with what is going on—who are tuned "out" rather than "in." The tuned out, rather than being strongly rejected by their peers, are simply ignored. This group includes the abnormally shy and withdrawn; it also includes those whose behavior might be described as immature. Thus, in this preschool group, many among the tuned out (the ignored) were more likely to pout, cry, shut their eyes, suck their fingers, shuffle, fall, flinch, be chased, crawl, whine, or use baby talk.

Sociometric rejectees are those who are not liked very much by any of their peers; they are actively rejected by everyone. These are the children who, in childhood, are the butts of cruel jokes and taunts. Gottman suggests it might be important for parents and teachers to know more about these socially rejected children. How do they become that way? What are the implications of social isolation? What can be done to help them?

It is important to note that there are wide individual differences in the *sociability* of different children. Not all are outgoing, talkative, expansive; many appear withdrawn and shy. We should not make the mistake of assuming that children who appear shy are also unfriendly and are likely to be rejected by their peers. In fact, countless children—and adults—who are not socially outgoing are nevertheless extraordinarily socially competent. Such children may have a large number of close friendships and might, in fact, be among Gottman's sociometric stars.

Functions of Peers

During the first years of school, children's peer groups have several important functions. One of these, discussed earlier in this chapter, has to do with the development of feelings of self-worth. As we saw, if children believe peers think highly of them, they are more likely to think highly of themselves (France-Kaatrude & Smith, 1985).

A second function of peer groups is *normative*—that is, the peer group serves to teach and reinforce key cultural *norms*. Thus peer groups are important for the formation of values and attitudes. In one study, Lamb, Easterbrooks, and Holden (1980) found that children as young as 3 reinforce their peers for sex-appropriate behavior but are quick to criticize what they perceive to be inappropriate cross-sex behavior. Not surprisingly, children who are reinforced tend to continue the behavior for which they received reinforcement. In contrast, most of those who are not reinforced or are criticized abandon their old behavior and go to some new activity within a minute or less.

This and a host of related studies leave little doubt that peers are extremely powerful sources of punishment and reinforcement. In addition, they are an important source of information about sex- and age-appropriate and inappropriate behaviors as well as about how to do things, what one should look and sound like, what music is good and bad, and on and on.

But peers are not the only source of influence on the child. The family, as we saw in Chapter 8, is another. So is the school.

The School

Outside of the family, say Asp and Garbarino (1988), the school is the most pervasive socializing influence in the life of the child. When children leave home and enter school, they leave behind much of their "play" and begin the serious "work" of childhood. Now the process of socializing takes on a new urgency—a new seriousness as the child is called upon to learn new rules and to adopt new roles. In Bronfenbrenner's terms, the transition from home to school is a transition from one microsystem (the family in face-to-face interaction) to another (teachers and peers in immediate interaction). The implications for the continued development of social, cognitive, and physical competence, as well as for the development of the child's sense of self and self-worth, can hardly be overestimated.

Schools are centrally involved in teaching children much that is necessary for their effective interaction in our increasingly complex world. They are fundamentally important as our formal, monolithic disseminators of culture. To simplify greatly, children acquire essential language and cognitive skills in schools, as well as developing the social skills and public personality that will characterize them throughout life.

Education and IQ

Schools do more than socialize children and teach them important information and skills; evidence shows that they also increase measured intelligence. For example, there has been a massive increase in IQ scores in the Netherlands since the 1950s. This increase, argue Husén and Tuijnman (1991), is due to changes in context, the most important of which may be formal schooling. Similarly, Flynn (1987) found that in 14 industrialized countries, IQ has increased about 15 points in one generation.

Additional evidence indicates that formal schooling is closely tied to measured intelligence. For example, Ceci (1991) reviews studies that show a relationship between level of schooling (grade attained) and IQ, between absences from school and declines in IQ, between delayed school entrance and lower IQ, and between increasing school attendance in a specific region and general increases in measured IQ.

The evidence, claim Husén and Tuijnman (1991), supports the conclusion "that not only does child IQ have an effect on schooling outcomes, but also that schooling per se has a substantial effect on IQ tests scores" (p. 22).

Teacher Expectations

One illustration of how schools can affect children is found in studies of the influence of teacher expectations, first investigated by Rosenthal and Jacobsen (1968a, 1968b). The study involved administering an intelligence test in the spring of the school year, telling teachers this was a test designed to identify academic "bloomers" (students *expected* to blossom next year), and later "accidentally" allowing teachers to see a list of likely bloomers. In fact, these bloomers were a randomly chosen group of about 20 percent of the school's population. No other treatment was undertaken.

Significantly, most teachers observed exactly what they expected. The experimental group not only scored higher on measures of achievement than a comparable

School has an impact not only on children's intellectual lives but also on their social and emotional lives. It is here that children develop much of the public personality and social skills that will characterize them through life. It is here, too, that they receive important information about their competence and about what others think of them—information that is critical to their development of self-esteem and self-confidence, and that contributes significantly to their happiness.

control group, but also scored higher on a general measure of intelligence.

Hundreds of replication studies have been undertaken since the Rosenthal and Jacobson research (see Meyer, 1985). Brophy and Good (1974) reviewed 60 of these studies and concluded that many were confusing and inclusive, and that none had results as dramatic as those first reported by Rosenthal and Jacobson. However, they point out that many of these studies reveal quite consistent patterns of teacher expectations that are probably linked in important ways to such crucial things as the student's self-concept and achievement. Similarly, Braun's (1976) review of the teacher-expectation literature supports the conclusion that many teachers develop consistent patterns of expectations. Specifically, teachers often develop more positive expectations for children from higher socioeconomic backgrounds, as well as for children who are obedient, attractive, and articulate, and who sit close to the teacher and speak clearly. Teachers also develop more

positive expectations for those given the most positive labels: *learning disabled* rather than *mentally retarded* (Rolison & Medway, 1985); *excellent* rather than *weak* (Babad, 1985). Thus the effects of teacher expectations have sometimes been invoked as a partial explanation for the poorer school performance of some minority group children.

Unfortunately, a cursory review of the results of studies such as these makes them seem far more dramatic and important than they actually are. In addition, there is a tendency to assume that negative expectations are more potent and more pervasive than more positive expectations. In fact, in most classrooms, the negative effects of teacher expectations are probably minor or even nonexistent. As Wineburg (1987) argues, the tremendous amount of attention that has been focused on the effects of teacher expectations probably exaggerates their significance. Changing social inequities would likely be more effective than trying to change teachers' expectations.

INTERACTIVE TABLE 10.6

Why Do You Succeed or Fail?

▶ *In Chapter 3, you were asked to figure out what Henry VIII didn't know that might have influenced his habit of beheading various wives who failed to give him sons. Did you succeed or fail? Why? Are you one of those who characteristically accept personal responsibility for successes and failures? Or are you more likely to invoke luck, the difficulty (or easiness) of the task, or other factors over which you have no control? How do you explain your high (or low) grades to yourself? Your reasons reveal important things about your personality and achievement motivation.*

External (not under personal control)	Internal (under personal control)
Difficulty (task easy or too difficult)	Ability (intelligence, skill, or lack thereof)
Luck (bad or good)	Effort (hard work, industriousness, self-discipline, or laziness, distraction, lack of time)

Self-Expectations

Teacher expectations can affect the performance of some students. Can the student's own expectations also have an effect?

Research that focuses on *attributions* suggests yes. An attribution is an assignment of cause. If I think my stupidity is due to my having hit my head on a low branch, then I *attribute* my stupidity to that event. Attribution theories look for predictable regularities in the ways in which we attribute causes to the things that happen around us (or to us) (see Weiner, 1980).

As we saw in Chapter 2, children appear to be very different in the ways in which they typically assign responsibility for their successes or failures. Some accept personal responsibility for the consequences of their behavior; they are *internally oriented* (Weiner, 1980) or, using Dweck's (1986) label, *mastery oriented*. Others are more likely to attribute successes and failures to circumstances or events over which they have no control; they are *externally oriented* (Weiner, 1980). In Dweck's terms, they are characterized by *helplessness* rather than by a mastery orientation (see Interactive Table 10.6).

Investigators have found several important differences between children who can be classed as helpless and those described as mastery oriented. First, mastery-oriented children tend to be more highly achievement oriented (Thomas, 1980). Second, mastery-oriented and helpless children react very differently to successes and failures. When Diener and Dweck (1980) arranged a problem so that all children would experience an unbroken sequence of eight successes, helpless children predicted that they would not do so well if they had to repeat the eight tasks. Children who see themselves as being helpless find it difficult to interpret success as indicating that they are capable. Even after succeeding, they not only continue to underestimate the number of likely future successes, but also overestimate the number of likely future failures. In contrast, mastery-oriented children were confident that they would continue to perform equally well. Even when mastery-oriented children are given a series of failures, they continue to see themselves as capable and to predict future success. It is as if notions of self-efficacy (effectiveness of behavior) and of self-worth are not affected when the outcomes of behavior are attributed to impersonal causes.

Changing Expectations and Attributions

Can expectations and attributions be changed, and will these changes be reflected in behavior? There is evidence that the answer to these questions is yes. Dweck and Repucci (1973) identified a group of *learned helpless* children—children who typically gave up after a single failure, even though they had both the motivation and the ability to succeed on subsequent tasks. Dweck (1975) then trained these children to take personal responsibility for failure and to attribute it to insufficient effort rather than to lack of ability. Subsequently, contrary to their earlier behavior, many of these children began to persist following failure.

A related study conducted by De Charms (1972) involves what the author terms *personal causation training*. De Charms uses his own labels: *pawns*, who characteristically see themselves as "pushed around," are *learned helpless; origins*, who see themselves as the originators of their own behaviors, are *mastery oriented*. De Charms then attempted to make pawns more like origins by giving teachers training in "personal causation"—training designed to encourage self-study, to foster the evaluation of personal motives, to bring about an understanding of the value of realistic goals and proper planning, and to highlight the importance of the distinction between origins and pawns. Subsequently, teachers helped design a series of classroom exercises for their sixth- and seventh-grade classes. These exercises were designed to achieve the same general goals as those of their own personal causation training. Final results showed an increase in both teacher and student motivation, as well as a significant increase in the academic achievement of students. It appears that children's expectations and attributions can be changed and that the effects might be highly beneficial.

What these programs have in common, Wittrock (1986) notes, is that they attempt to move the child in the direction of *effort* attributions. And there is increasing evidence they can be successful, at least in the short term. Still, several crucial questions remain unanswered. Perhaps the most important of these concerns the origins of helplessness. Although the majority of researchers think it is learned and can therefore be unlearned, the issue is still not clear (Wittrock, 1986). In addition, *helplessness* has been implicated in physical and psychological disorders, as well as in achievement

and adjustment problems, but its precise contribution to these has yet to be established (Seligman, 1975).

In summary, the influence of the school clearly goes well beyond simply imparting intellectual skills. It provides the child's first opportunity for meaningful and prolonged interaction with other significant adults and peers. It is a continuous source of information about the worth of self, as well as a constant source of models illustrating more or less acceptable behaviors.

The media, too, are a source of models.

Television

There is a fear in the hearts of many adults that mass media will taint their still naive and highly corruptible young. First to be feared were fairy tales, few of which have happy endings and even fewer of which are without violence. Next were comic books, whose primary characteristics have been described as "violence in content, ugliness in form, and deception in presentation" (Wertham, 1954, p. 90). Now there is television.

For some time now, prophets of doom have been decrying the influence of television on children. Their primary claims are that television is producing a generation of passive people or, alternatively, that the violence that pervades many television programs will produce a generation of violent people. Furthermore, claim the critics, television has harmful effects on family relationships, social and physical development, reading skills, and other areas. Although the evidence is incomplete, sufficient research exists to provide a partial response to these criticisms and to present a more balanced impression of the actual influence of television on the lives of children.

Viewing Patterns

By the early 1970s, more than 99 percent of homes with young children had television sets (Murray, 1973). Now many have two or more. A 1984 Nielsen report (Nielsen Television Index) indicates that preschool children spend almost 30 hours a week watching television. Figures for the 6- to 11-year-old group are very similar: 24.5 hours per week. A conservative estimate, Winn (1985) tells us, is that preschoolers spend more than a third of their waking time watching television. The

Is television producing a generation of passive individuals who are content to watch the world go by? Is it contributing to a society with a high tolerance for crime and violence? Or is it promoting positive behaviors such as friendliness, cooperation, empathy, and racial tolerance?

average male viewer will, between the ages of 2 and 65, watch television for almost nine years of his life. Singer and Singer (1983) point out that many young children spend more time watching television than they spend in conversation with adults or siblings. By age 18, many children will have spent about 50 percent more time watching television than going to school and doing schoolwork combined (Luke, 1988). Only sleeping will have taken more time (Huston et al., 1990).

Young children spend the greatest amount of time viewing television, followed by young adults, and elderly people. Preschoolers tend to prefer cartoons. As they get older, preferences shift to situation comedies and to action and adventure programs. During the school years, boys tend to prefer "mechanical" themes (science and action); nurturant themes (mothering and caring for) appeal more to girls (Mielke, 1983). These sex differences are not apparent in the preschool years (Anderson & Bryant, 1983).

Comprehension

What children see and understand from television might be quite different from what you or I see. As Winn (1985) points out, children do not have the same backlog of experiences and understanding that we do — their conceptual bases are more fragmented, less complete. We can evaluate television in terms of things we know and have experienced. Television reminds us of life. In contrast, children are less able to relate television's offerings to their knowledge about the world.

Collins and associates (1978) report that preschoolers respond to the most salient features of what is actually happening on television: the sights, the sounds, the action. In contrast, elementary school children become progressively more sensitive to motives and more attentive to implications of actions for the characters involved. They pay attention to *why* things happen and to the consequences of their happening, rather than simply to *what* happened. But even at the age of 5 or 6, children use fairly sophisticated cognitive skills to understand television's messages. And those with the most highly developed verbal skills have a higher level of comprehension (Jacobvitz, Wood, & Albin, 1991).

Commercial programs for young children seem to be based on the assumption that the best way to capture and hold the viewer's attention is through rapid action, constant change, high noise level, and slapstick violence (Huston & Wright, 1983). One very important question is, What are the effects of this violence on children?

PART

V

Adolescence

There is little of revivals and fires, or of theatres and sunrises, in the two chapters that summarize the adolescent experience — although there is something of scarification, circumcision, and the taboos of primitive *rites de passage*. There is also a good deal about one of the most important developmental tasks of this period: the selection and formation of an identity. It is in adolescence that we struggle to decide who we are, and that we begin to flesh out the dream of who we will be.

In these chapters, there is much, too, about newly expanding powers of mind and body — powers that make it possible to go flashing from one end of the world to the other, trying different manners, hearing chimes, and being converted at revivals.

And they make it possible to write halting verses, mostly about love.

CHAPTER 11

Physical and Cognitive Development: Adolescence

The old believe everything:
the middle-aged suspect
everything:
the young know everything.

Oscar Wilde,
*Phrases and Philosophies for
the Use of the Young*

There is an arrogance in the logic of the adolescent, an arrogance that stems from an unshakable belief in the power of logic. Adolescents do not yet have the wisdom of a more mature age. Their thinking is less influenced by social constraints or by pragmatics; it does not bow to intuition; it is absolute rather than relative.

Adolescents are intolerant of ambiguity. They are not what Basseches (1984) calls dialectical thinkers. To think dialectically is to recognize contradictions, to realize that knowledge is relative rather than absolute, to understand that the most effective thinking is contextual—that it should reflect real-life circumstances.

But the adolescent of whom we now speak is, like the child who came earlier, a mythical, idealized, *average* adolescent—a creation that does not actually exist. Many *real* adolescents are like this *average*; some are not. Not all adolescents are driven by an egocentric faith in the omnipotence of logic. Some would rather just play ball and let someone else do the thinking.

This Chapter

This chapter looks at the momentous physical changes that mark the transition from childhood to adolescence—changes that have tremendous implications for social development (covered in the next chapter). It discusses some of the implications of early and late maturation, and some of the physical concerns of adolescence that are sometimes manifested in eating disorders. Later sections in the chapter deal with the growth of logic and with manifestations of egocentrism in adolescence. The chapter concludes with a discussion of moral development and behavior.

A Period of Transition

Adolescence is the transition between childhood and adulthood—the period during which the child has achieved sexual maturity but has not yet taken on the roles and responsibilities, or the rights, that accompany full adult status.

In contemporary industrialized countries, adolescence is relatively easily defined, say Schlegel and Barry (1991): It spans the period of the teen years. But in preindustrial societies, it is not always clear that the period even exists.

Primitive Transitions

In some preindustrial societies, passage from childhood to adulthood is clearly marked by ritual and ceremony collectively termed **rites of passage**. Interestingly, even in totally unrelated societies, these rites often share several common features. Most rites of passage involve four steps. First, the child is separated from the group. A common **taboo** (forbidden behavior) during this period is that of brother–sister or mother–son contact. Second, prior to induction into adulthood, children are trained in behaviors expected of adults.

The third step is the **initiation** itself—the actual rituals that mark passage from childhood to adulthood. These ceremonies are often accompanied by feasting. They are a time of celebration; but they are also usually a time of pain and suffering. Thus many initiation ceremonies include fasting, scarification (the inflicting of wounds with resulting scars), and circumcision (Bloch & Niederhoffer, 1958).

The final step of the passage rite is **induction** (absorption into the tribe). Inductees now know, without any doubt, that they are full-fledged, adult members of their social group.

Rites of passage can serve a number of useful functions. They impart a sense of adult responsibility to children, and they lessen the ambiguity that might otherwise exist between childhood and adulthood. In addition, many primitive rites reinforce certain important taboos such as those having to do with incest. Bloch and Niederhoffer (1958) suggest this may be the main reason for separating boys and girls, as well as parents and their opposite-sexed children, prior to initiation.

High school graduations, some writers tell us, have many of the characteristics and functions of initiation rituals in some aboriginal societies. But they do not mark as clear a passage from childhood to adulthood. Society may not treat these adolescents very differently tomorrow than it did yesterday.

Another important function of a passage rite is that it creates a strong psychological bond between the initiate and the tribe, as well as among initiates. At the same time, it helps to sever bonds between the child and the immediate family. It is as if initiates are being told that they now belong to the tribe and not the family, that they can look to it for support and strength, but that they must also defend and protect it.

Contemporary Transitions

These nonindustrialized societies have no adolescence as we know it. There is only childhood, the passage, and adulthood.

We, on the other hand, have no formal rites of passage. Our young ones are exempted from the separation, the training, the initiation, and the induction. Instead, they are put through a period labeled adolescence—a period of life sometimes described as the most troubled, the most stressful, and the most difficult of all stages of development. The individual largely responsible for this description of adolescence is G. Stanley Hall (1916).

According to Hall's theory, all adolescents go through a period of *Sturm und Drang* (storm and stress). He believed that because this period of upheaval and turmoil is biologically based, it is largely inevitable, and it must also be common to all cultures. We now know that this view is fundamentally incorrect and misleading, and that this developmental period is not tumultuous for the majority of adolescents (Petersen, 1988).

In contemporary Western culture, there have not been formal rites of passage (except, perhaps, the Bar Mitzvah or the Bat Mitzvah, in which the Jewish boy or girl becomes an adult at the age of 13 through religious ceremony, and the "coming-out" party in certain social groups). Our "rites" of passage have historically been indefinite and confusing. They have included a wide range of events that can span many years: getting a driver's license, being old enough to vote or to drink, losing virginity, beginning work, growing (or trying to grow) a mustache, starting to date, and graduating from high school.

There are writers who claim that secondary schools now serve as *rites de passage* similar to the traditional rites of many nonindustrialized societies. They have all the same characteristics, Fasick (1988) argues. They exemplify *separation* (children are segregated into schools) and *training* (the adolescent is formally socialized for the responsibilities of adult life), and the high school graduation is an *initiation* and *induction* ceremony. Fasick suggests that this ceremony is almost universal for much

The Bat Mitzvah is a form of *rites de passage*. It tells children they have become adults. Graduation from secondary school may serve the same purpose for many children.

of the middle and working class; for many adolescents, it clearly marks passage from the world of childhood to a world of adult responsibilities.

In general, however, our society has been *continuous* (rather than *discontinuous*). It has not clearly demarcated passage from one stage to the next.

Physical Development

Clear, predictable biological change is the one universal feature of adolescence in all cultures (Montemayor & Flannery, 1990). Biologically, adolescence is the period from the onset of puberty to adulthood. *Puberty* signifies sexual maturity; **pubescence** refers to the changes that result in sexual maturity. These changes occur in late childhood or early adolescence. Adulthood cannot easily be defined but may arbitrarily be considered to begin at the age of 20. It would be convenient for this

text to say that adolescence begins at 12, because we have included the earlier ages in preceding developmental periods. However, it is more accurate to say that the beginning of adolescence is variable and that age 12 is a general approximation.

Age of Puberty

Puberty defines sexual maturity—the ability to make babies. As Jersild (1963) has observed, prior to puberty, individuals *are* children; afterward, they can *have* children. The problem is that it is almost impossible to determine exactly when a person becomes fertile. Past research has used the girl's first menstrual period (termed *menarche*) as the age at which puberty begins. However, a girl often is infertile for about a year after her first menstruation, so menarche is not an accurate index of puberty; nevertheless, it is a useful indication of impending sexual maturity (Malina, 1990).

It is nearly impossible to arrive at a clear index for boys, although first ejaculation (**spermarche**) is sometimes taken as a sign comparable to menarche in the girl. However, the probability that a boy can become a father immediately after first ejaculation is low—although not zero. The reason for this is that the concentration of sperm in the semen remains very low for the first year.

The average age for sexual maturity in North America is about 12 for girls and 14 for boys, immediately following the period of most rapid growth (the growth spurt). Consequently, the age of puberty may be established by determining the period during which the person grew most rapidly. The period of rapid growth may begin as young as 7¼ for girls compared with 9½ for boys. The actual range in age is wide, however. Some girls may not reach sexual maturity until age 16; some boys not until age 18 (Tanner, 1975).

The Secular Trend. In Western cultures, girls have been maturing earlier by as much as one third or one half a year per decade since 1850 (Tanner, 1955). Thus the average age of menarche has decreased from an average of approximately 17 to an average closer to 12 in the past hundred or so years. In addition, adolescents are often taller and heavier than they were several generations ago. There is evidence that this **secular trend** has slowed or stopped in most developed countries (Frisch & Revelle, 1970).

The reasons for the trend are unknown. However, it is not evident in a number of less developed parts of the world. For example, in New Guinea, menarche still occurs at ages ranging from an average of 15.5 to 18.4 (Eveleth & Tanner, 1976). This observation, coupled with the fact that the secular trend seems to be a phenomenon of the last century or so, suggests that improved health care and nutrition may be part of the explanation (Chumlea, 1982).

Pubescence

As noted, pubescence refers to all the changes that lead to sexual maturity. These changes, which are universal, are directly related to a dramatic increase in hormones (Inoff-Germain et al., 1988). Most signs of pubescence are well known. Among the first signs in both boys and girls is the appearance of unpigmented pubic hair, which is straight initially but becomes characteristically kinky and pigmented during the later stages of pubescence. At about the same time that pubic hair begins to appear, the boy's testes begin to enlarge, as do the girl's breasts. The girl then experiences rapid physical growth, her first menstrual period, the growth of axillary (armpit) hair, the continued enlargement of her breasts, and a slight lowering of her voice. The boy's voice changes much more dramatically; he, too, grows rapidly, particularly in height and length of limbs; he develops the capacity to ejaculate semen; he grows axillary hair, eventually develops a beard, and, if blessed by the gods who determine (cultural) signs of masculinity, begins to grow a matting of hair on his chest.

The changes of pubescence that relate directly to the production of offspring involve **primary sexual characteristics**. These include changes in the ovaries and the testes so that these organs are now able to produce mature ova and sperm. Changes that accompany the maturation of the sex organs but that are not directly related to reproduction involve **secondary sexual characteristics**. The appearance of facial hair in the boy and the development of breasts in the girl, voice changes, and the growth of axillary and pubic hair are all secondary sexual characteristics.

Although the age at which primary and secondary sexual characteristics develop varies a great deal, the sequence of their appearance is more predictable—although not entirely fixed. Interactive Table 11.1 summarizes that sequence.

Physical Changes

The rapid changes in height and weight characteristic of pubescence begin before the age of 12, and are shown in Figures 9.1 and 9.2 in Chapter 9. Figures 11.1 and 11.2 show average height and weight data for boys and girls ages 12–18. By the age of 11½, girls often surpass boys in height and maintain a slight advantage until 13½. Girls outweigh boys at approximately age 11, but by 14½, boys catch up to and surpass girls. An additional physical change, of particular significance to boys, is a rapid increase in the length of limbs. It is not uncommon for a boy to discover that his legs are suddenly several inches longer than they were a scant year ago and that he can reach an additional four or five inches. As a result of this growth, he acquires the gangling appearance so frequently associated with early adolescence, exaggerated by the fact that his rate of purchasing clothes is often considerably behind the rate at which he outgrows them.

INTERACTIVE TABLE 11.1

The Normal Sequence of Sexual Maturation for Girls and Boys in North America

▶ *Do you remember the timing of your puberty? Would you say it was early, average, or late? Would you have preferred a different timing? Why? (As explained in the text, early maturation is often seen as an advantage for boys, but not necessarily for girls.)*

Girls★		Boys†	
Sequence	Physiological Events	Sequence	Physiological Events
1	Beginning of adolescent growth spurt	1	Appearance of unpigmented pubic down; growth of testes and scrotum (sac containing testes)
2	Appearance of unpigmented pubic down	2	Beginning of adolescent growth spurt
3	Breast elevation ("bud" stage)	3	Enlargement of penis
4	Appearance of pigmented, kinky pubic hair	4	Appearance of pigmented, kinky pubic hair
5	Increase in size of vagina, clitoris, and uterus	5	Lowering of voice; appearance of "down" on upper lip
6	Decline in rate of physical growth	6	First ejaculations occur
7	Menarche	7	Decline in rate of physical growth
8	Development of axillary (armpit) hair; continued enlargement of breasts; slight lowering of the voice	8	Development of axillary (armpit) hair; growth of facial hair
9	Increase in production of oil; increased perspiration; possible acne	9	Increase in production of oil; increased perspiration; possible acne
		10	Growth of chest hair

★ The first of these changes may occur as young as age 7¼; the last may not be completed before age 16. Average age of menarche is 12.

† The first of these changes may occur as young as age 9½; the last may not be completed before age 18. Average age of first ejaculation is 13 to 14.

Early and Late Maturation

Figures 11.1 and 11.2 describe the physical growth of the average adolescent. But the average adolescent is no more real than the average child; both are inventions designed to bring some semblance of order to our understanding of a very complex subject. Hence, although the average adolescent matures at 12 or 14 (depending on sex), some mature considerably earlier and

some considerably later. Because maturity tends to be judged by physical appearance, the age at which the physical changes of adolescence take place are very important to the child.

In general, early-maturing boys suffer fewer psychological problems than those who mature later, largely because they often excel in activities and abilities that are highly prized in the adolescent peer culture. Not only are they larger and stronger, and therefore

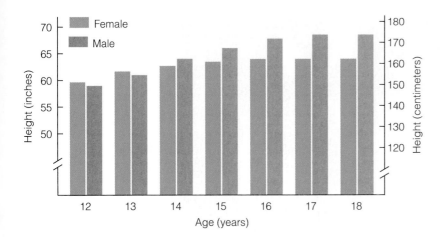

Figure 11.1 Height at 50th percentile for U.S. children. (From the Health Department, Milwaukee, Wisconsin; based on data by H. C. Stuart and H. V. Meredith, prepared for use in Children's Medical Center, Boston. Used by permission of the Milwaukee Health Department.)

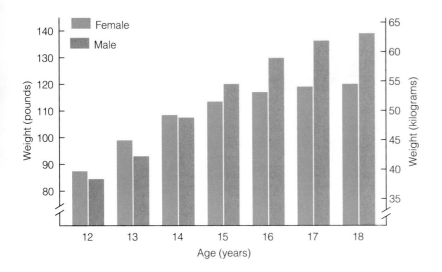

Figure 11.2 Weight at 50th percentile for U.S. children. (From the Health Department, Milwaukee, Wisconsin; based on data by H. C. Stuart and H. V. Meredith, prepared for use in Children's Medical Center, Boston. Used by permission of the Milwaukee Health Department.)

more likely to excel in athletic activities, but also they are more likely to serve as leaders in heterosexual activities. Longitudinal studies of early and late maturation in boys have usually provided clear and consistent findings. Early-maturing boys are typically better adjusted, more popular, more confident, more aggressive, and more successful in heterosexual relationships. In addition, they appear to have clear advantages with respect to more positive self-concepts (more about this in the next chapter). In contrast, adolescent boys who mature later than average are, as a group, more restless and more attention seeking; they are also less confident and have less positive self-concepts (Crockett & Petersen, 1987; Jones, 1957; Jones, 1965).

The apparent advantages of early maturation among boys are most evident *during* adolescence; and they apply primarily to social areas (adjustment, popularity,

and leadership). In later life, the advantages of early maturation are not nearly so apparent (Clausen, 1975).

Findings are more inconsistent for girls. Some studies indicate that early-maturing girls are initially at a disadvantage, a finding that directly contradicts the results of similar studies conducted with boys. In later adolescence, however, these disadvantages have often disappeared (Siegel, 1982). Thus the effects of early and late maturation in girls seem to depend on their ages. Early maturation is a disadvantage in the fifth or sixth grade, when most girls have not yet begun to mature and when the early-maturing girl is likely to find herself out of step with her peers and to be excluded from peer group activities. Because girls are also, on the average, two years ahead of boys, the early-maturing girl may well be four or more years in advance of like-aged boys, which would not contribute positively

Although they are the same age, these adolescent girls will reach sexual maturity at different times, some as early as 9 or 10, others as late as 16. For boys, early maturation is most often an advantage in terms of adjustment, popularity, leadership, and self-esteem. In contrast, early-maturing girls are initially at a disadvantage when their precocious development puts them out of step with their peers. The advantages and disadvantages of early or late maturation often disappear with age.

to her social life. However, starting around seventh or eighth grade, when most of her age-grade mates have also begun to mature, the early-maturing girl may suddenly find herself in a more advantageous position. Her greater maturity is now something to be admired.

In summary, the effects of early and late maturation appear to be different for males and females. As Petersen (1988) notes, pubertal change is most stressful when it puts the adolescent out of step with peers, especially if the change is not interpreted as desirable. And the consequences of maturational timing are most clearly understood in terms of their effects on relationships and interactions that are important to the adolescent. Thus early maturation may enhance peer relations for boys but is less likely to do so for girls. Furthermore, evidence suggests that relations with parents are

better for early-maturing boys and for *late*-maturing girls (Hill, 1988; Savin-Williams & Small, 1986).

From an ecological perspective, what we know of the implications of maturational timetables presents an excellent example of child characteristics interacting with each other (specifically, degree of sexual maturity interacting with age) to determine important elements of the child's ecology (namely, the nature of interaction with parents and peers). Still, the child's ecology is individualistic; every child–other interaction creates a unique microsystem. Thus, although some general advantages or disadvantages may be associated with the timing of pubescence, there are many individual exceptions to our generalizations. Not all early-maturing boys and girls are characterized by the same advantages or disadvantages; nor are all those who mature later affected in the same way.

Physical Concerns of Adolescents

Frazier and Lisonbee (1950) asked 10th-grade adolescents to indicate problems that concerned them and the degree to which they were worried about each. Items most frequently listed as the greatest worry for boys included the presence of blackheads or pimples, irregular teeth, oily skin, eyeglasses, and slight physical abnormalities such as too thin or too long noses, too dark skin, heavy lips, protruding chins, and so on.

Girls, like boys, were most concerned about the presence of blackheads or pimples. Scars, freckles, birthmarks, and moles were also a source of worry, as were fears about being homely, having oily skin, and wearing glasses.

Physical concerns for today's adolescent have changed little. Almost half of Canadian adolescents indicate that their physical appearance is a matter of much concern, and almost the same number are worried about their height or weight (Bibby & Posterski, 1985). In this survey, the adolescent's greatest worry concerned life beyond graduation—"What am I going to do after high school?"—a problem that affected approximately two thirds of all respondents. Other concerns had to do with money, achievement in school, boredom, loneliness, and the parents' marriage (see Interactive Table 11.2).

Interestingly, the adolescent's worries about physical changes typically do not include concerns about menarche or spermarche, *providing* the child has been prepared for these events. Gaddis and Brooks-Gunn (1985) interviewed 13 young adolescent boys and found that of the 11 who had experienced ejaculation, most had strong positive feelings about the event and none had been upset or ashamed. However, two of the boys had been unprepared for the event (often nocturnal upon first occurrence, and referred to as a "wet dream") and had been very frightened. Girls' recollections of their menarche are often not as positive, perhaps because of the lingering remnants of cultural attitudes that led to menstruation being labeled "the curse" (Morrison et al., 1980). However, menstruation is not a source of worry for most girls.

The adolescent's concern with the body is to be expected, not only because of the role that appearance plays in peer acceptance but also because of the way perception of the body affects self-concept. It is not surprising that the preferred body type for adolescent males is athletic—neither obese nor thin (Lerner &

Korn, 1972). Nor is it surprising to find that the desire of some young adolescent girls to be slim is sometimes so overwhelming that it can be reflected in serious eating disorders.

INTERACTIVE TABLE 11.2

Personal Concerns of Contemporary Adolescents

▶ *Were the concerns listed here* your *concerns when you were an adolescent? Are your current concerns—if you have any—different from these?*

Concern	Percentage Indicating Much or Some Concern
What am I going to do when I finish school?	68
Finances (40 percent of respondents worked part-time)	54
School concerns (relating to the fact that many do not find school enjoyable and to concerns over grades)	50
Time (do not feel they have enough time to do the things they want)	48
Appearance	44
What is the purpose of life?	44
Boredom	43
Height or weight	43
Loneliness	35
Feelings of inferiority (poor self-image)	29
Sex	28
Parents' marriage	20

Source: From *The Emerging Generation: An Inside Look at Canada's Teenagers* by R. W. Bibby and D. C. Posterski. © 1985, Irwin Publishing, Inc. Adapted by permission from Table 4.1, p. 60.

Surveys of adolescents indicate that future work and career is a predominant concern, as are more immediate problems relating to finances and to school. In addition, almost half of all adolescents express concern over their physical appearance and their height and weight. Among their physical worries are skin problems, irregular teeth, eyeglasses, and what they see as physical imperfections (noses too long, teeth too large, eyebrows too thin, and so on). The appearance of facial hair that needs to be shaved—or the lack thereof—can also be a source of concern.

Nutrition

Most adolescents, especially if they are very active physically, expend a large number of calories each day. In addition, during the rapid skeletal and muscular growth of pubescence—the growth spurt—their bodies require a high intake of protein and minerals, and especially of calcium, for normal growth. Calcium deficiencies, especially in women, sometimes become apparent in later life in the form of osteoporosis (a weakening and thinning of the bones). As a result, we should not be alarmed to see our adolescents consuming great mounds of hamburgers, devouring bowls of spinach and lentils and lettuce, and drinking gallons of milk.

But we should be concerned if they consume mostly "empty" snacks and sugar-laden drinks, or if

they eat too little of anything at all, or if they eat only in binges. Any of these might be a sign of a serious problem.

Obesity

As we saw in Chapter 9, obesity is the most common nutritional problem among children. Unfortunately, obese children often grow up to be obese adolescents. Consequently, obesity is also the most common nutritional problem among adolescents, affecting up to a quarter of all North American teenagers (Whitney & Hamilton, 1984).

The consequences of obesity are serious and far-reaching, which is not surprising given that physical appearance is probably the most important influence on the adolescent's feelings of self-worth (Harter, 1990). In addition to its negative effects on health, obesity contributes to peer rejection, to negative peer interactions, to low self-esteem, and to unhappiness (Baum & Forehand, 1984). It is also associated with poorer performance in school, although it isn't clear whether this is because obese adolescents are subject to discrimination, because they are expected to do less well, because they avoid participation, because teachers involve them less, because they lack self-esteem or independence, or because of other factors (Morrill et al., 1991).

At a superficial level, the causes and cures of obesity seem simple. Other than for rare glandular and metabolic problems, and genetic contributions notwithstanding, obesity in adolescents—and others—is caused by taking in more calories than are expended. Weight reduction can therefore be achieved by consuming fewer calories and by expending more.

Unfortunately, the problem is not so simple. Its alleviation requires nutritional information that not all adolescents have or are interested in acquiring; and it requires changing habits that are not only self-rewarding but encouraged by the media, and that are consequently extraordinarily persistent. As a result, obesity continues to be a very significant North American problem, and its alleviation a major industry.

Strangely, in spite of the prevalence of obesity, contemporary Western societies place tremendous emphasis on physical attractiveness, which, especially among girls, is clearly defined as *thinness*.

Anorexia Nervosa

Translated literally, *anorexia nervosa* means loss of appetite as a result of nerves. It describes a complex and only partly understood condition that may be increasing in frequency.

Definition. Anorexia is defined medically as involving a loss of at least 15–25 percent of "ideal" body weight, this loss not being due to any detectable illness. The American Psychiatric Association (1987) definition includes intense fear of gaining weight, disturbance in body image, and significant weight loss as criteria. An upcoming revision of its *Diagnostic and Statistical Manual* proposes to include a *bulimic* subtype characterized by usual symptoms of anorexia nervosa *plus* recurrent episodes of binge eating (Wilson & Walsh, 1991).

Prevalence. Crisp (1980) estimates that as many as 1 percent of girls ages 16–18 are anorexic; other estimates have been much higher. Pope and associates (1984) conducted a survey of 544 female college and secondary school students and found that somewhere between 1 and 4.2 percent could be described as anorexic, depending on the definitions used. Similarly, using very strict criteria for diagnosis of anorexia, Crisp, Palmer, and Kalucy (1976) found that 1 percent of the girls in nine London schools were severely anorexic.

In a study of more than 1,250 13- to 19-year-old adolescents, Lachenmeyer and Muni-Brander (1988) found that a full 13 percent of the girls reported significantly restricting their diets. These were girls who scored very high on a test designed to measure eating attitudes and behaviors that are known to be associated with anorexia. Although not every one of these "restricters" (see Tables 11.4 and 11.5) meets strict criteria for a diagnosis of anorexia, each is at risk. Although anorexia continues to be far more common among girls than boys, eating disorders are now more frequent among adolescent boys than had previously been suspected. Significantly, in this same comprehensive survey, 6.3 percent of the males in a lower socioeconomic sample (primarily black and Hispanic students) and 3.4 percent of a higher socioeconomic sample (primarily white) were also restricters. These rates for males are much higher than have traditionally been reported.

Causes. The causes of anorexia nervosa are neither simple nor well understood. Although there is some evidence of endocrine imbalances in anorexia (Walsh, 1982), as well as some indications that the disease may be genetically linked (Holland et al., 1984), the condition is acknowledged to be primarily psychological. Some speculate that anorexic individuals are typically those who do not feel that they are in control of their lives but who discover that they *can* control their body weight; in the end, control becomes an obsession. Other researchers suggest that lack of positive self-image, coupled with the emphasis that society places on thinness (particularly for females), may be manifested in anorexia in those cases where the person attempts to obtain parental and social approval by dieting.

Treatment. Anorexia nervosa is a particularly frightening and baffling condition for parents. It is frightening because it can be fatal; it is baffling and frustrating because it sometimes seems to parents that the

"Mirror mirror on the wall who is . . ." The message the mirror gives this girl can be tremendously important, given that her culture places extreme value on thin female bodies. Messages interpreted as unflattering may be related to some serious adolescent eating disorders. *Anorexia nervosa*, a sometimes fatal medical condition, is characterized by a loss of at least 15–25 percent of *ideal* body weight. It is often associated with a distorted body image (the very thin anorexic may still see herself as undesirably large). Even more common is *bulimia*, which is characterized by recurrent episodes of binge eating, often followed by self-induced vomiting, strict diets, and the use of laxatives.

anorexic adolescent *deliberately* and unreasonably refuses to eat. Neither pleas nor threats are likely to work. What is?

Because anorexia nervosa is not, in most instances, primarily a biological or an organic disorder, its treatment is often complex and difficult. There are no drugs or simple surgical procedures that can easily cure it, although in some instances, patients respond favorably to antidepressant drugs such as chlorpromazine (Walsh, 1982). Sometimes, it is necessary to force-feed anorexic

individuals to save their lives. In the main, however, successful treatments have typically involved one of several forms of psychotherapy. Among these, behavior therapy — the use of reinforcement or punishment, or both, in attempts to change behavior — has sometimes been dramatically effective, as have approaches that treat the entire family as a *system* that affects each of its individual members (Griffin, 1985). In addition, group therapies have sometimes been effective (Kline, 1985).

TABLE 11.3

Possible Medical Consequences of Bulimia and Bulimarexia

Excessive weight fluctuations.

Dehydration and fluid shifts, sometimes resulting in headaches and fainting. Problem more serious if diuretics are used or if bulimia or bulimarexia follow prolonged fasting.

Electrolyte imbalance, aggravated by laxative or diuretic use as well as by repeated vomiting.

Hypoglycemic symptoms.

Malnutrition-related problems (might include cardiovascular, kidney, gastrointestinal, or blood problems as well as insomnia).

Dental/oral problems sometimes associated with loss of enamel as a result of frequent exposure to stomach acids during vomiting episodes. Other possible gum, salivary duct, and tongue problems associated with emesis (vomiting).

Specific gastrointestinal difficulties, sometimes associated with ipecac abuse. Prolonged use can lead to cardiac problems and death.

Laxative-related problems that vary, depending on the nature of the laxative abused.

Insomnia resulting from malnutrition, nocturnal binges, or underlying depression.

Various neurological and endocrine problems.

Source: Based on "Medical Aspects of the Bulimic Syndrome and Bulimarexia" by E. T. Goode, 1985, *Transactional Analysis Journal, 15,* pp. 4–11.

Bulimia Nervosa

Whereas anorexia nervosa is characterized by not eating (in spite of the fact that some anorexics occasionally do go on eating binges), *bulimia nervosa* (or *bulimia*) involves recurrent episodes of binge eating.

Definition. The American Psychiatric Association (1987) defines bulimia in terms of *recurrent* episodes of binge eating, where the patient is aware that the eating pattern is not normal and where depression, or at least self-deprecation, follows the eating binge. In addition, criteria for diagnosing bulimia include a feeling of lack of control over eating behavior; inconspicuous eating; abdominal pain; self-induced vomiting; repeated attempts to lose weight through stringent diets, cathartics, diuretics, or self-induced vomiting; and persistent overconcern with body shape and weight. *Bulimarexia* is the term sometimes employed to describe a pattern of binge eating following by self-induced purge. (See Table 11.3 for a list of possible medical consequences.)

A proposed change in the new revision of the American Psychiatric Association's definitions would include *binge eating* as a separate disorder marked by recurrent eating binges without purging, exercising excessively, or using diuretics to reduce weight (Wilson & Walsh, 1991).

Prevalence. Bulimia is a more common eating disorder than anorexia. In Pope and associates' (1984) study of 544 female college students, between 1 and 4.2 percent of the sample could be classified as anorexic; a frightening 6.5–18 percent were bulimic. In another study, of a sample of 500 students who had gone to a university psychiatric clinic, 4.4 percent met all the criteria for classification of an eating disorder (Strangler & Printz, 1980). Of these, an astounding 86.4 percent were bulimic. Similarly, in the Lachenmeyer and Muni-Brander (1988) survey, 7.6 percent of the total *nonclinical* lower socioeconomic sample and 4.7 percent of the higher socioeconomic sample met *all* the criteria for a clinical diagnosis of bulimia! What is perhaps equally astounding is that the proportion of the clinically bulimic who are male is again much higher than expected: 5.7 percent of the lower socioeconomic group, compared with 9.7 percent female; and 2.1 percent of the higher socioeconomic group, compared with 7.6 percent female. Percentages of the sample who occasionally binged or induced vomiting, or both, and who used laxatives, diuretics, and diet pills, were also very high (see Tables 11.4 and 11.5).

Causes. The characteristics that most clearly differentiate bulimic girls from those who are nonbulimic include a greater desire to be thin, a higher degree of dissatisfaction with their bodies, and chronic dieting. In addition, bulimic girls are most likely to see themselves as being overweight and are far more concerned with being thin. In addition, they tend to be significantly more depressed (Post & Crowther, 1985).

TABLE 11.4

Prevalence Rates for Eating Disorders: Gender Comparison (Study I — Low Socioeconomic Sample)*

	Percentage		
	Female	Male	Total
Eating disorders			
Binge	51.8	49.7	50.0
Vomit	19.8	23.6	21.9
Binge and vomit	12.5	12.0	12.2
Clinical bulimia† (DSM-III)	9.7	5.7	7.6
Bulimia–1†	24.7	12.2	18.0
Bulimia–2†	12.5	5.7	8.8
Restricting	13.1	6.3	9.4
Laxatives	2.7	2.3	2.5
Diuretics	0.5	1.3	1.1
Diet pills	9.5	3.0	6.0

* Sample consisted of 328 females, 384 males, a total of 712.

† Clinical bulimics meet all DSM-III criteria for bulimia. Bulimia–1 individuals meet all criteria except one. Bulimia–2 individuals meet all criteria except two.

Source: From "Eating Disorders in a Nonclinical Adolescent Population: Implications for Treatment" by J. R. Lachenmeyer and P. Muni-Brander, 1988, *Adolescence 23* (90), pp. 303–312. Adapted by permission of Libra Publishers, Inc.

TABLE 11.5

Prevalence Rates for Eating Disorders: Gender Comparison (Study II — High Socioeconomic Sample)*

	Percentage		
	Female	Male	Total
Eating disorders			
Binge	65.6	57.9	62.3
Vomit	22.6	22.5	22.6
Binge and vomit	14.6	15.3	15.0
Clinical bulimia† (DSM-III)	7.6	2.1	4.7
Bulimia–1†	4.5	0.4	2.7
Bulimia–2†	22.0	5.9	15.0
Restricting	13.6	3.4	9.3
Laxatives	4.0	6.0	4.9
Diuretics	5.0	5.5	5.3
Diet pills	16.6	6.4	12.2

* Sample consisted of 314 females, 235 males, a total of 549.

† Clinical bulimics meet all DSM-III criteria for bulimia. Bulimia–1 individuals meet all criteria except one. Bulimia–2 individuals meet all criteria except two.

Source: From "Eating Disorders in a Nonclinical Adolescent Population: Implications for Treatment" by J. R. Lachenmeyer and P. Muni-Brander, 1988, *Adolescence 23* (90), pp. 303–312. Adapted by permission of Libra Publishers, Inc.

Marston and associates (1988) report that adolescents who are most at risk of compulsive overeating are those whose parents have the highest frequency of addictive problems (alcoholism, drug use, overeating, and gambling).

Polivy and Herman (1985) suggest that part of the explanation for bulimia may lie in the fact that dieting promotes the adoption of cognitive, rather than phys-iological, controls over eating. Whereas food intake would normally be regulated by the physiological mechanisms that have to do with hunger, the dieter deliberately takes conscious control of food intake and ignores physiological indicators of hunger. And perhaps the binges that follow dieting are partly facilitated by the awareness (cognition) that the individual can control the effects of the binge through a purge and through

TABLE 11.6

The Imaginary Audience Scale (IAS)

Instructions: Please read the following stories carefully and assume that the events actually happened to you. Place a check next to the answer that best describes what you would do or feel in the real situation.

TS scale   1. You have looked forward to the most exciting dress-up party of the year. You arrive after an hour's drive from home. Just as the party is beginning, you notice a grease spot on your trousers or skirt. (There is no way to borrow clothes from anyone.) Would you stay or go home?
_____ Go home.
_____ Stay, even though I'd feel uncomfortable.
_____ Stay, because the grease spot wouldn't bother me.

AS scale   2. Let's say some adult visitors come to your school and you are asked to tell them a little bit about yourself.
_____ I would like that.
_____ I would not like that.
_____ I wouldn't care.

TS scale   3. It is Friday afternoon and you have just had your hair cut in preparation for the wedding of a relative that weekend. The barber or hairdresser did a terrible job and your hair looks awful. To make it worse, that night is the most important basketball game of the season and you really want to see it, but there is no way you can keep your head covered without people asking questions. Would you stay home or go to the game anyway?
_____ Go to the game and not worry about my hair.
_____ Go to the game and sit where people won't notice me very much.
_____ Stay home.

AS scale   4. If you went to a party where you did not know most of the kids, would you wonder what they were thinking about you?
_____ I wouldn't think about it.
_____ I would wonder about that a lot.
_____ I would wonder about that a little.

Source: From "Imaginary Audience Behavior in Children and Adolescents" by D. Elkind and R. Bowen, 1979, *Developmental Psychology, 15* (1), pp. 38–44. Copyright 1979 by the American Psychological Association. Reprinted by permission.

How does research investigate beliefs such as these? How can psychology locate an imaginary audience? With an instrument—Elkind and Bowen (1979) have developed one—appropriately called the *Imaginary Audience Scale (IAS)*. It is based on the assumption that individuals will be *self-conscious* to the extent that their behaviors are subject to examination by an imaginary audience. The scale attempts to measure two areas of self-consciousness: *abiding* or relatively permanent aspects (labeled AS for *abiding self*) and temporary or transient aspects (labeled TS for *transient self*). One example of an abiding aspect of self is intelligence; a more transient characteristic is hairstyle or clothing.

Items for the IAS were selected from a pool of suggestions given by students who were asked to describe situations they might find embarrassing. The final scale consists of 12 items, the first 4 of which are reproduced in Table 11.6.

Elkind and Bowen administered the IAS to 697 students in grades 4, 6, 8, and 12. Two of their findings are noteworthy. First, young adolescents (eighth-grade students) were significantly more reluctant to reveal themselves to an audience than were younger children or older adolescents. Second, girls obtained higher scores than boys on the test. Adolescent girls seemingly are more concerned with imaginary audiences than are

At a Glance

Adolescent Risks and Violent Death

The risk-taking behavior of adolescents, especially of adolescent males, may be due in part to what Elkind labels the *personal fable* — the feeling that the adolescent is special and somehow invulnerable, that bad things happen only to other people. Risk-taking behavior is manifested in drug abuse, dangerous hobbies, and automobile and other accidents, and is especially evident in the incidence of violent death among white adolescent males. Violent death among blacks is more common than among whites and does not reveal the same pattern of higher incidence in adolescence, perhaps because it involves a higher proportion of homicides, which continue at a high rate after adolescence, and perhaps because of more limited access to automobiles. For both blacks and whites, violent death is considerably lower for females than for males.

| Age | White | | Black | |
	Male	Female	Male	Female
15–24	113.4	33.3	175.1	35.0
25–35	97.3	26.5	204.8	50.3
35–44	81.5	24.6	185.0	40.7
45–54	73.8	26.7	143.5	32.2
55–64	80.0	30.1	129.2	35.3
65 and older	156.3	84.1	193.7	84.0

Source: U.S. Bureau of the Census, 1991, p. 85.

Table 11.7 1988 U.S. Death Rates (per 100,000) by Age for Accidents, Suicides, and Homicides Combined

adolescent boys; and both are more responsive to these audiences than are younger or older subjects.

Some studies that have used Elkind and Bowen's IAS (or the Adolescent Egocentrism Scale developed by Enright, Shukla, and Lapsley, 1980) have found considerable variability in the ages at which children become egocentric, or have found less evidence of egocentrism (Buis & Thompson, 1989). Still, in the majority of cases, adolescents manifest some degree of egocentrism (Lapsley, 1990). But we don't yet understand its origins, and our instruments for measuring it need improvement.

Clarification of adolescent egocentrism might have practical implications, quite apart from how it might illuminate the adolescent experience for us. Elkind (1981b) suggests that it might contribute to our understanding of vandalism, teenage pregnancy, drug abuse, and other related behaviors. One of the motives that might underlie these behaviors may relate to what the adolescent expects the reaction of the imaginary audience to be. Teachers, parents, counselors, and friends are all members of that audience.

Personal Fable

Adolescent egocentrism is reflected not only in the creation of an imaginary audience but also in the elaboration of fantasies, the hero of which is, not surprisingly, the adolescent. These fantasies, labeled **personal fables**, have several identifying themes, the most common of which are "I am *special*"; "I will not get pregnant"; "I will not become addicted to these drugs that I take only for fun"; "Mom, you just don't understand what real love is"; "You don't either, Dad!"; "I will not have an accident."

One of the characteristics of the personal fable is a sense of invulnerability. Unfortunately, it is often sadly inappropriate, as is evident in the fact that adolescents—especially males—have the highest accident rate of all age groups except for those over 65 (U.S. Bureau of the Census, 1988) (see Table 11.7).

Elements of the personal fable run through the lives of most of us. We believe that we are somewhat different—just a little special. But these beliefs appear to be greatly exaggerated in adolescents and may account in part for the casualness with which they will take risks that they know *cognitively* to be horrendous—and perhaps even immoral.

Moral Development

With the conviction that frequently accompanies intuition, most of us believe that people are good or bad in differing degrees, that goodness or evil is an intrinsic part of what we are—of our *selves*. Are we really *good* or *bad*? Or do we simply behave well some of the time and badly at other times? Do we learn moral behavior and thinking? Does it develop as the child develops? Psychology says yes, morality is at least in part a decision-making process that develops and changes predictably from childhood to adolescence.

Behaving Morally

Carroll and Rest (1982) identify four separate components involved in behaving morally. First, moral behavior requires recognizing a moral problem and being sensitive to the fact that someone's welfare is involved. Second, the individual needs to make a judgment about what is right and wrong—about what ought to be done in a given situation. Third, the individual needs to make a plan of action that takes into account relevant ideals and values. Finally, the plan must be put into action.

It is entirely possible, Carroll and Rest argue, to fail to act morally because of a deficiency in only one of these components. Research on bystander intervention, stimulated by the now-famous murder of Kitty Genovese, is a case in point (Latané & Darley, 1970). Kitty was killed in full view of at least 38 of her neighbors, many of whom watched for the entire half hour during which the murder was taking place, and none of whom came to her assistance or even called for help. How can their behavior be interpreted in light of Carroll and Rest's analysis of what is required for moral behavior?

Clearly, some of the bystanders who failed to respond might not have recognized the seriousness of the situation ("It's only a lover's quarrel"); others might have been unable to devise a plan of behavior compatible with their ideals and values ("How can I save her life without endangering mine?"); still others might have felt incapable of implementing the plan they might have devised ("I should restrain the attacker physically, but I am not strong enough"); finally, there is the chilling possibility that some among the bystanders

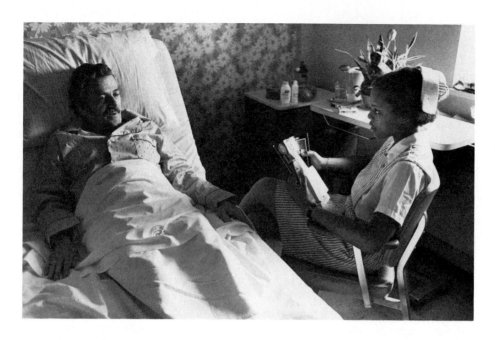

Carroll and Rest suggest that moral behavior involves four components: recognizing a situation or problem with implications for moral behavior, making a judgment about behavior that would be correct or moral, formulating a plan for behaving according to the values and ideals that apply in the situation, and putting the plan into action. One characteristic of highly moral individuals is altruism — selfless, helping behavior.

might have developed values that run counter to helping ("If he wants to kill her, hey, it's up to him").

To summarize, the four components of moral behavior are:

■ Moral sensitivity (recognition of a moral problem)

■ Moral judgment (deciding what *ought* to be done)

■ Moral values (conscience; ideals; that which guides moral action)

■ Moral action (moral or immoral behavior)

Two of these, moral values (conscience) and the development of moral judgment, are especially important in psychology and have been extensively researched. We look at them, and at their relationship to moral action, in the remaining sections of this chapter.

Conscience

What is a strong *conscience*? there are two historical approaches to answering this question. The psychoanalytic approach is based on the belief that the strength of the superego is the strength of conscience. It asserts that the stronger people's beliefs are about the immorality of an act, the less likely they are to engage in that act. But empirical evidence has not always supported this position. Several studies and reports (for example, Hendry, 1960) have indicated a low relationship between the strength of people's beliefs and actual behavior. Under some circumstances, the probability of behaving morally seems to have more to do with anticipated reward and with the probability of getting caught than with conscience.

The second approach, a more religious one, is based on the belief that a good conscience is a manifestation of strength of character and good habits that have become engrained in the individual, usually through religious training. Here, too, available evidence suggests that religious training has less to do with children's behavior than the likelihood of their being caught or the gains to be derived from transgression (Kohlberg, 1964). Other related factors are the individual's intelligence, ability to delay gratification (to choose long-range goals over short-range objectives), and self-esteem. Children who have favorable self-concepts apparently are less likely to engage in immoral behavior, presumably because they are more likely to feel guilty if they do.

Morality as a Cognitive Phenomenon

Based on these findings, Kohlberg argues that moral behavior is primarily a matter of strength of will (ego strength) rather than strength of conscience, superego, or character. In other words, **morality** is not a fixed behavioral trait but rather a decision-making capacity. Specifically, it refers to behaviors and judgments relating to broad issues of human justice, such as the value of human life, the ethics of causing harm to others or to their property, and the place of trust and responsibility.

Darley and Shultz (1990) speak of three different kinds of justice that might be considered when investigating moral development. *Retributive justice* relates to punishment; *distributive justice* has to do with fairness in the allocation of rewards; and *procedural justice* relates to the impartiality and fairness of the methods by which moral decisions are reached.

Because morality is viewed primarily as a decision-making process, it has been investigated mainly as a cognitive phenomenon. Not surprisingly, the models that have guided most of the research have been based closely on Piaget's work and, more recently, on information-processing theories. Clearly, however, morality includes not only thought but also emotion and behavior (Walker, 1988).

Piaget's Stages

Piaget (1932) investigated children's notions of evil by telling them stories and asking them to make judgments about the goodness or evil of the characters. For example, he told a story of a child who accidentally breaks 15 cups, asking the subject to compare this behavior with that of a child who deliberately breaks a single cup. From the children's responses to these stories, Piaget reached the general conclusion that there are two broad stages in the evolution of beliefs about guilt. In the first, lasting until about 9 or 10 years of age, the child judges guilt by the objective consequences of the act: The child who accidentally broke the larger number of cups is considered more evil than the one who deliberately broke only one cup.

Very young children do not respond in terms of abstract conceptions of right and wrong as might an adolescent, but rather in terms of the immediate personal consequences of their behavior. Thus a young child's morality is governed by the principles of pain and pleasure. Good behaviors are those that have pleasant consequences; bad actions have unpleasant consequences. Piaget's label for this first stage of moral development is *heteronomy*. During this stage, the child responds primarily to outside authority, since authority is the main source of reinforcement and punishment.

In the second stage, children's judgment becomes more adultlike—they are more likely to consider the motives behind an act. Thus morality comes to be governed more and more by principles and ideals. Moral judgments become more individual and more autonomous; hence Piaget's label, *autonomy*, for the second stage.

Piaget thought that the transition between heteronomy and autonomy likely happened by the age of 9 or 10. However, subsequent research indicates that children as young as 6 or 7 may consider the actor's intentions in judging the severity of an act (Darley & Shultz, 1990). Thus children will judge an act more harshly if it *intentionally* causes harm than if the harm is unintentional. Similarly, they will judge an actor more punishable if the harm should have been foreseen even if it was unintentional (Darley & Zanna, 1982). Also, children at this age have begun to consider other mitigating circumstances in their judgments of culpability. Thus various justifications such as necessity or provocation, or the fact that the transgressor has attempted restitution, serve to reduce the degree to which children think a transgressor should be punished.

In some ways, then, the moral judgments of children are somewhat similar to those of adolescents and adults. But, as Kohlberg's (1980) research shows, in other ways children think quite differently.

Kohlberg's Stages

Kohlberg (1969, 1980) describes three levels in the development of moral judgments, each consisting of two stages of moral orientation (see Interactive Table 11.8). The three levels are sequential, although succeeding levels never entirely replace preceding ones, making it almost impossible to assign ages to them.

Average children normally progress from an initial, preconventional stage, in which they respond mainly to punishment or reward, to a rule-based, highly conventional morality. The final, *postconventional* level, in which individuals respond to principles rather than to rules or to personal consequences, appears to be reached by only a handful of individuals. A reanalysis of Kohlberg's original data suggests, in fact, that only approximately one eighth of subjects in their twenties operate at a stage-5 level (Colby & Kohlberg, 1984). And evidence of stage-6 judgments (based on universal ethical principles) could not be found in that sample. Accordingly, although stage 6 is still included in Table 11.8 it

Kohlberg's Levels of Morality

▶ *Heinz's wife is dying, but the local pharmacist has discovered a drug that might save her life. Unfortunately, he charges such an exorbitant price that Heinz can't afford to buy it. Should he steal it? Why? Why not? Write out your answer and reasons, and then compare them with the sample responses given below to obtain a rough description of your moral orientation. The highest levels of moral judgment are rare or perhaps nonexistent in practice.*

Level 1 Preconventional	Stage 1: Punishment and obedience orientation	"If he steals the drug, he might go to jail." (Punishment.)
	Stage 2: Naive instrumental hedonism	"He can steal the drug and save his wife, and he'll be with her when he gets out of jail." (Act motivated by its hedonistic consequences for the actor.)
Level II Conventional	Stage 3: "Good-boy," "nice-girl" morality	"People will understand if you steal the drug to save your wife, but they'll think you're cruel and a coward if you don't." (Reactions of others and the effects of the act on social relationships become important.)
	Stage 4: Law-and-order orientation	"It is the husband's duty to save his wife even if he feels guilty afterwards for stealing the drug." (Institutions, law, duty, honor, and guilt motivate behavior.)
Level III Postconventional	Stage 5: Morality of social contract	"The husband has a right to the drug even if he can't pay now. If the druggist won't charge it, the government should look after it." (Democratic laws guarantee individual rights; contracts are mutually beneficial.)
	Stage 6: Universal ethical★	"Although it is legally wrong to steal, the husband would be morally wrong not to steal to save his wife. A life is more precious than financial gain." (Conscience is individual. Laws are socially useful but not sacrosanct.)

★ Stage 6 is no longer included among Kohlberg's stages. None of his sample reached it. However, it is still described as a *potential* stage.

Source: Based on Kohlberg, 1969.

exists as a *potential* stage rather than as one that has been discovered in behavior.

Preconventional. At the preconventional level, the child's judgment of right and wrong takes one of two orientations. In the first stage, the child believes that evil behavior is that which is likely to be punished, and good behavior is based on obedience or the avoidance of disobedience. The child does not evaluate right or wrong in terms of the objective consequences of the behavior or the intentions of the actor; judgment is based solely on the consequences to the child. Accordingly, the second moral orientation (stage 2) possible at this level is a hedonistic one, in which the child inter-

prets good as that which is pleasant and evil as that which has undesirable consequences. At this stage begins the reciprocity that characterizes morality at the second level, but it is a practical reciprocity. Children will go out of their way to do something good for someone if they themselves will gain by the deed.

Conventional. The second level, a morality of conventional role conformity, reflects the increasing importance of peer and social relations to the developing child. Stage 3, for example, is defined as morality designed to maintain good relations. Hence, moral behavior is behavior that receives wide approval from significant people: parents, teachers, peers, and society at large. Stage 4, conformity to rules and laws, is also related to the child's desire to maintain a friendly status quo. Thus, conforming to law becomes important for maintaining adults' approval.

Postconventional. At the highest level, the individual begins to view morality in terms of individual rights (stage 5) and as ideals and principles that have value as rules or laws, apart from their influence on approval. As we noted, however, stage-5 moral judgments are rare even among adults; stage-6 judgments, based on fundamental ethical principles, are even rarer. Colby and Kohlberg (1984) suggest that stage 6 is *potential* rather than actual.

A Seventh Stage? But Kohlberg (1984) also spoke of the possibility of a seventh stage—a mystical, contemplative, religious stage—a metaphorical stage in which, through the "logic of contemplation and mystical logic . . . we all know that the deepest feeling is love and the ultimate reality is life" (Hague, 1991, p. 283).

Generality of Kohlberg's Stages

Kohlberg's early research suggests that children progress through the stages of moral development in predictable sequence and at roughly the same ages. Theoretically, this makes sense, because moral judgments are mainly *cognitive* and would therefore be expected to reflect levels of cognitive development. As Walker (1988) explains, preoperational thought parallels stage-1 moral reasoning (physical consequences and authority determine morality); concrete operations make stage-2 morality possible (morality is instrumental and self-serving); and the beginning of formal operations is necessary for stage-3 morality (the emphasis is on being a "good" person; what is approved of is moral). Successively higher stages of moral judgment are made possible by the elaboration and consolidation of formal operations.

Note that the higher stages of moral development do not necessarily accompany advances in intellectual development. What Kohlberg and his followers maintain is that certain levels of cognitive performance are *essential* for corresponding levels of moral reasoning, but are not *sufficient*.

A number of researchers have criticized Kohlberg's concept of stages of moral development, and have challenged his belief that these stages parallel cognitive

development and that they are universal. For example, Holstein (1976) found that many subjects skipped stages, reverted to earlier levels of moral reasoning, or were so inconsistent in their responses to moral dilemmas that they could not easily be classified as being at any stage. Similarly, Kurtines and Grief (1974) and Fishkin, Keniston, and MacKinnon (1973) found few advances in moral reasoning among older children; they found that subjects often operated at different stages depending on the specifics of the moral questions to which they were responding.

Based on these criticisms, Kohlberg (1980) eliminated the sixth stage (no one ever reached it) and revised the scoring methods for the moral dilemma questions. He then reanalyzed his original data using the new scoring procedures (Colby & Kohlberg, 1984). What the reanalysis indicated was that progression through the stages takes much longer than had at first been thought and that postconventional morality is the exception rather than the rule, even among adults.

Ten-year-olds were typically either in stage 2 or still in transition between stages 1 and 2; young adolescents (ages 13–14) were usually still in transition between stages 2 and 3; and late adolescents as well as early adults were mainly in stage 3. As we noted previously, only one of every eight adults in this sample operated at a postconventional level.

Although Kohlberg's reanalysis indicates that the stages span a wide spread of ages, it also provides some support for his contention that these are legitimate stages in that they conform to the three common criteria for stages: (1) progression is upward, not backward; (2) there is no skipping of stages; and (3) the thinking that is characteristic of a stage is generally applied to all content areas while the individual is at that stage.

Walker (1988) subsequently analyzed and summarized a large number of studies that have examined Kohlberg's findings. He also concludes that there is little skipping of stages or regression to earlier stages.

Most of the research agrees, however, that the higher stages are not characteristic of adolescent—or even adult—thinking (Lapsley, 1990). Most young adolescents reason at a preconventional, stage-2 level (a self-serving, hedonistic morality), or at a conventional, stage-3 level (emphasis on conforming, being good, doing the expected). In fact, stage-3 reasoning is not very common until age 16–18, though it becomes more common in adulthood.

Some researchers suggest that Kohlberg's moral dilemmas are perhaps too verbal and too abstract for children. They require that the child understand and keep in mind very complex situations involving a number of actors and circumstances. Often, they do not provide enough information, but if they did, they would be even more complex. As a result, the Kohlberg dilemmas might underestimate children's moral reasoning. When questions are made simpler, or when children and adolescents are observed in naturalistic settings, researchers sometimes find evidence of very sophisticated moral reasoning at very young ages (Darley & Shultz, 1990; Lapsley, 1990).

Gilligan's Approach

In addition to the criticism that progression through Kohlberg's stages may not be as systematic as Kohlberg had thought, Gilligan (1977) suggests that Kohlberg's research suffers from at least two other important weaknesses. One is that all his subjects were male — and there is evidence of important male–female differences in morality. The second is that the moral dilemmas that he employed in his investigations are usually irrelevant to the lives of his subjects. A person's response to an abstract and hypothetical moral dilemma ("What would you do if you had to choose between letting your partner die and spending the rest of your life in jail?") might be quite different from that person's actual behavior in the case of a *real* dilemma.

Gilligan reasoned that subjects' apparent stages of moral reasoning might seem *higher* in the case of an abstract and impersonal moral dilemma such as Heinz's problem (see Interactive Table 11.8) than they would be in the case of a more immediate and perhaps more realistic dilemma.

Following this line of real rather than abstract reasoning, Gilligan (1982) examined morality in women by interviewing them while they were caught up in an actual moral dilemma. Her subjects were 28 women who had been referred to a counseling clinic for pregnant woman and who were currently facing the need to make a decision about having an abortion.

Following an analysis of the women's reasons for having or not having an abortion, Gilligan identified three stages in female moral development. In the first stage, the woman is moved primarily by selfish concerns ("This is what I want . . . what I need . . . what I should do . . . what would be best for me"). In the second stage, the woman progresses through a period of increasing recognition of responsibility to others.

And the final stage reflects a morality of caring and compassion. At this stage, the woman's decision is based on her desire to do the greatest good both for herself and for others.

If Gilligan's description of female moral development is accurate, it reflects several important differences between male and female morality. In contrast with Kohlberg's description of male moral progression from what are initially hedonistic (pain–pleasure) concerns toward a conventional, rule-regulated morality, Gilligan describes female moral progression from initial selfishness toward a recognition of social responsibility. Women's is a morality of *caring* rather than of *abstract justice*.

Nunner-Winkler (1984) elaborates Gilligan's position by reference to Kant's (1977 [1797]) distinction between *negative* and *positive* moral duties. Negative duties are illustrated in rules such as "Do not kill" and "Do not steal." These rules are absolute and clear; you follow them, or you do not. In contrast, positive duties are open-ended. They are reflected in rules such as "Be kind" and "Be compassionate." There are no boundaries to or limits on positive duties. They don't specify how kind, to whom, how often, when.

Negative duties, says Nunner-Winkler, reflect the justice orientation of males; females feel more obliged than males to fulfill positive duties, which relate more closely to caring and compassion.

Do women and men see the world differently, and make different moral judgments? Some research says yes. Stimpson and associates (1991) asked college students to rate 18 adjectives having to do with "interpersonal sensitivity" and "caring." Females consistently rated these adjectives higher in terms of goodness than did males. Similarly, Eisenberg and associates (1991) found that girls' prosocial reasoning was higher than boys' in late childhood and adolescence.

But other research has not found clear evidence of sex differences in morality. Muss (1988) reviewed a number of studies and concluded that the distinctions between male and female morality are not very clear. He reasons that if Gilligan's descriptions are correct, it follows that females should, on average, be more altruistic, more empathetic, more concerned with human relations; in contrast, males should be less altruistic. But research on altruism, cooperation, and other forms of prosocial behavior has not found these differences. Note, however, that these findings do not invalidate Gilligan's basic conclusions. Males and females may well be equally altruistic, but their altruism might stem from fundamentally different orientations, reflecting very different moralities. Females may, as Gilligan suggests, be altruistic because of their concern for humanity; males may be just as altruistic because of their adherence to principles and ideas that stress the injustice of being unkind.

One of the important contributions of Gilligan's approach is that it underlines the need to be aware of the possibility that many of our theories and conclusions about human development are not equally applicable to males and females. In Gilligan's (1982) words, the sexes speak *in a different voice*. Neither voice is louder or better; they are simply different.

Implications of Research on Moral Development

Some of the most important implications of our knowledge about morality relate to the observation that individuals who operate at the lowest levels (hedonistic) are more likely to be delinquent than those who operate at higher levels. As Gibbs (1987) notes, the delinquent's behavior generally reflects immature moral reasoning and egocentricity. Individuals who operate at higher levels of morality are more likely to behave morally (Kohlberg & Candee, 1984). By the same token, altruism in children is closely related to level of moral development. Children who are still at a hedonistic level (*good* things are those that lead to pleasant consequences) typically engage in less prosocial behavior (in this case, share less) than children at more advanced stages (Eisenberg-Berg, 1979). To the extent that these observations accurately describe reality, anything that schools, families, and other socializing influences can who employed arguments at a level higher than that at do to increase levels of moral orientation should be beneficial.

What, precisely, can schools and parents do? Although suggestions must still remain relatively abstract, research deliberately designed to increase levels of moral judgment or behavior in adolescents indicates that this is possible. Kohlberg reports, for example, that simply discussing moral dilemmas in the classroom can lead to an increase in levels of moral judgment (advancing approximately one third of a stage) (Kohlberg, 1978). And Arbuthnot (1975) reports an investigation in which older adolescents displayed higher levels of moral reasoning following role-playing situations involving moral dilemmas. In the Arbuthnot investigation, subjects played a role with a partner (opponent)

which the subject had been assessed. Modeling procedures have also been employed to increase morality (Damon & Colby, 1987).

Clearly, the development of morality is an important social and parental responsibility. Hoffman (1976) suggests four different types of activity that might be conducive to the development of altruistic, caring behavior:

- Situations in which children are allowed to experience unpleasantness rather than being overprotected
- Role-taking experiences in which children are responsible for the care of others
- Role-playing experiences in which children imagine themselves in the plight of others
- Exposure to altruistic models

One additional approach seems especially effective in fostering moral growth in adolescents: sociomoral discourse. Berkowitz, Oser, and Althof (1987) provide evidence that discussing moral problems and evaluating the ethical implications of behavior in groups can do much to elevate moral judgment and behavior.

In addition to what schools and educators might attempt to do, the values and behaviors of parents are highly instrumental in determining those of their children. For example, research reveals a clear relationship between parenting styles and children's morality. The internalization of moral rules is fostered by two things: (1) the frequent use of discipline that points out the harmful consequences of the child's behavior for others, and (2) frequent expression of parental affection (Hoffman, 1979). Most forms of parental discipline, Hoffman argues, contain elements of "power assertion" and "love-withdrawal." That is, discipline usually involves at least the suggestion of the possibility of loss of parental love as well as something such as deprivation of privileges, threats, or physical punishment. The main purpose of this "power assertion," according to Hoffman, is to get the child to stop misbehaving and pay attention. From the point of view of the child's developing morality, however, what is most important is that there now be an accompanying verbal component. The purpose of this verbal component is to influence the child cognitively and emotionally—perhaps by bringing about feelings of guilt or empathy, and by enabling the child to foresee consequences.

The future of this world depends on the morality of our children.

Main Points

1. In many nonindustrialized (discontinuous) societies, passage from childhood to adulthood is marked by *rites of passage*. Four common steps in these rites are separation, training, initiation (sometimes with scarification and circumcision), and absorption into the tribe. Continuous societies have no such rites, although some writers claim that secondary schools serve as rites of passage.

2. Puberty is sexual maturity. It results from pubescence — the period of change that includes the boy's ability to ejaculate semen and the girl's menarche. Most girls are unlikely to become pregnant for approximately one year following menarche. For the past several centuries, puberty has tended to occur earlier in succeeding generations in industrialized countries (due to improved health care, nutrition, and living conditions).

3. The changes of pubescence that make reproduction possible involve changes in *primary* sexual characteristics (menstruation and the capacity to ejaculate semen). Other changes that are not directly linked to reproduction involve *secondary* sexual characteristics (axillary hair, breasts, and voice changes, for example).

4. Early maturation appears to be initially advantageous for boys but may be less so for girls. Pubertal change is most stressful when it puts the adolescent out of step with peers, especially if it is not seen as desirable. Common adolescent concerns include worries about such things as the future, finances, school, appearance, feelings of inferiority, loneliness, the purpose of life, sex, the stability of the parental marriage, and lack of time.

5. Because of rapid muscular and skeletal growth during this period, adolescents require large amounts of protein and minerals such as calcium. Most also expend a relatively large number of calories, but obesity is still the most common nutritional problem of adolescence in North America. Alleviation of this problem requires nutritional information and important changes in attitudes and habits, and is often difficult.

6. *Anorexia* involves significant weight loss, refusal to maintain weight, and distorted body image. It is most common among adolescent girls (10 times more girls than boys). It is probably associated with our sociocultural emphasis on thinness. It can sometimes be treated with antidepressant drugs or with one of a number of psychotherapies.

7. *Bulimia* is defined in terms of recurrent episodes of binge eating that are accompanied by the realization that the behavior is not normal and by feelings of guilt or self-deprecation. The binges are sometimes followed by self-induced "purges" through laxatives, diuretics, or vomiting. Bulimia is more common than anorexia. Both are more common among girls than among boys and increasing in frequency. Bulimics sometimes respond to psychotherapy.

8. The intellectual development of the adolescent may culminate in thought that is potentially completely logical, is inferential, deals with the hypothetical as well as with the concrete, and is systematic. Formal operations make possible a type of intense idealism that may be reflected in adolescent frustration or rebellion, as well as in more advanced levels of moral orientation.

9. Information-processing views of development are concerned with the acquisition of a knowledge base, the development of information-processing strategies, and the development of metacognitive skills. Knowledge bases grow with experience (and schooling). Cognitive processing abilities develop by increasing capacity and through the acquisition of better and more appropriate processing strategies. Metacognitive skills relate to the child's increasing awareness of self as a processor of information and to an increasing understanding of the processes involved in learning and remembering.

10. Adolescent egocentrism describes a self-centeredness that often leads adolescents to believe that all others in the immediate vicinity are highly concerned with their thoughts and behaviors. It may be manifested in the creation of the *imaginary audience* (an imagined collection of people assumed to be highly concerned about the adolescent's immediate behavior) and the *personal fable* (a type of

fantasy whose themes stress the individual's invulnerability and uniqueness).

11. Carroll and Rest describe four components of moral behavior: (1) recognizing a moral problem (*moral sensitivity*), (2) deciding what ought to be done (*moral judgment*), (3) devising a plan of action according to ideals (*moral values*), and (4) implementing the plan (*moral action*). Failure to act morally may be the result of a deficiency in any one of these four components.

12. Kohlberg describes the development of morality as a sequential progression through three levels: *preconventional* (concerned with self—pain, pleasure, obedience, punishment), *conventional* (concerned with the group, with being liked, with conforming to law), and *postconventional* (concerned with abstract principles, ethics, social contracts). Each level consists of two stages.

13. Some evidence suggests that progression through these stages is not always sequential, that some subjects skip stages, and that subjects' responses are not always very consistent. Kohlberg's reanalysis of his original data using revised scoring procedures suggests that the stages are sequential and that subjects are consistent. However, none ever reaches the sixth stage, and the majority continue to operate in the second level throughout life—that is, at the conventional level ("I'll be a good boy/girl so you will like me; I'll obey the law because it's the law").

14. Gilligan's work suggests that men and women differ in their moral development. Whereas men become progressively more concerned with law and order, women respond more to social relationships and to the social consequences of behavior.

15. Various programs using indoctrination, role playing, and modeling have been successful in increasing levels of moral judgment and, sometimes, moral behavior in students. Two parenting-style variables are especially important in the internalization of moral rules: the use of discipline that points out the harmful consequences of the child's behavior for others, and the frequent expression of parental affection.

Further Readings

The following is an excellent collection of essays dealing with the transition from childhood to early adolescence. Especially pertinent to this chapter are Malina's essay on physical growth and performance, Eisenberg's essay on morality and prosocial development, and Lapsley's account of social/cognitive development:

Montemayor, R., Adams, G. R., & Gullotta, T. P. (Eds.). (1990). *From childhood to adolescence: A transitional period?* (Vol. 2). *Advances in adolescent development*. Newbury Park, CA: Sage.

The following volume is an excellent introduction to Kohlberg's ideas:

Kuhmerker, L. (Ed.). (1991). *The Kohlberg legacy for the helping professions*. Birmingham, AL: Religious Education Press.

An excellent account of contemporary adolescence, viewed against the backdrop of historical changes in adolescence, is provided by:

Kett, J. F. (1977). *Rites of passage: Adolescence in America, 1790 to the present*. New York: Basic Books.

Eating disorders are a subject of considerable current interest and research. An entire issue of the following journal is devoted to examining their nature and treatment:

Transactional Analysis Journal (1985), Vol. 15.

For a comprehensive collection of sometimes complex, although often fascinating, articles dealing with current approaches to cognition, see:

Chipman, S. F., Segal, J. W., & Glaser, R. (Eds.). (1985). *Thinking and learning skills* (Vol. 2). *Research and open questions*. Hillsdale, NJ: Erlbaum.

CHAPTER 12

Social Development: Adolescence

It's all that the young can do for the old, to shock them and keep them up to date.

George Bernard Shaw,
Fanny's First Play

One of my cousins, who should still remain nameless, is a good example of Shaw's "young." The summer she turned 16, she became pregnant—which was a totally unexpected turn of events especially since, just the summer before, she had been one of our gang, just as wild as the rest of us, but wild in a male kind of way. She was tough and strong and brash, and none of us thought of her that way at all.

But it wasn't so much because it was unexpected that we were shocked; it was because we were products of our families, of our religion, of our close-knit peer system. Our own peculiar small-town ecology had conspired with the larger social pressures of that age to produce a generation of adolescents and adults whose values condemned premarital intercourse, and whose morality was profoundly offended and scandalized by teenage pregnancy.

We felt shame for my cousin.

Had we been products of another context, we might have reacted very differently.

This Chapter

This chapter looks at adolescent social development not only in the North American context, but also in other more universal contexts. It deals with the evolution of the self, with emerging gender roles, with sexual beliefs and behaviors, and with some instances of adolescent turmoil and rebellion.

Keep in mind that change is a fundamental part of all of life through the entire lifespan. Our attitudes and our values are not fixed immutably, bound always to reflect the social, religious, political, educational, and family contexts from which we emerged at adolescence.

Even I would no longer be surprised or shocked by my cousin's pregnancy.

Contexts might be seen as exercising an equalizing influence. The pressure of a single ecology tends to produce individuals with similar values and attitudes. Clearly, however, we don't all turn out the same. Not a single one of us is average in every respect. Our selves and our identities are solely our own. Still, they, too, reflect our contexts.

Self and Identity

The self is central to a study of adolescence. But it is a difficult and complex notion, as is evident in the number of related expressions psychology has invented: self-concept, self-esteem, self-worth, self-image, identity.

The Self in Adolescence

In Chapter 10 we spoke of the evaluative aspects of *self* in childhood, often labeled self-worth or self-esteem. Self-worth (or self-esteem) is a reflection of how well one likes oneself. In childhood, self-evaluation is possible in a variety of areas, each of which is more or less important in determining global evaluations of self-worth. For example, Harter (1983) studied children's evaluations of self-worth in five areas: athletic, scholastic, social, physical, and behavioral. For those who think being a good athlete is most important for being liked, evaluations of their worth as athletes contributes significantly in determining global self-worth.

In adolescence, the evaluation of self becomes more cognitive, say Byrne and Shavelson (1987). It is based on a more objective (rather than emotional) understanding of who and what the self is—rather than mainly on how well adolescents like themselves or how competent they think they are in important areas. According to Byrne and Shavelson, adolescents make cognitive inferences about the *self* in different specific activities (playing ball, writing English compositions, solving arithmetic problems, playing the harpsichord, carrying on conversations) as they perceive and evaluate their behaviors in these areas. Inferences in specific areas lead, in turn, to inferences about the self in general areas (for example, athletics or academics). All these inferences lead ultimately to a general self-concept. And although this general self-concept is arrived at through a series of cognitive inferences, it is clearly evaluative. It is difficult to make judgments about what the self is

Teenagers who have positive self-images are often thought of highly by others; and those who are popular and well-liked tend to have positive self-images.

without also at least implicitly deciding whether that is good or bad, desirable or undesirable. Our notions of self-identity are always evaluative.

Self-Image and the Offer Questionnaire

The term *self-image* is used extensively in adolescent research. It means something very much like what we have taken self-esteem or self-worth to mean. Thus the *Offer Self-Image Questionnaire*, a widely used instrument for assessing self-image, has teenagers report on their attitudes toward and feelings about themselves in a number of different areas (Offer, Ostrov, & Howard, 1981).

Offer's Facets of Self. The questionnaire is based on the assumption that the adolescent has a multiplicity of selves that can be considered and evaluated separately:

- *Psychological self.* Composed of the adolescent's concerns, feelings, wishes, and fantasies. This self reflects adolescents' emotions, their conceptions of their bodies, their ability to control impulses.

- *Social self.* Consists of adolescents' perceptions of their relationships with others, their morals, their goals and aspirations.

- *Sexual self.* Reflects attitudes and feelings about sexual experiences and behavior.

- *Familial self.* Consists of adolescents' feelings and attitudes toward parents and other members of their family.

- *Coping self.* Mirrors psychological adjustment and emotional well-being, and taps, as well, how effectively the adolescent functions in the outside world.

The Offer questionnaire investigates each of these five facets of self by presenting adolescents with a series of statements (for example, "Being together with other people gives me a good feeling") and having them select one of six alternatives relating to how well the statement describes them (ranging from *describes me very well* to *does not describe me at all*). (See Table 12.1.) Each descriptor in the questionnaire is worded both positively and negatively.

The Offer questionnaire was developed more than 20 years ago (scoring procedures have changed since then) and has now been given to tens of thousands of adolescents. Results provide important data concerning the adolescent experience.

TABLE 12.1

Facets of Self in the Offer Self-Image Questionnaire

Important Aspects of Self★	Relevant Self-Evaluative Questions
Psychological self	Do I like my body? Am I in control of myself? What are my wishes? My feelings? My fantasies?
Social self	Am I friendly? Outgoing? Do people like me? What kind of morals do I have? What are my aspirations? Am I a loner?
Sexual self	How do I feel about sex? What do I think of pornography? Am I sexually attracted to others? Sexually attractive to them? Comfortable with my sexuality?
Familial self	How do I feel about my parents? Home? Siblings? Other relatives? Do I prefer to stay home? Do people at home like me? Need me? Want me?
Coping self	How effective am I? How well do I cope with what others demand? What school demands? What I demand? Am I well adjusted? Reasonably happy? How decisive am I?

★ *Note:* What the adolescent feels about each of these *multiple selves* has important implications for adjustment and happiness.

In a massive study, appropriate translations of the Offer Self-Image Questionnaire were administered to 5,938 adolescents in 10 different countries (Australia, Bangladesh, Hungary, Israel, Italy, Japan, Taiwan, Turkey, former West Germany, and the United States) (Offer et al., 1988). One of the objectives was to compare adolescents' self-images in each of these countries, and arrive at a better understanding of what is universal about adolescence in today's world and what might be specific to given cultural contexts. Adolescents included in the study were both male and female, classified into two age groups: younger (ages 13–15) and older (ages 16–19).

The Universal Adolescent. What is similar about adolescence in these ten countries? A surprising number of things. The "universal adolescent," to use Offer and associates' phrase, resembles most other adolescents in some ways with respect to each of the major facets of self-image:

■ *Psychological.* The universal adolescent is usually happy and optimistic, and enjoys being alive.

■ *Social.* The universal adolescent enjoys the company of others, is caring and compassionate, and places great value in school, education, and preparation for adult work.

■ *Sexual.* The universal adolescent is confident about the sexual self, and willing to talk and think about sex.

■ *Familial.* The universal adolescent expresses strongly positive feelings toward parents, a high degree of satisfaction with home lives, and good feelings about relationships at home.

■ *Coping.* The universal adolescent expresses confidence in his or her ability to deal with life, and feels talented and able to make decisions.

The Context-Bound Adolescent. But there are differences, too, across these cultures. Adolescents from Bangladesh, for example, were consistently lower on impulse control. Forty-two percent of the Bengali (Bangladesh) adolescents reported they were constantly afraid; many admitted feeling inferior to other people, as well as feeling sadder, lonelier, and more vulnerable. Why? Context seems the most plausible explanation. This was the poorest of the countries sampled. Lack of economic opportunities and adequate medical care, coupled with widespread disease and starvation, might well lead to feelings of vulnerability and fear.

Other cross-national differences included the very high value placed on vocational and educational goals by American adolescents and the very low value placed

---

▶ Subject   Female; age 14; ninth grade. (concerning worries, irritations, minor complaints, small concerns)

....

❝ *I don't really worry very much or have a lot of problems. I know you psychologists think we should have, but lots of us don't. I mean, we're not always 100 percent happy with everything but . . . well, there's a few things I would change if I could. My parents are pretty strict. I guess I'd change that. I'd like them to trust me more. Like on weekends, making me come home at 11 o'clock when my friends can all stay out (at a rollerskating rink) till they close. It's embarrassing being treated like a 12-year-old.* ❞

---

on them by Hungarian and Israeli teenagers—probably because vocational choice is a complex and important developmental task for American adolescents. For most Israeli and Hungarian adolescents, choices are more limited or are largely predetermined by society.

Not surprisingly, there were marked differences in the sexual attitudes of adolescents from some countries. In particular, Turkish and Taiwanese adolescents reported extremely conservative sexual attitudes and behaviors—clear evidence of the extent to which such attitudes are influenced by cultures (see Table 12.2). Similarly, Israeli adolescents reported the most positive family relationships, again not very surprising given the emphasis on family and community.

Sturm and Drang?   G. Stanley Hall believed that adolescence is a period of *sturm and drang* (storm and stress) for most adolescents in *all* cultures because the mood swings, the irritability, the conflict of this period are related directly to a dramatic increase in sex hormones. But when Buchanan, Eccles, and Becker (1992) examined the research, they found this supposition to be untrue. Adolescents are not victims of raging hor-

mones, they claim; in fact, nonbiological, contextual factors are more important influences on adolescent moods and behavior than are hormones. Not surprisingly, if the Offer and associates (1988) cross-national study were to be summarized in a single paragraph, it might read something like this: Contrary to what has been a popular view of adolescence since G. Stanley Hall's pronouncements about the storm and stress of this period, adolescence throughout the world is predominantly a positive, nonturbulent, energetic, growth-filled period.

At the same time, approximately 15 percent of North American adolescents describe themselves as anxious, depressed, confused, and emotionally empty (Offer, Ostrov, & Howard, 1984). True, this is a minority; but it is a relatively large one—and a very significant one. It includes adolescents whose notions of self-worth are largely negative but whose lives are only moderately unhappy; it includes, as well, those who are profoundly unhappy, who are delinquents and criminals, who seek out and instigate violence, who abuse drugs, who are depressed and prone to suicide. We speak again of these turmoil topics in the final section of this chapter.

Identity

The notion that one of the most important aspects of all development is the development of high self-esteem (self-worth) is shared by many psychologists. Erikson's (1968) work is probably the best example of a theory devoted to clarifying the importance of self or identity (see Chapter 2). By the term *identity*, Erikson (1968) means a sort of *wholeness* that derives from the past but that also includes future goals and plans. As Waterman (1984) puts it, identity means

> having a cleary delineated self-definition comprised of those goals, values, and beliefs to which the person is unequivocally committed. These commitments evolve over time and are made because the chosen goals, values, and beliefs are judged worthy of giving a direction, purpose, and meaning to life. (p. 331)

For Erikson, the development of strong feelings of identity—of clear feelings of who one is—is the most important developmental task of adolescence. Accordingly, the primary developmental crisis facing the adolescent is the conflict between accepting, choosing, or

TABLE 12.2

Sexual Self: Items Within Each Self Showing Consistent Intercountry Differences Across Age and Gender★

Number	Item	Percent Endorsement								
		Australia	Bangladesh	Hungary	Israel	Italy	Taiwan	Turkey	United States	West Germany
28	Dirty jokes are fun at times.	82	33	39	78	69	43	19	78	69
77	I think that girls/boys find me attractive.	53	63	58	68	55	41	59	73	63
91	Sexually I am way behind.	20	26	11	10	7	33	19	24	11
97	Thinking or talking about sex scares me.	7	50	13	6	7	27	22	10	6
117	Sexual experiences give me pleasure.	67	44	65	72	67	22	49	74	67
119	Having a girl-/boyfriend is important to me.	69	77	68	75	76	52	74	73	82

★ Items presented (1) were on a scale on which at least one country was consistently high (or low) in all four age-by-gender cells and (2) were consistently high (or low) for that country for that scale. Consistently high (or low) was defined in terms of being in the upper (or lower) third of nine countries in all four age-by-gender cells. Percentages shown are the average percent endorsement for that item for the country across four age-by-gender cells.

Source: From *The Teenage World: Adolescents' Self-Image in Ten Countries* by D. Offer, E. Ostrov, K. Howard, and R. Atkinson, 1988, New York: Plenum. Reprinted by permission of the author and publisher.

▶ Subject   Male; age 19; freshman college student. (concerning future plans)

66 *Well, no, I guess I really haven't decided what I'm going to be. There are lots of different things I think I'd like for a career. Something social, probably. I've thought of being a social worker or a psychologist even. Like maybe a counselor. But I've thought about going into business too, which is what I think my dad would like. It would probably be a lot easier and I'd maybe make a lot more money. Maybe that's important too, but I want to do something that I'd really like. Something that I'd be proud to say, "I'm a such and such!" I just don't know for sure what that's going to be.* 99

discovering an identity and the diffusion of the adolescent's energies resulting from conflict and doubt concerning choice of identities. Recall that the fifth of Erikson's eight developmental stages is labeled *identity versus role diffusion.*

Resolution of adolescents' identity crises can take a variety of forms, the most common of which is the selection of an identity that conforms to societal norms and to individuals' expectations of themselves. Erikson points out that one of the major social functions of prolonged adolescence is simply to serve as a breathing space (a moratorium, in his terms) during which adolescents can experiment with different roles in their quest for identity. He is not particularly alarmed that some of these roles constitute *negative identities* (delinquency and other forms of rebellion, for example), because in most cases they are temporary, eventually giving way to more acceptable and happier identities.

Waterman (1988) points out that even when the adolescent appears to have achieved an identity—that is, to have made firm commitments to career and lifestyle plans—further changes often occur. He notes that

some college students move in and out of identity crises before finally achieving a final commitment. And, as we will see in Chapter 13, the Peter Pans among us may never resolve our identity crises.

Erikson's description of this developmental stage has been clarified by Marcia's investigations of the development of identity in adolescence (Marcia, 1966; Marcia & Friedman, 1970; Raskin, 1984). Marcia describes the adolescent in terms of the extent to which a positive, stable identity has been achieved. Four distinct types of *identity status* have been identified. Distinctions among them are based on whether the adolescent has undergone (or is currently undergoing) a crisis and on whether a commitment has been made to a specific identity.

Identity Diffusion.   Adolescents in this state are characterized by a total lack of commitment, as well as no experience with an identity crisis. These are individuals whose political, social, and religious beliefs are ambiguous or nonexistent, and who have no vocational aspirations. Muuss (1975) suggests that whereas identity diffusion is common and normal in early adolescence, it is less normal in late adolescence. Individuals who have not developed a mature sense of identity by late adolescence are sometimes recognizable as full-time fun seekers (what Marcia calls "playboys") or as disturbed individuals characterized by high anxiety, low self-esteem, and lack of self-confidence (Marcia, 1980). Waterman (1988) also reports that these individuals are likely to be at the preconventional level of moral reasoning and are often social isolates.

Foreclosure.   Foreclosure is a strong commitment to an identity without having experienced a crisis. Foreclosure is clearly illustrated in instances where political, religious, and vocational decisions have been made for the adolescent and are accepted without question. This is often the case, for example, in close-knit religious or political communities where the roles and the beliefs of each individual are determined by others. It is also the case when adolescents simply allow parents or, sometimes, peers to make important identity-related decisions for them. These adolescents do not go through an identity crisis. Their most striking characteristics appear to be high adherence to authoritarian values (obedience and respect of authority) (Marcia, 1980).

Moratorium Individuals.   A large group of adolescents actively explore various roles and experiment

One of the most important developmental tasks of adolescence is the development of a strong sense of personal identity — of who and what and how worthwhile one is. The development of identity involves commitment to goals, values, and beliefs, which give direction and purpose to life, and is often reflected in career, occupational, and life-style choices. Even part-time occupational roles — such as working at the Fishin' Pier Grille — might be important in the development of this boy's notions of self.

with different commitments during a *moratorium*. According to Erikson, one of the important functions of adolescence is to serve as a time during which it is not essential to be fully committed to one life-style, one vocation, one set of beliefs — a period when the adolescent can explore the tremendous variety of alternatives that might be available. During the moratorium stage, adolescents have vague, changing commitments. In this sense, they are in crisis. But it is a useful crisis for most adolescents, because in the absence of a moratorium of

exploration, there is a danger of premature commitment (as in the case of foreclosure) or of continuing lack of commitment (as in identity diffusion). Côté and Levine (1988) point out that these are negative characteristics, and that the negative aspects of adopting a "ready-made" identity have been unfairly emphasized. On the positive side, some of the "foreclosed" choices that adolescents adopt are admirable. In addition, such individuals often manifest better adjustment, lower anxiety, and better relations with their parents.

Marcia's Descriptions of Identity Status in Terms of Crisis and Commitment*

Status	Characteristics
Identity diffusion	No crisis; no commitment (ambiguous belief systems; no vocational commitment)
Foreclosure	No crisis; strong commitment (commitment predetermined by political, social, or religious affiliation)
Moratorium	Crisis; no commitment (period of exploration of alternatives)
Identity achieved	Crisis finished; commitment made

★ *Crisis:* A period of active and conscious decision making during which various alternatives are examined and evaluated. *Commitment:* Acceptance of a combination of political, social, religious, or vocational alternatives.

Identity Achieved.   Adolescents who have experienced the moratorium—having experienced a *crisis* of some degree—and who have arrived at a choice—a commitment—may be described as *identity achieved.* Marcia (1980) reports that these adolescents are more independent, respond better to stress, have more realistic goals, and have higher self-esteem than adolescents in any of the other three categories. However, he also emphasizes that identities are never static and absolutely permanent.

The development of identity is summarized in Table 12.3.

Social Development in Context

The development of self does not occur in a vacuum—as our cross-cultural research so dramatically underlines. It occurs in a specific ecological context—a niche describable in terms of a wealth of interactions and

Three Stages of Socialization

Stage	Relationship with Parents	
Preadolescence	High dependence	Low conflict
Early adolescence	Decreasing dependence	High conflict
Late adolescence	High independence	Low conflict

influences. In Bronfenbrenner's (1989) terms, face-to-face interactions define the adolescent's microsystem—perhaps the single most important source of influence on the developing person. As we saw earlier, at every age through childhood, peers and parents are a fundamental part of the microsystem.

Parenting Adolescents

At the risk of oversimplifying, we can describe the socialization of the adolescent in terms of three stages based on changing roles of parents and peers (see Table 12.4). The first, a preadolescent stage, is marked by the child's social, emotional, and physical dependence on parents, and is characterized by low conflict. The second, spanning *early* adolescence, involves increasing independence and is a period of increasing conflict. And the third, beginning in later adolescence, is marked by declining conflict and the achievement of relative independence. Note, however, that there is a mutual interdependence between parents and their children that continues well beyond adolescence (Collins, 1991).

Roles of Parents.   Alvy (1987) proposes that parents of adolescents have several important responsibilities: providing basic resources and care (food, medical and dental care, shelter, clothing), protecting adolescents (monitoring activities, teaching self-protection skills, safeguarding from threats of all kinds), guiding and supporting development (providing opportunities for intellectual, social, emotional, and spiritual growth; fostering self-esteem), and advocacy (supporting and helping adolescents in relation to institutions or groups such as schools, employers, and various experts involved with their care).

As they develop, children progress from a state of high dependence on parents toward increasing independence. At the same time, peer groups and their activities become increasingly important.

Much of parenting involves protecting children from their own immaturity. For young children, whose immaturity is clearly reflected in their dependence, this role poses little conflict. But for adolescents, whose immaturity is less (and who, in most cases, do not recognize their immaturity), parenting is a far more difficult function.

There are several reasons, suggest Small and Eastman (1991), why rearing adolescents in contemporary society might be more difficult and might lead to more conflict. First, the period of adolescence has increased significantly in all industrialized countries. Hurrelman (1990) notes that most adolescents attend schools and postsecondary institutions through their teen years and beyond, and many remain economically dependent on the family for all or much of that time. This has led to greater uncertainty about the responsibilities of parents. Parents have also become confused about how best to prepare adolescents for entry into an increasingly complicated and rapidly changing world with competing sources of information and values. There are also more dangers about which to worry—high-risk and potentially harmful activities, substances, and influences, such as drugs and radical cults. Finally, increases in family breakup and increased mobility of family members have led to an erosion of the family, so that parents of adolescents have fewer sources of advice or support.

Partly because of the responsibilities and difficulties of parenting adolescents, and partly because of the changing roles and relationships of parents and adolescents, this period frequently involves conflict.

Parent–Adolescent Conflict. "The irrevocable giving-up of the love relationships of childhood," says Kaplan (1984), "entails an extended and painful emotional struggle" (p. 141). It is a period often characterized by varying degrees of conflict between parents and child. The current view is that conflict typically arises because the changing needs and interests of the adolescent require a readjustment in the family system. Paikoff and Brooks-Gunn (1991) note that the greatest conflict occurs in early adolescence (during puberty)—prior to adjustments in the family. Conflict typically declines in later adolescence.

Part of the "turbulence on the home front," say Bibby and Posterski (1985), relates to the adolescent's increasing allegiance to peers. In their survey of 3,600 adolescents, friendship ranked first in terms of importance; family life was a distant eighth (see Interactive Figure 12.1). Early in adolescence, children find themselves torn between two forces: On the one hand, there is former allegiance to their parents, their continued love for them, and their economic dependence on them; on the other hand, there is a need to be independent

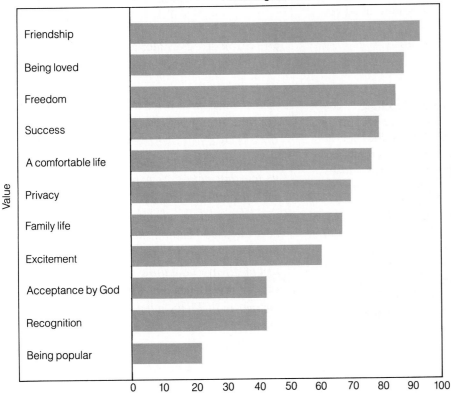

Percentage of adolescents

Interactive Figure 12.1 Most of us go through life without thinking very much about our values, without trying to sort them out. Our values are reflected in what we choose to do and in how we behave rather than in conscious decisions we make about what is important and what isn't. They are more concrete than abstract. Yet there might be some benefit in contemplating abstract values, both in terms of self-knowledge and in terms of guiding our real-life choices. One way of doing this is to rank values such as those given here in terms of their personal importance. Do so, and then compare your ranking with that of the 3,600 adolescents whose responses are represented in Figure 12.1.

and to be accepted by peers. Conflict between adolescents and their parents stems from their desire to associate more frequently and more closely with peer groups, and also from a variety of other sources. Adolescents often list such causes of strife as parental interference with social life, lack of adequate financial assistance, parental intrusion about schoolwork or criticism of grades, and parental criticism of friends (Sebald, 1984).

Petersen (1988) reports that areas of conflict have apparently not changed appreciably in the last 50 years, and that they still concern the more "mundane" things in life—chores, curfews, clothing, homework, and so on. Potentially more explosive matters such as those relating to sex and drugs are not usually discussed.

This does not mean that adolescence is generally a period of *storm and stress* for all youngsters. In fact, as the Offer and associates (1988) study of adolescent self-image showed, the majority of teenagers have very good relationships with their parents. And Meissner's (1965) investigation of parent–child relationships among 1,278 high school boys found that although there was some conflict between parents and their adolescents, there were many positive aspects as well.

The pattern, says Meissner, is one of "gradual **alienation**"; but rebellion is not a general feature of adolescent–parent interaction.

Peer Groups

"Adolescents have an urgent need to belong," says Drummond (1991, p. 283). Not only do the peer group and friends satisfy emotional needs, but they are an important source of information and opportunity for socialization. The adolescent peer group is, in many ways, like a separate culture that eases transition from childhood to adulthood.

Adolescent peer groups vary in size, interests, social backgrounds, and structure. They might consist of two or three like-sexed persons (buddies, pals, best friends), larger groups of like-sexed individuals, or couples, usually of opposite sexes, who currently find themselves in the throes of romantic love. Yet another type of peer group comprises persons of both sexes who "hang out" together. In addition, there are *gangs* (more about gangs later). Most adolescents belong to several groups at the same time. Indeed, friends (who are typically part of the peer groups) are the adolescent's most common source of enjoyment (Bibby & Posterski, 1985).

Peer groups change in predictable ways through adolescence, becoming both larger and more complex (Crockett, Losoff, & Petersen, 1984). At the same time, adolescents spend increasing amounts of time with peers whom they have chosen as friends, rather than simply with classmates. The intimacy of friendships also increases, with adolescents sharing more thoughts and feelings, rather than simply engaging in activities together (Gottman & Mettetal, 1987).

Figure 12.2 illustrates the development of groups in adolescence as they progress from small groups of like-sexed members to interaction between groups of different sexes, leading eventually to the formation of what Dunphy (1963) calls the "crowd"—a large heterosexual group that has evolved from the smaller single-sex groups. In later stages of adolescence, the earlier cohesiveness of the groups gradually disintegrates because of the pairing of boys and girls into couples. Brown and Lohr (1987) note that in American high schools, there are usually a number of different adolescent crowds: one involved in sports, an academic crowd, a social-success crowd, and perhaps a drugs-and-delinquent crowd. These crowds interact, and often

---

> ### INTERVIEW
>
> ▶ **Subject** Female; age 14; ninth grade. (concerning friends)
>
> **❝** *I have quite a lot of good friends. Lana is probably my best friend. And Sherri. The three of us always sit together in school and we go roller-skating. Jackie used to be with us too, but now she's going around with Phil. He's a hunk!*
>
> *I have lots of other friends at band and at school, too. I think that's one of the most important things in life, is your friends. I would always be willing to do whatever I can for my friends and I'm sure they would for me, too. That's what being friends is about.* **❞**

---

a single individual will be a member of several—for example an athlete who is also an honors student (Berndt, 1989).

One of Dunphy's important observations is that adolescent peer groups tend to consist of individuals of relatively similar ages. Age segregation, Hartup (1978) suggests, is pervasive throughout development—that is, when children have a choice, they are most likely to select friends similar to them in age (as well as ability and interests, which are both related to age). He suggests, as well, that age segregation is not necessarily good, a point also argued by Bronfenbrenner (1970) and others. These researchers maintain that it is important for children to have significant contact with a variety of age ranges. They suggest, for example, that contact with young children might help prepare adolescents for parenthood; by the same token, contact with older people is important for the socialization of children and adolescents.

The importance of being accepted by peers is highlighted in a large-scale study reported by Gronlund and Holmlund (1958). A group of 1,073 sixth-grade children were asked to select five people with whom they would like to sit, work, or play. Based on these socio-

Early adolescence

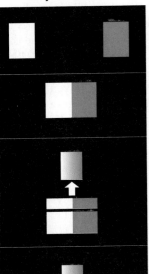

Stage 1: Precrowd stage. Isolated Single-sex cliques.

Stage 2: The beginning of the crowd. Single-sex cliques in group-to-group interaction.

Stage 3: The crowd in structural transition. Single-sex cliques with upper status members forming a heterosexual clique.

Stage 4: The fully developed crowd. Heterosexual cliques in close association.

Stage 5: Beginning of crowd disintegration. Loosely associated groups of couples.

Late adolescence

Figure 12.2 Stages in peer group development during adolescence. (Based on D. C. Dunphy, "The Social Structure of Urban Adolescent Peer Groups," *Sociometry, 26,* p. 236. Copyright 1963 by The American Sociological Association. Used by permission.)

metric data, the investigators divided the entire sample into two groups, designated the *high-status* group and the *low-status* group. High-status children were those selected most often — 27 or more times; low-status children were those selected fewer than 3 times. Seven years later, the records of some of the children in these groups were examined to determine how many had graduated from high school. It is significant that 82 percent of the high-status group, compared with 45 percent of the low-status group, had graduated, particularly because observed differences in intelligence between the two groups were too small to account for the higher dropout rate of the low-status children. However, this study cannot be interpreted as certain evidence that peer rejection is the causal factor in school

dropouts, delinquency, or other forms of social maladjustment. It is equally plausible to suppose that those factors responsible for maladjustment are the very factors that cause the child to be rejected by peers in the first place.

Gender Roles

As we saw in Chapter 8, the play of boys is often more boisterous, more aggressive, and more physical than that of girls. Also, the toys they select (and that parents select for them) tend to be "sex typed."

Differences between the sexes go far beyond the toys children might play with or their expressions of joy and physical movements while playing. They include a wide range of behaviors that are thought appropriate for boys and for girls—in other words, that are considered masculine or feminine. These behaviors, and the attitudes and personality characteristics associated with them, define *gender roles* (*sex roles*). Gender refers specifically to the psychological characteristics typically associated with biological sex. Thus there are two sexes, male and female, and two corresponding genders, masculine and feminine. Bem (1974) also argues that there are individuals who share relatively equally the characteristics of both genders, and labels these individuals *androgynous*. Androgyny implies a flexibility in gender roles, an ability to respond appropriately and adaptively regardless of gender (Hyde, Krajnik, & Skuldt-Niederberger, 1991). The learning of sex-appropriate behavior (of gender roles) is referred to as sex-typing or gender-typing (see Chapter 8).

Gender-Role Stereotypes

Very early in life, children begin to learn about the behaviors their culture finds acceptable and desirable for their sex. What do they learn in North America? Traditionally, males learn that it is masculine to walk without excessive buttock movement, to run fiercely with arms swinging free, to sit with legs sprawled, to throw a ball with full arm movement and a flexed wrist, to wrestle and fight (or at least to be playfully aggressive), to love sports, and to be interested in science and mathematics. Females learn that it is feminine to walk with more exaggerated buttock movement, to run limp-wristed with elbows tucked into the ribcage, to sit with legs crossed properly at the knee and hands tucked neatly in the lap, to throw a ball with a stiff-wristed motion, to sit quietly and demurely, to play the piano, to be interested in books and the arts, and to learn to cook and sew.

These sexual stereotypes are in some cases superficial and trivial; in others, they are more fundamental. Some might reflect basic anatomical differences; others are influenced more by context. In general, North American gender roles associate the male figure with active, work-oriented, and positively evaluated activities, and the female figure with more passive, home-oriented, and less positively evaluated roles. Boys and

girls still have little difficulty in identifying personality characteristics that are stereotypically masculine or feminine. Not only do they agree as to what boys and girls should be like, but they agree that masculine characteristics are more desirable (Shepherd-Look, 1982).

The Sex-Change Question. "If you woke up tomorrow and discovered that you were a *girl*, how would your life be different?" Tavris and Baumgartner (1983) asked a group of American boys. "Terrible," "a catastrophe," "I would immediately commit suicide" were some very typical answers. But when girls were posed the same question—that is, what would happen if they discovered they had become a boy?—they responded quite differently: "Great," "now I can do what I want," "now I can be happy."

Patterns of responses were clear: Girls often responded positively to the sex-change question; boys did extremely rarely. And this difference was evident in children as young as 8 and as old as 17. As of 1983, these sexual stereotypes appeared to be learned at a very young age and to be quite pervasive.

Intons-Peterson (1988) asked the same question of 11-, 14-, and 18-year-old Swedish and American adolescents—Sweden because, since 1968, the Swedish government has backed an explicit, family-based social program focused on the equalization of the sexes. As a result, Intons-Peterson expected that gender stereotypes would not be as marked in Sweden as in the United States, and that male and female reactions to the sex-change question would not reflect as decided a preference for the male sex.

Some aspects of her predictions are borne out. As expected, personality characteristics thought to be most descriptive of males in the United States reflect the "hard-driving, macho image of lore" (Intons-Peterson, 1988); females are seen as gentler and less aggressive. And although these differences are also apparent in the Swedish samples, they are not as extreme. Swedish respondents were more likely to see women as capable and effective, and men as being emotional and tender.

Responses to the sex-change question were essentially identical to those reported by Tavris and Baumgartner (1983). Although a majority of females were content with their gender, most responded by writing stories describing the positive aspects of becoming male. They wrote that they would now enjoy athletics more, that they would travel and stay out later at night, that they would study less but think more about a

Gender roles define patterns of behavior commonly associated with being male or female in a given culture. In North America, masculine gender roles have traditionally been more aggressive and more physical; feminine roles have been more passive and more home-oriented. Gender roles are evident in many areas of life: hobbies and interests, dress styles, career decisions, and social roles. Although recent social changes have begun to soften gender-role differences, they are still evident in many of the games and pastimes of adolescence, such as skateboarding.

career. They also felt they would be more aggressive and less emotional, that they would be less concerned about their appearance, and that they would need to become interested in fighting and in "showing off." Most males still reacted very negatively to the thought of becoming female. They saw themselves becoming burdened by menstruation, and concerned with contraception and pregnancy. They expected to be weaker and more passive, and to be restricted more to indoor activities. They thought, too, that they would become more interested in permanent sexual relationships, and more emotional.

Interestingly, these gender differences are more apparent for the 18-year-olds than for the younger group, especially in Sweden. This might be evidence that

attempts to eradicate sex stereotypes and to achieve greater gender equality are beginning to have an effect.

These evaluations reflect some of our culture's widely held beliefs about gender—in other words, they reveal our prevalent sexual stereotypes. *Stereotypes* are unquestioned beliefs based on category or group membership. For example, Turner and Turner (1991) show that gender stereotypes are affected not only by gender but also by age. With increasing age, men are seen as less *masculine* in that they are viewed as being less aggressive and less autonomous.

Stereotypes are sometimes partly valid; sometimes not. Rarely are they entirely one or the other. Gender stereotypes are no exception. What *are* some of the real differences between males and females?

Gender Differences

Physiology.

There are obvious biological and physical differences related to anatomical sex. These include differences in sexual characteristics as well as the fact that males are taller and heavier than females (except for a brief period in late childhood), and that females mature approximately two years earlier than males. Other differences are less readily apparent but no less real. Beginning from puberty, male blood pressure is higher than that of females; female heart rate is between two and six beats per minute higher than that of males; metabolic rate of males is higher than that of females, physical energy is greater, recuperative time is less, and muscle fatigue is slower (Shepherd-Look, 1982).

In many ways, however, males are the weaker sex — and from the very beginning as well. Males produce perhaps 50 percent more sperm bearing the male (Y) sex chromosome than the female sex chromosome, but there aren't 150 male infants born for every 100 females. Even before conception, the male sperm is more fragile. And thus it continues throughout life. At birth, there are perhaps 105 males for every 100 females, but males are more vulnerable to most infections and diseases, so that by adolescence, numbers of males and females surviving are approximately equal; by age 65, there are almost 150 females living for every 100 males!

Not only are males more fragile and less long-lived, they are also more prone to learning, speech, and behavior disorders, greatly overrepresented among the retarded and the mentally disordered, and more prone to bed-wetting, night terrors, and hyperactivity (Shepherd-Look, 1982).

Apart from these primarily physiological differences between the sexes, are there psychological differences?

The answer is yes, but it is not a simple yes; and it is not without controversy.

In an earlier review and summary of much of the important research in this area, Maccoby and Jacklin (1974) concluded that there are clear differences between the sexes in four areas: verbal ability (favoring females); visual/spatial ability (favoring males); mathematical ability (favoring males); and aggressiveness (lower among females).

But at least some of these gender differences no longer seem as pronounced in the early 1990s as they did in 1974 — evidence perhaps that because they resulted primarily from socialization processes, they re-flected a cultural context that has changed dramatically in the last several decades. Let's look briefly at research in each of these four areas.

Verbal Ability.

The research Maccoby and Jacklin (1974) summarized indicates that females have greater verbal ability than males. However, subsequent research has found that while the difference sometimes exists, it is not very general, is usually very small, and is not apparent at early ages (Shepherd-Look, 1982). In a large-scale survey of performance in high school (and beyond), Marsh (1989) found no significant differences between boys and girls on measures of verbal performance. Girls in this sample were somewhat more likely than boys to take additional English courses, but they were no less likely to take mathematics courses.

Visual/Spatial Ability.

Males often do better than females in tests of visual/spatial ability after early adolescence (see Hyde & Linn, 1986). Tests of spatial ability often require that the subject visualize three-dimensional objects and be able to rotate or otherwise manipulate them mentally. As Chipman (1988) notes, there isn't a great deal of information about the importance of spatial ability although some researchers argue that this gender difference may be related to differences in mathematics achievement (Pearson & Ferguson, 1989).

Mathematics and Science.

There is some evidence that males perform better than females in mathematical skills *from adolescence onward* (Randhawa, 1991), as well as doing better in science (Erickson & Farkas, 1991). Differences are most evident at the highest levels of mathematics achievement (such as university professorships, mathematics-related research positions, or prizes for college-level mathematics achievement) where males outnumber females more than 17 to 1 (Benbow & Stanley, 1983). However, gender differences in math and science are negligible in the earlier years. That females do not continue to do as well may be explained by culturally determined interest and motivational factors. Eccles and Jacobs (1986) found, for example, that student anxiety about math, its perceived value for the student, and parents' stereotyped views of how boys and girls typically perform in math — especially mothers' beliefs about how difficult math is — account for most of the observed gender differences in mathematics achievement.

Significantly, in the same way that gender differences in verbal performance have declined and, in many instances, completely disappeared, so, too, have differences in mathematics performance. Hyde, Fennema, and Lamon (1990) did a meta-analysis of 100 studies in this area, involving more than 3 million subjects. Their conclusion? Girls actually show a slight superiority in mathematical computation in elementary and junior high school; but differences in favor of males emerge in high school, and are most evident in problem solving. Becker (1990) reports very similar findings based on student performance on the SAT (Scholastic Aptitude Test). Only at the higher age levels do differences favor males. And, as Friedman (1989) concludes following a meta-analysis of research done between 1974 and 1987, differences in both mathematics and verbal ability are either nonexistent or very small and declining.

Aggression.   As we saw in Chapter 8, males are *generally* more aggressive than females. Following yet another meta-analysis (there has been a great deal of interest, and consequently of research, in this area), Hyde and Linn (1986) conclude that males are, *on average*, more aggressive both physically and verbally. This gender difference is assumed to have a biological as well as a cultural basis. But even if aggressiveness is related to anatomy and to hormones (hence to genes), it does not follow that observed gender differences would continue to exist in the same form in different sociocultural contexts.

A Conclusion.   Studies of gender differences reveal very small *average* differences — where there are any differences at all. They do not provide data that would be sufficient for making inferences about specific individuals. As Linn and Hyde (1989) point out, gender differences in height and strength are far more significant and far more stable. Interestingly, so are gender differences in career accessibility and in earning power. Other than perhaps for aggressiveness, not only are psychological gender differences very small, but they have been declining (Friedman, 1989; Jacklin, 1989). Important social changes likely are involved here; gender differences may become even smaller in coming decades, and may even disappear completely in some areas. And perhaps, as Chipman (1988) argues, these

small average sex differences are not very important in any case. Perhaps it would be far more useful to try to understand how interests and abilities develop and interact.

Sex

Sex is a profound preoccupation for many adolescents — an interest that consumes much of their time and energy and to which they sometimes devote themselves with rarely equaled ardor.

To begin with, sex is simply a category — male or female — that is usually easily defined by some obvious biological characteristics.

Sex is also a psychoanalytic term referring to thumb-sucking, defecation, masturbation, fantasies, repressions, and, indeed, to all of living. According to Freud, sex is the source of energy that motivates each of us from birth to death, whether by way of the "normal" psychosexual stages or through the labyrinth of neuroses and psychoses springing from the constant warring between our ids and our superegos. Needless to say, not all theorists agree with this Freudian notion.

Sex is also more than a psychoanalytic term or a simple biological dichotomy. It can mean (as it does in this section) nothing more or less complicated than the physical union between male and female, or variations thereof, or the wish thereto, or the fantasy thereof.

Sexual Beliefs and Behavior

There have been some major changes in sexual attitudes and behavior in recent decades. These are reflected in three areas, says Zani (1991): standards, attitudes toward sexual behavior, and age of sexual initiation.

The Double Standard.   First, the old *sexual double standard* has largely crumbled. This standard said, basically, "Boys will be boys, but girls, well, they should behave." In the 1950s, when Kinsey and associates (1948, 1953) first began to research sexual activity, the standard was in full force. At that time, most males reported experiencing orgasm before marriage, but only 30 percent of females reported doing so. By the mid 1960s, incidence of premarital intercourse among

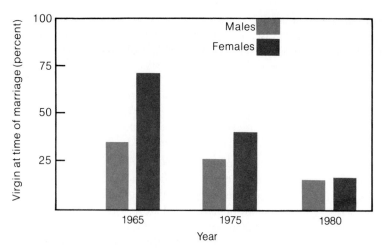

Interactive Figure 12.3 "If you woke up tomorrow and discovered that you were a *girl* (*boy*), how would your life be different?" Think about the question. Is your response positive or negative? As explained in the text, girls have often reacted very positively to the possibility of being male; boys have more typically reacted negatively to the possibility of being female. However, there have been important changes in sexual attitudes, stereotypes, and expectations. One example of this *sexual revolution* is the decrease in the percentage of people who are virgins when they marry—a change that has been far more dramatic for females than males.

girls had risen to about 40 percent—still some distance shy of males' reported 60 percent (Packard, 1968). By the 1980s, however, percentages were about equal at around 75 or 80 (Darling, Kallen, & Van Dusen, 1984) (see Interactive Figure 12.3).

Attitudes. Second, there have been important changes in *attitudes* toward sexuality. These are reflected not only in the demise of the double standard, but also in an increased openness about sexuality, and in a wider acceptance of premarital sex. This does not mean that sex has become totally casual and matter-of-fact among today's adolescents. In fact, the majority (almost 90 percent) of teenagers do not think it appropriate to have intercourse on the first date, but almost half believe it is quite appropriate after a few dates (Bibby & Posterski, 1985). For the majority of adolescents, the critical factor is whether the partners have a caring and committed relationship. The new standard holds that sexual activity is permitted for both sexes providing there is affection between partners (see Tables 12.5 and 12.6).

Age of Initiation. Third, average age of sexual initiation has declined in recent decades. A study of more than 600 Italian adolescents found that about one third of the girls and one quarter of the boys had had sexual intercourse before age 15 (Zani, 1991). Brooks-Gunn and Furstenberg (1989) report similar findings for the United States, but note that it is not uncommon for teenagers to have sex at 14 or 15 and then not to repeat the activity for another year or more.

Among the most obvious antecedents of sexual activity are the biological changes of pubescence. Changes in hormone levels affect sexual arousal directly. In addition, changes in secondary sexual characteristics, such as breast enlargement in the girl or lowering of the boy's voice, may serve as important sexually linked stimuli. Parental influences are also considered important factors in the sexual behavior of adolescents, although there isn't a great deal of research on the link between the two (Brooks-Gunn & Furstenberg, 1989). Similarly, peers probably influence whether an adolescent is likely to engage in sexual intercourse. In this

TABLE 12.5

What Adolescents Consider to Be Appropriate Dating Behavior★

"If two people on a date like each other, do you think it is all right for them to":

	Percentage		
	Male	Female	Total
Hold hands			
Yes, first date	92	91	92
Yes, after a few dates	7	9	8
No	1	0	0
Kiss			
Yes, first date	84	80	82
Yes, after a few dates	16	19	18
No	0	1	0
Neck			
Yes, first date	59	42	50
Yes, after a few dates	38	52	45
No	3	6	5
Pet			
Yes, first date	42	16	28
Yes, after a few dates	50	63	56
No	8	20	15
Have sexual relations			
Yes, first date	19	3	11
Yes, after a few dates	51	33	42
No	29	59	44
If they love each other	1	5	3

★ Based on a survey of 3,600 high school students, ages 15–19.

Source: From *The Emerging Generation: An Inside Look at Canada's Teenagers* by R. W. Bibby and D. C. Posterski, 1985. Copyright © 1985 Irwin Publishing Inc. Based on Table 5.1, p. 76.

connection, it is perhaps significant that adolescents often overestimate the amount of sexual activity engaged in by their peers, and underestimate the age of first intercourse (Zani, 1991).

The most common form of sexual outlet for adolescents is still **masturbation**.

Masturbation

Sorensen (1973) reports that 49 percent of all adolescents ages 13–19 have masturbated at least once. Males masturbate more frequently than females, reaching their peak sexual activity (*peak* is defined as frequency of orgasm, regardless of its cause) between ages 16 and 17. Among some adolescents, the practice may still be accompanied by totally unfounded fears of impotence, mental retardation, or other dire consequences. Early writers such as G. Stanley Hall (1905) treated masturbation as abnormal, debilitating, and sinful and provided parents with a number of suggestions for its avoidance or cure.

For males, masturbation, or a nocturnal emission, is usually the first sign of pubescence. But unlike the girl's menarche, it is usually a secretive affair. Also, because of males' reluctance to admit ignorance or innocence in sexual matters, many have little information about the event and seek none (Zani, 1991).

Although contemporary attitudes toward masturbation are that it is normal, pleasurable, and harmless, some adolescents continue to feel guilty and ashamed about masturbating, this being the case more among younger than among older adolescents (Hass, 1979).

Adolescent Pregnancy

Estimates suggest that as many as 12 million teenagers are sexually active in the United States—7 million male and 5 million female (Davis & Harris, 1982). Of the 5 million or so sexually active females, approximately 1 million become pregnant each year (Moore, 1990). The teenage birthrate in the United States accounts for 12.5 percent of all births (U.S. Bureau of the Census, 1991). It is now among the highest in the world—approximately 17 times higher than in Japan, 3 times higher than in the former Soviet Union, and about twice as high as in Canada (Jones, 1986). Who gets pregnant? Why? What are the outcomes and the implications of teenage pregnancy?

Who Gets Pregnant? Teenage pregnancies are not restricted to any particular social, economic, religious, or ethnic group. However, in the United States, pregnancies are about three times more common among black than among white teenagers (U.S. Bureau of the Census, 1991). They occur most often within six

425

TABLE 12.6

Teenagers' Beliefs About Sexual Behavior

Activity		Male Scale		Female Scale	
		N	Percent	N	Percent
1. I believe that kissing is acceptable for the male (female) before marriage if he (she) is engaged to be married.	Agree	693	85.7	775	95.8
	Disagree	116	14.3	34	4.2
	Total	809		809	
2. I believe that kissing is acceptable for the male (female) before marriage when he (she) is in love.	Agree	768	94.9	779	96.3
	Disagree	41	5.1	30	3.7
	Total	809		809	
3. I believe that kissing is acceptable for the male (female) before marriage when he (she) feels strong affection for his (her) partner.	Agree	785	97.0	783	96.8
	Disagree	24	3.0	26	3.2
	Total	809		809	
4. I believe that kissing is acceptable for the male (female) before marriage when he (she) is not particularly affectionate toward his (her) partner.	Agree	603	74.5	572	70.7
	Disagree	206	25.5	237	29.3
	Total	809		809	
5. I believe that petting is acceptable for the male (female) before marriage when he (she) is engaged to be married.	Agree	723	89.4	728	90.0
	Disagree	86	10.6	81	10.0
	Total	809		809	
6. I believe that petting is acceptable for the male (female) before marriage when he (she) is in love.	Agree	725	89.6	728	90.0
	Disagree	84	10.4	81	10.0
	Total	809		809	
7. I believe that petting is acceptable for the male (female) before marriage when he (she) is strongly affectionate for his (her) partner.	Agree	717	88.6	703	86.9
	Disagree	92	11.4	106	13.1
	Total	809		809	
8. I believe that petting is acceptable for the male (female) before marriage when he (she) is not particularly affectionate toward his (her) partner.	Agree	376	46.5	364	45.0
	Disagree	433	53.5	445	55.0
	Total	809		809	
9. I believe that full sexual relations is acceptable for the male (female) before marriage when he (she) is engaged to be married.	Agree	661	81.7	679	83.9
	Disagree	148	18.3	130	16.1
	Total	809		809	
10. I believe that full sexual relations is acceptable for the male (female) before marriage when he (she) is in love.	Agree	649	80.2	668	82.6
	Disagree	160	19.8	141	17.4
	Total	809		809	
11. I believe that full sexual relations is acceptable for the male (female) before marriage when he (she) is strongly affectionate toward his (her) partner.	Agree	586	72.4	603	74.5
	Disagree	223	27.6	206	25.5
	Total	809		809	
12. I believe that full sexual relations is acceptable for the male (female) before marriage when he (she) is not particularly affectionate for his (her) partner.	Agree	218	26.9	215	26.6
	Disagree	591	73.1	594	73.4
	Total	809		809	

Source: From *Teenage Sexuality* by S. Meikle, J. A. Peitchinis, and K. Pearce, 1985, San Diego, CA: College-Hill Press. Used by permission of the publisher.

Juvenile Delinquency and Violence

Random and unprovoked violence, sometimes perpetrated by gangs and sometimes by individuals, is as frightening as it is unpredictable. Violence that is not random, but that is based on allegiance to ideology and on hatred of identifiable groups (as is the case for some racist groups), is no less terrifying. Although the number of delinquency cases dealt with by U.S. courts has not changed very much in recent years (in the United States, 1.05 million cases in 1975 and 1.154 million in 1986; in Canada, 77,350 cases in 1987), incidence of juvenile violent offenses in the United States increased from 57,000 cases in 1982 to 70,000 cases in 1985. Male juvenile delinquents still outnumber females by a factor of more than 4 to 1; with respect to violent offenses, males outnumber females by approximately 7 to 1.

Table 12.7 Number (in 1,000s) and Types of Delinquency Cases Disposed of by U.S. Juvenile Courts in 1985.

| | Cases (thousands) | | |
Reason for Referral	Male	Female	Total
All delinquency offenses	912	205	1,117
Violent offenses	61	9	70
Criminal homicide	1	—	1
Forcible rape	4	—	4
Robbery	23	2	25
Aggravated assault	33	8	41
Property offenses	380	91	471
Burglary	124	9	133
Larceny	220	77	297
Motor vehicle theft	30	5	35
Arson	6	1	7
Delinquency offenses	472	105	577
Simple assault	62	22	84
Vandalism	74	8	82
Drug law violations	62	13	75
Obstruction of justice	48	16	64
Other★	226	48	274

— Indicates fewer than 500 cases.

★ Includes such offenses as stolen property offenses, trespassing, weapons offenses, other sex offenses, liquor law violations, disorderly conduct, and miscellaneous offenses.

Source: Adapted from U.S. Bureau of the Census, 1991, p. 192.

Parents. The father is perhaps the most influential parent with respect to delinquency (Biller, 1982). Fathers of delinquent boys are, on the average, more severe, more punitive, more prone to alcoholism, more rejecting, and more likely to have engaged in delinquent behavior themselves than are fathers of nondelinquent boys. Herzog and Sudia (1970) report a higher probability of delinquency among boys from fatherless homes. They speculate that absence of the father may contribute to delinquency in sons, perhaps by failure to provide adequate male models, perhaps as a function of protest against female domination, or perhaps simply because of inadequate supervision. Girls, too, appear to be more prone to delinquency in homes in which

Membership in adolescent groups is often marked by high conformity to dress codes. Less obvious but no less important, group members tend to share highly similar beliefs and values, and to reinforce each other for similar behaviors. Clearly, however, not all highly recognizable peer groups encourage delinquent values and behaviors.

the father is absent (Lynn, 1979) or where the mother is viewed as cold and rejecting (Kroupa, 1988).

Personality. Many studies have looked at the possibility that delinquency is at least partly a function of the individuals' personality characteristics. In one study, for example, Monachesi and Hathaway (1969) administered the Minnesota Multiphasic Personality Inventory (MMPI) — a widely used, very detailed, and comprehensive personality test — to more than 15,000 ninth-grade students. In later years, police and court records were checked routinely for the names of these students. Like a number of other researchers, Monachesi and Hathaway report that several personality variables appear to correlate most highly with later delinquency: namely, those having to do with psychopathic tendencies (evident in amorality and rebelliousness) and emotional instability (high scores on what is labeled *neuroticism*, which is manifested in high anxiety and mood fluctuations).

There is evidence as well that high impulsivity (low impulse control), high need for stimulation (danger-seeking orientation), and low self-esteem are related to delinquency (Binder, 1988).

Sex. The incidence of delinquency is approximately four times higher among boys than among girls. This may be partly explained by the male's greater aggressiveness and lesser acquiescence. Traditionally, delinquency among males has involved more aggressive transgressions, with girls being apprehended more often for sexually promiscuous behavior, shoplifting, and related activities. Drug-related offenses also account for an increasing number of detentions.

In summary, a complex set of psychological and social forces impinge upon the potential delinquent, although no single factor can reliably predict delinquent behavior. Social class, age, sex, home background, peer influences, intelligence, and personality are all impli-

for the development of social and intellectual adaptive skills. The emphasis should perhaps be less on preventing *use* than on preventing *abuse*.

The short-term implications of drug abuse among adolescents are sometimes painfully obvious. Alcohol, for example, is implicated in a staggering number of fatal teenage automobile accidents. Less dramatic, but no less real, drug abuse may be reflected in poorer school achievement, dropping out of school, failure to adjust to the career and social demands required for transition to young adulthood, deviance, and criminality. Watts and Wright (1990) report very high correlations between use of alcohol, tobacco, marijuana, and other illegal drugs, and delinquency. In their study of black, white, and Mexican-American adolescents, frequent drug use was the best predictor of both minor and violent delinquency.

The long-term implications of teenage drug abuse have been examined by Newcomb and Bentler (1988), who looked at seven different aspects of the lives of young adults (including family formation, stability, criminality, mental health, and social integration). They found that teenagers who had used large amounts of drugs were more likely to have left school early and to have consolidated family and career plans earlier. Those who had used a variety of drugs had often adopted adult roles less successfully; their attempted careers and marriages were more likely to have failed.

Specific Drugs

The long-term medical consequences of drugs such as nicotine and alcohol have also been extensively researched and are well known. In the following sections, we look at these and at some other commonly used drugs.

Marijuana. Marijuana is derived from hemp, a tall annual plant appearing in male and female forms. The specific chemical that accounts for its effects is **tetra-hydrocannabinol (THC)**. It is variously known as hashish, bhang, grass, ganja, charas, drawamesc, muta, grefa, pot, reefer, gauge, stick, Thai stick, Acapulco Gold, Columbian, Panama Red, Panama Gold, jive, Indian, Jamaican, tea, dope.

Marijuana is ordinarily smoked, although it can also be eaten or drunk. Its primary effect is a pleasant emotional state. If taken in sufficient doses and in sufficiently pure forms (which are extremely rare), it may evoke the same types of hallucinogenic reactions sometimes associated with stronger drugs, such as LSD.

Whether marijuana is physically addictive remains controversial. Gold (1989) suggests it may be addictive following prolonged use; others believe it has not been shown to be addictive or especially harmful (Royal College of Psychiatrists, 1987).

The physiological effects of marijuana use depend largely on the dosages used and the frequency of use. Cox and associates (1983) report an increased heart rate, even with very low doses. The respiratory system may be adversely affected by prolonged use and heavier doses, which seem to have more harmful effects than does prolonged smoking of tobacco (marijuana produces more tars than tobacco does, and these contain a higher concentration of certain cancer-causing agents) (Cox et al., 1983).

The fear that marijuana is the first step toward heroin addiction has generally been discounted. There is no evidence that tolerance to marijuana develops, as does tolerance to some of the so-called hard drugs. Hence, the marijuana user does not need to go to more powerful drugs to continue to achieve the same "high." Nor is there any evidence that using marijuana leads to a psychological craving for heroin.

LSD. **D-lysergic acid diethylamide tartrate**, or **LSD-25**, is the most powerful synthetic hallucinogen known. Common street names for LSD-25 are barrels, California sunshine, acid, blotters, cubes, wedges, purple haze, jellybeans, frogs, microdots, bluecaps, and window panes. Its use appears to have declined (U.S. Bureau of the Census, 1991).

LSD-25 (ordinarily referred to simply as LSD) is usually taken orally, commonly in the form of a white, odorless, and tasteless powder. Its effects vary widely from one person to another, as well as from one occasion to another for the same person. The predominant characteristic of an LSD experience (called an "acid trip") is the augmented intensity of sensory perceptions; color, sound, taste, and vision are particularly susceptible. On occasion, an acid trip is accompanied by hallucinations, which may be mild and amusing or sufficiently frightening to lead to serious mental disturbance in the subject (Slaby, 1989).

Alcohol. Alcohol, the most commonly used and abused drug in contemporary societies, is a central nervous system depressant. In relatively moderate doses, its primary effect is to suppress inhibition, which is

TABLE 12.9

Students Reporting Drinking with Friends

Age	"Never" (%)	"Sometimes" (%)	"Usually" (%)	"Always" (%)	At Least "Sometimes" (total %)	Total Number of Students
12	72	24	2	2	28	163
13	62	29	6	3	38	142
14	34	37	23	6	66	242
15	20	42	28	10	80	208
16	13	35	35	17	87	249
17	12	41	33	14	88	219

Source: Brown and Finn, 1982, p. 15.

why many individuals who have consumed alcohol behave as if they had taken a stimulant. In less moderate doses, the individual progresses from being "high" or "tipsy" to being intoxicated. Literally, to be "intoxicated" is to be *poisoned*. Behavioral symptoms of varying degrees of intoxication may include impaired muscular control, delayed reflexive reactions, loss of coordination and balance, impaired vision, uncertain speech, faintness, nausea, amnesia (blackouts), and, in extreme cases, paralysis of heart and lung muscles that sometimes leads to death (Reid & Carpenter, 1990).

Alcohol is physiologically addictive, although prolonged or excessive consumption is generally required before symptoms of physical addiction are present. Signs of psychological dependence (a strong desire to continue taking the drug) may appear considerably sooner. One of the major physiological effects of alcohol relates to its contribution to cirrhosis of the liver—a major cause of death in the United States. In addition, it is implicated in more than half of all motor vehicle deaths, a large number of which involve adolescents (Beatty, 1991).

Alcohol consumption among adolescents is widespread. Most surveys report that extremely few teenagers have not tried alcohol at least once (Torres, 1982). Close to 20 percent of those ages 14–17 are considered problem drinkers (see Table 12.9).

Why do adolescents drink? There are clearly many reasons, including social pressure, experimentation, insecurity and other personal problems, as well as simply for the sensation of being "tipsy," "high," or "drunk."

Why do adolescents want to get drunk? To feel good, have fun, celebrate, let off steam, cheer up, forget worries, feel less shy, and impress friends, they claim (Brown & Finn, 1982). But when they are asked what their actual behaviors and feelings are when they are drunk, while a large number do "feel good" and "laugh a lot," a significant number fall asleep, feel unhappy, cry, damage property, and get into fights. And approximately one third at all age levels occasionally get sick.

When does alcohol consumption by adolescents become deviant or a problem? Only when the adolescent gets into trouble? When alcohol consumption becomes habitual or excessive? When it interferes with normal social or physical functioning? Or is it always a problem, given that the behavior is generally illegal? There are no easy answers.

Cocaine. Cocaine is ordinarily a white powder derived from coca leaves. Also known as coke, big "C," snow, gold dust, star dust, flake, Bernice, or Corine, it is most commonly inhaled vigorously through the nostrils, although it can also be injected. Cocaine is sometimes purified to produce *freebase* cocaine (*crack*), which, when inhaled, has a more profound effect on the user. Some users mix it with heroin and inject it intravenously (called a *speedball*).

In moderate doses, the primary effect of cocaine, like that of other stimulants, is one of euphoria and high energy. In higher doses, it can lead to hallucinations and, sometimes, convulsions. For some decades, it was widely believed that cocaine is nonaddictive and largely harmless. It is now considered to be extremely dangerous (Cheung, Erickson, & Landau, 1991). Indications are that it may be as addictive as heroin (Ringwalt & Palmer, 1989).

Cocaine use has increased dramatically among high school populations, especially in its freebase form (U.S. Bureau of the Census, 1991). Next to marijuana, it is the most widely used *illegal* drug in North America (Gold & Giannini, 1989).

Crack appears to be particularly attractive to adolescents for several reasons. First, it is far cheaper than cocaine. Second, its effect is almost instantaneous and intensely euphoric. And third, so much glamour and misinformation have surrounded the so-called recreational use of cocaine that many adolescents think there is nothing to fear.

Crack is easily and quickly manufactured by *cooking down* ordinary powdered cocaine with bicarbonate of soda. Small pieces of the resulting solid are then smoked, usually in a waterpipe. The euphoric effect, or *rush*, occurs within 5 to 10 seconds and is far more intense than the effect of inhaling ordinary cocaine, the reason being that the concentrations of cocaine that reach the brain are many times higher than is the case with inhalation. Consequently, there is a far higher risk of overdosing with crack, of experiencing convulsions, or even of dying. Many users of crack experience an overwhelming compulsion to use it again as soon as possible, even after using it only once. The use of crack is also associated with psychological changes, the most common of which involve strong feelings of paranoia. Many users also become violent (Washton, 1989), and some commit suicide. (See Table 12.10 for some symptoms of drug use and abuse.)

Suicide

Suicide, the deliberate taking of one's life, is final — an end that is sought when individuals can see only two choices: life as it is now or death. Evidently they prefer to die. A male will probably shoot himself (three out of five cases in 1988 (U.S. Bureau of the Census, 1991);

a female is more likely to use poisoning (two out of five cases). There are obviously many other methods available, but some of these result in a death that appears accidental (drowning, a car accident) and is difficult to identify as suicide unless the person has left a note, letter, or other message. Because a suicide note appears in only 15 percent of all reported suicides, many apparent accidents are probably unidentified suicides.

Suicide is not a pleasant topic — it so violently contradicts our implicit belief in the goodness of life. Consequently, there is a powerful social stigma attached to the act, and the event is often covered over both by the information media and by the attending physician. As a result, people know only of suicides of people whom they have known, or of particularly prominent persons, or of people who commit the act so flagrantly that it compels attention. There are relatively few scientific investigations of suicide, its causes, and the personalities of those who deliberately choose their time and method of departure. Do children commit suicide? How often? How about adolescents, disillusioned idealists that they are, caught up in the stress and turmoil of the transition to adulthood? Here are some facts.

The suicide rate in the United States is approximately 12 per 100,000. Few children under the age of 15 commit suicide. Suicide rates increase slowly from adolescence, peaking at around age 65 for white males and at ages 45–55 for white females. Peaks are at younger ages for American blacks, and the numbers are also lower (U.S. Bureau of the Census, 1988). The most dramatic increase in suicide rates involves the 15- to 19-year-old age group, which almost doubled between 1970 and 1988 (U.S. Bureau of the Census, 1991) (see Table 12.11 on page 445).

Among adolescents, more girls than boys attempt suicide, but a higher percentage of the boys are successful. Some researchers have argued that this may be because boys who attempt suicide are more serious about wanting to die than are girls. It may also be because the more violent and instantaneous methods employed by males (guns, for example) do not provide much opportunity for intervention or other forms of help. In contrast, the slower and more passive methods most often used by females (such as pills) often provide time for rescue. Neiger and Hopkins (1988) report that the most likely predictors of suicide in adolescence include depression, poor family relationships, alcohol and drug use, failure in school, and recent serious loss. Shreve and Kunkel (1991) suggest that the *shame* that

TABLE 12.10

Symptoms of Drug Use and Abuse

Drug	Signs and Early Symptoms	Long-Term Symptoms
Narcotics	Medicinal breath	Loss of appetite
	Traces of white powder around nostrils (heroin is sometimes inhaled)	Constipation
	Red or raw nostrils	
	Needle marks or scars on arms	
	Long sleeves (or other clothing) at inappropriate times	
	Physical evidence may include cough syrup bottles, syringes, cotton swabs, and spoon or cap for heating heroin	
Sedatives	Symptoms of alcohol consumption with or without odor: poor coordination and speech, drowsiness, loss of interest in activity	Withdrawal symptoms when discontinued
		Possible convulsions
Stimulants	Excessive activity	Loss of appetite
	Irascibility	Possible hallucinations and psychotic reactions
	Argumentativeness	
	Nervousness	
	Pupil dilation	
	Dry mouth and nose, bad breath	
	Chapped, dry lips	
	Scratching or rubbing of nose	
	Long periods without sleep	
	Loss of appetite	
	Mood shifts	
	Changes in friends	
	"Hangover" symptoms	
Hallucinogens, marijuana	Odor on breath and clothing	None definite
	Animated behavior or its opposite	
LSD	Bizarre behavior	Possible contribution to psychoses
	Panic	Recurrence of experiences after immediate effects of drug
	Disorientation	
Inhalants	Odor of glue, solvent, or related substance	Disorientation
	Redness and watering of eyes	Brain damage
	Appearance of alcohol intoxication	
	Physical evidence of plastic bags, rags, glue, or solvent containers	

accompanies these conditions may be the determining motive.

Adolescent suicide, like most suicides, rarely occurs without warning. The most common warning is, simply, one or more unsuccessful attempts at suicide. Ladame and Jeanneret (1982) report that as many as four out of five adolescents who succeed in committing suicide have previously attempted to kill themselves at least once. Other warning signs include statements such as "I wish I were dead," "Nobody would miss me if I weren't here," and "I wish I'd never been born."

Suicide is still the solution of an isolated few. Most of us choose to wait for death and hope that it will be a long time in coming. And for most adolescents, life is only occasionally turbulent and stressful; most of the time, it abounds with joy and excitement.

Another Note

Suicide would not have been a very pleasant note upon which to end this chapter. Nor would it have been very realistic. Indeed, closing the chapter with the *turmoil topics*, as we have, is misleading.

It bears repeating that the adolescents whose lives are described in these closing pages are not our *average* adolescents. Our average adolescents are more joyful than sad, more exuberant than depressed, more confident than self-deprecating. They like order more than chaos, purpose more than dissipation—and junk food more than drugs.

And they laugh and smile a lot more than they cry. That's a better note upon which to end.

Main Points

1. Global self-worth (or self-esteem) reflects how well one likes oneself. Self-evaluations are possible in different areas (for example, scholastic or athletic; playing ball or playing poker). The Offer Self-Image Questionnaire assesses attitudes and feelings in five areas that contribute to global self-concept: psychological, social, familial, coping, and sexual.

2. Among the characteristics shared by adolescents in different countries (the universal adolescent) are general happiness and optimism; caring and concern for others, and the enjoyment of the company of others; confidence and openness about sexual matters; strongly positive feelings toward the family; and confidence in their ability to deal with life. Consistent differences among adolescents from different cultures (for example, lower confidence on the part of Bengali adolescents; very high values placed on educational and vocational goals by American adolescents; relatively conservative sexual attitudes among Turkish and Taiwanese adolescents) reflect historical and immediate context.

3. Contrary to Hall's belief, adolescence is not a period of storm and stress for the majority of the world's adolescents. In North America, approximately 15 percent of adolescents describe their lives as turbulent, confused, and unhappy.

4. According to Erikson, the major developmental task of adolescence is to develop a sense of identity. Marcia describes four possible identity statuses of the adolescent: *identity diffusion* (no commitment and no identity crisis—characteristic of early adolescence), *foreclosure* (strong commitment to an imposed identity), *moratorium individuals* (adolescents actively exploring alternative identities; vague, changing commitments), and *identity achieved* (commitment following the crisis of the moratorium).

5. Social development progresses from a stage of relative dependence on the parents to a stage of relative independence. The role of parents in adolescence is to provide resources, protect adolescents, guide their development, and serve as advocates for them. The prolongation of adolescence and uncertainty about how to prepare adolescents for adaptation to an increasingly complex world makes these tasks more difficult.

Suicide in the United States

Between 1970 and 1988, suicide rates in the United States increased for males but declined slightly for females. Close to two thirds of all male suicides, but only one third of female suicides, are committed with firearms. About as many women use poisoning as use firearms; only 20 percent as many men use poisons as use firearms. Hanging and strangulation account for between 10 percent and 15 percent of both male and female suicides.

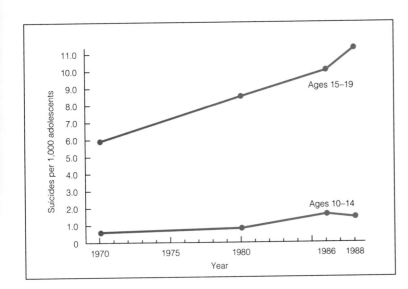

Figure 12.6 Changes in teenage suicide rates, 1970–1988.

Age (Years)	Total			Male White			Male Black			Female White			Female Black		
	1970	1980	1988	1970	1980	1988	1970	1980	1988	1970	1980	1988	1970	1980	1988
10–14	0.6	0.8	1.4	1.1	1.4	2.1	0.3	0.5	1.3	0.3	0.3	0.8	0.4	0.1	0.2
15–19	5.9	8.5	11.3	9.4	15.0	19.6	4.7	5.6	9.7	2.9	3.3	4.8	2.9	1.6	2.2
20–24	12.2	16.1	15.0	19.3	27.8	27.0	18.7	20.0	19.8	5.7	5.9	4.4	4.9	3.1	2.9
25–34	14.1	16.0	15.4	19.9	25.6	25.7	19.2	21.8	22.1	9.0	7.5	6.1	5.7	4.1	3.8
35–44	16.9	15.4	14.8	23.3	23.5	24.1	12.6	15.6	16.4	13.0	9.1	7.4	3.7	4.6	3.5
45–54	20.0	15.9	14.6	29.5	24.2	23.2	13.8	12.0	11.7	13.5	10.2	8.6	3.7	2.8	3.8
55–64	21.4	15.9	15.6	35.0	25.8	27.0	10.6	11.7	10.6	12.3	9.1	7.9	2.0	2.3	2.5
65 and over	20.8	17.8	21.0	41.1	37.5	45.0	8.7	11.4	14.0	8.5	6.5	7.1	2.6	1.4	1.6

Source: Adapted from U.S. Bureau of the Census, 1991, p. 86.

Table 12.11 Suicide Rates (per 100,000) in the United States by Sex, Race, and Age Group, 1970–1988.

6. Increasing allegiance to peers does not necessarily entail a high degree of parent–adolescent conflict. The majority of teenagers have good relations with their parents, although one of the developmental tasks of this period clearly involves increasing independence from parents.

7. Peer groups begin as small single-sex groups in early adolescence and progress through four additional stages: single-sex groups that interact as groups but remain intact; a stage when the crowd has begun to form but still consists of single-sex groups interacting in a closer fashion; large heterosexual groups form; and the crowd breaks into less cohesive groups of couples.

8. The adolescent's acceptance by peers is profoundly important for social and psychological well-being. Friendships tend to be highly age-segregated and to involve individuals who are more similar than dissimilar. High-status (well-liked) children tend to be happier, more cheerful, more active, and more successful.

9. The "sex-change" question ("What if you were a boy [girl]?") reveals predominantly positive evaluations of the male role and negative evaluations of the female role—by both males and females. Our predominant gender stereotypes see the male role as more active, aggressive, rational, and powerful; the female role is seen as more passive, emotional, and nurturant, and less aggressive.

10. Males appear to be the more fragile sex, as is revealed in substantially higher mortality rates and much lower life expectancies. In our culture, males have traditionally been more aggressive and females more submissive and nurturant. Gender differences in verbal ability (favoring females) are small and are not usually apparent prior to adolescence. Similarly, differences in mathematical ability (favoring males) are apparent only from adolescence onward, and are better explained in terms of culturally determined interests and opportunities than in terms of basic genetically ordained differences.

11. The sexual revolution among adolescents is evident in the number of adolescents reporting sexual intercourse before marriage; a much greater increase in sexual activity among females than among males; and a lowering of the age of first intercourse. Almost half of young adolescents consider sexual relations permissible if partners have been together

a number of times and have developed a caring relationship.

12. Approximately 20 percent of sexually active teenage girls become pregnant each year. Most of these pregnancies are accidental and occur within six months of the first sexual experience. Of those who do not choose abortion, 31 percent marry before the birth of the infant, and 69 percent have out-of-wedlock infants. Fewer than 4 percent of these infants are given up for adoption.

13. Teenage parents are more likely to divorce than people who marry later; their marriages are more likely to be associated with depression, suicide, infant mortality, child neglect, developmental problems among children, and other signs of inadequate parenting.

14. The most common sexually transmitted diseases are gonorrhea, herpes, and chlamydia; syphilis and AIDS are much rarer. Gonorrhea, chlamydia, and syphilis can be cured with drugs; herpes can sometimes be controlled, but it cannot be cured; AIDS is incurable and fatal.

15. Delinquency is a legal category defined by juvenile apprehension and conviction of a legal transgression; it appears to include more lower-class than middle-class adolescents. Other contributing factors include sex, self-esteem, intelligence, home, and peer influences (such as gang membership).

16. Incidence of drug use among adolescents appears to have leveled off in recent years, except for use of cocaine. Alcohol is still the drug of choice; nicotine is second; and marijuana is a close third. *Drug abuse* refers to the recreational use of drugs. *Drug dependence* is manifested in a strong desire to continue taking a drug. It may be *physiological* (organically based, also termed *addiction*), or *psychological* (urge to continue has to do more with psychological effects; also termed *habituation*).

17. Reasons for drug abuse include a complex set of genetic and social-environment factors. Predictors of the likelihood of drug abuse among teenagers include drug use among peers or parents; delinquency; stressful life changes; parental neglect, abuse, or abandonment; and low self-esteem.

18. Marijuana does not appear to be physiologically addictive, although it may lead to psychological dependence. LSD-25, a powerful synthetic halluci-

nogenic drug, can cause psychoticlike reactions. Alcohol is a highly addictive, central nervous system depressant. Cocaine, especially in freebase form, creates feelings of euphoria, and is potent, dangerous, and addictive.

19. Suicide is uncommon although its frequency among adolescents has more than doubled in recent decades. More girls than boys attempt suicide, but fewer are successful. Although adolescent suicides are often precipitated by a single event (such as the death of a friend, pregnancy, parental divorce, or arrest), few occur without warning.

20. For most adolescents, life is only occasionally turbulent and stressful; most of the time, it abounds with joy and excitement.

Further Readings

Offer and associates presented a self-image questionnaire to nearly 6,000 teenagers in 10 different countries. The result is a fascinating look at the thoughts and attitudes of teenagers around the world:

Offer, D. O., Ostrov, E., Howard, K., & Atkinson, R. (1988). *The teenage world: Adolescents' self-image in ten countries.* New York: Plenum.

A highly readable and insightful look into the world of early adolescence is:

Schave, D., & Schave, B. (1989). *Early adolescence and the search for self: A developmental perspective.* New York: Praeger.

Perkins and McMurtrie-Perkins present down-to-earth advice for parents concerned about drug use by their children:

Perkins, W. M., & McMurtrie-Perkins, N. (1986). *Raising drug-free kids in a drug-filled world.* Austin, TX: Hazelden.

The following two sources look at sexual behavior and pregnancy among adolescents. The first presents detailed information concerning rates of teenage pregnancy, abortion, childbirth, and marriage in more than 30 industrialized countries; the second presents a detailed look at a controversial topic—abortion:

Jones, E. F., et al. (1986). *Teenage pregnancy in industrialized countries.* New Haven, CT: Yale University Press.

Sachdev, P. (Ed.). (1985). *Perspectives on abortion.* Metuchen, NJ: Scarecrow Press.

Gender stereotypes are widely held beliefs about male–female characteristics and differences. The first of the following two references presents a balanced view of gender differences that psychology has actually found; the second examines the typical stereotypes and prejudices of American and Swedish adolescents:

Halpern, D. F. (1986). *Sex differences in cognitive abilities.* Hillsdale, NJ: Erlbaum.

Intons-Peterson, M. J. (1988). *Gender concepts of Swedish and American youth.* Hillsdale, NJ: Erlbaum.

Marc Chagall: *Forward!*, 1917. Art Gallery of Toronto, gift of Sam and Ayala Zacks.
Copyright © 1989, ARS/ADAGP, New York.

Sing on! sing on! I would be drunk
with life,

Drunk with the trampled vintage
of my youth.

Oscar Wilde, *The Burden of Itys*

VI

Early Adulthood

It's not always an easy thing to grow up, to leave one's childish toys and become an adult. There are important psychosocial tasks to be accomplished first, the psychologists tell us in their peculiar jargon. As we see in the next two chapters, there are competencies to be acquired, crises to be conquered, old attitudes and old ways of thinking to be discarded. There are mature commitments to be made to careers, to friends and spouses and family, perhaps even to dogs and horses and other beasts. There is intimacy to be explored and earned and given.

These are trappings of adulthood, not of adolescence and childhood. The things of childhood and adolescence must be left behind, trampled in the dust of childish years where wild oats were once sown.

If we do grow up, will our trampling of the vintage of our youth leave us with a wine so sweet it will make us want to sing with joy through our young adulthood?

Or will it leave us with only a vinegar to pucker our lips and furrow our brows and snatch the song from our hearts?

CHAPTER 13

Physical and Cognitive Changes: Early Adulthood

Peter: "Would you send me to school?"

Mrs. Darling (obligingly): "Yes."

Peter: "And then to an office?"

Mrs. Darling: "Very soon."

Peter (passionately): "I don't want to go to school and learn solemn things. No one is going to catch me lady, and make me a man. I want always to be a little boy and to have fun."

James Barrie, *Peter Pan*

Dan Kiley (1983) says that, like Peter Pan, he decided one day he would prefer not to grow up. He informed his grandmother of his decision. "That's nice, Danny," she answered. "Now get out in the garden and hoe the tomatoes."

Many of us flirt with the enchantment of not growing up, of living forever in the magic lands of carefree childhood. But for most of us, it is only a flirtation; the tomatoes, and sometimes the roses, in the gardens of our lives intervene. If we are to eat the tomatoes or smell the roses, harsh reality tells us, we must also hoe and weed, fertilize and prune — that is, we must accept and master the developmental tasks of adulthood.

Perhaps not all are willing to grow up. Kiley (1983) speculates that increasing numbers of young men — and perhaps women, too, although he speaks only of men — do not grow up. These individuals suffer from the *Peter Pan Syndrome*. They are unwilling or unable to accept the ordinary responsibilities that come with increasing maturity. Accordingly, they are reluctant to make career decisions, to become economically independent, or, even more, to become emotionally independent and to accept responsibility for others. They are also anxious and lonely because they do not relate well to others who have matured more normally.

But most of us cannot stay little boys and girls and just have fun. We have to go off and learn solemn things. We have to hoe our tomatoes.

This Chapter

The lifespan does not divide itself nicely into sections and chapters, organized neatly by age. That happens only in textbooks and theories where we sometimes stretch or squeeze to make things fit.

There are, of course, different ways of squeezing and stretching. The approach we have chosen organizes topics primarily by age. Within each age division, we consider the social, cognitive, physical, and emotional aspects of human development. In childhood and adolescence, change often seems to be tied quite closely to age. Hence, a chronological approach gives us a good sense of the sequence of important changes, and does not cause much fragmentation and distortion.

But in adulthood, it is more difficult to tie change to age. The adult part of the lifespan is, after all, an extremely large part of the entire span — far more than half of it in most cases. And the changes that characterize adulthood are often subtle and usually related to a complex of other changes and major events such as marriage or retirement; many are only loosely related to chronological age.

In some ways, it would be easier to organize the upper end of the lifespan by topic rather than by age: marriage, careers, parenting, and so on. But such an organization would hide the fundamental continuity of development. Accordingly, we continue with a chronological organization. In the next six chapters, we cover physical, cognitive, and social-emotional changes within three large chronological spans: youth and early adulthood (20 to 40–45), middle adulthood (40–45 to 65–70), and later adulthood (65–70 onward). Keep in mind, however, that although this forces us to treat separate topics at one age rather than another, many of the important activities and events of adulthood can occur at any age.

This chapter deals with important physical and cognitive changes of youth and early adulthood. It includes, as well, a discussion of work in the first third of the adult span.

Youth and Early Adulthood

As we saw in Chapter 11, adolescence is generally considered to begin with pubescence (changes leading to sexual maturity) and to end with adulthood. Unfortunately for those of us who would like things to be simple, both of these events can occur at very different times for individuals of the same sex and do occur about two years apart for individuals of different sexes. Thus adolescence, as a transition period, has rather fuzzy boundaries.

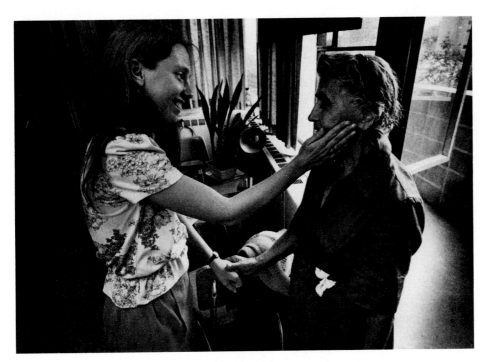

Growing up in a physical sense is not something about which we have any choice. Whether or not we want to, if we live long enough, we will eventually wither and stoop and wizen and sag. But growing up psychologically is a different matter. There are some who refuse to grow up. These "Peter Pans" think that if they do not accept the ordinary responsibilities of adulthood, they can avoid the troubles and cares of age. Others, like this social worker at a housing development for the elderly, joyfully accept the developmental tasks of adulthood.

Youth, also a transition period spanning the adolescent years, has somewhat clearer, although arbitrary, boundaries. Coleman (1974) defines it as the period from age 14 to age 24. He selects these boundaries because, as he puts it, nobody can be called an adult prior to the age of 14, and nobody can still be classed a child after the age of 24. That, of course, is not to say that all 14-year-olds are childish and all 24-year-olds mature — witness our Peter Pans. Our definitions are only definitions; they do not alter the exceptions that reality provides.

Early adulthood is generally considered to include the years between the end of adolescence (or sometimes, the end of youth) and about age 40 or 45 — which signals the beginning of middle adulthood. However, these periods are perhaps best understood in terms of the completion of important developmental tasks rather than simply in terms of having attained a given age. Accordingly, before looking at the physical changes of youth and early adulthood, we look at some important developmental tasks of this period.

Developmental Tasks

Developmental tasks are sequential milestones that reflect the acquisition of some major new competence, or the occurrence of a social event with important psychological consequences. For example, developmental tasks of infancy include learning to walk and talk; two developmental tasks of childhood are to learn how to get along with peers and to develop basic skills in reading, writing, and arithmetic (see Chapter 2). These are achievements with immediate and obviously important consequences for children.

Havighurst's Developmental Tasks

▶ *Developmental tasks are important social and psychological milestones in human development. Note that they are highly contextual — that is, they vary from one context to another. In contexts where accomplishing a task is seen as highly important (or essential), failure to do so may be linked with considerable distress and unhappiness. However, societies such as ours tolerate and encourage such a wide range of life-styles and values that failure to accomplish one or more tasks is sometimes totally inconsequential. How many of the tasks of adolescence — and young adulthood — have you now accomplished? Which of those that remain are important to you?*

Period	Tasks
Adolescence	1. Developing conceptual and problem-solving skills
	2. Achieving more mature relationships with male and female peers
	3. Developing an ethical system to guide behavior
	4. Striving toward socially responsible behavior
	5. Accepting the changing physique and using the body effectively
	6. Preparing for an economically viable career
	7. Achieving emotional independence from parents
	8. Preparing for marriage and family life
Young adulthood	1. Courting and selecting a mate
	2. Learning to live happily with partner
	3. Starting a family and assuming parent role
	4. Rearing children
	5. Assuming home management responsibilities
	6. Beginning career or occupation
	7. Assuming appropriate civic responsibilities
	8. Establishing a social network

Most of the developmental tasks of adolescence and of early adulthood have consequences that are not as immediate, that are more future oriented (Nurmi, 1991). Many of the tasks that are set for adolescents by teachers, parents, and social contexts have to do with expectations and goals for the future. Even the adoption of an identity is future oriented insofar as it involves *commitment* to career, life-style, and values.

The developmental tasks of youth and early adulthood, too, are transitional and future oriented: Most of them are important in terms of their *future* implications for career and family. And as adolescents age into young adulthood, Nurmi (1991) informs us, they become even more future oriented. Important descrip-

tions of developmental tasks in early adulthood are given by Havighurst and Coleman.

Havighurst's Tasks of Early Adulthood. Robert Havighurst's (1972) tasks for adolescence and young adulthood are shown in Interactive Table 13.1. (Later stages are shown in Tables 15.1 and 18.2.) Tasks that relate specifically to young adulthood have to do primarily with establishing a family, a career, and a place in the community — all future-oriented activities. They include things such as *courting and selecting a mate, learning to live happily with a partner, starting a family and assuming a parental role*, and *rearing children* (topics that we cover in the next chapter). They include, as well,

The important developmental tasks of young adulthood have traditionally centered around starting a family, choosing a career, and developing a place in the community. However, for many North Americans, the transition from adolescence to adulthood has been significantly prolonged in recent years. For these three college students, the requirements of formal education and an uncertain and changing employment market mean that career and family will wait much longer than they did for their parents and grandparents.

beginning a career or an occupation (a topic covered in the final sections of this chapter).

There are two important things to keep in mind when looking at developmental tasks. First, they are highly culture specific. They reflect competencies and achievements that are important and relevant primarily in North American societies, as well as in many industrialized societies elsewhere. However, many of these developmental tasks would be totally irrelevant in other societies. Among the native dwellers of the jungles of Cameroon, for example, selecting a career is largely meaningless. And although selecting a mate and starting a family are probably an important part of early adulthood in most of the world's societies, these events might entail very different responsibilities and might occur at much younger — or perhaps even older — ages elsewhere.

Second, although these sequential tasks describe what is *common and expected* in a given context, failure to achieve a developmental task, or achieving it earlier or later than expected, is not evidence of abnormality. Clearly, not all young adults want a mate. Similarly,

TABLE 13.2

Skills Required for Effective Transition to Adulthood

Self-Centered Skills	Useful for
Work and occupational skills	Attaining economic independence
Self-management skills	Making reasonable decisions in the face of wide choice
Consumer skills	Learning how to use and enjoy culture as well as goods
Concentrated involvement skills	Succeeding in undertakings; making significant contributions in many areas

Other-Centered Skills	Useful for
Social interaction skills	Effective commerce in a variety of situations with different people
Skills relating to management of others	Assuming responsibility for those who are dependent
Cooperative skills	Engaging in joint endeavors

Source: Based on Coleman, 1974.

some *cannot*, some *will not*, and some *should not* have children. Nor do all need to select and develop a career.

Coleman's Transitional Tasks. According to Coleman, a successful transition between childhood and adulthood requires meeting two classes of developmental objectives. The first concerns the individual's own capacities and abilities; the second has to do with how the individual relates to others. He refers to the first grouping of objectives as *self-centered* and to the second as *other-centered* (see Table 13.2).

The self-centered objectives have to do with the development of skills required for achieving economic independence. They include skills relating to specific occupations or careers. These skills might be acquired through postsecondary schooling, or through the cultivation of some special talent such as that of a musician or singer, for example.

Self-centered objectives also include skills relating to the management of one's own affairs—for example, handling financial affairs and resisting the lure of easy credit. Less obvious, but perhaps no less important, are tasks such as finding and looking after a living space, arranging for utilities, cooking, making decisions about leisure time, and on, and on.

A third self-centered objective has to do with acquiring the skills that are required to be an intelligent

consumer, not so much of goods as of the "cultural riches of civilization" (Coleman, 1974, p. 4). We all consume goods—although not all very intelligently; perhaps the same is true of culture. Presumably, consuming culture intelligently implies learning to enjoy both the more esoteric aspects of culture (plays, concerts, museums, literature) and the more mundane (sports, television dramas, and soap operas). Unfortunately, perhaps, schools and parents don't always do a great deal to prepare their charges to consume culture intelligently. Nor is it completely clear that doing so is highly desirable and beneficial, although we suspect this to be the case.

The final requirement for effective participation in adult society is the ability to engage in concentrated activity. By this, Coleman means that a completely successful transition to adulthood requires individuals to dedicate themselves to certain endeavors, unlike Peter Pan. In many cases, these endeavors will be job-related; in other cases, they might relate to community activities, specific hobbies, religious beliefs, or political interests. He suggests that the greatest of human achievements in all areas are usually the result of such concentrated activity.

Among other-centered objectives, Coleman lists three types of experiences that contribute significantly to the adoption of mature social roles. These include

The first years of early adulthood are often the peak of our lives in terms of strength, stamina, sensory functioning, and intellectual capacity — with no noticeable declines in functioning in any of these areas until the middle years and beyond. This camp counselor can run as fast and as far as any of his young charges; he can throw a ball a lot farther; and he is more skilled at paddling a canoe. And in the binder on his lap, there are tricks and amusements to amaze and astound these lads.

the opportunity to interact with a variety of individuals from many different social classes, races, age groups, religions, and occupations; experience in situations where the individual is *responsible* for others; and experience in activities where the outcomes depend on the cooperation of a number of individuals.

Acquiring these skills should facilitate the transition between youth and adulthood, and result in better-adjusted and happier adults.

The Transition

How do we know when the transition is complete? When does youth become adulthood? There is no simple, widely accepted answer. In general, however, the beginning of adulthood coincides roughly with attaining economic and emotional independence from the family. Accordingly, the most common manifestations of independence are finding some means of financial support (obtaining a job, for example) and establishing a new home, sometimes alone but very often with a mate.

Note that in the same way as adolescence is partly a cultural phenomenon, so too is youth. Youth is essentially a prolongation of adolescence that has been created by complex, technological societies where sim-

ply achieving puberty does not provide the child with the skills required for optimal participation in adult life. In the days of our grandparents, being able to make babies might have been sufficient qualification for admission to the rank of adulthood. Today, however, a great many of us are required to spend an increasing amount of time learning the skills — the "solemn things" — that we are likely to need later. And during this time, whether we are in college, in the military, unemployed or elsewhere, we are likely to be neither child nor adult but somewhere in between.

We should note again, however, that this swiftly brushed picture of youth paints only one of several possible scenes. Growing up in today's technological world does not always entail a prolongation of adolescence — a period of youth. There are many who still enter the work force during adolescence. And among these, many become adult in all significant ways far before others of identical age. Similarly, even in the time of our great-grandparents and beyond, during a period when we imagine life to have consisted largely of idyllic meanderings through pastoral scenes, many people prolonged their adolescence for long periods, unable or perhaps simply unwilling to become adult. Then, as today, there were some people who knew very clearly that we do not all have to become adults (in terms of work roles, responsibilities, and attitudes toward self, others, and life in general). There are those who can dream and play—like children—through the entire span. Let others hoe the tomatoes.

Physical Development

One of the reasons developmental psychology has traditionally been concerned with children and not with adults is simply that children change a great deal—sometimes very rapidly and dramatically; changes among adults are usually less dramatic and less uniform. Hence, the temptation is to think of adulthood as a *plateau*—a resting state following development and preceding decline. It is worth emphasizing again that contemporary models of development depart significantly from this conception.

In the area of physical development, adulthood clearly is not a plateau. Although change might not be as predictable or as dramatic as it was in earlier years, there are still some small mountains to climb and a few slopes to descend.

Performance

From childhood through adolescence, there is measurable improvement in various aspects of motor performance. For example, both boys and girls can run about 4 yards (3.64 meters) per second at the age of 4. By age 12, their speed has increased to about 6 yards (5.41 meters) per second. For boys, running speed continues to increase, reaching about 7 yards (6.37 meters) per second by age 17; but for girls, there is a slight decline after age 12 (Espenschade & Eckert, 1980). Haywood (1986) reports similar findings for motor tasks like throwing or vertical jumping. The pattern is of gradual improvement through childhood and into adolescence for males, with an earlier plateau and occasional slight decline for girls. Interestingly, this plateau is less apparent in more recent measures, probably because of increased female participation in sports (Haywood, 1986). It is also not apparent among competitive male or female athletes—evidence, says Haywood, of the social and practice factors involved in motor performance.

Note that measures of running speed and of distance an object is thrown are *quantitative*. Qualitative assessment of motor performance is difficult and inexact. One technique is to use high-speed film to yield super-slow-motion pictures. Sequences can then be ana-

lyzed and judged on different qualitative dimensions. When motor performance is evaluated *qualitatively*, a slightly different developmental pattern emerges, especially for complex and highly practiced skills. Motor skills required for high-level performance in sports such as basketball, hockey, and football, for example, continue to improve into adulthood.

Flexibility

Improvements in motor performance after adolescence are highly dependent on practice. Perhaps nowhere is this more evident than in measures of range of joint motion (flexibility). In fact, without training, flexibility begins to decline at about the age of 12 (Clarke, 1975). Decline is gradual and often goes unnoticed, but, in the absence of training, continues through early adulthood. Boone and Azen (1979) measured flexibility in males ages 18–54 and found, for example, that range of hip rotation decreases by about 5 degrees each decade.

Flexibility often diminishes even for athletes and others who work physically, simply because few sports and occupations require a full range of motion in all joints. It is *not* the case for gymnasts and dancers whose training is directed toward maintaining flexibility, and who typically retain a high range of motion in all joints through early adulthood. The evidence is that flexibility can be maintained through training, and perhaps increased through appropriate exercises, even when these are begun very late in life. For example, Munns (1981) increased flexibility in participants ages 65–88 through a program of dance and exercise.

Declining flexibility results largely from the fact that certain motions are not generally required in ordinary life. As a result, the individual is often unaware that range of joint movement is gradually decreasing. When it becomes most apparent—for example, in the shorter steps and reduced pelvic rotations of older walkers—it is often dismissed as one of the inevitable consequences of aging. But it may not be completely inevitable given continued high-flexing activity throughout life, says Adrian (1981).

Strength and Stamina

Early adulthood is potentially the peak of our physical development in terms of speed, strength, coordination, and endurance, as well as in terms of general health

(Newman, 1982). If we remain fit and active during our twenties and early thirties, we can lift more, run faster, throw farther, work longer, climb higher, and crawl lower than at any other time in our lives. It is not surprising that Lehman's (1953) studies of the ages at which people were most likely to achieve in a variety of fields found that the twenties and sometimes the early thirties were periods of highest achievement for sports requiring strength, stamina, and coordination (see Table 13.3).

The normal developmental pattern with respect to physical strength sees a very gradual decline following the peak years. This decline is often not particularly noticeable until the forties and is most apparent with respect to back and leg strength. Clement (1974) reports that loss of upper body strength (particularly arm strength) is often no more than 10 percent by the age of 60.

In addition to a gradual loss of strength following the peak in early adulthood, there is a more noticeable loss of stamina, usually related to poorer aerobic functioning (heart–lung efficiency) (Brooks & Fahey, 1984). Few 40-year-olds can still compete with younger individuals in athletic events and sports requiring strength and endurance (marathons or hockey, for example). For this reason, in the same way that competitions in childhood are made more fair by assigning competitors to age-determined classes, so adult competitions are sometimes separated into age classes. But whereas the older age groups typically outperform the younger groups in childhood, the opposite is true in adulthood. Masters' class (over 40) marathons are won with slower times than the open classes.

It is important to note that here, as elsewhere, many of the changes and declines of age are neither dramatic nor inevitable. As Troll (1985) points out, declines in physical endurance and strength before the age of 50 are scarcely noticeable. And with proper exercise and training, many individuals are able to continue performing physically at high levels well into old age. Some, like Gordie Howe, who still played professional hockey after the age of 50, can even compete successfully with individuals far younger. Many a well-conditioned 50- or 60-year-old marathoner can put an untrained 20- or 30-year-old to shame.

In conclusion, although peak strength and stamina, maximum cardiac output, and maximum pulmonary functioning are typically achieved in the twenties, and although there is measurable decline in many aspects of physical functioning after this peak, the decline is generally sufficiently gradual that the period of early

TABLE 13.3

Age Ranges: Peak Athletic Achievement

	Age Range (years)
Professional football players	22–26
Professional prizefighters	25–26
Professional hockey players	26
Professional tennis players	25–29
Leading chess contestants	29–33
Professional golfers	31–36
World billiards records	31–36

Source: From *Age and Achievement* by H. C. Lehman, 1953, Princeton, NJ: Princeton University Press. Copyright 1953, © 1981 by the American Philosophical Society. Reprinted by permission of the publisher.

adulthood is best described as a period of *stability* rather than one of decline.

The Senses

There are no dramatic age-related changes in the functioning of our senses through early adulthood: All our senses continue to function about as well at the end of early adulthood as they did at the beginning.

However, there are a number of more subtle changes. Their effects are generally felt so gradually that they are seldom noticed as they are occurring. Visual acuity, for example, declines very slowly until about 50 (Kline & Schieber, 1985). Similarly, the lens in the eye is subject to the effects of aging almost from birth. It becomes progressively less flexible, and its shape changes so that most individuals become increasingly farsighted as they age (Timiras, 1972).

Hearing, like vision, changes only slightly in early adulthood but, *on average*, begins to decline in the thirties and accelerates after middle age (Belsky, 1990). Losses that do occur are typically more common for men than for women. Hearing losses in early adulthood are most often the consequence of environmental factors, such as prolonged exposure to noisy environments, rather than the effects of age (Troll, 1985).

Changes in touch sensitivity, as well as in taste and smell, are not apparent in early adulthood.

Health

In the same way that early adulthood is characterized by the peak of physical strength and endurance, as well as of sensory capacity, so is it characterized by the peak of physical health. In particular, many of the infections of childhood become far less common in early adulthood and remain so throughout life. With increasing age, however, there is increased susceptibility to chronic (recurring) medical complaints, such as back and spine problems, heart ailments, and so on. Whereas the leading causes of death among young adults are accidents, heart disease and cancer are the leading causes of death among older adults, particularly after the ages of 35 for men and 45 for women (U.S. Department of Health and Human Services, 1986). In this connection, there have been some dramatic changes in the most common causes of death during the last several decades. In 1940, the leading cause of death was pneumonia and influenza, followed closely by tuberculosis. Thirty years later, influenza and pneumonia were a distant fifth, and tuberculosis had become almost inconsequential as a cause of death. Heart disease and cancer now lead the list (U.S. Bureau of the Census, 1991).

Bayer, Whissell-Buechy, and Honzik (1981) have looked at health during early and middle adulthood by summarizing data from three major longitudinal studies: the Oakland Growth Study (ages 11–50), the Berkeley Growth Study (birth–36), and the Berkeley Guidance Study (birth–42). They found that the majority of adults (over 80 percent) consider themselves to be in "good-to-excellent" health in early adulthood. Toward the end of this period, however, there is a gradual increase in the number who suffer from a variety of complaints. As noted previously, these complaints tend to be chronic rather than instances of acute infections such as colds and influenza. Among women, the most common complaints relate to the reproductive system. These may involve attempts to become pregnant, pregnancy itself, problems relating to menstruation, ovarian cysts and tumors, and infections. Among men, the most common complaints relate to the digestive system; men have three times the incidence of stomach ulcers that women do.

Another sex difference with respect to adult health is that women generally report more illnesses than do men. Ironically, their life expectancies continue to be significantly higher. Some theorize that women are more sensitive to their bodies and perhaps less likely to dismiss symptoms as inconsequential. Accordingly, they are more likely to seek medical help and thus to report more illnesses. Also, they are more likely to receive assistance when it will be most effective.

Exercise

Participate! Play tennis! Play racquetball! Play squash! Dance! Join a spa! Take an exercise class! Skate! Ski! Swim! Run! Jog! At least walk.

Literally millions of adults, many of whom had engaged in virtually no unnecessary physical activity since high school or college—and perhaps not even then—have now embarked on exercise programs. And many undertake these programs with the same dedication and determination that they bring to their careers—and perhaps to other aspects of their lives. Why? Simply, to be happy and healthy. That is, after all, what most of us want. Exercise, we are told, will make us healthier, may enable us to live longer, and should make us trimmer, more fit, and perhaps even more attractive, given our contemporary cultural standards of physical attractiveness.

How valid are these claims? Research leaves little doubt that exercise contributes significantly to good health. Numerous studies of cardiovascular fitness have repeatedly found higher levels of fitness and lower incidence of coronary heart disease among those who exercise regularly than among those whose lives are more sedentary (Sinclair, 1989). In addition, exercise is important in reducing the percentage of body fat and in increasing muscle and bone density.

But does exercise make us happier? Does it affect us psychologically? Blumenthal and associates (1982) provide some answers, based on an investigation of the effects of exercise on a group of 16 subjects who had registered for a 10-week adult fitness program. The average age of this group was 45 years; the youngest subject was 25, and the oldest 61. At the beginning of the program, all subjects were administered a battery of three psychological tests to assess mood, anxiety, and some general aspects of everyday functioning such as sleep patterns and social habits. A control group, consisting of healthy but sedentary individuals of similar age, was also administered these same tests.

The exercise program for the 16 experimental subjects consisted of a 10-minute routine of stretching exercises, followed by 45 minutes of walking or running, three times a week over a period of 10 weeks.

Research leaves little doubt that regular exercise increases cardiovascular fitness, strength, stamina, and endurance, and that it contributes significantly to health and longevity. The evidence also indicates that exercise can relieve stress and anxiety, and improve one's general sense of well-being and happiness.

All exercise periods were under medical supervision. Control-group members continued as before, without any regular exercise program.

At the end of the 10-week period, individuals in both the experimental and the control groups were again administered the three psychological instruments. The results are clear and striking. Whereas the groups had initially been similar on each of these instruments, the experimental group now felt less tension, fatigue, depression, and confusion, and experienced significant reductions in immediate and general anxiety. And, as expected, physiological measures indicated significant improvements in the experimental groups.

Apparently, adults who are inactive but basically healthy can increase their well-being, as well as their *sense* of well-being, through exercise.

Drugs and Stress

Whereas exercise generally has a positive effect on health and well-being, recreational drugs and excessive stress typically do not. Of the drugs used by young adults, alcohol and nicotine are by far the most common. In fact, they are the two that show only slight decline after age 25; marijuana, cocaine, stimulants, and

all others show a marked decline (U.S. Bureau of the Census, 1991). The health consequences of nicotine use and heavy alcohol consumption are well known.

The effects of stress on the health of the young adult are not as clear as those of drugs such as alcohol and nicotine. This is largely because stress is far more difficult to define and measure than is alcohol or nicotine use. In addition, its effects are more subtle and may involve a greater number of systems.

As we saw in Chapter 10, stress may be defined in terms of stimuli that make excessive demands on the individual, or in terms of responses that are accompanied by the physiological changes of high arousal (Johnson, 1986). We saw, too, that in some ways a stress response is an adaptive response. The physiological changes of arousal — the sudden spurt of adrenaline, for example — are useful in mobilizing the individual's systems for responding. However, prolonged exposure to stress can eventually lead to a "stress overload" and to a consequent breakdown of the adaptive response (Selye, 1974). Excessive stress in childhood is sometimes evident in sleeping or eating disturbances, depression, and a variety of physical complaints (Johnson, 1986).

Clearly, not all children respond to stress in the same way. Some capitulate early; others remain unperturbed, perhaps even strengthened, in the face of stress.

The consequences of stress for adults are perhaps not very different from those in children. In general, high stress is often associated with anxiety, and high anxiety is one of the most common of all psychiatric symptoms (American Psychiatric Association, 1980). In addition, stress is linked to several physical complaints that sometimes appear in early adulthood, including gastrointestinal problems such as ulcers, heart problems, and high blood pressure (Krantz, Grunberg, & Baum, 1985).

Like children, not all adults respond to stressful events in the same way. Psychology and medicine have sometimes found it useful to distinguish between two types of individuals identifiable largely in terms of the level of stress that seems to permeate their lives. These types, well popularized in literature, are labeled Type A and Type B (Friedman & Rosenman, 1974).

Type A individuals are hard-driving, loud, aggressive, achievement oriented, and impatient. These are individuals who drive themselves mercilessly, who sense most keenly the unrelenting pressures of time and the urgency of their lives. In contrast, Type B individuals are slow, relaxed, easygoing. They speak more softly, tend to impose few deadlines on themselves, and do not, in general, respond to life with the same sense of urgency that drives Type A's.

Type A and B individuals can be identified by means of questionnaires that ask questions such as "Do people sometimes tell you that you eat too fast?" or "Do the people with whom you work see you as being aggressive and achievement oriented?" (Jenkins, Zyzanski, & Rosenman, 1971). Using such questions, researchers have found that perhaps 40 percent of the population is Type A; the remainder is Type B. Clearly, however, the types are less a dichotomy than a continuum: Some Type A individuals would manifest extremes of Type A behavior and others would be only slightly different from Type B individuals.

The medical profession has found this typology particularly useful because of an apparent relationship between Type A behavior and coronary problems (Corse et al., 1982). Some studies indicate that Type A individuals are approximately twice as likely as Type B individuals to suffer fatal heart attacks. And if they survive the first attack, they are more likely to have a second (Rosenman et al., 1975). In addition, approximately three fourths of all men suffering from hypertension (high blood pressure) are Type A's ("Down with Type A!" 1983). Small wonder that being a Type A individual has sometimes been accorded the same weight as a contributor to coronary problems as high blood pressure, high cholesterol level, smoking, and obesity. However, subsequent research has not always found as high a relationship between Type A behavior and coronary problems as did earlier research (Matthews, 1984). But what this research has been finding is that certain components of the Type A personality are more important than others in contributing to health problems. In particular, Type A individuals who are hostile and angry seem to be more coronary-prone than Type A's who are simply highly achievement oriented, aggressive, and fast-paced.

It is also worth noting that through training in relaxation, and with proper motivation, Type A individuals can become more like Type B's (Ovcharchyn, Johnson, & Petzel, 1981). At the very least, such individuals might learn to relax sufficiently that they can effectively rid themselves of the damaging effects of stress, although they continue to be hard-driving Type A's in the workplace.

Sources of stress in everyday life might include a variety of frustrations, demands, and conflicts having to do with social relationships, spouse and children, career, and so on. They might also include significant events or changes. Several theorists suggest that *all* change is stressful—even pleasant changes such as going on vacation. In Chapter 10, there is a scale of potential changes in the lives of children ranked in terms of their probable stressful impact. Interactive Table 13.4 presents a similar scale for adults. In an early study involving 400 subjects, Rahe (1972) reported that those who reported scores of 150 or lower in the preceding year were likely to remain healthy; those whose scores were above 300 were much more likely to develop physical as well as mental problems.

Sex and Reproduction

The most dramatic changes in the reproductive system throughout the entire lifespan are those that occur in adolescence. It is then, as we saw, that profound hormonal changes trigger the well-known series of developments that define pubescence and that lead eventually to puberty (sexual maturity). Within approximately a year of the girl's first menstrual period and the boy's first ejaculation of semen (although sometimes sooner), each is capable of becoming a parent.

Social Readjustment Rating Scale

▶ *Major, and even minor, changes can be sources of stress. Some theorists suggest that all change is stressful, and that its effects are cumulative. You can obtain a rough estimate of the stress in your own life using the scale reproduced here. Simply total the life-change unit values associated with each of the life events you have experienced during the past 12 months. Scores of 150 or less are associated with continued health and happiness; scores above 300 are sometimes associated with later problems. However, these generalizations are based on averages, and do not reflect countless individual exceptions. Some people are remarkably resistant to stress; others buckle more easily.*

Rank	Life Event	Mean Value (life-change units)	Rank	Life Event	Mean Value (life-change units)
1	Death of spouse	100	23	Son or daughter leaving home	29
2	Divorce	73	24	Trouble with in-laws	29
3	Marital separation	65	25	Outstanding personal achievement	28
4	Jail term	63	26	Wife begins or stops work	26
5	Death of close family member	63	27	Begin or end school	26
6	Personal injury or illness	53	28	Change in living conditions	25
7	Marriage	50	29	Revision of personal habits	24
8	Fired at work	47	30	Trouble with boss	23
9	Marital reconciliation	45	31	Change in work hours or conditions	20
10	Retirement	45	32	Change in residence	20
11	Change in health of family member	44	33	Change in schools	20
12	Pregnancy	40	34	Change in recreation	19
13	Sex difficulties	39	35	Change in church activities	19
14	Gain of new family member	39	36	Change in social activities	18
15	Business readjustment	39	37	Mortgage or loan less than $10,000	17
16	Change in financial state	38	38	Change in sleeping habits	16
17	Death of close friend	37	39	Change in number of family get-togethers	15
18	Change to different line of work	36	40	Change in eating habits	15
19	Change in number of arguments with spouse	35	41	Vacation	13
20	Mortgage over $10,000	31	42	Christmas	12
21	Foreclosure of mortgage or loan	30	43	Minor violations of the law	11
22	Change in responsibilities at work	29			

Source: From "The Social Readjustment Rating Scale" by T. H. Holmes and R. H. Rahe, 1967, *Journal of Psychosomatic Research, 11*, pp. 213–218. Reprinted by permission of Pergamon Press, Ltd.

Normal Sexual Responses

Masters and Johnson (1966) describe the normal sexual response in both males and females as a four-stage event: excitement, plateau, orgasm, and resolution. Excitement is a preparatory phase leading to sexual arousal. Major changes that mark the excitement phase in females include vaginal lubrication and expansion and distension of the vagina; in males, excitement is characterized by erection of the penis.

The plateau is a period of continuing sexual arousal following initial excitement, but preceding orgasm. Among women, the plateau entails continued swelling of the vagina, some changes in the *labia* ("lips" surrounding vaginal opening), breast enlargement and sometimes nipple erection, increased heart rate and blood pressure, and occasionally a flushing of chest, neck, and face. Among men, the plateau is marked by a maintenance of the erection, enlargement of the testes, occasional nipple erection, and a sharp increase in pulse rate, blood pressure, and respiration rate.

The orgasmic phase in women entails between 5 and 15 contractions of the outer third of the vagina, some uterine contractions, some muscle spasms, and a marked increase in respiration. Orgasm in men involves explosive contractions of the urethra as sperm is ejaculated, muscle spasms, rapid increase in respiration rate, and maximum heart and blood pressure levels.

In both males and females, resolution involves a rapid return to a preexcitement state.

There are two important differences between male and female response patterns. First, immediately following the male orgasm, there is a period, termed *refractory*, during which the male is incapable of a second orgasm. This period may be as short as a few minutes or as long as several hours. (See Figure 13.1.)

Second, whereas the usual male pattern of sexual response is a single excitement–plateau–orgasm–resolution cycle, there are three common patterns of female sexual response. The first (A in Figure 13.2) involves excitement, the plateau, an ensuing orgasm, and the possibility of one or more subsequent orgasms (without recycling through the excitement phase), followed by the resolution after the final orgasm. The second (B) is marked by a longer plateau and a slower resolution, but no orgasm. And the third (C) is a faster response cycle that goes relatively directly from excitement to orgasm and returns equally rapidly to a normal state.

In both men and women, the entire sexual response cycle is typically accompanied by physical sensations that vary from mildly to intensely pleasurable. In light of this, and given its biological significance, it is little wonder that sexuality is among the most important of human motivations and behaviors.

There are two kinds of problems that can interfere with sexual responsiveness and reproduction: sexual dysfunctions and infertility.

Sexual Dysfunctions

The most common sexual dysfunction among men who consult sex therapists is *erectile dysfunction* or *impotence*—the inability to achieve or to maintain an erection (Hawton, 1985). This condition is more common with increasing age. In as many as 50 percent of all cases, it may have physical or medical origins; in others, its roots are more psychological.

Premature ejaculation—the inability to control ejaculation—is a relatively common sexual dysfunction among men in early adulthood, but becomes less common with increasing age.

Retarded ejaculation, essentially the opposite of premature ejaculation, is characterized by an inability to achieve orgasm during sexual intercourse. In many cases, retarded ejaculation is situational—that is, it is manifested in some situations, but not others. Evidence suggests that stress and anxiety are often involved.

Female sexual dysfunctions include inability to derive pleasure from sexual intercourse; *vaginismus*, or involuntary contractions of the vagina that make intercourse painful or impossible; and inability to achieve orgasm. Inability to achieve orgasm is *not* viewed as a problem unless the woman expects that she *should* experience one. As we saw, a female sexual response cycle without an orgasm is common and pleasurable for many women.

All of these sexual dysfunctions can be treated, sometimes by means of psychological-sexual therapy, sometimes medically. Of them, only severe vaginismus, retarded ejaculation, and impotence are likely to be causes of infertility—the inability to produce children.

Infertility

With puberty, men and women not only acquire the capacity to respond sexually, but also develop strong urges to do so. There appear to be few major changes in these urges or in the capacity to respond through

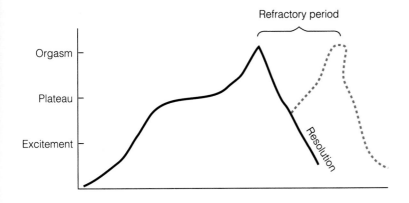

Figure 13.1 Male sexual response. (Based on Masters and Johnson, 1966.)

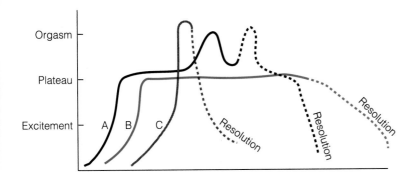

Figure 13.2 Three female sexual response cycles. (Based on Masters and Johnson, 1966.)

early adulthood—although frequency of sexual intercourse declines rapidly within the first few years of marriage (see Chapter 14). Some evidence indicates that men might, on the average, be slightly less easily aroused toward the end of early adulthood, and achieve orgasm more slowly. At the same time, through early adulthood, women apparently become more capable of achieving orgasm during intercourse (Sloan, 1985).

Biologically, women and men are capable of producing healthy infants throughout early adulthood. As we saw in Chapter 3, however, the probability of genetic and birth complications increases with advancing age of both parents, but especially the mother.

Infertility, however, is a relatively common problem among both men and women. Among women, it is most often due to blocked fallopian tubes, the blockage usually resulting from infections. Recall that chlamydia is a relatively common cause of this type of infertility. In addition, fertility in women drops slowly from the age of 20. One reason is that ovulation, which may initially occur regularly, sometimes becomes less predictable as menstrual cycles become less regular.

Nor does ovulation always occur with every cycle. Thus, *on the average*, even when they are fertile, older women do not become pregnant as easily as younger women.

Fertility among men also decreases very gradually through early adulthood, largely because of a decrement in the production of sperm. However, this decrement is very slight before middle age—most men in very late adulthood still produce sperm. However, the number of viable sperm produced by elderly men is ordinarily too small to make conception very likely.

It's important to note that decreasing fertility among men and women in early adulthood is not a *primary* aging process—that is, it is not an inevitable consequence of age. In fact, the principal causes of changes in fertility rate during this period are infections and diseases. And although these become more probable with advancing age, they are not a result of aging.

As is discussed in Chapter 14, many women are now having children somewhat later than in the past. Morris (1988) reports that although the overall birthrate has scarcely risen in North America in recent decades, the number of first births to women over the age of 30 has increased by more than 35 percent.

One reason for this is that recent decades have seen some profound changes in female work and career patterns.

Work and Careers

One of the most important developmental tasks in making a successful transition from youth to adulthood is finding some sort of "adult" employment. But finding employment is far more than simply a mundane developmental task; it is fundamentally important to who and what we are. And the ease with which we make the transition from nonwork to work, either at the beginning of our adult years or at the end (or, perhaps, even in the middle) is fundamentally important to our well-being.

Employment: Some Definitions

Although terms such as *career, vocation, job*, and *occupation* are often used interchangeably, their precise meanings are somewhat different. The narrowest of these terms is *job*, which refers to the specific tasks or duties that the worker performs. Thus one of the jobs undertaken by a caretaker might be to empty wastebaskets. In much the same way, there are jobs associated with being a lawyer or a dentist — specific tasks that are part of the individual's **work**.

Occupation is a more general term than job; it refers to a broad employment classification such as accounting, clerking, selling, being a mechanic, and so on. Occupations are categories of work that cover a variety of related jobs.

The term *career* is far broader than either occupation or job. It does not refer to any specific occupation or employment but to an entire range of related occupations. Thus a career will often span an entire lifetime of work and may include a host of related occupations (each with its own jobs). A career in food services, for example, might include such occupations as busboy, waiter, bartender, food manager, convention manager, and chain food-services supervisor. Similarly, a career in law might include a variety of employments (occupations) for different legal firms or government agencies, private practice, and so on. It is possible, of course, to have more than one career in a single lifetime.

In its strictest sense, the term *vocation* refers to a "calling" and has traditionally been restricted to the clergy and to certain white-collar professions. Thus one can have a vocation for the ministry, a vocation for medicine, or a legal vocation; it is less appropriate to refer to a laborer's or a secretary's vocation.

In this text, as in many other contexts, *work* is often used as a general term to include all manner of occupations, careers, professions, jobs, and vocations.

Why Work?

At the most basic and obvious level, the majority of us work to earn a living. However, it would be highly misleading to suggest that that is the only, or even the most important, reason for working. A majority of men and women claim that they would continue to work even if they did not have to (Crowley, Levitin, & Quinn, 1973).

Work serves a variety of purposes. Herr and Cramer (1985) divide these into three areas: *economic, social*, and *psychological*. The economic functions of work include what we usually mean when we speak of "making a living" — that is, they have to do with the satisfaction of physical needs. In industrialized societies such as ours, however, the economic benefits of work often go considerably beyond putting a chicken (or a zucchini, for those who prefer) in our pots. Many people can put a dozen or more chickens in their pots. That's one sign of "success."

The social purposes of work are reflected in opportunities for social interaction and the development of friendships. More than this, work provides people with status and responsibility, and gives them reasons for feeling important and wanted.

The psychological purposes of work, closely related to its social purposes, have a lot to do with the development of confidence and self-esteem. It is through working and earning that people achieve a sense of self-worth and satisfaction. More than this, it is from our work that many of us derive important aspects of our identities. It is no accident that many of us answer the question "What do you do for a living?" with "I am a(n) _____." In a sense, we *are* what we do.

Changes in the Work Ethic

The traditional work ethic of the Western world has been described as the Protestant ethic — one that places tremendous value on hard work and that, by the same

How we earn a living has a significance that goes far beyond the chickens it provides for our pots and the shoes it puts on our children's feet. Work gives many of us opportunities for social interaction and for the development of important friendships; it also contributes in important ways to our confidence and self-esteem. Who we are is often inextricably tied to what we do. This man does not simply work at a computer; he *is* a computer programmer.

token, views leisure as potentially dangerous and detrimental to society. In its most extreme applications, this ethic holds that idleness is sinful and hard work ("the sweat of one's brow") is especially meritorious in a religious sense.

But perhaps the work ethic that drove our grandparents has lost some of its power. In the 1960s, Yankelovich (1981; Yankelovich & Lefkowitz, 1982) tells us, there were four major themes that served as common reasons for working and that characterized the Protestant work ethic. The first was that of the *good provider*. Good people are those who provide well for their families. The second was that of the *independent person*— the person who can stand alone, and "make it" alone. The third was the *success* theme—the belief that hard work will be rewarded. The fourth was the *self-respect* theme—the belief that there is dignity in hard work and that people's worth is reflected in how hard they work. If eulogists could think of nothing else to say about the "dearly departed," it might be sufficient sim-

ply to say, "One thing you have to say about our friend is that he was a hard worker!"

Yankelovich reports that in the early 1980s these themes no longer seemed dominant. First, people seemed to be less concerned with economic security. Achieving economic security was no longer seen as entirely the individual's responsibility but had become at least partly the government's.

A second fundamental change was related to the entry of women into the work force in numbers that might have been viewed as startling from the perspective of the 1960s. And increasingly, their entry into jobs and careers, like that of many men, was motivated as much by social and psychological factors as by economic factors. Working is no longer a harsh duty or even a privilege; it is a right!

Yankelovich describes other changes of the early 1980s: a growing tendency to place less value on efficiency, productivity, high income, and other indicators of "success." Instead, increasing emphasis is placed on

INTERVIEW

▶ Subject   Male; age 24; single; high school dropout; varied history of short-term employment, primarily as laborer for construction firms.

▶ Question   "What do you want out of life? What do you dream of being or doing? Say, when you're 40 or so."

....

66 *Well, I sure wouldn't want to be doing what I'm doing now. And I won't be. No way, Jose! Maybe I'll win the lottery. . . . What would I do then? Heck, nothing. Drink beer and party. Have a good time.* 99

mechanizes production and services; it thrives on the collection, storage, analysis, and dissemination of information; and it creates a vast array of new jobs while at the same time eliminating a great many others.

Job Trends.   Today's "high-tech" society presents an incredible array of jobs, an increasing number of which have replaced unskilled, low-education occupations. Furthermore, the nature of these jobs is in a constant state of flux, as are the markets that provide employment. For example, since 1976, there has been an increase of more than 50 percent in technical and related occupations, as well as in managerial and administrative jobs—and similar increases in professional specialities and in marketing. During the same period, service occupations increased by only 28 percent, and manufacturing and labor jobs by only 3 percent; meanwhile, forestry, farming, and fishing occupations *declined* by 8 percent (Silvestri & Lukasiewicz, 1989).

Forecasts of future occupations have been controversial and unreliable, notes Bailey (1991). On the one hand are those who argue that rapid technological advances leading to increasing automation will greatly reduce the demand for unskilled, low-level employment, and that most of the jobs created in the future will require education and training beyond the high school level (Johnston & Packer, 1987). On the other hand are those who note that modern technology is increasingly successful in reducing the need for trained and educated workers, and that the ultimate effect of this is that *less* rather than more education will be required of many workers in the future—witness the "dumbing-down" of cashier jobs as one example, where electronic bar-code readers automatically enter prices; or the use of icons of tiny hamburgers, fries, or sodas on multikeyed, computerized registers, so that fast-food employees need not even know how to read or recognize numbers (let alone add or subtract).

Our best guess, says Bailey, is that there will be a gradual increase in the need for highly educated workers, in spite of the fact that lower-skill occupations such as sales, janitorial and cleaning work, and food or beverage service occupations are projected to have a very large absolute growth (see Figure 13.3). And the need for upgrading within occupations will become greater as workers are forced to keep up with rapidly changing technology.

Other Job Changes.   Other important changes in employment include the fact that more than half of all

quality-of-life issues. Workers no longer negotiate simply, or even primarily, for higher income but ask, instead, for "fringe benefits." They are no longer interested only in earning great piles of money but in such things as leisure time during which to enjoy the benefits of smaller piles of money.

Whether these important changes are descriptive of today, and how general they are, cannot easily be answered. But clearly, there are many reasons to work. And even today, there are many people for whom quality of life is not as important as how big the final pile of money is.

Changes in Work Opportunities

Apart from changing attitudes toward work, in recent decades, we have seen some startling changes in the nature of the work that people do in Western societies. We went very rapidly from societies that were primarily agricultural to societies that were increasingly industrial. Now we have entered a third phase—that of the technological society. The technological society

Projected Job Trends for the Year 2000

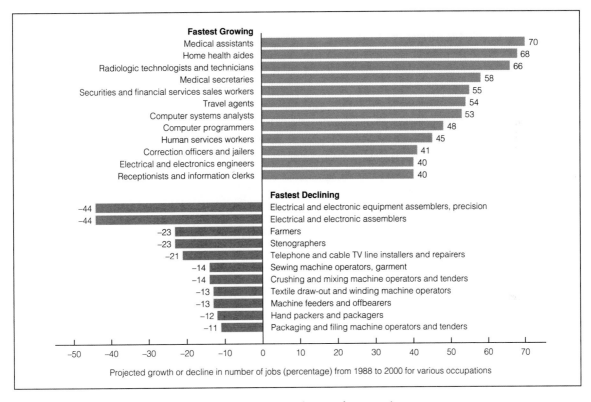

Figure 13.3 Fastest-growing and fastest-declining jobs: moderate estimates, 1988–2000. (Based on U.S. Bureau of the Census, 1991, p. 398.)

There are hundreds of jobs today that did not exist a mere one or two decades ago. Yet the fastest-growing job markets are those that have existed for centuries. Many of these are related to medicine — a direct result of our aging population coupled with advances in medical knowledge and technology. The most rapidly declining job markets include equipment and electronic manufacturing and assembling, and stenographers — both a result of the use of computers in the workplace. Retail salespersons is the single largest job category at present, and is projected to be the largest in 2000; second is general managers and top executives.

A Job–Person Matching Model Based on Holland's Coping Styles

▶ *You who have recently made (or may soon make) a career decision might find it interesting to examine the goodness-of-fit between your characteristics and interests and the decision you have made (may make). If you have a realistic notion of your characteristics and interests (shown in column 2), you can assess your type (column 1) and see whether what you plan to do is anything like the corresponding list in column 3. If the match seems strained, don't be alarmed; perhaps you don't know yourself very well. Besides, global matching models of this kind are not sufficiently sensitive to slot everybody into the very best of all possible careers; and, for many, there may be a very wide range of nearly best of all possible careers.*

Type	Characteristics and Interests	Recommended Job Settings
Realistic	Concrete Mechanically oriented Motor activity	Gas station Construction Labor Skilled trade Farm
Intellectual	Abstract Creative Introverted	Research Academics
Artistic	Subjective Creative Intuitive Emotional	Performing arts Visual arts
Social	Extroverted Socially concerned High verbal ability High affiliative needs	Social work Teaching Counseling
Enterprising	Domineering Adventurous Impulsive Extroverted	Leadership roles Planning roles Real estate development
Conventional	Unimaginative High self-control Want social approval Systematic	Accounting Banking Business/clerical

adult women are now in the work force (U.S. Bureau of the Census, 1991); an increase in part-time work; significantly higher educational levels among workers; and a reduction in the number of people available for lower-paying jobs. In addition, there is a vastly increased job turnover rate and much higher job mobility, not only among different occupations within a single career but also among different careers. As Toffler (1970) suggests, present conditions dictate that many of us should be looking not at a single career but at *serial* careers. Not only is there time in a single lifetime to engage successfully in more than one career, but doing so may be required by the rate at which old jobs disappear and new ones take their place. But through it all, we must be prepared for adjustments and adaptations that were not likely to be demanded of our grandparents, lest we, too, be overcome by *future shock*.

How is the young adult (or adolescent) to choose from among so many careers? Or the older adult, for that matter? Do we *naturally* drift toward a career? Do our personal talents and interests urge us gently down the right paths? Or should we be guided? And if we are to be guided, how should it be done?

Theories of Career Choice

There are two general groups of theories that influence much of the thinking in career guidance. One is based on the notion that individuals and jobs should be matched with respect to the individual's interests and talents and the job's requirements. This approach is sometimes referred to as *job–person matching*. The other emphasizes the development of career-related abilities rather than simple job–interest matching and includes what are termed *developmental models of guidance*. A third *family-based model* combines aspects of these two basic models, but pays more attention to the individual's context.

Job–Person Matching. Guidance counselors who adopt the job–person matching model attempt to identify talents that are essential for specific occupations, administer batteries of tests to discover talents, and then try to match the two. The matching generally takes into account the individual's interests as well as talents.

One well-known example of this trait-interest, job-matching approach is that of Holland, who developed the Holland Vocational Preference Inventory (Holland, 1975). It identifies six specific combinations of traits

TABLE 13.6

Ginzberg's Developmental Guidance Model

Stage	Approximate Ages	Major Career Events
Fantasy	To 10 or 12	Unrealistic notions of career possibilities; child wants to be a president, an astronaut, a ballerina, an actress, a famous explorer, a cowboy.
Tentative	10–12 to about 16	Growing awareness of requirements of different careers; increasing realization of personal interests and capabilities; keener awareness of the status and rewards associated with different careers.
Realistic	Late adolescence through early adulthood and even later	Involves beginnings of career decisions through active *exploration* of alternatives; commitment to a clear career choice (*crystallization*); undertaking series of activities necessary for implementing choice (*specification*). For many individuals, the process of career evaluation continues through life, and different career choices may be made in midladder.

and interests, labeled *coping styles: realistic, intellectual, social, conventional, enterprising*, and *artistic*. These styles, and recommended occupations, are summarized in Interactive Table 13.5.

Trait-interest matching approaches to career guidance have proved highly useful and continue to be widely used both in schools and in placement and employment offices. Computer-assisted career guidance (CACG) systems are widely used to match individuals with careers, to suggest alternatives, or to permit exploration of various careers. There are a large number of such systems available (Sampson & Reardon, 1990; Sampson, Reardon, & Lenz, 1991).

Developmental Models. Developmental models of career selection are concerned less with matching jobs and persons than with understanding and facilitating the chronological development of career decisions. These models typically view career choices as beginning in childhood and as involving a gradual, decision-making process. Among the best known of developmental guidance models are those advanced by Ginzberg (1951, 1972) and Super (1957, 1974; Super & Hall, 1978). Ginzberg's model describes three sequential preadult stages in career development: the *fantasy* period, the *tentative* period, and the *realistic* period (see Table 13.6).

The fantasy period lasts until approximately age 10 or 12 and is often characterized by highly unrealistic notions of career choice. This is the stage during which children want to be astronauts, baseball players, physicians, or presidents.

During the tentative period (ages 11–16), adolescents gradually become aware of the requirements of different careers, as well as of their own personal interests and capabilities. Slowly and *tentatively*, they begin to think about matches between their interests and abilities and the various career opportunities that might be open to them. They also become increasingly aware of the values and rewards attached to different occupations, and they evaluate these as well.

The realistic period begins about age 17 and involves the beginnings of career decisions. However, final decisions might be some distance in the future, particularly in view of the extent to which postsecondary education extends adolescence and often postpones the need to enter the work world. Even after a career choice has been made, it will remain tentative for some time.

Ginzberg speaks of three substages within the realistic period. The first, *exploration*, consists of actively investigating, and even trying out, some of the various options. Exploration often occurs when first entering the job market or in the early years of college or other postsecondary education. The individual then moves from exploration to *crystallization*, which entails a relatively firm commitment to a career. The final stage, *specification*, involves doing the things required to implement the career decision.

According to Ginzberg's developmental model, career evaluation occurs first in early adulthood and often continues through much of the remainder of the lifespan. Increasingly, when people's evaluations of their

---

INTERVIEW

▶ Subject   Male; age 46; divorced; no children; involved in film business.

▶ Question   "How or why did you become a _____? And is this the type of work (career) that you think you would have chosen when you were in high school?"

....

66 *Sure. When I was in high school we had a communications course and everybody made little 8-millimeter films. I guess I had some talent which the teacher recognized. I'll never forget that teacher. It's probably because of him that I went into this business. I mean, it wasn't just an accident. I decided this is what I wanted, and I've been working at it ever since. I haven't done everything I want to yet, but it's shaping up. It's a lot of work and learning and contacts. This is a tough business, but I wouldn't want to be anything else.* 99

INTERVIEW

▶ Subject   Male; age 26; single; recent university graduate; permanent employment with government department.

▶ Question   "What do you want out of life? What do you dream of being or doing? Say, when you're 40 or so."

....

66 *You're sure this is going to be anonymous? . . . Okay. What I'd really like, I guess, is a good administrative position in this department or in another one. It doesn't really matter. As long as I'm in charge. Of people and decisions. I know I've got the right background, and if I play my cards right I should be assistant director by the time I'm 35. I'll be in line for a supervisor's job by next summer. But there's lots of politics, and if it doesn't work out—like if I don't go as fast as I think I should—then I'd move. Transfer to another department, or maybe even run for politics. If the situation looks right. I don't want to waste my time and run if it doesn't look like I can win. Here you have to be in the right party. But mostly I think I can make a heck of a good career here if I play my cards right.* 99

---

careers reveal less satisfaction and happiness than had been anticipated, alternate career decisions are made; this can occur at almost any time throughout the lifespan. As is discussed later, middle-of-the-lifespan career choices are made not only by women returning to the work force after raising children or entering it for the first time, but also by men who might already have devoted many of their working years to climbing the ladders of a career whose summits they no longer wish to reach—or whose slopes they find too steep or too unrewarding.

A Family-Based Lifespan Model.   Most approaches to career exploration and development have several assumptions in common, say Grotevant and Cooper (1988); and these assumptions are not always valid. They assume, for example, that the young adult will leave home to establish a commitment to work—and to intimacy as well. But in many industrialized societies, it has become increasingly common to delay leaving home—or to return after initially leaving—so that career plans and intimate relationships are sometimes highly developed before the young adult leaves. And even after the young adult leaves, the family continues to be an important source of influence on careers.

Many career development models also assume that adolescents and young adults have a relatively unlimited number of options from which to select a career. While this may be true for many, it does not take into consideration various constraints that factors such as economic opportunity, gender, race, and intelligence sometimes place on career choice.

These models also assume that career exploration begins late in adolescence, that career choice and development progresses in a linear and irreversible fashion, and that the process is complete with the adoption of a career. But, say Grotevant and Cooper (1988), career exploration may start in early childhood, may involve a variety of abandoned choices that require starting over again, and in many cases is a lifelong process. Hence the need for a career exploration model that takes into account the influence of interactive *contextual* factors such as the family, the social environment, and the individual's characteristics.

The family influences career choice not only by providing models of occupational roles, educational levels, and life-styles, but also through parental attitudes, which might strongly affect the developing person's values and, ultimately, career choice. Parental attitudes toward female achievement and leadership, for example, may be reflected in a daughter's career choice (Nadelson, 1990); aspirations, career choices, and accomplishments of siblings might also exercise profound influences.

Family influences can have a wide range of more subtle and less easily identified influences on career choices as well. Grotevant and Cooper (1988) point out, for example, that the nature of the individual's attachment as a child might later be reflected in a tendency to explore—or not to explore—as well as in quality of interpersonal relationships in young adulthood. Also important in career choice are individual qualities such as self-esteem, self-confidence, and creativity, which are strongly influenced by *mutual interactions* between growing children and their family contexts. Similarly, factors such as intellectual and motor ability are important, as are contextual factors. In certain geographical, social, or ethnic contexts, for example, or for different sexes in some contexts, choice of occupations might be more limited or at least different.

Taking these interactive factors into account does not clarify or simplify our career choice models very much; but it does make them more realistic and more complete.

Work Selection

It would be naive and misleading to suggest that most of us make our career choices following well-reasoned decisions based on what we know of our interests and abilities—that each of us undertakes a careful examination of available careers and a thoughtful analysis of their requirements as well as of their potential contributions to our eventual growth and satisfaction. In fact, many of us select our careers (or are selected for them) in very different ways. As we saw, the occupations of our parents, our sex, our socioeconomic status, and other personal and contextual factors may each contribute significantly to what we eventually become.

Fortune, too, may play a role. It might provide a variety of chance happenings that mold great chunks of our lives. A father dies and leaves his child a business, a farm, or a family to look after; a teenage girl becomes pregnant; a dedicated young doctor marries into great wealth. Events such as these can profoundly influence the course of an individual's career, as can the simple availability of jobs. For those who attempt to enter the labor market directly from high school, or even before completing high school, the first job obtained is likely to be the one that is first available. And in many cases, the individual's eventual career may be related to this first accidental job.

Sex, too, has much to do with career choice as well as with career availability. Despite rapidly changing social conditions, stereotypes of appropriate male-female career divisions are still prevalent (Intons-Peterson, 1988). These stereotypes may limit the number of choices girls think they have (Tittle, 1982). However, the proportion of women in management and administrative positions has risen from around one quarter in the early 1970s to more than one third in the mid-1980s (Bloom, 1986).

Socioeconomic background also influences choice of careers, with people from higher levels being most likely to obtain postsecondary education or training, and consequently being most likely to select professional, white-collar, and high-technology occupations. People from lower levels are more likely to be found

---

INTERVIEW

▶ **Subject**   Female; age 48; widowed; two children, both independent; manager of a cleaning business.

▶ **Question**   "How or why did you become a _____? And is this the type of work (career) that you think you would have chosen when you were in high school?"

....

❝ *Not bloody likely (laughter). I mean, working my fingers to the bone like this (laugh). I would of been a princess like that, what's her name, Grace Kelly. Married a prince if I could of. But I married this guy when I got pregnant and I never found no prince. Just this guy who cleaned rugs and stuff. Till he got a heart attack. That's how come.* ❞

---

in blue-collar occupations. Similarly, parental occupation often has a strong bearing on the child's selection of careers.

Job Satisfaction

Not many decades ago, the primary motivations for work were money, perhaps security, and often duty. And the emphasis was on being a successful, productive worker. But when Yankelovich (1972) interviewed youths about their attitudes toward work, he found overwhelming agreement that the financial aspects of an occupation are far less important than its nature, its purpose, its social significance, and the extent to which growth and happiness are likely to be associated with it. As Kuder (1977) notes, it is no longer sufficient just to have a job; we also want to be *happy* in our work and to feel that our contributions are worthwhile. In

Terkel's (1972) words, work is "a search for daily meaning as well as daily bread, for recognition as well as cash, for astonishment rather than torpor; in short, for a sort of life rather than a Monday through Friday sort of dying. Perhaps immortality, too, is part of the quest" (p. xiii).

How satisfied and happy are most of us with what we do? Here, as in the more general areas of satisfaction with their lives, few adults are willing to describe themselves as very dissatisfied or very unhappy (see Chapter 16). In a widescale study of workers, Quinn, Staines, and McCullough (1974) found that at least three quarters of all workers at any age level describe themselves as being satisfied with their jobs and happy. Interestingly, however, workers tend to report greater job satisfaction the longer they work (Rhodes, 1983). In the Quinn and associates survey, for example, 75 percent of those under the age of 21 describe themselves as happy; 84 percent of those between 20 and 30, and an amazing 90 percent of those above 30, also describe themselves as happy.

Why do we become progressively more happy with our jobs? In addition to the fact that work gives meaning to a great many lives and that we therefore *want* to be satisfied, perhaps finding it difficult to admit even to ourselves that we might not be, there are at least three reasons why people seem to become happier with their work as they age. The first and most obvious is that those who are truly unhappy with their careers will often change them early in their lives. The second is that it is possible to grow to love (or at least accept) a career that at first seems unpleasant. And third, as we age, many of us might modify our original *dream*, dropping our aspirations, lowering our estimates of what our contributions and rewards should be; perhaps we become satisfied with less as it becomes clearer that we are unlikely to be given more.

Not all people are bound to succeed as success is commonly defined in the economically driven corporate world. Not all will climb the high ladders of corporate achievement to accumulate great power and status, to become, as Kanter (1981) puts it, "fast trackers." Many more will simply be "dead enders"—those who never reach the summits toward which the "fast trackers" climb so rapidly. Dead enders, Kanter tells us, include those who initially enter occupations that have low ceilings, those who are in high-ceiling employment but who fail somewhere along the line, and those who simply take the wrong paths. Low-ceiling jobs are those that do not ordinarily lead to advancement and include many labor and clerical jobs. High-ceiling occupations include opportunities for advancement. Dead enders in low-ceiling employment are relatively satisfied; those in high-ceiling employment but who fail to climb upward are most unsatisfied. And those who simply climb the wrong ladders in the beginning find themselves at an intermediate level of satisfaction. There are, of course, other definitions of success. And "dead ender," because of its negative connotations, is not a good label for all those who enter low-ceiling occupations. There are sources of job satisfaction that have absolutely nothing to do with climbing corporate ladders.

Clausen (1981) identifies three factors that appear to be closely related to the satisfaction workers experience with their occupations. Most important is the extent to which the job reflects personal interests. Also crucial is the extent to which it requires full use of the worker's capabilities and provides an opportunity to develop ideas. Finally, income also contributes to job satisfaction. It is revealing that although each of these factors was important for both white- and blue-collar workers in Clausen's sample, more than half of the blue-collar workers also indicated that job security was extremely important. In contrast, fewer than 20 percent of those in white-collar occupations thought job security was critical. Clausen speculates that this might be because a common characteristic of white-collar occupations is that job permanence or security is seldom an issue. Such is not the case for blue-collar occupations, particularly during economic recessions.

Cognitive Change

Our predominant models of human development, as we noted, have traditionally been based on the assumption that the major developmental changes through the lifespan occur in infancy, childhood, and adolescence. This has been especially true for theories that have looked at cognitive and moral development—but perhaps less true for theories concerned more with social-emotional development. It had somehow seemed reasonable to admit that adults are capable of profound and sometimes systematic social or personal changes, but it had seemed less likely that they would also experience systematic developmental changes in cognition. However, recent research and theorizing have identified some important positive changes that occur later in the lifespan; much of development is not complete at adolescence.

Moral development presents one clear example of a developmental progression that continues into adulthood. Postconventional morality is extremely rare among adolescents; indeed, it is very rare among adults in their twenties. And Kohlberg's final stage, that of universal ethical principles, may be so advanced developmentally that even among adults it remains potential rather than actual.

So, too, with Piaget's formal operations. Only the easiest of the formal operations tasks can be performed by young adolescents; many of the more difficult must wait for adulthood. And some researchers have suggested that a fifth stage be added to Piaget's theory—what Arlin (1975) describes as a *problem-finding stage*, and Riegel (1976), as a *dialectical stage*.

Dialectical Thinking

Webster's Third New International Dictionary defines *dialectics* as "the process of self-development or unfolding (as of an action, event, idea, ideology, movement, or institution) through the stages of thesis, antithesis, and synthesis. . . ." It further defines *dialectical* as being "marked by a dynamic internal tension, conflict, and interconnectedness of its parts or elements." The central ideas in dialectics are conflict and change (Tolman, 1983).

Riegel's Conflict Resolution.
And what might dialectics have to do with adults' human development? A great deal, according to Klaus Riegel (1970, 1972, 1976), who argues that our conventional views of development as a series of stages or plateaus characterized by a state of balance or equilibrium are incorrect and misleading. According to Riegel, lifespan human development is best viewed as sequences of conflicts, crises, or contradictions and their continued resolution. The concept of *dialectics* is implicit in the view that conflicts or crises arise from contradictory actions and reactions—the classical situation of a thesis leading to an antithesis and finally being resolved in a synthesis.

Whereas most developmental theories deal mainly with a single facet of development, Riegel's theory applies to development in four dimensions: inner-biological, individual-psychological, cultural-sociological, and outer-physical. Human development may be seen as progressions in each of these four areas. For example, we grow physically even as hormonal changes lead us to sexual maturity, our intellectual processes alter, and our social positions and interests shift. However, these changes do not always occur in synchrony.

For example, sexual maturity might lead a young adolescent toward behaviors that are culturally difficult. From this lack of synchrony conflict arises, and conflict is the root of dialectical processes. Resolution of conflicts may lead to new developments, some of which require major reorganizations in one or more of the four areas of development. And when the reorganization is sufficiently dramatic, we might be tempted to recognize a *stage* or a *plateau*. But a dialectical view does not emphasize the plateau or the equilibrium—as does Piaget's theory, for example. Instead, it views development as a continuous process because the organism and society are never static. Change is constant, and complete synchrony is rare and fleeting.

Riegel (1973a) proposes a fifth Piagetian stage—a dialectical stage similar to one described by Arlin (1975) as a problem-finding stage. In this fifth stage, there are no clear plateaus—no levels of cognitive accomplishment clearly evident in the ability to solve a new class of problems. Instead, there is a renewed realization that development occurs on different levels, that it is replete with contradictions, and that different levels of behavior are entirely appropriate. As Riegel notes, a laborer might remain at the level of concrete operations, and a dancer at a sensorimotor level.

"The developmental and aging processes . . . are founded upon the ability to tolerate contradictions and insufficiencies in action and thought," Riegel informs us; he adds, "this ability has been buried as a consequence of physical restrictions, normative social pressure, and especially, formal education" (1973b, p. 482).

Basseches's Dialectical Schemata.

In close agreement with Riegel is Basseches (1984), who argues that the thought processes that our cognitive and developmental theories have described are not nearly as relevant for adults as they are for children and adolescents. Cognitive development continues after adolescence, Basseches insists, and much of it is dialectical. Dialectical thought, in Basseches's (1984) words, "represents a development beyond Piaget's formal operations stage. . . . [It] describes a more epistemologically powerful way of making sense of the world" (p. 15).

What the dialectical view of development provides is the recognition that there are no static levels—no stages—toward which the individual strives and that, once reached, represent the culmination of that age's developmental progress. The adult dialectical thinker struggles to create meaning and order, but is always aware of conflict—of thesis and antithesis. Unlike Piaget's formal operations adolescent (or adult), logic

is not omnipotent; it does not invariably lead to the one, unique, correct solution for all of life's problems. In fact, the most important problems in life are those that demand the application of values and the examination of alternatives.

Basseches proposes that through early adulthood, cognitive growth, to the extent that it occurs, may take the form of *dialectical schemata*. These schemata are patterns of thought that are involved in dialectical thinking. Some of these schemata, for example, draw the thinker's attention to relationships and interactions, some have to do with change and movement, and some deal with form or pattern. All relate to the recognition and resolution of conflict.

Basseches proposes that dialectical thinking is a uniquely adult form of reasoning that places the adult in the world of changing systems, and that allows the application of thought and of values to an analysis and interpretation of these systems. In the same way as concrete operations made it possible for the schoolchild to reason about real classes and objects, so dialectical operations makes it possible for the adult to reason about social and political systems, interpersonal relationships, and so on. But, even as formal operations remains a *potential* stage for many adolescents, so too does dialectical thought remain merely potential for many adults.

In summary, dialectical thinking is a mode of thinking that involves recognition of ambiguities and contradictions, *and* increasing tolerance of these. Unlike formal reasoning, which is highly constrained in the sense that it is limited by rules of logic, dialectical thinking is more intuitive, more subject to value judgments. Formal reasoning, claims Basseches, is rarely used in the real world, although it might occasionally be used in science or in a formal testing situation—or perhaps to confirm the results of intuition. Dialectical thought, on the other hand, can be applied to problems relating to intimate personal interactions, artistic activities, business transactions, the sciences, and so on.

Labouvie-Vief's Pragmatic Wisdom.

Much adult reasoning, Labouvie-Vief (1980) argues, occurs in very different contexts than does child and adolescent reasoning. Reasoning that involves the manipulation of classes or the consideration of all possible alternatives might be entirely appropriate for many of the problems that children face, especially in schools. But these ways of thinking are not very suitable or useful for many of the situations that the adult faces. Because of the realities of adult responsibilities, because of the practical demands of certain contexts, and because of ethical constraints, the reasoning that evolves in adulthood is different from the reasoning of the preadult. It is, in Labouvie-Vief's (1980) words, a form of reasoning that is "marked by specialization, concrete pragmatics, and pressures towards social system stability" (p. 141). As a result, in adult thought, there is often a trade-off between the most scientific or most logically correct of possible alternatives and a desire for social stability—or for the most ethical alternative. It is as though age and experience grant adults a kind of wisdom—a dialectical wisdom—that allows them to factor *more* variables into their problem-solving activities than formal operations allows.

A Summary. Riegel, Basseches, Labouvie-Vief, and others who are concerned with the cognitive processes of adults present a compelling argument that the logic of systems such as Piaget's do not adequately describe the thinking of adults (Stevens-Long, 1990). They argue that with adulthood there may come an increasing recognition of ambiguity and contradiction, greater tolerance for these, and the learning of new dialectical schemata. These schemata are ways of thinking that allow the ongoing resolution of problems, but that bring into play a variety of important considerations other than simple logic—for example, ethics, feasibility, social implications, and so on.

Although it is still too early to evaluate the impact and the usefulness of these ideas, their emphasis on aspects of development that have largely been ignored may lead to important insights about changes in thinking through the lifespan. These notions might also do much to resolve what has been an ongoing controversy about the nature of age-related changes in intellectual ability.

Intelligence

There are those who have believed that one of the inevitable consequences of aging is a marked decline in intellectual functioning; others insist that this decline has been greatly exaggerated, that it does not involve most areas of cognitive functioning, and that even where it is apparent, it is trivial into very old age. Since most of the negative changes that are alleged to occur (or not to occur) do not begin until middle or later adulthood, the controversy and its resolution are not discussed here, but are covered in Chapters 15 and 17. Here, we look briefly at a theory of adult intelligence.

Sternberg's Triarchic Theory of Intelligence. In Chapter 9, we spoke of a *contextual* theory of intelligence. This theory maintains that behavior is intelligent if it is adaptive in the context in which it occurs. In some contexts, it might be intelligent to fight when confronted by an enemy (if, for example, not fighting would lead to a great loss, or even death); in other situations, *not* fighting might be far more intelligent (if, for example, fighting would almost certainly mean losing or dying—or both).

Sternberg's theory of intelligence is not only contextual, but also *componential*. As we saw in Chapter 9, the theory describes intelligence in terms of three major components: metacomponents (cognitive skills having to do with recognizing a problem, selecting a strategy for its solution, and monitoring cognitive activity), performance components (skills actually used in solving problems), and knowledge-acquisition components (relating to what is actually learned or decided).

There is a third aspect to Sternberg's theory of intelligence—hence his label *triarchic theory of intelligence*. The first two arches of this theory are the componential theory and the contextual theory; the third is *experiential*. It deals primarily with the application in new situations of what has been learned through experience. (See Table 13.7.) Hence, it is a dimension of intelligence that is highly dependent on the individual's exposure to a variety of situations. Accordingly, experiential intelligence is likely to be greater in adults than in children.

Sternberg and Berg (1987) asked a sample of 152 adults to *list* behaviors that they thought might characterize extremely intelligent and extremely unintelligent 30-, 50-, and 70-year-olds. Subsequently, they asked a second sample to *rate* the importance of the factors identified by the first sample. Later, a third sample was asked to rate the likelihood of intelligent and unintelligent 30-, 50-, and 70-year-olds engaging in the behaviors ranked in the second study.

There were two striking findings from this investigation: First, people seem to have clear and remarkably consistent notions of what intelligence is; and second, these notions vary systematically according to the age for which the judgment is being made. All groups typically placed greater weight on the more conventional indicators of intelligence for the younger age group; and the majority agreed that social and contextual features of intelligence—those that relate to the everyday requirements of living—are more important for the 70-year-olds. (See Table 13.8.)

Conventional measures of intelligence typically tap a number of processes and capabilities that compose what Sternberg has labeled the componential aspect of intelligence; they do not ordinarily sample behaviors that might reflect contextual intelligence or the application of experience in novel but *real* situations. As a result, such tests may be unfair to those whose intelligence is more practical and more intuitive. If the dialectical theorists are correct, such tests are unfair to adults.

Researchers have now begun to identify a number of important cognitive changes that occur with age and that appear to lend support to those who argue that thought processes are dialectical—or at least *different*, perhaps in the sense that they are more pragmatic. Additional evidence suggests that adults emphasize different aspects of intelligence in their behavior.

We look at these topics again in Chapter 15.

A Contextual Reminder

This chapter is clearly rooted in the Western industrialized world, as, of course, is most of this book. That is probably as it should be since I am of that world; and most of you are as well. But it is worth repeating once more than much of what we have to say about human development reflects the contexts in which we live and work. Thus what we believe about the vigor and health of young adulthood, the excellent functioning of the senses, the benefits of exercise, and the relative absence of disease, may well be true and important in our Western industrialized world, but not the least bit true in some jungle tribe where the average life expectancy is 40 and a woman's child-bearing period is over by 30. There, the normal course of physical development is quite different.

Similarly, we can make grand pronouncements about how work must not only put chickens in our pots but also fill our souls with a sense of value and purpose. But these assertions would mean nothing if we were speaking of the natives of the Amazon basin. These people have no careers; they have no corporate ladders to climb—or from which to fall. What they have is a compelling need to go out into the jungle every day of their lives and find enough food to survive yet another day.

Do you suppose their thoughts are dialectic? Do you think they struggle to balance pragmatics and morals in the resolution of issues of profound social and economic importance?

Or is their thinking different, their intelligence more *of their context*?

TABLE 13.7

Main Aspects of Intelligence According to Explicit (Triarchic) Theory

I. Componential Subtheory
  A. Metacomponents
    1. Recognizing existence of a problem
    2. Defining nature of the problem
    3. Selecting lower-order components to solve problem
    4. Selecting strategy into which to combine components
    5. Selecting a mental representation upon which strategy acts
    6. Allocating mental resources
    7. Solution monitoring
    8. Utilizing external feedback
  B. Performance Components (partial list)
    1. Encoding stimuli
    2. Inferring relations between stimuli
    3. Mapping higher-order relations between relations
    4. Applying old relations to new stimulus domains
    5. Comparing stimuli
    6. Justifying selected solutions
    7. Responding to stimuli
  C. Knowledge-Acquisition Components
    1. Selective encoding of information
    2. Selective combination of information
    3. Selective comparison of new to old information

II. Experiential Subtheory
  A. Dealing with relative novelty
  B. Automatizing information processing

III. Contextual Subtheory
  A. Adaptation to environment
  B. Shaping of environment
  C. Selection of environment

Source: From "What Are Theories of Adult Intellectual Development Theories Of?" (p. 11), by R. Sternberg and C. Berg, 1987. In *Cognitive Functioning and Social Structure Over the Life Course*, C. Schooler and K. W. Schaie (Eds.). Reprinted by permission of Ablex Publishing Corporation.

Main Aspects of Intelligence According to Implicit Theories

30-Year-Old

I. Novelty in Problem Solving
   A. Is interested in gaining knowledge and learning new things
   B. Displays curiosity
   C. Challenges what is presented to him or her in the media
   D. Is able to learn and reason with new kinds of concepts
   E. Is able to analyze new topics in new and original ways
II. Crystallized Intelligence
   A. Is experienced in his or her field
   B. Is competent in career choice
   C. Is able to draw conclusions from information given
   D. Displays clarity of speech
   E. Displays the knowledge to speak intelligently
III. Everyday Competence
   A. Displays good common sense
   B. Adjusts to life situations
   C. Is able to adapt to disastrous life situations
   D. Is interested in his or her family and home life
   E. Is able to adapt well to the environment

50-Year-Old

I. Novelty in Problem Solving
   A. Is able to analyze topics in new and original ways
   B. Is able to perceive and store new information
   C. Is able to learn and reason with new kinds of concepts
   D. Challenges what is presented to him or her in the media
   E. Displays curiosity
II. Everyday Competence
   A. Adjusts to life situations
   B. Is perceptive about people and things
   C. Is able to adapt to disastrous life situations
   D. Is able to adapt well to the environment
   E. Is aware of events beyond his or her area of expertise
III. Social Competence
   A. Acts in a mature manner
   B. Has high moral values
   C. Is interested in his or her family and home life
   D. Displays good common sense
   E. Is experienced in his or her field

70-Year-Old

I. Composite Fluid and Crystallized Intelligence
   A. Displays a good vocabulary
   B. Reads widely
   C. Is able to understand feedback and act upon it
   D. Is able to sift out relevant from irrelevant information
   E. Is able to draw conclusions from information given
II. Everyday Competence
   A. Displays wisdom in actions and thoughts
   B. Is perceptive about people and things
   C. Thinks before acting or speaking
   D. Is able to adapt to disastrous life situations
   E. Is aware of what is going on around him or her
III. Cognitive Investment
   A. Displays curiosity
   B. Is competent in career choice
   C. Appreciates young and old individuals
   D. Is interested in his or her family and home life

Source: From "What Are Theories of Adult Intellectual Development Theories Of?" (pp. 17–18), by R. Sternberg and C. Berg, 1987. In *Cognitive Functioning and Social Structure Over the Life Course*, C. Schooler and K. W. Schaie (Eds.). Reprinted by permission of Ablex Publishing Corporation.

Main Points

1. The Peter Pan Syndrome describes men who have not finished growing up in that they have refused or avoided completing the important developmental tasks of youth. Youth is a developmental period (ages 14–24, according to Coleman) that serves as a transition between childhood and adulthood.

2. Developmental tasks are sequential milestones that reflect the acquisition of important competencies and capabilities. Havighurst's developmental tasks for early adulthood have to do primarily with establishing a family, a career, and a place in the community.

3. According to Coleman, a successful transition from youth to adulthood requires the development of "self-centered" competencies (relating to economic independence, management of one's affairs, intelligent consumption of culture as well as of goods, and the ability to engage in concentrated activity), and "other-centered" capabilities (having to do with social interaction, cooperation with others, and assuming responsibility for those who are dependent).

4. Although we have sometimes been tempted to view adulthood as a *plateau* between childhood and old age—a period characterized by *no* change following the rapid growth of childhood and preceding the rapid declines of very old age—our current models suggest that this view is misleading.

5. Motor performance among males, measured quantitatively (speed of running; distance thrown) usually improves through childhood and adolescence; among females, there is sometimes a plateau or decline after puberty, associated with limited practice. Qualitative measures show continued improvement of motor performance into adulthood.

6. In the absence of training, flexibility declines gradually from about age 12, but can be maintained and even improved into adulthood with training. The twenties are the peak of physical functioning in terms of stamina and strength for those who remain fit and active. Exercise is closely related to physical *and* mental well-being.

7. There are no dramatic age-related changes in the functioning of the senses through early adulthood, but there are subtle changes in the flexibility of the lens, and gradual, mostly noise-induced hearing loss, especially in men. Health is generally good throughout early adulthood, with a decreased susceptibility to common infections, but a somewhat greater incidence of chronic complaints (such as back problems). Accidents are the principal cause of death prior to age 35; after that, heart disease and cancer become the leading causes of death.

8. Alcohol and nicotine use does not decline dramatically in early adulthood, as does use of other common nonprescription drugs. Stress is implicated in physical complaints (ulcers, hypertension, cardiovascular problems) as well as in psychological complaints (Type A individuals, who are aggressive and hard-driving, are more likely to suffer from coronary heart disease than Type B's, who are more easy-going and relaxed).

9. The human sexual response, of which three patterns are common in women, cycles through excitement (preparation), plateau (mounting arousal), orgasm, and resolution. Sexual dysfunctions in the male include premature ejaculation, retarded ejaculation, and erectile dysfunction; in the female, common dysfunctions are inability to attain orgasm or pleasure from sexual intercourse, and vaginismus. Infertility increases gradually through early adulthood. The most common causes are blocked fallopian tubes in the female, often as a result of infections (sometimes from chlamydia), and low sperm count in men.

10. Work serves three sets of purposes: economic (it puts chickens in our pots), social (it provides an opportunity for social interaction and for establishing friendships), and psychological (it allows us to achieve a sense of self-worth, and it provides us with important aspects of our identities; in a sense, we *are* what we do).

11. *Jobs* are specific tasks or duties; *occupation* refers to broad employment classifications such as accounting or being a mechanic; *career* refers to a range of closely related occupations; *vocation* refers to a "calling," and is generally used for such things as the ministry.

12. The work ethic that motivated our forebears made a virtue of hard work and emphasized the themes of good provider, independence, success, and self-respect. Our increasing concern with quality of life, a decline in emphasis on security, and fundamental changes in gender roles indicate that the traditional work ethic is changing. There is some controversy about whether increasing technology will increase demand for highly educated, skilled workers, or whether it will succeed in "dumbing-down" vast numbers of jobs so they can be filled by the illiterate and mathematically incompetent.

13. The job–person matching theory of career choice argues that we should select occupations on the basis of a match between interests and work requirements; developmental guidance models suggest that we explore and develop careers through sequential stages (Ginzberg lists three: fantasy, tentative, realistic). Interest inventories and computer-assisted guidance systems are useful. In practice, family and other contextual influences are fundamental to career choice, career development is often a lifespan process, and our choices are constrained by factors such as race, sex, economics, and so on. Fortune also plays a role.

14. We ask not only that our jobs fill our bellies but also that they make us happy. Job satisfaction is related to personal interest in the work, the extent to which it requires use of the individual's capa-bilities, and income. Job security is also important for blue-collar workers.

15. Dialectical thinking involves the recognition and tolerance of ambiguities, and the development of ways of resolving contradictions. Riegel suggests that dialectical thinking is, in a sense, a fifth Piagetian stage. Like Riegel, Basseches argues that the logic of formal operations is not relevant to adult problem solving, but that the adult may progress, instead, to the development of *dialectical schemata* — thought patterns directed toward the resolution of contradictions. Labouvie-Vief, also a proponent of an adult level of dialectical thinking, suggests that because of the practical demands and the ethical constraints that impinge on adult decision making, preadult (that is, formal or concrete operations) forms of thought are not applicable.

16. Sternberg's *triarchic* view of intelligence is componential (intelligence consists of metacomponents, performance components, and knowledge-acquisition components), contextual (intelligence is adaptive in a specific context), and experiential (intelligence may be manifested in the application of old learning to new situations). Indications are that contextual and experiential intelligence become more important as individuals age.

17. Our observations and conclusions are context specific.

Further Readings

The following collection is a good source for current research and theory about differences between adult and preadult thought:

Schooler, C., & Schaie, K. W. (Eds.). (1987). *Cognitive functioning and social structure over the life course*. Norwood, NJ: Ablex.

A detailed and comprehensive look at career education and vocational guidance is provided by the following text, which should be of particular value for those who are concerned with career education at different stages in the lifespan:

Herr, E. L., & Cramer, S. H. (1985). *Career guidance through the life span: Systematic approaches* (2nd ed.). Boston: Little, Brown.

Dialectical thinking and other forms of postadolescent thought are examined in:

Stevens-Long, J. (1990). Adult development: Theories past and future. In R. A. Nemiroff & C. A. Colarusso (Eds.), *New dimensions in adult development*. New York: Basic Books.

Those interested in sexual functions and dysfunctions, and in sexual therapies, might consult:

Hawton, K. (1985). *Sex therapy: A practical guide*. Oxford: Oxford University Press.

CHAPTER 14

Social Development: Early Adulthood

Lord, how ashamed I should be of not being married before three and twenty!

Jane Austen, *Mansfield Park*

In Jane Austen's day, there were few socially desirable life-style choices other than marriage or a religious vocation; but there are many other choices in today's contexts. Those who do not marry need no longer feel the shame of which Jane Austen spoke.

Still, two basic themes seem to be common in all our lives: *love* and *power*. These themes surface repeatedly in the fantasies and dreams in which we are the larger-than-life heroes, says McAdams (1984). The love theme is revealed in our concern with personal relationships and in our need to be liked and wanted. The power theme manifests itself in our wish that others recognize our strength and leadership.

The importance of these themes, McAdams tells us, is that they reveal two of our most important motives. First, we are driven by an *intimacy* motive, revealed in our "preference for close, warm, communicative exchange with another" (p. 166). Second, we respond to a *power* motive, evident in a desire to establish or maintain impact, control, or influence over others, and apparent, as well, in our strivings for prestige and recognition.

As Kegan (1982) put it, in the cognitive sphere, we strive to make sense of the world—to construct meaning. And in the social sphere, we strive to become meaningful. In becoming meaningful, we achieve both intimacy and power.

This Chapter

Intimacy and power are two fundamental human motives that have a long history in psychology. They often appear under different names: For example, *agency* and *communion*, or *control* and *affiliation* (Henry, 1988). What these pairs of motives have in common is that they deal with human relationships. Adult socialization and relationships are the topics of this chapter.

Socialization begins in infancy and continues through childhood and adolescence. It results from complex interactions between children, parents, schools, peers, and other aspects of context. Throughout, it is enormously facilitated by the acquisition of language.

But socialization does not end with childhood or adolescence. The child may learn to speak, understand, read, and write, all of which are important for social roles not only in childhood but also in adulthood. But with adulthood come new roles, new statuses, new expectations. The child who has read comic books now reads journals; the adolescent who has written poetry now writes legal briefs. And the child whose socialization has gone awry, note Elkin and Handel (1989), may end up in a *re*socialization context such as a prison or a mental institution.

Continued social adjustment requires that we remain socially malleable into old age—not only because of the changing requirements of our adult roles, but also because we continue to meet *new* significant others throughout our lives. There are important relationships to be maintained, new ones to be formed, some to be changed.

We look at relationships in this chapter, beginning with a discussion of some theoretical descriptions of development in early adulthood; then we turn to the complex and sometimes perplexing topic of love; finally, we focus on contemporary life-styles, marriage, and the family.

Erikson's Psychosocial Theory

Recall from Chapter 2 that Erikson's theory describes a series of eight stages through which individuals progress as they develop (Erikson, 1959) (see Figure 14.1). Each of these stages involves the resolution of an important conflict that arises out of the individual's *social* interaction—hence the label *psychosocial* theory. Progression from one stage to the next requires the resolution of this conflict, an achievement that evolves through the development of a new competence. But

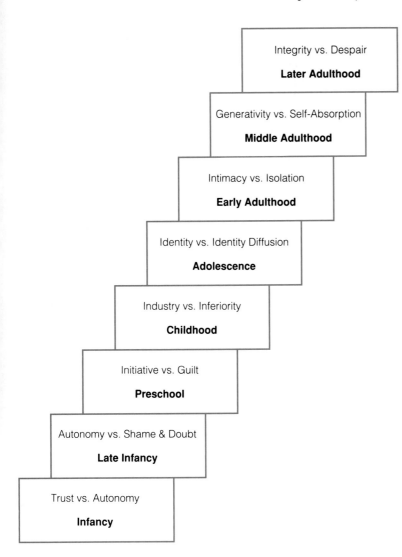

Figure 14.1 Overview of Erikson's psychosocial theory.

the conflicts specific to each stage are never completely resolved during that stage; they continue, in one form or another, throughout life. As we develop and grow, our social environments change, and as a result, so do our most important conflicts.

With the advent of adulthood, the adult is faced with a series of new social demands that require additional adjustments. These, too, may be expressed in terms of competing tendencies that give rise to crises of greater or lesser severity and that will be resolved through the development of new competencies. Erikson describes three developmental stages that span adulthood and old age: (1) intimacy and solidarity versus isolation, (2) generativity versus self-absorption, and (3) integrity versus despair (the last two of these are discussed in Chapters 16 and 18, respectively).

Intimacy Versus Isolation

The search for identity does not end with puberty but continues through adolescence and beyond. One of the primary functions of adolescence is to serve as a period during which the child need not make a final decision concerning a self. "Negative identities," identities that are not ordinarily conducive to normal adjustment to society, can be experimented with during this period. Essentially, a negative identity simply retains negative aspects of earlier crises: mistrust, guilt, and so on. In a real sense, adolescents must incorporate into their identities the notion that at times they are also guilty and incompetent.

Relationships with the Opposite Sex. One of the principal ways in which adolescents and young adults arrive at a sense of worth and personal identity is through the development of feelings of intimacy with others. For the majority of young adults, Erikson claims, the intimacy they seek will come through a relationship with someone of the opposite sex.

But here, as in other stages of the lifespan, there is a conflict—in this case, a conflict between the need to make a commitment and an unwillingness to do so. The individual has an urge to remain independent, to retain a hard-won sense of personal identity; in addition, there is a fear of commitment. Both of these mitigate against intimacy. As a consequence, young adults commonly enter into sexually intimate relationships that involve little emotional commitment. Erikson and Hall (1983) describe these relationships as primarily *genital* (phallic or vaginal), and claim that they may lead to feelings of extreme isolation.

The culmination of this developmental period, and the resolution of the conflict between a need for intimacy and a drive for independence, is to be found in a balance that permits the commitment and the *mutuality* of love, but that also allows the individual to retain an independent identity.

Relationships with Parents. The young adult's search for intimacy and independence requires a redefinition and realignment of relationships with parents. As we saw, this process begins in early adolescence and is sometimes marked by conflict—although conflict is not the main characteristic of most parent—adolescent relationships.

Miller and Lane (1991) note that the adolescent's happiness is more closely related to the quality of relationships with parents than with peers. Adolescents who describe their relationships with parents as supportive and emotionally warm have a higher sense of well-being than those who see themselves in conflict. Might this also be the case for young adults?

Miller and Lane presented questionnaires to 72 college undergraduates in an attempt to discover the nature and importance of their relationships with parents.

One of their clearest findings is that these students, both male and female, felt closer to their mothers and spent more time with them than with their fathers. Both parents appeared to have considerable emotional influence on their young adult children. "Adolescents achieve autonomy by asserting themselves in a context of close and supportive relations with parents," claim Miller and Lane, "rather than by distancing themselves from them" (p. 180). In early adulthood, close parental relationships continue to be important; but the development of a close relationship with someone else is also very important.

According to Erikson, the crowning achievement of early adulthood is most often found in marriage and child rearing. This view has been criticized and is often rejected. There are many individuals who lead happy, well-adjusted lives, but who do not express their need for intimacy in a lifelong marital commitment. And although Erikson describes a social pattern that is still relatively common, it is perhaps no longer as common in the late 20th century as it was in the middle of the century.

A Test of Erikson's Model

Although a theory such as Erikson's cannot easily be tested, several studies have attempted to confirm some of its most important beliefs. Among these is a longitudinal study conducted by Vaillant and Milofsky (1980). The study involved a sample of 94 male college students, originally chosen to examine some of the factors related to mental health in men (Vaillant, 1978), and a second sample of 392 noncollege, inner-city residents, first selected as a control group in Glueck and Glueck's (1950) study of juvenile delinquency. The control group were nondelinquent males who came from the same social and economic background as a group of delinquents.

Although a variety of measures was available for each of the subjects in these groups, the most important ones were the results of questionnaires given to each subject once every two years over a period of almost three decades, as well as the results of in-depth interviews that occurred at the beginning of the study (when the men were in their early twenties) and twice more, at approximately 10-year intervals.

One of the objectives of these questionnaires and interviews was to determine which of Erikson's devel-

According to Erikson, one of the major achievements of early adulthood is often found in child rearing and marriage. For parents who must juggle career responsibilities with home and child-caring tasks, the adjustments required may be especially difficult. But for many, the addition of new roles is more a joy than a burden.

opmental stages most accurately described individual subjects. For example, assignment to stage 4 (industry versus inferiority) would reflect the extent to which the subject "did things beside and with others" and would be determined by summing scores assigned for doing home chores, adjusting to school academically, and participating in extracurricular jobs and related tasks. Assignment to stage 5 required that the subject have achieved some sense of identity, most often evident in the fact that he would now be self-supporting and relatively independent of the family. Stage 6 (intimacy), as defined by Erikson, requires that the subject be involved in a long-lasting and interdependent relationship. For the men in this study, cohorts of the early- to mid-1920s, this relationship typically involved marriage.

Vaillant and Milofsky introduce an additional stage between Erikson's sixth and seventh (appropriately numbered stage 6a), labeled *career consolidation versus self-absorption*. Erikson had originally believed that career consolidation occurred during the fifth stage (identity formation), an observation that might have been more accurate in an early sociocultural context where career decisions were often made earlier than they are now.

Assignment to the seventh stage, generativity, was based on evidence of the individual's having assumed responsibility for others. The most common indication of generativity in this study involved caring for adolescents, as well as various wider community involvements.

Once the results of the questionnaires and interviews had been sorted, the investigators looked at three hypotheses. First, they reasoned that if Erikson's model is open-ended, as he maintains, then people should reach the various stages at different ages. Second, if the model is to be useful and generalizable, it should be relatively independent of social class and education. And third, if the model is developmental, progression through each of the stages should be sequential. That is, an individual should not reach stage 6 or 7 before having achieved stage 4 or 5.

The results of the study support each of these hypotheses. First, assignment to stages cannot be made on the basis of age. For example, although between 30 and 40 percent of the middle-aged men (around age 47) could be described as generative, almost 20 percent were still struggling with the identity issues of adolescence.

Second, social-class membership and educational level were not related to the subject's developmental level. Although there were very marked contrasts between the two major groups involved in this study (a juvenile delinquency sample on the one hand, raised in an inner-city high-crime, low-status area; and a college sample on the other), approximately equal proportions of each of these groups were assigned to each stage at any given age.

Third, progression through the stages appeared to be remarkably sequential. Achieving identity and being self-supporting seemed to be a requirement for developing a committed and intimate relationship. By the same token, intimacy seemed to precede career consolidation, which, in turn, preceded generativity.

Vaillant and Milofsky conclude that the Erikson model is a useful, open-ended description of a sequential pattern of development that is relatively unaffected by education and social-class membership. Because it is an open-ended model, however, aging does not in any way guarantee the achievement of psychosexual maturity. They caution, as well, that the term *stage*, which Erikson uses to describe sequential developmental achievements, is metaphorical rather than literal. These are less stages than organized and somewhat predictable changes in commitments and relationships. Accordingly, terms such as *developmental level* or *developmental task* would probably be more appropriate.

In summary, the single most important developmental task of early adulthood, Erikson tells us, is to achieve intimacy. By intimacy, he means something very close to what others call love.

Love

Freud (1935) put it very simply: There are two things that are essential to be a healthy adult: love and work. (We look at work in Chapters 13 and 15.)

Love was the province of the poet long before science claimed it. And even now, science may have less to say about love itself than the poets do.

Still, science, with its penchant for measurement and investigation, provides us with ways of measuring, if not of completely understanding, love. Rubin's (1970) Loving and Liking Scales attempt to provide a way of separating interpersonal attraction into two categories (see Table 14.1). The scales are based on the assumption that when we like people, we sense that we have things in common with them, we evaluate them positively, we appreciate their company. But loving is not simply more of liking, according to Rubin. Loving involves

three components: caring, attachment, and intimacy. It also implies a degree of emotional interdependence, a quality of exclusiveness and absorption. If you simply like someone, that person does not dominate your thoughts and your dreams; nor are you concerned that someone else might also like the same person. Love, on the other hand, often brings with it a measure of fierce possessiveness and possibilities for jealousy and pain — perhaps possibilities for ecstasy as well.

A Model of Love

But there is more to interpersonal attraction than simply liking or loving, Sternberg (1986) informs us. There are at least eight varieties of this thing, including non-

---

TABLE 14.1

Several Items from Rubin's Loving and Liking Scales★

Loving-Scale Items

1. I feel that I can confide in _____ about virtually everything.
2. If I could never be with _____, I would feel miserable.
3. One of my primary concerns is _____'s welfare.

Liking-Scale Items

1. I think that _____ is unusually well adjusted.
2. I would highly recommend _____ for a responsible job.
3. _____ is the sort of person whom I myself would like to be.

★ Each scale is ranked 1 to 9 to indicate degree of agreement.

Source: From "Measurement of Romantic Love" by Z. Rubin, 1970, *Journal of Personality and Social Psychology, 16,* pp. 265–273. Copyright 1970 by the American Psychological Association. Reprinted by permission of the author.

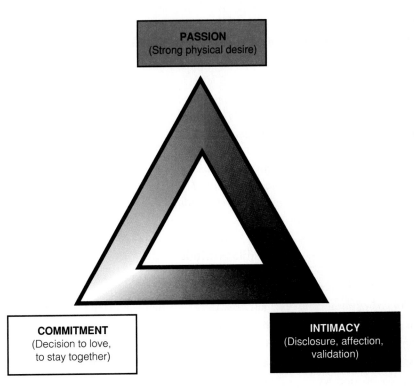

PASSION
(Strong physical desire)

COMMITMENT
(Decision to love,
to stay together)

INTIMACY
(Disclosure, affection,
validation)

Figure 14.2 Sternberg's Triangle of Love. Different combinations of these three components determine the nature of the love relationship (see Table 14.2).

love, romantic love, liking, fatuous love, infatuation, companionship, empty love, and consummate love (see Interactive Table 14.2). What differentiates these states from one another is the combination of *intimacy, passion,* and *commitment* involved in each. Accordingly, Sternberg, who, as we saw in Chapter 13, has presented us with a *triarchic* theory of intelligence, has also given us a *triangular* theory of love. But the triangle in this theory is not the classical male–male–female or female–female–male love triangle. It is the intimacy–passion–commitment triangle (see Figure 14.2).

In this model, intimacy refers to emotions that bring people closer together — emotions such as respect, affection, and support. Feelings of intimacy are what lead two people to want to share things, perhaps to disclose personal, private things.

Passion is a strong, sometimes almost overwhelming, desire to be with another person. Passion is often, although not always, sexual. Sternberg suggests that passion is a feeling that builds rapidly, but then gradually subsides.

Commitment implies a decision-making process, and may involve either a short-term or a long-term decision. On a short-term basis, commitment requires making the decision that one is in love. From a long-term point of view, commitment involves deciding to cultivate and maintain the loving relationship. In practice, this most often implies a decision to share living arrangements and perhaps the raising of a family, either in marriage or otherwise.

Sternberg's (1986) theory of love holds that it is the particular combination of these three components — intimacy, passion, and commitment — that determines the nature of the relationship. As Interactive Table 14.2 shows, for example, *empty love* involves commitment but is devoid of passion or of intimacy ("By $%#, we'll stay together until the children are gone. Then *adios!*") *Consummate love*, on the other hand, has all three components.

There is a pattern to the development of many relationships, Sternberg suggests. Thus two individuals might begin with *nonlove* — no passion, commitment,

INTERACTIVE TABLE 14.2

Sternberg's Model of Love

▶ *Do you have a main relationship? Is it love? How can you tell for sure? One way, says Rubin, is to use scales with items such as those in Table 14.1, which attempt to separate loving from merely liking. Another way is to analyze the dimensions of your relationship. The Sternberg model describes eight possible relationships, each of which is defined in terms of the balance among passion (physical attraction), intimacy (affection, mutual disclosure), and commitment (conscious decision to love, to share, to be together). Does your main relationship fit one of these categories?*

Relationship	Balance of Components	Possible Attitude
Nonlove	No passion, no intimacy, no commitment	"Who? I didn't notice him."
Infatuation	Passion; no intimacy or commitment	"I just want to be with him — physically, you know."
Liking	Intimacy; no passion or commitment	"She's nice to talk to."
Romantic love	Passion and intimacy; no commitment	"He's for me; he's the one! At least for the time being."
Companionate love	Intimacy and commitment; no passion	"She's like a sister! We're in it for the long haul."
Fatuous love	Commitment and passion; no intimacy	"I need him . . . can't leave. But I need to talk to you."
Empty love	Commitment; no passion or intimacy	"We'll stick it out. But just because of the kids."
Consummate love	Intimacy, passion, and commitment	"I want him. I like him. I'm his. Forever."

★ The model describes eight possible relationships, each of which is defined in terms of a balance of passion (physical attraction), intimacy (affection, mutual disclosure), and commitment (conscious decision to love, to stay together).

or intimacy. In time, as intimacy grows, nonlove might give way to infatuation, which has passion but no commitment or intimacy — or perhaps to romantic love, which now adds intimacy but is still short of commitment. Eventually, consummate love might evolve as commitment is brought into the relationship. And perhaps the end result will be marriage or some other long-term commitment, reflecting the resolution of the crisis Erikson describes for early adulthood.

But even consummate love is not a static, unchanging thing. Sternberg (1986) points out that passion is usually very high early in a consummate relationship. But with the passage of time, it diminishes; at the same time, however, commitment and intimacy might increase. Sternberg reports that intimacy and commitment are generally seen as being more important for a lasting love relationship than is passion.

Interpersonal Attraction

How does this thing called love begin? And when it has happened, how does one know that it is love? True love and not puppy love? A romance and not a crush? An *amour* and not an infatuation?

It begins, social psychologists tell us, with interpersonal attraction; and interpersonal attraction seems to be strongly influenced by three things: *physical attraction, similarity,* and *proximity.* The first of these, physical attractiveness, is important in determining whether people want to see each other again after they have met. Following an elaborate dating experiment involving 376 computer-arranged "blind date" pairs where members of each pair had been ranked as ugly, attractive, or average, Walster and associates (1966) questioned and interviewed participants. Not surpris-

TABLE 14.3

Measures of Subjects' Desire to Date Their Partners, Arranged According to Physical Attractiveness

	Date's Physical Attractiveness		
	Ugly	Average	Attractive
Percentage of subjects saying they wanted to date partner again			
According to ugly male subjects	.41	.53	.80
According to average male subjects	.30	.50	.78
According to attractive male subjects	.04	.37	.58
According to ugly female subjects	.53	.56	.92
According to average female subjects	.35	.69	.71
According to attractive female subjects	.27	.27	.68

Source: From "Importance of Physical Attractiveness in Dating Behavior" by E. Walster, V. Aronson, Q. Abrahams, and L. Rottman. *Journal of Personality and Social Psychology,* 1966, *4,* p. 513. Copyright 1966 by the American Psychological Association. Reprinted by permission of E. Walster Hatfield.

ingly, they found that the more attractive individuals were far more likely to have been asked out again (see Table 14.3). Note, however, that physical attractiveness appears to be more important to men than women. Walster reports that although women also prefer physically attractive men, they are attracted as well to power, leadership, status, maturity, and similar qualities.

Similarity and physical proximity (often referred to as *propinquity* in social psychology) are related variables. People who are in close proximity are typically those who attend the same schools, churches, or colleges, or who frequent the same country clubs, bars, or bingo parlors. By the same token, people who attend the same social and educational milieus are likely to be similar in a lot of important ways. Accordingly, there is a high tendency for individuals to select mates from very similar backgrounds and who are, therefore, very similar in social class, race, age, education, and religious background (Morgan, 1981). Marrying within one's group is referred to as *homogamy; heterogamy* involves marriage outside one's religious, racial, educational, or social class. As Lamanna and Riedmann (1988) point

out, even where marriage partners come from different races, they will likely be of similar educational or social backgrounds; and if their religions are different, their races, educational levels, and most important values will be the same.

Mate Selection

Physical attraction, propinquity, and similarity. Put the three together and *voilà*, a potential mate!

Perhaps. But often, it isn't quite so simple. You see, there are dozens, perhaps hundreds, of potential candidates who might all, at one time or another, be sufficiently attractive, sufficiently near, and sufficiently similar to become a potential mate for any given person — well, perhaps not *any* given person but *many* given persons.

There is, Murstein (1976) suggests, a three-stage filtering process involved in selecting a mate. The process begins with the initial *stimulus*: the potential mate. This is where propinquity and physical attractiveness come into play. The first is, of course, essential.

Interpersonal attraction is a complex emotional phenomenon ranging from mild attraction to all-consuming love. It may be described in terms of passion (a strong, often sexual, urge to be with another), intimacy (emotions, such as respect and affection, that bring people together), and commitment (a decision to share important aspects of life with another). Passion is often most important early in a relationship; later, intimacy and commitment may become more important.

In the second stage, potential mates examine each other's *values*. This is when they talk to each other about their goals and aspirations, their likes and dislikes — their selves. It is a period of the revelation of identities through the self-disclosure that, as we saw, is fundamental to the development of intimacy. And as identities are revealed, it is possible for the partners to make judgments about how similar they are.

Finally, Murstein suggests that partners begin to develop *roles* relative to each other. These roles might reflect one partner's leadership and initiative in one or more areas; they might also reflect traditional roles in the partners' families. They are often evident in the usually unconscious decisions people make about who should do what. The development of roles acceptable to both partners is sometimes a difficult task, and resulting conflict may lead to a disruption of the mate selection process — or, later, of the marriage, should one result.

There is much more to our intimacy motives than might be apparent in these few pages. Certainly, there is more to liking and loving than simple physical attractiveness, propinquity, and similarity. And there is more to mate selection than Murstein's three-stage filtering process. There may even be *chemistry*, about which psychology is ill-equipped to comment.

And mate selection followed by marriage is not the only choice, although it is the most common.

Life-Style Choices

At some point, usually in early adulthood or even before (although sometimes much later), many young adults make a very basic life-style choice: to marry or not to marry. More than 90 percent of all adults marry at least once (Thornton & Freedman, 1983). This figure

In most industrialized societies, courtship is an important and highly absorbing process that varies in duration, but for which there are few explicit rules.

has shown a slight decrease from approximately 95 percent in the early 1970s.

Cohabitation, homosexuality, singlehood (with or without children), and a variety of communal living arrangements are among the other life-styles young adults might select. We look briefly at each of these before turning to the most common adult life-style: marriage.

Cohabitation

Cohabitation, living together without being married, was a rare and scandalous occurrence a mere one or two generations ago. For today's cohorts, it is less rare and more widely accepted.

Incidence. A survey at Cornell University in 1983 revealed that one third of a large sample of senior and sophomore students shared accommodations with a member of the opposite sex (Macklin, 1983), and more than 95 percent of the sample, whether or not they

lived alone, considered cohabitation of unmarried couples totally acceptable. In the United States, about 1 out of 25 couples is unmarried, and many of those who are married lived together before marriage (U.S. Bureau of the Census, 1991). In Sweden, more than 1 out of every 8 couples is not married, and close to 40 percent of all infants are born to unmarried couples (Trost, 1981).

Throughout much of Europe, the number of unmarried cohabiting couples has increased far more rapidly than it has in North America. But even here, the numbers of cohabiting couples almost quadrupled after 1970, so that by 1989, almost 2.8 million American couples were ummarried (U.S. Bureau of the Census, 1991). The majority of these were between ages 25 and 44. Approximately two thirds of these couples included at least one member who had previously been married.

Reasons. Couples live together without marrying for several reasons. Among college students, for example, it has become increasingly common to share accommodations for financial reasons. Sexual relations

INTERVIEW

▶ Subject   Female; age 31; never married; university education; successful career in a helping profession. (concerning a recently ended relationship with a man with whom she had been living)

66 *I read an article which described a couple making love. They both liked different music, so she would listen to one thing on headphones and he would listen to something else. Sometimes making . . . well, not even making love with him reminded me of that article. It was like we both wanted to be listening to something else. We were so different we never heard or saw the same things even when we were together . . .*

I don't think I will get married now. At least not for a while. I'm not saying no, period. I might like to have a child someday. But I guess it wouldn't really matter if I was married or not. 99

might or might not be part of the arrangement. Among couples whose relations are intimate, cohabitation is sometimes preferred over marriage because the legal obligations are different, partners want intimacy and passion without long-term commitment, or marriage is simply being delayed. In many cases, cohabitation serves as a sort of "trial marriage" during which couples explore their compatibility and assess the rewards that each is likely to obtain from a permanent relationship.

Few cohabiting couples view their arrangement as long-term and permanent (Macklin, 1983). Most plan either to eventually marry the person with whom they currently live or to marry someone else. In fact, however, perhaps as many as two thirds of all cohabiting couples do *not* marry each other (Clayton & Voss, 1977).

Who Cohabits?   Based on a review of the literature, Macklin (1983) identifies several very general characteristics of individuals who cohabit. First, such individuals tend to be younger. They are also, on average, less religious (in terms of church attendance, for example). In the United States, more blacks than whites and more individuals from large population centers than from smaller or more rural areas cohabit. Education and employment levels tend to be lower among men who cohabit than among married men. Interestingly, the opposite is true for women. Cohabitant women tend to be better educated and are more often employed than married women. Finally, and perhaps not entirely surprisingly, cohabiting couples tend to be less conventional and less traditional in their values than married couples.

Other important differences between cohabiting and married couples include the observation that there is usually less commitment in cohabitation. That is, unmarried couples typically do not have the same personal commitment to continuing the relationship over the long term or to maintaining it through difficulty; also, unmarried couples usually do not have the same impediments to terminating the relationship. Often, there are few possessions that need to be divided or disposed of, no continuing financial obligations, and no ongoing responsibilities for children.

Common Law.   In some jurisdictions, cohabitation does have legal status and can, therefore, entail the same sorts of legal responsibilities that are more explicit in conventional marriage. Where cohabitation defines a legally recognized union of partners, it is termed a *common-law marriage.* Common-law marriages apparently originated on the frontier, where ministers, priests, rabbis, and ships' captains were scarce, and where couples were often forced to exchange "marriage" vows, sometimes in the presence of witnesses but often in private as well. Subsequently, these common-law marriages were upheld as being valid in the courts (Leslie, 1979). The result is that, to this day, if it can be established that a couple intend to live together with the same commitments as a married couple, theirs may be a legal, common-law marriage.

A word of caution is appropriate at this point. There is a danger, when summarizing research of this nature, to mistakenly assume that what is generally true must also be true in individual cases. That, of course, is clearly not the case. To say that unmarried couples are, on the average, younger than married couples is not to deny the fact that there are 50-, 60-, and

Homosexual relationships may differ from heterosexual relationships in important ways, but the need to love and be loved is common to all people regardless of sexual orientation.

even 90-year-old couples living together but unmarried. Similarly, to say that unmarried couples typically do not share the same kind and degree of commitment as do married couples is not to deny the fact that there are many couples who are firmly committed to their relationship but who have decided not to marry.

Homosexuality

Several life-styles are available to those whose sexual preferences are directed toward members of their own sex (*homo*sexual) rather than toward members of the opposite sex (*hetero*sexual). Here, as elsewhere, however, things are seldom simply an either/or proposition. The research of Kinsey, Pomeroy, and Martin (1948) revealed that sexual preference is, in many respects, a continuum, with the vast majority of individuals being primarily attracted to members of the opposite sex, a small minority being attracted primarily to members of the same sex, and others falling in between. Estimates of the number of people who can be considered to be homosexual vary a great deal and tend to be highly unreliable. Many still view homosexuality as deviant and unnatural, although it has now been deleted from the American Psychiatric Association's manual of mental disorders. Accordingly, given that many homo-

sexuals have preferred to remain incognito, some surveys have probably provided underestimates. In contrast, the 1960s and 1970s witnessed a dramatic increase in a sense of community among homosexual groups and a sometimes militant tendency to agitate for rights and recognition. And estimates of homosexuality that have been provided by outspoken members of this community have perhaps sometimes been overestimates.

Indications are that perhaps fewer than half of homosexual men live as couples, whereas approximately three quarters of lesbians are coupled (Harry, 1983). Research on the nature of homosexual couples reveals that, contrary to a popular stereotype, it is uncommon for one partner to adopt the "feminine" role, and the other the "masculine." In Bell and Weinberg's (1978) investigation of 686 gay couples, only 10 percent were found to conform to what might be considered traditional roles among heterosexual couples. When interviewed, the majority of gay couples place high value on equality of roles, whether sexual, economic, or decision making (Peplau, 1981). Equality is perhaps easier to achieve among homosexual than heterosexual couples because most homosexual relationships involve economic equality to begin with. Typically, neither member assumes the exclusive role of housekeeper/homemaker, and both work at careers outside the home.

In addition to obvious differences in sexual orientation, there are several notable differences between homosexual and heterosexual couples. First, most of the literature indicates that couple relationships among homosexuals, especially among gay males, tend to involve younger individuals and not to last as long. Harry (1983) cautions, however, that many of these studies might have underrepresented older and longer-lasting relationships by drawing most of their samples from gay bars and gay associations, both of which tend to be frequented by younger people.

A second difference concerns sexual exclusivity. Whereas contemporary standards within marriage stress the importance of sexual fidelity, this appears to have been less the case among gay men and women (Peplau, 1981). However, fear of AIDS seems to have reduced promiscuity among gay males, a fact that has resulted in a decline in the number of other sexually transmitted diseases in the gay population (see Lamanna & Riedmann, 1988).

Approximately 20 percent of gay men and 33 percent of gay women have been or are married. Of these, many have children. Gay fathers who leave their wives very seldom gain custody of their children. However, some who are admittedly gay remain married. In many cases, their relationships with their children remain close and caring even after the children have been told of their father's sexual orientation (Miller, 1979). The same appears to be true of lesbian mothers, far more of whom retain custody of their children after they have divorced and established a homosexual couple relationship.

Contrary to what some people have feared, available evidence does not reveal a greater tendency for children raised by a homosexual couple to themselves develop a homosexual orientation (Hotvedt & Mandel, 1982). However, the evidence is still skimpy. Moreover, as Harry (1983) points out, if homosexual couple relationships last an average of three years, children being brought up by such couples likely will be subjected to major disruptions perhaps not unlike those associated with the divorce of heterosexual parents. We can only guess at the eventual effects on children of a series of such disruptions.

Singlehood

Single adults include not only those who have never married but also those who are divorced, separated, or widowed. There is strong evidence that each of these categories is growing. The age of marriage has increased dramatically in the last several decades, thereby prolonging the period of singlehood before marriage. In 1960, only 30 percent of women ages 20–24 had not yet married, but by 1980, that figure had risen to 50 percent; by 1989, it had reached 77 percent (U.S. Bureau of the Census, 1991). As we saw previously, the number of unmarried couples living together in the United States quadrupled between 1970 and 1989. In addition, during that period, the number of one-parent families also increased dramatically. More than one out of every five children under the age of 18 is now in a one-parent home—twice as many as in 1970 (U.S. Bureau of the Census, 1991).

Never-Marrieds. Close to 5 percent of the population never marries (95 percent do at least once) (Schulz & Rodgers, 1985). The never-marrieds make up the largest group of singles, accounting for almost 20 percent (see Figure 14.3).

Among the never-marrieds are those who have deliberately chosen never to marry, those who have temporarily postponed marriage for one reason or another, and those who have been unsuccessful in finding a mate. Accordingly, several social factors have contributed to the increasing number of never-marrieds, as well as to the rising age of first marriage. Among them, Stein (1983) includes the greater number of women going to college and beginning careers before marriage; expanding career opportunities for women; a greater number of women than men at the "most marriageable age"; the increasing divorce rate, which, for some, has reduced the appeal of marriage; and the increasing availability of birth control methods. One additional factor may well be the increased social acceptance of cohabitation.

One of the important implications of these social changes is that many of the never-married who have deliberately postponed marriage, often for an education or a career, and who see their singlehood as temporary, may end up in a state of involuntary, rather than voluntary, singlehood. This may be especially true of women whose increasing age and increasing educational, social, or professional status may serve to dramatically reduce the number of men who are likely to be suitable mates.

We should hasten to point out that unlike Jane Austen, who exclaims, "Lord, how ashamed I should be of not being married before three and twenty!" today's generation typically sees no shame in singlehood. Indeed, among men it is not uncommon to take

The Never-Marrieds

Singlehood includes adults who have never married, as well as the widowed, separated, and divorced. Numbers in all these categories have increased in recent decades. In 1970, by the age of 29, about 80 percent of all males and 90 percent of all females had been married. By 1989, these figures had been reduced to about 55 percent for males and 70 percent for females.

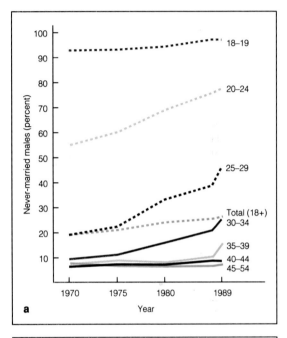

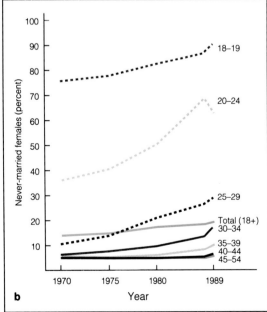

Figure 14.3 Percentage of (a) males and (b) females over 18 who have never married, by age. (From U.S. Bureau of the Census, 1991, p. 44.)

pride in being "*le gai bachelor*"; and perhaps with the advent of the newly liberated woman, these attitudes will become increasingly common among women as well.

The Separated and Divorced.

As we have seen, there are many among the never-married who are voluntarily single, either temporarily or permanently. The singlehood characteristic of the separated and divorced, although it may well result from a deliberate and completely voluntary decision to end a marriage, was initially unplanned and may not be quite so voluntary.

Chances of a marriage ending in separation or divorce have increased dramatically in recent decades. More than one in three marriages now end in divorce; indications are that this proportion may soon reach 50 percent (O'Leary & Smith, 1991). The majority of those who divorce, however, will remarry. More men remarry than women, and they tend to remarry sooner after divorce (five out of six men and three out of four women typically remarry within three years). Obviously, divorce does not disillusion those who have already been married. And happiness ratings are about the same for people in a second marriage as for comparable people in their first. However, people who have divorced and remarried often report more happiness in their second than in their first marriage (Benson-von der Ohe, 1984).

Because more divorced men than women remarry, because they do so sooner, and because men die sooner than women, there are more separated, divorced, widowed, and never-married women than men in all age groups, but especially at the upper age levels.

Cold statistics do not reveal the potential emotional impact of divorce. In Chapter 8, we looked at this impact on children, noting, among other things, that very few children are left unaffected. However, there are large individual variations in the extent to which children are chagrined or disturbed by their parents' divorce; these differences are sometimes related to the child's age and sex.

There are large variations in adult reactions to divorce as well. For women, the effects of divorce often include substantial, and sometimes very serious, reductions in income. In Ferri and Robinson's (1976) investigation of divorce, more than half of a sample of 168 divorced mothers relied primarily on social assistance for their livelihood. Weiss (1984) reports that divorce reduces a mother-headed family's income by between one third and one half.

In addition to having to cope with reduced income, divorced women must adjust to different living arrangements, establish new social relationships, and sometimes assume a new work role in addition to the old homemaker role.

The lives of men are often changed less by divorce than those of women, particularly if they continue in the same work roles. But men, too, need to adjust to new living arrangements and a continued need for intimacy. It is worth noting that studies of happiness typically find that married men are happier than those who are not married, and among the least happy are those who are divorced (Campbell, 1981).

Clearly, however, divorce is not inevitably difficult and traumatic for everyone. And, as we noted in Chapter 8, there are conflict-ridden and unhappy marital relationships where the partners involved, and the children, may be far better off in different situations. It is perhaps significant, nevertheless, that when Lopata (1981) looked at adjustment among widows and divorcées, they found that the divorcées were unhappier and had a more negative attitude toward life than the widows. Strangely, the divorcées were more likely to feel they had been taken advantage of, that they had been treated unfairly, and that they had lost status. Or perhaps it isn't so strange. We have no choice concerning death and little need to accept any blame or guilt for its coming to our spouses. And although we might mourn their passing, we are hardly likely to feel bitter or angry at them for leaving.

Communes

Communes are yet another possible life-style. But unlike most other choices, this one does not necessarily exclude any other life-style. Communes are, by definition, *communities*—joint, cooperative attempts to carve a happy or useful life-style. Although they present a life-style that is different from, and hence an alternative to, the life-styles we have looked at thus far, they are compatible with any of them. Thus there are communes for conventionally married couples as well as for people involved in group marriages; there are homosexual and heterosexual communes, religious and political communes, utopian communes, and all manner of other possible communal arrangements. As Ramey (1972) notes, so many communes are possible that "being a commune is almost a state of mind" (p. 477). Some communes are established so that members can do their own, presumably unconventional, "thing";

others function primarily to pool individual resources as a means of coping more effectively with society. And still others result from fundamental religious beliefs that can more easily be encouraged and practiced in relative isolation from society.

Marriage

Although we have a choice of many life-styles, marriage is the choice of the vast majority. It is perhaps notable, however, that we choose it somewhat later than did our parents — and they later than theirs. The average age of first marriage for men is 25.3, and for women it is 23.6 (U.S. Bureau of the Census, 1991) (see Figure 14.4).

For most of us, there is only one officially approved form of marriage: that where each partner is entitled to only one other partner — *monogamy*. Having more than one wife or husband is illegal in North America and is termed *bigamy* by the courts. **Polygamy** is a more general expression for the same state of affairs. It includes *polygyny*, where the man is permitted to have more than one wife, and *polyandry*, where a wife is permitted more than one husband. Murdock (1957) looked at 554 of the world's societies and found that only 24 percent sanctioned only monogamy. The vast majority (75 percent) permit polygyny; only 1 percent permit polyandry (see Table 14.4). Note, however, that even in those societies that permit one or more forms of polygamy, these are typically the exception rather than the rule. Often only the old and the wealthy can afford more than one wife (or husband). Often, too, only the very highly placed in the social hierarchy are permitted polygamy.

Although contemporary Western societies do not permit polygamy, they do permit what Mead (1970) calls *serial monogamy*: We are free to marry, divorce, and remarry an unlimited number of times. In addition, various group-sex arrangements, mate swapping, open marriages, and other forms of sexual and emotional permissiveness, while not a dominant part of the current social mainstream, are nevertheless not altogether uncommon.

Premarital Sex

Indications are clear that monogamy is not what it used to be. This is particularly true for the many women

TABLE 14.4

Common Forms of Marriage Among 554 of the World's Societies

Type of Marriage	Number of Societies	Percentage
Monogamy	135	24
Polygamy	419	76
Polyandry	4	1
Polygyny	415	75

Source: Based on data reported in "World Ethnographic Sample" by S. P. Murdock, 1957, *American Anthropologist,* 59, pp. 664–688. Reprinted by permission of the American Anthropological Association.

whose roles were determined largely by the well-known double standard that was rampant until recently and that still rears its head on occasion in various male bastions: "Boys will be boys, you know." It went without saying that "girls will not be girls; if they must be anything, they will be angels." As we saw in Chapter 12, approximately as many women as men are now nonvirgins when they marry (see Figure 12.3, Chapter 12). Contrary to some popular reports, however, the sexual revolution did not translate itself into widespread, indiscriminate, totally recreational sex, although there is clearly more of this type of sexual activity now than there was when my grandfather sowed his particular species of oats. True, the sexual revolution of these past decades does manifest itself in greater sexual permissiveness. But it is a permissiveness that, with some notable exceptions, insists on *affection*. Miekle, Peitchinis, and Pearce (1985) asked more than 1,300 teenagers ages 13–18 about the circumstances under which intercourse would be acceptable. Approximately 80 percent thought that as long as the partners were in love or engaged, sexual relations were acceptable. Almost 75 percent felt that as long as there was strong affection between partners, intercourse would be acceptable. But only about 25 percent thought that sexual relations without affection were acceptable (see Table 12.6, Chapter 12).

As Scanzoni and Scanzoni (1981) explain, there are four categories of premarital sexual behavior. The first,

Changes in Marriage

Marriage is as popular an institution as ever, but recent years have seen significant changes. Both men and women are now marrying later than they were a few decades ago, and fewer marriages are the first marriage for either partner (more are remarriages). Interestingly, for marriages that end in divorce (approximately half), the median duration has not changed in almost two decades — it is still about seven years. (Does this prove the existence of the seven-year-itch?)

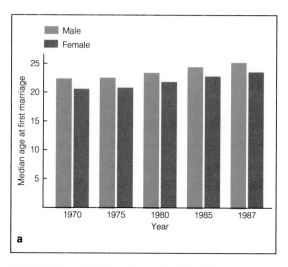

a

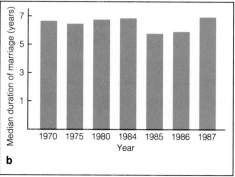

b

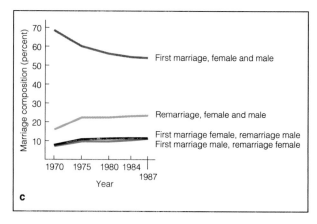

c

Figure 14.4 (a) Median (midpoint) age of first marriage, (b) duration of first marriage, and (c) changes in composition of first and subsequent marriages, 1970–1987. (From U.S. Bureau of the Census, 1991, p. 87.)

TABLE 14.5

Alternative Nonexclusive Marital Life-Styles

Type	Characteristics
Open marriage (O'Neills)	Major concern is with the independence and growth of individual partners and the development of mutually accepted rules governing the relationship
Extramarital sex	Mostly nonconsensual, secretive, clandestine "sexual affairs" that tend to be of short duration
Nonsexual extramarital relationships	More open, nonsexual opposite-sex relationships involving dinners and movies, for example; apparently widely approved by college populations
Sexually open marriage	An open arrangement designed to permit sexual adventuring by either or both partners with other individuals in independent relationships that do not threaten the marriage
Swinging	Concerned with recreational sex rather than with relationships and often involves groups and mate swapping
Group marriage	An uncommon alternative usually involving four adults (two spouse pairs)

Source: Based on "'Open' Marriage and Multilateral Relationships: The Emergence of Nonexclusive Models of the Marital Relationship" by D. L. Weis, 1983. In *Contemporary Families and Alternative Lifestyles: Handbook on Research and Theory* (pp. 194–215), E. D. Macklin and R. H. Rubin (Eds.), 1983, Beverly Hills, CA: Sage. Used by permission of the publisher.

abstinence, belongs largely to another age. The second, the *double standard*, was recently common and still lingers, although it is a battered and torn standard, ravaged by the forces of the feminist movement. The third, *permissiveness with affection*, appears to be increasingly common. The last, *permissiveness without affection*, also has its place in the contemporary world, although sexual activity is a long way from having become as indiscriminate, as matter of fact, and as casual as many had feared.

Extramarital Sex

Through the last several decades, several writers have advocated alternatives to the traditional marital relationship (for example, Rimmer, 1972, 1977; O'Neill & O'Neill, 1972). What most of these alternatives have in common is that they propose sexual nonexclusivity. Put another way, these are alternatives that provide for extramarital sexual relations (see Table 14.5).

Although extramarital sex (*adultery*, if a spade is to be called a shovel) is apparently not uncommon, most societies discourage its practice, often on the grounds that it threatens the family unit. There is ample evidence, however, of a powerful double standard here, as there is with respect to premarital sex. In Japan and in many European countries, it is quite acceptable for a man to have a mistress, providing he is reasonably discreet about the affair and continues to meet his familial obligations. The same behavior is far less easily tolerated among married women and, indeed, is often grounds for punishment or divorce; such is seldom the case when the man is the adulterer.

In North American societies, the mistress and the male lover are less clearly condoned or condemned. Approximately 30 percent of adult men and women say they approve of extramarital sex. Those who approve tend to be young, male, not highly religious, well educated, unhappy with their marriages, and politically liberal. In addition, they are more likely to believe in sexual equality and are more likely to have engaged in premarital sex (Weis, 1983).

Affairs. Although some 70 percent of married people say they disapprove of extramarital sex, the *affair* is still common. An affair is a sexual-emotional episode of varying duration and intensity involving two people, one or both of whom are married to someone else. It implies an element of deception, such that if the other partner were to "find out," there would follow some consequences of greater or lesser severity. How common are affairs?

More than 30 years ago, Kinsey and associates (Kinsey et al., 1953) reported that by the age of 40, 26 percent of all married females and almost half of all males had engaged in at least one extramarital affair. More than 20 years later, Maykovich (1976) reported an increase to 32 percent for females. Major surveys conducted by Hunt (1974) and Athanasiou (1973) report that the incidence of adultery has become almost as common among women as it is among men (somewhere between 33 and 50 percent by middle age). And although affairs might be implicated in the breakup of some marriages, Strean (1980) suggests that it is relatively rare that a husband or wife will disrupt a marriage specifically to live with the lover.

Open Marriages. Affairs, by definition, are clandestine and secretive, and are seldom tolerated by the other marriage partner. One type of marriage that does tolerate extramarital encounters is labeled *open* and is described by O'Neill and O'Neill (1972) as providing both freedom and the "relatedness" that we all crave. But the freedom of the successful open marriage is not the freedom of the unmarried "swinger"—a freedom without responsibility. "Freedom in open marriage does not mean freedom to 'do your thing' without responsibility. It is the freedom to grow to the capacity of your individual potential through love—and one aspect of that love is caring for your partner's growth and welfare as much as your own" (p. 258). We have little evidence that truly open marriages are common. Nor is there reliable information about the frequency of marriages where partners engage in group sex or in mate swapping (also termed *consensual adultery*).

Good and Bad Marriages

We know that 30–50 percent of all new marriages now end in divorce. We know, too, that between one third and one half of all married people, even if they remain married all their lives, will not always be sexually faithful. But we also know that married people describe their lives in more satisfactory terms and see themselves as being happier than those who remain single (or who are separated, divorced, or widowed).

To describe marriages as being either good or bad would be oversimplistic. There can be much that is good and much that is bad in any marriage. But it might be important to know what a "good" marriage can be like. Cuber and Harroff (1965) provide us with the beginnings of some answers. They studied 211 men and women—all upper-middle-class and highly successful professionals. Each had been married for at least 10 years and *none* had ever seriously contemplated separation or divorce—the marriages were *good* at least to that extent. Cuber and Harroff identified five different types of relationships among these couples.

The *conflict-habituated* marriage is characterized by a continuously stormy atmosphere of domestic disagreement and conflict, as if each of the partners wants and perhaps even needs constant disagreement, so that, in spite of the quarrels, the marriage endures.

The *devitalized* marriage is a lifeless affair; it has no fire, no passion, and little intimacy—only commitment. Couples in this type of marriage typically remember that they were quite madly in love when younger, that their relationship was intense and fiery, that they were deeply intimate. Now habit and memory bind them in an apathetic but enduring relationship.

Those in a *passive-congenial* marriage are trapped in the same dull, lifeless relationship that characterizes the devitalized marriage. Sadly, however, a passive-congenial marriage is one that was devoid of any of the sweet excesses of romantic love from its beginning. Such marriages are often simply convenient arrangements for both parties, socially expected, proper, and sometimes useful for advancing careers or for clinging to the proper rungs in the social ladder; but they are emotionally barren.

A *vital* marriage is one in which the marriage relationship is fundamentally important to both partners and in which there is a genuine sharing of important experiences and values. While both husband and wife devote much of their time to the marriage rela-

At the turn of the century, almost all marriages lasted until the death of one partner; now, close to half of all marriages end in divorce. We expect our marriages to make us happy, and if they don't, we try again . . . and again. What is perhaps most remarkable, however, is that half of all new marriages do last until the death of one of the spouses. And although some of these enduring marriages are not entirely happy, many — like the one pictured here — are marked by lasting satisfaction.

tionship and are genuinely happy with it, the partners retain their individuality.

A *total* marriage describes a relationship that is very similar to that characteristic of the vital marriage, except that it involves a greater commitment to the relationship, much closer and more intense agreement on most issues, and a total, unreserved, and intimate sharing of all aspects of life. For those in a total relationship,

the marriage and the marriage partner are the absolutely dominant fact of life. (See Table 14.6 on page 506.)

These five types of marriages describe the nature of the relationships that are possible between husband and wife, but they do not describe whether a marriage is good or bad. However, because the sample studied by Cuber and Harroff did not include any obvious instances of serious marital discord, we can conclude

Marriage and Divorce

Divorce rates in the United States more than doubled between 1960 and 1975, and have remained relatively constant since then. At present, close to 50 percent of all marriages end in divorce. The majority of those who divorce remarry. Most remarriages occur within three years of divorce. Although marriage rates have declined slightly in very recent years, marriage is still more common than divorce.

that each of these relationships can be characteristic of an enduring marriage.

Marital Discord

Marital discord can be an extremely serious problem, say O'Leary and Smith (1991). Not only do difficulties with relationships cause great distress and unhappiness among married couples, as well as among their children, but they are the most important factor in many suicides. Relationship problems are also involved in a large number of family homicides. And a survey of small businesses in Ohio indicates that marital problems may be a more important contributor to lack of productivity than either alcohol or drug abuse (American Psychological Association, 1990).

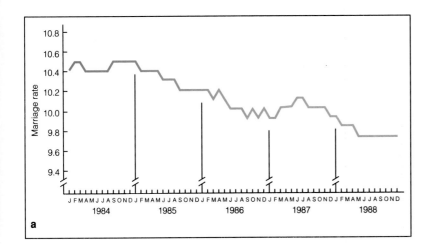

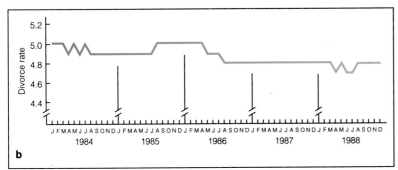

Figure 14.5 (a) Marriage rate and (b) divorce rate per 1,000 population. (From U.S. Department of Health and Human Services, 1989, p. 4.)

If nearly 50 percent of all marriages end in separation or divorce, then almost half of all marriages are eventually characterized by discord. The reasons for this are complex and varied. O'Leary and Smith (1991) review a number of studies suggesting that marriage partners tend to select each other for similarity of personality traits, values, goals, and other important characteristics. Apparently, a basic wisdom guides this selection process, since degree of similarity is predictive of marital adjustment and satisfaction; by the same token, dissimilarity may be associated with marital discord.

Also related to marital discord are certain personality variables associated with *neuroticism* — characteristics such as impulsivity, emotional instability, fearfulness, and poor social adjustment. In addition, there is

TABLE 14.6

Cuber and Haroff's Five Kinds of Marriages*

Label	Description
Conflict-habituated	Constantly stormy; riddled with conflicts
Devitalized	Once full of passion and intimacy; now only commitment is left
Passive-congenial	A marriage of convenience, never characterized by the passion and intimacy of the devitalized marriage
Vital	High intimacy and commitment; partners share but retain their individuality
Total	Similar to the vital marriage but more extreme; for each partner, the marriage is absolutely central

* Note that each of these types of marriage may be an *enduring* relationship.

Source: Based on Cuber and Haroff, 1965.

evidence that the nature of childhood (and infant) attachments may later be reflected in adult attachments. Feeney and Noller (1990) found that persons who were securely attached as children are more prone to stable, positive, and lasting relationships. In contrast, anxious attachments are associated with suspicious, insecure relationships; and avoidant attachments are related to demanding, one-sided relationships.

About one third of all divorces occur within the first four years of marriage (National Center for Health Statistics, 1990). Not surprisingly, research indicates that marital dissatisfaction tends to increase over the early years of marriage as partners are required to make difficult adjustments, and perhaps to reassess their expectations of continuing, idealized romantic love (Belsky & Rovine, 1990). Kurdek (1991) studied 310 couples over the first three years of their marriages in an attempt to uncover factors most closely related to increments in marital discord. He found that for both men and women, low education level is one such factor.

Perhaps, suggests Kurdek, this is because people with less education have had less opportunity to develop verbal and social skills involved in conflict resolution, and are less well prepared for changes that occur in the early years of a marriage.

Interestingly, in Kurdek's study, couples who maintained separate rather than joint bank accounts were more likely to experience conflict—as were couples with lower incomes and those where stepchildren were involved.

Marital discord is often characterized by misunderstanding among partners, poor communication, misinterpretation of actions and intentions, and limited engagement in shared activities. A large number of *marriage enhancement* programs have arisen to remedy these conditions and restore harmony to discordant marriages. Many of these, note O'Leary and Smith (1991), have not been systematically investigated and may have no beneficial effects. However, others have sometimes been shown to be effective for some couples.

Marital Satisfaction

There is, of course, a great deal more to marital satisfaction than might be evident in the simple longevity of a marriage. Indeed, a great many abjectly miserable marriages endure; and a number of perfectly contented marriages may end too abruptly.

We ask a great deal of our marriages. Our forebears asked mostly that marriage bring them a workable, child-rearing arrangement with a clear division of duties and responsibility. Now we expect marriage to make us *happy*; we think happiness is our right. And if it does not come sooner, we seldom wait for it to come later. We simply try again.

But are the married happier? More satisfied? The evidence suggests yes. When compared with unmarried individuals, married people at all ages report higher levels of satisfaction and happiness (Campbell, 1981). Coombs (1991) reviewed 130 studies of the relationship between marriage and well-being. He concludes, "married men and women are generally happier and less stressed than the unmarried" (p. 97).

Happiness in marriage is not a static, unchanging thing. Although some studies find little relationship between age and happiness in marriage, most studies indicate that there is a curvilinear relationship between happiness and the stage of marriage (Cole, 1984). Couples tend to report highest levels of satisfaction in the early, prechildbearing years of marriage, least satisfaction through the childbearing years, and a return to higher levels of satisfaction in later years (see Figure 14.6). Researchers have hypothesized that the presence of children puts considerable strain on a couple. The requirements associated with raising children make tremendous demands on the time and energy of parents (Bigras, LaFrenière, & Lacharité, 1991). In addition, in the traditional family, this is often the time when career demands on the father are greatest. As a result, time for interaction between spouses and for leisure activities becomes scarce.

In spite of the fact that marital happiness often declines in midmarriage, absolute levels of happiness, as we saw earlier, tend to be higher for the married than for the single, although perhaps not markedly so. And happiness, of course, is relative and highly individualistic. It does not allow itself to be easily measured.

A Study of Marital Happiness.
Skolnick (1981) provides some insights into who among the married might be happier and why. Her findings are based on intensive interviews with 232 members of the Oakland Guidance Study and the Berkeley Guidance Study, conducted in 1958 and 1979, respectively. Members of these longitudinal samples were born in 1920 or 1921 and in 1928 or 1929, and were therefore between 29 and 38 in 1958 and 50 and 59 in 1979. Seventy-five percent of the members were still in their first marriage; 19 percent had divorced, and more than half had remarried. Only 6 women and 5 men of the original 232 had not married. Data concerning marital satisfaction and happiness were based on self-reports as well as on more objective assessments by teams of experienced raters.

Several social factors appeared to be closely related to marital satisfaction. For women, the most important of these is age at first marriage. In general, the older the woman, the more likely she is to be happily married later on. That teenage marriages break up twice as frequently as older marriages is additional corroboration of this finding. For men, the social variable most highly related to marital satisfaction is occupation, with socioeconomic status, a closely related variable, being almost equally important. In general, executives and professionals tend to be more happily married than other men.

For both men and women, amount of education is positively related to marital satisfaction, as is socioeconomic status. The number of marriages relates positively to satisfaction for men (second marriages are hap-

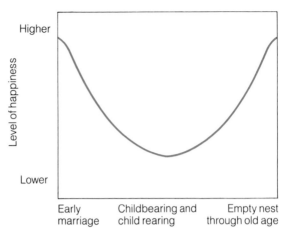

Figure 14.6 Graphic representation of U-shaped curvilinear relationship between level of marital happiness and stage in family life cycle. Note that the lower levels of reported happiness through the child-rearing years do not indicate unhappiness. Note, too, that happiness is highly individualistic and highly varied. Clearly, not all marriages follow this idealized pattern.

pier) but is negatively related to satisfaction for women (second marriages are less happy) (Skolnick, 1981).

In addition to these social variables, Skolnick also looked at personality variables. Like most other researchers, she found that opposites do not attract and complement each other or live happy lives because the strengths of one make up for the weaknesses of the other. Quite the contrary, similar people are attracted to each other. Indeed, the more similar members of a pair were, the more likely they were to report high marital satisfaction. This was particularly true of cognitive variables such as intelligence and impulsiveness or reflectiveness. It is also true of social characteristics. Couples in which both members share some major social characteristic (for example, both are highly aggressive or highly sociable) tend to live in greater harmony than those in which each is the opposite of the other.

In Skolnick's study, marital satisfaction did not appear to decline with age *on the average*, although it sometimes changed a great deal over time for any given couple. In a study of 80 middle-aged couples, Abrioux and Zingle (1979) found, for example, that a majority of these couples considered their present marriages to be better than they had ever been. Among these couples, those whose last child had been gone from home

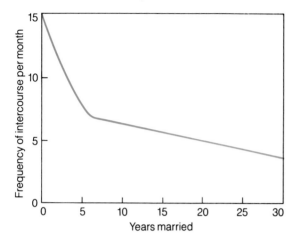

Figure 14.7 Average frequency of intercourse per month according to years of marriage. (Based on L. A. Westoff and C. F. Westoff, *From Now to Zero*, 1971. Reprinted by permission of Little, Brown & Co., Inc.)

for more than one complete year reported somewhat more satisfaction than those whose last child had left home within the year immediately preceding. These findings are in agreement with Cole's (1984) conclusion that marital satisfaction is related to the marriage cycle in U-shaped fashion, with highest levels of happiness occurring before and after the child-rearing phase (see Figure 14.6).

In Skolnick's (1981) investigation, certain observations seemed consistently to be *most characteristic* of those marriages that were rated satisfactory. For example, spouses who liked, admired, and respected each other were most likely to be happily married. In contrast, spouses who had discordant personalities, who were critical of each other, and who saw their relationship as utilitarian (rather than as personally close) were more likely to have unhappy marriages.

Sex and Marital Happiness. Sex, too, appears to be related to marital happiness, with both men and women selecting it as one of their favorite activities — and many singling out unsatisfactory sexual relations as the reason for unhappy marriages (DeBurger, 1967). On the average, frequency of sexual intercourse is highest for the first few years after marriage and then declines rapidly for the next few years. Subsequent average declines are more gradual (see Figure 14.7). Initial declines probably have more to do with the woman becoming pregnant and with the resulting pressures,

time constraints, and lack of privacy associated with child rearing, than with declining sexual interest. Most evidence suggests, in fact, that males do not experience a noticeable reduction in sexual interest until about 50 and then again about 70 (Pfeiffer, Verwoerdt, & Davis, 1972). Women, too, report little reduction in sexual interest or, indeed, in sexual responsiveness through the bulk of their adult years. Solnick and Corby (1983) report that some women are still capable of orgasm well into their seventies and eighties.

Marriage and the Family: A Life-Cycle Approach

A marriage is simply the legal union of two individuals. Its social function, however, goes considerably beyond these two individuals; it makes possible the *family*.

As we saw in Chapter 8, there have historically been two types of families. The one most common in Western societies consists of parents and their immediate children, and is termed *nuclear*. That which is most prevalent throughout the world includes grandparents and assorted other relatives in addition to children and their parents, and is labeled *extended*.

Among recent changes in the family in North America are a reduction in its longevity, a decrease in the absolute number of *intact* nuclear families, and a corresponding increase in one-parent families. These changes are due largely to divorce rates that have increased dramatically in the past several decades.

In spite of these changes, the nuclear family continues to be the most prevalent child-rearing unit in North America. In 1970, 85 percent of American children lived with both parents. In 1989, the percentage was still 70 (73 percent of whites, 67 percent of Hispanics, and 38 percent of blacks in 1989; U.S. Bureau of the Census, 1991). Chapter 8 examines the importance of the family and discusses the impact of divorce and of one-parent families from the child's point of view. In the remaining pages of this chapter, we look at the family as a sociological unit and at the impact of children *on parents*.

Duvall's Model

One way to approach a study of the family is to look at it in terms of the series of relatively predictable

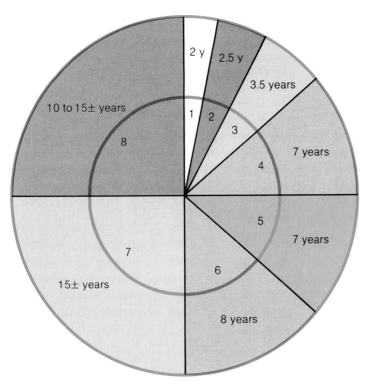

2 y

2.5 y

3.5 years

10 to 15± years

8

1 2

3

7 years

4

7

5

7 years

6

15± years

8 years

▶ **Interactive Figure 14.8**
Duvall's eight stages of the family life cycle. At which stage of the cycle is your parents' family? Your family, if you are married? What are the tasks and responsibilities of those stages? (From Duvall, 1977, p. 148. Based on data from the U.S. Bureau of the Census and from the National Center for Health Statistics, Washington, DC.)

1. Married couples without children

2. Childbearing families
   (oldest child birth–30 months)

3. Families with preschool children
   (oldest child 30 months–6 years)

4. Families with schoolchildren
   (oldest child 6–13 years)

5. Families with teenagers
   (oldest child 13–20 years)

6. Families launching young adults
   (first child gone to last child leaving home)

7. Middle-aged parents
   (empty nest to retirement)

8. Aging family members
   (retirement to death of both spouses)

changes that occur in the traditional family from its beginning to its end. This is the **family life-cycle** approach, of which there are many examples (Vinovskis, 1988). One example, described here, is provided by Duvall (1977), who identifies eight sequential stages in the evolution of the family. These stages often overlap and can also be very different for different families. In the main, however, they describe a relatively common progression premised, at least in part, on Duvall's belief that families, like individuals, are exposed to a series of important developmental tasks. But whereas individual developmental tasks, described by theorists such as Erikson, relate to the resolution of personal conflicts and the development of individual competencies, family-based tasks relate to child rearing. Thus all but the last of Duvall's stages of the family life cycle

deal specifically with the family in relation to its children. These stages, together with the amount of time the *average* couple spends in each, are summarized in Interactive Figure 14.8. Note, however, that the family cycle described here applies primarily to the "traditional" family—that is, to first-marriage, child-rearing families. In addition, this approach neglects the many important influences on the family other than children—such as careers as well as relationships with parents, friends, siblings, and spouse. Also, it concentrates on the influence of the first, and thus oldest, child, and ignores the impact of other children (Vinovskis, 1988). However, other approaches that include more factors become too complex to be very practical.

The first five of Duvall's eight stages span the period of early adulthood, and are described briefly here. The sixth and seventh last through middle adult-hood and are discussed in Chapter 16; the eighth stage is covered in Chapter 18.

Stage 1: To Have Children?

Most families begin as a childless couple, a period that, in Duvall's model, lasts for approximately two years. In fact, however, it lasts until the birth of the first child; and because increasing numbers of women are post-poning having their first child — or are deciding not to have children — the first stage (sometimes called the *honeymoon* stage) might last much longer.

The first stage brings with it several developmental tasks. These may include finding and keeping a job for the man and sometimes for the woman as well. In addition, both partners are faced with important tasks relating to sexual fulfillment and the development of a harmonious marriage.

One of the most important decisions that needs to be made early in the marriage (if it has not already been made) is whether to have one or more children, and when. The decision is more complicated in families where both partners have careers. As Wilk (1986) points out, in the dual-career family, the decision to start a family (or not to do so) will be affected by at least four groups of considerations. The first two of these, *life-style* and *career* issues, are most relevant to women who work. The other two, *marriage* and *psychological* issues, affect all potential parents.

Life-style issues involve questions relating to how the presence of children might change the partners' activities, the impact of potential reduction of income coupled with the costs associated with child rearing, and decisions that have been made or are being made by important reference groups such as friends and co-workers.

Career issues relate to whether the wife is satisfied with her career and her future career prospects, and whether the development of her career can survive one or more interruptions. The transition to a parenting role is sometimes more difficult for dual-career families, and especially for mothers in these families (Doxey, 1990).

Marriage issues have to do with how happy each of the partners is with their marriage, how stable they think it is, and how they think it will respond to the introduction of children. As we noted earlier, the family is a dynamic system. It changes as its composition changes; and it changes, as well, in response to changes in its larger context. It is, in the jargon of this age,

an *ecological* system, composed of complex and ever-changing relationships that give it a life of its own. The strength and viability of this system, its likely effects on children, and the likely effects of children on it, are all important factors — not only for dual-career families but also for others.

Psychological factors that are important in making a childbearing decision affect all potential mothers — and all potential fathers as well. They have to do with individual values and preferences, and are related to a host of other variables, the most important of which might be the potential parents' relationships with their own parents when they were children. There are some who do not *want* children for personal reasons. (Wilk's [1986] decision-making model is summarized in Figure 14.9.)

There are those for whom the question is difficult; sometimes it is simply put off as a result. There are some, too, who do not ask or answer the question, but who simply let nature or luck answer it for them. And there are others for whom the answer is so clear that they scarcely need to ask themselves the question.

Stages 2–5: Child Rearing

Stage 2: Infancy. If the couple decides to and is successful in having a family, they enter the second of Duvall's eight stages of the family life cycle. This stage begins with the birth of the first child and lasts approximately two and a half years. This time of very rapid changes and adjustments in the family brings with it a variety of demands for both mother and father. Among other things, the mother is called upon to develop and clarify her roles as mother, wife, and person; she needs to learn how to care for and cope with infants and young preschoolers; she needs to maintain a satisfying relationship with her husband; and she must, through all this, nevertheless maintain some sense of personal autonomy (Duvall, 1977). The father, too, is required to make numerous adjustments, including reconciling conflicting conceptions of his role as father, accepting new responsibilities for parenting, conforming to changes in schedules, coping with the reduced time and attention that the wife can now devote to him, and maintaining a satisfying marital relationship and a sense of autonomy and self-worth.

Stage 3: Preschool. As the first child reaches the preschool age, the family enters the third stage of Duvall's family life cycle. It begins when the first child

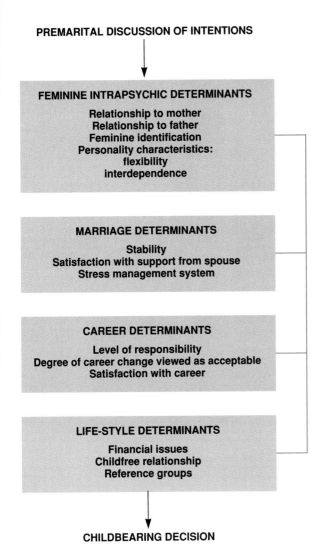

PREMARITAL DISCUSSION OF INTENTIONS

FEMININE INTRAPSYCHIC DETERMINANTS

Relationship to mother
Relationship to father
Feminine identification
Personality characteristics:
flexibility
interdependence

MARRIAGE DETERMINANTS

Stability
Satisfaction with support from spouse
Stress management system

CAREER DETERMINANTS

Level of responsibility
Degree of career change viewed as acceptable
Satisfaction with career

LIFE-STYLE DETERMINANTS

Financial issues
Childfree relationship
Reference groups

CHILDBEARING DECISION

Figure 14.9 A dual-career childbearing decision model. (From C. A. Wilk, *Career Women and Childbearing.* © 1986 Van Nostrand Reinhold. Used by permission.)

tention, as well as a new set of child-rearing responsibilities and problems. And to complicate matters, only those families with a single child can be described as being in only one developmental phase at one time. For many families, there is considerable overlap among stages as additional children are born.

Stage 4: Preteen School Years. The fourth stage, much longer than any of the first three, spans the preteen school years of the oldest chid (6–13). It brings three important developmental tasks, none of which is exclusive to this developmental phase, but all of which are fundamentally important to the happy and effective functioning of the family. These include providing for children's special as well as ordinary needs, enjoying life with children, and encouraging children's growth. And although these tasks are difficult and demanding, most parents raise their children without a great deal of deliberation or guidance, relying primarily on intuition, folk wisdom, and their recollection of the child-rearing techniques of their parents (Lunde & Lunde, 1980). Interestingly, a study of 454 couples indicates that parents who had more socialization experiences related to child rearing (for example, babysitting, teaching, being a camp counselor, looking after siblings, or taking parenting courses) were happier parents who more easily made the transition to parenthood (Gage & Hendrickson Christensen, 1991).

Stage 5: Teen Years. The fifth phase in the family life cycle spans the teen years of the oldest child (13–20) and brings with it the occasional parenting problems of adolescence. These present many family developmental tasks, including working out possible financial problems, reallocating the sharing of responsibilities, bridging the communication gap between generations, and, all the while, continuing to maintain the marriage relationship (Duvall, 1977).

An Evaluation of the Life-Cycle Approach

It is important to keep in mind that life-cycle approaches such as Duvall's describe common patterns in *traditional* families. However, increasing numbers of families are no longer traditional. As a result, many of the important events that serve as transitions from one stage to another in the evolution of the family now occur much later than they once did. Not only are

is 2½, ends with school age (6), and brings with it a continuation of most of the developmental tasks that were first introduced in the preceding stage. Few of these tasks are ever completely resolved during any one phase of the cycle. Indeed, such important tasks as maintaining a sense of autonomy and worth while striving for the development of a mutually satisfying and happy marriage continue from the beginning to the very end of the family life cycle. In addition, the presence of preschoolers in the family brings additional demands for income, space, equipment, time, and at-

The family is a dynamic social organization. It changes dramatically with the advent of children and changes again as children grow and leave home. Accordingly, the average family can be described in terms of a series of stages defined largely by the presence and age of its children. However, because the size and composition of families vary so much, the stage-based approach, so useful in describing the average family cycle, is not very meaningful in describing the nonaverage family, such as this five-child family.

young adults getting married at later ages, but also many are delaying the start of a family.

Approaches such as this also tend to oversimplify very complex and highly dynamic relationships. They are based on assumptions that might not always be correct—for example, that families with more than one child go through the same sorts of changes as families with only one child. Nor can they take into account the impact of family crises such as death and divorce; and they say little about the vast number of families that do not fit the traditional mold of working father and homemaking mother. Divorce, one-parent families, career mothers, and a variety of other family situations that have become increasingly common in recent decades present different sets of problems and tasks. In spite of this, however, we should not forget that no matter the nature of their families, children still progress in similar ways through their infancies and

childhoods, into their adolescence, and finally into the world. And it is children who, after all, define the very existence and nature of the family.

Violence in the Family

Prophets and others who specialize in gloom and related states have been warning us for some time that violence is rapidly becoming a way of life in contemporary societies. And perhaps they are correct. Certainly, police reports indicate that incidence of violent crimes in Western industrialized nations has increased sharply during recent decades, as has international terrorism. However, wife abuse, defined in terms of physical violence by the husband, appears to have decreased

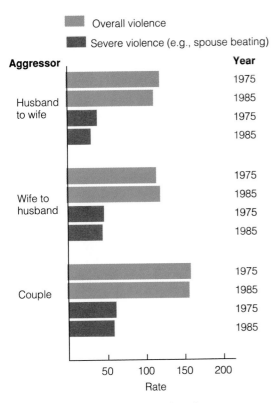

Figure 14.10 Rate of marital violence per 1,000 couples. (From Straus & Gelles, 1986.)

Violence in the family takes a variety of forms. It is perhaps most evident in the observation that more than 9 out of 10 parents admit to using physical force to punish children (Martin, 1978). It is even more dramatically apparent in instances of child abuse (discussed in Chapter 10). And it is present, as well, in countless episodes of violence among siblings. Indeed, violence among siblings seems to be highly prevalent among young children, although it diminishes rapidly with increasing age. In a sample of 2,143 families, Straus (1980b) found that 74 percent of all 3- to 4-year-old children who had siblings occasionally resorted to some form of physical aggression in their interactions. Only 36 percent of those ages 15–17 behaved in similar fashion.

Spouse Battering

Violence in the family is also apparent in instances of wife and husband beating. And surprisingly, the latter is almost as common as the former. In Straus and Gelles's (1986) investigation of American families, 3.8 percent of all husbands admitted to activities that the authors define as wife beating. These activities include kicking, biting, hitting with the fist or some other object, threatening with a knife or a gun, or actually using a knife or a gun. And an amazing 4.6 percent of all wives admitted to similar activities with respect to their husbands. However, Straus cautions that wife beating tends to be hidden and secretive more often than is husband beating, and that wives are, in fact, far more often *victims* than are husbands.

The picture presented by surveys such as these is probably only a partial sketch, given the privacy of the family. Its affairs are not easily accessible to social science or to law enforcement agencies. In addition, our prevailing attitudes concerning the *right* of parents to punish their children physically, the normality of siblings fighting, and, yes, even the right of a husband to beat his wife, tend to obscure the prevalence and seriousness of violence in the family. Thus, when Shotland and Straw (1976) staged a series of events where one individual attacked another, bystanders almost invariably tried to assist the victim unless the attack involved a man and a woman. When a man attacked a woman, bystanders usually assumed that the couple was married and that they should therefore not interfere.

Why do some husbands beat their wives? There is no simple answer. Some, probably a minority, might

by approximately 27 percent between 1975 and 1985 (Straus & Gelles, 1986).

Although it might be tempting to assume that violence typically involves strangers and that surrounding ourselves with friends and family will therefore protect us, that, sadly, does not appear to be the case. Indeed, more than 25 percent of all assaults and homicides that are reported to police involve members of the same *family* (U.S. Bureau of the Census, 1991). And a large percentage of the remainder involve friends or at least acquaintances. More than half of all rapes, crimes that most of us attribute to disturbed strangers in dark parking lots, are committed by acquaintances or relatives — or "dates." One third of all female murder victims are killed by boyfriends or husbands (U.S. Department of Justice, 1984). As Gelles (1978) puts it: "We have discovered that violence between family members, rather than being a minor pattern of behavior, or a behavior that is rare and dysfunctional, is a patterned and normal aspect of interaction between family members" (p. 169) (see Figure 14.10).

Interspouse Violence

Two large-scale surveys of domestic violence conducted 10 years apart show little change in violent acts between husband and wife during this period, although Straus and Gelles note a trend toward a reduction in the incidence of family violence. They speculate this reduction may result from (1) differences in the two studies, (2) a greater reluctance to report violence in 1985, or (3) an actual reduction in family violence, perhaps because of programs designed to combat child and wife abuse, or because of social changes that make such behavior less acceptable and less likely. Still, overall incidence of family violence is shockingly high. Projections of these figures led to an estimate of some 1.6 million battered wives in the United States in 1985. A surprising finding, first reported in 1975 and confirmed again in 1985, is that as many wives beat their husbands as vice versa.

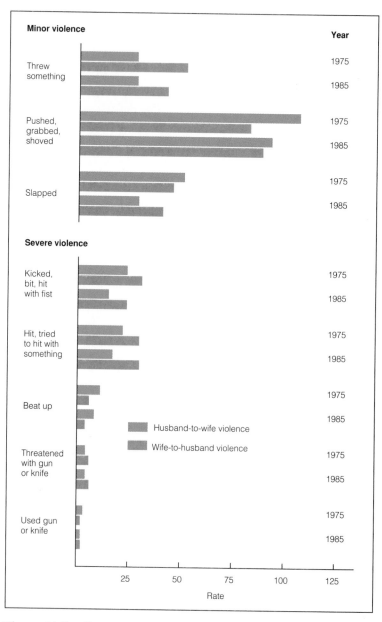

Figure 14.11 Comparison of interspouse violence rates per 1,000 couples, 1975–1985. (From M.A. Straus and R. Gelles, "Societal Change and Change in Family Violence from 1975 to 1985 as Revealed by Two National Surveys," *Journal of Marriage and the Family, 48.* Copyright 1986 NCFR. Reprinted by permission.)

be classified as suffering from a psychological disorder. In one study involving 100 battered wives, 25 percent of the husbands had received psychiatric help in the past. And, according to the wives, many more were in need of such help (Gayford, 1978). Many of these husbands came to their marriages with a history of violence. Many had been physically abused and beaten as children. And compared with the general population, more of them were chronically unemployed and poorly educated.

Other factors that contribute to violence in the family include the high incidence of violence in society, cultural attitudes that accept violence as a legitimate reaction in certain situations, and our predominantly sexist attitudes toward the roles of husband and wife in contemporary marriage. These and other contributing factors are summarized in Figure 14.12.

Sexual Assault

One form of violence that is not restricted to the family, but that is pertinent there as well, is sexual assault. Sexual assault can range from sexual innuendo and unwanted suggestions to forcible rape. It is an increasingly common problem with a range of sometimes extremely negative consequences.

Rape is ordinarily defined as forcible sexual intercourse with someone *other* than a spouse (Gelles, 1979). In 1989, 89.3 out of every 100,000 American women over the age of 12 was subjected to forcible rape — a total of more than 90,000 incidents. This represents an increase of more than 50,000 cases since 1970, when the rate per 100,000 women was 46.3 (U.S. Bureau of the Census, 1991).

Note that the legal definition of rape specifically excludes the wife as victim. In this definition is an implicit acceptance of a husband's right to use physical force on his wife — and an explanation for the reluctance of law enforcement agencies to charge husbands with assault when wives are victims (Straus, 1980a). English common law maintains that a man is still king in his castle, however humble that castle might be.

In many jurisdictions, then, it is legally impossible for a man to rape his wife — although he might well be guilty of sexual violence variously labeled *sexual aggression, sexual coercion,* or *sexual victimization*. It is *not* legally impossible for a friend, a date, or an acquaintance to rape his partner. In fact, such behaviors are shockingly common. Estimates of instances of what is

sometimes called *courtship violence* range from 15 to 25 percent of all women when the violence is restricted to actual or attempted intercourse (Koss, 1988; Rivera & Regoli, 1987). Estimates of other forms of courtship violence are much higher.

Rape on Campus. Ward and associates (1991) speak of four different kinds of rape that occur on college and university campuses (and elsewhere, too, of course): (1) the *stranger* incident in which the perpetrator attacks an unknown victim, (2) the *party* incident in which victim and perpetrator know each other from a single social function during or after which the assault occurs, (3) the *acquaintance* incident in which the man and woman know each other casually, and (4) the *date* incident in which the man and woman have an ongoing relationship.

Prevalence of sexual assault on college campuses is difficult to ascertain, as it is elsewhere. There are problems of definition, as well as problems having to do with underreporting. Koss (1988) found that only 58 percent of rape victims reported the incident *to anyone at all*; a mere 5 percent went to the police. Many women are uncertain or ambiguous about the seriousness of the incident; and many think that little or nothing can be done.

A self-report questionnaire survey of 524 women and 337 men on a college campus presents interesting and useful findings about acquaintance rape (Ward et al., 1991). During the less-than-one-year period covered by the study, 34 percent of the women in this group had experienced unwanted sexual contact (kissing, fondling, or touching in a sexual way); 20 percent had been subjected to attempted sexual intercourse; and 10 percent had experienced unwanted completed sexual intercourse. The majority of these episodes occurred with an acquaintance at a party; about three quarters involved alcohol use by the male and one half involved alcohol use by the female; and in almost half the cases of unwanted intercourse, no one was told later (see Table 14.7).

It is perhaps striking that in this sample, men's recollections of sexual incidents were dramatically different from the women's. Only 9 percent of the males recalled having sexual contact with an unwilling woman, and another 9 percent claimed they had attempted intercourse with an unwilling partner (woman reported 34 and 20 percent, respectively); a mere 3 percent of men admitted they had actually completed intercourse (women reported 10 percent).

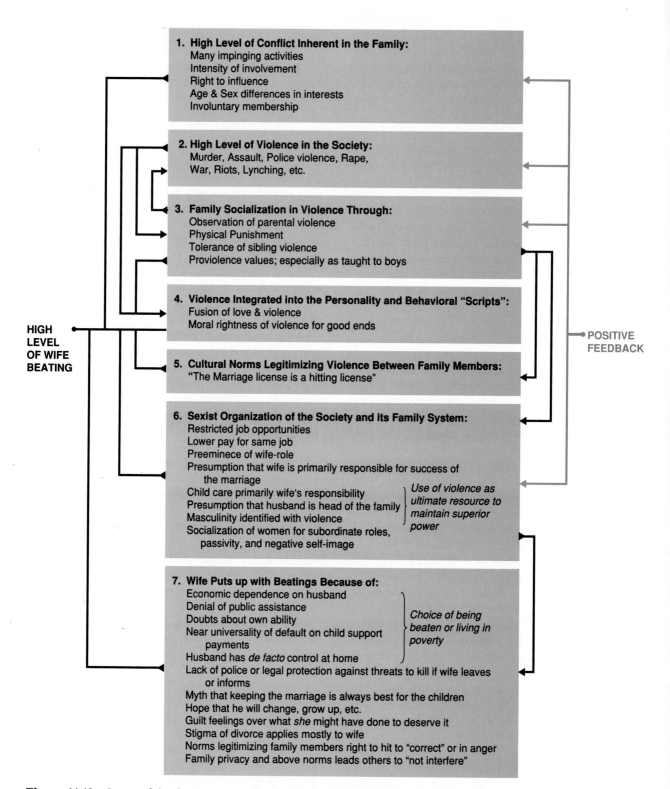

Figure 14.12 Some of the factors accounting for the high incidence of wife beating (solid lines) and positive feedback loops maintaining the system (dashed lines). (From Straus, 1980a. Used by permission of the University of Minnesota Press.)

TABLE 14.7

Characteristics of "Most Serious" Sexual Incidents

	Type of Experience		
	Contact (N = 176)	Attempted Intercourse (N = 102)	Intercourse (N = 50)
Location			
Dorm	32%	41%	50%
Fraternity	28	10	8
Apartment	29	43	36
Other	11	6	6
Occasion			
Date	9%	8%	14%
Party	68	65	57
Other	24	27	29
Alcohol Use			
Male use	80%	77%	76%
Female use	57	54	65
Relationship			
Stranger	18%	9%	12%
Acquaintance/friend	66	57	47
Boyfriend	14	30	33
Other	2	5	8
Male Tactics			
Just did it	77%	62%	46%
Verbal	15	28	33
Force	8	10	21
Female Response★			
Too frightened	6%	6%	20%
Said no	76	91	70
Cried	5	9	22
Struggled/fought	17	16	28
Other protests	17	7	12
What Resulted★			
Physical injury	0%	3%	10%
Psychological injury	18	30	51
Required counseling	2	2	8
Who Was Told★			
No one	23%	30%	41%
Roommate	41	38	25
Close friend	59	54	41
Counselor	< 1	< 1	4

★ Percentages do not add to 100 because of multiple responses.
Source: From Ward, S. K., Chapman, K., Cohn, E., White, S., & Williams, K. (1991). Acquaintance rape and the college social scene. *Family Relations, 40,* 65–71. Copyright 1991 by the National Council on Family Relations. Reprinted by permission.

Attitudes and Violence. Sexual assault is a form of violence that reflects an attitude of male dominance and female passivity, and an implicit assumption of the man's rights to sexual satisfaction under certain circumstances. In date or acquaintance rape, for example, there is often a misperception of sexual cues coupled with the man's attitude that he is entitled to sex.

Wife battering and child abuse also reflect similar stereotypes of male dominance. The attitudes of men who batter their wives, says Bograd (1988), are more sexist; these men are socialized into power and control over women. Eisikovits and associates (1991) report that their sample of wife beaters in Israel had different attitudes about wife beating, and that they tended to be more impulsive and less self-controlled. They argue that attempts to alleviate the problem need to be more ecological in the sense that they take into account multiple rather than single contributing factors.

The Continuing Evolution of Self

Family violence and sexual assault would not have been a happy topic with which to end this chapter. It is shocking and distressing to consider that more than 3 million men and women and more than 2 million children in the United States are victims of *severe* violence each year. The topic smacks too much of power and too little of love.

Love and power are the two themes that run through our dreams. They are the themes that unify the stories of our lives, that give purpose and direction to our actions. It is through expressions of love and power that we achieve meaning — that we become meaningful. Being meaningful is the essence of Kegan's (1982) view of the evolution of the self.

Kegan describes five stages in the evolution of the self — five major transformations in the relationships that link individuals and their contexts. The first, the age of the *impulsive self*, describes a self that is embedded in impulses and perceptions. This is the self of Piaget's sensorimotor and preoperational child. But the correspondence to these periods is only conceptual, not chronological. There are many adults whose selves do not evolve beyond this level, and whose preoccupations through life remain fixed at the level of gratification of impulses.

The second self, the *imperial self*, struggles to take over the power and the control that were previously held by parents. The imperial self strives toward the development of personal competence and the achievement of personal control. Much energy is directed toward gaining power and becoming self-sufficient. Developmentally, this self corresponds to Piaget's period of concrete operations and to Erikson's initiative versus guilt. The imperial self's meaning making derives from relationships with school, family, and peers.

As the self continues to evolve, the imperial self gradually transforms into the *interpersonal self* — a self that recognizes the mutuality of relationships and searches for reciprocity. Whereas the imperial self is oriented toward power and control, the interpersonal self orients itself around inner feelings and interpersonal relationships. Self-definition — being meaningful — is no longer expressed simply in competence and control but is now found in the feelings others have toward the self.

The self of the transition through adolescence to young adulthood is the *institutional self*. It is a self that is embedded in culture, work, and love. In Erikson's view, it is a self that creates its meaning through the selection and cultivation of a personal identity.

The self of early adulthood is a more *interindividual self* — a self oriented toward adult relationships. It is the interindividual self that searches for the special combination of passion, intimacy, and commitment that make up consummate love.

The interindividual self of the young adult, like all of Kegan's other selves, is all that has come before it. At every stage, we retain elements of the selves that we have been. Thus the interindividual self continues to develop the abilities and the competencies that admission to the public world of adulthood demand; at the same time, it retains an orientation toward independence and reciprocal interpersonal relationships. And through all of young adulthood, as through all of life, the self struggles to remain meaningful — to *mean something*.

If we are loved and have power, do we not mean something?

Main Points

1. According to Erikson's psychosocial, ego-oriented theory of human development, the individual progresses through a series of stages characterized by basic conflicts, the resolution of which results in the appearance of new capabilities and attitudes. The stage that spans young adulthood is *intimacy versus isolation*. During this period, the young adult strives to achieve intimacy most often through a reciprocated love relationship with someone of the opposite sex.

2. Liking implies positive evaluation and perhaps friendship; loving implies a degree of absorption, attachment, and intimacy. Love is often marked by a fierce possessiveness and brings with it the capacity for jealousy and pain as well as ecstasy. Sternberg's model describes eight varieties of love (or nonlove) identifiable on the basis of combinations of *passion* (strong physical desire), *intimacy* (affection, disclosure), and *commitment* (a decision to *be* in love, to stay together).

3. Important antecedents of interpersonal attraction (which underlies love) include physical attractiveness, similarity, and propinquity (physical proximity).

4. Mate selection, according to Murstein, involves a three-stage filtering process: reaction and attraction to the *stimulus* (the potential mate), a comparing of *values* (a revelation of identities, which makes possible judgments about similarity), and the development of *roles* relative to one another. *Chemistry* may also be involved.

5. Our one fundamental choice of life-style is to marry or not to marry. If we opt not to marry, we might select from among singlehood, cohabitation, homosexuality, or one of a variety of communes. About 10 percent of the adult population is single by choice.

6. Approximately 1 out of 25 couples in the United States lives together unmarried for economic and sexual benefits, the elimination of the legal responsibilities of marriage, and the possibility of using cohabitation as a "trial marriage."

7. Singlehood includes the never-married, divorced or separated, and widowed. Some singles are temporarily and voluntarily single, having postponed marriage for educational, career, or other reasons; some are involuntarily single, having failed to find a mate or having been widowed; and some are single after the dissolution of a marriage.

8. More than one in three marriages ends in divorce, but the majority of those divorced remarry within three years (five of six men and three of four women). The emotional, social, and economic impact of divorce is sometimes severe and often affects women more than men, although both are usually affected.

9. Marriage is our most commonly selected adult life-style (95 percent).

10. Social standards governing premarital sex have moved from a period that encouraged total abstinence, through a period characterized by a double standard that condoned sexual activity among males but not among females, and finally to a period where premarital sexual activity is seen as being permissible for women as well as men, providing there is affection between partners.

11. A double standard governs the attitudes of many societies toward extramarital sex (adultery). In North America, extramarital affairs are engaged in by between one third and one half of men and women at least once. Marriages that tolerate extramarital sexual encounters may be *open* or may deliberately engage in group sex or mate swapping.

12. Enduring marriages may be *conflict-habituated* (continual disagreement and conflict), *devitalized* (no passion remains), *passive-congenial* (where there never was any fire), *vital* (couples share intimately but each remains an individual), and *total* (the most important thing is the relationship).

13. We ask not only that our marriages provide a social institution for raising our children but also that they make us happy. Factors contributing to marital satisfaction among women include age at first

marriage (later is better), education, and socioeconomic status. Among men, occupation, socioeconomic status, and education contribute to marital satisfaction.

14. Opposites do not attract, but similars do. The more alike two people are, the more likely they are to describe their marriage as a happy one. Sexual compatibility is related to marital happiness. Frequency of sexual intercourse is highest for several years immediately following marriage. Unsatisfactory sexual relations are often implicated in marriage dissolution.

15. The contemporary North American family can be described in terms of a life cycle with several stages, each reflecting different developmental tasks that occur as children are born, grow up, and leave home. Duvall's eight stages in the family life cycle include the initial childless years, the first child, the phase of the preschool child, a school-aged phase (7 years), a teenager phase (7 years), a "launching" phase (8 years), the empty nest to retirement period (15 years), and a retirement-until-death phase.

16. An important first-stage decision is whether to have children and when. Important considerations include life-style issues (How will children affect income and leisure?), career issues (What will the effect be on careers?), psychological issues (Do we *want* children?), and marriage issues (Do we like each other enough?).

17. Although this life-cycle approach is useful, it cannot easily take into account the increasingly common single-parent families that result from unwed parenthood, divorce, and death. Nor is it sensitive to differences among families that might relate to the parents' occupations, to the family's socioeconomic status, to parents' attitudes toward each other and their children, or to the number of children in the family.

18. The incidence of violence in the family does not appear to have increased in recent years; however, more than 1.6 million women were victims of severe physical violence in the United States in 1985. About 90,000 were victims of forcible rape. Perhaps 5 percent were victims of unwanted sexual actions. Prevailing social attitudes toward the permissibility of physical punishment and the reluctance of individuals as well as of law enforcement agencies to become involved in "domestic disputes" contribute to violence in the family.

19. Kegan's five selves, in order of their evolution, are *impulsive* (concerned with gratification of impulses), *imperial* (oriented toward developing personal competence and achieving control), *interpersonal* (concerned with reciprocal relationships), *institutional* (embedded in work, love, and culture), and *interindividual* (oriented toward adult relationships).

20. If we have love and power, do we not mean something?

Further Readings

The following are two good texts on marriage and the family. The first is somewhat more comprehensive and detailed than the second, a highly readable text, which relies less on research:

Lamanna, M. A., & Riedmann, A. (1988). *Marriages and families: Making choices and facing change* (3rd ed.). Belmont, CA: Wadsworth.

Schulz, D. A., & Rodgers, S. F. (1985). *Marriage, the family, and personal fulfillment* (3rd ed.). Englewood Cliffs, NJ: Prentice-Hall.

Excellent accounts of changes in the family are contained in:

Arnold, L. E. (Ed.). (1985). *Parents, children and change.* Lexington, MA: D. C. Heath.

Vetere, A., & Gale, A. (1987). *Ecological studies of family life*. New York: John Wiley.

A well-known textbook that presents an Eriksonian, developmental-task analysis of the family through its various cycles is:

Duvall, E. M. (1977). *Marriage and family development* (5th ed.). New York: Harper & Row.

A comprehensive, research-based look at life-style choices, including singlehood in all of its variations, traditional marriage, remarriage, stepparenting, homosexuality, open marriages, commuter marriages, and others, is:

Macklin, E. D., & Rubin, R. H. (1983). *Contemporary families and alternative lifestyles: Handbook on research and theory*. Beverly Hills, CA: Sage.

A detailed analysis of the factors involved in reconciling career demands with the demands of raising children is presented in:

Wilk, C. A. (1986). *Career women and childbearing: A psychological analysis of the decision process*. New York: Van Nostrand.

Kegan's book is an intriguing, sometimes poetic, look at the self and at our attempts to make meaning and to be meaningful:

Kegan, R. (1982). *The evolving self: Problem and process in human development*. Cambridge, MA: Harvard University Press.

John Singer Sargent: *In the Generalife, Granada,* c. 1912. The Metropolitan Museum of Art, purchase, Joseph Pulitzer bequest, 1915 (15.142.8).

Women sit or move to and fro, some old, some young.

The young are beautiful — but the old are more beautiful than the young.

Walt Whitman, *Beautiful Women*

VII

Middle Adulthood

Are the old really more beautiful than the young? Much that we see and hear in this century's youth-worshiping context would have us think not. "Think young!" "Feel young!" "Be young!" we are told. When your face begins to fall, you must lift it. Cream and rejuvenate your wrinkles. Restretch your sagging skin. Color your graying hair. Starve yourself if that's what is needed to maintain your hips and your belly. Dance and drink and sing all night even if you would rather dream by the fire.

We struggle so desperately to delay or hide the signals of aging. We do not mature gracefully.

Yet, as we see in Chapters 15 and 16, the middle-aged have more of almost everything we work so hard to achieve—hence more of everything we value. On average, it is the middle-aged who have the most money, the greatest number of possessions, the most power, perhaps even the most love.

In many ways, middle adulthood is the very peak of life's mountain.

But how steep is the downhill side?

CHAPTER 15

Physical and Cognitive Development: Middle Adulthood

To youth I have but three words of counsel — work, work, work.

Otto von Bismarck

Youth does not always take Bismarck's counsel very seriously. In the transition between childhood and adulthood, there is often time and inclination for childhood games. Youth is sometimes like the man in Jerome K. Jerome's *Three Men in a Boat* who declared, "I like work; it fascinates me. I can sit and look at it for hours. I love to keep it by me: the idea of getting rid of it nearly breaks my heart."

Not so for much of middle age. Working, acquiring, succeeding, climbing the slippery rungs of career ladders — these consume much of the middle years.

This Chapter

Work is one of the important topics of this chapter — although we look at leisure as well. The chapter deals with the physical changes of this period: changes in appearance, in the senses, in organ functioning, in general health; and major changes in the reproductive system, particularly in women. It looks, as well, at cognitive changes and at the controversy over whether some aspects of intellectual functioning suffer from the ravages of age. It examines the changing workplace and the role of careers in the lives of men and women before turning, finally, to leisure.

Middle Adulthood

To keep things clear and simple, middle adulthood is defined as the two-decade span from the age of 40 or 45 to around 60 or 65. Unfortunately, however, age does not tell us very much about the social and emotional lives of most adults — nor even all that much about their physical lives. Here, as elsewhere in the lifespan, there are those we think of as being old before their time; and there are those we consider young for their age. In general, however, the very old think of the middle-aged as young; and the very young think of the 40-year-old as very old.

And those who are middle-aged? How do *they* see themselves and their lives?

The answer depends, of course, on the individual. For those whose identities are closely bound to their physical selves, the advent of the middle years can be a source of consternation and perhaps even grief. As is discussed in this chapter, there are, in the middle years, some subtle but largely inevitable and irreversible changes in the body — changes that, given our contemporary *contextual* definitions of physical attractiveness, are often viewed as negative. But for those whose identities — whose personal meaningfulness — stems more from relationships, from knowledge and intelligence, from cultural competence and success, and from the power that results, the middle years can be a source of profound happiness.

For most adults, the middle years are very busy years. From a career point of view, these are often the most productive and the most successful years of adulthood. Middle-aged workers, on average, already earn and possess more than younger workers, continue to earn and accumulate more, have more competence, and wield more power.

From a social point of view, middle adulthood often involves more close interpersonal relationships than any other period in the lifespan — relationships with aging parents, with children and grandchildren, with siblings and co-workers, and with half a lifetime's worth of friends and acquaintances.

But it is also in the middle years that something happens to our perceptions of time — something initially quite subtle, but nevertheless significant. Our psychological perceptions of time are tied to our ages; they are also very personal. For the very young, days last forever. As Wordsworth put it in "To a Butterfly," "Sweet childish days, that were as long as twenty days are now." But as we get older, the opposite happens, and 20 days now seem no longer than one used to be. And when we reach a point close to the middle of life, Neugarten (1968) tells us, our perception of time changes in yet another way: We stop thinking in terms of how long we have lived; now we begin to think in terms of how much time we have left.

And if there is much we still want to do, perhaps we must now run a little faster. But alas, we get tired more easily. Besides, the days have shrunk.

Do they lengthen again in old age? We look at this question in Chapter 18.

Developmental Tasks of Middle Adulthood

Developmental tasks are culturally determined responsibilities that represent competencies or achievements important for happiness and adjustment. Havighurst describes a series of such tasks at every stage of the lifespan (see Chapters 2 and 13). Those that are important for middle adulthood are summarized in Table 15.1. They include problems of adjusting to physiological changes, as well as to work and leisure; these are the subjects of this chapter. In addition, Havighurst's developmental tasks for the middle years deal with relationships with children, parents, spouse, and the community; these are the focus of Chapter 16.

TABLE 15.1

Havighurst's Developmental Tasks

Challenges in Middle Adulthood

1. Assisting children in transition from home to world
2. Developing adult leisure activities
3. Relating to spouse as a person
4. Reaching adult social and civic responsibility
5. Maintaining satisfactory career performance
6. Adjusting to physiological changes of middle age
7. Adjusting to aging parents

Physical Changes

Aging is a linear, time-bound, biological process. Some of its consequences are apparent; others are hidden. Loss of hair or hair pigmentation is clearly visible; reduction in the efficiency of various organs is not so obvious.

Appearance

Although the normal changes in appearance that occur in the middle years typically bear little relationship either to health or physical functioning, for those whose meaning is closely bound to their physical selves, they can be tremendously important.

Our cultural standards of beauty and attractiveness, closely tied to physical appearance, dictate that peak attractiveness will generally occur during early adulthood. This is particularly true for females and is evident in the physical appearance of the models employed by the advertising industry. It is also evident in the enormous salaries that many of these models command between ages 16 and 25, as well as in the observation that the period of peak income for movie actresses and models has traditionally been near the beginning of early adulthood, or between ages 23 and 27. Men, whose attractiveness (or ugliness) seems, for cultural reasons, not to be so close to the skin, fare somewhat better as actors. Their average periods of peak income, according to Lehman (1953), were between 30 and 34. Note, however, that the Lehman study was conducted in the early 1950s. There is some indication that patterns have changed somewhat since then.

Physical changes that account for our progressively changing appearance are highly varied and initially very subtle. The most obvious are changes in height and weight. After the late teens or early twenties, height does not generally increase. However, after the age of 45 (sometimes earlier and sometimes later), there are frequently decrements in height. On the average, these decrements are greater for women than for men. Rossman (1977) reports average lifetime losses of 4.9 centimeters (almost 2 inches) for women and 2.0 centimeters (about ¾ inch) for men.

Although changes in height occur late in adulthood and are usually so gradual that they are not often detected, changes in weight are often far less subtle. As Bischof (1976) notes, after we stop growing at the ends, we begin to grow in the middle. Thus adulthood is often accompanied by the accumulation of fatty tissue, which tends to be distributed differently in men and women. Typically, excess fat first finds its way around the middles of men; it is more likely to be deposited on the hips among women. In general, percentage of body weight that is fat is higher for women than for men throughout the adult years. Figure 15.1 presents the results of a study that looked at relative distributions

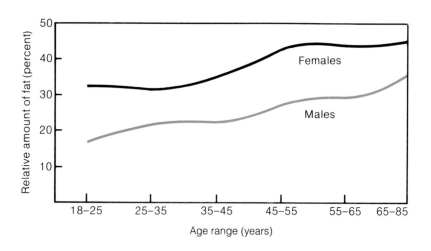

Figure 15.1 Relative amounts of body fat by age and sex. (From Novak, 1972, p. 440. Reprinted by permission of the Gerontological Society of America.)

INTERVIEW

▶ Subject   Male; age 33; first marriage; two children; university education; professional career.

▶ Question   "When do you think the 'prime of life' is?"

....

❝ *"The prime of life. It depends exactly what you mean . . .*

Okay. Well, generally, the prime of life is right at the peak. I'd say it probably goes from the time you're grown up and finished with education — 20 or 25 maybe — right up until you're "over the hill," and I suppose for most people that wouldn't happen for quite a long time. Retirement, maybe. Sixty or sixty-five . . .

Well, if I had to narrow it down to just five years, I'd say maybe around . . . well it depends. My physical prime is different. Probably from 25 to 30. But intellectually and in my work, I haven't reached my prime yet. Maybe around 45 years. ❞

---

of fat among 520 adults (215 males, 305 females) between the ages of 18 and 85.

Other physical changes that contribute to the adult's changing appearance include loss of skin elasticity, thinning of hair, loss of muscle tone, loss of flexibility in joints, gradual recession of gums (hence the expression "long in the tooth"), and the appearance of longer, stiffer hair in the eyebrows, ears, and nose (Spence, 1989). In addition, even among adults who remain trim, there is a gradual thickening of the torso but an eventual thinning of the legs and arms. It is partly for this reason that, as Troll (1982) notes, a skinny old person does not look like a skinny young person.

Most of these physical changes are very gradual and seldom dramatic while they are occurring; yet, we resist them with incredible passion and vigor, especially early in the middle years.

We have made a cult of being and looking youthful. Americans spend an estimated $10 billion plus a year for lotions, creams, potions, herbs, toupees, dyes, tonics, salves, pigments, tinctures, and unguents designed to make them at least *look* young — not to mention the countless billions more spent on other chemical, surgical, or natural cosmetic aids and on various exercise, weight-reducing, and rebuilding and repair programs for aging bodies.

There are, of course, extremely wide individual variations, not only in the speed with which we age physically but also in the ways we age. Some of us will lose all our hair; the hair of others will turn snowy white. And some, like my paternal great-grandfather,

As we age, we are subjected to a series of gradual physical and sensory changes. Our hair thins, recedes, loses color; our skin becomes less elastic, more wrinkled, perhaps more discolored; our strength and stamina decline; and our vision changes so that a single pair of glasses is no longer sufficient. For those whose sense of self-worth is closely tied to their physical selves, these changes are sometimes very difficult.

will retain a thick head of raven-black hair right into their tenth decade of life.

The Senses

Like most of our physical systems, our senses are subject to the influences of time. Vision, for example, appears to be best at around age 20 and typically remains relatively constant until age 40. Because of gradual thickening of the lens, loss of lens elasticity, and increased lens density, most individuals become more farsighted beginning in middle age. In one longitudinal study of aging, it was found that by the age of 50, 88 percent of the women and all of the men had at least one pair of eyeglasses (Bayer, Whissell-Buechy, &

Honzik, 1981). Glaucoma, (increased pressure in the eye that can cause blindness if not treated), and cataracts (clouding of the lens caused by fibers) are also associated with aging. Both become more common after age 50 (Spence, 1989).

Hearing losses are also very gradual during the early years of adulthood but are typically more severe for men than for women. *Presbycusis* is the term used for hearing losses associated with age. It is most apparent in an inability to hear high-pitched sounds. Bayer, Whissell-Buechy, and Honzik (1981) report that hearing complaints at the age of 30 are very few (2 percent of the men and none of the women in the sample). By the age of 42, however, while very few women had experienced noticeable hearing loss, 14 percent of the men had—a figure that had risen to 32 percent by the age of 50.

Changes in the ability to taste appear to be very slight until later adulthood, although by the age of 50, some individuals are less sensitive to spices, salts, and sugars—a fact that most are not likely to have noticed. Loss ot taste sensitivity is common during adulthood—a condition that might be linked to heavy drinking and smoking as well as to the excessive use of salt. In later adulthood, loss of taste sensitivity often leads individuals to flavor their foods with quantities of salt and pepper that children would find almost unpalatable.

Health and Organ Function

Although health generally continues to be good through the middle years, there is a gradual decline in the efficiency of most major organ systems. For example, beginning in early adulthood, the volume of blood the heart pumps declines very slowly. At the same time, there is frequently a gradual accumulation of plaque on the insides of blood vessels (*atherosclerosis*) and a progressive hardening of artery walls (*arteriosclerosis*). This increases blood pressure and also increases the probability of a stroke (caused by the blockage of flood flow to part of the brain) and heart attack (the result of a blockage of blood flow to the heart muscle).

Other organs that become less efficient through the middle years include lungs, stomach, and liver. The lungs, for example, take in progressively less air with each breath as the person ages. This is mainly because the amount of air that remains in the lungs after expelling a breath increases from about 20 percent at the age of 20 to about 35 percent by age 65 (Klocke, 1977). Part of the reduced lung efficiency of older people is due to loss of lung tissue elasticity, as well as to increasing rib cage stiffness (Spence, 1989). As a result of declines in lung efficiency, middle-aged adults suffer from more chronic complaints such as *emphysema, bronchitis, pneumonia,,* and *tuberculosis.*

Various diseases to which individuals become more susceptible with age include cancer, arthritis, cirrhosis, hypertension (high blood pressure), and *osteoporosis*, a thinning and weakening of the bones. Women are much more prone to this latter condition than are men. And although it does not commonly become serious until later adulthood, it often begins in midlife or earlier. A diet rich in calcium (low-fat milk products, vegetables such as broccoli and turnips, and seafood products such as sardines and salmon) can help prevent osteoporosis or reduce its seriousness—as can exercise, which contributes to bone growth and strength. In addition, **estrogen replacement therapy (ERT)** is sometimes recommended after menopause (discussed shortly) or after a woman's ovaries have been surgically removed. However, estrogen therapy is somewhat controversial, given the possibility that it may be linked with a higher incidence of cancer (Katchadourian, 1987). DeLorey (1984) points out that the combination of appropriate nutrition and exercise may, in fact, be more effective than ERT for reducing the risk of osteoporosis.

Diet and Exercise

Not all middle-aged persons experience the same declines in organ functioning; nor are all equally susceptible to various diseases and infections. Genes continue to be extremely important influences on health at all stages in the lifespan. We know that susceptibility to many forms of heart disease, as well as to cancer, the two leading causes of death in the middle years, is partly inherited. At the same time, however, exercise and diet can each play a significant role in preventing disease and in delaying the effects of age. Obesity, for example, is clearly implicated in heart disease. There is evidence, too, that certain cholesterols contribute to atherosclerosis; that alcohol is a prime cause of cirrhosis of the liver; that cigarette smoking contributes to emphysema, to lung cancer, and to other forms of cancer; and that excessive salt intake is related to heart disease.

Exercise, for its part, can do a great deal to keep the middle-aged strong and healthy. The best defense against loss of muscle mass and strength is exercise. We know that exercise can also increase cardiac output, improve circulation and decrease fatty accumulation in blood vessel walls, help keep arteries and veins flexible, and prevent obesity (Spence, 1989). And, as we saw in Chapter 13, it can also contribute significantly to a general sense of well-being. In short, research leaves little doubt that a regular exercise program can improve both physical and cognitive functioning (Stones & Kozma, 1988).

The Climacteric

One area of physical change that is important for understanding the adult years involves changes in the sex glands and is popularly referred to as the *change of life* or, more properly, the **climacteric**. The term origi-

Physical exercise can help to keep joints supple, improve cardiopulmonary functioning, and maintain clear, flexible arteries and veins. In addition, it can help prevent obesity and bone loss. A regular exercise program can also do much to improve our sense of well-being and perhaps even to improve cognitive functioning. It may contribute something to the health of the family pooch as well.

nates from two Greek words meaning "critical time" and "rung" (as of a ladder). Use of the expression is perhaps unfortunate; it implies too strongly that the rung is critical — that it might break or not be reached, or cause pain and suffering.

A Biological Event.

Among women, the climacteric involves *menopause*, the cessation of menstruation. Among men, the climacteric is more subtle, which has

led to some debate concerning whether it is fruitful or even appropriate to speak of a male climacteric or change of life.

The secretion of the sex hormones by the ovaries (primarily estrogen) and the testes (primarily testosterone) is among the most important changes of pubescence (see Chapter 11). These hormones are closely involved in the development of secondary sexual characteristics (breasts, facial hair, voice changes, and

► Subject Female; age 31; never married; university education; successful career in a helping profession.

► Question "When do you think the 'prime of life' is?"

....

66 *I'm not sure. Some people say around 40. I think maybe it's earlier. Like around . . . in the twenties. That's when you're the strongest and everything, and all your goals and your life is still ahead of you. But maybe men are in their prime later than women, because after the age of 40 or maybe even 50 women are getting old, but men don't seem that old even when they're 40 or even 50. Men can get married and have children when they're pretty old; when a woman is past 35, she's pretty well finished. If she hasn't had any yet, too bad. Her prime, at least for having kids, is finished.* 99

so on), as well as in sexual interest and behavior. Their production continues, relatively unabated, from puberty through early adulthood. But by the late thirties or early forties among women, and perhaps by the early fifties for men, the production of sex hormones begins to decrease. Among men, this decrease is often very gradual and not easily noticed.

Among women, changes in production of sex hormones are considerably less gradual and far more noticeable and are linked with the woman's declining store of ova (Finch, 1988). Women are born with about seven or eight hundred thousand immature ova. By puberty, half of these have died; and by the early forties, few—if any—are left.

Among the first signs of menopause in women are changes in menstrual pattern: irregularity, skipping of

menstrual periods, or noticeably reduced discharge during menstruation. Eventually, menstruation stops entirely.

A Psychological Event?

Strictly speaking, menopause is a biological event with discernible causes and clear biological effects—specifically, cessation of ovulation and menstruation, and consequent permanent infertility. But in many of the world's cultures, it is also a psychological event. In industrialized Western societies, for example, menopause is sometimes accompanied by a number of symptoms and complaints such as "hot flashes," dizziness, headaches, mood fluctuations, tremors, and weakness. In as many as one third of all women, these symptoms are serious enough to cause the women to consult a physician (Katchadourian, 1987).

However, evidence from cross-cultural studies suggests that the occasional negative consequences of menopause may be largely contextual. Datan, Rodeheaver, and Hughes (1987) report, for example, that among five different Israeli subcultures, the psychological consequences of menopause are quite different from North American patterns. In these cultures, loss of fertility is a *welcome* event, and its consequence is typically positive. Similarly, Flint (1975) found the Rajput women of East India manifested none of the negative psychological and physical complaints normally associated with menopause elsewhere. Women of this caste, too, openly look forward to menopause. Flint suggests this is perhaps because prior to menopause, they are not allowed to associate publicly with men; after menopause, however, they can visit and socialize freely. As a result, menopause leads to an elevation of their status. In contrast, in many Western societies, loss of fertility may be viewed as an implicit loss of status. Thus many women await it with resignation rather than anticipation; and once it has occurred, a sizable proportion experience negative emotions and related physical complaints.

Beyene (1989), who studied menopause among Mayan and Greek peasant women, also found evidence that many of its symptoms are context specific. For example, the most common menopausal symptom among the Greek women was hot flashes. Cold sweats, insomnia, and irritability were also relatively common; depression was rare, but did occur occasionally. In contrast, *none* of the Mayan women experienced *any* of these symptoms. About one third of them experienced headaches and dizziness (more than 40 percent of the

Greek women reported these symptoms); and about one fifth experienced hemorrhaging (12 percent of the Greek women reported hemorrhaging).

These differences, claims Beyene, cannot be accounted for solely in terms of role changes or cultural expectations given marked similarities among the peasant women in their attitudes toward menopause and in the social implications of the event. In other areas such as diet and childbearing patterns, however, the women were very different. Mayan women typically had protein-deficient diets, consisting primarily of corn and very rarely of meat or eggs; Greek women ate meat and cheese, and a variety of legumes. Also, more than half of the Mayan women had five or more children (one in five had eight or more); more than 60 percent of the Greek women had two children or fewer. More cross-cultural studies are needed to clarify the role of these and other variables, says Beyene.

Treatment.   Where problems accompanying menopause are sufficiently serious, they are sometimes treated with estrogen replacement therapy (ERT). In effect, this therapy serves to replace some of the estrogen that is no longer being produced after menopause. As we saw, ERT is also sometimes used in an attempt to reduce the risk and seriousness of osteoporosis, but remains a controversial therapy given its possible association with cancer.

A summary of research on the psychological consequences of menopause in North America suggests four important conclusions (Parlee, 1984): (1) The negative symptoms traditionally associated with menopause do *not* affect the majority of women; (2) changes in women at midlife are affected in important ways by changes in women's social roles, and by changing relationships with spouse, children, and parents; (3) the psychological effect of the climacteric cannot easily be disentangled from the psychological effect of other normal changes of the aging process; and (4) menopause is often used, both by physicians and by others, as an explanation for symptoms that have other causes.

Although symptoms similar to those that occasionally accompany menopause have sometimes been reported by men, there is little evidence that they might be tied to hormonal changes that are common to most men. In fact, hormonal changes among men are seldom sufficient to lead to infertility, although they often do lead to a reduction in the number of viable sperm that are produced.

Sexuality

Sexual functioning among men and women does not normally change with the climacteric. Most women continue to be interested in sex and capable of orgasm, although there might be some reduction in vaginal lubrication following arousal. Among men, changes in sexual interest and functioning are gradual and vary a great deal from one individual to another. It may now take longer for the man to achieve an erection, both before and after intercourse, and the erection might not always be as firm as it was some decades ago. In addition, ejaculation itself will typically be less forceful. Unfortunately, these highly common changes are seldom discussed openly and are often interpreted as evidence of rapidly declining sexual prowess—an event that can lead to considerable anxiety concerning sexual performance and that is often implicated in the man's resulting impotence. In fact, among men, the process of aging does not entail the loss of ability to perform sexually.

Cognitive Changes

Many of the physical changes of aging are obvious. We can *see* the wrinkles and the sags, the graying and the thickening, the bending and the slowing. Cognitive changes, however, are not so obvious. Do they even occur? We have had little difficulty in answering this question with respect to childhood and adolescence when, at every succeeding age, we could detect increases in comprehension and reasoning, and in the ability to analyze, synthesize, and solve problems. The task is not so simple with respect to adults and has led to considerable controversy. Does cognitive ability, like strength, vision, and the elasticity of our skin, reach a peak in early or middle adulthood, enter a period of stability, and then begin a downhill slide—slow and imperceptible at first but gradually more rapid until, in the words of Shakespeare, we reach again our "second childishness"? Or does it continue to grow so that, when we are finally old, we might also be truly wise?

Controversy About IQ Changes

At first glance, it might not seem very difficult to answer these questions. After all, if cognitive ability is reflected in measured IQ, all we should need to do is

TABLE 15.2

Mean Scores for Five Primary Mental Abilities for Mean Ages 25–88

	Primary Mental Ability				
Mean Age	Verbal Meaning	Spatial Orientation	Inductive Reasoning	Number	Word Fluency
25	54.38	56.25	59.11	48.87	55.06
32	54.53	55.40	58.15	51.44	55.11
39	56.17	55.21	57.84	51.39	54.93
46	55.68	55.69	56.23	51.77	53.64
53	53.90	53.46	54.17	50.98	52.58
60	52.65	51.44	51.43	52.31	50.09
67	49.31	48.27	47.44	50.67	48.06
74	44.59	44.63	43.37	48.80	46.58
81	39.14	41.53	38.74	44.15	43.53
88	34.42	37.54	36.31	41.29	40.58

Source: From "Variability in Cognitive Function in the Elderly: Implications for Social Participation" by K. W. Schaie, December 1986. Paper presented at the Symposium on Phenotypic Variation in Populations: Relevance to Risk Assessment. Upton, NY: Brookhaven National Laboratory. Reprinted by permission.

administer appropriate tests to the appropriate people, and *violà*, an answer: Intelligence increases fantastically with age; intelligence decreases with age; intelligence doesn't change; or intelligence changes this way to begin with, then that way, and then that way.

What do the experts tell us? They tell us that some intellectual decline with age is inevitable. In Horn and Donaldson's (1976) words, "the evidence suggests that if one lives long enough, decrement in at least some of the important abilities of intelligence is likely to occur" (p. 701).

But Horn and Donaldson are not the only experts, and not all other experts share their views. In an article appropriately titled "The Myth of the Twilight Years," Baltes and Schaie (1974) challenge the long-held traditional belief in the inevitability of intellectual decline with age. In their words: "In the field of aging, we have argued that there was a myth, both among laymen and among professionals, that much or most of the development of intelligence in adulthood and old age is one of decline" (Baltes & Schaie, 1976).

Why the controversy? Does the evidence not provide an answer for so simple a question?

The Evidence

It turns out that the question is not so simple, and the evidence is not so clear. And much of the controversy stems from the fact that the complexity of the question and the inadequacy of the evidence have not always been recognized.

Cross-Sectional Studies. The first studies that looked at changes in intelligence associated with age were typically cross-sectional; they compared the performance of groups of individuals of different ages. Almost invariably, when the intelligence test scores of older subjects were compared with those of adolescents or young adults, the adults did less well (Schaie, 1986). On general intelligence tests such as the Stanford-Binet and the WAIS (Wechsler Adult Intelligence Scale), the highest scores are almost always obtained by adolescents (or young adults), with progressively lower scores for older age groups. The same is also true of measures of specific mental abilities such as knowledge of verbal meaning, inductive reasoning, number concepts, and so on (see Table 15.2).

But the implications of these cross-sectional studies were not quite so clear-cut. Although they almost invariably found a significant decline in measured IQ beginning in the late twenties or thirties, patterns of decline were not consistent across all abilities. Some abilities (for example, verbal ones) declined less than others (inductive reasoning, for example) (Bromley, 1990).

There are, in fact, several reasons other than lower intelligence that might explain apparent decline. Many of these have to do with the fact that the studies upon which conclusions of decline are based are primarily cross-sectional. As we saw in Chapter 1, cross-sectional studies have significant weaknesses—and, of course, significant strengths.

Perhaps most important among their weaknesses is the fact that they cannot take into account the influence of cohort variables. A cross-sectional study that presents intelligence tests to groups of 70-year-olds and 20-year-olds in 1990 is comparing different cohorts—in this case, a cohort born in 1970 with one born in 1920. Clearly, these cohorts have been exposed to dramatically different environmental influences. Among other things, individuals born in 1920 have spent considerably less time in school than those born in 1970, were not exposed to television and computers in their childhood, are often totally unfamiliar with the types of items in most intelligence tests, may never have been exposed to electronically scored answer sheets with their fine print and their demand for careful eye–hand coordination, and might be quite intimidated by the entire testing procedure.

Longitudinal Studies.   Longitudinal studies do not bring with them the same problems that cross-sectional research does. Recall that a longitudinal study compares the performance of the same individuals at different times. For example, a study that presents intelligence tests to a group of 20-year-olds in 1944 and presents the same test to the same individuals in 1964 and again in 1984 is longitudinal. It provides far better data for reaching conclusions with respect to changes that are age-related rather than specific to cohort variables

(Schaie, 1988). However, their findings might be valid for only one cohort.

Sequential Studies.   Sequential designs combine elements of longitudinal and cross-sectional studies and avoid some of the disadvantages of each. One good example is Schaie's (1983c) investigation of intelligence mentioned in Chapter 1. To review briefly, the study was a 28-year longitudinal study (the Seattle Longitudinal Study), with intelligence testing of all subjects at 7-year intervals and the addition of new samples at each of the five testing times. Subjects ranged in age from 25 to 88. Thus the study permitted comparison of different cohorts (cross-sectional) as well as the investigation of each of four cohorts over a 28-year period.

The results of the cross-sectional part of the study were as expected: There appears to be an age-related decline in performance on the Primary Mental Abilities Test (see Table 15.2). However, when different cohorts are compared with each other, it becomes apparent that the earlier-born cohorts are generally at a disadvantage. This suggests that at least part of the decline in intellectual functioning is due to cohort-related influences (such as schooling, for example) rather than to age. And this possibility is further supported by the results of the longitudinal part of the investigation. Vastly simplified, these results show very little decline within cohorts over the 28-year period prior to the age of 67! In fact, for some abilities such as verbal meanings, performance continues to increase slightly after age 25; at age 88, individuals still perform as well as at age 25 (see Figure 15.2). But for other abilities such as spatial orientation, there is, in fact, some decline (see Figure 15.3).

A Conclusion

There are two conclusions supported by the current evidence:

- There is a decline in some measures of intellectual capacity or performance with age.

- Some measures of intellectual capacity are stable or continue to increase through early and middle adulthood and sometimes even into old age.

The two conclusions are clearly not contradictory but complementary. Taken together, they might do

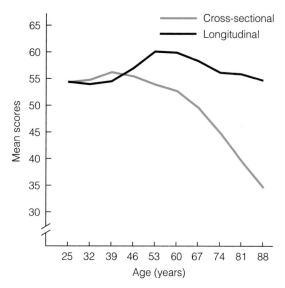

Figure 15.2 Comparison of cross-sectional and longitudinal age differences for verbal meaning. (Adapted from Schaie, 1986. Used by permission of Brookhaven National Laboratory.)

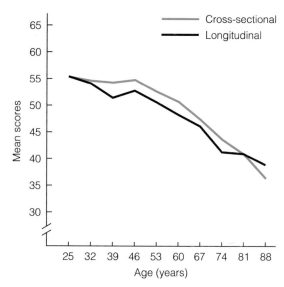

Figure 15.3 Comparison of cross-sectional and longitudinal age differences for spatial orientation. (Adapted from Schaie, 1986. Used by permission of Brookhaven National Laboratory.)

much to resolve the Baltes/Schaie–Horn/Donaldson controversy that opened this section.

An important question asks what aspects of intellectual performance increase or remain stable, which decline, and why. The answer appears to be that those capacities that depend on underlying physiological mechanisms—on a smoothly functioning nervous system, for example—are mostly likely to decline with age. These capacities define what Cattell calls *fluid* intelligence. Fluid abilities are not dependent on experience but seem to depend more on some underlying, basic capacity. They are reflected in general reasoning, memory, attention span, and analysis of figures.

Capacities that depend more on experience are most likely to remain stable or even to increase. After all, why shouldn't general information, vocabulary, and the other legacies of experience not continue to increase with increasing experience? These capacities define *crystallized* intelligence. Crystallized abilities are those that are influenced by culture. They depend on education and experience, and are reflected in measures of vocabulary, general information, and arithmetic skills. Our reasoning suggests that fluid abilities would decline with age and that crystallized abilities would remain

stable or perhaps increase. That, in fact, is the case, as is shown in Figures 15.4 and 15.5.

Back to the Controversy

Although it is generally true that some capacities decline with age while others either remain stable or increase slightly, it is not true that global measures of intellectual performance, such as IQ scores, inevitably decline through middle adulthood. For some individuals in the Berkeley Growth Studies, there were significant increases in measured IQ between ages 17 and 18, and again between ages 36 and 48 (Honzik, 1984). As might be expected, these increases are related primarily to better performance on crystallized (culture-influenced) measures. Not surprisingly, the people most likely to continue to perform well or even to improve their performance as they age are those whose spouses were significantly more intelligent than they themselves were to begin with (in terms of measured IQ). There appears to be little doubt that continued intellectual stimulation and opportunity to stretch the capacities

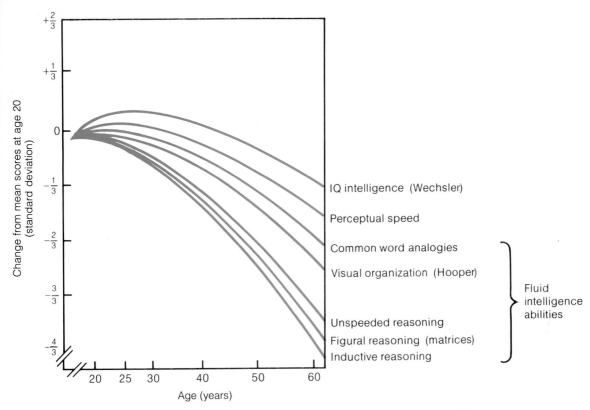

Figure 15.4 Smoothed curves summarizing several studies on aging and fluid intelligence. (From Horn & Donaldson in Brim & Kagan, 1980, p. 469.)

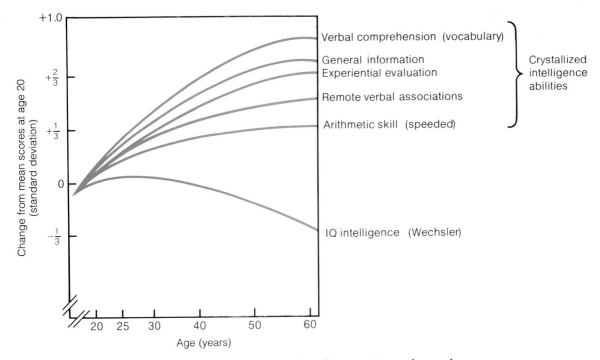

Figure 15.5 Smoothed curves summarizing several studies on aging and crystallized intelligence. (From Horn & Donaldson in Brim & Kagan, 1980, p. 471.)

that define intelligence are closely related to maintaining or improving peak performance. It is worth noting, as well, that those who experienced the greatest intellectual declines in the Berkeley studies often were heavy drinkers or had suffered some illness.

The controversy? In retrospect, it seems that it can be resolved relatively easily, although it has been a hotly debated issue (see the Further Readings section at the end of this chapter for a pertinent reference). There is no direct contradiction, in fact, between the Baltes/ Schaie and the Horn/Donaldson statements included at the beginning of this section. Horn and Donaldson argue that there is "decrement in at least some important abilities of intelligence" if we live long enough; Baltes and Schaie counter that the belief that "much or most of the development of intelligence in adulthood and old age is one of decline" is a "myth."

The disagreement is more one of degree and emphasis than of directly opposing beliefs. Although most researchers do not deny that decline is frequently observed, the majority maintain that belief in its inevitability and irreversibility is not warranted. As Bromley (1990) notes, the reasons for decline may often be physical factors such as reduced oxygen supply to the brain—which may in turn be due to reversible conditions such as illnesses, stress, or even lack of exercise.

The most sensible conclusion at this point is an optimistic one. Decline in important areas such as verbal ability, reasoning, and numerical skills is usually inconsequential until well into the sixties and appears to be occurring later for succeeding generations (Schaie & Labouvie-Vief, 1974). Given appropriate environmental stimulation, not only will many cognitive abilities not decrease with age, but some may actually continue to increase well into old age. Wisdom, which we discuss in Chapter 17 (along with other aspects of cognitive change), may be a case in point.

To the extent that there *are* cognitive changes with age, it is reasonable to expect that these changes will be reflected in the ways in which information is processed—that is, in changes in learning, remembering, and problem solving.

Thinking in Middle Adulthood

As we saw in Chapter 13, current views of adult thinking have changed remarkably in recent decades. We know that adults continue to learn through much of the lifespan, both formally and incidentally (Rossing,

1991). It is inevitable that this learning should be reflected in their thinking.

Researchers such as Labouvie-Vief and Basseches argue that the problems that adults face, and the circumstances of their lives, exercise a profound influence on their cognitive processes. The formal logic of a Piagetian system might be suitable in an academic setting, or perhaps even for the adolescent who has not yet learned that there are reasons why logic is not always the only—or even the best—approach. Real-life problems often require experience as much as logic, and their solutions need to reflect practical realities. As Hoyer (1985) notes, a comprehensive and useful model of the cognitive competence of adults must consider "experience-based real knowledge and acquired competencies . . . while recognizing that some elementary information processing skills and their control processes may show selective deficits with age" (p. 82).

Basseches (1984) also argues that a uniquely adult form of reasoning evolves through early adulthood and into the middle years. It is a form of thinking that is *dialectical*. Not only are adult dialectical thinkers more sensitive to contradictions—and more tolerant of them—but they have learned a series of procedures (*dialectical schemata*) for dealing with them. Thus they have an ability to reason about political and social systems, as well as about interpersonal relationships, that is not commonly found in younger individuals. And perhaps that is why, for many adults, the middle years are the most creative of the entire lifespan.

Creative Output

Perhaps the most convincing evidence of the middle-aged person's continuing ability to learn, solve problems, and remember is found in the creative output of adults. Among the first studies in this area were Lehman's (1953) estimates of the age ranges during which peak creativity, leadership, and achievement occurred. Results of these studies indicated that the peak in most areas (the sciences, mathematics, music) occurred in the thirties, except for the writing of novels and other books (excluding poetry), which peaked in the forties. Achievement in athletics, as we noted earlier, peaks during the twenties.

Later analyses revealed that Lehman's studies had used some questionable procedures (including failing to take subject mortality into account) and that his estimates of ages of peak performance were therefore

TABLE 15.3

Creative Output by Decade for Persons Living to Age 79 or More

Area	Number of Men	Number of Works	Decade					
			20s	30s	40s	50s	60s	70s
Scholarship								
History	46	615	3	19	19	22	24	20
Philosophy	42	225	3	17	20	18	22	20
Scholarship	43	326	6	17	21	21	16	19
Sciences								
Biology	32	3456	5	22	24	19	17	13
Botany	49	1889	4	15	22	22	22	15
Chemistry	24	2420	11	21	24	19	12	13
Geology	40	2672	3	13	22	28	19	14
Invention	44	646	2	10	17	18	32	21
Mathematics	36	3104	8	20	20	18	19	15
Arts								
Architecture	44	1148	7	24	29	25	10	4
Chamber music	35	109	15	21	17	20	18	9
Drama	25	803	10	27	29	21	9	3
Librettos	38	164	8	21	30	22	15	4
Novels	32	494	5	19	18	28	23	7
Operas	176	476	8	30	31	16	10	5
Poetry	46	402	11	21	26	16	16	10

Source: From "Creative Productivity Between the Ages of 20 and 80" by W. Dennis, 1966,
Journal of Gerontology, 21, pp. 1–18. Reprinted by permission of the publisher.

biased toward the younger age groups. (Many creative individuals in his samples didn't live long enough to demonstrate that it is possible to be creative in old age.) Subsequent investigations undertaken by Dennis (1966) found that the age of peak achievement in most areas is substantially higher than Lehman had estimated (see Table 15.3). Peak production seldom occurs before the forties, and sometimes even the fifties and sixties. In fact, in many areas, it continues well into the seventies.

And when peak production declines during the middle years, this does not always mean that the capacity for creative production has also declined. Diamond (1986) points out that many highly successful adults find their creative output reduced precisely because of their success. In many fields, those who are the highest producers are also those who are most likely to be promoted. Administrative responsibilities might then severely reduce the individual's output.

In many areas, creative production is based not only on the special predispositions and talents that make up the creative personality (see Chapter 9) but also on a large store of relevant information and experience. Dennis's finding that creative output in most areas seldom peaks before the forties should come as no surprise. In fact, there are some who believe that creativity in later life is unique in that it is based not only on talent but also on wisdom (Hildebrand, 1990).

A Summary

There is a rapidly accumulating body of information concerning systematic cognitive changes in middle adulthood. These include significant increases in measured IQ, particularly for individuals whose lives expose them to intellectual stimulation; a gradual shift

U.S. Women in the Work Force

At the turn of the century, fewer than 20 percent of American women were in the work force. By midcentury, the percentage had doubled, and by 1989, it had almost tripled. During this time, the percentage of men in the work force hardly changed.

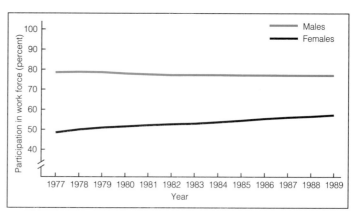

Figure 15.6 Female increase and (slight) male decrease in work force participation, 1977–1989. (From U.S. Department of Labor, 1988, p. 7, and U.S. Bureau of the Census, 1991, p. 384.)

from an egocentric reliance on logic to a more prag-matic form of reasoning more firmly grounded in social reality; changes in intellectual functioning related to the nature of the abilities involved, with experience-dependent (crystallized) abilities improving with age; and an indication that the thought processes of the adult are more sensitive to contradictions, more tolerant of them, and better able to resolve them dialectically, em-ploying modes of thinking not ordinarily available to younger thinkers. Furthermore, the middle years are often the most creatively productive period of the entire lifespan.

Work

Not only are the middle years the most *creatively* pro-ductive, they are also the most productive in the area of careers and jobs. Middle-aged adults hold more ad-ministrative positions than younger workers and they earn more. In general, they are more competent.

In Chapter 13, we discussed the nature and rewards of work, changes in attitudes toward work as well as in employment opportunities, and processes involved in selecting and preparing for careers. As we saw, there have been major changes in employment opportunities in recent decades. No one has been more affected by these changes than women.

Women in the Workplace

Between 1900 and 1970, the percentage of adult women working for a salary in North America more than doubled (from 20 to 45 percent; Sheppard, 1976). By 1988, about 75 percent of women between 18 and 44 were employed (U.S. Bureau of the Census, 1991) (see Figure 15.6). Age groups most likely to work outside the home include young adults prior to marriage and those whose children have left home (ages 45–64). In addition, black women and those from poorer groups have always been more likely to work than more afflu-ent, white middle-class women. Figure 15.7 shows the relative distribution of the U.S. work force in 1989 by age, sex, and marital status. Note that the curve for females is bimodal. That is, there are two age periods of peak employment for females rather than a single period as for males—one occurs shortly after 20 (prior

to marriage or children) and the other shortly after 45 (after children have left home).

Male–Female Differences at Work

Fewer women than men work for a salary—75 percent of all women between 18 and 44 in 1988, compared with over 90 percent of all men (U.S. Bureau of the Census, 1991). As mentioned previously, typical female occupations are not yet on a par with male occupations in terms of status, prestige, or income. For example, 80 percent of clerical workers, 63 percent of service workers, and 62 percent of retail sales workers are females. In contrast, only 6 percent are craft workers, and only 28 percent are managers and administrators (Tittle, 1982).

Average income for females is about 65 percent that of males (Statistics Canada, 1992, see Figure 15.8). In 1988, women with four years of college earned less than men who had only completed high school (U.S. Bureau of the Census, 1991). Those with high school diplomas earned less than men who had not completed elementary school (see Figure 15.9).

The reasons women work are often not very dif-ferent from the reasons men work, although many women are not as career-oriented as men, a fact that may well be due to the greater number of low-status jobs that many women occupy (Lopata & Barnewolt, 1984).

Research on job satisfaction reveals that working women are, on the average, happier than those who do not work outside the home. In addition, middle-aged career women tend to have higher self-esteem than other women, whether they are single or married (Joshi, Garon, & Lechasseur, 1984). Also, work satis-faction appears to increase with age, even for those women who are responsible for the dual roles: career, on the one hand, and homemaking and child rearing, on the other (Huston-Stein & Higgins-Trenk, 1978). There appears to be relatively little conflict between being a mother and working at the same time, although there is a possibility of work overload (see the section on dual careers).

Social Changes

In the relatively recent past, women who continued their education after 12th grade or who took one of various job-training courses often claimed that they

Inequity in the Workplace

Despite dramatic changes in the workplace, certain forms of employment are still primarily male, and others female. In the United States in 1989, for example, more than 10 million precision production jobs (mechanics, construction trades, repairs) were held by males, and fewer than 1 million by females. In contrast, more than 11 million clerical, support, and office administration positions were held by females, and only 3 million by males. In the United States, the average income of female workers in 1988 was only 63.1 percent that of males. The ratio of female–male earnings for all full-time workers in Canada in 1987 was 65.3. Gains since 1967 have been small (see Figure 15.8); and a woman with four years of college can still expect to earn *less* than a man with no more than a secondary school education (see Figure 15.9).

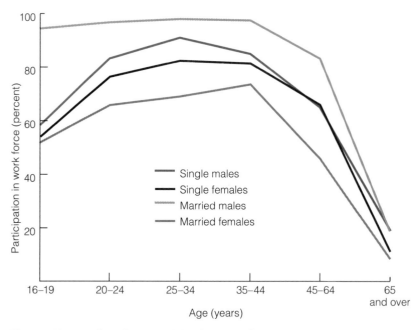

Figure 15.7 Labor force participation rates by age, sex, and marital status in the United States, 1989. (From U.S. Bureau of the Census, 1991, p. 390.)

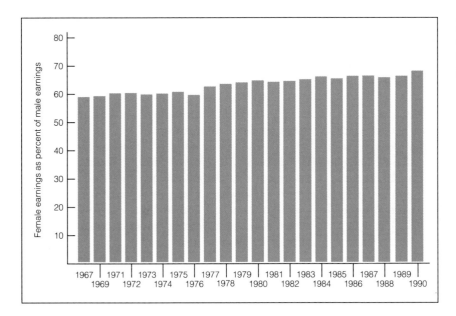

Figure 15.8 Changes in ratio of female-to-male earnings in Canada, 1967–1990. (Based on Statistics Canada, 1992, p. 12.)

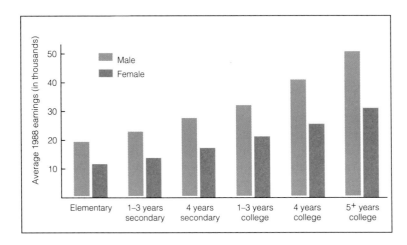

Figure 15.9 U.S. male and female earnings by educational attainment in 1988. (Based on U.S. Bureau of the Census, 1991, p. 459.)

were doing so in order "to have something to fall back on later." The implicit, and sometimes explicit, assumption that these women made was that they would marry, and bear and raise their children while the husband earned their bread. Having to "fall back" was something that would happen only in the wake of some great misfortune that would make it impossible for the husband to provide for his wife and children.

Not so any longer. Few people still believe that the home is woman's only rightful place. And an increasing number of women continue their education, not to have something to fall back on but so that they can pursue their own careers. However, because close to 50 percent of all young-adult marriages eventually end in divorce, there is sometimes a real need to have "something to fall back on."

Changing social conditions are reflected not only in the increasing numbers of women who have entered the work force but also in the fact that the *expected* family pattern, where the man works outside the home and the woman inside, describes fewer than 20 percent of all contemporary American families. Approximately 55 percent of two-parent families also have two wage earners (U.S. Department of Labor, 1988). Increasing numbers of families have deliberately chosen not to have children. Furthermore, single-parent families headed by a woman are now as common as the more traditional two-parent family, where the male is the sole wage earner (Eisenstein, 1982). Clearly, there have been some profound changes in the American family.

Dual Careers

Families with two wage earners now appear to be the norm rather than the exception. However, a two-earner family is not necessarily a dual-career family. A career, as we saw, is defined by a relatively systematic progression through a series of related occupations. Unlike a simple job, a career demands commitment and loyalty; typically, it requires a greater investment of time and energy.

A dual-career family is one in which both the husband and the wife have separate careers and the career of neither is sacrificed for the other — or for the family. Among college populations, the notion of a dual-career family has apparently become increasingly popular. In one survey, more than 80 percent of both male and female college students indicated they were interested in having a dual-career family (Nadelson & Nadelson, 1980).

Surveys of dual-career couples reveal that they often share several common characteristics. Typically, for example, the husband and the wife have very similar values, possess relatively high-level job skills, are self-reliant and independent, and have high incomes. It is also quite common for these couples either not to have children or to have small families, which are typically started only after the wife has already established her career (Hertz, 1986).

Double Careers. Dual-career families sometimes present their members with unique sets of problems. One of the best known of these affects the wife rather than the husband, and results from the fact that many wives not only are members of a dual-career partnership but also are involved in a double career (also referred to as a *double-track* career). The difference between a dual career and a double career is simple. Dual careers exist where two people develop separate and individual careers; a double career exists where a *single* person assumes the responsibilities of two careers at the same time.

Double careers are common among wives who are responsible for their careers outside the home and who must also assume responsibility for a tremendous range of home-related tasks: cooking, cleaning, supervising, child rearing, and so on. What is perhaps surprising is that most college students and, indeed, most young couples believe strongly that if both husband and wife are to have individual careers, each should share domestic responsibilities equally. Ironically, however, this is not often the case in practice. There are still pervasive and often unconscious gender-role stereotypes that view the woman's career as secondary to the husband's and that also view child rearing and domestic tasks as primarily female responsibilities (Pleck, 1985).

One of the possible results of the tremendous burden of responsibilities that the double-tracked woman carries is *burnout* — a term used to describe a situation where the individual no longer feels able to cope. Ways of preventing burnout, or of relieving its effects, might include abandoning or postponing the wife's career, enlisting the husband's help with domestic duties (difficult in practice), making children increasingly responsible for their own care, or hiring domestic help or "nannies."

Working Women in Canada

In 1984 in Canada, slightly more lone (single) female parents than wives living with husbands were in the work force (61 and 57 percent, respectively). Interestingly, the percentage of wives in the work force does not change appreciably between ages 25 and 54; however, the number of working lone female parents increases dramatically, peaking at 83 percent between ages 40 and 44, and then declining again. At most ages, there appears to be a greater need for lone parents to work.

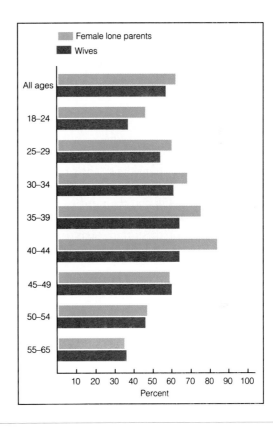

Figure 15.10 Working wives and lone ("single") parents in Canada, 1984. (Based on Pool & Moore, 1986, p. 37.)

Children of Working Mothers

In the United States, more than 70 percent of mothers in two-parent families now work outside the home (Hoffman, 1989). Figures for lone parents are even higher. (See Figure 15.10 for statistics on working mothers in Canada.) Among those who have firmly believed that the mother's place is at home with her children, this has been a source of alarm. There have been fears that the wholesale entry of women into the workplace not only would erode traditional family values but also might have highly negative effects on children. There may indeed be instances of child neglect and abuse that can be related to the mother's working. But overall, as we saw in Chapter 8, children of working mothers who are placed in day-care facilities during working hours suffer no measurable disadvantages relative to other children. Similarly, children of career mothers do not seem to be at a disadvantage and might even have a small advantage in some areas.

One advantage that children in dual-career families appear to have relates to the benefits of having fathers who are more involved in parenting than might otherwise be the case. Boys in these families often develop fewer gender-role biases and tend to have a more egalitarian view of male–female roles (Hoffman, 1989). In addition, dual-career families present children with a wider range of role models and tend to foster independence, achievement, and high feelings of self-worth (Nadelson & Nadelson, 1980).

Voluntary Career Changes

In Levinson's (1981) description of the seasons of our lives, there are three major transitions: The first occurs between adolescence and adulthood (ages 17–22); the second is at midlife (40–45); and the third is between middle adulthood and late adulthood (60–65). According to Levinson, each of these transitions entails an analysis and evaluation of our dreams and often results in important adjustments in how we view ourselves and our lives. One of the more radical of the adjustments that people sometimes make is that of a midlife career change.

Not all career changes occur at midlife, however, and not all such changes are voluntary. As Isaacson (1986) points out, there are involuntary career changes as well as those that are undertaken deliberately.

There are many reasons people might choose to change careers. As Levinson (1978) and Sheehy (1981) suggest, changes that occur at midlife might well result from the resolution of the crises that sometimes mark that period. The individual might reevaluate the present and find that reality hasn't measured up to the *dream* that motivated earlier choices. Or perhaps the dream itself will have changed, and goals that seemed important at 25 might now seem trivial. (See Chapter 16 for a summary of Sheehy and Levinson.)

In Chapter 16, we look at evidence that indicates that, for men, the midlife trend is often one of increasing concern with social and emotional issues, with family and friends, with relationships. Accordingly, careers that have demanded a tremendous investment of time and energy, and that do not allow sufficient time for these new concerns, might be abandoned in favor of more gentle, less aggressive pursuits. For women, the midlife trend is often opposite to that of men; they become more career-oriented, more aggressive, more interested in exploring their strengths and talents, and in testing their limits in different settings. Their career changes might be motivated accordingly.

There are many other reasons people might voluntarily change careers through the lifespan. Technological changes sometimes make people restless about the permanence and value of their present careers; alternatively, these changes can open up exciting new fields and, rather than chasing people from careers, might attract them instead. Thus new opportunities can attract people to different careers, even as changed circumstances in existing careers might drive some people away.

Heald (1977) suggests that another relatively common reason for voluntary midlife career changes is the emptying of the family nest. When the little ones have flitted away, the parents are freed. They have less reason to fear the risks that might come with career changes. In addition, mothers who have interrupted their schooling or their careers to raise children can now resume the interrupted activity. If the mother begins to earn a second family income, the resulting reduction in the financial risk involved will sometimes lead to the father's changing careers. Interestingly, however, career changes are seldom made specifically to increase income (Atchley, 1985).

Not surprisingly, studies that have looked at the characteristics of people who voluntarily decide to change careers have often found these people to be more self-reliant, somewhat more willing to take risks, and generally characterized by feelings of control and power (Heath, 1976). This is not to say, however, that all people who change careers are more in control, more self-reliant, and less characterized by feelings of powerlessness. In Vaitenas and Wiener's (1977) investigation of career changes, for example, a significant number of those who made many career changes had fluctuating and unstable interests, had a high fear of failure, and suffered from emotional problems. Their reasons for changing careers likely would be quite different from those who are more self-reliant and in control.

Beyene, Y. (1989). *From menarche to menopause: Reproductive lives of peasant women in two cultures.* New York: State University of New York Press.

Pan American Health Organization. (1989). *Midlife and older women in Latin America and the Caribbean.* Washington, DC: PAHO; World Health Organization.

A collection of views of changes that occur in cognitive function with age is:

Schooler, C., & Schaie, K. W. (Eds.). (1987). *Cognitive functioning and social structure over the life course.* Norwood, NJ: Ablex.

Changes in the employment of women, and issues relating to dual careers, are discussed in:

Hertz, R. (1986). *More equal than others: Women and men in dual-career marriages.* Berkeley: University of California Press.

Pleck, J. H. (1985). *Working wives/working husbands.* Beverly Hills, CA: Sage.

CHAPTER 16

Social Development: Middle Adulthood

Spring still makes spring in
the mind

When sixty years are told.

Ralph Waldo Emerson,
The World Soul

But the spring in the mind may have a different reality than the spring of earlier years. You see, the seasons of our lives follow each other, nose to tail, in a straight line. In childhood, when all our seasons stretch unbroken before us, we know that they will last forever. Even as adolescents, we continue to believe that our personal winters will never come — that we are special. That's part of adolescent egocentrism — part of our own personal fable of invulnerability.

But somewhere in the middle years, Neugarten (1968) tells us, there is a change in our perception of personal time. Age is no longer simply a question of how long we have lived, but more a question of how much — or how little — there is still to come. And our youthful myth of immortality and invulnerability crumbles.

Perhaps middle age is only the autumn of our lives; but our springs and summers are gone.

Still, as we see in Chapters 17 and 18, our winters might yet be our very best seasons.

This Chapter

Chapter 16 looks at some of the theories that try to clarify the seasons of our lives, and especially the stages and transitions of the middle adult years (40 or 45 to about 60 or 65). It looks in turn at theories described by Erikson, Peck, Levinson, Sheehy, and Gould; and then it asks the question: Is there a period in our middle years when, overwhelmed by existential anguish, we struggle more desperately with the meaningfulness of our lives? Is there, in the popular jargon, a **midlife crisis**?

The chapter then looks at the importance of relationships with spouse, with children, with aging parents, with friends; it examines personality changes in middle adulthood; and finally, it presents a recipe for happiness and satisfaction.

Theories and Descriptions of Middle Adulthood

Our intuitive notions about the life cycle, says Nanpon (1991), agree remarkably well with those of the experts — except that younger people tend to view the later stages of life as occurring at earlier ages. He asked 100 beginning psychology students to trace a "life" line across a sheet of paper, mark it off into major life stages with specific age boundaries, label each of these stages, and describe the key characteristics of each. Students were free to describe as many or as few stages as they wished.

Most students described the expected preadult stages: infancy, the preschool period, preadolescence, and adolescence. Many described adulthood as beginning at 18, and a large number thought age 25 represented a significant transition to life as a couple (or its equivalent). The next important transition was age 40, which students saw as the beginning of a transition between adulthood and old age. For a remarkable number (25 of the 100), age 50 was seen as the end of professional life and the beginning of old age. Another 48 thought old age began later, at about age 60.

According to Nanpon's students, the key characteristics of the middle years (beginning at around age 40) are those of maturity linked with responsibility, work, and family. According to the respondents, it is also a period of transition marked by growing ambivalence: "People want to be mature and responsible, but they want to stay young." "People are afraid to age." "It's a difficult transition." "People try to start over again." "People try to start living again."

Those who saw age 50 as an important middle-age boundary used the world "old age" 14 times when describing the stage. Key concepts associated with this age include menopause, retirement, and end of professional activity. On a more positive note, a number of participants described the stage as one involving the marriage of children, grandparenting, and the continuation of life.

Our intuitive notions of stages of the life cycle, says Nanpon, are typically tied to important sociocultural events—for example, access to school, voting or drinking age, average ages of marriage and retirement. Erikson's theory, too, is tied to social and cultural demands.

Erikson's Psychosocial Development

Erikson's theory of psychosocial development describes *crises* at every developmental stage—crises that arise primarily from social demands placed on the individual. Progress at each stage requires acquiring a competence or an attitude that resolves the conflict underlying the crisis. In early adulthood, for example, the individual confronts the profoundly important task of achieving intimacy and, at the same time, overcoming an urge to remain independent, to retain the autonomy and the personal identity that have been achieved in earlier developmental stages. These urges make it difficult to achieve the commitment that is required for genuine, mutual intimacy—the kind of intimacy that, according to Erikson, is most often found in a marital relationship. Hence the conflict; and hence, too, the stage's label: *intimacy versus isolation.*

In the middle years, individuals are faced with a new developmental task and a new crisis: *generativity versus self-absorption*. With increasing maturity, the adult needs to establish the sorts of caring and work relationships that will benefit the world and the community—that is, to be generative or productive rather than absorbed in self. People can become productive in different areas. One is work. As we note in Chapter 13, for many, work is far more than a means of earning a living or of "killing time." It can be a way of *being* someone, a means of self-discovery and self-expression, an essential aspect of feeling worthwhile, as well as a means of contributing to family and society in significant ways.

Another way of expressing generativity is through the establishment of a family, by producing children and acting as a parent. Note, again, Erikson's continuing emphasis on the individual's relationship to the sociocultural environment.

As in all of Erickson's stages, there is a crisis, a conflict here. Generativity requires a concern for others. People are generative when they rear and guide their children or the children of others; when they contribute to the community through political, social, or eco-

nomic involvement; and when they contribute through their work. But even the most selfless and the most *generative* of individuals are occasionally tempted to turn and look inward at themselves. There is an urge to become preoccupied with things that affect the self—things such as health, the accumulation of money, the enjoyment of life. Resolution of the crisis does not require abandoning all thoughts of self, but rather achieving a balance between self-interests and the interests of others.

Peck's Elaboration of Erikson

Several theorists have criticized the global and rather vague descriptions of development provided by Erikson, particularly with respect to the adult years. Among them, Peck (1968) suggests that the last two stages, spanning the last 40 or 50 years of life, are not detailed enough to account for some of the critical issues during those years. He suggests there are several additional crises related primarily to the physical and mental changes of adulthood, as well as to some of the more common social changes. These crises describe an additional seven stages, the first four of which are applicable primarily to middle age; the last three relate to old age (see Figure 16.1).

Valuing Wisdom Versus Valuing Physical Powers.
Among the important physical changes of middle age is a gradual decline in stamina, elasticity, muscle tone, and other components of strength, endurance, and athletic prowess. Thus it becomes progressively more difficult for laborers to toil without pain, for professional athletes to continue participating in their sports, or for fathers to beat their sons at racquet sports or Indian leg wrestling. As these changes occur, it becomes more important for individuals to place greater emphasis on qualities that do not relate solely to the physical. The athlete must develop other competencies; the laborer must work differently or change employment; and the father might consider less physically demanding sports, such as bowling, curling, or billiards, or more cerebral competitions, such as chess or poker—hence the label for this particular psychosocial conflict.

Socializing Versus Sexuality.
In the same way that physical powers decline, so there are often changes in sexual interest, behavior, or capability. And some of

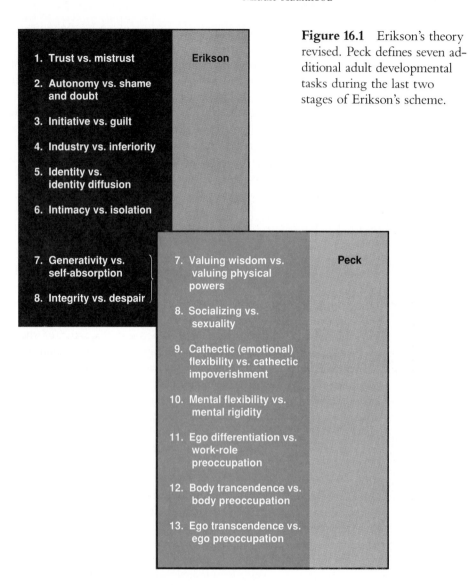

Figure 16.1 Erikson's theory revised. Peck defines seven additional adult developmental tasks during the last two stages of Erikson's scheme.

Erikson

1. Trust vs. mistrust
2. Autonomy vs. shame and doubt
3. Initiative vs. guilt
4. Industry vs. inferiority
5. Identity vs. identity diffusion
6. Intimacy vs. isolation
7. Generativity vs. self-absorption
8. Integrity vs. despair

Peck

7. Valuing wisdom vs. valuing physical powers
8. Socializing vs. sexuality
9. Cathectic (emotional) flexibility vs. cathectic impoverishment
10. Mental flexibility vs. mental rigidity
11. Ego differentiation vs. work-role preoccupation
12. Body trancendence vs. body preoccupation
13. Ego transcendence vs. ego preoccupation

the important interpersonal relationships that characterize early adulthood, and that might initially have had a strong sexual component, change accordingly. Friendship, trust, emotional and moral support, companionship, and other dimensions of social relationships become more important as sexuality becomes less so.

Emotional Flexibility Versus Emotional Impoverishment. The various crises and conflicts described by Erikson and Peck stem, in large part, from social and physical changes in the lives of individuals. These changes, in turn, require adaptation and change. The third of Peck's stages is a good illustration of this need for adaptability. Through middle age (sometimes much earlier and sometimes much later), many of our emotional ties are strained or ruptured for any of a variety of reasons: People die, children leave home, couples separate and get divorced, careers end, and dogs run away. Adjusting to these emotional changes often requires considerable emotional flexibility.

Mental Flexibility Versus Mental Rigidity. In the same way that changes in our emotional lives require us to be able to form new relationships and sometimes to forget old ones, so a variety of social and cultural changes require us to accept new ideas and sometimes to reject old ones. Hence the need for mental flexibility. We cannot always rely on old beliefs and opinions or on old attitudes.

Erikson and Peck: A Summary

Erikson and Peck present a theory that describes human development as progression through a series of stages, each of which is characterized by a basic conflict requiring resolution. This process generally involves the development of a new set of attitudes, behaviors, or preoccupations—in Erikson's terms, some new social competence. None of the conflicts is ever completely resolved at a given stage, so that each of us, throughout life, carries remnants of old fears, insecurities, and conflicts (Freudian influence).

The first five of Erikson's eight stages deal specifically with development from infancy through adolescence; the last three relate to adulthood and old age. Peck's elaboration of Erikson's theory involves the description of seven stages (psychosocial conflicts) to replace the last two of Erikson's eight stages—an attempt to provide a more detailed and more realistic portrayal of the many important developmental events that fill the long spread of years from the onset of adulthood to death.

Theories such as those of Erikson and Peck do not lend themselves easily to specific age-related predictions for any given individual. Nor can they easily be validated experimentally. Their principal usefulness lies in the insights they provide for understanding the concerns and preoccupations of adults. That, too, is the principal usefulness of the two descriptions we consider next: Levinson's seasons and Sheehy's passages.

Levinson's Seasons of Life

In a widely read book, Levinson (1978) attempts to organize the lives of 40 men around common, universal themes and changes. These men, ages 35–45, belong to four occupational groups, with 10 subjects in each group: novelists, biologists, business executives, and industrial workers. Each subject was interviewed in depth during a series of between 5 and 10 separate meetings, each lasting an hour or more, and all were interviewed again 2 years after the initial series of interviews. In Levinson's (1978) term, these were *biographical interviews*, intended to uncover the sequence of each man's life, the major changes in that sequence, and the forces underlying these changes.

Following these interviews, Levinson (1977, 1978, 1981) advanced a description of adult development, an account of the *seasons of a man's life*. Like Erikson's and Peck's accounts, this description deals primarily with psychological and social change, and their relationship to one another.

Levinson (1981) suggests that the human lifespan divides itself roughly into five major *eras* or *ages*: pre-adulthood (birth–22); early adulthood (17–45); middle adulthood (40–65); late adulthood (60–85); and late late adulthood (80–death). Within these eras, he identifies a sequence of stages that appear to be common to each of the 40 subjects. These are described here and summarized in Figure 16.2 on page 559.

Early Adulthood. Each of Levinson's stages involves a major developmental task. The transition into early adulthood requires separating from the family and establishing a separate identity. *Entering the adult world* involves exploring career roles as well as establishing stable adult roles.

Of major significance toward the end of this period—at around age 30—is the adoption of what Levinson refers to as a "dream." This dream is an idealized fantasy that includes the goals and aspirations of the dreamer. In one sense, the dream is a tentative blueprint for the dreamer's life. In Levinson's (1978) words:

> These are neither night dreams not casual daydreams. A "dream" of this kind is more formed than a pure fantasy, yet less articulated than a fully thought-out plan. . . . In its primordial form, the Dream is a vague sense of self-in-adult-world. It has the quality of a vision, an imagined possibility that generates excitement and vitality. (p. 91)

The majority of men's dreams have to do with occupations. Some men also include marriage and family goals in their dreams, or sometimes personal growth or spiritual goals (Gooden & Toye, 1984). Women's dreams are more likely to involve marriage and family goals (Roberts & Newton, 1987).

▶ Subject   Male; age 46; divorced;
             no children; involved in
             film business.

▶ Question   "Do you think you
             experienced a midlife
             transition or crisis?"

....

❝ *Do I? I have a couple every week.
Seriously, though, sure. Doesn't everybody? I
mean, there was a period, there, just about the
time I turned 40, when I figured — I guess I
just wasn't that certain anymore. Here I was,
40, I'd been divorced for about three years,
and I was feeling an awful lot of pressure
about deciding if I was ever going to get
married again and about whether I was going
to have kids. I mean, at 40 it didn't seem
like I had forever left anymore, and whatever
I was going to do I better get on and do it.
And then I thought, 'What the heck, Bob,
you're doing exactly what you want to do,
so go with the flow.' Maybe that's my
philosophy. 'Go with the flow.'* ❞

▶ Subject   Female; age 48; widowed;
             two children, both
             independent; manager of
             a cleaning business.

▶ Question   "Do you think you
             experienced a midlife
             transition or crisis?"

....

❝ *What the heck is that? My whole life is
a bloody crisis! . . . I get'cha, but the answer
is no, I never had no crisis like that. I was
too bloody busy bringin' up the kids and
tryin' to make ends meet which they never
did. If my husband hadn't of died, I might've
had enough time. No, I'm afraid I can't help
you there at all.* ❞

---

to grips with successes and failures relative to the dream. Otherwise, suggests Tamir (1982), the dream may continue to exercise the same power it held when the dreamer had more time, energy, and perhaps opportunity to achieve it.

Drebing and Gooden (1991) looked at the importance of the dream in the lives of 68 men ages 36–55. They found that 78 percent of these men had formed a dream in early adulthood. Of the men who had developed a dream (primarily occupational in nature), 38 percent claimed to have been largely successful in fulfilling it while 10 percent had failed. Others were in the process of trying to alter their dreams, either by changing them or by adding to them.

The most important findings from this study have to do with the importance of the dream's outcome to the individual's sense of well-being. The most depressed, anxious, and purposeless individuals in this sample (that is, those who most clearly were experiencing a crisis) were those who had never developed a dream. And those who had failed in their dreams were also significantly more depressed and anxious, and had lower scores on a measure of *purpose in life* than those

Individuals often reexamine career and life-style choices during early adulthood, and especially during the *age 30 transition*, and reevaluate them in terms of the dream. Divorce and career changes sometimes result.

The next period, *settling down* (late thirties), is marked by major efforts to lay the groundwork for accomplishing the dream in all important areas: career-related, social, economic, political, family-related, and so on.

The Midlife Transition.   Probably the most highly popularized of all adult developmental stages is the *midlife transition* — often referred to as the *midlife crisis*. The main developmental task of this period is to come

who had been successful in their dreams. Interestingly, those who were still pursuing dreams, often modified from earlier aspirations, were also characterized by higher levels of emotional well-being.

The urgency of the need to reexamine the dream in midlife is aggravated by the fundamental change that now occurs in the individual's perception of time. As Neugarten (1968) described it, people change from a perspective of "time from birth" (age, in other words) to one preoccupied with "time until death." Any of a variety of what Levinson calls "marker events" can contribute dramatically to this change in time perspective: death of parents, children leaving home, death of friends and age peers, sickness, and so on. Following these and other less dramatic events (such as being beaten at tennis or golf by one's son), individuals become progressively more conscious of their own mortality and of the idea that there may not be enough time to achieve the dream. For many, it now becomes fundamentally important to modify the dream — to change commitments and life-styles and to emphasize those aspects of life that might have been neglected. For some men, the result is a resolution to spend more time with family and friends — and perhaps less with work and career. For others, it might involve a complete abdication of earlier responsibilities and commitments — and new commitments to what are sometimes dramatically different life-styles. Some middle-aged individuals do "drop out."

Entering Middle Adulthood. Individuals enter middle adulthood at about age 45. Some bring with them renewed commitment to family and career; others, following the crises of the preceding period, enter middle adulthood with new commitments and new life-styles. All, according to Levinson (1978), experience fundamental change following the midlife transition, even if they continue in the same external roles. Detailed examinations of the lives of his subjects leads him to observe that there are typically changes in relationships with work, family, and others — sometimes for better and sometimes for worse. Thus there is tremendous variation in the extent to which men find their lives satisfactory during this period.

Age 50 Transition. Levinson (1986) provides only a quick sketch of developmental phases after the age of 45. He suggests that about age 50, another period of transition involves tasks very similar to those of the

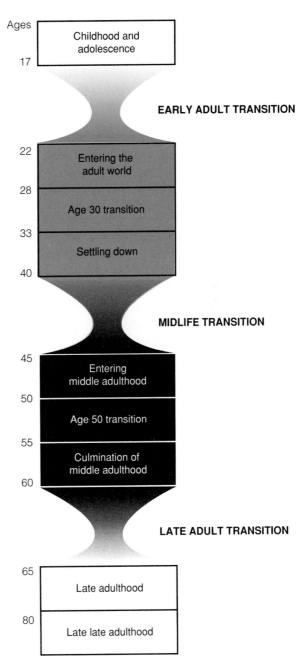

Figure 16.2 Levinson's description of major developmental periods through early and middle adulthood. (From D. J. Levinson, *The Seasons of a Man's Life.* Copyright © 1978 by Daniel J. Levinson. Reprinted by permission of Alfred A. Knopf, Inc.)

midlife transition: namely, to reexamine accomplishments and relationships in relation to the dream espoused in early adulthood. For those who have accomplished this task inadequately in their early forties, there may be a crisis similar to that of the midlife; for others, the period may be relatively free of turmoil.

Culmination of Middle Adulthood.

Following this period of transition, there is a relatively stable "settled" period during which the individual's career will begin to wind down. In a final period of transition, bridging middle and late adulthood, the key tasks will involve reconciling the dream with reality, accepting again the notion of one's own mortality, and preparing for what are sometimes drastic changes brought about by retirement and all that it entails.

A Summary of Levinson's Description

Levinson's account of the adult lifespan describes major tasks during developmental phases that last between five and seven years. These tasks typically involve making important choices concerning life-style and career.

In an overly simplified sense, the primary preoccupation during early adulthood revolves around work: climbing the "ladder," being recognized, achieving success, being somebody in the community. Between ages 40 and 45, the individual confronts his or her dreams and evaluates life in relation to earlier goals and ambitions. This confrontation often translates itself into a crisis ("Where am I going? What do I want out of life? What is really important?"). Subsequently, work and external marks of success may become less important; the self and the family, more so.

It is revealing that other studies of the lifespan present a global picture highly similar to that advanced by Levinson. For example, Vaillant's (1977) study of 95 Harvard graduates (classes of 1922–1924) reveals a period of commitment to work and success during early adulthood, a critical period of reappraisal at midlife, and a tendency to become more concerned with "the world within" following this midlife crisis. Similarly, Sheehy's (1976) journalistic account of the lives of 115 men and women also describes a developmental progression very much like that described by Levinson. We look at Sheehy's descriptions next.

Sheehy's Passages

Sheehy (1976, 1981), a journalist, suggests that the word *crisis* is often misinterpreted—that we interpret it too seriously. It hints of impending catastrophe, of calamity just around the corner. For this reason, *crisis* is not entirely appropriate to describe most of the events that characterize the adult lifespan—hence her substitution of the term *passages*. Sheehy's early stages are very similar to Levinson's, but the labels have been changed (see Interactive Table 16.1).

It is in her description of entry into middle adulthood, the *deadline decade*, that Sheehy departs most significantly from Levinson. This phase, corresponding to Levinson's midlife transition, is accorded a longer age span by Sheehy (ages 35–45, compared with 38–43). Other researchers tend to support Sheehy's observation that midlife crises can occur during a much wider age range than Levinson suggests. For example, Vaillant (1977) argues that critical midlife changes can occur at any time between ages 30 and 50.

Male–Female Differences at Midlife.

A second important observation made by Sheehy concerns male–female differences. Although the general developmental pattern of men and women is highly similar, says Sheehy, the midlife *passage* often occurs considerably earlier for women—frequently at about age 35 (compared to 40 or 45 for men). Perhaps most important, resolution of this crisis sometimes takes a dramatically different form for men than for women.

As we saw earlier, both Levinson and Vaillant describe very similar patterns of development among men up to the midlife crisis. To oversimplify somewhat, men spend much of their early twenties deciding on a "life structure," commit themselves to their early decisions during their thirties, subject their lives to profound reexamination at about age 40, and frequently end up more concerned with family and self than with aggressive, achievement-related goals after the midlife crisis.

In contrast to this general male pattern, Sheehy suggests not only that women begin their reexamination of goals and priorities considerably earlier, but also that the resolution of any resulting crisis often takes the form of greater assertiveness and more achievement-oriented goals. Thus, whereas many men become more passive, more oriented toward *feeling*—perhaps more "feminine"—many women become more active, more aggressive—

INTERACTIVE TABLE 16.1

Sheehy's Adult Transitions

▶ *Each transition of the lifespan entails far more tasks than can be described here. Where do you fit in Sheehy's sequence? What do you see as the most important psychological tasks you now face? Look, as well, at Gould's transformations, described in Table 16.2. To what extent do you still hold the false assumptions of earlier ages? Or did you ever?*

Passages	Principal Tasks and Characteristics
Pulling Up Roots (18–22)	Separating individuality from that of parents; leaving security of parental home.
The Trying Twenties (23–27)	Trying on life's alternatives; developing capacity for intimacy; career and life-style choices.
Catch 30 (28–33)	Emphasis on stability and on "making it"; *rooting and extending*; first sense of stagnation.
Deadline Decade (35–45)	Midlife crisis; realization of mortality; reexamination of youthful illusions and dreams; turmoil.
The Comeback Decade (46–55)	Danger zone; need to balance work and play, time lived with time left, and changes in placement within generations.
The Freestyle Fifties (50s)	Phenomenon of second life; movement from stagnation to peak excitement; for men, more interest and enjoyment in environment and social relationships; for women, more aggressive, managerial commitments.
The Selective Sixties (60s)	Ability to separate the truly important from the trivial; development of distinctive personality; possibility of high excitement about life.
The Thoughtful Seventies (70s)	Healthiest and happiest individuals are independent, highly involved, and plan ahead. Highly developed ability to think abstractly.
The Proud-to-Be Eighties (80s)	Detached contemplation; need to find balance between demanding and giving help and comfort; pride in survival and in continued competence.

Source: Based on Sheehy, 1976, 1981.

perhaps a little more "masculine" (Hyde, Krajnik, & Skuldt-Niederberger, 1991).

Gutmann (1975), in his investigations of the lifespan, has made essentially the same observation as Sheehy. He notes that the transition from the parental to the postparental phase of life, a transition that generally occurs somewhere between 40 and 55, has different implications for the sexes. During this period, men often give up or modify their active, aggressive, and production-centered stance, and turn their attention and energy to the more socioemotional aspects of existence (relationships and feelings). In contrast, women are more likely to enter middle age with a newfound interest in political, managerial, and production-oriented endeavors. As Gutmann puts it, this period often sees a "return of the repressed." Specifically, the man's repressed femininity and the woman's repressed masculinity begin to assert themselves in a gradual movement toward the androgyny that researchers such as Gutmann believe to be part of old age (Gutmann, 1990).

As Sheehy notes, one of the ways in which couples can sometimes resolve their midlife dilemmas and find new excitement and meaning in the next decades is to "renegotiate" traditional roles. Perhaps the wife can contribute salary and vacations to the family—and the husband can provide nurturance, laundered clothing, and pot roasts.

TABLE 16.2

Gould's Transformations

Age	Major False Assumptions	Major Tasks
16–22	"My parents will always be my parents. I'll always believe in them."	Move away from home; abandon idea that parents are always right.
22–28	"If I want to succeed, I need to do things the way my parents do." "If I make mistakes and need rescuing, they'll rescue me."	Become independent; explore adult roles; abandon idea that things will always turn out right if done in the manner of parents.
28–34	"Life is pretty straightforward, especially if you're on the right track. There aren't too many contradictions."	Explore aspects of inner self; become more sensitive to emotions; begin to realize inner contradictions.
34–45	"I have all the time I need. I am doing the right thing."	Recognize and accept idea of one's own mortality; develop strong sense of personal responsibility; reassess values and priorities.

The *freestyle fifties* is characterized by individuals who have accepted who they are. Transition through the *selective sixties* frequently involves a new recognition of what is most important in life — friends, family, loving, caring, sharing. These attitudes carry on into the *thoughtful seventies*, when individuals are in an excellent position to contemplate important philosophical, religious, social, and political abstractions — and on into the *proud-to-be eighties*, when some individuals find new vigor and pride in existence. In Sheehy's (1981) words: *"The approach of the final passage transforms the grains in the hour-glass to the dust of gold and cinnamon — precious enough to be spent well and to be savored in the smallest ways" (p. 53).*

Gould's Transformations

One final description of the adult phase of the human lifespan is presented here: that formulated by Gould (1972, 1978). Gould studied a large sample (more than 500 individuals) and included both men and women between the ages of 16 and 60. What was most unusual about his sample, however, was that members were outpatients at a psychiatric clinic (at the University of California, Los Angeles) involved in group therapy. Subjects in this sample were divided into different groups according to age and were interviewed by psy-

chiatrists, who attempted to uncover feelings and statements that would be most characteristic of each age group. In this way, Gould hoped to arrive at a sequential description of important changes in the adult lifespan. Following these initial interviews, questionnaires were sent to a sample of 524 individuals who were *not* psychiatric patients. These questionnaires were based primarily on patients' statements that appeared to be characteristic of specific age groups. This aspect of the study was intended simply to corroborate initial findings and to establish that the patient population was not fundamentally different from a nonpatient population.

Gould's description of adult development is summarized in Table 16.2. At first glance, it appears to be very similar to that advanced by Levinson and Sheehy. Thus early preoccupations center on separating from the family and establishing an adult identity (work, family, social responsibility); crises occur about age 30 and again at 40, the latter being tied to a recognition of mortality and a sense of urgency with respect to goals.

Closer examination reveals that Gould's *transformations* present a different emphasis from that of Levinson's seasons or Sheehy's passages. Gould, a psychiatrist, is concerned less with the individual's relationship to work, career, dreams, and family, and more with the person's *self-consciousness* — that is, with the individual's understanding of the self and with the gradual transformations that change a child's consciousness into adult consciousness. Thus development is described through developmental tasks that involve getting rid of the false, "childish" assumptions of early years and replacing them with more adult assumptions. For example, between ages 16 and 22, the principal false (or immature) assumption that dominates the individual's life concerns the rightness of parents: "I'll always want to be with my parents and believe in them—and they can always rescue me if I need help." Accordingly, the major developmental task of this early period is that of leaving home—but not simply in a physical sense. To really "leave" home is to discard these false assumptions concerning the rightness and potency of parents and to accept that parents can be wrong. We do this *intellectually*, says Gould (1990), long before we are successful in doing it emotionally.

In a similar fashion, progress through the lifespan requires shedding a variety of other false assumptions and adopting others that are more realistic (see Table 16.2). The result, according to Gould, is greater self-understanding and greater self-acceptance.

Is There a Midlife Crisis?

Popular literature, rather than psychological research, may be largely responsible for the currency of the expression *midlife crisis* or *midlife identity crisis*. Unfortunately, books such as Levinson's and Sheehy's are not based on the kind of investigation that science demands (see Loevinger, 1987). But they are nevertheless intriguing and suggestive, and sometimes they can lead to important insights. Still, what does science say about the midlife crisis?

In this case, the findings of science do not entirely agree with our popular conceptions. Costa and McCrae (1980) looked at distress among men ages 30–70. Distress is presumably an emotion that would accompany a serious midlife crisis. In this study, however, distress did not peak in the middle years. In fact, younger adults reported *more* distress than did older subjects. Similarly, Long and Porter (1984) cite evidence indicating that for many women, the changes that occur at midlife (children leaving home; perhaps resuming a career) are often liberating. True, these changes require major readjustments, but the eagerness with which many women embrace them hardly connotes a crisis. But for some, of course, there may be a crisis.

Farrell and Rosenberg (1981) developed a "midlife crisis scale" to study midlife *identity* crises in a group of men. This scale ranks responses to statements such as "I find myself wondering what I really want in life." Although they found some degree of dissatisfaction and conflict in more than half their group, only 12 percent of the men could be classified as having genuine midlife crises.

Steinberg and Silverberg (1988) used Farrell and Rosenberg's scale to look at the midlife crisis among 129 couples. Although they were more interested in factors that contribute to marital satisfaction than in the midlife crisis, their study indicates that for some men and women, concerns about life, career, and the future are a significant preoccupation. Interestingly, among this sample, there was a significant relationship between marital satisfaction and measures of the midlife crisis for women but not for men. That is, those wives who were most concerned about identity issues were also the *least* satisfied. This, of course, could mean that marital dissatisfaction leads to a midlife identity crisis rather than that the crisis leads to marital dissatisfaction.

Vaillant (1977), like many other researchers, agrees that the middle years involve major transitions that require change if the individual is to cope and remain reasonably happy. During this period, the increasing frailness of aging parents, or their death, underline for the middle-aged their own potential frailty, and their own inevitable mortality. Sometimes the realization leads to a difficult adjustment—and sometimes to a crisis. However, there are important transitions throughout the lifespan, and major adjustments to be made at all levels. Furthermore, crises are tied less to age than they are to events. Hence, crises that occur in midlife for some might occur much earlier or much later for others. Accordingly, it is misleading to refer to the midlife as a period of crisis. However, it may not be misleading to suggest that at some point in middle adulthood, many individuals will reevaluate their lives, and some will suffer frustration and regret at the outcome. For some, the situation may evolve into a crisis; for others, it may be interpreted as simply another opportunity for growth.

Family Relationships

Of all the stages in the span of our lives, the middle years have the potential for the greatest number of different family relationships. A middle-aged couple

The middle years involve major physical and psychological transitions brought about by changes in the family, by physical decline, and by a mounting awareness of mortality. Most individuals adjust well to these changes, but for some, they lead to conflict and turmoil, popularly labeled the *midlife crisis*. Some individuals try to resolve their midlife crises by acting and dressing young, hoping to recapture the feelings they once had, when all life's possibilities lay ahead.

can have relatively young children, or children who are themselves on the threshold of the middle years. They can have grandchildren who are infants and some who are old enough to have given them great-grandchildren. They can have parents who are still in the upper reaches of middle adulthood, or parents who are very old. Add to this all the possibilities of aunts and uncles, cousins and nephews and nieces, brothers and sisters, in-laws, and so on, and the web of relationships becomes very tangled indeed.

The launching phase in the family life cycle begins when the oldest child leaves home and ends when the youngest is gone. This phase is followed by the empty nest, a period that, contrary to what we might expect, is among the happiest for married couples.

Relationships with Children

In Duvall's eight-stage description of the family life cycle, there are two stages that span the middle years: the *launching* phase and the *empty nest* phase (see Figure 14.8). Recall from Chapter 14 that Duvall's approach describes the most common child-rearing patterns in *traditional* families. Accordingly, it does not take into consideration the possibility that the major events and tasks that define the stages might occur much later, or sometimes earlier, in many families. Nor is it suitable for cultural contexts different from ours. In addition, there is a tendency to oversimplify when discussing complex relationships within simple stages. At the same time, however, the simplification is sometimes an advantage, providing a way to organize and understand facts.

Launching. The *launching* phase, the sixth in Duvall's cycle of the family, begins with the first child's leaving home and ends when the youngest child departs. The launching phase lasts as long as the space between the oldest and youngest child, which averages approximately eight years. It, too, brings new demands on the family, including those relating to the rearrangement of physical facilities and resources, additional ex-penses relating to the launching (college or wedding expenses, for example), and reassigning responsibilities among grown and growing children. Clearly, the launching phase will be longer, more expensive, and perhaps more difficult in those families in which there are many children in which the space between the oldest and youngest child is greatest. By the same token, it will be far shorter for those families in which there is a single child.

The Empty Nest. The "empty nest" phase, the seventh in the family life cycle, begins with the launching of the last child and lasts perhaps 15 or more years. The average age of the contemporary mother at the beginning of this stage is about 52 (54 for the average father). Although the family continues to function as an important social unit and to encourage the development of autonomy among its sons and daughters, its primary developmental tasks shift away from children and refocus on the husband and wife. Among these tasks are those that relate to maintaining a sense of well-being, developing and enjoying career responsibilities, dealing with aging parents, and establishing and maintaining a useful or enjoyable position in the community.

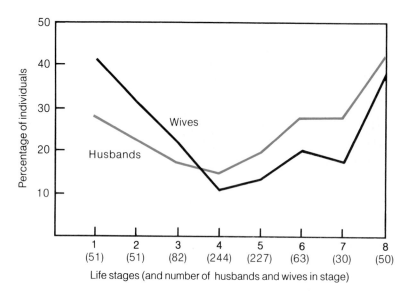

Figure 16.3 Percentage of individuals at each stage of the family life cycle (from stage 1, "beginning families," to stage 8, "retirement") reporting their marriage was going well "all the time." (Figures in parentheses indicate the number of husbands and wives in each stage. There was a total of 1,598 cases.) (From Rollins and Feldman, 1981, p. 308. Used by permission of Columbia University Press.)

Although folklore has often associated the departure of children with unhappiness and even depression among parents, especially among mothers, remarkably consistent research findings contradict this belief. As an example, Rollins and Feldman (1981) looked at marital satisfaction through Duvall's stages among 850 couples. Like other researchers, they found that the majority (around 80 percent) of husbands and wives thought their marriages were "going well" either all or most of the time. But they also found that happiness and satisfaction tend to be highest in the first stage of the cycle (prior to the advent of children) and begin to decline with the first child, reaching a low at about the time that the oldest child is entering adolescence. By the time of the empty nest stage, happiness and satisfaction again begin to increase, and continue to do so until the retirement years (see Figure 16.3).

Following a massive study of 1,746 couples at all stages of Duvall's family life cycle, Nock (1979) concludes that two family variables are most important for predicting factors such as satisfaction with the marriage, as well as satisfaction with self, occupation, living standard, and so on. The first of these is simply the presence or absence of children; the second is length of marriage. Specifically, the most happily married couples are those *without* children, whether they are couples who have not yet had children, couples who will never have children, or couples whose children have already left home. In addition, childless couples are least likely

to contemplate divorce. And the longer couples have been married, the more likely they are to express satisfaction with their lives, their spouses, and their marriages, and the less likely they are to contemplate divorce, to disagree over finances or child-rearing practices, or to be unhappy with their standard of living.

When Rubin (1978) interviewed 160 middle-aged women whose nests had recently emptied, she found some understandable sadness; but she found no depression. Seemingly, although the launching of the last child *can* bring about considerable sorrow, and may sometimes even trigger a severe midlife crisis or lead to serious depression, this is not ordinarily the case. In fact, many parents look forward to their children's leaving and establishing their own independent lives as adults. And many are distressed when, because of economic and employment conditions, their adult children either do *not* empty the nest as expected or return after having left (Glick & Lin, 1986).

In the majority of cases, relationships with children who have left home remain very close and very positive, and both mothers and fathers evaluate the nest-emptying experience positively more often than negatively (Borland, 1982). Parents continue to support their children, advising them on all kinds of subjects ranging from careers to child rearing. When Frank, Avery, and Laman (1988) analyzed the relationships of 142 young adults (ages 22–32) with their parents, they found a

Dramatic increases in life expectancy mean that middle-aged parents—and their children—are far more likely to know their aging parents and grandparents than was the case several decades ago. For most, this brings joy, but it also brings new responsibilities. However, even if Grandpa is very old and very wise, it is not necessary to sell him Boardwalk for $100!

remarkable degree of closeness. They also found that before the age of 24, about half of these young adults had serious doubts about their ability to cope with all aspects of their lives without relying on their parents; only 20 percent felt completely confident. But by the age of 28, the majority felt completely competent to cope with all of life's problems without their parents. Interestingly, however, when children and their parents interact and advise one another, most of the advice flows from parent to child no matter whether the children are 20 or 50 (Cohler & Grunebaum, 1981).

Relationships with Aging Parents

The socialization of children in many Asian societies is quite different from that which characterizes most of North America. In Chinese society, for example, one of the most important values acquired in childhood is that of *filial piety*—a concept that is the cornerstone of Confucian ethics. Filial piety denotes something more than respect; it means, in fact, something close to reverence. "Filial piety," Ho (1983) tells us, "defines one's proper relationship with one's parents and ancestors" (p. 41).

One manifestation of filial piety is found in the love and respect that is traditionally accorded Chinese parents. Consequently, it is not a mere duty to look after and care for aging parents; instead, it is an honor and a source of great pride.

North America does not socialize the same degree of respect and piety relative to ancestors, or even to parents. Yet the parent–child bond that is forged in infancy stretches across the entire lifespan. As we saw, when young adults leave the nest, they do not abandon all the emotions that bind them to their parents. And links still remain when young adults have become middle-aged, and their parents older still.

Given the dramatic increase in life expectancy in recent decades, there are now proportionally more older adults than there have ever been (U.S. Bureau of the Census, 1991). This may be a source of joy for middle-aged adults; but sometimes it is a source of frustration and anxiety, especially if the middle-aged adult and the aging parent do not get along well.

In North America, aging adults do not commonly move in with their children unless financial need or health problems compel them to do so—although they often move closer to them. That more elderly parents once lived with their children than is now the case is not evidence that today's middle-aged children care less for their parents. Aizenberg and Treas (1985) point out that parents have seldom lived with their children unless economic or social circumstances forced them to. It is the parent generation, and not the children, who most insist on independence, says Shanas (1980). However, as parents become more frail, there is a greater need for children to provide assistance and support—sometimes financial, often emotional and physical. In addition, there is sometimes the need to adjust to the death of one or both parents.

For most of us, the realization that our parents are not the strongest and the wisest people in the whole world is a reluctant discovery. In childhood, we have little doubt about what father and mother are, and what they can do. Even through adolescence, when logic and experience should teach us better, we remain convinced that in at least some ways, our parents are still the biggest and the best. And so it continues through early adulthood.

But finally there comes a day, usually some time in the middle years, when we look at our parents, when we actually *realize* what they think and *hear* what they say, and are shocked to discover that our childhood convictions were an illusion. It is a sobering and sometimes distressing realization.

Divorce and Remarriage

We have looked at divorce at several stages in the life-span. In Chapter 6, we looked at its implications for infants and young children; in Chapter 8, we examined how children of different ages react to the separation of their parents; and in Chapter 14, we looked at the effects of divorce on husbands and wives. We noted, there, that currently about 50 percent of all marriages end in divorce, and that the vast majority of those who divorce will also remarry, most within three years.

Remarriage in middle adulthood is not as common as it is at younger ages. This is partly because the majority of divorces take place within three years of first marriage, so that many remarriages will already have occurred prior to middle age. It is also because happiness in and satisfaction with marriage tend to increase through the middle years, especially after the nest has emptied, so that there are fewer divorces then (Rollins & Feldman, 1981).

Research suggests that divorce in middle age can be difficult for both the husband and the wife. In general, the longer the couple has been married, the more difficult the adjustment. Lingering unhappiness, bitterness, and even depression are not uncommon (Chiriboga, 1982).

Divorce is often more difficult for middle-aged women than for men, for several reasons. The fact that men often receive more emotional and psychological support outside the home, particularly in a one-wage-earner family, may make it easier for the man to make the transition out of a marital relationship (Whiting, 1984). In addition, women are more likely than men to suffer economic hardship following divorce. And perhaps most important, the chances of finding someone suitable for an intimate relationship or for remarriage are lower for middle-aged women than men (Spurlock, 1984). For one thing, by middle age, more men than women have died, so that the total pool of men has been reduced; for another, our contemporary standards of physical attractiveness penalize women more than men (Katchadourian, 1987). Not surprisingly, middle-aged men tend to remarry younger women.

Among the adjustments and changes that are sometimes required following remarriage in middle age are those having to do with the marital relationship itself. Often, difficult interpersonal adjustments are required of two individuals who have had half a lifetime to establish their own habits and expectations. In addition, there may be the need to establish relationships with an entirely new set of in-laws, as well as perhaps stepchildren.

We should note, however, that these adjustments and changes are not necessarily problems, although they can be challenges. And divorce in middle age is not always traumatic. In addition, remarriage and the creation of stepfamilies has some definite benefits. For example, whereas divorce often brings economic hardship, remarriage generally eliminates that hardship.

Marriage and Divorce

Taking into account population increases, wedding bells ring about as often now as they did in the days of our grandparents. In any given year, around 10 or 11 marriages take place for every 1,000 people. But when our grandparents or great-grandparents agreed to marry and remain married "until death do us part," they were far less likely to break the agreement. In 1910, there was less than 1 divorce per 1,000 population; 76 years later, that number had increased by a factor of more than 5. In the meantime, birthrates have been cut in half.

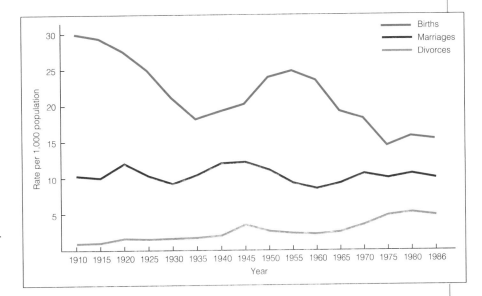

Figure 16.4 Changes in marriage, divorce, and birthrates per 1,000 population, 1910–1986. (From U.S. Bureau of the Census, 1988, p. 59.)

Quality of family life

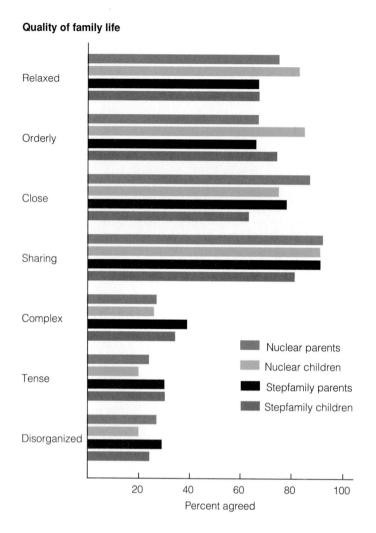

Figure 16.5 Percentage of parents and children who agreed that their family life conformed with the listed descriptions in the preceding few months. (From Furstenberg, 1987, p. 50. Reprinted by permission of The Guilford Press.)

Furstenberg (1987) reports that remarried women are about as well off as women in their first marriage. They are about as likely to work, and no more likely to consider their economic situation a problem. At the same time, on the average, remarried women are far better off than those who have not remarried, largely because the majority of divorced fathers do not pay significant amounts toward family support (Weitzman, 1985).

In addition to the possible economic benefits of remarriage, there are clearly some emotional benefits. Not surprisingly, remarried men and women consider themselves to be happier than do those who are divorced. In fact, the happiness ratings of remarried couples is about the same as that of those who are still in their first marriage (Glenn & Weaver, 1977).

Stepparenting

Remarriage where one or both of the partners have children from a previous marriage can sometimes lead to complicated patterns of relationships among members of the resulting stepfamily. Understandably, there are often signs of strain. Furstenberg and Spanier (1984) found, for example, that remarried parents frequently do not consider stepchildren part of their family system. Similarly, stepchildren tend not to consider the stepparent part of their family. And even with the passage of time, this situation often remains unchanged. When members of stepfamilies were asked for their subjective impressions of family life, both parents *and* children who were members of stepfamilies had somewhat more negative evaluations than those who belonged to intact nuclear families (Furstenberg, 1987). Stepfamilies are seen as less relaxed and less close, and as more tense, complex, and disorganized, than traditional families. (See Figure 16.5.)

In spite of these findings, on the whole, both children and parents have positive evaluations of life in a stepfamily. And when the stepfamily consists of their biological mother and a stepfather (rather than their biological father and a stepmother), stepchildren rate their stepfamilies about as positively as do children with both biological mother and father.

The stepfamilies that result from remarriages in middle age, if they include children at all, are more likely to include older rather than younger children. Even when older children have been living with one of the partners prior to the remarriage, it is not uncommon for them to move out at the time of remarriage. Giles-Sims (1987) reports a number of case studies that illustrate this pattern, and that illustrate, as well, that the greatest amount of adjustment occurs during the first year or two of the new marriage. These first years are a time of negotiation and bargaining; they are a time for establishing roles and defining norms.

But ultimately, as we have seen, the majority of those who have remarried will rate their lives as "very happy."

Personality Changes in Middle Age

We are *persons; personalities* are what make us what we are. As personalities, we can be described in terms of several characteristics, or *traits*. Some people are bold and assertive; others are retiring and submissive. Some are anxious; others, secure. Some are depressive; others, optimistic; conservative or experimenting; emotional or stable; trusting or suspicious; relaxed or tense; practical or imaginative; and on and on.

One way to simplify the study of human personality is to group related traits together into what are sometimes called *types*. Extraversion and introversion, for example, are broad personality types that Jung (1923) thought might include a host of related traits.

One suggestion for organizing traits into related groupings is Costa and McCrae's (1978) NEO typol-

ogy: *N* for neuroticism, *E* for extraversion, and *O* for openness. Their analyses of various personality tests suggest that the NEO model includes most of the personality variables that would be of greatest interest to those doing research on personality characteristics and changes through the lifespan. Neuroticism, for example, includes such traits as anxiety and depression. And a common folk belief, sometimes supported by research, has been that many older people become more depressed with age.

Extraversion includes traits such as those sometimes labeled *sensation seeking* (adventurousness) and *activity*. Again, we have often assumed that both adventurousness and activity decline with age.

Openness refers primarily to the individual's receptivity to new experiences and might also be reflected in measures of dogmatism, rigidity, and authoritarianism.

An important question in the developmental study of personality concerns the extent to which people change with age. Is the cheerful, outgoing 20-year-old likely to be a cheerful, outgoing 60-year-old? Are there major developmental changes in personality traits that occur with age, and if so, are these changes predictable?

Cross-Sectional Research

In a widely reported study of aging, Neugarten (1964) identified some general patterns of changes in personality. The study involved a group of more than 700 subjects between 40 and 70, and a second group of more than 300 individuals between 50 and 90. Among the findings of this study was the tendency of men and women to alter their dominant approaches to life in middle adulthood. As we saw earlier, Neugarten observed a tendency for males to become less aggressive, more passive, and more concerned with emotions and with internal states—in short, to become somewhat more "feminine." In contrast, women frequently become more aggressive, more active, and more concerned with achieving personal goals (Gutmann, 1990).

A similar study, also conducted by Neugarten (1968), looked at the *self-concepts* of 100 middle-aged men and women. All these individuals were highly articulate, well-educated, successful business and professional leaders. Interviews revealed that most felt that middle age is "the prime of life." As one of the subjects put it, "There is a difference between wanting to *feel* young and wanting to *be* young" (Neugarten & Datan, 1981, p. 281). Although subjects would have liked to retain the appearance and the vigor of youth, most would have been reluctant to give up the competence, confidence, power, and other rewards that had come with maturity.

Middle age, Neugarten informs us, is characterized by a tremendous increase in self-awareness and introspection and by greatly heightened self-understanding. Accordingly, the prevalent theme of these middle years is the reassessment of self. And, as we saw, the result of this reassessment often takes the form of greater femininity for males and greater masculinity for females.

How valid are Neugarten's observations with respect to male–female personality changes in midlife? Other evidence provides corroboration. Gutmann (1977) studied personality changes in several different cultures (American, Israeli, Navaho, and Mayan, among others) and found patterns very similar to those described by Neugarten. He reports that in all these cultures, by age 55, women had become noticeably more aggressive and men more passive. His tentative explanation is that the roles that men and women play with respect to child rearing during their early adulthood require that women be unaggressive and nurturant if they are to be good mothers, and that men be aggressive and active if they are to be successful breadwinners. Following midlife, when men and women are finally freed from parenting roles, they are able to concentrate on those aspects of their personalities that had previously been repressed.

Two important points must be noted here. First, these patterns of personality change are far from universal, and they are not usually very dramatic. In other words, most men do not become highly (or even noticeably) feminine after age 55, and most women do not become dramatically more aggressive. In fact, in an important longitudinal study of personality changes (discussed in more detail shortly), Costa, McCrae, and Arenberg (1983) point out that although there were declines in masculinity scores for their male subjects, these were so slight that at current rates of decline it would take 136 years for an "average" 75-year-old man to reach the average masculine score of the women in the sample!

Second, if Gutmann's explanation for this slight change in gender roles after the midlife is accurate, it follows that changing male–female roles with respect to parenting, economic support of families, and decision making may do a great deal to lessen personality differences that now exist between younger males and females. In the end, it may no longer be possible for males to become less aggressive or for females to become more active and aggressive. Put another way, male–female personality differences in adulthood, and the changes described by Neugarten and Gutmann, might well be cohort specific rather than age-related. This, of course, makes them no less real or important, but might significantly alter our explanations and our understanding.

Longitudinal Research

Although a number of cross-sectional studies, such as the Neugarten studies described here, report some small but relatively consistent changes in personality with age, these studies do not warrant the conclusion that change is a function of age. It bears repeating that cross-sectional studies cannot separate the effects of age from those of the cohort.

Using data from the Baltimore Longitudinal Study, Costa, McCrae, and Arenberg (1983; McCrae & Costa, 1987) performed a series of studies employing sophisticated sequential designs (see Chapter 1). These designs allow researchers to separate age effects from those related only to the specific cohorts being examined, as well as from the effects of time of testing.

A variety of personality tests were employed in the Baltimore study, with testing occurring every one or two years after 1958, and including samples spanning all age decades between 20 and 80.

The results of these studies can be summarized very simply: For almost all the personality scales used, there is no consistent change related to age. In fact, not only is there no consistent change, but there is firm evidence of considerable stability through the entire age range for all important traits that make up the NEO model (neuroticism, extraversion, and openness to experience), plus two new traits, conscientiousness and agreeableness. Two exceptions are scores on the general activity and masculinity scales of the Guilford-Zimmerman Temperament Survey. As we noted earlier, masculinity scores tend to decline for males and increase for females. Similarly, measures of general ac-

satisfaction with their marriages (compatibility with their husbands) and satisfaction with their husbands' jobs. For men, the most important early predictors of later happiness are health, stamina, energy level, their wives' emotional stability, job satisfaction, and marital compatibility.

From the Campbell research, psychology would conclude that health and marriage are important for happiness. Research reported by Markides and Martin (1979) agrees; health, income, and activity level are three common correlates of happiness. The Sears (Sears & Barbee, 1977) longitudinal study would add that for men, working into the sixties and maintaining an intact marriage are important for happiness; and for women, working and being married are also important. The Morganti and associates (1988) study found that satisfaction increases with age (until very old age), and that it is highly correlated with health, self-concept, and personal autonomy (control). (See Interactive Table 16.3.)

Psychology's recipe for happiness might include all the foregoing and might add, as well, that we should try to die at least as early as our spouses. But psychology would not yet dare be so bold or so flippant.

Main Points

1. Erikson describes eight psychosocial stages, each characterized by a major conflict, the resolution of which is manifested in a new competence, attitude, or ability. The stage that spans the middle years, *generativity versus self-absorption*, presents the task of becoming generative (productive) and overcoming a temptation to become self-absorbed.

2. Peck proposes seven additional psychosocial crises that occur during Erikson's last two major stages. His self-explanatory labels for the stages for middle adulthood are valuing wisdom versus valuing physical powers, socializing versus sexuality, emotional flexibility versus emotional impoverishment, and mental flexibility versus mental rigidity.

3. Following biographical interviews with 40 men, Levinson describes uniformities that characterize the *seasons* of our lives. Early and middle adulthood are characterized by several developmental phases with important developmental tasks (for example, leaving home and making life-style decisions). Between these major phases are important transition periods, occurring at approximately the turn of each decade (ages 20, 30, 40, and so on).

4. The most highly popularized of transition periods is the *midlife transition*—also called the *midlife crisis*. Levinson suggests it occurs at about age 40 and that it entails a serious reexamination of the individual's life, particularly in relation to earlier goals and ambitions ("dreams").

5. Sheehy describes *passages* through the lifespan, which differ from Levinson's seasons in that (1) the midlife crisis spans a wider age range (30–50 rather than 4 or 5 years around age 40) and occurs earlier for women than for men, and (2) resolution of the midlife crisis often results in a "turning inward" among men (becoming more concerned with self, family, and emotion); the opposite is often true among women.

6. Sheehy's investigations suggest that happiness ("psychological well-being") is associated with age (older is better), love (married people are happier), and enjoyment of work (professionals are happier than blue-collar workers).

7. Gould describes several *transformations* whereby a childish consciousness, characterized by false and immature assumptions (particularly concerning the infallibility and power of parents), is gradually replaced by a more adult consciousness.

8. Research suggests that crises are tied more to events than to age and that the majority of individuals do *not* have a full-blown crisis during middle age. But some do.

9. In Duvall's eight-stage description of the traditional family life cycle, two stages span the middle years: the launching phase, which begins when the first child leaves home and ends when the last one is gone; and the empty nest phase, which begins when the last child is gone and ends with retirement. The empty nest does not ordinarily lead to serious unhappiness or depression but most often brings an increase in happiness.

10. Relationships with departed children tend to remain close, especially when the children are still in their twenties. Relationships of middle-aged individuals with their aging parents vary but tend to be warm and highly supportive.

11. Divorce in middle age is less common than at earlier ages; the longer two people have lived together, the less likely they are to separate. Remarriage is more common for men than for women after a middle-age divorce, partly because the pool of available men is smaller than the pool of women.

12. Remarriages in the middle years bring substantial emotional, and sometimes economic, benefits. They can also require major readjustments, especially if children are involved. Neither stepparents nor stepchildren easily accept stepkin emotionally as an integral part of their family.

13. Cross-sectional investigations of age-related personality changes suggest that males and females become less gender-typed and more androgynous through middle age. The magnitude of these changes is very small.

14. Sophisticated longitudinal investigations of personality change using sequential designs support the hypothesis that there is far more stability than change with age.

15. Satisfaction relates to the extent to which various objective aspects of our lives correspond with our goals and aspirations. Happiness is an emotional state, susceptible to fluctuations of mood; it is not necessarily closely tied to satisfaction.

16. Isolated findings from happiness surveys include the following: Married individuals report more happiness than those who are alone (single, widowed, or divorced); childless couples report as much happiness as those with children; couples whose children have left home (the "empty nest") do not, as a result, report lower levels of happiness; and perceived health is closely related to happiness.

17. Psychology does not yet have a complete recipe for happiness.

Further Readings

Belsky's book is a straightforward account of important changes that occur in adulthood and old age. Especially relevant for this chapter are sections on personality changes and the family:

Belsky, J. K. (1990). *The psychology of aging* (2nd ed.). Pacific Grove, CA: Brooks/Cole.

Probably the best sources of additional information with respect to models of the lifespan are original books written by Levinson, Sheehy, and Gould. Jacobs's much shorter account is based on the lives of women and provides some interesting insights into female adult development:

Gould, R. L. (1978). *Transformations: Growth and change in adult life.* New York: Simon & Schuster.

Jacobs, R. H. (1979). *Life after youth.* Boston: Beacon Press.

Levinson, D. J. (1978). *The seasons of a man's life.* New York: Alfred A. Knopf.

Sheehy, G. (1976). *Passages: Predictable crises of adult life.* New York: E. P. Dutton.

Sheehy, G. (1981). *Pathfinders.* New York: Morrow.

The following is an excellent, although frequently technical, collection of essays dealing with a variety of topics relevant to middle age. Among them are essays on physical health, mental health, and drinking, as well as on marriage, parenting, and careers — topics that we examine in the next chapter:

Eichorn, D. H., Clausen, J. A., Haan, N., Honzik, M. P., & Mussen, P. H. (Eds.). (1981). *Present and past in middle life*. New York: Academic Press.

The classic studies of satisfaction and happiness in the United States, conducted by Campbell and his associates beginning in 1957, are summarized in:

Campbell, A. (1981). *The sense of well-being in America: Recent patterns and trends*. New York: McGraw-Hill.

David Fredenthal: *The People*, c. 1930–1940. The University of Arizona Museum of Art, Tucson, gift of Mr. and Mrs. Leonard Pfeiffer.

The years like great black oxen tread the world,

And God, the herdsman goads them on behind,

And I am broken by their passing feet.

William Butler Yeats,
The Countess Cathleen

VIII

Late Adulthood

In our youths, we scarcely know there are great black oxen that tread the world. We believe we are alone, gifted and special, with our paths stretching out forever before us. In those carefree years, we know with the certainty of youth that there will always be roses along the way, and that we will always know to smell them.

But even then, if we allow ourselves to think of it, we realize that the great black oxen march relentlessly and that they will catch up to us one day. Even as children, if we look to the horizon, we can see their shadow. It is inescapable.

They are not malevolent, God's great beasts. It is not that they have singled us out, you and I, that they have decided it is us upon whose bones they will tread. But they cannot slow down, the oxen of our years; and we can go no faster.

In Part VIII, the breaths of God's great black oxen are hot upon the backs of our subjects. But the bones that are broken in these chapters are accidental. And it would be a mistake to think that the beasts that age brings rumbling behind us always bring pain and fear. There is much of late adulthood that is hopeful and wonderfully happy.

When, as old men and old women, our years have finally caught up with us and the beasts are no longer simply shadows, perhaps they will have become our friends. Maybe then we will see that they do not care to chew on our roses.

In the end, they will break our bones, God's great black oxen. But that won't be until Part IX.

CHAPTER 17

Physical and Cognitive Development: Late Adulthood

"You are old, Father William,"
the young man said,
"And your hair has become
very white;
And yet you incessantly stand on
your head—
Do you think, at your age, it
is right?"

Lewis Carroll, *Alice in Wonderland*

I cannot imagine my grandparents standing on their heads—or even my mother or father. I think it would make me feel strangely uncomfortable if I were to surprise my father standing on his white hair, or my mother sitting cross-legged on the bed smoking a cigar and listening to rock music at 90 decibels.

They have their feet planted firmly on the ground, my silver-haired parents—which seems right. We don't expect our old people to stand on their heads.

Nor do we expect our youth to sit in rocking chairs, reminiscing about the good old days. We expect that people will act their ages. And we have certain widely held beliefs about what is appropriate behavior for different ages.

This Chapter

Unfortunately, the expectations our society has for old people are sometimes inaccurate, and prejudicial (for example, the belief that old people are narrow-minded, rigid, and prejudiced). *Negative* expectations of this kind that are based solely on age define **ageism**. Ageism is the first topic in this chapter.

The chapter looks as well at important changes in the demographics of old age, brought about by dramatic increases in life expectancy (although not in life-span). It discusses various explanations for why we age, and examines some of the important physical changes that are part of the aging process. Finally, it looks at intellectual changes in old age, and at the growth of wisdom.

Ageism

"How old are you?" Few questions are more important to any of us when we first meet someone. Of course, it isn't always proper to ask; there are many for whom age is very private.

But if we do ask and find out how old someone is, what have we actually discovered? A great deal, most of us think, for we all have definite opinions about what people of different ages *should* be like. We know, for example, that children should be immature and impulsive; that adolescents should be moody and sometimes rebellious; that young adults should be adventurous, bold, and energetic; that middle-aged adults should be responsible, controlled, and strong; and that older adults should be cautious, rigid, and narrow-minded. Armed with these tidbits of folk knowledge, we glibly judge people to be "old" or "young" for their age. And, in fact, our judgments are probably often accurate and useful. At other times, however, our age-based expectations are inaccurate and highly prejudiced. Recall that ageism is the term employed to describe *negative* attitudes toward a group that are based solely on age.

Examples of Ageism

Ageism is most common with respect to old age, which is often described by the young in terms such as "used up," "ready to die," "narrow-minded," "prejudiced," "worn," and "incompetent." When Ng, Giles, and Moody (1991) asked people what kind of information they would ask of a driver involved in an automobile accident so that they might assign responsibility, they found that responses were highly dependent on the *age* of the driver—but not the *sex*. Younger drivers would be asked about their driving conduct (Had they been drinking? Had they been in previous accidents? How fast were they going?). But older drivers would be asked about their *competence* (How was their vision? Their health? Were they licensed to drive? Were they mentally capable? Were they physically capable?). Implicit in these questions are negative age-related stereotypes of the old.

Social Treatment and Media Portrayal. Negative attitudes such as these are sometimes manifested in age discrimination, in which older and younger people are treated differently simply on the basis of age. Kalish (1982) notes, for example, that the medical treatment of the elderly often reflects ageism. Not only do the medical professions assign a much lower priority to geriatrics and to research dealing with diseases associated with aging, but the actual care that medical facilities provide for the aged is often inferior to that which would be provided for a younger person in the same circumstances. Another example of ageism may be found in immigration policies, which have traditionally favored the young and which, earlier in U.S. history, allowed parents to bring their children from foreign countries but often did not permit them to bring their parents (Gruman, 1978). Similarly, ageism is illustrated in those customs and rulings that have made retirement mandatory at a specific age. Finally, it is evident in the negative media portrayals of the old as doddering, feebleminded, wrinkled, and laughable men and women, standing weakly and foolishly on the last of their worn legs.

Child-Directed Speech.   The speech of mothers to their infants and young children is consistently different from speech directed to adults or older children. As we saw in Chapter 5, speech is higher-pitched, sentences are shorter, ideas are presented in their simplest forms and are often repeated, and delivery is slower and more careful. In addition, child-directed speech (or *motherese*) makes more use of body language such as widening of the eyes and exaggerated gestures and expressions (Warren-Leubecker & Bohannon, 1984).

Child-directed speech is also common with the very old, and has essentially the same characteristics as when it is used with the very young. This, say Bunce and Harrison (1991), reflects a view of the elderly as helpless and incompetent. Ryan and associates (1986) speculate that the lowered expectations and negative stereotypes communicated by such speech might lead to lower self-esteem on the part of the elderly, withdrawal from social interaction, and poorer performance. Many among the elderly find child-directed speech degrading. There is some evidence, however, that the performance of some older people might be *better* when instructions are child- rather than adult-directed—perhaps because child-directed instructions are clearer and simpler, and because they communicate lower expectations and do not increase arousal as much (Bunce & Harrison, 1991).

Prevalence and Implications of Ageism

Is ours the only society that sometimes views its elderly in these terms? Was it always this way? Although it might be tempting to suggest that we honored our old

---

INTERVIEW

▶ Subject   Female; age 14; ninth grade.

▶ Question   "How would you describe old people? What do you think they are really like?"

....

66 *It depends how old, I mean, really old people . . . well, the physical things you can see, like being bald or gray and wrinkled. Other than that, maybe they're pretty different. Like my grandma, she bowls and goes curling and has a good time. Lots of other old people just sit and rock or they lie around in old folks' places. I probably shouldn't say it, but it's like they're waiting to die.* 99

---

ones more in days past, when the family was strong and our roots stretched lovingly among our kinfolk, Ward (1979) cautions against doing so. In the first place, only recently have the old become numerous. Only a century ago, less than 1 percent of the population was over 65. Being old in such unlikely circumstances might have been somewhat more prestigious than being old now. Thus our social attitudes toward the old might well have something to do with their numbers. In addition, Ward (1979) suggests that these attitudes often reflect environmental, economic, political, and social conditions. For example, in harsh and demanding environments, where survival is at a premium, the old quickly become a burden. And, in the same way that children who were an economic burden were sometimes killed during the Middle Ages, there are societies in which the elderly were also killed or customarily committed suicide (Mowat, 1952; Simmons, 1960).

Lest this paint too cynical a picture, let me hasten to point out that perhaps no more than one quarter of us are actually guilty of ageism with respect to the old

(McTavish, 1971). Furthermore, the rapidly increasing number of old people in contemporary society is having a profound effect on public opinion as well as on social policy. And the middle-aged and the elderly are increasingly breaking traditional age barriers. Many go back to school, begin new careers, marry for the first time, or devote themselves to dramatically new life-styles at ages that many would have considered far too advanced only a few decades ago. People such as Andres Segovia, who, at 93, continued to play the guitar with unbelievable emotion and skill, do much to relieve us of lingering age-related negative stereotypes ("Guitar Still Segovia's Passion," 1986).

Ageism describes negative attitudes that are prejudicial because they are based on age alone. Attitudes that are based on fact, even though they might be negative, do not illustrate ageism. Thus the sometimes gloomy pictures that we have of social, physical, and psychological changes in very old age might, to some extent, be fact—negative and uncomfortable fact, to be sure, but fact nevertheless. And social policies that appear to favor the young might often be based not on a stereotyped and prejudiced ageism but on the sometimes painful recognition that the elderly present much greater risks of decline in all areas. Indeed, they are at much greater risk of death, and it would be a pointless exercise in wishful thinking to behave as if this were not the case. But, as is made clear in this chapter, all is not sudden gloom with the advent of old age.

Definitions and Demography of Late Adulthood

When does old age actually begin? Most of us think of age 65 as the boundary between middle and old age, perhaps because 65 has been a common retirement age. In addition, Social Security programs for the aged, "old age" pension plans, and the various concessions that some public and private entities grant the "elderly" are typically for those aged 65 and above. In fact, however, variability among individuals is at least as great at age 65 as it is at any other time in the lifespan. It is important to keep in mind that there are 65-year-olds whose interests, activities, and vitality are comparable to those of an average 50-year-old. And, of course, there are some who are "old before their time."

Although it is convenient and simple to group all those above age 65 in a single category, we should also bear in mind that there is a tremendous spread of years between a 65-year-old and an 85- or 90-year-old. With this in mind, several researchers have proposed different divisions within this part of the lifespan. For example, Neugarten (1978) suggests that it might be fruitful to consider two major periods during old age. The "young-old" are those who are still highly active physically, mentally, and socially, although they might already have retired from their main careers. The young-old are found between the ages of 55 and 75. Beyond this age are the "old-old"—those for whom physical activity is more limited and among whom the effects of decline have become more apparent and more rapid. These unimaginative and somewhat clumsy labels reflect our lack of more common terms with which to discuss the elderly, and are another indication of how we have historically had little interest in aging. Unfortunately, being called "old-old" or even "young-old" may not be looked on with great favor by those who are now often labeled *seniors* or *senior citizens*.

As noted earlier, the numbers of older people have increased dramatically, both in absolute terms and as a proportion of the overall population. For example, while the population of the United States increased almost two and a half times during the first six decades of this century, the number of people over the age of 65 increased by a factor of five (Blau, 1973). This tremendous increase is due in part to a high birthrate early in the century as well as to immigration policies that increased the number of young people in North America. Initially, therefore, there were relatively few old people. Dramatic increases resulted not only because the children of the high-birthrate group had grown up but also because medical advances, as well as changes in nutrition, have contributed to our increased life expectancies. The net result was that, by 1989, more than 12 percent of the population of the United States was age 65 or older—almost 31 million individuals (see Figure 17.1). And the percentage continues to increase. Projections are that by the year 2000, almost 14 percent of the population will be over 65; that percentage is expected to increase to 20 percent by the year 2030 (U.S. Bureau of the Census, 1988). At present, the fastest growing age group in the United States is above age 80.

One of the reasons for predicting a continued increase in the proportion of older people is the effect of the population bulge created by the postwar baby boom (evident in Figure 17.3). As this bulge moves

The Demographics of Aging

The demography of old age has changed dramatically in the last 30 years. Between 1960 and 1989, the number of people age 65 and older in the United States increased from 16.7 to almost 30 million, an increase from 9.2 to 12.4 percent of the total population. The greatest percentage increase occurred at the upper levels: The percentage of those age 85 and older more than tripled. Because of increased longevity, percentages of those widowed declined during that period; but the percentage of those divorced more than doubled.

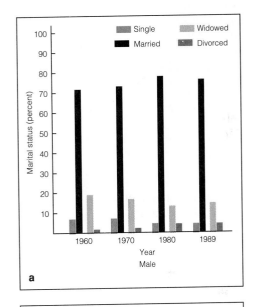

a

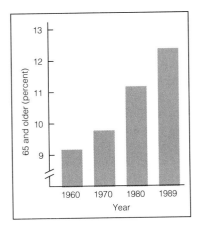

Figure 17.1 Percentage of total population age 65 and older. (From U.S. Bureau of the Census, 1991, p. 13.)

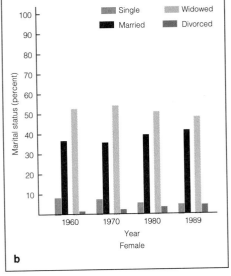

b

Figure 17.2 Marital status of (a) males and (b) females age 65 and older. (From U.S. Bureau of the Census, 1991, p. 37.)

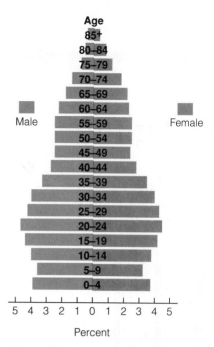

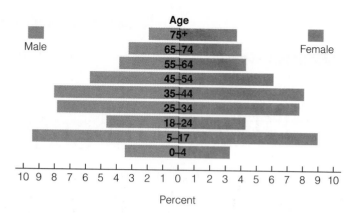

Figure 17.4 Age–sex population pyramid projected for 1995, based on 1991 data. (From U.S. Bureau of the Census, 1991, p. 16.)

Figure 17.3 Age–sex population pyramid for the United States: 1980. (From U.S. Bureau of the Census, initial tabulation, May 6, 1983.)

into old age, the numbers of old people relative to younger people will increase dramatically. The net effect is increased even more by declining birthrates. As a result, the age–population pyramids shown in Figures 17.3 and 17.4 are not pyramids at all—as they would be if birthrates remained relatively constant and if deaths occurred primarily from "natural" causes (rather than as a result of wars or other events that can kill primarily within selected age groups).

Lifespan and Life Expectancy

In North America, life expectancy has increased by almost one quarter of a century in little more than three quarters of a century. At the turn of the century, the average individual did not live 50 years; now we can reasonably expect to live to about age 75—less if we are male, more if we are female. Table 17.1 on page 590 presents life-expectancy data for 19 countries. Note

the tremendous variation for different countries, as well as the consistent differences between males and females in all countries. In Canada and the United States, for example, women live an average of between 7 and 8 years longer than men, a fact that is partly explained in terms of the greater susceptibility of men to stress-related disease (heart disease, for example) and to their traditionally less restrained life-styles (more automobile accidents, for example) (see Figure 17.5). But part of the explanation must also lie elsewhere, because male infants and children are also more likely to die than are female infants and children. Although approximately 105 males are born for every 100 females, the numbers of each still alive are equal by early adulthood. And by age 65, fewer than 70 males are still alive for every 100 females. Social and cultural sex biases may have favored males; nature has been less kind.

Although improved nutrition and medical care have given us 25 more years than our late-19th-century predecessors, our lifespans still remain virtually identical to what they have always been. If we live until age 65, our life *expectancy* is another 14.9 years for males and 18.6 for females (U.S. Bureau of the Census, 1991)—only a few years more than it was almost a century ago. In other words, while it is now far more likely that we will reach old age (approximately two thirds of us can expect to reach age 70), the very oldest among us will, in the end, live no longer than the very oldest who lived a long time ago. If disease, accident, or boredom do not claim us, old age surely will.

Male and Female Longevities

From the very beginning, men are more fragile than women. There are slightly more males than females born, but more male than female infants die—and more male children and adolescents also die. By the time men and women reach the age of 65, there are approximately three women alive for every two men. In the past half-century, life expectancy has increased by some 10 years for both men and women, but on average, life expectancy for women has remained approximately 7 years beyond that for men.

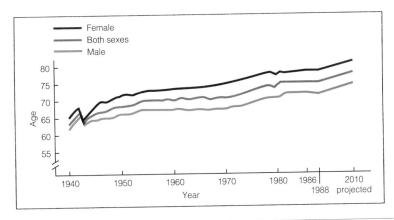

Figure 17.5 Life expectancy for women and men in the United States, 1940–1988, with projections for 2010. (From U.S. Department of Health and Human Services, 1988, p. 4, and U.S. Bureau of the Census, 1991, p. 73.)

TABLE 17.1

Life Expectancies at Birth of Men and Women in Selected Countries

Country	Date	Men	Women
Algeria	1970–1975	52.9	55.0
Belgium	1968–1972	67.8	74.2
Canada	1970–1972	69.3	76.4
Chile	1969–1970	60.5	66.0
China	1970–1975	60.7	64.4
Costa Rica	1972–1974	66.3	70.5
Egypt	1960	51.6	53.8
France	1976	69.2	77.2
The Gambia	1970–1975	39.4	42.5
Kuwait	1970	66.4	71.5
Mexico	1975	62.8	66.7
Morocco	1970–1975	51.4	54.5
Netherlands	1977	72.0	78.4
Pakistan	1962	53.7	58.8
Peru	1960–1965	52.6	55.5
Poland	1976	66.9	74.8
Senegal	1970–1975	39.4	42.5
Switzerland	1968–1973	70.3	76.2
United States	1988	71.5	78.3

Source: From *Demographic Yearbook, 1978* by the Statistical Office of the United Nations, 1979, Department of Economic and Social Affairs. New York: United Nations, and U.S. Bureau of the Census, 1991.

Theories of Biological Aging

Contrary to what we might like to believe, age is probably fatal. We all suffer from the same terminal condition: life. Although **life expectancy** (the average anticipated years of life) might continue to increase for some time, it is not likely to go beyond the **lifespan** (the maximum length of life in the absence of disease or accident). The span of human life is not likely to be increased until (and unless) we achieve control over the biological processes of aging (Cristofalo & Hayflick,

1985). And even if we could control the biology of aging, whether we *should* do so remains a highly debatable point.

Genetic Theory. Although we do not yet know exactly why we age, there are several theories of biological aging. A *genetic* theory holds, for example, that cells are programmed to die—that, in other words, the limits to life are biological and are inherent in the cells of which we are composed or in the protein matter that binds the cells (collagen) (Brouwer, 1990). When tissue cultures are raised in the laboratory, these cultures initially regenerate and multiply at a high rate. But they do not do so indefinitely; eventually, they begin to atrophy and finally die. What is perhaps most striking about this observation is that while cultures based on human embryonic lung tissue regenerate perhaps 15 times before dying, cultures from animals with shorter lives regenerate correspondingly fewer times. And when cultured cells are taken from an adult organism rather than from an embryo, they, too, multiply fewer times before dying. In fact, there is an almost perfect relationship between the normal lifespan of the organisms and the number of times that cultures derived from their tissue will regenerate (Cristofalo & Hayflick, 1985). Only certain defective, usually cancerous, cells regenerate indefinitely.

Cell-Malfunction Theories. Several other theories of aging also relate directly to body cells. *Error* theory suggests that, with the passage of time, certain changes occur in DNA material so that the cell eventually ceases to function. These changes are seen as errors rather than as genetically preprogrammed occurrences (Cristofalo, 1988).

The *toxin* theory of cell malfunction maintains that there is a gradual buildup of foreign material in the cell. Although much of this material is poisonous, initially it is present in insufficient quantities and does not affect cell function. With the passage of time, however, it continues to accumulate until the cell dies. One of the consequences is a reduced ability to combat infections and disease (Horan, Hendricks, & Brouwer, 1990).

The *free-radical* theory argues that portions of cells sometimes become detached during normal metabolic processes. Many of these "free radicals" are highly unstable chemical compounds that may interact with various enzymes and proteins in the body, and significantly affect the cell's ability to function normally (Brouwer, 1990).

TABLE 17.2

Theoretical Explanations for Why We Will Die in Any Case★

Theory	Explanation
Genetic	Cells are preprogrammed to die.
Error	Cellular changes lead to cells becoming nonfunctional as a result of errors that occur in DNA material over time.
Toxin	The gradual buildup of foreign material in the cells eventually becomes toxic and the cell dies.
Free-radical	Portions of cells become detached, interact with various chemicals and enzymes, and eventually impede the cells' ability to function normally.
Cross-linking	Bonds form among cells, changing their properties and altering their functioning.
Immune system breakdown	Immune system weakens with age and provides less protection against viral and bacterial invasion or, in a process known as autoimmunity, loses the ability to recognize foreign invaders and begins to attack the system it previously protected.

★ Aging and dying may well result from the combined effects of all these possibilities. Comfort (1978) suggests that we may not be very far from discovering ways to reprogram genetic programs, to prevent or delay cellular misbehaviors and errors, to guard against immune system breakdown, or to cleanse the cells of accumulated toxins. If these things occur, the lifespan may reach somewhat further.

A last cell-related theory refers to *cross-linking*, a process whereby bonds ("cross-links") form between molecules or parts thereof, changing the properties of the component cells and altering their functioning.

Organ and System Theories. In addition to these genetic and cell-based theories of biological aging, other theories speculate that various body systems undergo age-related changes that eventually lead to their breakdown or malfunction. Such theories sometimes argue that aging results from reductions in the efficiency of body systems that control temperature, blood-sugar level, and so on (Davies, 1990). Perhaps best known among these theories is that involving our immune systems. These are the systems in our bodies designed to guard against foreign invaders. They protect us from cancer, for example, as well as from a variety of infections. With advancing age, however, not only do our immune systems weaken so that they can less effectively protect us from infection and disease, but they also sometimes make errors and interpret some of our own cells as invaders. This process, known as **autoimmunity**, leads to the production of antibodies that may attack the body itself. Autoimmunity is thought to be involved in some diseases of aging, such as rheumatoid arthritis (Szewczuk & Mackay, 1985).

As (Brouwer, 1990) notes, aging is an extremely complex process that probably cannot be well understood within the context of any single theory. It is likely that various processes are involved and that genetic factors, cellular changes, and failing or weakening body systems are all implicated. Furthermore, these explanations are probably largely interdependent. That is, genetic factors may well account for many of the cellular changes that occur with age; cellular changes may, in turn, be responsible for functional changes in body systems. (See Table 17.2.)

Longevity in North America

As of this writing, and as far as science knows, our life*spans* are the upper biological limits of our lives. But our life *expectancies* will seldom reach the limit of our spans. Some of us will die sooner, others later. Why these differences in longevity?

INTERACTIVE TABLE 17.3

A Recipe for Longevity

▶ *How long can you expect to live? On average, the U.S. Bureau of the Census (1991) tells us, if you are a white American female age 20, about 59.9 more years (55.1 years if black). If you are a white American male age 20, your average life expectancy is another 53.6 years (47.0 if black). But some of us will live longer; others will die sooner. Sex and race are only two of the factors that influence longevity. You cannot control your sex or race; and you have only limited control over the possibility of accidental death. But perhaps you can control some of the other factors associated with longevity, listed here.*

You may live longer if:
1. You are female.
2. Your ancestors lived long lives.
3. You are a large tortoise and not a housefly.
4. You remain physically active well into old age.
5. You are highly educated.
6. Your employment is high-status.
7. You continue to be employed well into old age.
8. You are a monk or a nun.
9. You are married or cohabit full-time.
10. You exercise moderately on a regular basis.
11. You drink moderately and do not smoke.
12. You avoid wars, accidents, and homicidal maniacs.
13. Your job requires physical activity.
14. You are not overweight.
15. You sleep less than 9 hours per night.
16. There is no incidence of cardiovascular diseases, cancer, chronic bronchitis, or thyroid disorders among your close relatives.
17. You live in the country rather than in the city.
18. You undergo regular medical examinations.

Several factors contribute to longevity. As we saw in Table 17.1, sex and culture are two such factors. Women live longer than men, whites longer than blacks, and Americans longer than Senegalese. Some of the reasons for this are clearly environmental and relate to nutrition, medical care, health habits, and various vices and virtues having to do with life-style—exercising, drinking, smoking, and so on. Other reasons for longevity are genetic and relate to inherited susceptibility to various diseases, as well as to other genetically linked strengths and weaknesses.

A variety of other factors have also been found to be linked to longevity. These include physical condition (overweight individuals have shorter life expectancies; those who exercise are more likely to live longer), nature of occupation (people whose jobs require little physical activity live less long on the average), locale (rural people live longer than those in urban environments), wars (life expectancies of those actively engaged in such contests are understandably less), and religious calling (nuns live longer than monks; other things being equal, both live longer than you and I) (see Interactive Table 17.3).

So should we all become athletic monks and nuns, and move to the country? Perhaps not. Birren and Renner (1977) caution that the most important factors in determining a long life are those over which we do not have any control—namely, genetic factors, the environments of our grandmothers and of our mothers before and during pregnancy, and our own experiences in early childhood. Sadly, we can far more easily shorten our lives than lengthen them. That is, the good that we might do by not smoking or drinking is not likely to be equal, in terms of years, to the bad that we might do were we to smoke and drink. And perhaps living a long time is not very important. We have to be concerned with the quality of our lives as well as with their length.

Longevity Elsewhere

In most parts of the world, only 2 or 3 people out of every 100,000 live to be 100; 1 in 1 million reach 105; and only 1 in 40 million live to be 110 (Hayflick, 1975). Occasionally, however, the popular press tantalizes us with visions of healthy old people, sometimes 120 or more years of age, living in some faraway place. There are at least three such groups of people: the Vilcabambans in Ecuador, the Hunzukuts in the Karakoram Range of Kashmir, and the Abkhasians in parts of the Caucasus of the Georgian Republic of the former Soviet Union. Scientists have visited each of these parts of the world, interviewed the inhabitants, and attempted to determine what they might have in common (Leaf, 1973). They found, for example, that some long-lived individuals smoked and drank rum and never bathed; others climbed up and down mountains and bathed in ice-cold streams. Some ate chicken but no pork or other fatty meats; others ate mutton and goat; still others were largely vegetarian. Most were illiterate, medical care was primitive or nonexistent, and infant mortality was high.

Unfortunately, none of this information is very valuable because scientists were unable to verify the ages of the older people in these societies. None had valid birth records, and many of the older people seemed to systematically exaggerate their ages by as many as 40 years (Hayflick, 1975).

Models of Aging

Although there is no undisputed proof that people in these cultures live longer than North Americans or Western Europeans, their aging nevertheless appears to be very different. Old Abkhasians, for example, are vigorous and strong. They continue to work, they walk up and down the mountain slopes, they swim in icy streams. Among the Abkhasians, there is no thought of retirement, although the very old reduce their workday somewhat; and men sometimes father children at remarkable ages (Benet, 1976).

Why do the Abkhasians age so well? Benet explains that both genetic and environmental factors are clearly important. In a harsh, physically demanding environment, it is reasonable to expect that, historically, those who have survived are also those who are genetically stronger. Hence, the harshness of the mountain country may have served to select for a better genetic pool. At the same time, the Abkhasian culture stresses the importance of physical work but sees no virtue in overexertion. It also sees virtue in thinness, a condition that is perhaps simpler to maintain among people who are as physically active as the Abkhasians and whose diet consists primarily of fruit, vegetables, and meat.

There is perhaps one additional reason becoming older in cultures such as this takes a different course than it often does in North American societies: the prevailing attitudes toward aging. The Western model of aging, described by Havighurst, Neugarten, and Tobin (1968), demands little of the individual for the first 20 or so years of life (other than cultural preparation, primarily through schooling); for the middle 30 or 35 years, it asks for the individual's contribution; and after age 60 or 65, it says the individual now may do nothing—or, as we see in Chapter 18, sometimes it says "now you *will* do nothing."

This *discontinuity* between productive and nonproductive life, is, in effect, a clear social signal that differentiates between being useful and being useless, between being culturally valued and not being valued, between being wanted and not being wanted.

Societies such as those of the Abkhasians do not manifest this discontinuity. Abkhasians feel useful throughout life; no one retires or feels useless; no one loses status with age. In fact, there is no word for the old in their language, although there is sometimes reference to those who are "long-living" (Benet, 1976).

As Fry (1985) notes, although the longevity data from studies of people such as the Abkhasians are suspect, they lead to an important question: Under what circumstances do people exaggerate their ages? The answer seems to be: When being old is valued positively by a society.

It is highly revealing that in societies such as ours, we are, like Jack Benny, more likely to claim we are 39 than 79 when we find ourselves somewhere in between. It is also revealing that "looking one's age" is considered negative (as in "He's sure been looking his age lately"). Many people only reluctantly allow themselves to look their age, resorting first to facelifts, skin tonics, hair transplants, and the hundreds of other means that our culture defines as cosmetic improvement.

Still, many people genuinely look forward to aging. Perhaps, as the proportion of the aged continues to increase, many more will do so.

Physical Changes in Later Adulthood

Those who study aging sometimes speak of three great stages in human development. The first, from conception to early adulthood, is ordinarily described as a stage of growth and development. The second, from early adulthood to age 50 or 60, is sometimes seen as a plateau—a period during which relatively few dramatic changes occur. And the final stage is marked by physical, social, and cognitive changes. Many of these changes in the upper years involve decline. The technical term for this period of decline is **senescence**. Senescence can begin at very different ages for different individuals, and the losses it entails are not always dramatic or rapid. In addition, manifestations of aging are not identical for all individuals. Some results of aging are nearly universal and are sometimes referred to as *primary aging*. Loss or atrophy of brain cells is one primary change of senescence, as is gradual loss of cells from all organ systems (Sinclair, 1989). Various forms of degeneration are also part of senescence. One example is the loss of calcium in bones, leading to osteo-

porosis. Another is arteriosclerosis—a gradual hardening of the arteries—which begins very early in life and becomes progressively more serious, although its severity varies greatly among different individuals.

Note that arteriosclerosis is *not* universal but *nearly* so. Cox (1988) points out that biologists have not yet found any completely universal characteristic of aging. In other words, all the possible physical changes of old age do not affect everybody. But the probability of undergoing them increases greatly with age (for example, such diseases as cancer, arthritis, Parkinson's disease, osteoporosis, and acute brain syndrome).

Appearance

Most of the physical changes characteristic of old age begin well back in middle age and progress slowly through the remainder of the lifespan. For example, as we saw in Chapter 13, both strength and endurance peak in early adulthood (through the twenties and sometimes early thirties), and begin to decline very slowly from that point. In the same way, height usually reaches its maximum in early adulthood and begins to decline very slowly after age 45, partly because of tendons that shrink and harden, feet that become flatter, a spinal column that shortens, and muscles that have begun to atrophy. The combined result of these changes can often be seen in the characteristically stooped posture of the very old.

Among the many changes that contribute to the appearance of age, perhaps none are more apparent than those that occur in the skin, on the face, and on the head. Our skins are truly marvelous things. Indeed, it is difficult to imagine a better wrapping for our bodies—totally flexible, self-regenerating and self-repairing, sensitive to heat and cold as well as to pain, highly elastic, porous yet impervious to wind and rain, and totally washable. But with age, these wrappings become thinner and far less elastic, and are often flecked with little splotches of brown pigment (popularly called "liver spots") as well as with warts, bristly hairs, and the blackish bruises of tiny leaks in blood vessels. As fatty cells die, old skin is no longer sufficiently elastic to cover the loss; it sags and droops under our arms and chins, and it creases and wrinkles. And the wrinkles of the very old are quite different from those of the middle-aged. No longer do they follow the contours of muscles that have repeatedly stretched the skin

Our skin clearly shows the signs of aging. It becomes thinner, less elastic, and dotted with patches of brown pigment. As this photograph shows, the predominant wrinkles follow definite patterns near the eyes and mouth and on the forehead. Only among the very old do wrinkles become more random.

in the same way—the laugh lines on the cheek, the "crow's feet" at the corners of the eyes, and the frown lines on the forehead. The wrinkles of the very old are an almost random arrangement of tiny little creases running in all directions between larger crevices. But these are the wrinkles of the very old; there is a long space of time between the appearance of our first wrinkles and the wizening of very old age. Some people have a surgical retightening of the skin in the interim—a "face-lift."

Other physical changes that have begun in middle age (or earlier) also continue. Hair becomes thinner or loses pigment; wear on remaining teeth (if any still remain) becomes more apparent, and gums continue to recede. Thus the caricature of the "old codger" might be either "toothless" or "long in the tooth."

The timing and the exact manifestations of these changes are sometimes very different in different individuals. Nutrition and physical activity can affect their appearance, as can genetic background.

Health and Strength

As we noted in Chapter 13, muscular strength may begin to decline very slowly in the thirties or the forties, particularly in the back and the lower body; the upper body (arms and torso) retains it strength for a longer time. But with the advent of old age, there is a progressive decline in strength. This relates not only to the gradual deterioration of muscles but also to the shortening and stiffening of tendons and ligaments, and to the weakening of bones (Spence, 1989). The bones of the old are more brittle than those of the young; consequently, they break more easily, and mend more slowly and with more difficulty—the condition of osteoporosis. As we saw in Chapter 15, osteoporosis is far more common among women than men, and is sometimes treated with estrogen. Both diets rich in calcium and exercise (earlier in adulthood) can do much to reduce osteoporosis.

We noted earlier that susceptibility to diseases changes from childhood through middle adulthood. Whereas the young are more susceptible to acute infections (colds, for example), those who are older suffer more from chronic complaints (back problems, heart disease). This pattern continues into old age. In addition, whereas the old are perhaps less susceptible to acute infections, they experience greater difficulty in coping with them. Upper respiratory infections are not often fatal among children, but they sometimes are among the very old.

With age, the entire cardiovascular system becomes less efficient, slower, and less able to cope with strenuous demands. In the same way, lungs typically do not function as well, kidneys and the liver are less efficient, and there may be changes in glandular functioning as well as in nervous system activity (Bromley, 1990).

The most common chronic conditions in people above the age of 65 include arthritis, hypertension, hearing impairment, heart conditions, visual impairments, and arteriosclerosis. Other diseases to which the elderly are susceptible include Parkinson's disease, which is linked to a deficiency in the neurotransmitter dopamine and which is often characterized by coarse tremors, generalized weakness, slow movement, sleep disturbances, and sometimes depression; cancer; kidney and urinary problems; osteoporosis; and acute brain syndrome, which may be characterized by confusion, speech disturbances, hysteria, paranoia, or other symptoms of mental disturbance, but which, to the extent that it is acute (as opposed to *chronic*, or recurring), will

generally respond to treatment. Acute brain syndrome often results from drug overdoses, toxic drug combinations, or excessive ingestion of alcohol. The elderly are particularly susceptible to acute brain syndrome, not only because of age-related changes in the brain and nervous system but also because many of the elderly take an alarming number and variety of prescription drugs (Cristofalo & Hayflick, 1985).

There is a danger, when listing the possible ailments of the aged, that we will confound aging with disease. Some diseases become more common with age; but they are not caused by age, and are therefore not an inevitable consequence of aging. Our focus, claims Butler (1989), should be on the extraordinary potential of the elderly.

Fitness and Exercise

When older adults were asked to throw tennis balls as hard and as well as they could, investigators found that they threw with about the same motions and velocities as 9- or 10-year-old children (Williams, Haywood, & Vansant, 1991). Clearly, with age, there is ordinarily a steady decline in flexibility, strength, stamina, and various aspects of physical performance. The important point, however, is that much of this decline does *not* result from primary aging processes. Hence, much of it is avoidable; and some is reversible.

In the absence of sustained training, for example, flexibility declines gradually from about age 12 (Haywood, 1986). But when Munns (1981) had groups of 65- to 88-year-olds participate in 1-hour exercise programs three times a week over a 3-month period, their flexibility improved on six different measures.

Evidence of the benefits of fitness and exercise are perhaps most dramatic in the case of older athletes. Many older adults cannot perform a single sit-up, or a modified push-up; yet competitors at a Seniors' Games event, which included such activities as track and field, tennis, swimming, golf, softball, and horseshoes, performed at levels far beyond expectations. O'Brien and Conger (1991) studied 199 of these elite senior athletes. They found these athletes generally exceeded performance levels of groups between 10 and 30 years younger. In fact, 70-year-old male athletes demonstrated higher grip strength than 60 percent of 17- to 19-year-olds. And 70-year-old women were as flexible as teenagers. The authors conclude, "Seniors who are physically active in late life are advantaged in terms of

O'Brien and Conger studied more than a hundred senior athletes and found that their performance levels generally exceeded those of groups as much as 30 years younger. With exercise and training, strength, muscular endurance, and joint flexibility can be maintained well into late adulthood.

strength, muscular endurance, and joint flexibility into their years beyond age seventy" (p. 78). It is also worth noting that these athletes were remarkably positive about life: They had plans and goals for the future, and they felt useful, important, and wanted.

Alzheimer's Disease

Alzheimer's is a brain disorder that occurs more in older than younger individuals. It was first found in a female patient by Dr. Alois Alzheimer in 1906 and may occur in people as young as 40 or as old as 80 or more. Physiologically, it involves a tangling and plaquing of nerve fibers visible under microscopic examination of the brain, as well as a gradual shrinking of the brain, and cannot be conclusively diagnosed without neurological examination after death (Goudsmit, Fliers, & Swaab, 1990). In general, the earlier the onset of the disease, the more rapid its progression (Bondareff, 1985).

Among the earliest symptoms of Alzheimer's is progressive loss of memory. Individuals suffering from the disorder gradually forget all sorts of information, including how to do things they have done all their lives. They can become confused and disorganized, easily lost—even in their own homes—and bewildered. Perhaps even more frightening, in the early stages of the disease, which can run over an 8- to 20-year course, they are often fully aware of what is happening to them. Eventually, they may not recognize people they have always known, and in advanced cases, they may lose all sense of their own personal identity. Affected individuals eventually revert to a speechless childishness; it is necessary to feed them, dress them, sit them on the toilet, and lead them around by the hand. It has been described as a type of "living death" in which the doors of the mind close one by one (CBC Television, 1986).

Alzheimer's is estimated to affect as many as 2 percent of individuals over the age of 65 and as many as 5 percent of those over 75 (Sloane, 1983). Its causes are still unknown, although various theories and findings implicate any of a combination of viruses (perhaps contracted in childhood but inactive or ineffectual until old age); genetic factors (incidence is much higher among people who have Down syndrome and among their relatives [Goldgaber et al., 1987]); metals (higher concentrations of zinc and aluminum have been found in the brains of some Alzheimer's victims (Goudsmit, Fliers, & Swaab, 1990); defects in brain neurotransmitter substances (there may be less acetylcholinesterase activity); and malfunctions of the immune system. In fact, probably each of these can be implicated because there appear to be different forms of Alzheimer's. Some of these are more genetically linked than others (Finch, 1989).

Alzheimer's remains a progressive and irreversible condition. There are several potential treatments including diet control of aluminum, attempts to reduce aluminum concentrations in victims, and the delivery of neurotransmitter substances to patients' brains by means of tiny pumps and plastic tubes that are surgically implanted. A control or perhaps even a cure may not be very far in the future.

Lest this brief examination of the health consequences of aging paint too grim a picture, let me hasten to point out that although some 86 percent of the elderly suffer from one or more major conditions, the majority do not consider their health to be a very serious problem. Remarkably few are bedridden, dependent, or hospitalized. In fact, only 5 percent of those over 65 and 17 percent of those over 85 are in any kind of institution (Troll, Miller, & Atchley, 1979).

Sensory Changes

As we saw in Chapter 15, beginning in early adulthood, there are very gradual changes in most of the sensory systems.

Vision. Virtually all individuals require at least one pair of prescription eyeglasses by the end of middle age, with men generally requiring them at younger ages than women. The most common problem is farsightedness, which is related to decreasing elasticity and thickening of the lens, and its consequent inability to focus clearly on nearby objects. The lens also becomes less transparent with age (Spence, 1989). Peripheral vision, depth perception, color vision, and adaptation to the dark also become poorer. In addition, approximately 90 percent of all people over 70 have at least the beginning of cataracts (Spence, 1989). However, most of these vision problems can be corrected with surgery, although over half of the blind are found among the elderly (Belsky, 1990). Blindness often results from glaucoma—increased pressure in the eyeball.

In spite of these potential problems, the vast majority of old people function very well with glasses.

Hearing. One of the major sensory changes associated with aging is *presbycusis*, the loss of hearing due to aging. Symptoms of presbycusis often begin in midlife and become more serious after the age of 60. They are more common for men than for women and are most evident in decreased sensitivity to higher tones and in difficulty in discriminating among different sounds (Belsky, 1990). It is partly for this reason that older people sometimes find it very difficult to follow conversations when there is background noise (other conversations, radio or television, or children playing, for example). The desire that many older people have for quiet environments may well be related not to an aversion to noise so much as to a desire to follow normal conversation without strain.

Loss of hearing among the elderly is caused at least in part by changes in the inner ear, including the loss of hair cells, which are closely involved in translating vibrations into nerve impulses (Olsho, Harkins, & Lenhardt, 1985), and also the loss of nerve cells along auditory pathways.

The psychological consequences of a hearing loss can be quite serious. Elderly people whose impairment is severe enough to seriously limit the ability to understand speech may be prevented from enjoying such pastimes as playing cards, watching television, attending movies and concerts, and so on. Even more serious, hearing-impaired elders may deliberately avoid social interaction and also suffer loss of self-esteem. The result may be loneliness and depression.

The physical changes that lead to hearing loss among the elderly can sometimes be corrected simply by removing earwax, or occasionally through surgery. In other cases, they are irreversible and irremediable. However, the auditory receiver (the hearing system) is only one of four components involved in the communication of oral messages. Fortunately, something can be done about the other three: the sender, the acoustic environment, and the acoustic signal (Olsho, Harkins, & Lenhardt, 1985). The acoustic signal, for example, can be amplified and sometimes clarified by means of a hearing device. The acoustic environment can be altered to eliminate background noise. In addition, something as simple as placing furniture so that speakers must face each other can be highly helpful. And the speaker can take pains to speak loudly (without shouting), to face the listener with mouth and lips in full view and uncovered, and to enunciate clearly and distinctly.

Other Senses. Many older people frequently find that food does not taste as good as it once did. Some use far more salt, pepper, and other spices than they did when younger, because both smell and taste become less acute in old age (Botwinick, 1984). In fact, in one study, subjects over 65 were about 10 times less sensitive to odors than subjects between 18 and 26 (Murphy et al., 1991). This diminishment is due to a combination of loss of nerve cells, changes in parts of the brain related to smell and taste, and the cumulative effects of life-style factors such as drinking alcohol, smoking, and perhaps eating spicy foods.

There is evidence, too, that some people may be somewhat less sensitive to pain in old age, although there are marked variations in the sensitivities of different people (Botwinick, 1984).

Changes in Reaction Time

Late adulthood comprises a substantial portion of the lifespan; it can last more than 30 years. As a result, it is highly misleading to make general statements about capacities and declines of this period as if they were common to the entire period. It is extremely important to keep in mind that the sensory losses and the physical changes that we have described thus far may be undetectable at the very beginning of late adulthood, and often occur so gradually that they are not easily noticed until very late in life—if at all.

Changes in reaction time are no different. Although it has long been established that reaction time slows significantly in late adulthood, it is *not* true that all elderly people are markedly slower than younger people.

On the average, however, people over 65 do not react as rapidly, either physically or mentally (Botwinick, 1984). That is, they do not reach conclusions or make decisions as rapidly; nor do they respond as quickly. As we see later in this chapter, this is one explanation for their poorer performance on timed cognitive measures. It is also part of the explanation for their worsening performance in sports that require rapid reactions (such as tennis, for example). And it explains in part why older people have proportionally more traffic accidents. There are, of course, other explanations for each of these observations, including changes in both physical functioning and sensory abilities.

Salthouse (1985) suggests that the most plausible explanations for the general age-related slowing of behavior do not involve *peripheral* processes—that is, processes relating to sensory and motor functioning as such. Instead, slowing is most likely related to changes in *central* processes, and especially to a slowing in cycletime—the amount of time required for neural activity. One of the important implications of this hypothesis is that it might also explain changes in cognitive functioning.

Reassuringly, exercise and activity can do a great deal to preserve optimal functioning in old age. As Salthouse (1985) notes, "it is now clear that healthier adults (particularly with respect to cardiovascular function) have faster reaction times than less healthy adults of comparable age" (p. 402).

Sexuality

One of the myths that we have long entertained with respect to the old is that they are essentially sexless—affectionate and emotional, perhaps, but generally devoid of either the desire or the ability for sexual expression. It bears repeating that this view *is* a myth, but as Cox (1988) points out, whereas society encourages sexuality among the young, it tends to disapprove of sexuality among the old.

Whereas society encourages sexuality among the young, it discourages its expression among the old. We tend to think of the very old as being much like children: affectionate but sexless. Yet research indicates that although sexual activity does decline with very old age, most older people with partners continue to be sexually active: These newlyweds are 84 and 76!

As we saw in Chapter 15, the climacteric does bring with it some important changes in sexual functioning. Most notably, it brings a cessation of reproductive capacity for women—an event that has generally occurred by age 50. Total loss of reproductive capacity for males may not occur until very old age, if at all. But in both sexes, the climacteric involves a significant reduction in the production of the sex hormones that are most closely associated with sexual interest and behavior in early years. Does that mean that the old must therefore lose their sexual interest?

Our best evidence indicates that this is not the case. Although sexual activity *does* decline with age, most people with partners remain sexually active into their seventh and eighth decades—and perhaps even later (Solnick & Corby, 1983). But there are some differences in sexual responsiveness between the young and the old. In the female, for example, after the climacteric there is a gradual shrinking and loss of elasticity in the uterus, a thinning of the walls of the vagina, and a loss of fatty tissue and elasticity surrounding the vagina. In addition, lubrication may occur more slowly and be less plentiful. As a result, some women may experience pain and irritation during intercourse. However, these changes are much less noticeable in some women than in others. Furthermore, in most women, the clitoris

remains sensitive to stimulation, so that the vast majority of women who were capable of orgasm when younger will not lose this capability.

Among men, there is a higher incidence of impotence with advancing age (Masters & Johnson, 1970). Indications are that as many as three out of four men above the age of 80 are impotent; however, in the sixties, impotence affects perhaps only one out of four men. This may be related less to age than to other factors such as heart or circulatory disease, diabetes, or certain types of surgery or medication (Solnick & Corby, 1983). In addition, older men often require more time and stimulation to achieve an erection, tend to be less active sexually than younger men, and may experience less intense orgasms.

Although sexual activity, defined in terms of intercourse or orgasm, clearly declines with advancing age, there is little evidence that sexual interest does likewise. When the definition of sexual activity is broadened to include a variety of activities such as caressing and holding, it becomes clear that sexuality can continue to be important through the upper reaches of the lifespan. How important it is appears to be related to three factors: age, sex, and previous sexual experience (Solnick & Corby, 1983). The youngest among the elderly are most active sexually; males are

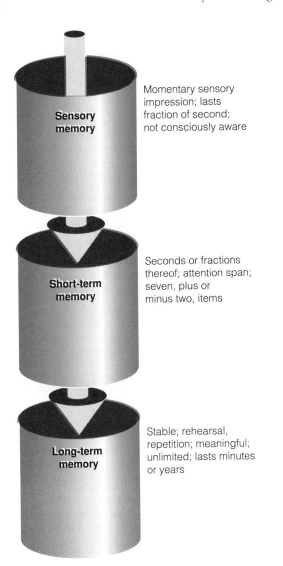

Sensory memory — Momentary sensory impression; lasts fraction of second; not consciously aware

Short-term memory — Seconds or fractions thereof; attention span; seven, plus or minus two, items

Long-term memory — Stable; rehearsal, repetition; meaningful; unlimited; lasts minutes or years

Figure 17.6 Model of an information-processing system of memory.

more active than females; and those who have been most sexually active through life are more likely to be active longer (Ludeman, 1981). We should note, however, that sexual behavior is a highly private matter for many, and perhaps even more so for the cohorts that have thus far reached old age. In addition, among these cohorts, extramarital sexual activity has not been widely accepted. Because the majority of very old women are *not* married but the majority of very old

men are, opportunities for sexuality in old age may be very limited for many women and less so for men. Succeeding cohorts may tell a different story.

Cognitive Changes

Physical changes are only one aspect of development in late adulthood, although they are often the most obvious. Intellectual changes, reflected primarily in changes in remembering, thinking, and problem solving, are a second important aspect of development.

Memory

We are, in effect, what we remember. To lose one's memory is also to lose one's identity. But loss of one's identity through memory loss is relatively rare, although it is sometimes the eventual outcome of Alzheimer's disease. Less extreme losses of memory, however, may not be uncommon with age. Indeed, one of our stereotypes of old age is the belief that old people have considerable difficulty learning new things and remembering recent events. Another related belief is that old people can remember things that happened long ago better than things that happened recently. We examine the validity of some of these beliefs in the following sections.

Information-Processing Model.
Our contemporary views of the human information processor, described in Chapter 9, are based on a three-stage model of information storage (see Figure 17.6). *Sensory memory* relates directly to the sensory systems (vision, taste, touch, and so on) and consists of the momentary impressions created by stimulation. Activity at this level is highly dependent on physiological systems associated with the senses.

Short-term memory (sometimes called *primary* or *working memory*) describes something like attention span. When we pay attention to information at the sensory level, it is momentarily transferred to short-term memory, where we can deal with it consciously.

Everything that we remember for longer periods of time is said to be stored in *long-term memory* (sometimes called *secondary memory*). Organization and elaboration are two important processes involved in storing information over a long period of time.

In practice, it is very difficult to separate learning from memory, although the ways in which each is studied are often different. Thus, although evidence that something has been learned is identical to evidence that it is remembered, studies of memory often look at the effects of experience after a time lapse, whereas studies of learning are generally more concerned with the immediate effects of experience. What is often unclear in memory research, however, is whether the inability to remember something is due to faulty memory or because it was never learned.

Sensory Memory. Differences between younger and older subjects with respect to sensory memory do not appear to be very significant before the age of 60 or more (Walsh & Thompson, 1978). Some of these differences may be associated with changes in the effectiveness of the sensory systems themselves (Poon, 1985). As we saw earlier, both vision and hearing (as well as taste, smell, and touch) become less sensitive with increasing age. And even though functioning of the senses that are our most important sources of information can be improved with glasses and hearing aids, the older person's sensitivity to sights and sounds will, on the average, be inferior to that of young people. Thus there may be less information to process in the first place. There is also some indication that neurological functioning may be slower in older people (Salthouse, 1985). Nevertheless, most researchers do not believe that differences in sensory memory capacity are sufficiently large to be very important in the business of processing and storing information.

Short-Term Memory. There are few differences in short-term memory between younger and older adults before age 60. One of the most common measures of short-term memory is a digit-span test, which is also part of many intelligence tests. It typically involves reading a series of unrelated numbers at 1-second intervals and having the individual recall as many as possible. Whereas a 5-year-old child might be capable of recalling three or four numbers, a young adult may remember seven or more, as will a middle-aged adult. However, there is an average loss of one digit during the decade of the sixties and loss of another digit during the seventies (Poon, 1985). These losses, in themselves, are probably not very significant decrements. And it is not clear whether they represent an actual loss in attention span (recall that short-term memory defines span of attention) or whether they relate,

instead, to a reduction in the speed with which the older person processes new information (Cunningham, 1989).

Long-Term Memory. So far, the evidence suggests that any differences in memory between middle-aged and younger adults are probably not due to differences in sensory or short-term memory (although some of the differences between the very old and the much younger might be). These differences are more likely due to changes in long-term memory.

There are several different ways of assessing long-term memory. If I want to know whether you remember the people in your first-grade class, I might ask you to name them for me. This illustrates a *recall* procedure; you simply retrieve material from memory as best you can. Alternatively, I might show you photographs of different individuals, among whom are the members of your first-grade class, and ask you to point your classmates out to me. This method relies on *recognition* rather than recall. A third method for assessing memory is to have individuals *relearn* material that was previously learned. To the extent that it takes less time to relearn than to learn initially, there is evidence of memory from the initial learning.

Of these three methods—recall, recognition, and relearning—the last is the most sensitive. That is, it is most likely to provide evidence of memory. The first, recall, is the least sensitive (the most difficult); it is most likely to provide no evidence of memory. The fact that we can recognize more than we can recall (without hints or clues) suggests that much of what we apparently forget is really not forgotten at all but simply cannot be retrieved. Put another way, many memory problems are problems of retrieval rather than problems of storage.

The distinctions between methods of measuring memory are particularly important when comparing the memories of older and younger people because apparently they change in different ways with age. Following a review of relevant research, Troll (1982) concludes that our abilities to *recognize* do not suffer from the ravages of time in the same way as our ability to *recall* does. For example, Bahrick, Bahrick, and Wittlinger (1975) found virtually no changes in the ability of individuals to recognize the names and photographs of those with whom they went to high school, whether they were tested 3 months or almost 50 years after leaving school. During the entire span, recognition hovered around 90 percent.

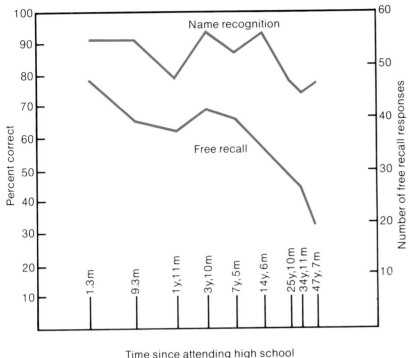

Interactive Figure 17.7 Free recall and name recognition as a function of age. How many of the names of your 12th-grade classmates can you recall and write down at this moment? Of your 8th-grade classmates? How many of those you have forgotten do you suppose you would *recognize* if you were shown a list of names that included them? The graph depicts the results of a study in which subjects who had left school between 1.3 months and 50 years earlier were asked either to recall the names of their former classmates or to recognize them from lists. (From Bahrick, Bahrick, and Wittlinger, 1975, pp. 62, 66. Reprinted by permission of The American Psychological Association and H. P. Bahrick.)

Unfortunately, our ability to recall does not appear to fare quite as well as does our ability to recognize. In the Bahrick, Bahrick, and Wittlinger (1975) study, recall of high school colleagues was less than 80 percent accurate after only 3 months, had dropped to around 60 percent after 4 years, and was below 50 percent 20 years later (see Interactive Figure 17.7).

Long-term memory in old age is clearly not as good as it once was (Light, 1991). Older people see themselves as more likely to foreget, as more absent-minded, as slower. Some use memory aids like pill alarms and whistling tea kettles to help them remember (Petro et al., 1991). But not all forget as much or as easily as we have sometimes imagined. Even among the very old, there are sometimes remarkable memories (Perlmutter, 1988).

Task Meaningfulness. Much of the research that has investigated age changes in long-term memory has looked at the ability to recall lists of words, most often memorized under laboratory conditions. In addition, this research has not usually taken into account important individual characteristics of learners such as verbal ability. Some researchers have argued that the material used in these studies is typically not meaningful for older subjects and that factors such as verbal ability or educational level — which might be related to cohort differences — might account for the apparently poorer

INTERVIEW

▶ Subject   Male; age 75; retired schoolteacher.

▶ Question   "Do you notice any difference in how well you remember things now compared to, say, 20 or 30 years ago?"

....

" *No. To be quite honest, I don't really. Maybe little things once in a while but nothing really important. Everybody forgets some things no matter how old they are. I think if I've forgotten more than, say, somebody your age, it's just because I've had that much more time to forget. What I mean is the saying that your memory goes when you get older isn't right. Your memory doesn't get poorer — except maybe if you're really old. What happens is that you forget a lot of things that happened 20 or 30 years ago. And when you're 50 or 60, the same thing happens. Everybody forgets what happened a long time ago no matter what their age unless it's something important. Then you remember it no matter how old you are. That's what I think.* "

ages 67.9 and 20.9, respectively) on a nonverbal task involving a series of events. These researchers conclude that memory for day-to-day happenings, especially if they are novel, is not as affected by age as are other memory tasks.

Other studies have also looked at the possibility that older subjects do not learn as efficiently. Some of these studies, for example, simply require subjects to organize or rehearse words until they can recall all of them (Moenster, 1972). Under these conditions, older subjects often remember as well as younger subjects when tested later, although they sometimes require more trials initially before they can recall all the words. Following a series of experiments, Howe (1988) concludes that both younger and older subjects are able to store more easily than retrieve. Typically, however, younger subjects (around age 22) performed better than older subjects (around age 70) on most storage and retrieval tasks (Light, 1991). One of the main differences between younger and older subjects is that older subjects process information more slowly (Salthouse & Babcock, 1991).

Some Conclusions.   The most important conclusions warranted by the evidence are the following:

- Sensory and short-term memory are not dramatically affected by the passage of time, although attention span (short-term memory span), which is normally somewhere around seven plus or minus two items, declines at an average of perhaps one item per decade after age 60.

- Long-term memory does decline with age after around age 65.

- There are important changes in the brain that probably underlie memory loss in old age. By age 90, the brain weighs about 10 percent less, largely because of loss of neurons (Spence, 1989). This reduction in brain mass is related to declining speed of responding in the elderly.

Several important observations can be made about these three conclusions. First, observed memory declines are seldom very noticeable before age 70 or beyond. Second, studies that have found the greatest differences between older and younger subjects have generally looked at the *speeded* recall of *unfamiliar* material. Many researchers have suggested that studies of this type may well be unfair to older people, who are usually not highly motivated to learn and remember

memories of older individuals. Accordingly, some have looked at memory using more meaningful stimuli and considering individual learner characteristics. For example, Cavanaugh (1983) compared the extent to which 20- and 60-year-old subjects understood and remembered segments from television programs. He found that while older subjects who were low on verbal ability did not do as well as younger subjects, those who were high on verbal ability understood and remembered as much as the 20-year-olds.

Ratner, Padgett, and Bushey (1988) compared the performances of older and younger subjects (average

lists of nonsense syllables or pairs of unrelated words (Belsky, 1984). Not surprisingly, age differences in long-term memory are not nearly so apparent when the materials are more meaningful and relevant to people's lives (Ratner, Padgett, & Bushey, 1988). Consequently, an increasing number of researchers in this area have begun to emphasize problems and tasks that are immediately relevant to their subjects. This *contextual* approach looks at such things as the ability to understand sentences, to recall meaningful instructions, and to employ available information in the solution of realistic problems. Under most circumstances, older subjects (usually 70 or older) do *not* perform as well on these tasks as do younger subjects (see Howe & Brainerd, 1988). However, on measures of what is called *personal* memory (the ability to recall events from one's life), there do not appear to be age-related deficits (Rybash, Hoyer, & Roodin, 1986).

The general pattern of declining memory in old age is *not* universal; there are many older people who maintain remarkable cognitive skills throughout life. It is continuing potential we should emphasize, says Perlmutter (1988), and not deficits.

Intelligence

In Chapter 15, we reviewed the most important concepts and findings with respect to changes in measured intelligence. Also, we examined the controversy between those who believe that intellectual capacity inevitably declines with age and those who think decline is not inevitable.

Decline or Stability. The research is far from conclusive, but it does reveal the following:

- Cross-sectional comparisons of intellectual performance have typically found far more striking evidence of intellectual decline than longitudinal studies. This suggests that cohort (or generational) influences may be responsible for some of the apparent difference in performance between older and younger subjects. Among other things, older cohorts are typically less well educated, did not grow up with television and computers, and have had considerably less exposure to the types of tasks that make up most intelligence tests. In the same way as height has increased over recent decades, there also seems to have been a trend toward generally higher measured IQs (Flynn, 1987).

- Longitudinal studies of changes in intelligence find little general decline in performance before age 67. For some specific abilities, there is little measurable decline prior to the ninth decade of life (Schaie et al., 1989).

- Intellectual abilities that are most likely to decline in old age are those that Cattell labeled *fluid*. These are reflected in measures of attention span, memory, or analysis of figures, and seem to be highly dependent on intact physiological systems but relatively independent of experience. Hence, their decline may be associated with physiological changes such as loss of neurons in the brain and reduced delivery of oxygen to the brain (Spence, 1989).

- Abilities that are least likely to decline and that may, in fact, continue to improve well into old age are the *crystallized* abilities. These are highly dependent on culture and experience, and are evident in verbal and numerical skills (see Figure 15.2 and Table 15.2 in Chapter 15). Thus older people sometimes do less well on the *performance* scales of the Wechsler tests; these require motor coordination, speed, dexterity, and spatial-visual abilities. In contrast, they continue to do as well and sometimes even better on the *verbal* scales of the Wechsler tests (vocabulary, information, comprehension) (Bromley, 1990). These scales deal with familiar, rather than unfamiliar, items and do not reward speed (or punish slowness) as do the performance scales.

In summary, there is some decline in intellectual performance with advancing age *on the average*. It must be stressed, however, that decline is not usually significant until near age 70 or beyond and that it is not universal in two senses: First, it does not affect all aspects of intellectual functioning equally; second, it does not affect all individuals equally.

When summarizing research of this nature, there is always the danger of mistakenly assuming that what is *generally* and *on the average* true must apply to all, or at least most, individuals. Not so. There are, in fact, 30-year-olds who experience measurable and sometimes very rapid and highly significant declines in intellectual functioning. In the same way, there are 60-, 70-, and 80-year-old people who also experience declines in intellectual functioning. Is age the cause, always and inevitably, in the case of the older people?

The simple answer is no. There is evidence, for example, that intellectual decline can occur throughout the lifespan as a result of illness (Belsky, 1990). Because

INTERVIEW

▶ Subject   Female; age 62; married; three children; four grandchildren; not working outside home; husband recently retired.

▶ Question   "Do you think old people are as intelligent as younger people?"

66 *That's a hard one. I guess probably not. I wouldn't do as well in school even at my age, let alone when I'm old. What I really think is old people just slow down an awful lot and their memory isn't as quick. Not that . . . well, there's some really smart old people too. But maybe not that many. We slow down when we get older.* 99

the elderly are more at risk of chronic illness than the young, observed differences in intellectual performance might conceivably be related to illness, or perhaps to drugs taken to counteract the illness, rather than to age itself.

Terminal Drop.   One curious observation based on studies of intellectual change in old age concerns the phenomenon labeled **terminal drop**. Some 3 decades ago, Kleemeier (1962) noticed that among subjects who died during the course of his longitudinal study, there were many whose measured intelligence dropped noticeably before death. Subsequently, other researchers noticed much the same thing: Many people experience a sudden drop in intellectual performance 1 or 2 years prior to dying (Riegel & Riegel, 1972). This finding has sometimes been explained in terms of a general decline in functioning that might be associated with poorer health preceding death (Palmore & Cleveland, 1975). Thus, sudden declines in IQ scores might be an early indication of a physical change and impending illness. However, not all cognitive declines are *terminal* in the sense that they herald death (Bromley, 1990).

Many older people deliberately *disengage* themselves from life. One manifestation of this disengagement might be a drastic reduction in motivation to do well on measures of intelligence.

Problem Finding and Intuition

Some evidence suggests that older people might approach problems at a lower level of abstraction than do adolescents or younger adults. For example, with respect to the Piagetian tasks that are typically used to investigate formal operations, older subjects *on the average* do less well than young adults (Denney, 1979). And in the game 20 Questions, adolescents and middle-aged adults typically ask general, abstract questions that allow them to eliminate large numbers of alternatives at once ("Is it alive?" "Is it vegetable?"); in contrast, the young and the elderly are more likely to ask very specific questions to test concrete hypotheses immediately ("Is it my baseball cap?" "Is it my gold star?"). In Bromley's (1990) words, "Old subjects tend to pay attention to irrelevant information, to miss or forget the point of the exercise, to let personal experience substitute for logical reasoning" (p. 198).

These findings do not necessarily mean that older persons are less *capable* of abstract and rational thought than adolescents. Newman and Newman (1983) argue that older adults may be as capable of rational thinking and abstract problem solving as younger adults, but that they simply approach problems differently. As we saw in Chapter 15, the thinking of older adults may be more pragmatic and more attuned to social and economic realities (Labouvie-Vief, 1980). As a result, abstract questions might not seem very meaningful or important to the elderly.

Datan, Rodeheaver, and Hughes (1987) note that when older adults are faced with abstract formal reasoning tasks, they tend to personalize them. Instead of applying the logico-deductive system that would lead directly to the correct solution, they rely on more personal and intuitive ways of thinking. Labouvie-Vief (1986) labels this approach *mythos* (for mythical, as opposed to *logos* for logic). Mythos is a form of thinking that is subjective, personal, and intuitive. But it is *not*, she insists, inferior to a formal, logical approach; it is simply different. The two types of thinking coexist, and in some adults, they reach a balance. In others, perhaps, there is an imbalance — an overreliance on intuition and pragmatics, and an underreliance on logic. It is as if the pendulum has now swung fully from the other extreme that once characterized adolescence, where the thinker believed in the omnipotence of logic.

Life, perhaps a little like school, is full of problems that require solutions and that demand decisions. But the problems presented to us in school are well defined and conform nicely to the methods of solution that we have been carefully taught. They have reassuringly simple answers, unique solutions that fit and that earn check marks and gold stars and smiles and hugs and pretty rainbows.

Many of life's problems are not so simple. Nobody presents them to us clearly defined; nobody teaches us the precise and appropriate methods for solving them; they have no simple, unique solutions; they tend to be long-term problems requiring long-term decisions, rather than short-term problems with immediately available solutions. Life's problems are open-ended and context-bound. Problems of human relationships, of history, of politics, of economics, cannot neatly be factored and solved. And there isn't always someone there to give us our gold stars and our hugs or to stamp neat check marks on our life's work.

In many ways, adulthood requires a different kind of thinking—not a schoolchild's thinking, which accepts teacher-determined problems and applies pre-learned strategies in an attempt to reach *the* correct solution, but thinking that is concerned more with identifying problems, with deciding which ones are in need of solution, and with determining which solutions are pragmatic and ethical. Accordingly, Arlin (1975) suggests that there might be a fifth Piagetian stage—one that goes beyond formal operations and that is concerned as much with *finding* as with *solving* problems. In this stage, the thinker is concerned less with the systematic application of the rules of logic than with the practical and pragmatic aspects of problems and their solutions. Thus, although older persons might not play the game of 20 Questions at as abstract and complex a level as the young adult, their solutions to real-life problems might be just as effective.

Some Cautious Conclusions

The research leaves little doubt that there are decrements in cognitive functioning with advancing age. But that most (or any) of these changes are the inevitable consequences of aging has not been established. And whether the changes are as large as research sometimes indicates or whether they are as significant in the lives of the elderly as we might think also is not entirely clear.

At least four important points must be considered when trying to interpret this research. First, we need to keep in mind that *performance* and *competence* are not identical (Baltes & Willis, 1979). Many reasons other than incompetence might lead an individual to perform poorly on some measure. These include fatigue, to which the elderly are susceptible; the low education of many older samples; physical and sensory problems such as poor hearing, vision, or motor control; differences in motivation; unfamiliarity with laboratories or testing instruments; and timidity.

Second, cognitive abilities are so complex that we cannot justifiably arrive at single, all-encompassing generalizations that will still be accurate. As we saw, for example, research indicates that some cognitive abilities do *not* decline but that others do. In the same way, sensory memory (immediate recognition of auditory or visual stimuli) does not appear to change much with age, but longer-term memory does (Poon, 1985).

Third, there are vast cognitive differences among individuals at *all* ages, and, in addition, there are some fundamentally important cohort differences. Not only is there a tremendous variability within a single age group (one cohort), but there may also be great variability between two different cohorts. These observations make it clear that many observed differences in cognitive competence and performance are related to factors other than age.

Finally, an increasing number of studies demonstrate that intellectual performance can be improved, sometimes dramatically, through various training programs (Denney, 1979). To the extent that this is the case, intellectual decline is not a primary aging process.

Adult Learning

The reality of *eventual* decline in the performance of physical and intellectual tasks cannot be denied. However, in most cases, these declines do *not* significantly affect the older person's ability to adjust to changes or to cope with the demands of everyday life throughout most of late adulthood. For most individuals, learning can, and does, continue throughout the lifespan. In fact, as noted above, it is possible to significantly improve the memories of older people through systematic training programs (Rybash, Hoyer, & Roodin, 1986).

Later adulthood increasingly is a time for new learning. Proliferating adult education programs specialize in high-interest courses: woodcarving, bird watching, dog training, hydroponics, creative writing, painting, gardening, dancing, weaving, ceramics . . .

Increasingly, older people are going back to school after retirement. As a result, adult education programs are proliferating. Many of these specialize in high-interest courses, responding to the fact that many older people take courses primarily out of personal interest. For many, retirement means that they can finally do what they have wanted to do for a long time.

There are others, too, who undertake programs for more practical reasons, who see potential economic benefit from learning. For example, it is increasingly common for a retired person to take courses in order to launch a cottage industry—market gardening, hydroponics, ceramics, freelance accounting, writing, and on and on. Second careers often begin in middle adulthood, but there are some that begin in late adulthood as well.

Learning programs that are geared to the very old need to consider some of the possible differences between the old and the young. For example, the learning environment needs to be comfortable, well lighted, and free from distracting background noises. The stimuli used should consider the probability that some learners will have hearing or vision losses. Accordingly, speech should be clear, distinct, and unhurried; printed materials should be nonglossy (to reduce glare), and typefaces should be bold and high-contrast; and steps should be taken to ensure that the material presented is interesting, personally relevant, and not overly demanding.

It is a social failing that our culture, unlike that of the Chinese (Ho, 1983), does not encourage reverence for the elderly. The old can contribute a great deal to society—witness Picasso, Segovia, and George Burns.

Even if they do not paint, play, act, write, or grow orchids, the elderly are perhaps much wiser.

Wisdom

Wisdom is a particular quality of human behavior and understanding that has long been associated with old age. This quality appears to combine the types of intuition, emotion, and knowledge that are not easily available to those whose experiences span only a few years. Thus it is that we believe the ancients — the old ones — to be wise.

Wisdom is not a highly obvious and easily measured human characteristic, which might account for its relative absence in psychological literature. Peck (1968), in his elaboration of Erikson's theory, is one of the few developmental theorists to mention wisdom specifically as an age-related characteristic. According to Peck, as physical strength and endurance decline, one of the important developmental tasks that faces the adult is that of valuing wisdom rather than physical powers. But what, precisely, is wisdom? How does it develop? And does it truly belong only to the old?

Philosophical Conceptions

Psychology suggests a few tentative answers for these questions, but in the main, biblical history and ancient philosophy deal most thoroughly with wisdom. Clayton and Birren (1980) present a review of some of the important literature. Among other things, they note that although wisdom is universally acknowledged as a quality most commonly found in older persons, Eastern and Western beliefs concerning how it is most likely to be acquired differ somewhat.

In the West, there have been three paths to wisdom — all of which need to be followed if the individual is to be truly wise. The first is that of formal education, which historically emphasized the ability to make intelligent judgments and thoroughly reasoned decisions. The second path involved listening to and learning from parents or other important and influential mentors. The third path to wisdom is that of faith — in some ways a far easier path than the first two: Some individuals are simply chosen to be wise. These people are given wisdom in the same way that others are given long noses or curly hair.

Eastern conceptions concerning paths to wisdom are somewhat different. In the main, these are tied to religion, but unlike the Western belief that having faith might be sufficient to be granted wisdom, most Asian religions require great sacrifice and dedication on the part of those who would be wise. These religions often prescribe specific behaviors and regimens, such as meditation or fasting, that must be followed by those who are disciples of wisdom. Most have in common the belief that wisdom (often referred to as enlightenment) requires long periods in the presence of a *master* teacher.

Both Western and Eastern conceptions of wisdom view it as a type of knowledge that leads to a greater understanding of reality (of life, its meaning and purpose, and so on). And if the descriptions of its development provided by East and West are accurate, it is unlikely that the young will be very wise.

Psychological Conceptions

The adult thinker, Basseches (1984) informs us, does not always apply the straightforward rules of logical, deductive thought to the solution of real-life problems. Instead, the mature thinker may bring to bear a form of thought that is uniquely adult: dialectical thinking. To think dialectically is to recognize contradictions and to deal with them. The adult thinker understands that knowledge is relative rather than absolute, that reality abounds with contradictions, and that the most effective kind of thinking is contextual — that is, it arises from the practical, real-life circumstances that surround contradictions.

Interestingly, these characteristics of dialectical thinking are very similar to Dittmann-Kohli and Baltes' (1986) description of what is involved in the ability to make wise decisions. Specifically, they suggest that wise decision making requires (1) some level of skill or expertise relevant to the problem at hand, (2) emphasis on the practical aspects of solutions, (3) a related emphasis on the problem's context, (4) a recognition of uncertainty, and (5) relativism in judgment and behavior. In other words, wisdom is a sort of marriage between knowledge and a pragmatic or practical intelligence. Dittmann-Kohli and Baltes suggest that as a result of the wisdom that older people acquire, they are better able to resolve complex interpersonal problems.

Clayton and Birren (1980) conducted a study designed to determine how wisdom is seen by individuals of different ages and whether it is typically associated with the elderly. Their sample consisted of 21-year-olds, 49-year-olds, and 70-year-olds. Subjects were presented with 15 terms that might be considered to be related to wisdom (for example, *intuitive, pragmatic, understanding, gentle, sense of humor,* and so on). These were presented in 105 pairs, and subjects were asked to judge how similar each pair was. (For example, are *wise* and *aged* highly similar? Are *experienced* and *knowledgeable* alike?)

Wisdom is a particular combination of knowledge, gentleness, patience, and intelligence that is more often associated with age than with youth. This marriage of knowledge and intelligence requires a recognition of life's uncertainty and an ability to draw from one's life experiences and apply those lessons to new challenges.

In general, this study revealed that most subjects do tend to associate wisdom with age. Strikingly, however, older subjects are less likely to see themselves as being wise, although younger subjects view them that way. Thus older subjects were less likely to associate *experience* and *aged* with *wise*; they were more likely to judge emotional qualities such as *empathetic* and *understanding* as being more closely related to wisdom. Does this mean that the wise do not recognize their own wisdom? Or does it mean that the wisdom that the young attribute to the old is merely an illusion?

It is perhaps significant that, historically, positions of greatest responsibility requiring fundamentally important decisions are seldom entrusted to the young. With some notable exceptions, presidents, popes, emperors, and kings and queens have generally been older rather than younger. Lehman (1953) found that even in industry and commerce, the peak age for leadership was above 65. Perhaps even more significant, Dennis (1966) reports that maximum creative output in the

fields of history and philosophy occurs in the sixties, seventies, and beyond. And there are countless examples of outstanding achievement in art (Pablo Picasso, Anna "Grandma" Moses), music (Andres Segovia), and literature (Laura Wilder, Goethe, Shakespeare) by individuals well into old age.

The Implications of Physical and Cognitive Change

Although it might be somewhat distressing to contemplate the increasing probability of decline with age, most of us will in the end cope successfully and even happily with aging—should we be lucky enough to live that long. We are, after all, human, and part of being human is being resilient, remembering the good things, and always having hope. There is little evidence that age robs us of any of these qualities.

There are other reasons, too, why the aged might cope successfully with whatever declines and losses they experience. To begin with, changes often occur so slowly that it is often possible to adapt to them without making any major adjustments. In addition, other people of the same age also experience similar changes, and that, presumably, makes life easier. Even

more dramatic and perhaps more personal changes that might initially appear to be totally devastating (knowledge of a serious health problem or death of a spouse, for example) can usually be adapted to. It is important to keep in mind that physical and cognitive decline is only one feature of the lives of the very old. Increasing wisdom and peaceful reflectiveness may be others.

As the studies of life satisfaction that we review in the next chapter clearly show, happiness and joy can continue to come from many sources.

Main Points

1. The elderly are frequently the object of *ageism* (negative prejudices that are based solely on age), evident in media portrayals, in expected behaviors, and in child-directed speech.

2. Old age is socially defined as beginning at age 65. The proportion of people over 65 in the United States has increased fivefold in this century, while the entire population has slightly more than doubled. In many industrialized countries, life expectancies (but not lifespans) have increased nearly 50 percent since the turn of this century. In the United States, women can expect to live an average of 8 years longer than men.

3. Theories of aging include genetic theory (lifespan limits are programmed in cells), cell-malfunction theory (cell errors, toxins, free-radicals, or cross-linked cells hamper normal cell functioning), or autoimmunity theory (our immune systems become defective and attack the wrong cells).

4. Longevity is related to sex, race, mobility, education, occupation, employment, locale, heredity, and other factors. In some cultures, people age better than in others, remaining vigorous, employed, and socially useful throughout life. In the Western model, there is sharp discontinuity between the "useful" years and retirement; in more *continuous* models, there is no loss of status attached to aging.

5. *Senescence* describes biological decline as a function of age. Although biologists have not identified any completely universal characteristic of aging, certain changes eventually affect most individuals (for example, arteriosclerosis and increased susceptibility to cancer, arthritis, and acute brain syndrome).

6. Age-related changes that affect appearance include changes in posture, loss of skin elasticity and consequent wrinkling, loss of hair or hair pigmentation, and loss of teeth or recession of gums. Other changes include lower susceptibility to acute infections and higher susceptibility to chronic conditions (arthritis, hearing losses, heart disease, visual impairment, and arteriosclerosis).

7. Alzheimer's disease is a brain disorder marked by deterioration of brain tissue (tangling and plaquing of nerve fibers). Alzheimer's is characterized by a gradual loss of memory and resulting confusion, disorientation, and eventual loss of sense of personal identity.

8. Changes in sensory functioning with age include increasing farsightedness, hearing impairment, and loss of taste and smell sensitivity. On average, people over the age of 65 do not react as quickly mentally or physically.

9. Age-related changes in sexual functioning among women include diminished lubrication and loss of

vaginal elasticity; in males, greater time for achieving an erection and orgasm, and decline in the force of ejaculation and the intensity of orgasm. Old age brings some decline in sexual interest and activity, but in most cases, sexual activity can continue well into old age.

10. Sensory and short-term memory are not dramatically altered by the passage of time, although attention span is reduced by an average of one item per decade after age 60. Long-term memory declines after age 65. When older people are tested under unspeeded conditions with familiar and meaningful material, age differences in long-term memory are less significant.

11. Older–younger differences in intellectual performance in cross-sectional studies reflect cohort differences that are probably related to educational and other environmental differences between older and younger generations.

12. Longitudinal studies of intellectual performance find little general decline before the age of 67. Decline is most apparent for abilities highly dependent on physiology rather than experience (*fluid*: memory or attention span, for example); they are least apparent for abilities highly dependent on experience and education, which sometimes continue to increase in old age (*crystallized*: verbal and numerical skills).

13. Measured IQ appears to drop, sometimes dramatically, in some individuals within 1 or 2 years of their deaths; labeled *terminal drop*, this phenomenon is sometimes a sign of health problems.

14. Older adults often do not do as well as younger individuals on tasks requiring abstract reasoning. Labouvie-Vief describes the thinking of older adults as more intuitive and more personal (*mythos*) rather than formal and logical (*logos*).

15. Declines on measures of intelligence might reflect problems of *performance* rather than lack of *competence* and can perhaps be partly explained in terms of the greater susceptibility of the old to fatigue, differences in motivation and education, physical and sensory problems, and their unfamiliarity with contemporary tests and testing procedures.

16. Adult learning is a fast-growing field of education that reflects well the capabilities, interests, and enthusiasm of many older people. Courses for the elderly are often of a personal interest and self-improvement type; some are designed to facilitate late-adulthood career or avocation changes.

17. Wisdom is one of the positive qualities we typically associate with old age. The characteristics of dialectical thinking (openness to contradiction, recognition of the relative nature of knowledge, emphasis on context and pragmatics, acceptance of uncertainty) are closely related to what psychologists think of as *wise* decision making.

18. Elderly adults, on average, adjust well to aging. The majority continue to experience joy and happiness in their lives.

Further Readings

A moving look at creativity and learning among the old is presented in:

Koch, K. (1977). *I never told anybody.* New York: Random House.

Physiological changes of old age are clearly outlined in Spence's book. Especially relevant for this chapter is his account of theories of aging, and his discussion of sensory changes:

Spence, A. P. (1989). *Biology of human aging.* Englewood Cliffs, NJ: Prentice-Hall.

Far more complete accounts of aging than can be contained in a single chapter may be found in the following books:

Belsky, J. K. (1990). *The psychology of aging* (2nd ed.). Pacific Grove, CA: Brooks/Cole.

Cox, H. G. (1988). *Later life: The realities of aging* (2nd ed.). Englewood Cliffs, NJ: Prentice-Hall.

The following three books are good sources of information about cognitive changes in late adulthood. Bromley's book deals with some of the social implications of aging in contemporary society; Howe and Brainerd's book is a collection of research-based, somewhat technical chapters dealing with memory and cognition; and the Rybash, Hoyer, and Roodin book is a somewhat simpler synthesis of thinking in this area:

Bromley, D. B. (1990). *Behavioural gerontology: Central issues in the psychology of ageing.* New York: John Wiley.

Howe, M. L., & Brainerd, C. J. (Eds.) (1988). *Cognitive development in adulthood: Progress in cognitive development research.* New York: Springer-Verlag.

Rybash, J. M., Hoyer, W. J., & Roodin, P. A. (1986). *Adult cognition and aging: Developmental changes in processing, thinking, and knowing.* New York: Pergamon.

that comes with having enough money and partly because those who are healthy and who have sufficient money are more easily able to remain actively involved (Kelly & Westcott, 1991).

Another factor that appears to be related to happiness is *educational level* (Dillard, Campbell, & Chisolm, 1984). Again this may be related to the opportunities that education provides for continued involvement in interesting activities, such as reading or doing crossword puzzles, sometimes well beyond the time that physical strength, energy, or general well-being allows more physical involvements.

It is noteworthy that in DeGenova's (1992) study, in response to the question "What would you do differently if . . .?" participants most regretted not having spent more time on education and intellectual self-improvement.

There are several personality characteristics that also appear to contribute to happiness. Costa and McCrae (1984), in a longitudinal investigation of psychological well-being, identified three such characteristics: *emotional stability, objectivity*, and *friendliness*. Those high on measures of emotional stability are, by definition, less likely to suffer serious depression. Those who are characterized by objectivity rather than subjectivity are less concerned with internal states, perhaps less preoccupied with declining capacities, and, by the same token, more likely to be involved in external activities. And those high on friendliness are more likely to have more friends and to satisfy continuing needs for intimacy.

Close friendships are extremely important to maintaining what Lowenthal and Haven (1981) refer to as *high morale* — a quality closely related to what we have been calling happiness. In a study of morale, these researchers looked at the importance of intimate friends (confidants) in the lives of 280 individuals above the age of 60. All resided in the community rather than in institutions, and many were divorced or widowed. Some had intimate friends in whom they could confide; others did not. For those who were married, the confidant was often, although not always, the spouse.

Results of the study indicate strongly that the presence of a confidant can be of tremendous importance in maintaining morale, even in the face of serious and tragic events such as the death of a spouse or serious illness. Perhaps equally important, in the absence of a confidant, progressive social disengagement (withdrawal from old social roles — for example, retirement) was often associated with depression. This was far less likely to be the case for those individuals who had access to an intimate friend. Indeed, even those who *increased* their social roles but had no confidants were more likely to become depressed than those who decreased their roles but did have confidants.

In conclusion, we cannot easily say that old age is a happier or a sadder time than any other in the lifespan. For some, it may indeed be happier, or at least as happy; for others, it might be much sadder. But whether it brings sorrow, joy, or simple resignation, it will also bring new roles and new problems, and it requires a whole new set of adjustments. Perhaps none of these adjustments is more difficult or painful than the need to face the certainty of death. We look at this topic in Chapter 19.

Main Points

1. Cohler's *personal narrative* approach argues that our lives are not nearly as predictable or as orderly as stage theories imply, but that we maintain a sense of continuity and stability by constructing a sensible personal narrative out of our lives.

2. Erikson's late-adulthood stage, *integrity versus despair*, requires a positive evaluation of life and a decision that its final outcome is natural, inevitable, and acceptable. In the absence of these outcomes, despair may result.

3. Peck details three psychosocial conflicts that compose the final Erikson stage: *ego differentiation versus work-role preoccupation* (need to shift preoccupations from career to self at retirement), *body transcendence*

versus body preoccupation (danger of becoming preoccupied with declining physical and mental powers), and *ego transcendence versus ego preoccupation* (an acceptance of death).

4. The life review is an active process wherein the older adult recalls important aspects of the past, including unresolved conflicts, evaluates these, and synthesizes them. A positive outcome of this process is the view that life has been at least satisfactory.

5. Retirement is a 20th-century phenomenon made possible by a high standard of living, high worker productivity, and a surplus of labor. Increasing numbers of older people, declining birthrates, and continued inflation may change the retirement scene.

6. Attitudes toward retirement are important predictors of satisfaction and healthy adjustment after retirement. Retirement is most likely to be positive if it is voluntary rather than forced, if work is not the only thing in the person's life, if health and income are sufficient to permit the enjoyment of newly created leisure, and if retirement has been planned.

7. Atchley describes several phases of retirement: *pre-retirement* (fantasies about retirement), *honeymoon* (vigorous doing of things not done before), *rest and relaxation* (a quiet period), *disenchantment* (a relatively rare period of disillusionment), *reorientation* (coming to terms with disenchantment), *routine* (establishing satisfying routines), and *termination* (withdrawal from the retirement role).

8. Most of the elderly cope with the processes of aging and continue to find contentment and joy in their lives. *Disengagement* theory suggests that, with failing physical and mental capabilities, the elderly seek to withdraw from active social roles and that they should be allowed, perhaps encouraged, to do so. *Activity* theory argues that continued social, physical, and emotional involvement is important to physical and emotional well-being.

9. Family relationships are ordinarily the most important of all social relationships throughout the entire lifespan—and other than that with a spouse, the most important are with children.

10. There are several possible roles of grandparents: *surrogate parent* (caring for children), *fun-seeking* (indulgent playmate), *distant figure* (occasional gifts), *reservoir-of-family-wisdom* (awe, fear-, and obedience-inspiring patriarch or matriarch of extended family), and *formal* (nonintrusive but emotionally involved).

11. Marriages tend to become happier with the empty nest and remain happy into old age. Sexual interest and responsiveness often decline in very old age. Among women, a decline in sexual activity is most often due to lack of a suitable partner.

12. In late adulthood, close friends serve important roles relating to intimacy, social and intellectual stimulation, confiding, relieving stress, and support during crises.

13. Filial responsibility is a common feature of most family systems. In contemporary Western societies, filial responsibility may be manifested in doing things with and for elderly parents, in caring for them, and sometimes in sharing living accommodations.

14. Alternatives to institutional care include arrangements involving filial responsibility as well as various forms of community-based assistance that make it possible for the elderly to continue to live in their homes in relative independence. Most of the elderly prefer to remain independent.

15. Although satisfaction with life appears to increase with age (we achieve our goals or become resigned to not doing so), happiness may decrease for some individuals. Health, income, friendships, and personality appear to be important for later happiness and high morale.

Further Readings

The processes and implications of reminiscence in old age are considered in:

Coleman, P. G. (1986). *Aging and reminiscence processes: Social and clinical implications*. New York: Wiley.

This candid, short, and highly readable book deals specifically with many of the problems of aging, including loneliness, illness, spirituality, and relationships with aging parents:

Weininger, B., & Menkin, E. L. (1977). *Aging is a lifelong affair*. Lost Angeles: Guild of Tutors Press.

A highly insightful look at the personal experience of aging is the following:

Breytspraak, L. M. (1984). *The development of self in later life*. Boston: Little, Brown.

Atchley's book provides a comprehensive look at aging in contemporary North America. Especially pertinent to this chapter is his chapter on employment and retirement:

Atchley, R. C. (1985). *Social forces and aging: An introduction to social gerontology* (4th ed.). Belmont, CA: Wadsworth.

The following is an interesting collection of articles dealing with aging and the care of the elderly in Britain:

Bytheway, B., Keil, T., Allatt, P., & Bryman, A. (Eds.). (1989). *Becoming and being old: Sociological approaches to later life*. London: Sage.

Winslow Homer: *Sunlight on the Coast*, 1890. The Toledo Museum of Art, gift of Edward Drummond Libbey.

"People can't die, along the coast," said Mr. Peggotty, "except when the tide's pretty nigh out. They can't be born, unless it's pretty nigh in — not properly born, till flood. He's a going out with the tide."

Charles Dickens, *David Copperfield*

IX

The End

Chapter 19 Dying and Grieving

A book is a little like a life. It has a beginning, a middle, and an end. And sometimes it seems to have a willfulness, a vitality, that are reminiscent of life.

But if it has life, then it must also have death. Because one is surely the price to be paid for the other. Much as we would like not to think so, they are two sides of the same coin, are they not? Is there ever one without the other?

Sadly, the tide is nigh out for this book. There remains only one last chapter in this, the final section.

Throughout this book, the coin of life has lain faceup on the table of our reason. Now, in this final chapter, we must pick it up, turn it, and look at the other side.

Dying and Grieving

Do not go gentle into that good night,
Old age should burn and rave at close of day;
Rage, rage against the dying of the light.

Dylan Thomas, *Do Not Go Gentle*

Old man! 'Tis not so difficult to die.

Lord Byron, *Manfred*

Dying is a highly personal thing. For some, perhaps it is not so difficult, but there are many who burn and rave and rage at its coming. My grandfather tried to go more gently and with a little humor. Having probably read a translation of Viscount Henry John Temple Palmerston's famous last words, he paraphrased them for my grandmother: "Die?" he is reported to have said, "That's the last thing I'm gonna do!" Which he then did.

That, of course, is the problem with dying. Once we have done it, we can no longer write textbooks — or even letters — about it. We take its secrets to our graves.

But science has ways to pry the dusty grave, ways to define, analyze, and measure even this most private, unique, and ultimate of all events.

This Chapter

Science's mutterings about death and dying are the subject of this chapter. It looks at what death is, at how medicine and common sense define it. It examines developmental changes in our beliefs about dying. It traces the stages that death may take. And it deals with the effects of death on those who are left to mourn.

And in the end, the chapter turns and looks once more at the themes that were presented at the very beginning of the text — themes that underlie our study and understanding of development through the lifespan.

Death

I remember my first, childish experience with death. Mouche, Marc Voisin's dirty-yellow dog, cornered a bear in the raspberries, whereupon the bear clouted him on the side of the head. We found him lying there among the raspberry canes. "I think he's dead," Marc announced gravely.

"How can you tell?" I asked.

"My dad showed me," he answered. "Wait." And off he ran, leaving me alone with the dog. I waited a long time standing in the raspberry canes, looking at Mouche but not quite daring to touch him; I wasn't absolutely certain that death isn't catching.

When Marc came back, he had a small mirror, which he held in front of the dog's nostrils. "If he's still alive, it'll cloud over," Marc said. "That's what my dad showed me."

Mouche was dead; we had proved it. Then we proved we were still alive by repeatedly clouding the mirror. And for a while after that, I took to carrying a small mirror around with me in case I should ever need it — until Robert Gaudry tripped me and I fell into the river and broke my mirror and maybe almost died in the process, which I wouldn't have had a mirror to prove.

Some Definitions

Science doesn't need a mirror to prove death, but in some ways, the medical sciences have complicated our notions of dying. Not very many years ago, if someone stopped breathing, or the heart stopped beating, everybody agreed that that person was dead. Doctors noted, as well, that the pupils dilated when someone died, that being the reason, in so many movies, the possibly dead person's eyelids are lifted by someone who then peers intently at the eyeball. Other changes that characterize death include eventual rigor mortis (stiffening of the corpse) and relaxation of the sphincter muscle.

Now, however, there is a new concept of **death** in the medical professions: that of neurological, or brain, death. When the dying person's heart and lungs stop functioning, the brain is quickly deprived of oxygen, and electrical activity of the brain, detected by means of an electroencephalogram (EEG), eventually stops. Death is said to have occurred following complete cessation of brain activity for a certain period of time. However, recent medical advances now make it possible to restart heart and lung action or to substitute for their normal functioning by means of life-sustaining equipment. In fact, it is now possible to keep some people alive in the physiological sense — that is, their bodies consume and process nutrients and oxygen, and eliminate wastes, even though they have suffered irreparable brain damage as a result of temporary cessation of heart and lung activity. Defining death in such circumstances presents serious medical and ethical problems.

Bereavement is the term used to describe the loss suffered by those who are friends and relatives of the person who has died. The bereaved are those left behind—those from whom something has been taken. Bereavement is typically accompanied by **grief**—the bereaved person's emotional reaction to the loss. Grief reactions may include feelings of anger, guilt, anxiety, depression, or preoccupation with thoughts of the deceased (Parkes, 1972). In addition, grief reactions sometimes include physical components such as shortness of breath, dizziness, heart palpitations, loss of appetite, sighing, and so on. As we saw in Chapter 18, there is also a slight reduction in life expectancy for the widowed person for a few years immediately following death of the spouse (we look at grief in more detail later in this chapter). The term **mourning**, which describes external manifestations of grief, is often used to indicate a period of time during which the bereaved person grieves.

Notions of Death Through the Lifespan

Cox (1988) suggests that the most common attitude toward death is fear. We do not easily resign ourselves to the inevitability of our ends. We deny death in countless ways. We seldom speak seriously about it—and we speak of it in a *personal* way even less often. Nor are we willing to admit our fear of dying, says Belsky (1990); somehow, it embarrasses us. When death does come, we often pretend that it is an accident—especially if it came before the end of what we expect will be a normal lifespan. We use expressions such as *untimely* or *sudden* or *unexpected* to describe it. And we invent euphemisms to replace the harsh reality of the words *dead* or *died*: "Passed away," we say, or "dearly departed," or "departed loved ones," or "gone beyond."

Contemporary society distances itself from death not only in its language, but also in the way funerals are generally handled. For example, it has become increasingly less common for the deceased to be kept at home, or even in churches, for a brief period of mourning. Close to 90 percent of all funerals now occur in funeral parlors, with brief periods of visitation by family members and friends (Kephart, 1950).

The process of dying, itself, is often very private. Many hospitals go to great lengths to isolate patients who are expected to die, and then remove the bodies as unobtrusively as possible. Unless we have been in wars, or have witnessed automobile accidents or other similar events, most of us have not had a great deal of exposure to human death and dying. For many, all there has been is a brief glimpse of the deceased in a well-lined casket. Ironically, under these circumstances, the dead are carefully arranged to look as *lifelike* as possible.

Given our society's widespread denial and avoidance of death, what do children—to say nothing of adolescents and adults at all stages of adulthood—know of dying?

Early Childhood

Many children's first real exposure to death comes when a family pet dies. But for most, there is a great deal of secondhand exposure to death and dying in the media. Television is especially prone to presenting vivid and dramatic portrayals of death—especially of violent death. Its depictions of grief and remorse are considerably more rare.

Do children, as a result of personal and vicarious experience, understand death?

Early research and theorizing indicated that they typically know very little. Nagy (1948) interviewed children and identified three stages in their understanding of death. The first (ages 3–4) is marked by the beginning of an understanding, although at this stage, children do not understand the finality of death. They believe, for example, that those who are dead are simply "not here"—that they continue to breathe and eat—that they are, in other words, something and somewhere. During the next stage (ages 5–9), children begin to *personify* death. It becomes a "bogeyman," a "witch," or some other wicked something that is capable of taking people away. In the third stage (age 9 onward), children begin to understand that the end of life is a biological process, that its cause lies within the body rather than with some outside force.

Although subsequent research has often found evidence corroborating the unfolding of stages such as these, children apparently can develop an understanding of death at considerably earlier ages. Bluebond-

Langner (1977) suggests that the reason children do not understand the nature of death is not that they are *incapable* of understanding but simply that they have not had experiences with death. This interpretation seems particularly appropriate, because more recent research indicates that children are not nearly as naive as was once thought (Tallmer, Formanek, & Tallmer, 1974). Television has done a great deal to provide children with vicarious experiences that contribute to their early understanding of death and dying. And it is perhaps partly for the same reason that so many adolescents and young adults *expect* to die within a few years, most from violent causes (Teahan & Kastenbaum, 1970).

The fact that children's answers to questions about death and dying reveal only a primitive awareness of what dying is does not mean that they do not understand or respond to *loss*. The ability to verbalize an understanding of death presupposes some relatively advanced cognitive *and* language skills. Perhaps because infants and young children do not yet possess these skills, their cognitive understanding of death seems undeveloped. In fact, overwhelming behavioral evidence indicates that loss does have profound meaning for them (Bloom-Feshbach & Bloom-Feshbach, 1987). Even very young infants experience profound distress at the loss of a caregiver, evident in disturbances in feeding and sleeping, in clinging behavior, and in crying. For example, Bowlby (1980) describes how a 12-month-old infant spent days crying for his mother after she had died, how he turned in the direction of every sound that might be her. Eventually, in Bowlby's words, such a child "becomes apathetic and withdrawn, [characterized by] a despair broken only perhaps by an intermittent and monotonous wail. He is in a state of unutterable misery" (p. 9).

Later Childhood

As children become older and more sophisticated intellectually, their understanding of death becomes progressively more adultlike. But for most of them, thoughts of death are remote and abstract. There is little reason to be concerned with dying when the future stretches ahead seemingly forever.

Kastenbaum (1985) suggests that people's understandings of death at any age may have as much, or more, to do with their life experiences than with their age. Thus, although active, healthy children do not

ordinarily think very much about death, and do not necessarily develop very sophisticated notions of what it means, those who are terminally ill seem to have an understanding of dying that goes well beyond their years. Bluebond-Langner (1977) reports that terminally ill children understand the inevitability and the absolute finality of death even in early childhood. At ages when healthy children still suspect that death might be a witch or a bogeyman who can take people away, but who will not necessarily keep them forever, the terminally ill child has begun to understand the biological and irreversible nature of dying.

The time orientation of terminally ill children changes dramatically, notes Bluebond-Langner. As death nears, conversations about the distant future disappear from their speech. Now the future that concerns them is very immediate—the next birthday, Christmas, Easter. Some children pay a lot of attention to these upcoming events, almost as though trying to rush them, to make them more real and immediate by talking about them.

Adolescence

By adolescence, children understand the finality and the biological nature of death. But, as we saw in Chapter 11, many have developed *personal fables*. These fables stress adolescents' specialness, the concern others have for them, and their invulnerability. It might follow from this that they would not be very concerned about dying. Yet evidence indicates that thoughts of dying and accompanying fears are common in adolescence (Zeligs, 1974). This may be at least partly due to the fact that violent and unexpected deaths occur quite frequently in adolescence, especially among males. As we saw in Chapter 11, the majority result from accidents of various kinds—a fact that is sometimes explained as a manifestation of an age-related propensity for risk-taking behavior.

Kastenbaum (1985) notes that the literature on adolescent attitudes toward death is scarce and contradictory. Some studies have reported little concern about death among adolescents; others have suggested that adolescents are extremely preoccupied with and worried about death. The contradiction may be at least partly due to the reluctance of adolescents (and others) to talk about dying. Talking about death in a personal way, admitting fears and concerns, requires, in a very real sense, an admission of what we are socialized to deny at every turn. We do not easily admit that death is something that might happen to us personally — either in adolescence or later; for most, the thought is very frightening. So we repress it and tell each other that it is wise to smell the roses.

Deep down, that, too, may be an admission of fear of death.

Early and Middle Adulthood

Through adulthood, many events generally conspire to emphasize the transitory nature of living. These include the sometimes painful observation that with every passing decade, more and more of our friends, acquaintances, and relatives die. In addition, many adults experience the loss of their own parents or observe signs of aging and impending loss. And, as Kalish (1981) notes, because we all know that parents are supposed to die before children, we perhaps fear death less while our parents still live — and more after they die. Research does indicate that young adults are more concerned about death and more afraid to die than the middle-aged (Kalish & Reynolds, 1976). Kalish suggests that this might be because having lived less, they sense that they have more time coming and have more to lose if they die.

With passing years, the inevitability of death becomes clearer and we begin to think in terms of the number of years we have yet to live rather than of the time we have lived (Neugarten, 1968). This change in orientation is often one aspect of the midlife crisis described in Chapter 16.

Late Adulthood

How do old people feel about dying? Reassuringly, they often report less fear of death than at earlier ages. Kalish (1981) suggests several reasons this might be so. In the first place, the elderly have usually had far more experience with death than younger people, and many of these experiences have involved close friends, relatives, perhaps even a spouse. They have therefore been repeatedly compelled to think about death. In addition, progressive changes in their own bodies, often accompanied by one or more diseases, continue to emphasize that their own end is imminent, forcing them to adjust gradually to thoughts of dying. Kalish (1981) also suggests that our knowledge of what normal life expec-

tancy is has led us to accept a lifespan of 70 or so years as one over which we have few legitimate complaints (see Figure 19.1).

Fear of Dying.   It would be misleading to imply that fear of dying gradually diminishes and finally vanishes altogether in old age. Although the majority of adults do not report a morbid fear of death, death anxiety is found at all age levels including late adulthood. We no longer believe in the bogeyman that we invented in our childish minds, the one we feared might come one dark night and get our parents — or, worse yet, us. Yet, if we think about it, the bogeyman still lurks there in the shadows, and deep down we know that we are never completely safe.

It is not a happy thought. Say what we will, few of us are not afraid of dying; few of us can remain perfectly calm at the thought of the bogeyman — which is why we keep him in the shadows.

There are at least seven reasons why we might fear death, claim Schultz and Ewen (1988):

- Fear of physical suffering and pain
- Fear of the impact of death on those left behind
- Fear of the deaths of those we love
- Fear of eternal punishment
- Fear of not achieving important goals
- Fear of humiliation and cowardice
- Fear of not existing

This last source of fear, fear of not existing, may be what has driven so many to search for some form of immortality. Arnett (1991) describes how the kings of ancient Assyria tried to achieve a form of immortality by emphasizing the continuity and importance of the family tree, and especially of the males in this line. Each king took great pains to remember the achievements and glories of past kings, to praise their names — expecting, in turn, that succeeding kings would do the same for them. Thus could kings buy a hint of immortality in the memories of generations to come.

Ego Integrity.   Freud is said to have become increasingly preoccupied with dying in his later years. "On March 13 of this year," he writes, "I quite suddenly took a step into real old age. Since then the thought of death has not left me. Sometimes I have the impression that seven of my internal organs are fighting to have the honor of bringing my life to an end"

Life Expectancies

In 1989, the average life expectancy in the United States for all races and sexes combined was 75.2 years — a full 12.5 years longer than in 1940 (U.S. Bureau of the Census, 1991). When we are young, Neugarten says, we think in terms of how old we are — how long we have lived. But starting in mid-life, we begin to think more about how long we have left to live. Reassuringly, the longer we have lived, the longer we can expect to live — up to a point. Thus, although our life expectancy at birth might be 75, if we actually reach the age of 75, we can reasonably expect to live about 11 more years.

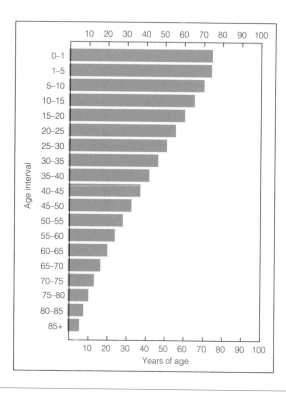

Figure 19.1 Average life expectancy in the United States, 1988, for individuals of given age. (From U.S. Bureau of the Census, 1991, p. 74.)

(quoted in Jones, 1957, p. 78). In spite of his constant thoughts of death, however, Freud was reportedly not overwhelmed or depressed at the prospect of dying. "Still, I have not succumbed to this hypochondria," he continues, "but view it quite coolly . . ." (p. 79).

Our reactions to dying, says Bromley (1990) are highly individual. They include calm acceptance, grim determination to fight, or profound depression. One of the important developmental tasks of late adulthood is to confront our mortality while still maintaining a sense of integrity, a feeling that life has been worthwhile. In Erikson's terms, the major crisis of old age involves achieving this sense of ego integrity, often through a life review process, and overcoming the despair that might result instead. Those who have truly achieved ego integrity do not fear death.

Not everyone resolves the crisis in the same way, or equally effectively. To realize the inevitability of our ends is not necessarily to become reconciled to death. There are some who, in Dylan Thomas's words, "Do not go gentle into that good night" but instead "Rage, rage against the dying of the light."

TABLE 19.1

Kübler-Ross's Sequential Stages of Dying

Stage	Illustration
Denial	"Not me! I don't believe it! There must be a mistake!"
Anger	"Why me? Lots of people smoked more than I did, and look at them! It isn't fair!"
Bargaining	"Okay, I *might* die. Just let me live a little longer so I can wrap up the business and see my new grandson."
Depression	"Yes, it's happening. There's nothing I can do. I wish I had died a long time ago."
Acceptance	"Let it happen. It's okay. I'm not interested in anything anymore. I'm not unhappy, just tired."

Dying

Psychologists have divided much of our lifespans into stages. There is nothing magical about these stages, nor is there anything intrinsically correct about them. They are simply inventions. They simplify our understanding, they make it easier to organize and to remember important observations, and sometimes they lead to important theoretical and practical insights.

Stages of Dying

Must we also die in stages? Some theorists suggest that this might sometimes be the case. Clearly, we need not resort to stages to understand the immediate and senseless finality of a gun, a bomb, or a plane crash. But perhaps a stage approach might be useful for understanding the process of dying when the person *knows* that death is near. (Figure 19.2 lists the most common causes of death in the United States.)

Elisabeth Kübler-Ross (1969, 1974) describes five stages through which a patient progresses after learning of a terminal illness. In the first, *denial*, the patient often

rejects the diagnosis and its implications: "This can't happen to me. There must be some mistake." Denial is sometimes followed by *anger*: "Why me? It shouldn't be me." The third stage, labeled *bargaining*, is characterized by the patient's attempts to look after unfinished business (with God, for example), promising to do well in exchange for a longer life or less suffering. The fourth stage, *depression*, frequently follows. Finally, the patient may arrive at an *acceptance* of death. (See Table 19.1.)

Kübler-Ross's main concerns have been with the needs of the dying and with those who are left to mourn. Accordingly, much of her work deals less with a description of stages of dying than with advice concerning practical questions related to dying: When should a patient be told? Who should do the telling? How can we reduce fear of death? Nevertheless, her description of the stages of dying has had a tremendous impact on the various professions that deal with death, as well as on the lay public. However, these stages have been extensively criticized. Not only are they a highly subjective interpretation of the process of dying, but

Causes of Death

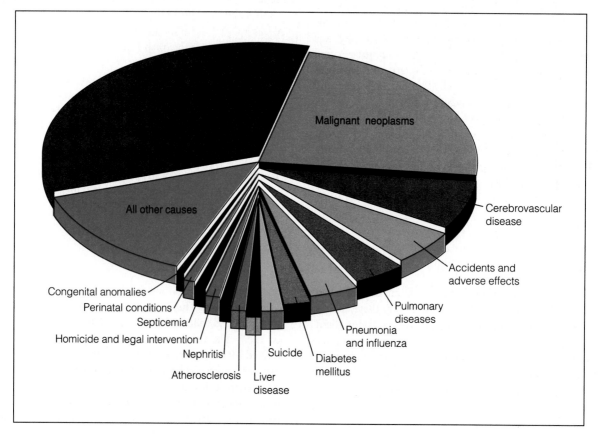

Figure 19.2 The 15 leading causes of death in the United States, 1989. (From U.S. Bureau of the Census, 1991, p. 79.)

In 1989, almost 90 percent of all deaths in the United States were assigned to 15 leading causes. Of these, heart disease remains the most common killer, especially among men; cancer (malignant neoplasms) is second. For many of these diseases, there is some indication of reduced death rates in recent years. Between 1970 and 1989, deaths from atherosclerosis declined from 15.6 to 7.7 per 100,000. Deaths from heart disease have also been declining since 1950; those due to liver disease and cirrhosis have declined since 1979. However, between 1985 and 1989, there were increases in deaths from AIDS, pulmonary diseases, suicide, and homicide.

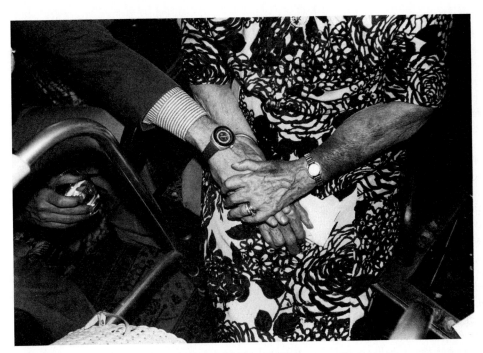

Although the elderly spend more time thinking about death than do those who are younger, they also report less fear of dying. Perhaps this is because they have had more experience with death, and because their declining physical powers have gradually led them to accept that they, too, must die. Perhaps, too, it is because many of the elderly have successfully accomplished one of the final developmental tasks of life: confronting mortality and overcoming the despair that can result.

there is little empirical evidence to support the claim that people typically pass through these five stages and in the order prescribed. Shneidman (1976) observes, for example, that many patients alternate between different stages, vacillating between acceptance and denial, sometimes depressed and other times resigned. Moreover, Kübler-Ross's stages do not consider that one of the recurring emotions characterizing many of the terminally ill is *hope* (Metzger, 1979–80).

Life's Trajectories

Kübler-Ross's stages provide one way to understand the process of dying; trajectories are a second. A *trajectory* implies something quite different from a stage. Stages are like steps, small plateaus that must be successively scaled. They imply a marked degree of discontinuity. Hence, each stage can be labeled differently, and each can be compared and contrasted with preceding and succeeding stages. One of the main values of stages is that they tell us very specific and sometimes very important things about people at each plateau or level. And sometimes they tell us things about the process of getting from one stage to another as well.

A trajectory is a continuous path. It has a beginning and an end, and it can usually be described as ascending or descending (or sometimes both). But it is not described in steps or stages. A missile's path or the flight of a baseball represent trajectories; a journey from my basement to my kitchen represents stages.

Our lives, as we have seen repeatedly throughout this book, can be conceived of in terms of stages, as can our dying. They can also be thought of in terms of trajectories. These are, after all, only metaphors.

Neither conception need be evaluated in terms of correctness; it need only provide insight.

Pattison (1977) defines the life trajectory as the expected span of life. It is our life's trajectory about which we construct personal narratives and in which we are the incomparable heroes. And it is also our life's trajectory about which we reminisce, analyze, and evaluate when, in old age, we conduct our life review.

Dying Trajectories.

When, either in old age or sometime earlier, something happens that informs us that the ends of our spans are imminent, our life trajectories become **dying trajectories**. The phrase *dying trajectory* is used in medicine and psychology to refer to the speed of dying. Glaser and Strauss (1968) identified several distinct dying trajectories as they are labeled by medical personnel. For example, *expected swift death* describes a trajectory often found in emergency wards; *expected lingering while dying* describes a trajectory that is sometimes characteristic of diseases such as cancer. *Expected temporary recovery* is another possible trajectory. Belsky (1990) points out that misdiagnosed trajectories or trajectories that change during the patient's illness can have serious implications for both the patient and his or her relatives. Patients who linger far longer than expected might occasionally be given less care than required because they have been expected to die. And going from an "expected to die within weeks" to "in temporary remission" complicates the process of accepting death as well as that of advance grieving undertaken by survivors.

Reactions to Dying.

Pattison (1977) describes three phases that characterize our personal trajectories when we discover (because of illness or accident, for example) that we will die sooner than we had hoped or expected. The first, the *acute crisis phase*, begins with knowledge of impending death and is often marked by extreme anxiety and depression. It is during this phase that the denial and perhaps the anger of which Kübler-Ross speaks are most likely.

The *chronic phase* involves a gradual adjustment to the thought of dying. Most professionals in this field now advocate that the certainty of impending death should not be denied—that there should be open communication among family members and spouses (Kalish, 1981). As Atchley (1984) points out, longer dying trajectories provide more time for the dying person to adjust and to die with some measure of acceptance; perhaps as important, they provide survivors

with an opportunity to grieve in advance and to begin to make their own adjustments.

The final portion of our dying trajectories, the *terminal phase*, follows final acceptance of the inevitability of dying.

Like stages, trajectories do not describe patterns or movements that are common to everyone. Both leave little room for individual differences. Not all of us go through stages or phases in this order and with these emotions. Dying is a highly individualistic process.

So is living.

Terminal Care

In much the same way that most people try to avoid thinking about their personal deaths, so too do most try to avoid the death of others. Kastenbaum (1985) cites several studies indicating that hospitalized patients who have been diagnosed as terminal are often not afforded the same care as those who are expected to recover. Nurses take longer answering their buzzers, visitors spend less time in their rooms, and physicians are less likely to try different treatments or even to continue current treatments. Similarly, when terminal patients seem to want to talk about their dying, when they try to express their anger and their fear, both hospital attendants and relatives are likely to change the subject (Kastenbaum & Aisenberg, 1976).

The ultimate objective of care for terminally ill individuals is to ease their dying as much as possible. It seems likely that those who have accepted the inevitability of death and who have reconciled themselves to it will have the easiest time of dying. But this does not mean that those who care for the dying must expend all their efforts on getting the person to accept death.

Hospices.

Concerted attempts to offer the best possible care to the dying are found in the hospice movement. A hospice might be a medical or housing facility specifically dedicated to the care of the terminally ill; or it might be the terminally ill patient's own home. When the home is used as a hospice—that is, as a place to die in dignity—hospice workers, who are trained medical personnel, usually visit the home daily. When dying patients are brought into a separate hospice facility, members of their families are ordinarily expected to provide much of the needed care, sometimes being required to remain in the hospice with the terminally ill person on a full-time basis. Hospices of this kind provide medical attention, including pain-relieving drugs, but they do not ordinarily use any life-prolonging measures. Their goals are not only to ease the process of dying for the person involved but also to ease the process for friends and relatives.

Mor (1985) describes the growth of hospice care in North America as spectacular. He attributes this growth largely to a new sensitivity to death and dying. It is a movement that is characterized by a "hands-on" type of care, very similar to that which a terminally ill person might receive in a private home. Hospice care is intended only for short-term patients. In a large-scale survey of 40 hospices over a 2-year period (more than 13,000 patients), Mor (1985) found that the average length of stay was 35 days. Whereas hospices provide short-term care for the terminally ill whose dying trajectories are of expected imminent death, longer-care is sometimes found in nursing homes or in private homes.

The majority of the 13,000 patients in these hospices were older adults. Sixty-five percent were over 65; 30 percent were over 75. Note, however, that a full 35 percent were under age 65. Hence, these hospices are not care facilities designed solely for the aged. One of the reasons for this is that many hospices require that someone from the patient's family (or some hired caregiver) be available. As a result, almost half of hospice patients are male, despite the fact that they represent a much smaller percentage of the older adult population; elderly males are more likely to have a caregiver available for them (typically, a spouse or sister) than are elderly females.

The hospice movement is not without critics. Because it shifts the burden of medical care for the terminally ill from hospital facilities, where care is very expensive, to the home, where care is relatively inexpensive, there is a danger that hospices may become dumping grounds for certain patients who require a lot of care, but little of which is medically complicated (Mor, 1985). However, the fact that hospice care is restricted to those diagnosed as terminally ill reduces this risk somewhat. By the same token, however, restricting hospices in this way makes them inappropriate for many of the dying. Only if both the patient and the patient's family have completely accepted the inevitability of death is the patient eligible for hospice care. Accordingly, entering a hospice requires giving up whatever vestige of hope might have been left. And

even at the very end—even after complete acceptance of the inevitability of imminent death—there is always room for a little hope.

Perhaps there *is* hope for a miracle, for those who believe in such things; perhaps the wish is simply for a happy day or a happy hour—or maybe just for one last sniff of the rose.

Euthanasia

In May 1985, Roswell Gilbert, then age 76, was convicted of first-degree murder for shooting his 73-year-old wife. Suffering from both Alzheimer's disease and a painful bone disease, she had begged him to shoot her. He was sentenced to 25 years in prison.

In June 1985, Joe Wilson killed his 80-year-old wife. She had been in a coma for more than 6 years, and he had looked after her during this time. The court accepted a bargained plea of guilty of attempted murder. He was given a 3-year suspended sentence and required to perform 250 hours of community service ("Mercy Killing," 1985).

Popularly referred to as *mercy killing*, euthanasia encompasses a complicated and controversial collection of issues, which are presented here starkly, with little evaluative comment; our consciences make their own comments.

Definitions.   The term *euthanasia* is of Greek origin and means, literally, "good death." A distinction is often made between passive and active euthanasia. *Active* euthanasia involves deliberately doing certain things to shorten life, such as administering a lethal injection or removing a patient from life-support systems. *Passive* euthanasia involves *not* doing certain things that might have prolonged life and is illustrated in those instances where heart surgery is *not* performed or blood transfusions are *not* given.

Active euthanasia is dramatically illustrated in the case of 22-year-old Karen Ann Quinlan, whose brain no longer functioned, but whose body was being kept alive artificially. Her parents were successful in obtaining a U.S. Supreme Court ruling permitting them to remove her from life-sustaining equipment. In effect, the Court ruled that the state should not interfere in such decisions but that they should be made by the family in consultation with their physicians. The Quinlan's lawyer, Paul Armstrong, has handled more than 100 similar cases since Karen Ann's case and has won

ADVANCE DIRECTIVE
Living Will and Health Care Proxy

*D*eath is a part of life. It is a reality like birth, growth and aging. I am using this advance directive to convey my wishes about medical care to my doctors and other people looking after me at the end of my life. It is called an advance directive because it gives instructions in advance about what I want to happen to me in the future. It expresses my wishes about medical treatment that might keep me alive. I want this to be legally binding.

If I cannot make or communicate decisions about my medical care, those around me should rely on this document for instructions about measures that could keep me alive.

I do not want medical treatment (including feeding and water by tube) that will keep me alive if:
- I am unconscious and there is no reasonable prospect that I will ever be conscious again (even if I am not going to die soon in my medical condition), <u>or</u>
- I am near death from an illness or injury with no reasonable prospect of recovery.

I do want medicine and other care to make me more comfortable and to take care of pain and suffering. I want this even if the pain medicine makes me die sooner.

I want to give some extra instructions: [Here list any special instructions, e.g., some people fear being kept alive after a debilitating stroke. If you have wishes about this, or any other conditions, please write them here.]

**The legal language in the box that follows is a health care proxy.
It gives another person the power to make medical decisions for me.**

I name _____ , who lives at _____

_____ , phone number _____ ,

to make medical decisions for me if I cannot make them myself. This person is called a health care "surrogate," "agent," "proxy," or "attorney in fact." This power of attorney shall become effective when I become incapable of making or communicating decisions about my medical care. This means that this document stays legal when and if I lose the power to speak for myself, for instance, if I am in a coma or have Alzheimer's disease.

My health care proxy has power to tell others what my advance directive means. This person also has power to make decisions for me, based either on what I would have wanted, or, if this is not known, on what he or she thinks is best for me.

If my first choice health care proxy cannot or decides not to act for me, I name _____

_____ , address _____

phone number _____ , as my second choice.

(over, please)

LWGEN

I have discussed my wishes with my health care proxy, and with my second choice if I have chosen to appoint a second person. My proxy(ies) has(have) agreed to act for me.

I have thought about this advance directive carefully. I know what it means and want to sign it. I have chosen two witnesses, neither of whom is a member of my family, nor will inherit from me when I die. My witnesses are not the same people as those I named as my health care proxies. I understand that this form should be notarized if I use the box to name (a) health care proxy(ies).

Signature _____

Date _____

Address _____

Witness' signature _____

Witness' printed name _____

Address _____

Witness' signature _____

Witness' printed name _____

Address _____

Notary [to be used if proxy is appointed] _____

Drafted and Distributed by Choice In Dying, Inc.—the National Council for the right to Die. Choice In Dying is a National not-for-profit organization which works for the rights of patients at the end of life. In addition to this generic advance directive, Choice In Dying distributes advance directives that conform to each state's specific legal requirements and maintains a national Living Will Registry for completed documents.

**CHOICE IN DYING INC.—
the national council for the right to die**
(formerly Concern for Dying/Society for the Right to Die)
200 Varick Street, New York, NY 10014 (212) 366-5540

5/92

Figure 19.3 A living will. (Reprinted with permission from Choice in Dying, 200 Varick Street, New York, NY 10014.)

them all. Ironically, however, Karen Ann Quinlan defied all medical predictions and was still alive, though comatose, more than 7 years after being removed from artificial life-support systems ("Quinlans Have No Regret," 1983). She has since died.

Some Questions. Do we have a moral or a legal right to decide when we shall die? (Suicide has historically been illegal.) Do we have the right to decide when others shall die? Do conditions such as severe and irreversible pain, coupled with inevitable and imminent death, justify euthanasia? Is passive euthanasia less objectionable than active euthanasia? Are there significant ethical or biological issues that clearly separate suicide, euthanasia, and perhaps even abortion?

These questions are far easier to ask than to answer. But for those whose answers are clear and who believe they would want to choose death under certain circumstances, the Euthanasia Education Council provides a document that can be used to formalize these wishes. It is called a *living will* and is reproduced in Figure 19.3. This is merely a sample form. State-specific forms are available, free of charge, from Choice in Dying.

Bereavement and Grieving

Bereavement, as we saw earlier, is the loss of something or someone important. *Grief* is an intense emotional reaction to bereavement. *Mourning* is what is done as a result of grief—for example, crying, praying, or, as at some Irish wakes, singing and drinking, and perhaps even fighting and dancing, in addition to crying and praying.

Bereavement can have a variety of short-term effects, including a higher risk of mental and physical complaints, and even a higher risk of death. Depression following bereavement is quite common but is not usually as severe or as long-term as depression resulting from other causes. Recovery from bereavement appears to be more rapid and more complete among those who mourn openly than among those who deny their sorrow or try to hide it.

In some cultures and in some religions, length of mourning is predetermined. Often, too, certain ritual behaviors are undertaken by the bereaved. Some of these behaviors, like wearing the black colors of "widow's weeds" or sprinkling ashes on one's head, may serve as external symbols of loss. They are also a sign of homage for the deceased. But perhaps even more importantly, they provide a ritualized and acceptable way of displaying grief, and they may accelerate the eventual acceptance of the loss.

Effects of Bereavement

Bereavement appears to have both long-term and relatively short-term effects.

Short-Term Effects.   The short-term effects of bereavement are sometimes described in terms of stages, but there is considerable variation in the ways in which different people express grief, as well as in the length of time required for recovery.

Lindemann (1944), among the first to systematically investigate grief reactions, identified a number of symptoms and behaviors that appear to be quite general following the death of someone close. Among these are physiological signs of distress such as crying and eating and sleeping disturbances, and other physical symptoms such as constriction of the throat, heart palpitations, trembling, and sighing. Lindemann also reports that feelings of guilt are quite common during this stage. Often, the bereaved person feels guilty about things that were done or not done for the deceased. Also, many who are recently bereaved are constantly preoccupied with the image of the dead person, almost as though it were a hallucination. Some hear the dead person's voice, or think they have caught glimpses of the deceased among crowds. Others feel a sort of *presence*, and become fearful that they are losing their minds. Still others become obsessed with details of the dead person's last days or hours.

Other investigations of grief reactions have confirmed that these symptoms are not uncommon, nor are they pathological. For example, Kastenbaum (1977) reports that elderly widowers are prone to loss of appetite, sleep disturbances, headaches, dizziness, and feelings of guilt. In addition, many are preoccupied with constant reminiscing about past events with the deceased. However, feelings of guilt and self-blame do *not* appear to be highly common among the elderly who are bereaved (Breckenridge et al., 1986).

Long-Term Effects. The longer-term effects of bereavement are sometimes evident in mental and physical complaints, and sometimes even in decreased life expectancy. La Rue, Dessonville, and Jarvik (1985) cite several studies that indicate significantly higher incidence of physical illness and mortality among those recently bereaved. Other studies suggest that severe depression requiring medical or psychiatric attention is more common following bereavement (Turner & Sternberg, 1978). Depression after bereavement, however, is not ordinarily as severe as depression resulting from other causes, and usually responds to treatment (Clayton, Halikas, & Maurice, 1972). And 5 years following bereavement, there is no longer higher incidence of illness or of mortality.

The long-term effects of bereavement vary considerably from one person to another, depending partly on individual personality characteristics and partly on the nature of the bereavement. Loss of a child is especially difficult for parents, particularly if it is unanticipated (Doka, 1984–85). In contrast, loss of an elderly parent is more easily accepted.

Stages of Grief

Grieving, like all other aspects of human development, involves change and adjustment.

Parkes's Stages of Acute Grief. Parkes (1972) describes four stages in the expression of acute grief. These are relatively common, although there is considerable variation in their intensity and duration.

The first stage is marked by a sort of *numbness* or disbelief, often described as shock. This stage may include strong feelings of anger or denial. The physiological symptoms described by Lindemann—weeping, dizziness, loss of appetite, and so on—are common during this stage.

Following the initial numbness, grief is manifested in intense *yearning*. The bereaved longs to be with the deceased. As Lindemann (1944) observed, the image of

the deceased is constantly in mind, and there may even be hallucinations centered around that person.

The third stage is one of *depression*, and perhaps of apathy. Occasionally, this phase occurs later, following a period during which the bereaved seemed to have begun to adjust to the loss. At other times, it alternates with the second phase, *yearning*, so that the two cannot always be clearly identified as sequential stages.

In time, grief becomes less intense, and the mourner enters the final phase, a period of *recovery* or reorganization. Parkes (1972) notes that long after the bereaved person seems to have become reconciled to the loss and to have reengaged into a relatively happy life, grief can often be recalled through various reminders such as Christmas or birthdays (sometimes termed *anniversary* grief).

Anticipatory Grief. An important form of grieving not included among these stages is *anticipatory grief*, the grief reactions people experience in the time between learning that someone is terminally ill and the actual death. Anticipatory grief can be very profound, and is often accompanied by many of the physiological and psychological symptoms that follow actual bereavement. However, some evidence suggests that anticipatory grief can sometimes temper the severity of the grief reaction following death, and reduce the length of the grieving period (Doka, 1984–85).

Clearly, working through grief (often referred to as *grief work*) and recovering from loss is extremely important to happiness and well-being. Unfortunately, however, there are no easy recipes for alleviating the pain and agony of the bereaved. Formal periods of mourning that are dictated and sanctioned by society appear helpful. And Parkes's (1972) investigation of grief among widows suggests that those who mourn openly adjust more easily to bereavement than those who deny their sorrow, or who try to hide it. As a result, counselors often suggest that the bereaved be allowed and even encouraged to express their emotions. There is a great deal that concerned friends, spouses, children, and other relatives can do to help the recovery.

Final Themes

Dying and grieving are not happy notes upon which to end a chapter—or a book; birth would have been happier. Unfortunately, however, the chronology of our lives must inevitably run in the same womb-to-tomb direction. And *The Lifespan* has been structured along that same chronology.

But this is a book, not real life. We can end where and how we please. If we wanted to, we could slap a birth right onto the tail end of this tale, pretend life is a huge cycle, and start all over again, full of joy and optimism.

Instead, we end not with a new birth but with a brief summary of the most important themes that have run through this book, giving it continuity. These themes, which define the lifespan perspective, are presented as an introduction in Chapter 1. Here, they are a summary.

■ *Development is continuous.* It isn't something that happens only to infants, children, and perhaps adolescents, and then ceases with adulthood. There are important *positive* changes throughout the entire lifespan. Sadly, there are negative changes, too.

■ *Maturity is relative.* Lifespan human development does not eventually culminate in a predetermined and final state of maturity. Hence, the developmental psychologist is interested as much in the *processes* of development as in *states* of competence. Our competencies are relative; they do not always endure. A mature and fully competent 2-year-old can pull my baseball cap over her ears, but cannot tie her shoes; a mature 10-year-old can tie his shoes, but cannot solve an abstract problem of Boolean algebra; a mature 65-year-old may solve the problem in Boolean algebra, but will be hard-pressed to explain the final and absolute meaning of existence.

■ *Development is contextual.* What we become and how we think, feel, and act are bound to the contexts from which we have emerged and in which we continue to interact. The conclusions of developmental psychology need to be interpreted in light of what we know of the lives, the cultures, and other aspects of the contexts of those whose behaviors led to the conclusions. Intelligence in North America presupposes the ability to acquire high levels of facility with symbol systems such as written language; elsewhere, intelligence might be more closely related to the ability to recognize slug tracks in the sand.

■ *Developmental influences are bidirectional.* We are part of our contexts. We carry them around with us. They shape us; we shape them. Sharon's parents bought her a set of encyclopedias—which helped her prove to them (and others) that she was as intelligent as they suspected. That they suspected she was intelligent influenced them to buy the books in the first place. Her behavior influenced their suspicions, which influenced their behavior, which influenced her . . .

■ *Heredity and environment interact through the lifespan.* Gene–environment interactions affect all aspects of human functioning: physical, social, and intellectual. Alone, neither explains very much at all.

■ *There is no average person.* Each of us is unique, very special, quite wonderful.

And perhaps even after our mirrors no longer cloud over, we may still continue to be very special and wonderful.

Perhaps God's great black oxen will not trample our bones after all. Maybe when they reach us, they will pause for a moment so that we might scramble onto their broad backs. And then they will carry us through eternity, stopping as often as we wish so that we can smell the new roses.

Main Points

1. Neurological, or brain, death signifies cessation of electrical activity in the brain. With life-sustaining medical equipment, it is sometimes possible to keep physiologically alive, people whose brains have been irreversibly damaged.

2. *Bereavement* describes a loss; *grief* is an intense emotional reaction to bereavement; and *mourning* describes the things people do when they are grieving.

3. Very young children often do not understand the finality of death, slightly older children may understand its finality but may personalize it in the form of some "bogeyman," and older children understand it as an irreversible biological phenomenon. Fear of death appears to be more common among adolescents and young adults than it is later in life.

4. Kübler-Ross describes five stages of dying (when the person knows that death is imminent): *denial* ("not me"), *anger* ("why me?"), *bargaining* ("let me suffer less and I will . . ."), *depression*, and *acceptance*. Not all people go through these stages and in this order.

5. Our life's trajectories are our expected spans of life. When something happens to inform us that our trajectories will end, our perspectives change from life trajectory to dying trajectory. Medically, the phrase *dying trajectory* refers to the speed with which a person is expected to die.

6. A longer dying trajectory may give the dying person more time to adjust and may also provide survivors with an opportunity for anticipatory grieving and the beginnings of later readjustment.

7. Care for the terminally ill is designed to ease their dying as well as to make things easier for the bereaved. Hospice care is short-term care for the terminally ill outside a hospital setting, sometimes in the patient's home or in centers designed specifically for that purpose.

8. Euthanasia, popularly called mercy killing, is a controversial procedure that can be either passive (*not* doing something that would prolong life) or active (deliberately doing something to shorten life).

9. The longer-term effects of bereavement can include psychological and physical problems.

10. Parkes describes short-term effects of bereavement in four stages: *numbness* or disbelief (often accompanied by physical symptoms such as crying, sleeplessness, loss of appetite, dizziness), *yearning* (an intense longing to be with the deceased, sometimes accompanied by hallucinations), *depression* (sometimes alternates with yearning), and *recovery* (an acceptance of the loss, often with lingering sadness).

11. Working through grief (grief work) seems important for mental and psychological well-being. Sometimes *anticipatory* grief (profound grief that results when the bereaved first learns about the impending death) may be useful in reducing both the severity of the grief reaction following death and the length of time required for recovery.

12. There are always new roses.

Further Readings

Kalish's book presents a comprehensive look at our understanding of death throughout the lifespan and at the process of dying and of grieving. A classic layperson's book on death and dying is the one by Kübler-Ross:

Kalish, R. A. (1981). *Death, grief, and caring relationships*. Pacific Grove, CA: Brooks/Cole.

Kübler-Ross, E. (1969). *On death and dying*. New York: Macmillan.

The following is an excellent collection intended specifically for those involved in helping families cope with death and dying:

Hansen, J. C. (Ed.). (1984). *Death and grief in the family*. Rockville, MD: Aspen.

Glossary

This glossary defines the most important terms and expressions used in this text. In each case, the meaning given corresponds to the text usage. (The number after each definition indicates the page on which the term is first discussed.) For more complete definitions, consult a standard psychological dictionary.

Abortion A miscarriage occurring usually before the 20th week of pregnancy when the fetus normally weighs less than 1 pound. 131

Accommodation The modification of an activity or an ability that the child already has in order to conform to environmental demands. Piaget's description of development holds that assimilation and accommodation are the means by which an individual interacts with and adapts to the world. 59

Acquired Immune Deficiency Syndrome (AIDS) An incurable and fatal sexually transmitted disease, transmitted through the exchange of body fluids. 122

Adaptation Changes in an organism in response to the environment. Such changes are assumed to facilitate interaction with the environment. Adaptation plays a central role in Piaget's theory. 59

Adolescence A general term for the period from the onset of puberty to adulthood and typically including the teenage years. 378

Affiliation A positive emotional relationship. Affiliative behavior is evident in behavior designed to make friends and includes talking, smiling, and playing with others. Affiliation implies a weaker relationship than does attachment. 210

AFP test A screening test designed to detect the likelihood of a fetal neural tube defect by revealing the presence of *alphafetoprotein* in the mother's blood. 90

Afterbirth The placenta and other membranes that are expelled from the uterus following the birth of a child. 133

Ageism Stereotyped prejudice with negative attitudes based on age. Ageism with respect to the elderly is common. 584

Alienation In both existential philosophy and psychology, an individual's feelings of separation from people and things that are important to that individual. 418

Alzheimer's disease A disease associated with old age (but also occurring as young as 40), marked by progressive loss of memory and of brain function and eventual death. 91

Ambivalent Describes infants who are profoundly upset when the principal caregiver leaves and who are often angry when that person returns. 208

Amniocentesis A procedure in which amniotic fluid is removed by a hollow needle from around the fetus in a pregnant woman. Subsequent analysis of this fluid may reveal chromosomal aberrations (Down syndrome, for example) and other fetal problems. 92

Amniotic sac A sac filled with dark, serous fluid (amniotic fluid) in which the fetus develops in the uterus. 132

Anal stage The second of Freud's psychosexual stages of development, beginning at approximately 8 months and lasting until around 18 months. It is characterized by the child's preoccupation with physical anal activities. 42

Anoxia A condition in which there is an insufficient supply of oxygen to the brain. 139

Arousal A term with both physiological and psychological meaning. Physiologically, arousal refers to changes in heart rate, respiration, brain activity, and so on. Psychologically, it refers to corresponding changes in alertness or vigilance. 58

Artificial insemination A breeding procedure often used in animal husbandry and sometimes with humans. The procedure eliminates the need for a physical union between male and female. 81

Assimilation The act of incorporating objects or aspects of objects to previously learned activities. To assimilate is, in a sense, to ingest or to use something that is previously learned; more simply, it is the exercise of previously learned responses. 59

Association Relates to associationism, a term employed almost synonymously with stimulus–response learning. Associationism refers to the formation of associations or links between stimuli, between responses, or between stimuli and responses. 50

Authoritarian A highly controlling, dogmatic, obedience-oriented parenting style in which there is little recourse to reasoning and no acceptance of the child's autonomy. 278

Authoritative A moderately controlling parenting style in which value is placed on independence and reasoning, but where parents impose some regulations and controls. 278

Autism A serious childhood mental disorder that is usually apparent by age 3 and that is characterized by social unresponsiveness, poor or nonexistent communication skills, and bizarre behavior. 219

Autoimmunity A malfunction in the body's disease-fighting capabilities whereby the body's own benign cells are identified as harmful and thus attacked. Autoimmunity is thought to be involved in some age-related diseases. 591

Autosome Any chromosome in mature sperm and ova other than the sex chromosome. Each of these cells therefore contains 22 autosomes. 82

Avoidant Describes infants who are *anxiously* attached to a caregiver, who show little signs of distress when that person leaves, and who initially *avoid* reestablishing contact when the person returns. 208

Babbling The relatively meaningless sounds that young infants make or repeat. 178

Babinski reflex A reflex present in the newborn child but disappearing later in life. When infants' feet are tickled in the center of their soles, the toes fan outward. Normal adults curl their toes inward. 113

Basic need An unlearned physiological requirement of the human organism. Specifically, the need for food, drink, and sex. 70

Behavioristic theory A general term for those theories of learning that are primarily concerned with the observable components of behavior (stimuli and responses). Such theories are labeled S–R learning theories and are exemplified in classical and operant conditioning. 54

Behavior modification A general term for the application of behavioristic principles (primarily those of operant conditioning) in systematic and deliberate attempts to change behavior. 54

Bereavement A term used to describe the *loss* suffered by friends and relatives of a person who has died. 643

Bidirectionality Describes the reciprocal effects on one another of people or people and their environment. 8

Birth order The position that a child occupies in a family (for example, first-, second-, or third-born). 283

Blind procedure When an observer of or participant in an experiment does not know the conditions or variables being tested. 23

Breech birth An abnormal presentation of the fetus at birth with the buttocks first rather than the head first. 133

Canalization Waddington's term to describe the extent to which genetically determined characteristics are resistant to environmental influences. A highly canalized trait (such as hair color) remains unchanged in the face of most environmental influences; less canalized characteristics (such as manifested intelligence) are highly influenced by the environment. 86

Cephalocaudal Referring to the direction of development, beginning with the head and proceeding outward toward the tail. Early infant development is cephalocaudal because children acquire control over their heads before gaining control over their limbs. 113

Cervix The small circular opening to the womb (uterus) that dilates considerably during birth to allow passage of the child. 132

Cesarean delivery A common surgical procedure in which the fetus is delivered by means of an incision in the mother's abdomen and uterus. 133

Chorion biopsy A procedure in which samples of the membrane lining the uterus are used to permit prenatal diagnosis of potential birth defects. 92

Chromosomal disorders Abnormalities, inconsistencies, or deformities in chromosomes, sometimes involving absent or extra chromosomes. 90

Chromosome A microscopic body in the nucleus of all human and plant cells containing genes—the carriers of heredity. Each mature human sex cell (sperm or ovum) contains 23 chromosomes, each containing countless numbers of genes. 82

Chunking A type of memory strategy (cognitive strategy) whereby related items are grouped into more easily remembered "chunks" (for example, a prefix and four digits for a phone number rather than seven unrelated numbers). 311

Classical conditioning Also called *learning through stimulus substitution*, it involves the repeated pairing of two stimuli so that a previously neutral (conditioned) stimulus eventually elicits the same (conditioned) response that was previously evoked by the first (unconditioned) stimulus. Pavlov was the first to describe this type of conditioning. 50

Climacteric Popularly called the "change of life" that accompanies middle age. It involves reduced reproductive capabilities in both men and women and culminates in menopause for women. 530

Cognition To *cognize* is to know. Hence, cognition deals with knowing, understanding, problem solving, and related intellectual processes. 59

Cognitive Descriptive of mental processes such as thinking, knowing, and remembering. Cognitive theories attempt to explain intellectual development and functioning. 54

Cognitive strategies Procedures, knowledge, and information that relate to the processes involved in learning and remembering rather than to the content of what is learned. Cognitive strategies are used to identify problems, select approaches to their solution, monitor progress, and use feedback. Cognitive strategies are closely related to metacognition and metamemory. 315

Cohort A group of individuals born within the same specific period of time. For example, the 1920s cohort includes those born between 1920 and 1929. 26

Communication The transmission of messages. Communication does not require language, although it is greatly facilitated by it. Nonhuman animals communicate even though they do not possess language. 174

Compensation A logical rule stating that certain changes can compensate for opposing changes, thereby negating their effects. For example, as a square object becomes thinner, it also becomes longer; increases in length compensate for decreases in width. These changes combine to negate any actual changes in the object's mass. 305

Concept A collection of perceptual experiences or ideas related by virtue of their common properties. 236

Conception The beginning of human and other animal life. Also called *fertilization*, conception occurs with the union of a sperm cell with an egg cell. 110

Conceptualization The forming of concepts (ideas or meanings). An intellectual process leading to thinking and understanding. 160

Concrete operations The third of Piaget's four major stages, lasting from age 7 or 8 to approximately 11 or 12, and characterized primarily by the child's ability to deal with concrete problems and objects, or objects and problems easily imagined in a concrete sense. 61

Conditioned response A response that is elicited by a conditioned stimulus. In some obvious ways, a conditioned response resembles its corresponding unconditioned response, although they are not identical. 50

Conditioned stimulus A stimulus that either does not elicit any response or initially elicits a global orienting response. As a result of being paired with an unconditioned stimulus and its response, the conditioned stimulus comes to elicit the same response. For example, a stimulus that is always present at the time of a fear reaction may become a conditioned stimulus for fear. 50

Conditioning A term that describes a simple type of learning. (See also *classical conditioning; operant conditioning*.) 50

Conscience An internalized set of rules governing an individual's behavior. 41

Conservation A Piagetian term implying that certain quantitative attributes of objects remain unchanged unless something is added to or taken away from them. Mass, number, area, and volume are capable of being conserved. 239

Contextual model A developmental model that emphasizes the importance of environmental variables such as culture, cohort, family, and historical events. This model maintains that in order to explain and understand human development, the *context* in which development occurs must be considered. 38

Contextual theory of intelligence The label for Sternberg's belief that intelligence involves adaptation in real-life contexts (in contrast with the view that intelligence is best measured by means of abstract timed questions and problems). 317

Control group A group of subjects who are not experimented with but who are used as comparisons to an experimental group to ascertain whether an experimental procedure affected the experimental group. 23

Correlational study A study that looks at the relationship (correlation) between two or more variables — for example, home background and delinquency, or achievement and intelligence. 24

Critical period The period during which an appropriate stimulus must be presented to an organism for imprinting to occur. 63

Cross-sectional study A technique in the investigation of human development that involves observing and comparing different subjects at different age levels. For example, a cross-sectional study might compare 4- and 6-year-olds by observing two different groups of children at the same time, one group consisting of 4-year-old children and the other of 6-year-old children. A longitudinal study would require that the *same* children be examined at age 4 and again at age 6. 25

Crystallized abilities Cattell's term for intellectual abilities that are highly dependent on experience (verbal and computational skills and general information, for example). These abilities may continue to improve well into old age. (See also *fluid abilities*.) 317

Culture fair A general label for intelligence tests that are less heavily biased in favor of the cultural groups for which the tests were initially designed and on which they have been normed — in other words, tests that are more fair to certain cultures. 320

Death Cessation of vital functioning. Medically, death is usually defined in terms of cessation of brain activity. 642

Defense mechanism A relatively irrational and sometimes unhealthy method used by people to compensate for their inability to satisfy basic desires and to overcome the anxiety accompanying this inability. 43

Deferred imitation Imitating people or events in their absence. Deferred imitation is assumed by Piaget to be critical to developing language. 174

Dependent variable The variable that may or may not be affected by manipulations of the independent variable in an experimental situation. 22

Development The total process whereby individuals adapt to their environment. Development includes growth, maturation, and learning. 20

Developmental psychology The study of changes in the behavior and thinking of human beings over time. 6

Developmental theory A body of psychological theories concerned with the development of children from birth to maturity. 48

Diabetes An insulin deficiency disease, some forms of which are associated with a recessive gene. 90

Diary description As a method of child study, it involves recording sequential descriptions of a child's behavior at predetermined intervals (daily or weekly, for example). Sometimes useful for arriving at a better understanding of general developmental patterns. 21

Dilation and curettage (D & C) A surgical procedure that involves scraping the walls of the uterus. It is occasionally necessary after birth if all of the placenta has not been expelled. 133

Disinhibitory effect See *inhibitory–disinhibitory effect*. 55

Dizygotic Resulting from two separate eggs and forming fraternal (nonidentical) twins. 98

DNA (deoxyribonucleic acid) A substance assumed to be the basis of all life, consisting of four chemical bases arranged in an extremely large number of combinations. The two strands of the DNA molecule that compose genes are arranged in the form of a double spiral (helix). These double strands are capable of replicating themselves as well as crossing over from one strand of the spiral to the other and forming new combinations of their genetic material. The nuclei of all cells contain DNA molecules. 81

Dominant gene   The gene (carrier of heredity) that takes precedence over all other related genes in genetically determined traits. Because all genes in the fertilized egg occur in pairs (one from the male and one from the female), a dominant gene as one member of the pair of genes means that the related hereditary characteristic will be present in the individual. 83

Double-blind procedure   An experimental method in which experimenters collecting or analyzing data do not know which subjects are members of experimental or control groups. Double-blind procedures are used as a safeguard against experimenter bias. 29

Down syndrome   The most common chromosomal birth defect, related to the presence of an extra 21st chromosome (technically labeled *trisomy 21*) and sometimes evident in mild to severe mental retardation. 90

Drug abuse   The recreational use of drugs. The APA considers drug abuse a disorder when it impairs functioning. 436

Drug dependence   A strong, sometimes overwhelming desire to continue taking a drug. (See also *physiological dependence; psychological dependence.*) 436

Drugs   Chemical substances that have marked physiological effects on living organisms. 435

Drug tolerance   A change resulting from drug use in which the user requires more frequent or stronger doses of the drug to maintain its initial effects. 436

Dying trajectories   An expression used in reference to the process of dying. Dying trajectories are temporal—that is, described in terms of time (for example, *expected swift death, expected lingering while dying,* or *expected temporary recovery*). 650

Dyslexia   A form of learning disability manifested in reading problems of varying severity. Dyslexia

may be evident in spelling errors that are erratic rather than consistent. 325

Ecology   The study of the interrelationships between organisms and their environment. In developmental psychology, ecology relates to the social context in which behavior and development occur. 8

Egg cell   See *ovum.* 81

Ego   The second stage of the human personality, according to Freud. It is the rational, reality-oriented level of human personality that develops as the child becomes aware of what the environment makes possible and impossible, thereby serving as a damper to the id. The id tends toward immediate gratification of impulses as they are felt, whereas the ego imposes restrictions that are based on environmental reality. 41

Egocentric   Adjective based on Latin words for *self* (ego) and *center.* Literally, it describes a self-centered behavior, attitude, or personality characteristic. Although egocentrism often has negative connotations of selfishness, it is simply descriptive when applied to the child's perception of the world. For example, egocentric perception is characterized by an inability to assume an objective point of view. 239

Elaborated language code   A phrase used by Bernstein to describe the language of middle- and upper-class children. Elaborated language codes are grammatically correct, complex, and precise. 256

Electra complex   A Freudian development stage during which a girl's unconscious sexual feelings toward her father lead to jealousy of her mother. (See also *Oedipus complex.*) 42

Elicited response   A response brought about by a stimulus. The expression is synonymous with the term *respondent.* 51

Eliciting effect   That type of imitative behavior in which the observer does not copy the model's responses but simply behaves in a related manner. 56

Embryo   The second stage of prenatal development, beginning around the first week after conception and ending after six weeks. 112

Emitted response   A response not elicited by a known stimulus but simply by the organism. An emitted response is an operant. 51

Environment The significant aspects of an individual's surroundings. Includes all experiences and events that influence the child's development. 78

Epigenesis The developmental unfolding of genetically influenced characteristics. 86

Episiotomy A small cut made in the vagina to facilitate the birth of a child. An episiotomy prevents the tearing of membranes and ensures that once the cut has been sutured, healing will be rapid and complete. 132

Equilibration A Piagetian term for the process by which we maintain a balance between assimilation (using old learning) and accommodation (changing behavior; learning new things). Equilibration is essential for adaptation and cognitive growth. 168

Estrogen replacement therapy (ERT) A medical treatment in which women whose production of hormones has declined or ceased—often because of menopause or surgical removal of the ovaries—are given estrogen. ERT has been found to reduce risk of osteoporosis but remains controversial given a possible link with cancer. 530

Ethologists Scientists who study the behavior of animals in their natural habitats. 63

Eugenics A form of genetic engineering that selects specific individuals for reproduction. Although widely accepted and practiced with animals, as applied to humans, the concept raises many serious moral and ethical questions. 96

Event sampling A method of child study in which specific behaviors are observed and recorded and unrelated behaviors are ignored. 21

Exceptionality A category used to describe physical, social, or intellectual abilities and performance that are significantly above or below average. 217

Exosystem Interactions between a system in which the child is involved (microsystem) and another system that does not ordinarily include the child (father relationships with employers, for example). 68

Experiment A procedure for scientific investigation that requires manipulation of some aspects of the environment to determine the effects of this manipulation. 22

Experimental group A group of subjects who undergo experimental manipulation. The group to which something is done in order to observe its effects. 23

Extended family A large family group consisting of parents, children, grandparents, and sometimes uncles, aunts, cousins, and so on. 278

Fallopian tube One of two tubes that link the ovaries and the uterus. Fertilization (conception) ordinarily occurs in the fallopian tubes. From there, the fertilized egg cell moves into the uterus and attaches to the uterine wall. 111

Family life cycle A sociological term referring to the stages through which typical families progress (for example, early marriage, raising children, raising adolescents, postchildren and dissolution). 509

Feral children Those raised by animals in the wild and away from human contact. 79

Fertilized ovum The first stage of prenatal development, beginning at fertilization and ending at approximately the second week. 112

Fetal alcohol syndrome (FAS) A pattern of birth defects associated with alcohol consumption by pregnant women. FAS symptoms include mental retardation, retarded physical growth, and facial and cranial deformities. 120

Fetoscopy A surgical procedure that allows the physician to see the fetus while obtaining tissue samples to determine its status. 93

Fetus The final stage of prenatal development, which begins approximately six weeks after conception and lasts until the baby's birth. 112

Fluid abilities Cattell's term for intellectual abilities that seem to underlie much of our intelligent behavior and that are not highly affected by experience (general reasoning, attention span, memory for numbers). Fluid abilities are more likely to decline in old age than are crystallized abilities. (See also *crystallized abilities.*) 317

Forceps Clamplike instruments that sometimes assist in a baby's delivery. 138

Formal operations The last of Piaget's four major stages, beginning around the age of 11 or 12 and lasting until about 14 or 15. It is characterized by the child's increasing ability to use logical thought processes. 61

Fragile X syndrome   A sex-linked, primarily male disorder that is often manifested in mental retardation. Susceptibility increases with the mother's age. 92

Fraternal twins   Twins whose genetic origins are two separate eggs. Such twins are as genetically dissimilar as average siblings. (See also *dizygotic*). 98

Galvanic skin response (GSR)   A measure of the skin's electrical conductivity. With increases in emotional reaction (arousal), conductivity increases; hence, GSR measures may be considered indexes of arousal or emotion. 157

Gametes   Mature sex cells. In humans, the egg cell (ovum) and the sperm cell. 81

Gender roles   Attitudes, personality characteristics, behavior, and other qualities associated with being male or female in a specific culture. Gender roles are, in effect, the groupings of qualities that define masculine and feminine. Because they are largely culturally defined, gender roles may be quite different in different cultures. 216

Gender-typing   Learning behavior appropriate to the sex of the individual. The term refers specifically to the acquisition of masculine behavior by a boy and feminine behavior by a girl. 275

Gene   A carrier of heredity. Each of the 23 chromosomes contributed by the sperm cell and the ovum at conception is believed to contain 50,000–100,000 genes. 82

General factor theory   A theory of intelligence based on the assumption that there is a basic underlying quality of intellectual functioning that determines *intelligence* in all areas. This quality is sometimes labeled *g*. 316

Generalizability   The extent to which conclusions, rules, and principles are applicable to new situations—in short, their generality. 28

Genitalia   A general term referring to sex organs. 113

Genital stage   The last of Freud's stages of psychosexual development, beginning around age 11 and lasting until around 18. It is characterized by involvement with normal adult modes of sexual gratification. 42

Genome   One set of single chromosomes with the genes they contain; considered an organism's genetic map. 87

Gestation period   The time between conception and birth (typically 266 days for humans). 111

Grief   An emotional reaction to loss. Grief reactions are sometimes accompanied by both physical and psychological symptoms (shortness of breath, heart palpitations, sighing, loss of appetite, and so on, as well as anxiety, depression, anger, and guilt). 643

Growth   In the study of children, a term that ordinarily refers to physical changes, which are primarily quantitative because they involve addition rather than transformation. 20

Head turning reflex   A reflex elicited in infants by stroking the cheek or the corner of the mouth. Infants turn their heads toward the side being stimulated. 157

Heredity   The transmission of physical and personality characteristics and predispositions from parent to offspring. 78

Herpes   An incurable sexually transmitted viral disease whose symptoms usually include sometimes painful or itchy lesions in the genital area. 122

Heterozygous   Refers to the presence of different genes with respect to a single trait. One of these genes is dominant and the other is recessive. 88

Homozygous   Refers to an individual's genetic makeup. Individuals are homozygous with respect to a particular trait if they possess identical genes for that trait. 88

Huntington's disease   An inherited neurological disorder characterized by neural degeneration typically beginning between the ages of 20 and 40, and usually leading to death. 88

Hypothesis   A prediction based on partial evidence of some effect, process, or phenomenon that must be experimentally verified. 23

Id   One of the three levels of the human personality, according to Freudian theory. The id is defined as all the instinctual urges to which humans are heir; it is the level of personality that contains human motives. A newborn child's personality, according to Freud, is all id. 40

Identical twins   Twins whose genetic origin is a single egg. Such twins are genetically identical. (See also *monozygotic*.) 98

Identification A general term referring to the process of assuming the goals, ambitions, mannerisms, and so on of another person — of identifying with that person. (See also *imitation*.) 42

Identity A logical rule specifying that certain activities leave objects or situations unchanged. 45

Imaginary audience One manifestation of adolescent egocentrism. A reflection of the adolescent belief that a wide range of individuals are always aware of the adolescent's behavior and are very concerned about it. 394

Imaginative play Activities that include make-believe games; these are particularly prevalent during the preschool years. 270

Imitation The complex process of learning through observation of a model. 55

Immature birth A miscarriage occurring sometime between the 20th and 28th weeks of pregnancy and resulting in the birth of a fetus weighing between one and two pounds. 131

Imprinting An instinctlike type of learning that occurs shortly after birth in certain species and which is seen in the "following" behavior of young ducks and geese. 63

Independent variable The variable in an experiment that can be manipulated to observe its effects on other variables. 22

Induction As an aspect of rites of passage, acceptance into adult status. 378

Infancy A period of development that begins a few weeks after birth and lasts until approximately the age of 2. 10

Infant state An expression used to describe the general, current condition of an infant — for example, sleeping, crying, drowsy, or alert. 190

Information-processing approach A psychological orientation that attempts to explain cognitive processes such as remembering, decision making, or problem solving. This orientation is primarily concerned with how information is acquired and stored (acquisition of a knowledge base), as well as the development of both cognitive strategies and notions of the self as a processor of information (metacognition). 309

Inhibitory–disinhibitory effect Imitative behavior that results in either the suppression (inhibition) or appearance (disinhibition) of previously acquired deviant behavior. 55

Initiation Ceremonies and rituals that, in some societies, mark entry into adulthood. 378

In utero A Latin term meaning inside the uterus. 113

Labor The process during which the fetus, placenta, and other membranes are separated from the woman's body and expelled. The termination of labor usually is birth. 131

Language Complex arrangements of arbitrary sounds that have accepted referents and can therefore be used for communication among humans. 175

Language Acquisition Device (LAD) A label used by Chomsky to describe the neurological something that corresponds to grammar and which children are assumed to have in their brains as they learn language. 252

Lanugo Downy, soft hair that covers the fetus. Lanugo grows over most of the child's body sometime after the fifth month of pregnancy and is usually shed during the seventh month. However, some lanugo is often present at birth, especially on the infant's back. 113

Latency stage The fourth of Freud's stages of psychosexual development, characterized by both the development of the superego (conscience) and loss of interest in sexual gratification. This stage is assumed to last from ages 6 to 11. 42

Learning Changes in behavior resulting from experience rather than from the maturational process. 20

Libido A general Freudian term denoting sexual urges. The libido is assumed to be the source of energy for sexual urges. Freud considered these urges the most important force in human motivation. 40

Life expectancy The expected duration of a human life. An average of the ages at which individuals die. 590

Life review A dynamic process whereby an individual remembers, analyzes, and evaluates past experiences in an effort to resolve and accept personal conflicts. The life review is common in late adulthood but also occurs throughout life. 617

Lifespan The total length of an individual life; not an expectancy, but the maximum attainable in the absence of accident and disease. 590

Lifespan developmental psychology The area of psychology concerned with the development of individuals from conception to death—that is, with the entire lifespan. 6

Longitudinal study A research technique in the study of child development that observes the same subjects over a long period of time. 25

Long-term memory A type of memory whereby with continued rehearsal and recoding of sensory input (processing in terms of *meaning*, for example), material will be available for recall over a longer period of time (minutes to years). 311

LSD-25 (d-lysergic acid diethylamide tartrate) A particularly powerful hallucinogenic drug, this inexpensive, easily made synthetic chemical can sometimes have profound influences on human perception. In everyday parlance, it is often called "acid." 439

Macrosystem All interactive social systems that define a culture or subculture. 68

Marker genes A length of DNA material that seems to be identical in all individuals with a specific characteristic. 87

Masturbation The self-stimulation of one's genitals for sexual gratification. 425

Maturation A term used to describe changes in human development that are relatively independent of the environment. 20

Mature birth The birth of an infant between the 37th and 42nd weeks of pregnancy. 131

Mechanistic model A model of human development based on the belief that it is useful to view human beings in terms of their reactive, *machine-like* characteristics. 37

Meiosis The division of a single sex cell into two separate cells, each consisting of 23 chromosomes rather than 23 pairs of chromosomes. Meiosis therefore results in cells that are completely different, whereas mitosis results in identical cells. 82

Menarche A girl's first menstrual period, an event that transpires during pubescence. 28

Menopause The cessation of menstruation in women. Menopause may begin in the early forties or late thirties and usually is complete around age 50. 81

Menses A monthly discharge of blood and tissue from the womb of a mature female. The term refers to menstruation. 110

Mental retardation A global term referring to the mental state of individuals whose intellectual development is significantly slower than that of normal individuals and whose ability to adapt to their environment is therefore limited. 322

Mesosystem Interactions among two or more microsystems (for example, family and school). 68

Metacognition Knowledge about knowing. As we grow and learn, we develop notions of ourselves as learners. Accordingly, we develop strategies that recognize our limitations and that allow us to monitor our progress and take advantage of our efforts. 309

Metamemory The knowledge that we develop about our own memory processes—knowledge about how to remember rather than simply about our memories. 235

Metaneed Maslow's term for a "higher" need. In contrast to a basic need, a metaneed is concerned not with physiological but with psychological functions. It includes the "need" to know truth, beauty, justice, and to "self-actualize." 70

Microsystem Defined by immediate, face-to-face interactions, where everybody affects everybody (for example, child and parent). 68

Middle childhood An arbitrary division in the sequence of development beginning somewhere around age 6 and ending at approximately 12. 298

Midlife crisis A popular expression for the potential emotional turmoil that sometimes occurs in middle age with the individual's growing recognition of mortality and with the realization that the dreams of younger years may never be achieved. 554

Mitosis The division of a cell into two identical cells. Mitosis occurs in body cells rather than in sex cells. 82

Model A pattern for behavior that can be copied by someone else. (See also *symbolic models*.) Alternatively, a model is a representation, usually abstract, of some phenomenon or system. Thus we might have a model of the universe or a model of some aspects of behavior. 37

Modeling effect Imitative behavior involving the learning of a novel response. 55

Monozygotic Twins resulting from the division of a single fertilized egg. The process results in identical twins. 98

Morality The ethical aspect of human behavior. Morality is intimately bound to the development of an awareness of acceptable and unacceptable behaviors. It is therefore linked to what is often called conscience. (See also *conscience*.) 398

Moro reflex The generalized startle reaction of a newborn infant. It characteristically involves throwing out the arms and feet symmetrically and then bringing them back in toward the center of the body. 157

Morpheme Combination of phonemes that make up the meaningful units of a language. 175

Mother–infant bonding Expression for a biological and physiological process involved in the very early formation of emotional links between mother and infant. 202

Motivation Our reasons for behaving as we do. What initiates, directs, and accounts for the cessation of behavior. 315

Mourning The external manifestations of grief. Many cultures and religions have prescribed periods of mourning—periods during which the bereaved are expected to show their grief. 643

Muscular dystrophy A degenerative muscular disorder, most forms of which are genetic, usually manifested in an inability to walk and sometimes fatal. 90

Nature–nurture controversy A long-standing psychological argument over whether genetics (nature) or environment (nurture) is more responsible for determining development. 19

Negative reinforcement A stimulus that increases the probability of a response when the stimulus is removed from the situation. A negative reinforcer is usually an unpleasant or noxious stimulus that is removed when the desired response occurs. 51

Neonatal abstinence syndrome Neonatal symptoms associated with narcotics use by the mother that has resulted in the newborn also being addicted. Severe cases may be fatal. 121

Neonate A newborn infant. Newborns typically lose weight immediately after birth, but regain it within 2 weeks. The neonate period terminates when birth weight is regained. 133

Neural tube defects Spinal cord defects often linked with recessive genes, sometimes evident in failure of the spine to close (spina bifida), or in absence of portions of the brain. 90

Nonstandard language A variation (different dialect) of the dominant *standard* language. Nonstandard dialects are often ungrammatical and colloquial. 256

Norm An average or standard way of behaving. Cultural norms, for example, refer to the behaviors expected of individuals who are members of that culture. 159

Normal curve A mathematical function represented in the form of a symmetrical bell-shaped curve that illustrates how a large number of naturally occurring or chance events are distributed. 86

Nuclear family A family consisting of a mother, a father, and their offspring. 277

Observational learning Learning through imitation. 55

Obstetrics A sophisticated medical term for what grandmothers called midwifery. It involves the medical art and science of assisting women who are pregnant, both during pregnancy and at birth. 129

Oedipus complex A Freudian stage of development during which a boy unconsciously has sexual desires for his mother and a consequent resentment of his father. (See also *Electra complex*.) 42

Ontogeny Systematic changes that occur in the lives of individuals. Changes that define lifespan development. (See also *phylogeny*.) 79

Open systems A theory that recognizes the interactive nature of biological, psychological, and social systems, and the impossibility of predicting final outcomes with absolute confidence (in contrast to a *closed* system, which is completely predictable). 38

Operant The label used by Skinner to describe a response not elicited by any known or obvious stimulus. Most significant human behaviors appear to be operant. Such behaviors as writing a letter or going for a walk are operants if no known specific stimulus elicits them. 51

Operant conditioning A type of learning involving an increased probability of a response occurring as a result of reinforcement. Much of B. F. Skinner's experimental work investigates the principles of operant conditioning. 51

Operation Piaget's term for mental activity. An operation is a thought process characterized by certain rules of logic. Preoperations are more intuitive and egocentric and less logical. 61

Oral stage Freud's first stage of psychosexual development, lasting from birth to approximately 8 months of age. The oral stage is characterized by preoccupation with the immediate gratification of desires. This is accomplished primarily with the mouth, by sucking, biting, swallowing, playing with the lips, and so on. 41

Organismic model This model in human development assumes that it is useful to view people as active rather than simply reactive, as more like biological organisms than machines. 37

Orienting response The initial response of humans and other animals to novel stimulation. Also called the *orienting reflex* or *orientation reaction*. Components of the orienting response include changes in EEG patterns, respiration rate, heart rate, and conductivity of the skin to electricity. 156

Ovary A female organ (most women have two) that produces ova (egg cells). 111

Ovum (plural *ova*) The sex cell produced by a mature female approximately once every 28 days. When mature, it consists of 23 chromosomes as opposed to all other human body cells (somatoplasm), which consist of 23 *pairs* of chromosomes. It is often referred to as an egg cell. 81

Palmar reflex The grasping reflex that a newborn infant exhibits when an object is placed in its hand. 158

Peer group A group of equals. Peer groups may be social groups, age groups, intellectual groups, or work groups. When the term applies to young children, it typically refers to age and grade mates. 346

Perception Reaction to and interpretation of physical stimulation (sensation). A conceptual process, dependent on the activity of the brain. 160

Permissive A parenting style that may be characterized as "laissez-faire." Permissive parents are nonpunitive and undemanding. Their children are autonomous rather than obedient, and thus are responsible for their own decisions and actions. 278

Personal fable The belief that we are unique, special, and right. This belief is sometimes exaggerated in adolescence as a function of adolescent egocentrism. 397

Personality The set of characteristics that we typically manifest in our interactions with others. It includes all the abilities, predispositions, habits, and other qualities that make each of us different. 197

Phallic stage The third stage in Freud's theory of psychosexual development, beginning at 18 months and lasting to approximately 6 years of age. During this stage, children become concerned with their genitals and may show evidence of the much-discussed *Oedipus* and *Electra* complexes. 42

Phenylketonuria (PKU) A genetic disorder associated with the presence of two recessive genes. 88

Phoneme The simplest unit of language, consisting of a single sound such as a vowel. 175

Phonology One of the four major components of language. Phonology has to do with the sounds (phonemes) of a language. 175

Phrase structure rules A modern grammatical phrase referring to the implicit (or explicit) rules that govern the formation of correct phrases. For example, a phrase structure rule might specify that correct noun phrases may consist of an article and a noun; an article, an adjective, and a noun; an adjective and a pronoun; and so on. 249

Phylogeny Changes that occur in a species over generations. Evolutionary changes. (See also *ontogeny*.) 79

Physiological dependence Also known as *addiction*. The desire to continue using a drug for organic or physiological reasons, and where unpleasant reactions result when the drug is not taken. 436

Placenta A flat, thick membrane attached to the inside of the uterus and to the developing fetus during pregnancy. The placenta connects the mother and the fetus by the umbilical cord. 112

Play May be defined as activities that have no goal other than the enjoyment derived from them. 270

Polygamy Forms of marriage that permit a husband to have more than one wife (polygyny) or a wife to have more than one husband (polyandry). 499

Positive reinforcement   A stimulus that increases the probability of a response recurring as a result of being added to a situation after the response has occurred. It usually takes the form of a pleasant stimulus (*reward*) that results from a specific response. 51

Postmature birth   The birth of an infant after the 42nd week of pregnancy. 131

Practice play   See *sensorimotor play*. 270

Pragmatics   One of four components of language, relating to the practical aspects of language. Pragmatics includes all the implicit rules that govern when and how speakers interact in conversation, as well as the subtle rules of intonation, accent, emphasis, and other variations that give rise to different meanings. 175

Preconcept   The label given to the preconceptual child's incomplete understanding of concept, resulting from an inability to classify. 236

Pregnancy   The condition of a woman who has had an ovum (egg cell) fertilized and who, nature willing, will eventually give birth. 110

Premature birth   The birth of a baby between the 29th and 36th weeks of pregnancy. A premature baby weighs between 2 and 5½ pounds (1,000 to 2,499 grams). 131

Prenatal development   The period of development beginning at conception and ending at birth. That period lasts approximately nine calendar months in the human female (266 days). Chickens develop considerably faster. 110

Preoperational thought   The second of Piaget's four major stages, lasting from about 2 to 7 or 8 years. It consists of two substages: intuitive thinking and preconceptual thinking. 61

Pretend play   See *imaginative play*. 270

Primary circular reaction   An expression used by Piaget to describe a simple reflex activity such as thumb-sucking. 171

Primary sexual characteristics   Sexual characteristics directly associated with reproduction (for example, ovaries and testes). 381

Prolapsed cord   A condition that sometimes occurs during birth when the infant's umbilical cord becomes lodged between the body and the birth canal, thereby cutting off the supply of oxygen. This may result in brain damage of varying severity, depending on the length of time until delivery following prolapsing of the cord. 139

Proteins   Molecules made up of chains of one or more amino acids. In a sense, proteins are the basis of organic life. 81

Proximodistal   Literally, from near to far. Refers to a developmental progression in which central organs develop before external limbs and the infant acquires control over muscles close to the center of the body before acquiring control over those that are more peripheral. 113

Psycholinguist   Those who study the relationship between language (linguistics) and development, thinking, learning, and behaving (psychology). 175

Psychological dependence   Drug dependence in which the desire to continue taking a drug is related primarily to its psychological rather than its physical effects (for example, a strong sense of well-being). 436

Psychology   The science that examines human behavior (and that of animals as well). 6

Psychosexual   A term used to describe psychological phenomena based on sexuality. Freud's theories are psychosexual in that they attribute development to sexually based forces and motives. 45

Psychosocial   Pertaining to events or behaviors that relate to the social aspects of development. Erikson's theory is psychosocial in that it deals with the resolution of social crises and the development of social competencies (independence or identity, for example). 45

Puberty   Sexual maturity following pubescence. 81

Pubescence   Changes that occur in late childhood or early adolescence and that result in sexual maturity. In boys, these changes include enlargement of the testes, growth of axillary hair, deepening of the voice, and the ability to ejaculate semen. In girls, pubescence is characterized by rapid physical growth, occurrence of the first menstrual period (*menarche*), a slight lowering of the voice, and enlargement and development of the breasts. 380

Punishment   Involves either the presentation of an unpleasant stimulus or the withdrawal of a pleasant stimulus as a consequence of behavior. Punishment should not be confused with negative reinforcement because punishment does not increase the probability of a response occurring; rather, it is intended to have the opposite result. 52

Pupillary reflex An involuntary change in the size of the pupil as a function of brightness; it is present in the neonate. 162

Quickening The name given to the first movements of the fetus in utero. Quickening does not occur until after the fifth month of pregnancy. 110

Rapid eye movement (REM) sleep A stage of sleep characterized by rapid eye movements. Most of our dreaming occurs during REM sleep, which accounts for approximately 25 percent of an adult's sleep time and as much as 50 percent of an infant's. 191

Recessive gene A gene whose characteristics are not manifest in the offspring unless it is paired with another recessive gene. When a recessive gene is paired with a dominant gene, the characteristics of the dominant gene will be manifest. 83

Reinforcement The effect of a reinforcer. Specifically, to increase the probability of a response recurring. 51

Reinforcer A reinforcing stimulus. A consequence, such as a reward, that increases the probability of a behavior recurring. 51

Reliable A measure is reliable to the extent that it measures accurately whatever it measures. 316

Respondent A response elicited by a specific known stimulus, used by Skinner to contrast with *operant*. 51

Response Any organic, muscular, glandular, or psychic reaction resulting from stimulation. 50

Restricted language code A term used by Bernstein to describe the language typical of the lower-class child. Restricted language codes are characterized by short and simple sentences, general and relatively imprecise terms, idiom and colloquialism, and incorrect grammar. 256

Retarded A description of abnormally slow development or those people who have not developed either physically or intellectually as rapidly as normal. (See also *mental retardation*.) 323

Reversibility A logical property manifested in the ability to reverse or undo activity in either an empirical or conceptual sense. An idea is said to be reversible when a child can unthink it and re-alize that certain logical consequences follow from doing so. 305

Reward An object, stimulus, event, or outcome that is perceived as pleasant and may therefore be reinforcing. 51

Rites of passage A collective term for the ceremonies and rites that accompany transition from one stage to another within a culture. The most dramatic examples of rites of passage include the *initiation* or *puberty* rites of some "primitive" cultures. 378

Rooting reflex A neonatal reflex manifested, for example, in the infant's attempts to find a breast. 157

Scheme (also *schema* or *schemata*) The label used by Piaget to describe a unit in cognitive structure. In one sense, a scheme is an activity together with its structural connotations. In another sense, a scheme may be thought of as an idea or a concept. It usually labels a specific activity: the looking scheme, the grasping scheme, the sucking scheme. 59

Schizophrenia A serious mental disorder that may take a variety of forms, sometimes characterized by bizarre behaviors, obsessions, distorted views of reality, and so on. Schizophrenia in infants and children is sometimes confused with autism, although it does not ordinarily begin as early. 219

Script A term used to describe our knowledge of what goes with what and in what sequence. Scripts are a part of cognitive structure, which deals with the routine and the predictable. 312

Secondary circular reaction Infant responses that are circular in the sense that the response serves as a stimulus for its own repetition and secondary because the responses do not center on the child's body, as do primary circular reactions. 171

Secondary sexual characteristics Sex-linked features not directly linked with reproduction (for example, facial hair or breast development). 381

Secular trend A trend over succeeding generations toward earlier physical maturation in adolescence. 381

Securely attached Describes infants who are strongly and positively attached to a caregiver, who are distressed when that person leaves, and who quickly reestablish contact when the person returns. 207

Self-actualization   The process or act of becoming oneself, developing one's potential, achieving an awareness of one's identity, fulfilling oneself. The term *actualization* is central to humanistic psychology. 70

Self-concept   The concept that an individual has of him- or herself. Notions of the self are often closely allied with individuals' beliefs about how others perceive them. 46

Self-efficacy   Personal estimates of our effectiveness in dealing with the world. 57

Self-esteem   See *self-worth.* 340

Self-referent   Pertaining to the self. Self-referent thought is thought that concerns our own mental processes (for example, thoughts that evaluate our abilities or that monitor our progress in solving problems). 57

Self-worth   The desire to be held in high esteem by others and to maintain a high opinion of one's own behavior and person. 340

Semantics   The component of language that relates to meaning or significance of sounds. 175

Senescence   Technically, the period in later adulthood marked by physical and cognitive decline. It begins at different ages for different individuals, and is not always characterized by very dramatic changes. 594

Sensation   The physical effect of stimulation. A physiological process dependent on activity of the senses. 160

Sensitive period   A period during which specific experiences have their most pronounced effects — for example, the first 6 months of life during which the infant forms strong attachment bonds to the mother or caregiver. 64

Sensorimotor period   The first stage of development in Piaget's classification. It lasts from birth to approximately age 2 and is so called because children understand their world primarily through their activities toward it and sensations of it. 61

Sensorimotor play (also called *practice play*)   Activity involving the manipulation of objects or execution of activities simply for the sensations that are produced. (See also *play.*) 270

Sensory memory   The simple sensory recognition of stimuli (also called *short-term sensory memory*). Sensory memory requires no cognitive processing and does not involve conscious awareness or attention. 310

Sequential designs   Research strategies that involve taking a sequence of samples at different times of measurement in order to reduce or eliminate biases that may result from confounding the effects of the age of subjects, the time of testing, and the cohort to which subjects belong. 27

Seriation   The ordering of objects according to one or more empirical properties. To seriate is essentially to place in order. 307

Sex chromosome   A chromosome contained in sperm cells and ova that is responsible for determining the sex of offspring. Sex chromosomes produced by the female are of one variety (X); those produced by the male are either X or Y. At fertilization (the union of sperm and ovum), an XX pairing will result in a girl, and an XY pairing will result in a boy. The sperm cell is essentially responsible for determining the offspring's sex. 82

Sex roles   See *gender roles.* 216

Sexual abuse   A form of maltreatment in which the victim is forced — physically or by virtue of the abuser's status and power — to submit to sexual behaviors (ranging from talking, looking, or touching to actual intercourse or other sexual acts). Children are relatively often victims of sexual abuse. 363

Short-term memory   A type of memory in which material is available for recall for a matter of seconds. Short-term memory primarily involves rehearsal rather than more in-depth processing. It defines our immediate consciousness or awareness. 311

Siblings   Offspring whose parents are the same; brothers and sisters. 98

Socialization   The complex process of learning those behaviors that are appropriate within a given culture as well as those that are less appropriate. The primary agents of socialization are home, school, and peer groups. 266

Social play   Activity that involves interaction between two or more children and frequently takes the form of games with more or less precisely defined rules. 273

Sociobiology   The systematic study of the biological basis of all social behavior. 65

Sociogram   A pictorial or graphic representation of the social structure of a group. 349

Sociometry   A measurement procedure used extensively in sociological studies. It attempts to determine patterns of likes and dislikes in groups; it also plots group structure. 348

Special abilities theory   A theory of intelligence based on the assumption that intelligence consists of several separate factors (for example, numerical, verbal, memory) rather than a single underlying factor common to performance in all areas. (See also *general factor theory*.) 316

Specimen description   As a method of child study, it involves recording detailed, specific instances of a child's behavior. Useful for in-depth studies of individual children. 21

Spermarche   A boy's first ejaculation. Often a nocturnal event. (See also *menarche*.) 381

Sperm cell   The sex cell produced by a mature male. Like egg cells (ova), sperm cells consist of 23 chromosomes rather than 23 *pairs* of chromosomes. 81

Stage   An identifiable phase in the development of human beings. Developmental theories such as Piaget's are referred to as stage theories because they describe behavior at different developmental levels. 19

Standard language   The current (hence standard) form of a society's dominant language; the form that is taught in schools and against which other dialects are judged for correctness. (See also *nonstandard language*.) 256

Stethoscope   A medical instrument that amplifies the sound of a heartbeat. 111

Stimulus (plural *stimuli*)   Any change in the physical environment capable of exciting a sense organ. 50

Sucking reflex   The automatic sucking response of a newborn child when the mouth is stimulated. Nipples are particularly appropriate for eliciting the sucking reflex. 113

Sudden infant death syndrome (SIDS)   Unexplained and unexpected infant death. The leading cause of infant death between ages 1 month and 1 year. (Not really a cause, because it is unknown; *SIDS* is simply a label.) 155

Superego   The third level of personality according to Freud. It defines the moral or ethical aspects of personality and, like the ego, is in constant conflict with the id. 41

Symbolic   The final stage in the development of a child's representation of the world. Bruner uses the term to describe a representation of the world through arbitrary symbols. Symbolic representation includes language, as well as theoretical or hypothetical systems. 55

Symbolic models   Nonhuman models such as movies, television programs, verbal and written instructions, or religious, literary, musical, or folk heroes. 270

Syncretic reasoning   A type of semilogical reasoning characteristic of the classification behavior of the very young preschooler. In syncretic reasoning, objects are grouped according to egocentric criteria. These criteria change from object to object. In other words, children do not classify on the basis of a single dimension but change dimensions as they classify. 237

Syntax   Part of the grammar of a language that consists of the set of implicit or explicit rules that govern the combination of words that compose a language. 175

Taboo   A prohibition imposed by social custom or as a protective measure. 378

Tay-Sachs disease   A fatal genetic enzyme disorder that can be detected before birth, but that cannot yet be prevented or cured. 90

Temperament   The biological basis of personality — its hereditary components. 198

Teratogen   An external influence (as opposed to an inherited genetic influence) such as a virus or a drug that is capable of producing defects in a fetus. 114

Teratology   The study of birth defects. 114

Terminal drop   A label for the observed decline in measured intelligence that sometimes occurs a year or two before a person's death. 606

Tertiary circular reaction   An infant's response that is circular in the sense that the response serves as the stimulus for its own repetition, although the repeated response is not identical to the first response. This last characteristic, the altered response, distinguishes a tertiary from a secondary circular reaction. 173

Tetrahydrocannabinol (THC)   The active ingredient in marijuana and related substances (hashish, bhang). 439

Theory In its simplest sense, an explanation of observations. Theories emphasize which facts (observations) are important for understanding and which relationships among facts are most important. 36

Time-lag study A research design in which subjects of the same age but belonging to different cohorts are compared (for example, 40-year-olds in 1985 are compared with other cohorts of 40-year-olds in 1990 and 1995). 27

Time sampling A method of child observation in which behavior is observed during specific time intervals, frequently with the aim of recording instances or frequency of specific behaviors. 21

Transductive reasoning The type of semilogical reasoning that proceeds from particular to particular rather than from particular to general or from general to particular. One example of transductive reasoning is the following: (1) Cows give milk, (2) goats give milk, (3) therefore, goats are cows. 237

Transformational rules An implicit (or explicit) grammatical rule that governs the alteration of expressions and their resulting meanings. For example, one transformational rule specifies that a declarative sentence may be transformed into a question by altering the order of the words (as in transforming "I can go" to "Can I go?"). 249

Transitional objects A general term for objects such as blankets and bears that are temporary objects of attachment and affection for some children while they are in *transition* between high dependence on parents and growing personal independence. 212

Transverse presentation A crosswise presentation of the fetus at birth. 133

Trauma An injury or nervous shock. Traumas are usually intense and unpleasant. 139

Ultrasound A diagnostic technique in medicine whereby high-frequency sound waves are used to provide images of internal body structures. Ultrasound recordings are used extensively to evaluate the condition of the fetus. 92

Umbilical cord A long, thick cord attached to what will be the child's navel at one end and to the placenta at the other. It transmits nourishment and oxygen to the growing fetus from the mother and carries away waste material from the fetus. 112

Unconditioned response A response elicited by an unconditioned stimulus. 50

Unconditioned stimulus A stimulus that elicits a response prior to learning. All stimuli capable of eliciting reflexive behaviors are examples of unconditioned stimuli. For example, food is an unconditioned stimulus for the response of salivation. 50

Uterus The organ in which the embryo or fetus is contained and nourished during pregnancy; also called the womb. 111

Valid A measure is said to be valid to the extent that it measures what it is intended to measure. (See also *reliable*.) 316

Variable A property, measurement, or characteristic that is susceptible to variation. In psychological experimentation, qualities of human beings such as intelligence and creativity are referred to as variables. (See also *dependent variable; independent variable*.) 22

Vegetative reflex A reflex pertaining to the intake of food (for example, swallowing and sucking). 157

Version Turning the fetus manually to assist delivery. 133

Visual-spatial ability Ability to see relationships among objects in space, to identify objects, in short, to deal with the world of physical space as it is perceived through vision. The ability to maintain orientation in a strange place is sometimes a manifestation of visual-spatial ability. 422

Work Activities engaged in for gain rather than primarily for the pleasure derived from them. 466

Zone of proximal development Vygotsky's phrase for the individual's current potential for further intellectual development — a capacity not ordinarily measured by conventional intelligence tests. He suggests that hints and questions might help in assessing this zone. 252

References

Abel, E. L. (1984). *Fetal alcohol syndrome and fetal alcohol effects*. New York: Plenum.

Abram, M. J., & Dowling, W. D. (1979). How readable are parenting books? *The Family Coordinator, 28*, 365–368.

Abramson, L. (1991). Facial expressivity in failure to thrive and normal infants: Implications for their capacity to engage in the world. *Merrill-Palmer Quarterly, 37*, 159–182.

Abrioux, M. L., & Zingle, H. W. (1979). An exploration of the marital and life-satisfactions of middle-aged husbands and wives. *Canadian Counsellor, 13*, 85–92.

Abroms, I. F., & Panagakos, P. G. (1980). The child with significant developmental motor disability (cerebral palsy). In A. P. Scheiner & I. F. Abroms (Eds.), *The practical management of the developmentally disabled child*. St. Louis: C. V. Mosby.

ACOG Technical Bulletin. (1988). *Human Immune Deficiency Virus Infections*. (No. 123). Washington, DC, December.

Acredolo, L. P., & Hake, J. L. (1982). Infant perception. In B. B. Wolman et al. (Eds.), *Handbook of developmental psychology*. Englewood Cliffs, NJ: Prentice-Hall.

Adams, R. E., Jr., & Passman, R. H. (1979). Effects of visual and auditory aspects of mothers and strangers on the play and exploration of children. *Developmental Psychology, 15*, 269–274.

Adams, R. E., Jr., & Passman, R. H. (1983). Explaining to young children about an upcoming separation from their mother: When do I tell them? *Journal of Applied Developmental Psychology, 4*, 35–42.

Adams, R. G. (1986). Friendship and aging. *Generations, 10*, 40–43.

Adrian, M. J. (1981). Flexibility in the aging adult. In E. L. Smith & R. C. Serfass (Eds.), *Exercise and aging: The scientific basis*. Hillside, NJ: Enslow.

Ahammer, I. M., & Murray, J. P. (1979). Kindness in the kindergarten: The relative influence of role playing and prosocial television in facilitating altruism. *International Journal of Behavior Development, 2*, 133–157.

The AIDS threat: Who's at risk? (1988, March 14). *Newsweek*, pp. 42–52.

AIDS virus strain beats pill; scientists scramble for new cure. (1989, March 15). *Edmonton Journal*, p. A2.

Ainsworth, L. L. (1984). Contact comfort: A reconsideration of the original work. *Psychological Reports, 55*, 943–949.

Ainsworth, M.D.S. (1973). The development of infant–mother attachment. In B. M. Caldwell and H. N. Ricciuti (Eds.), *Review of child development research* (Vol. 3). Chicago: University of Chicago Press.

Ainsworth, M.D.S. (1979). Infant–mother attachment. *American Psychologist, 34*, 932–937.

Ainsworth, M.D.S., Blehar, M. C., Waters, E., & Wall, S. (1978). *Patterns of attachment*. Hillsdale, NJ: Erlbaum.

Aizenberg, R., & Treas, J. (1985). The family in late life: Psychosocial and demographic considerations. In J. E. Birren & K. W. Schaie (Eds.), *Handbook of the psychology of aging* (2nd ed.). New York: Van Nostrand Reinhold.

Alba, F., & Potter, J. E. (1986). Population and development in Mexico since 1940: An interpretation. *Population and Development Review, 12* (March), 47–75.

Albert, R. S., & Runco, M. A. (1986). The achievement of eminence: A model based on a longitudinal study of exceptionally gifted boys and their families. In R. J. Sternberg & J. E. Davidson (Eds.), *Conceptions of giftedness*. New York: Cambridge University Press.

Aldis, O. (1975). *Play fighting*. New York: Academic Press.

Allen, M. C., & Jones, M. D. (1986). Medical complications of prematurity. *Obstetrical gynecology, 67*, 427.

Allison, P. D., & Furstenberg, F. F., Jr. (1989). How marital dissolution affects children: Variations by age and sex. *Developmental Psychology, 25*, 540–549.

Als, H., Tronick, E., Lester, B. M., & Brazelton, T. B. (1979). Specific neonatal measures: The Brazelton neonatal behavior assessment scale. In J. D. Osofsky (Ed.), *Handbook of infant development*. New York: John Wiley.

Alvy, K. T. (1987). *Parent training: A social necessity*. Studio City, CA: Center for the Improvement of Child Caring.

Amato, P. R., & Keith, B. (1991). Parental divorce and the well-being of children: A meta-analysis. *Psychological Bulletin, 110*, 26–46.

American Association for Protecting Children (1987, October 23). *National estimates of child abuse and neglect reports 1976–1986*. Denver, CO: American Humane Association.

American Humane Association. (1983). *Highlights of official child neglect and abuse reporting*. Denver, CO: American Humane Association.

American Psychiatric Association. (1980). *Diagnostic and statistical manual of mental disorders*. Washington, DC: American Psychiatric Association.

American Psychiatric Association. (1987). *Diagnostic and statistical manual of mental disorders* (3rd ed., rev.). Washington, DC: American Psychiatric Association.

American Psychological Association. (1990). *Practitioner. Focus, 4*, 7.

Anastasi, A. (1958). Heredity, environment, and the question "how"? *Psychological Review, 65*, 197–208.

Anastasiow, N. (1984). Preparing adolescents in child bearing: Before and after pregnancy. In M. Sugar (Ed.), *Adolescent parenthood* (pp. 141–158). New York: SP Medical and Scientific Books.

Anderson, D. R., & Bryant, J. (1983). Research on children's television viewing: The state of the art. In J. Bryant & D. R. Anderson (Eds.), *Children's understanding of television: Research on attention and comprehension* (pp. 331–353). New York: Academic Press.

Anderson, J. R. (1980). *Cognitive psychology and its applications*. San Francisco: Freeman.

Anisfeld, M. (1991). Review: Neonatal imitation. *Developmental Review, 11*, 60–97.

Anthony, E. J. (Ed.). (1975). *Exploration in child psychiatry*. New York: Plenum.

Appel, L. F., Cooper, R. G., McCarrell, N., Sims-Knight, J., Yussen, S. R., & Flavell, J. H. (1972). The development of the distinction between perceiving and memorizing. *Child Development, 43*, 1365–1381.

Arber, S., & Gilbert, G. N. (1989). Transitions in caring: Gender, life course and the care of the elderly. In B. Bytheway, T. Keil, P. Allatt, & A. Bryman (Eds.), *Becoming and being old: Sociological approaches to later life*. London: Sage.

Arbuthnot, J. (1975). Modification of moral judgment through role playing. *Developmental Psychology, 11*, 319–324.

Ariès, P. (1962). *Centuries of childhood: A social history of family life* (R. Baldick, Trans.). New York: Alfred A. Knopf. (Original work published 1960.)

Arlin, P. K. (1975). Cognitive development in adulthood: A fifth stage? *Developmental Psychology, 11*, 602–606.

Arnett, W. S. (1991). Growing old in the cradle: Old age and immortality among the kings of ancient Assyria. *International Journal of Aging and Human Development, 32*, 135–141.

Asher, S. R. (1983). Social competence and peer status: Recent advances and future directions. *Child Development, 54*, 1427–1434.

Asher, S. R., & Renshaw, P. (1981). Children without friends: Social knowledge and social skill training. In S. R. Asher & J. M. Gottman (Eds.), *The development of children's friendships*. New York: Cambridge University Press.

Askew, S., & Ross, C. (1988). *Boys don't cry: Boys and sexism in education*. Milton Keynes, Philadelphia: Open University Press.

Aslin, R. N. (1987). Visual and auditory development in infancy. In J. D. Osofsky (Ed.), *Handbook of infant development*. New York: John Wiley.

Aslin, R. N., Pisoni, D. P., & Jusczyk, P. W. (1983). Auditory development and speech perception in infancy. In M. H. Haith & J. J. Campos (Eds.), *Handbook of child psychology* (Vol. 2): *Infancy and developmental psychology*. New York: John Wiley.

Aslin, R. N., & Smith, L. B. (1988). Perceptual development. *Annual Review of Psychology, 39*, 435–473.

Asp, E., & Garbarino, J. (1988). Integrative processes at school and in the community. In T. D. Yawkey & J. E. Johnson (Eds.), *Integrative processes and socialization: Early to middle childhood.* Hillsdale, NJ: Erlbaum.

Atchley, R. C. (1974). The meaning of retirement. *Journal of Communications, 24*, 97–101.

Atchley, R. C. (1982). Retirement: Leaving the world of work. *Annals of the American Academy of Political and Social Sciences, 464*, 120–131.

Atchley, R. C. (1984). *The social forces in later life* (4th ed.). Belmont, CA: Wadsworth.

Atchley, R. C. (1985). *Social forces and aging: An introduction to social gerontology* (4th ed.). Belmont, CA: Wadsworth.

Atchley, R. C. (1989). A continuity theory of aging. *Gerontologist, 29*, 183–190.

Athanasiou, R. (1973). A review of public attitudes on sexual issues. In J. Zubin & J. Money (Eds.), *Contemporary sexual behavior: Critical issues in the 1970's.* Baltimore: Johns Hopkins University Press.

Atkinson, R. C., & Shiffrin, R. M. (1971). The control of short-term memory. *Scientific American, 225*, 82–90.

Aylward, E. H. (1991). *Understanding children's testing: Psychological testing.* Austin, Tex: Pro-Ed.

Babad, E. Y. (1985). Some correlates of teachers' expectancy bias. *American Educational Research Journal, 22*, 175–183.

Babies without Dads: Single women turning to artificial insemination. (1992, January 16). *The Edmonton Journal*, p. B9.

Babson, S. G., Pernoll, M. L., Benda, G. I., & Simpson, K. (1980). *Diagnostics and management of the fetus and neonate at risk: A guide for team care* (4th ed.). St. Louis: C. V. Mosby.

Bahrick, H. P., Bahrick, P. O., & Wittlinger, R. P. (1975). Fifty years of memory for names and faces: A cross-sectional approach. *Journal of Experimental Psychology: General, 104*, 54–75.

Bailey, T. (1991). Jobs of the future and the education they will require: Evidence from occupational forecasts. *Educational Researcher, 20*, 11–20.

Baillargeon, R. (1987). Object permanence in 3½- and 4½-month-old infants. *Developmental Psychology, 23*, 655–664.

Baker, R. L., & Mednick, B. R. (1984). *Influences on human development: A longitudinal perspective.* Boston: Kluwer-Nijhoff.

Baker, S. A., Thalberg, S. P., & Morrison, D. M. (1988). Parents' behavioral norms as predictors of adolescent sexual activity and contraceptive use. *Adolescence, 23*, 265–282.

Bakwin, H. (1949). Psychologic aspects of pediatrics. *Journal of Pediatrics, 35*, 512–521.

Balow, B. (1980). Definitional and prevalence problems in behavior disorders of children. *School Psychology, 18*, 348–354.

Baltes, P. B., & Schaie, K. W. (1974, March). The myth of the twilight years. *Psychology Today*, pp. 35–40.

Baltes, P. B., & Schaie, K. W. (1976). On the plasticity of intelligence in adulthood and old age: Where Horn and Donaldson fail. *American Psychologist, 31*, 720–725.

Baltes, P. B., & Willis, S. L. (1979). The critical importance of appropriate methodology in the study of aging: The sample case of psychometric intelligence. In F. Hoffmeister & C. Muller (Eds.), *Brain functions in old age.* Heidelberg: Springer-Verlag.

Bancroft, R. (1976). Special education: Legal aspects. In P. A. O'Donnell & R. H. Bradfield (Eds.), *Mainstreaming: Controversy and consensus.* San Rafael, CA: Academic Therapy Publications.

Bandura, A. (1969). *Principles of behavior modification.* New York: Holt, Rinehart & Winston.

Bandura, A. (1977). *Social learning theory.* Englewood Cliffs, NJ: Prentice-Hall.

Bandura, A. (1981). Self-referent thought: A developmental analysis of self-efficacy. In J. H. Flavell & L. Ross (Eds.), *Social cognitive development: Frontiers and possible futures.* Cambridge, England: Cambridge University Press.

Bandura, A. (1986). *Social foundations of thought and action: A social cognitive theory.* Englewood Cliffs, NJ: Prentice-Hall.

Bandura, A. (1989). Regulation of cognitive processes through perceived self-efficacy. *Developmental Psychology, 25*, 729–735.

Bandura, A., Ross, D., & Ross, S. A. (1963). Vicarious reinforcement and imitative learning. *Journal of Abnormal and Social Psychology, 67,* 601–607.

Bandura, A., & Walters, R. (1963). *Social learning and personality development.* New York: Holt, Rinehart & Winston.

Banks, M. S. (1980). The development of visual accommodation during early infancy. *Child Development, 51,* 646–666.

Baran, S. I., Chase, L. I., & Courtright, J. A. (1979). Television drama as a facilitator of prosocial behavior: "The Waltons." *Journal of Broadcasting, 23,* 277–285.

Baratz, J. D. (1969). A bi-dialectical task for determining language proficiency in economically disadvantaged Negro children. *Child Development, 40,* 889–901.

Baron, M., Risch, N., Hamburger, R., Mandel, B., Kushner, S., et al. (1987). Genetic linkage between X-chromosome markers and bipolar affective illness. *Nature, 326,* 289–292.

Barr, H. M., Streissguth, A. P., Darby, B. L., & Sampson, P. D. (1990). Prenatal exposure to alcohol, caffeine, tobacco, and aspirin: Effects on fine and gross motor performance in 4-year-old children. *Developmental Psychology, 26,* 339–348.

Barratt, M. S., Roach, M., & Colbert, K. K. (1991). Single mothers and their infants: Factors associated with optimal parenting. *Family Relations, 40,* 448–454.

Barrett, G. V., & Depinet, R. L. (1991). A reconsideration of testing for competence rather than for intelligence. *American Psychologist, 46,* 1012–1024.

Barss, V. A. (1989). Obstetrical management. In J. W. Hare, (Ed.), *Diabetes complicating pregnancy: The Joslin Clinic Method.* New York: Alan R. Liss.

Basseches, M. (1984). *Dialectical thinking and adult development.* Norwood, NJ: Ablex.

Bates, E. (1976). *The emergence of symbols.* New York: Academic Press.

Bates, E., Bretherton, I., Shore, D., & McNew, S. (1981). Names, gestures, and objects: The role of context in the emergence of symbols. In K. E. Nelson (Ed.), *Children's language* (Vol. 3). New York: Gardner Press.

Bates, E., O'Connell, B., & Shore, C. (1987). Language and communication. In J. D. Osofsky (Ed.), *Handbook of infant development.* New York: John Wiley.

Bates, E., Thal, D., Whitesell, K., Fenson, L., & Oakes, L. (1989). Integrating language and gesture in infancy. *Developmental Psychology, 25,* 1004–1019.

Baum, C. G., & Forehand, R. (1984). Social factors associated with adolescent obesity. *Journal of Pediatric Psychology, 9,* 293–302.

Baumrind, D. (1967). Child care practices anteceding three patterns of pre-school behavior. *Genetic Psychology Monographs, 75,* 43–88.

Baumrind, D. (1977). Some thoughts about child rearing. In S. Cohen & T. J. Comiskey (Eds.), *Child development: Contemporary perspectives.* Itasca, IL: F. E. Peacock.

Baumrind, D. (1989). Rearing competent children. In W. Damon (Ed.), *Child development today and tomorrow,* San Francisco, CA: Jossey-Bass.

Baxter, G., & Beer, J. (1990). Educational needs of school personnel regarding child abuse and/or neglect. *Psychological Reports, 67,* 75–80.

Bayer, L. M., Whissell-Buechy, D., & Honzik, M. P. (1981). Health in the middle years. In D. H. Eichorn, J. A. Clausen, N. Haan, M. P. Honzik, & P. H. Mussen (Eds.), *Present and past in middle life.* New York: Academic Press.

Beatty, P. (1991). Foreword. *The Journal of Drug Issues, 21,* 1–7.

Becker, B. J. (1990). Item characteristics and gender differences on the SAT-M for mathematically able youths. *American Educational Research Journal, 27,* 65–87.

Bell, A., & Weinberg, M. (1978). *Homosexuality: A study of diversity among men and women.* New York: Simon & Schuster.

Belmont, J. M. (1989). Cognitive strategies and strategic learning: The socio-instructional approach. *American Psychologist, 44,* 142–148.

Belsky, J. (1980). Child maltreatment: An ecological integration. *American Psychologist, 35,* 320–335.

Belsky, J. (1981). Early human experience: A family perspective. *Developmental Psychology, 17,* 3–23.

Belsky, J. K. (1984). *The psychology of aging: Theory, research, and practice.* Pacific Grove, CA: Brooks/Cole.

Belsky, J. K. (1990). *The psychology of aging: Theory, research, and interventions* (2nd ed.). Pacific Grove, CA: Brooks/Cole.

Belsky, J., Lerner, R. M., & Spanier, G. B. (1984). *The child in the family.* Reading, MA: Addison-Wesley.

Belsky, J., & Rovine, M. J. (1988). Nonmaternal care in the first year of life and the security of infant-parent attachment. *Child Development, 59,* 156–167.

Belsky, J., & Rovine, M. (1990). Patterns of marital change across the transition to parenthood: Pregnancy to three years postpartum. *Journal of Marriage and the Family, 52,* 5–20.

Bem, S. L. (1974). The measurement of psychological androgyny. *Journal of Consulting and Clinical Psychology, 42,* 155–162.

Benbow, C. P., & Stanley, J. C. (1983). Sex differences in mathematical reasoning: More facts. *Science, 222,* 1029–1031.

Benet, S. (1976). *How to live to be 100.* New York: Dial.

Benson-von der Ohe, E. (1984). First and second marriages: The first three years of married life. In S. A. Mednick, M. Harway, & K. M. Finello (Eds.), *Handbook of longitudinal research* (Vol. 2): *Teenage and adult cohorts.* New York: Praeger.

Bentley, K. S., & Fox, R. A. (1991). Mothers and fathers of young children: Comparison of parenting styles. *Psychological Reports, 69,* 320–322.

Berdine, W. H., & Blackhurst, A. E. (Eds.). (1985). *An introduction to special education* (2nd ed.). Boston: Little, Brown.

Bereiter, C. (1991). Implications of connectionism for thinking about rules. *Educational Researcher, 20,* 10–16.

Bereiter, C., & Engelmann, S. (1966). *Teaching disadvantaged children in the preschool.* Englewood Cliffs, NJ: Prentice-Hall.

Berg, W. K., & Berg, K. M. (1987). Psychophysiological development in infancy: State, startle, and attention. In J. D. Osofsky (Ed.), *Handbook of infant development* (2nd ed.). New York: John Wiley.

Berkowitz, L. (1975). *A survey of social psychology.* Hinsdale, IL: Dryden Press.

Berkowitz, M. W., Oser, F., & Althof, W. (1987). The development of sociomoral discourse. In W. M.

Kurtines & J. L. Gewirtz (Eds.), *Moral development through social interaction.* New York: John Wiley.

Berndt, T. J. (1979). Developmental changes in conformity to peers and parents. *Developmental Psychology, 15,* 608–616.

Berndt, T. J. (1981). *Prosocial behavior between friends and the development of social interaction patterns.* Paper presented at the annual meeting of the Society for Research in Child Development, New Orleans, LA.

Berndt, T. J. (1988). The nature and significance of children's relationships. In R. Vasta (Ed.), *Annals of child development* (Vol. 5). Greenwich, CT: JAI Press.

Berndt, T. J. (1989). Friendships in childhood and adolescence. In W. Damon (Ed.), *Child development today and tomorrow.* San Francisco, CA: Jossey-Bass.

Berne, E. (1964). *Games people play.* New York: Grove Press.

Bernstein, B. (1958). Social class and linguistic development: A theory of social learning. *British Journal of Sociology, 9,* 159–174.

Bernstein, B. (1961). Language and social class. *British Journal of Sociology, 11,* 271–276.

Bertalanffy, L. von. (1950). The theory of open systems in physics and biology. *Science, 111,* 23–29.

Beyene, Y. (1989). *From menarche to menopause: Reproductive lives of peasant women in two cultures.* New York: State University of New York Press.

Bibby, R. W., & Posterski, D. C. (1985). *The emerging generation: An inside look at Canada's teenagers.* Toronto: Irwin.

Bigras, M., LaFrenière, P. J., Lacharité, C. (1991). L'impact de la présence de l'enfant sur la relation conjugale. *Journal international de psychologie, 26,* 281–298.

Bijou, S. W. (1989). Psychological linguistics: Implications for a theory of initial development and a method for research. In H. W. Reese (Ed.), *Advances in child development and behavior.* New York: Academic Press.

Biller, H. B. (1982). Fatherhood: Implications for child and adult development. In B. B. Wolman et al. (Eds.), *Handbook of developmental psychology.* Englewood Cliffs, NJ: Prentice-Hall.

Binder, A. (1988). Juvenile delinquency. *Annual Review of Psychology, 39*, 253–282.

Birren, J. E., & Renner, V. (1977). Research on the psychology of aging: Principles and experimentation. In J. E. Birren & K. W. Schaie (Eds.), *Handbook of the psychology of aging*. New York: Van Nostrand Reinhold.

Bischof, L. J. (1976). *Adult psychology* (2nd ed.). New York: Harper & Row.

Black, C., & DeBlassie, R. R. (1985). Adolescent pregnancy: Contributing factors, consequences, treatment, and plausible solutions. *Adolescence, 78*, 281–290.

Blackwelder, D. E., & Passman, R. H. (1986). Grandmothers' and mothers' disciplining in three-generational families: The role of social responsibility in rewarding and punishing grandchildren. *Journal of Personality and Social Psychology, 50*, 80–86.

Blau, Z. S. (1973). *Old age in a changing society*. New York: New Viewpoints.

Bloch, H. A., & Niederhoffer, A. (1958). *The gang: A study of adolescent behavior*. New York: Philosophical Library.

Bloom, D. E. (1986). Women and work. *American Demographics, 8*, 25–30.

Bloom, L., Beckwith, R., Capatides, J. B., & Hafitz, J. (1988). Expression through affect and words in the transition from infancy to language. In P. B. Baltes, D. L. Featherman, & R. M. Lerner (Eds.), *Life-span development and behavior* (Vol. 8). Hillsdale, NJ: Erlbaum.

Bloom-Feshbach, J., & Bloom-Feshbach, S. (1987). *The psychology of separation and loss: Perspectives on development, life transitions, and clinical practice*. San Francisco: Jossey-Bass.

Bluebond-Langner, M. (1977). Meanings of death to children. In H. Feifel (Ed.), *New meanings of death*. New York: McGraw-Hill.

Blumenthal, J. A., Sanders Williams, R., Needels, T. L., & Wallace, A. G. (1982). Psychological changes accompany aerobic exercise in healthy middle-aged adults. *Psychosomatic Medicine, 44*, 529–536.

Bograd, M. (1988). Feminist perspectives of wife abuse. In K. Yllo & M. Bograd (Eds.), *Feminist perspectives on wife abuse*. Newbury Park, CA: Sage.

Boisvert, M. J. (1972). The battered child syndrome. *Social Casework*, 475–480.

Boldizar, J. P. (1991). Assessing sex typing and androgyny in children: The Children's Sex Role Inventory. *Developmental Psychology, 27*, 505–515.

Bolton, P. J. (1983). Drugs of abuse. In D. F. Hawkins (Ed.), *Drugs and pregnancy: Human teratogenesis and related problems* (pp. 128–154). London: Churchill Livingstone.

Bondareff, W. (1985). The neural basis of aging. In J. E. Birren & K. W. Schaie (Eds.), *Handbook of the psychology of aging* (2nd ed.). New York: Van Nostrand Reinhold.

Boone, P. C., & Azen, S. P. (1979). Normal range of motion of joints in male subjects. *Journal of Bone and Joint Surgery, 61*, 756–759.

Boring, E. G. (1923). Intelligence as the tests test it. *New Republic, 35*, 35–37.

Borkowski, J. G., Milstead, M., & Hale, C. (1988). Components of children's metamemory: Implications for strategy generalization. In F. E. Weinert & M. Perlmutter (Eds.), *Memory development: Universal changes and individual differences*. Hillsdale, NJ: Erlbaum.

Borland, D. C. (1982). A cohort analysis approach to the empty-nest syndrome among three ethnic groups of women: A theoretical position. *Journal of Marriage and the Family, 11*, 117–128.

Bornstein, M. H. (1984). Perceptual development. In M. H. Bornstein & M. E. Lamb (Eds.), *Developmental psychology: An advanced textbook* (pp. 81–132). Hillsdale, NJ: Erlbaum.

Bornstein, M. H. (1988). Perceptual development across the life cycle. In M. H. Bornstein & M. E. Lamb (Eds.), *Developmental psychology: An advanced textbook* (2nd ed.). Hillsdale, NJ: Erlbaum.

Bornstein, M. H., & Marks, L. E. (1982, January). Color revisionism. *Psychology Today, 16*, pp. 64–72.

Botwinick, J. (1984). *Aging and behavior* (3rd ed.). New York: Springer-Verlag.

Bouchard, T. J., Jr., & McGue, M. (1981). Familial studies of intelligence: A review. *Science, 212*, 1055–1059.

Bower, T.G.R. (1989). *The rational infant: Learning in infancy*. New York: W. H. Freeman.

Bowes, W. A., Jr., Brackbill, Y., Conway, E., & Steinschneider, A. (1970). The effects of obstetrical medication on fetus and infant. *Monographs of the Society for Research in Child Development, 35*(4).

Bowlby, J. (1940). The influence of early environment. *International Journal of Psychoanalysis, 21,* 154–178.

Bowlby, J. (1953). Some pathological processes set in train by early mother–child separation. *Journal of Mental Science, 99,* 265–272.

Bowlby, J. (1958). The nature of the child's tie to his mother. *International Journal of Psychoanalysis, 39,* 350–373.

Bowlby, J. (1969). *Attachment and loss* (Vol. 1): *Attachment.* New York: Basic Books.

Bowlby, J. (1979). *The making and breaking of affectional bonds.* London: Tavistock Publications.

Bowlby, J. (1980). *Attachment and loss* (Vol. 3): *Loss, sadness and depression.* New York: Basic Books.

Bowlby, J. (1982). *Attachment and loss* (Vol. 1): *Attachment* (2nd ed.). London: Hogarth Press.

Bowman, J. M. (1990). Maternal blood group immunization. In R. D. Eden, F. H. Boehm, & M. Haire (Eds.), *Assessment and care of the fetus: Physiological, clinical, and medicolegal principles.* Norwalk, CT: Appleton & Lange.

Boyd, G. A. (1976). *Developmental processes in the child's acquisition of syntax: Linguistics in the elementary school.* Itasca, IL: F. E. Peacock.

Bradshaw, G. L., & Anderson, J. R. (1982). Elaborative encoding as an explanation of levels of processing. *Journal of Verbal Learning and Verbal Behavior, 21,* 165–174.

Braine, L. G., Pomerantz, E., Lorber, D., & Krantz, D. H. (1991). Conflicts with authority: Children's feelings, actions, and justifications. *Developmental Psychology, 27,* 829–840.

Bransford, J. D. (1979). *Human cognition: Learning, understanding and remembering.* Belmont, CA: Wadsworth.

Braun, C. (1976). Teacher expectations. Sociopsychological dynamics. *Review of Educational Research, 46,* 185–213.

Brazelton, T. B. (1973). *Neonatal behavior assessment scale.* Philadelphia: Lippincott.

Brazelton, T. B., Nugent, J. K., & Lester, B. M. (1987). Neonatal behavioral assessment scale. In J. D. Osofsky (Ed.), *Handbook of infant development.* New York: John Wiley.

Breast milk prevents disease. (1984). *Glimpse, 6*(2).

Breckenridge, J. N., Gallagher, D., Thompson, L. W., & Peterson, J. (1986). Characteristic depressive symptoms of bereaved elders. *Journal of Gerontology, 41,* 163–168.

Brendt, R. L., & Beckman, D. A. (1990). Teratology. In R. D. Eden, F. H. Boehm, & M. Haire (Eds.), *Assessment and care of the fetus: Physiological, clinical, and medicolegal principles.* Norwalk, CT: Appleton & Lange.

Brennan, P. L., & Steinberg, L. D. (1984). Is reminiscence adaptive? Relations among social activity level, reminiscence, and morale. *International Journal of Aging and Human Development, 18,* 99–109.

Brenner, J., & Mueller, E. (1982). Shared meaning in boy toddler's peer relations. *Child Development, 53,* 380–391.

Bridges, L. J., Connell, J. P., & Belsky, J. (1988). Similarities and differences in infant–mother and infant–father interaction in the strange situation: A component process analysis. *Developmental Psychology, 24,* 92–100.

Brock, D.J.H. (1982). *Early diagnosis of fetal defects.* London: Churchill Livingstone.

Broderick, P. (1986). Perceptual motor development in children's drawing skill. In C. Pratt, A. F. Garton, W. E. Tunmer, & A. R. Nesdale (Eds.), *Research issues in child development.* Boston: Allen & Unwin.

Bromley, D. B. (1990). *Behavioural gerontology: Central issues in the psychology of ageing.* New York: John Wiley.

Bronfenbrenner, U. (1970). *Two worlds of childhood: U.S. and U.S.S.R.* New York: Russell Sage Foundation.

Bronfenbrenner, U. (1977a). Is early intervention effective? In S. Cohen & T. J. Comiskey (Eds.), *Child development: Contemporary perspectives.* Itasca, IL: F. E. Peacock.

Bronfenbrenner, U. (1977b, May). Nobody home: The erosion of the American family. *Psychology Today,* pp. 41–47.

Bronfenbrenner, U. (1989). Ecological systems theory. In R. Vasta (Ed.), *Annals of child development* (Vol. 6). Greenwich, CT: JAI Press.

Bronfenbrenner, U., Belsky, J., & Steinberg, L. (1977). Daycare in context: An ecological perspective on research and public policy. In *Policy issues in daycare*. Washington, DC: U.S. Department of Health & Human Services.

Bronson, G. W. (1971). Fear of the unfamiliar in human infants. In H. R. Schaffer (Ed.), *The origins of human social relations*. London: Academic Press.

Bronson, G. W. (1972). Infants' reactions to unfamiliar persons and novel objects. *Monographs of the Society for Research in Child Development, 37*(3).

Brooks, J. B. (1981). *The process of parenting*. Palo Alto, CA: Mayfield.

Brooks, G. A., & Fahey, T. D. (1984). *Exercise physiology: Human bioenergetics and its application*. New York: John Wiley.

Brooks-Gunn, J., & Furstenberg, F. F., Jr. (1989). Adolescent sexual behavior. *American Psychologist, 44*, 249–257.

Brophy, J. E., & Good, T. L. (1974). *Teacher–student relationships: Causes and consequences*. New York: Holt, Rinehart & Winston.

Brouwer, A. (1990). The nature of ageing. In M. A. Horan & A. Brouwer (Eds.), *Gerontology: Approaches to biomedical and clinical research*. London: Edward Arnold.

Brown, B. B., & Lohr, M. J. (1987). Peer group affiliation and adolescent self-esteem: An integration of ego identity and symbolic interaction theories. *Journal of Personality and Social Psychology, 52*, 47–55.

Brown, J., & Finn, P. (1982). Drinking to get drunk: Findings of a survey of junior and senior high school students. *Journal of Alcohol and Drug Education, 27*, 13–25.

Brown, J. L. (1964). States in newborn infants. *Merrill-Palmer Quarterly, 10*, 313–327.

Brown, K., Covell, K., & Abramovitch, R. (1991). Time course and control of emotion: Age differences in understanding and recognition. *Merrill-Palmer Quarterly, 37*, 273–287.

Brown, R. (1973). *A first language: The early stages*. Cambridge, MA: Harvard University Press.

Brownell, K. D., & Walden, T. A. (1984). Confronting obesity in children: Behavioral and psychological factors. *Pediatric Annals, 13*, 473–480.

Browne Miller, A. (1990). *The day care dilemma: Critical concerns for American families*. New York: Plenum.

Bruner, J. S. (1977). Early social interaction and language acquisition. In H. R. Schaffer (Ed.), *Studies in mother–infant interaction*. London: Academic Press.

Bruner, J. S. (1978, September). Learning the mother tongue. *Human Nature*, pp. 43–49.

Bruner, J. S. (1983). *Child's talk*. New York: W. W. Norton.

Bruner, J. S. (1985). Models of the learner. *Educational Researcher, 14*, 5–8.

Buchanan, C. M., Eccles, J. S., & Becker, J. B. (1992). Are adolescents the victims of raging hormones: Evidence for activational effects of hormones on moods and behavior at adolescence. *Psychological Bulletin, 111*, 62–107.

Buhler, C. (1961). Old age and fulfillment of life with considerations of the use of time in old age. *Acta Psychologica, 19*, 126–148.

Buis, J. M., & Thompson, D. N. (1989). Imaginary audience and personal fable: A brief review. *Adolescence, 24*, 773–781.

Bulcock, J. W., Whitt, M. E., & Beebe, M. J. (1991). Gender differences, student well-being and high school achievement. *Alberta Journal of Educational Research, 37*, 212–222.

Bullinger, A. (1985). The sensorimotor nature of the infant visual system: Cognitive problems. In V. L. Shulman, L.C.R. Restaino-Baumann, & L. Butler (Eds.), *The future of Piagetian theory: The neo-Piagetians* (pp. 19–32). New York: Plenum.

Bunce, V. L., & Harrison, D. W. (1991). Child- or adult-directed speech and esteem: Effects on performance and arousal in elderly adults. *International Journal of Aging and Human Development, 32*, 125–134.

Burns, B., & Lipsitt, L. P. (1991). Behavioral factors in crib death: Toward an understanding of the sudden infant death syndrome. *Journal of Applied Developmental Psychology, 12*, 159–184.

Bush calls for unprecedented increase in Head Start program. (1992, January 22). *The Monterey Herald*, p. A3.

Buss, A. H., & Plomin, R. (1985). *Temperament: Early developing personality traits.* Hillsdale, NJ: Erlbaum.

Butler, J. R., & Burton, L. M. (1990). Rethinking teenage childbearing: Is sexual abuse a missing link? *Family Relations, 39,* 73–80.

Butler, R. N. (1963). The life review: An interpretation of reminiscence in the aged. *Psychiatry, 26,* 65–76.

Butler, R. N. (1989). Productive aging. In V. L. Bengtson & K. W. Schaie (Eds.), *The course of later life: Research and reflections.* New York: Springer.

Butler, R. N., & Lewis, M. I. (1982). *Aging and mental health* (3rd ed.). St. Louis: C. V. Mosby.

Byrne, B. M., & Shavelson, R. J. (1987). Adolescent self-concept: Testing the assumption of equivalent structure across gender. *American Educational Research Journal, 24,* 365–385.

Bytheway, B., Keil, T., Allatt, P., & Bryman, A. (Eds.), (1989). *Becoming and being old: Sociological approaches to later life.* London: Sage.

Cairns, R. B. (1983). The emergence of developmental psychology. In P. H. Mussen (Ed.), *Handbook of child psychology* (4th ed.) (Vol. 1): *History, theory, and methods* (pp. 41–102). (W. Kessen, Ed.). New York: John Wiley.

Cairns, R. B., Gariépy, J. L., & Hood, K. E. (1990). Development, microevolution, and social behavior. *Psychological Review, 97,* 49–65.

Caldwell, B. M. (1989). Achieving rights for children: Role of the early childhood profession. *Childhood Education, 66,* 4–7.

Calfee, R. (1981). Cognitive psychology and educational practice. In D. C. Berliner (Ed.), *Review of Research in Education* (Vol. 9). Washington, DC: American Educational Research Association.

Campbell, A. (1976). Subjective measures of well being. *American Psychologist, 31,* 117–124.

Campbell, A. (1981). *The sense of well being in America: Recent patterns and trends.* New York: McGraw-Hill.

Campbell, A., Converse, P. E., & Rodgers, W. L. (1976). *The quality of American life: Perceptions, evaluations, and satisfactions.* New York: Russell Sage Foundation.

Campbell, B. A., & Randall, P. J. (1977). Paradoxical effects of amphetamine on preweanling and post-weanling rats. *Science, 195,* 888–991.

Campbell, S. (1974). Cognitive styles and behavior problems of clinic boys. *Journal of Abnormal Child Psychology, 2,* 307–312.

Campbell, S. B., & Cohn, J. F. (1991). Prevalence and correlates of postpartum depression in first-time mothers. *Journal of Abnormal Psychology, 100,* 594–599.

Campos, J. J., Langer, A., & Krowitz, A. (1970). Cardiac response on the visual cliff in prelocomotor human infants. *Science, 170,* 196–197.

Canning, P. M., & Lyon, M. E. (1991). Misconceptions about early child care, education and intervention. *Journal of Child and Youth Care, 5,* 1–10.

Carey, S. T. (1987). Reading comprehensions in first and second languages of immersion and Francophone students. *Canadian Journal for Exceptional Children, 3,* 103–108.

Carey, W. B. (1989). Introduction: Basic issues. In W. B. Carey & S. C. McDevitt (Eds.), *Clinical and educational applications of temperament research.* Berwyn, PA: Swets North America.

Carlson, P., & Anisfeld, M. (1969). Some observations on the linguistic competence of a two year old child. *Child Development, 40,* 572–574.

Carroll, J. C., & Rest, J. R. (1982). Moral development. In B. B. Wolman et al. (Eds.), *Handbook of developmental psychology.* Englewood Cliffs, NJ: Prentice-Hall.

Cartwright, D. S., Tomson, B., & Schwartz, H. (1975). *Gang delinquency.* Pacific Grove, CA: Brooks/Cole.

Case, R. (1991). Stages in the development of the young child's first sense of self. *Developmental Review, 11,* 210–230.

Case, R., Hayward, S., Lewis, M., & Hurst, P. (1988). Toward a neo-Piagetian theory of cognitive and emotional development. *Developmental Review, 8,* 1–51.

Cattell, R. B. (1971). *Abilities: Their structure, growth, and action.* Boston: Houghton Mifflin.

Cavanaugh, J. C. (1983). Comprehension and retention of television programs by 20- and 60-year-olds. *Journal of Gerontology, 38,* 190–196.

CBC Television (1986, April 16). *Fifth Estate*.

Ceci, S. J. (1991). How much does schooling influence general intelligence and its cognitive components? A reassessment of the evidence. *Developmental Psychology, 27,* 703–722.

Chalfant, J. C. (1989). Learning disabilities: Policy issues and promising approaches. *American Psychologist, 44,* 392–398.

Chase, N. F. (1975). *A child is being beaten.* New York: Holt, Rinehart & Winston.

Chase-Lansdale, P. L., Brooks-Gunn, J., & Paikoff, R. L. (1991). Research and programs for adolescent mothers: Missing links and future promises. *Family Relations, 40,* 396–403.

Chasnoff, I. J. (1986). Perinatal addiction: Consequences of intrauterine exposure to opiate and nonopiate drugs. In I. J. Chasnoff (Ed.), *Drug use in pregnancy: Mother and child.* Boston: MTP Press.

Chasnoff, I., Burns, W., Schnoll, S., & Burns, K. (1985). Cocaine use in pregnancy. *New England Journal of Medicine, 313,* 666–669.

Chassin, L., Rogosch, F., & Barrera, M. (1991). Substance use and symptomatology among adolescent children of alcoholics. *Journal of Abnormal Psychology, 4,* 449–463.

Chess, S., & Thomas, A. (1989). The practical application of temperament to psychiatry. In W. B. Carey & S. C. McDevitt (Eds.), *Clinical and educational applications of temperament research.* Berwyn, PA: Swets North America.

Chess, S., & Thomas, A. (1989a). Temperament and its functional significance. In S. I. Greenspan & G. H. Pollock (Eds.), *The course of life: Vol II Early Childhood.* Madison, Conn.: International Universities Press.

Cheung, Y. W., Erickson, P. G., & Landau, T. C. (1991). Experience of crack use: Findings from a community-based sample in Toronto. *Journal of Drug Issues, 21,* 121–140.

Chez, R. A., & Chervenak, J. L. (1990). Nutrition in pregnancy. In R. D. Eden, F. H. Boehm, & M. Haire (Eds.), *Assessment and care of the fetus: Physiological, clinical, and medicolegal principles.* Norwalk, CT: Appleton & Lange.

Chi, M.T.H., & Glaser, R. (1980). The measurement of expertise: Analysis of the development of knowledge and skill as a basis for assessing achievement. In E. L. Baker & E. S. Quellmalz (Eds.), *Educational testing and evaluation: Design, analysis and policy.* Beverly Hills, CA: Sage.

Chilman, C. S. (1983). Remarriage and stepfamilies: Research results and implications. In E. D. Macklin & R. H. Rubin (Eds.), *Contemporary families and alternative life-styles: Handbook on research and theory* (pp. 147–163). Beverly Hills, CA: Sage.

China fears sexual imbalance. (1983, March 14). *Edmonton Journal.*

Chipman, S. F. (1988). Far too sexy a topic. *Educational Researcher, 17,* 46–49.

Chiriboga, D. A. (1982). Adaptation to marital separation in later and earlier life. *Journal of Gerontology, 37,* 109–114.

Chlamydia — More common than gonorrhea. (1988, November 24). *Folio* (p. 6). Edmonton, Alta: University of Alberta.

Chomsky, N. (1957). *Syntactic structures.* The Hague: Mouton.

Chomsky, N. (1965). *Aspects of the theory of syntax.* Cambridge: MA: M.I.T. Press.

Christopher, F. S., & Roosa, M. W. (1990). An evaluation of an adolescent pregnancy prevention program: Is "Just say no" enough? *Family Relations, 39,* 68–72.

Christopherson, V. A. (1988). The family as a socialization context. In T. D. Yawkey & J. E. Johnson (Eds.), *Integrative processes and socialization: Early to middle childhood.* Hillsdale, NJ: Erlbaum.

Chugani, H. T., & Phelps, M. E. (1986). Maturational changes in cerebral function in infants determined by FGG positron emission tomography. *Science, 231,* 840–843.

Chumlea, W. C. (1982). Physical growth in adolescence. In B. B. Wolman et al. (Eds.), *Handbook of developmental psychology.* Englewood Cliffs, NJ: Prentice-Hall.

Cicirelli, V. (1983). A comparison of helping behavior to elderly parents of adult children with intact marriages. *Gerontologist, 23,* 619–625.

Clarke, H. H. (1975). Joint and body range of movement. *Physical Fitness Research Digest, 5,* 16–18.

Clark, H. H., & Clark, E. V. (1977). *Psychology and language: An introduction to psycholinguistics.* New York: Harcourt Brace Jovanovich.

Clarke-Stewart, A. (1984). Day care: A new context for research and development. In M. Perlmutter (Ed.), *The Minnesota Symposia on Child Psychology* (Vol. 17): *Parent–child interaction and parent–child relations in child development*. Hillsdale, NJ: Erlbaum.

Clarke-Stewart, K. A. (1989). Infant day care: Maligned or malignant? *American Psychologist, 44*, 266–273.

Clausen, J. A. (1975). The social meaning of differential physical and sexual maturation. In S. E. Ragastin & G. H. Elder (Eds.), *Adolescence in the life cycle: Psychological change and social context*. New York: John Wiley.

Clausen, J. A. (1981). Men's occupational careers in the middle years. In D. H. Eichorn, J. A. Clausen, N. Haan, M. P. Honzik, & P. H. Mussen (Eds.), *Present and past in middle life*. New York: Academic Press.

Clayton, P. J., Halikas, J. A., & Maurice, W. L. (1972). The depression of widowhood. *British Journal of Psychiatry, 120*, 71–78.

Clayton, R. R., & Voss, H. L. (1977). Shacking up: Cohabitation in the 1970's. *Journal of Marriage and the Family, 39*, 273–283.

Clayton, V. P., & Birren, J. E. (1980). The development of wisdom across the life span: A reexamination of an ancient topic. In P. B. Baltes & O. G. Brim, Jr. (Eds.), *Life-span development and behavior* (Vol. 3). New York: Academic Press.

Clement, F. J. (1974). Longitudinal and cross-sectional assessments of age changes in physical strength as related to sex, social class, and mental ability. *Journal of Gerontology, 29*, 423–429.

Cohler, B. J. (1982). Personal narrative and life course. In P. B. Baltes & O. G. Brim, Jr. (Eds.), *Life-span development and behavior* (Vol. 4) (pp. 205–241). New York: Academic Press.

Cohler, B. J., & Grunebaum, H. V. (1981). *Mothers, grandmothers and daughters: Personality and childcare in three-generation families*. New York: John Wiley.

Colby, A., & Kohlberg, L. (1984). Invariant sequence and internal consistency in moral judgment stages. In W. M. Kertines & J. L. Gewirtz (Eds.), *Morality, moral behavior, and moral development* (pp. 41–51). New York: John Wiley.

Cole, C. L. (1984). Marital quality in later life. In W. H. Quinn & G. A. Hughston (Eds.), *Independent aging: Family and social systems perspectives*. Rockville, MD: Aspen.

Cole, P. M. (1986). Children's spontaneous control of facial expression. *Child Development, 57*, 1309–1321.

Coleman, J. S. (1974). *Youth: Transition to adulthood*. Chicago: University of Chicago Press.

Coleman, P. G. (1986). *Aging and reminiscence processes: Social and clinical implications*. New York: John Wiley.

Collins, W. A. (1983). Interpretation and interference in children's television viewing. In J. Bryant & D. R. Anderson (Eds.), *Children's understanding of television: Research on attention and comprehension* (pp. 125–150). New York: Academic Press.

Collins, W. A. (1991). Shared views and parent–adolescent relationships. *New Directions for Child Development, 51*, 103–110.

Collins, W. A., & Gunnar, M. R. (1990). Social and personality development. *Annual Review of Psychology, 41*, 387–416.

Collins, W. A., Wellman, H., Keniston, A. H., & Westby, S. D. (1978). Age-related aspects of comprehension and inference from a televised dramatic narrative. *Child Development, 49*, 389–399.

Comfort, A. (1978). A biologist laments and exhorts. In L. F. Jarvik (Ed.), *Aging into the 21st century*. New York: Gardner Press.

Condon, W. S. & Sander, L. W. (1974). Neonate movement is synchronized with adult speech: Interactional participation and language acquisition. *Science, 183*, 99–101.

Confrey, J. (1991). Steering a course between Vygotsky and Piaget. *Educational Researcher, 20*, 28–32.

Connell, B. (1985). A new man. In *The English Curriculum, ILEA*. London: English Centre Publication.

Cooke, B. (1991). Family life education. *Family Relations, 40*, 3–13.

Cooley, C. H. (1902). *Human nature and the social order*. New York: Scribner's.

Coombs, R. H. (1991). Marital status and personal well-being: A literature review. *Family Relations, 40*, 97–102.

Copans, S. A. (1974). Human prenatal effects: Methodological problems and some suggested solutions. *Merrill-Palmer Quarterly, 20*, 43–52.

Corbin, C. B. (1980). The physical fitness of children: A discussion and point of view. In C. B. Corbin (Ed.), *A textbook of motor development*. Dubuque, IA: Brown.

Corse, C. D., Manuck, S. B., Cantwell, J. D., Giordani, B., & Matthews, K. A. (1982). Coronary-prone behavior pattern and cardiovascular response in persons with and without coronary heart disease. *Psychosomatic Medicine, 44*, 449–459.

Costa, P. T., Jr., & McCrae, R. R. (1978). Objective personality assessment. In M. Storandt, I. C. Siegler, & M. F. Elias (Eds.), *The clinical psychology of aging*. New York: Plenum.

Costa, P. T., Jr., & McCrae, R. R. (1980). Still stable after all these years: Personality as a key to some issues in aging. In P. B. Baltes & O. G. Brim (Eds.), *Life-span development and behavior* (Vol. 3). New York: Academic Press.

Costa, P. T., Jr., & McCrae, R. R. (1984). Personality as a lifelong determinant of wellbeing. In C. Z. Malatesta & C. E. Izard (Eds.), *Emotion in adult development* (pp. 141–158). Beverly Hills, CA: Sage.

Costa, P. T., Jr., McCrae, R. R., & Arenberg, D. (1983). Recent longitudinal research on personality and aging. In K. W. Schaie (Ed.), *Longitudinal studies of adult psychological development* (pp. 222–265). New York: Guilford Press.

Costabile, A., Smith, P. K., Matheson, L., Aston, J., Hunter, T., & Boulton, M. (1991). Cross-national comparison of how children distinguish serious and playful fighting. *Developmental Psychology, 27*, 881–887.

Côté, J. E., & Levine, C. (1988). A critical examination of the ego identity status paradigm. *Developmental Review, 8*, 147–184.

Court to decide right of surrogate mother. (1992, January 24). *Monterey Herald*, p. A8.

Coustan, D. R. (1990). Diabetes mellitus. In R. D. Eden, F. H. Boehm, & M. Haire (Eds.), *Assessment and care of the fetus: Physiological, clinical, and medicolegal principles*. Norwalk, CT: Appleton & Lange.

Cowen, E. L., Work, W. C., Hightower, A. D., Wyman, P. A., Parker, G. R., & Lotyczewski, B. S. (1991). Toward the development of a measure of perceived self-efficacy in children. *Journal of Clinical Child Psychology, 20*, 169–178.

Cox, H. G. (1988). *Later life: The realities of aging* (2nd ed.). Englewood Cliffs, NJ: Prentice-Hall.

Cox, T. C., Jacobs, M. R., Leblanc, A. E., & Marshman, J. A. (1983). *Drugs and drug abuse: A reference test*. Toronto: Addiction Research Foundation.

Cratty, B. J. (1978). *Perceptual and motor development in infants and children* (2nd ed.). Englewood Cliffs, NJ: Prentice-Hall.

Creasy, R. K. (1988). Preterm labor and delivery. In R. K. Creasy & R. Resnik (Eds.), *Maternal-fetal medicine: Principles and practice*. Philadelphia: W. B. Saunders.

Creasy, R. K. (1990). Preterm labor. In R. D. Eden, F. H. Boehm, & M. Haire (Eds.), *Assessment and care of the fetus: Physiological, clinical, and medicolegal principles*. Norwalk, CT: Appleton & Lange.

Crisp, A. H. (1980). *Let me be*. New York: Grune & Stratton.

Crisp, A. H., Palmer, R. L., & Kalucy, R. S. (1976). How common is anorexia nervosa: A prevalence study. *British Journal of Psychiatry, 128*, 549–554.

Cristofalo, V. J. (1988). An overview of the theories of biological aging. In J. E. Birren & V. L. Bengtson (Eds.), *Emergent theories of aging*. New York: Springer.

Cristofalo, V. J., & Hayflick, L. (1985). Basic biological research in aging: An overview. In G. L. Maddox & E. W. Busse (Eds.), *Aging: The universal human experience*. New York: Springer.

Crockett, L. J., Losoff, M., & Petersen, A. C. (1984). Perceptions of the peer group and friendship in early adolescence. *Journal of Early Adolescence, 4*, 155–181.

Crockett, L. J., & Petersen, A. C. (1987). Pubertal status and psychosocial development: Findings from the early adolescence study. In R. M. Lerner & T. T. Foch (Eds.), *Biological-psychosocial interactions in early adolescence: A life-span perspective*. Hillsdale, NJ: Erlbaum.

Crowell, J. A., & Feldman, S. S. (1991). Mothers' working models of attachment relationships and mother and child behavior during separation and reunion. *Developmental Psychology, 27*, 597–605.

Crowley, J. E., Levitin, T. E., & Quinn, R. P. (1973, September). Seven deadly half-truths about women. *Psychology Today, 6*, pp. 94–96.

Crowley, P. A. (1983). Premature labour. In D. F. Hawkins (Ed.), *Drugs and Pregnancy: Human tera-*

togenesis and related problems. New York: Churchill Livingstone.

Cuber, J. F., & Harroff, P. B. (1965). The significant Americans. New York: Appleton-Century-Crofts.

Culbertson, J. L. (1991). Child advocacy and clinical child psychology. Journal of Clinical Child Psychology, 20, 7–10.

Cumming, E., & Henry, W. H. (1961). Growing old. New York: Basic Books.

Cummins, J. (1986). Empowering minority students: A framework for intervention. Harvard Educational Review, 56, 18–36.

Cummins, J., & Swain, M. (1986). Bilingualism in education: Aspects of theory, research and practice. London: Taylor & Fry.

Cunningham, W. R. (1989). Intellectual abilities, speed of response, and aging. In V. L. Bengtson & K. W. Schaie (Eds.), The course of later life: Research and reflections. New York: Springer.

Curtiss, S. (1977). Genie: A psycholinguistic study of a modern-day wild child. New York: Academic Press.

Cusack, R. (1984). Dietary management of obese children and adolescents. Pediatric Annals, 13, 455–464.

Dalton, K. (1980). Depression after childbirth. Oxford: Oxford University Press.

Damon, W., & Colby, A. (1987). Social influence and moral change. In W. M. Kurtines & J. L. Gewirtz (Eds.), Moral development through social interaction. New York: John Wiley.

Danilewitz, D., & Skuy, M. (1990). A psychoeducational profile of the unmarried mother. International Journal of Adolescence and Youth, 2, 175–184.

Dansky, J. L. (1980). Make-believe: A mediator of the relationship between play and associative fluency. Child Development, 51, 576–579.

Darley, J. M., & Shultz, T. R. (1990). Moral rules: Their content and acquisition. Annual Review of Psychology, 41, 525–556.

Darley, J. M., & Zanna, M. P. (1982). Making moral judgments. American Scientist, 70, 515–521.

Darling, C. A., Kallen, D. J., & Van Dusen, J. E. (1984). Sex in transition, 1900–1980. Journal of Youth and Adolescence, 13, 385–394.

Darwin, C. (1877). A biographical sketch of an infant. Mind, 2, 285–294.

Das, J. P., & Dash, U. N. (1990). Schooling, literacy and cognitive development: A study in rural India. In C. K. Leong & B. S. Randhawa (Eds.), Understanding literacy and cognition: Theory, research, and application. New York: Plenum.

Dasen, P. R. (Ed.). (1977). Piagetian psychology: Cross-cultural contributions. New York: Gardner Press.

Datan, N., Rodeheaver, D., & Hughes, F. (1987). Adult development and aging. Annual Review of Psychology, 38, 153–180.

David, C. B., & David, P. H. (1984). Bottle feeding and malnutrition in a developing country: The "bottle-starved" baby. Journal of Tropical Pediatrics, 30.

Davies, I. (1990). A physiological approach to ageing. In M. A. Horan & A. Brouwer (Eds.), Gerontology: Approaches to biomedical and clinical research. London: Edward Arnold.

Davis, S. M., & Harris, M. B. (1982). Sexual knowledge, sexual interests, and sources of sexual information of rural and urban adolescents from three cultures. Adolescence, 17, 471–492.

DeBurger, J. E. (1967). Marital problems, helpseeking, and emotional orientation as revealed in helpseeking letters. Journal of Marriage and the Family, 29, 712–721.

DeCasper, A. J., & Fifer, W. P. (1980). Of human bonding: Newborns prefer their mother's voices. Science, 208, 1174–1176.

De Charms, R. (1972). Personal causation training in the schools. Journal of Applied Social Psychology, 2, 95–113.

DeGenova, M. K. (1992). If you had your life to live over again: What would you do differently? International Journal of Aging and Human Development, 34, 135–143.

DeLorey, C. (1984). Health care and midlife women. In G. Baruch & J. Brooks-Gunn (Eds.), Women in midlife. New York: Plenum.

DeMause, L. (1975, April). Our forebears made childhood a nightmare. Psychology Today, pp. 85–88.

Dempter, F. N. (1985). Short-term memory development in childhood. In C. J. Brainerd & M. Pressley (Eds.), Basic processes in memory development: Progress in cognitive development research. New York: Springer-Verlag.

DeMyer, M. K., Barton, S., DeMyer, W. E., Norton, J., Allen, J., & Steele, R. (1973). Prognosis in autism: A follow-up study. *Journal of Autism and Childhood Schizophrenia, 3,* 199–246.

Denney, N. W. (1979). Problem solving in later adulthood: Intervention research. In P. B. Baltes & O. G. Brim, Jr. (Eds.), *Life-span development and behavior* (Vol. 2). New York: Academic Press.

Dennis, W. (1941a). Infant development under conditions of restricted practice and of minimum social stimulation. *Genetic Psychology Monographs, 23,* 143–191.

Dennis, W. (1941b). The significance of feral man. *American Journal of Psychology, 54,* 425–432.

Dennis, W. (1951). A further analysis of reports of wild children. *Child Development, 22,* 153–158.

Dennis, W. (1960). Causes of retardation among institutional children: Iran. *Journal of Genetic Psychology, 96,* 47–59.

Dennis, W. (1966). Creative productivity between the ages of 20 and 80. *Journal of Gerontology, 21,* 1–18.

deRegt, R. H., Minkoff, H. L., Feldman, J., & Schwartz, R. H. (1986). Relation of private or clinic care to the Cesarean birth rate. *The New England Journal of Medicine, 315,* 619–625.

Desor, J. A., Maller, O., & Greene, L. S. (1978). Preference for sweet in humans: Infants, children and adults. In J. M. Weiffenbach (Ed.), *Taste and development: The genesis of sweet preference.* Bethesda, MD: National Institute of Dental Research, DHEW Publication 77–1068.

deVries, M. W. (1989). Difficult temperament: A universal and culturally embedded concept. In W. B. Carey & S. C. McDevitt (Eds.), *Clinical and educational applications of temperament research.* Berwyn, PA: Swets North America.

deVries, M. W., & Sameroff, A. J. (1984). Culture and temperament: Influences on infant temperament in three East African societies. *American Journal of Orthopsychiatry, 54,* 83–96.

Diamond, A. M. (1986). The life-cycle research productivity of mathematicians and scientists. *Journal of Gerontology, 41,* 520–525.

Diaz, R. M. (1983). Thought and two languages: The impact of bilingualism on cognitive development. In E. W. Gordon (Ed.), *Review of Research in Education* (Vol. 10). Washington, DC: American Educational Research Association.

Diaz, R. M., Neal, C. J., & Vachio, A. (1991). Maternal teaching in the zone of proximal development: A comparison of low- and high-risk dyads. *Merrill-Palmer Quarterly, 37,* 83–108.

Dick-Read, G. (1972). *Childbirth without fear: The original approach to natural childbirth* (4th ed.) (H. Wessel & H. F. Ellis, Eds.). New York: Harper & Row.

Didion, J. (1979). *The white album.* New York: Simon & Schuster.

Diener, C. I., Dweck, C. S. (1980). An analysis of learned helplessness: II. The processing of success. *Journal of Personality and Social Psychology, 39,* 940–952.

DiLalla, L. F., & Watson, M. W. (1988). Differentiation of fantasy and reality: Preschoolers' reactions to interruptions in their play. *Developmental Psychology, 24,* 286–291.

Dillard, J. M., Campbell, N. J., & Chisolm, G. B. (1984). Correlates of life satisfaction of aged persons. *Psychological Reports, 54,* 977–978.

Dinkmeyer, D., & McKay, G. (1976). *Systematic training for effective parenting (S.T.E.P.).* Circle Pines, MN: American Guidance Service.

Dittmann-Kohli, F., & Baltes, P. B. (1986). Towards a neo-functionalist conception of adult intellectual development: Wisdom as a prototypical case of intellectual growth. In C. Alexander & E. Langer (Eds.), *Beyond formal operations: Alternative endpoints to human development.* New York: Oxford University Press.

Dix, T. (1991). The affective organization of parenting: Adaptive and maladaptive processes. *Psychological Bulletin, 110,* 3–25.

Doby, J. (1980). Firstborn fallacies. *Science, 80,* 4–10.

Doka, K. (1984–85). Expectation of death, participation in funeral arrangements, and grief adjustment. *Omega, 15(2).*

Doman, G. J. (1984). *How to multiply your baby's intelligence.* Garden City, NY: Doubleday.

Donaldson, M. (1978). *Children's minds.* London: Fontana/Croom Helm.

Donate-Bartfield, E., & Passman, R. H. (1985). Attentiveness of mothers and fathers to their baby's cries. *Infant behavior and development, 8,* 385–393.

Donnelly, B. W., & Voydanoff, P. (1991). Factors associated with releasing for adoption among adolescent mothers. *Family Relations, 40,* 404–410.

Donovan, C. M. (1980). Program planning for the visually impaired child. In A. P. Scheiner & I. F. Abroms (Eds.), *The practical management of the developmentally disabled child.* St. Louis: C. V. Mosby.

Down with Type A! (1983, January). *Health*, pp. 14–15.

Doxey, I. M. (Ed.). (1990). *Child care and education: Canadian dimensions.* Scarborough, Ont.: Nelson Canada.

Drebing, C. E., & Gooden, W. E. (1991). The impact of the dream on mental health functioning in the male midlife transition. *International Journal of Aging and Human Development, 32,* 277–287.

Dreyer, P. H. (1982). Sexuality during adolescence. In B. B. Wolman (Ed.), *Handbook of developmental psychology.* Englewood Cliffs, NJ: Prentice-Hall.

Drugan, A., Johnson, M. P., & Evans, M. I. (1990). Amniocentesis. In R. D. Eden, F. H. Boehm, & M. Haire (Eds.), *Assessment and care of the fetus: Physiological, clinical, and medicolegal principles.* Norwalk, CT: Appleton & Lange.

Drummond, W. J. (1991). Adolescent relationships in a period of change: A New Zealand perspective. *International Journal of Adolescence and Youth, 2,* 275–286.

Duffty, P., & Bryan, M. H. (1982). Home apnea monitoring in "near-miss" Sudden Infant Death Syndrome (SIDS) and in siblings of SIDS victims. *Pediatrics, 70,* 69–74.

Duncan, S., & Fiske, D. W. (1977). *Face-to-face interaction: Research methods and theory.* Hillsdale, NJ: Erlbaum.

Dunphy, D. C. (1963). The social structure of urban adolescent peer groups. *Sociometry, 26,* 230–246.

Duvall, E. M. (1977). *Marriage and family development* (5th ed.). New York: Harper & Row.

Dweck, C. S. (1975). The role of expectations and attributions in the alleviation of learned helplessness. *Journal of Personality and Social Psychology, 31,* 674–685.

Dweck, C. S. (1986). Motivational processes affecting learning. *American Psychologist, 41,* 1040–1048.

Dweck, C. S., & Repucci, N. D. (1973). Learned helplessness and reinforcement responsibility in children. *Journal of Personality and Social Psychology, 25,* 109–116.

East, P. L. (1991). The parent–child relationships of withdrawn, aggressive, and sociable children: Child and parent perspectives. *Merrill-Palmer Quarterly, 37,* 425–444.

Eastman, P., & Barr, J. L. (1985). *Your child is smarter than you think.* London: Jonathan Cape.

Eccles, J. S., & Jacobs, J. E. (1986). Social forces shape math attitudes and performance. *Signs, 11,* 367–389.

Eckerman, C. O., & Whatley, J. L. (1975). Infants' reactions to unfamiliar adults varying in novelty. *Developmental Psychology, 11,* 562–566.

Eckland, B. K. (1977). Darwin rides again. *American Journal of Sociology, 82,* 693–697.

Eden, R. D., Blanco, J. D., Tomasi, A., & Gall, S. A. (1990). Maternal-fetal infection. In R. D. Eden, F. H. Boehm, & M. Haire (Eds.), *Assessment and care of the fetus: Physiological, clinical, and medicolegal principles.* Norwalk, CT: Appleton & Lange.

Egeland, B., & Sroufe, L. (1981). Attachment and early maltreatment. *Child Development, 52,* 44–52.

Egeland, B., & Vaughn, B. (1981). Failure of "bond formation" as a cause of abuse, neglect, and maltreatment. *American Journal of Orthopsychiatry, 51,* 78–84.

Egeland, J. A., Gerhard, D. S., Pauls, D. L., Sussex, J. N., Kidd, K. K., et al. (1987). Bipolar affective disorders linked to DNA markers on chromosome 11. *Nature, 325,* 783–787.

Eiger, M. S., & Olds, S. W. (1987). *The complete book of breastfeeding.* New York: Workman.

Eilers, R. E., & Minifie, F. D. (1975). Fricative discrimination in early infancy. *Journal of Speech and Hearing Research, 18,* 158–167.

Eilers, R. E., & Oller, D. K. (1988). Precursors to speech. In R. Vasta (Ed.), *Annals of child development* (Vol. 5). Greenwich, CT: JAI Press.

Eisenberg, N. (1989). Empathy and sympathy. In W. Damon (Ed.), *Child development today and tomorrow*, San Francisco, CA: Jossey-Bass.

Eisenberg, N., Miller, P. A., Shell, R., McNalley, S., & Shea, C. (1991). Prosocial development in adolescence: A longitudinal study. *Developmental Psychology, 27,* 849–857.

Eisenberg-Berg, N. (1979). Development of children's prosocial moral judgement. *Developmental Psychology, 15*, 38–44.

Eisenstein, Z. R. (1982). The sexual politics of the new right: Understanding the "crisis of liberalism" for the 1980's. *Signs, 7*, 567–588.

Eisikovits, Z. C., Edleson, J. L., Guttmann, E., & Sela-Amit, M. (1991). Cognitive styles and socialized attitudes of men who batter: Where should we intervene? *Family Relations, 40*, 72–77.

Eisler, T. A. (1984). Career impact on independence of the elderly. In W. H. Quinn & G. A. Hughston (Eds.), *Independent aging: Family and social systems perspectives* (pp. 256–264). Rockville, MD: Aspen.

Elder, G. H., Jr. (1974). *Children of the great depression.* Chicago: University of Chicago Press.

Elder, G. H., Jr. (1979). Historical change in life patterns and personality. In P. B. Baltes & O. G. Brim, Jr. (Eds.), *Life span development and behavior* (Vol. 2). New York: Academic Press.

Elder, G. H., Jr., Nguyen, T. Van, & Caspi, A. (1985). Linking family hardship to children's lives. *Child Development, 56*, 361–375.

Elkin, F., & Handel, G. (1989). *The child and society: The process of socialization* (5th ed.). New York: Random House.

Elkind, D. (1967). Egocentrism in adolescence. *Child Development, 38*, 1025–1034.

Elkind, D. (1981a). *The hurried child: Growing up too fast too soon.* Reading, MA: Addison-Wesley.

Elkind, D. (1981b). Understanding the young adolescent. In L. D. Steinberg (Ed.), *The life cycle: Readings in human development.* New York: Columbia University Press.

Elkind, D. (1987). *Miseducation: Preschoolers at risk.* New York: Alfred A. Knopf.

Elkind, D., & Bowen, R. (1979). Imaginary audience behavior in children and adolescents. *Developmental Psychology, 15*(1), 38–44.

Emery, A.E.H. (1984). Introduction — The principles of genetic counseling. In E. H. Emery & I. Pullen (Eds.), *Psychological aspects of genetic counselling.* New York: Academic Press.

Emery, R. E. (1989). Family violence. *American Psychologist, 44*, 321–328.

Endsley, R. C., & Bradbard, M. R. (1981). *Quality day care: A handbook of choices for parents and caregivers.* Englewood Cliffs, NJ: Prentice-Hall.

Enright, R., Shukla, D., & Lapsley, D. (1980). Adolescent egocentrism–sociocentrism in early and late adolescence. *Adolescence, 14*, 687–695.

Erickson, G., & Farkas, S. (1991). Prior experience and gender differences in science achievement. *Alberta Journal of Educational Research, 37*, 225–239.

Erickson, M. T. (1987). *Behavior disorders of children and adolescents.* Englewood Cliffs, NJ: Prentice-Hall.

Erikson, E. H. (1956). The problems of ego identity. *Journal of the American Psychoanalytic Association, 4*, 56–121.

Erikson, E. H. (1959). Identity and the life cycle: Selected papers. *Psychological Issue Monograph Series, I* (No. 1). New York: International Universities Press.

Erikson, E. H. (1961). The roots of virtue. In J. Huxley (Ed.), *The humanist frame.* New York: Harper & Row.

Erikson, E. H. (1968). *Identity, youth and crisis.* New York: W. W. Norton.

Erikson, E., & Hall, E. A. (1983, June). A conversation with Erik Erikson. *Psychology Today, 17*, pp. 22–30.

Erikson, J. D., & Bjerkedal, T. (1981). Down's syndrome associated with father's age in Norway. *Journal of Medical Genetics, 18*, 22–28.

Ernst, C., & Angst, J. (1983). *Birth order: Its influence on personality.* New York: Springer-Verlag.

Espenschade, A. S., & Eckert, H. D. (1980). *Motor development* (2nd ed.). Columbus, OH: Charles E. Merrill.

Evans, R. I. (1989). *Albert Bandura: The man and his ideas — a dialogue.* New York: Praeger.

Eveleth, P. B., & Tanner, J. M. (1976). *Worldwide variation in human growth.* Cambridge, England: Cambridge University Press.

Eysenck, H. J., & Kamin, L. (1981). *Intelligence: The battle for the mind.* London: Macmillan.

Fagan, J., Piper, E., & Moore, M. (1986). Violent delinquents and urban youths. *Criminology, 24*, 439–468.

Falek, A. (1975). Ethical issues in human behavior genetics: Civil rights, informed consent, and ethics of intervention. In K. W. Schaie, V. F. Anderson, G. E. McClearn, & J. Money (Eds.), *Developmental human behavior genetics*. Lexington, MA: D. C. Heath.

Fantz, R. L. (1963). Pattern vision in newborn infants. *Science, 140,* 269–297.

Farrell, M. P., & Rosenberg, S. D. (1981). *Men at midlife*. Boston: Auburn House.

Fasick, F. A. (1988). Patterns of formal education in high school as *Rites de Passage. Adolescence, 23,* 457–471.

Feeney, J. A., & Noller, P. (1990). Attachment style as a predictor of adult romantic relationships. *Journal of Personality and Social Psychology, 58,* 281–291.

Feingold, B. F. (1975a). Hyperkinesis and learning disabilities linked to artificial food flavors and colors. *American Journal of Nursing, 75,* 797–803.

Feingold, B. F. (1975b). *Why your child is hyperactive*. New York: Random House.

Feldman, D. H. (1989). Creativity: Proof that development occurs. In W. Damon (Ed.), *Child development today and tomorrow*. San Francisco, CA: Jossey-Bass.

Fernald, A., & Mazzie, C. (1991). Prosody and focus in speech to infants and adults. *Developmental Psychology, 27,* 209–221.

Ferri, E., & Robinson, H. (1976). *Coping alone*. Windsor, Berks., Great Britain: NFER Publishing.

Feuerstein, R., (1979). *The dynamic assessment of retarded performers: The learning potential assessment device, theory, instruments, and techniques*. Baltimore: University Park Press.

Finch, C. E. (1988). Aging in the female reproductive system: A model system for analysis of complex interactions during aging. In J. E. Birren & V. L. Bengtson (Eds.), *Emergent theories of aging*. New York: Springer.

Finch, C. E. (1989). The brain, genes, and aging. In V. L. Bengtson & K. W. Schaie (Eds.), *The course of later life: Research and reflections*. New York: Springer.

Finkelhor, D., et al. (1986). *A sourcebook on child sexual abuse*. Beverly Hills, CA: Sage.

Fischer, K. W., & Pipp, S. L. (1984). Development of the structures of unconscious thought. In K. Bowers & D. Meichenbaum (Eds.), *The unconscious reconsidered*. New York: John Wiley.

Fischer, K. W., & Silvern, L. (1985). Stages and individual differences in cognitive development. *Annual Review of Psychology, 36,* 613–648.

Fishkin, J., Keniston, K., & MacKinnon, C. (1973). Moral reasoning and political ideology. *Journal of Personality and Social Psychology, 27,* 109–119.

Flanagan, J. C. (1982). *New insights to improve the quality of life at age 70*. Palo Alto, CA: American Institutes for Research.

Flavell, J. H. (1982). On cognitive development. *Child Development, 53,* 1–10.

Flavell, J. H. (1985). *Cognitive development* (2nd ed.). Englewood Cliffs, NJ: Prentice-Hall.

Flint, M. (1975). The menopause: Reward or punishment. *Psychosomatics, 16,* 161–163.

Flynn, J. R. (1987). Massive IQ gains in 14 nations: What IQ tests really measure. *Psychological Bulletin, 17,* 171–191.

Fogel, A. (1984). *Infancy: Infant, family, and society*. St. Paul, MN: West.

Fogel, A., Toda, S., & Kawai, M. (1988). Mother–infant face-to-face interaction in Japan and the United States: A laboratory comparison using 3-month-old infants. *Developmental Psychology, 3,* 398–406.

Follman, J. (1991). Teachers' estimates of pupils' IQs and pupils' tested IQs. *Psychological Reports, 69,* 350.

Foner, A., & Schwab, K. (1981). *Aging and retirement*. Pacific Grove, CA: Brooks/Cole.

Fox, R. A. (1990). Assessing parenting of young children. Bethesda, MD: National Center for Nursing Research of the National Institutes of Health. (Contract 1 RO1 NRO160901A1.)

France-Kaatrude, A., & Smith, W. P. (1985). Social comparison, task motivation, and the development of self-evaluative standards in children. *Developmental Psychology, 21,* 1080–1089.

Francis, P. L., Self, P. A., & Horowitz, F. D. (1987). The behavioral assessment of the neonate: An overview. In J. D. Osofsky (Ed.), *Handbook of infant development*. New York: John Wiley.

Frank, S. J., Avery, C. B., & Laman, M. S. (1988). Young adults' perceptions of their relationships with their parents: Individual differences in connectedness, competence, and emotional autonomy. *Developmental Psychology, 24,* 729–737.

Frankenburg, W. K., Fandal, A. W., Sciarillo, W., & Burgess, D. (1981). The newly abbreviated and revised Denver Developmental Screening Test. *Journal of Pediatrics, 99,* 995–999.

Franklin, J. T. (1985). Alternative education as substance abuse prevention. *Journal of Alcohol and Drug Education, 30,* 12–23.

Frazier, A., & Lisonbee, L. K. (1950). Adolescent concern with physique. *School Review, 58,* 397–405.

Freud, S. (1935). *A general introduction to psychoanalysis* (rev. ed.). (J. Riviere, Trans.). New York: Liveright.

Freyberg, J. T. (1973). Increasing the imaginative play of urban disadvantaged kindergarten children through systematic training. In J. L. Singer (Ed.), *The child's world of make-believe.* New York: Academic Press.

Fried, P. A. (1986). Marijuana and human pregnancy. In I. J. Chasnoff (Ed.), *Drug use in pregnancy: Mother and child.* Boston: MTP Press.

Friedman, L. (1989). Mathematics and the gender gap: A meta-analysis of recent studies on sex differences in mathematical tasks. *Review of Educational Research, 59,* 185–213.

Friedman, M., & Rosenman, R. H. (1974). *Type A behavior and your heart.* Greenwich, CT: Fawcett.

Frisch, R. E., & Revelle, R. (1970). Height and weight at menarche and a hypothesis of critical body weights and adolescent events. *Science, 169,* 397–398.

Fry, C. L. (1985). Culture, behavior and aging in the comparative perspective. In J. E. Birren & K. W. Schaie (Eds.), *Handbook of the psychology of aging* (2nd ed.). New York: Van Nostrand Reinhold.

Fry, P. S. (1991). Individual differences in reminiscence among older adults: Predictors of frequency and pleasantness ratings of reminiscence activity. *International Journal of Aging and Human Development, 33,* 311–326.

Furstenberg, F. F., Jr. (1987). The new extended family: The experience of children and parents after remarriage. In K. Pasley and M. Ihinger-Tallman (Eds.), *Remarriage and stepparenting: Current research and theory.* New York: Guilford Press.

Furstenberg, F. F., Jr., Brooks-Gunn, J., & Chase-Lansdale, L. (1989). Teenaged pregnancy and childbearing. *American Psychologist, 44,* 313–320.

Furstenberg, F. F., Jr., & Spanier, G. B. (1984). *Recycling the family: Remarriage after divorce.* Beverly Hills, CA: Sage.

Furth, H. G. (1973). *Deafness and learning: A psychosocial approach.* Belmont, CA: Wadsworth.

Furth, H. G. (1980). Piagetian perspectives. In J. Sants (Ed.), *Developmental psychology and society.* London: Macmillan.

Furth, H. G. (1981). *Piaget and knowledge* (2nd ed.). Englewood Cliffs, NJ: Prentice-Hall.

Gaddis, A., & Brooks-Gunn, J. (1985). The male experience of pubertal change. *Journal of Youth and Adolescence, 14,* 61–72.

Gage, M. G., & Hendrickson Christenson, D. (1991). Parental role socialization and the transition to parenthood. *Family Relations, 40,* 332–337.

Galef, B. G., Jr. (1991). A contrarian view of the wisdom of the body as it relates to dietary self-selection. *Psychological Review, 98,* 218–223.

Galjaard, H. (1982). Basic research, early diagnosis and prenatal analysis of congenital disorders: A survey. In H. Galjaard (Ed.), *The future of prenatal diagnosis* (pp. 1–10). London: Churchill Livingstone.

Galler, J. R. (Ed.). (1984). *Human nutrition: A comprehensive treatise* (Vol. 5): *Nutrition and behavior.* New York: Plenum.

Gallistel, C. R. (1989). Animal cognition: The representation of space, time and number. *Annual Review of Psychology, 40,* 155–189.

Galton, F. (1896). *Hereditary genius: An enquiry into its law and consequences.* London: Macmillan.

Gamble, T. J., & Zigler, E. (1986). Effects of infant day care: another look at the evidence. *American Journal of Orthopsychiatry, 56,* 26–42.

Gardner, H. (1983). *Frames of mind: The theory of multiple intelligences.* New York: Basic Books.

Garmezy, N. (1976). *Vulnerable and invulnerable children: Theory, research, and intervention.* Master lecture on developmental psychology, American Psychological Association.

Garvey, C. (1977). *Play.* Cambridge, MA: Harvard University Press.

Gayford, J. J. (1978). Battered wives. In J. P. Martin (Ed.), *Violence and the family.* New York: John Wiley.

Gelles, R. J. (1978). Violence in the American family. In J. P. Martin (Ed.), *Violence and the family*. New York: John Wiley.

Gelles, R. J. (1979). *Family violence*. Beverly Hills, CA: Sage.

Gelles, R. J., & Straus, M. A. (1979). Violence in the American family. *Journal of Social Issues, 35*, 15–38.

Gelman, R. (1978). Cognitive development. In M. R. Rosenzweig & L. W. Porter (Eds.), *Annual review of psychology* (Vol. 29). Palo Alto, CA: Annual Reviews.

Gelman, R. (1982). Basic numerical abilities. In R. J. Sternberg (Ed.), *Advances in the psychology of human intelligence* (Vol. 1). Hillsdale, NJ: Erlbaum.

Gelman, R., & Gallistel, C. R. (1978). *The young child's understanding of number*. Cambridge, MA: Harvard University Press.

Gelman, R., Meck, E., & Merkin, S. (1986). Young children's numerical competence. *Cognitive Development, 1*, 1–29.

The gene hunt. (1989). *Time*. March 20, pp. 54–61.

Genesee, F. (1985). Second language learning through immersion: A review of U.S. programs. *Review of Educational Research, 55*, 541–546.

Genuis, M., Thomlison, B., & Bagley, C. (1991). Male victims of child sexual abuse: A brief overview of pertinent findings. *Journal of Child and Youth Care* (Special Issue), 1–6.

Gerber, M. (1958). The psycho-motor development of African children in the first year and the influence of maternal behavior. *Journal of Social Psychology, 47*, 185–195.

Gerbner, G. (1972). Violence in television drama: Trends and symbolic functions. In G. A. Comstock & E. A. Rubenstein (Eds.), *Television and social behavior* (Vol. 1). Washington, DC: U.S. Government Printing Office.

Gerbner, G., & Gross, L. (1980). The violent face of television and its lessons. In E. L. Palmer & A. Dorr (Eds.), *Children and the faces of television*. New York: Academic Press.

Gesell, A. (1925). *The mental growth of the preschool child*. New York: Macmillan.

Getzels, J. W., & Jackson, P. W. (1962). *Creativity and intelligence*. New York: John Wiley.

Gewirtz, J. L. (1965). The course of infant smiling in four child-rearing environments in Israel. In B. M. Foss (Ed.), *Determinants of infant behavior III*. London: Methuen.

Giambra, L. M. (1977). Daydreaming about the past: The time setting of spontaneous thought intrusions. *The Gerontologist, 17*, 35–38.

Gianino, A., & Tronick, E. Z. (1988). The mutual regulation model: The infant's self and interactive regulation coping and defense. In T. Field, P. McCabe, & N. Schneiderman (Eds.), *Stress and coping*. Hillsdale, NJ: Erlbaum.

Gibbs, J. C. (1987). Social processes in delinquency: The need to facilitate empathy as well as sociomoral reasoning. In W. M. Kurtines & J. L. Gewirtz (Eds.), *Moral development through social interaction*. New York: John Wiley.

Gibson, E. J., & Walk, R. D. (1960). The "visual cliff." *Scientific American, 202*, 64–71.

Gil, D. G. (1970). *Violence against children: Physical child abuse in the United States*. Cambridge, MA: Harvard University Press.

Giles-Sims, J. (1987). Social exchange in remarried families. In K. Pasley and M. Ihinger-Tallman (Eds.), *Remarriage and stepparenting: Current research and theory*. New York: Guilford Press.

Gilligan, C. (1977). In a different voice: Women's conceptions of self and morality. *Harvard Educational Review, 47*, 481–517.

Gilligan, C. (1982). *In a different voice: Psychological theory and women's development*. Cambridge, MA: Harvard University Press.

Ginzberg, E. (1972). Toward a theory of occupational choice: A restatement. *Vocational Guidance Quarterly, 20*, 169–176.

Ginzberg, E., et al. (1951). *Occupational choice*. New York: Columbia University Press.

Gitomer, D. H., & Pellegrino, J. W. (1985). Developmental and individual differences in long-term memory retrieval. In R. F. Dillon (Ed.), *Individual differences in cognition* (Vol. 2) (pp. 1–34). New York: Academic Press.

Glaser, B., & Strauss, A. L. (1968). *A time for dying*. Chicago: Aldine.

Glenn, N., & Weaver, C. (1977). The marital happiness of remarried divorced persons. *Journal of Marriage and the Family, 39*, 331–337.

Glick, P. C. (1989). Remarried families, stepfamilies, and stepchildren: A brief demographic profile. *Family Relations, 38*, 24–27.

Glick, P. C., & Lin, S. L. (1986). More young adults are living with their parents: Who are they? *Journal of Marriage and the Family, 42*, 19–30.

Glueck, S., & Glueck, E. (1950). *Unravelling juvenile delinquency*. New York: The Commonwealth Fund.

Gold, M. S. (1989). *Drugs of abuse: A comprehensive series for clinicians*. Vol. 1: *Marijuana*. New York: Plenum.

Gold, M. S., & Giannini, A. J. (1989). Cocaine and cocaine addiction. In A. J. Giannini & A. E. Slaby (Eds.), *Drugs of abuse*. Oradell, NJ: Medical Economics Books.

Goldberg, S. (1983). Parent–infant bonding: Another look. *Child Development, 54*, 1355–1382.

Goldgaber, D., Lerman, M. I., McBride, O. W., Saffiotti, U., & Gajdusek, D. C. (1987). Characterization and chromosomal localization of a DNA encoding brain amyloid of Alzheimer's disease. *Science, 235*, 877–880.

Goldsmith, J. P. (1990). Neonatal morbidity. In R. D. Eden, F. H. Boehm, & M. Haire (Eds.), *Assessment and care of the fetus: Physiological, clinical, and medicolegal principles*. Norwalk, CT: Appleton & Lange.

Göncz, L., & Kodžopeljic, J. (1991). Exposure to two languages in the preschool period: Metalinguistic development and the acquisition of reading. *Journal of Multilingual and Multicultural Development, 12*, 137–142.

Gooden, W., & Toye, R. (1984). Occupational dream, relation to parents and depression in the early adult transition. *Journal of Clinical Psychology, 4*, 945–954.

Gordon, T. (1975). *P.E.T.: Parent effectiveness training*. New York: New American Library.

Gordon, T. (1976). *P.E.T. in action*. New York: Bantam Books.

Gottesman, I. I. (1974). Developmental genetics and ontogenetic psychology: Overdue detente and propositions from a matchmaker. In A. Pick (Ed.), *Minnesota Symposia on Psychology* (Vol. 12) (pp. 55–180).

Gottesman, I. I. & Shields, J. (1982). *The schizophrenic puzzle*. New York: Cambridge University Press.

Gottlieb, G. (1991). Epigenetic systems view of human development. *Developmental Psychology, 27*, 33–34.

Gottman, J. M. (1977). Toward a definition of social isolation in children. *Child Development, 48*, 513–517.

Gottman, J., & Mettetal, G. (1987). Speculations about social and affective development: Friendship and acquaintanceship through adolescence. In J. M. Gottman & J. Parker (Eds.), *Conversations of friends*. New York: Cambridge University Press.

Gould, R. L. (1972). The phases of adult life: A study in developmental psychology. *American Journal of Psychiatry, 129*, 521–531.

Gould, R. L. (1978). *Transformations: Growth and change in adult life*. New York: Simon & Schuster.

Gould, R. L. (1990). Clinical lessons from adult development theory. R. A. Nemiroff & C. A. Colarusso (Eds.), *New dimensions in adult development*. New York: Basic Books.

Gould, S. J. (1981). *The mismeasure of man*. New York: W. W. Norton.

Graham, J. M., Jr. (1985). The effects of alcohol consumption during pregnancy. In M. Marois (Ed.), *Prevention of physical and mental congenital defects*. New York: Alan R. Liss.

Grant, J. P. [Executive Director of the United Nation's Children's Fund (UNICEF)] (1986). *The state of the world's children: 1986*. New York: Oxford University Press.

Green, K. D., Forehand, R., Beck, S. J., & Vosk, B. (1980). An assessment of the relationship among measures of children's social competence and children's academic achievement. *Child Development,* 1149–1156.

Greenacre, P. (1959). Play in relation to creative imagination. *Psychoanalytic Studies of the Child, 14*, 61–80.

Greenspan, S. I., & Lieberman, A. F. (1989). A quantitative approach to the clinical assessment of representational elaboration and differentiation in children two to four. In S. I. Greenspan & G. H. Pollock (Eds.), *The course of life*. Vol. II: *Early Childhood*. Madison, CT: International Universities Press.

Greer, J. V. (1991). A child is a child is a child. *Exceptional Children, 57*, 198–199.

Grieser, D. L., & Kuhl, P. K. (1988). Maternal speech to infants in a tonal language: Support for universal prosodic features in motherese. *Developmental Psychology, 24*, 14–20.

Griffin, S. (1985). Eating issues and fat issues. *Transactional Analysis Journal, 15*, 30–36.

Griffiths, M. D. (1991). Amusement machine playing in childhood and adolescence: A comparative analysis of video games and fruit machines. *Journal of Adolescence, 14*, 53–73.

Grindstaff, C. F. (1988). Adolescent marriage and childbearing: The long-term economic outcome, Canada in the 1980s. *Adolescence, 23*, 45–58.

Gronlund, N. E., & Holmlund, W. S. (1958). The value of elementary school sociometric status scores for predicting a pupil's adjustment in high school. *Educational Administration and Supervision, 44*, 255–260.

Grossman, J. J. (Ed.). (1983). *Manual on terminology and classification in mental retardation, 1983 revision.* Washington, DC: American Association on Mental Deficiency.

Grotevant, H. D., & Cooper, C. R. (1988). The role of family experience in career exploration: A lifespan perspective. In P. B. Baltes, D. L. Featherman, & R. M. Lerner (Eds.), *Life-span development and behavior* (Vol. 8). Hillsdale, NJ: Erlbaum.

Grotevant, M. D., Scarr, S., & Weinberg, R. A. (1977, April). *Intellectual development in family constellations with adopted and natural children: A test of the Zajonc and Markus model.* Paper presented at a meeting of the Society for Research in Child Development, New Orleans, LA.

Grow, L. J. (1979). *Early childrearing by young mothers: A research study.* New York: Child Welfare League of America.

Gruman, G. J. (1978). Cultural origins of presentday age-ism: The modernization of the life cycle. In S. F. Spicker, K. M. Woodward, & D. D. Van Tassel (Eds.), *Aging and the elderly: Humanistic perspectives in gerontology.* Atlantic Highlands, NJ: Humanities Press.

Guidubaldi, J., & Cleminshaw, H. (1985). Divorce, family health, and child adjustment. *Family Relations, 34*, 35–41.

Guilford, J. P. (1950). Creativity. *American Psychologist, 5*, 444–454.

Guilford, J. P. (1959). Three faces of intellect. *American Psychologist, 14*, 469–479.

Guitar still Segovia's passion at 93. (1986, March 22). *Edmonton Journal,* p. B1.

Gustafson, G. E., & Harris, K. L. (1990). Women's responses to young infants' cries. *Developmental Psychology, 26*, 144–152.

Gutmann, D. (1975). Parenthood: A key to the comparative psychology of the life cycle. In N. Datan & L. Ginsberg (Eds.), *Lifespan developmental psychology: Normative life crises.* New York: Academic Press.

Gutmann, D. (1977). The cross-cultural perspective. In J. E. Birren & K. W. Schaie (Eds.), *Handbook of the psychology of aging.* New York: Van Nostrand Reinhold.

Gutmann, D. (1990). Psychological development and pathology in later adulthood. In R. A. Nemiroff & C. A. Colarusso (Eds.), *New dimensions in adult development.* New York: Basic Books.

Hague, W. J. (1991). Kohlberg's legacy—More than ideas: An essay review. *The Alberta Journal of Educational Research, 37*, 277–294.

Haight, B. K. (1991). Reminiscing: The state of the art as a basis for practice. *International Journal of Aging and Human Development, 33*, 1–32.

Haith, M. M. (1980). *Rules that babies look by: The organization of newborn visual activity.* Hillsdale, NJ: Erlbaum.

Haith, M. M. (1986). Sensory and perceptual processes in early infancy. *Journal of Pediatrics, 109*, 158–171.

Hakuta, K., & Garcia, E. E. (1989). Bilingualism and education. *American Psychologist, 44*, 374–379.

Hall, G. S. (1891). The contents of children's minds on entering school. *Pediatric Seminars, 1*, 139–173.

Hall, G. S. (1905). *Adolescence, two.* New York: Appleton-Century-Crofts.

Hall, G. Stanley. (1916). *Adolescence* (2 volumes). New York: Appleton-Century-Crofts.

Hall, G. S. (1922). *Senescence: The last half of life.* New York: Apple-Century-Crofts.

Hall, W. G., & Oppenheim, R. W. (1987). Developmental psychobiology: Prenatal, perinatal, and early postnatal aspects of behavioral development. *Annual Review of Psychology, 38*, 91–128.

Hallahan, D. P., & Kauffman, J. M. (1986). *Exceptional children: Introduction to special education* (3rd ed.). Englewood Cliffs, NJ: Prentice-Hall.

Halonen, J. S., & Passman, R. H. (1978). Pacifier's effects upon play and separations from the mother for the one-year-old in a novel environment. *Infant Behavior and Development, 1,* 70–78.

Hare, J. W. (Ed.). (1989). *Diabetes complicating pregnancy: The Joslin Clinic Method.* New York: Alan R. Liss.

Hargrove, L. J., & Poteet, J. A. (1984). *Assessment in special education: The education evaluation.* Englewood Cliffs, NJ: Prentice-Hall.

Harlow, H. F. (1958). The nature of love. *American Psychologist, 12,* 673–685.

Harlow, H. F. (1959). Love in infant monkeys. *Scientific American, 200,* 68–74.

Harris, P. L., & Gross, D. (1988). Children's understanding of real and apparent emotion. In J. W. Astington, P. L. Harris, & D. R. Olson (Eds.), *Developing theories of mind.* New York: Cambridge University Press.

Harris, T. (1973). *I'm OK — You're OK.* New York: Avon Books.

Harrison, L. (1985). Effects of early supplemental stimulation programs for premature infants: Review of the literature, *Maternal–Child Nursing Journal, 14,* 69–90.

Harry, J. (1983). Gay male and lesbian relationships. In E. D. Macklin & R. H. Rubin (Eds.), *Contemporary families and alternative lifestyles: Handbook on research and theory* (pp. 216–233). Beverly Hills, CA: Sage.

Harter, S. (1983). Developmental perspectives on the self-system. In P. H. Mussen (Ed.), *Handbook of child psychology* (4th ed.) (Vol. 4): *Socialization, personality, and social development* (E. M. Hetherington, Ed.). New York: John Wiley.

Harter, S. (1985a). Processes underlying the construct, maintenance and enhancement of the self-concept in children. In J. Suls & A. Greenwald (Eds.), *Psychological perspectives on the self* (Vol. 3). Hillsdale, NJ: Erlbaum.

Harter, S. (1985b). *The self-perception profile for children: Revision of the perceived competence scale for children.* Denver, CO: University of Denver.

Harter, S. (1987). The determinants and mediational role of global self-worth in children. In N. Eisenberg (Ed.), *Contemporary topics in developmental psychology.* New York: John Wiley.

Harter, S. (1988). Developmental processes in the construction of self. In T. D. Yawkey & J. E. Johnson (Eds.), *Integrative processes and socialization: Early to middle childhood.* Hillsdale, NJ: Erlbaum.

Harter, S. (1990). Processes underlying adolescent self-concept formation. In R. Montemayor, G. R. Adams, & T. P. Gullotta (Eds.), *From childhood to adolescence: A transitional period?* (*Advances in adolescent development,* Vol. 2). Newbury Park, CA: Sage.

Hartup, W. W. (1978). Children and their friends. In H. McGurk (Ed.), *Issues in childhood social development.* London: Methuen.

Hartup, W. W. (1983). Peer relations. In P. H. Mussen (Ed.), *Handbook of child psychology* (4th ed.) (Vol. 4): *Socialization, personality, and social development* (pp. 103–196). (E. M. Hetherington, Ed.). New York: John Wiley.

Hartup, W. W. (1989). Social relationships and their developmental significance. *American Psychologist, 44,* 120–126.

Harway, M., Mednick, S. A., & Mednick, B. (1984). Research strategies: Methodological and practical problems. In S. A. Mednick, M. Harway, & K. M. Finello (Eds.), *Handbook of longitudinal research* (Vol. 1): *Birth and childhood cohorts* (pp. 22–30). New York: Holt, Rinehart & Winston.

Haskins, R. (1989). Beyond metaphor: The efficacy of early childhood education. *American Psychologist, 44,* 274–282.

Hass, A. (1979). *Teenage sexuality: A survey of teenage sexual behavior.* New York: Macmillan.

Hauser, R. M., & Sewell, W. H. (1985). Birth order and educational attainment in full sibships. *American Journal of Educational Research, 22,* 1–23.

Havighurst, R. J. (1972). *Developmental tasks and education.* New York: D. McKay.

Havighurst, R. J. (1979). *Developmental tasks and education* (4th ed.). New York: D. McKay.

Havighurst, R. J. (1982). The world of work. In B. B. Wolman (Ed.), *Handbook of developmental psychology.* Englewood Cliffs, NJ: Prentice-Hall.

Havighurst, R. J., Neugarten, B. L., & Tobin, S. S. (1968). Disengagement and patterns of aging. In B. L. Neugarten (Ed.), *Middle age and aging.* Chicago: University of Chicago Press.

Hawton, K. (1985). *Sex therapy: A practical guide.* Oxford: Oxford University Press.

Hayflick, L. (1975, September). Why grow old? *Stanford Magazine,* pp. 36–43.

Haywood, K. M. (1986). *Life span motor development.* Champaign, IL: Human Kinetics.

Hazen, N. L., & Lockman, J. J. (1989). Skill and context. In J. J. Lockman & N. L. Hazen (Eds.), *Action in social context: Perspectives on early development.* New York: Plenum.

Heald, J. (1977). Mid-life career influences. *Vocational Guidance Quarterly, 25,* 309–312.

Heath, D. H. (1976). Adolescent and adult predictors of vocational adaptation. *Journal of Vocational Behavior, 9,* 1–19.

Hebb, D. O. (1966). *A textbook of psychology* (2nd ed.). Philadelphia: W. B. Saunders.

Heisel, B. E., & Ritter, K. (1981). Young children's storage behavior in a memory for location task. *Journal of Experimental Child Psychology, 31,* 250–364.

Held, D. F. (1984). *The intuitive approach to reading and learning disabilities: A practical alternative.* Springfield, IL: Charles C. Thomas.

Henderson, G., & Henderson, B. B. (1984). *Mending broken children: A parent's manual.* Springfield, IL: Charles C. Thomas.

Hendricks, J., & Hendricks, C. D. (1986). *Aging in mass society.* Cambridge, MA: Winthrop.

Hendry, L. S. (1960). *Cognitive processes in a moral conflict situation.* Unpublished doctoral dissertation, Yale University, New Haven, CT.

Henker, B., & Whalen, C. K. (1989). Hyperactivity and attention deficits. *American Psychologist, 44,* 216–223.

Henry, J. P. (1988). The archetypes of power and intimacy. In J. E. Birren & V. L. Bengtson (Eds.), *Emergent theories of aging.* New York: Springer.

Herbst, D. S., & Miller, J. R. (1980). Nonspecific X-linked mental retardation. II: The frequency in British Columbia. *American Journal of Medical Genetics, 17,* 461.

Herr, E. L., & Cramer, S. H. (1985). *Career guidance through the life span: Systematic approaches* (2nd ed.). Boston: Little, Brown.

Hertz, R. (1986). *More equal than others: Women and men in dual-career marriages.* Berkeley: University of California Press.

Herzog, E., & Sudia, C. (1970). *Boys in fatherless homes.* Washington, DC: U.S. Department of Health & Human Services.

Hess, G. C. (1990). Sexual abstinence, a revived option for teenagers. *Modern Psychology, 1,* 19–21.

Hetherington, E. M., Cox, M., & Cox, R. (1979). Play and social interaction in children following divorce. *Journal of Social Issues, 35,* 26–49.

Hetherington, E. M., Stanley-Hagen, M., & Anderson, E. R. (1989). Marital transitions: A child's perspective. *American Psychologist, 44,* 303–312.

Higbee, K. L. (1977). *Your memory: How it works and how to improve it.* Englewood Cliffs, NJ: Prentice-Hall.

Hildebrand, H. P. (1990). The other side of the wall: A psychoanalytic study of creativity in later life. In R. A. Nemiroff & C. A. Colarusso (Eds.), *New dimensions in adult development.* New York: Basic Books.

Hill, J. P. (1988). Adapting to menarche: Familial control and conflict. In M. R. Gunnar & W. A. Collins (Eds.), *Development during the transition to adolescence (Minnesota Symposia on Child Psychology,* Vol. 21). Hillsdale, NJ: Erlbaum.

Hinde, R. A. (1983). Ethology and child development. In P. H. Mussen (Ed.), *Handbook of child psychology* (4th ed.) (Vol. 2): *Infancy and developmental psychobiology* (pp. 27–94) (M. M. Haith & J. J. Campos, Eds.). New York: John Wiley.

Hinde, R. A. (1989). Ethological and relationship approaches. In R. Vasta (Ed.), *Annals of child development* (Vol. 6). Greenwich, CT: JAI Press.

Hindelang, M. J. (1981). Variations in sex-race-age-specific incidence of offending. *American Sociological Review, 46,* 461–474.

HLA Consultants (1992). *Moderately priced retirement housing.* Edmonton, Alberta: HLA Consultants.

Ho, D. (1983). Asian concepts in behavioral science. *Bulletin of the Hong Kong Psychological Society, 10,* 41–49.

Ho, D.Y.F. (1987). Fatherhood in Chinese culture. In M. E. Lamb (Ed.), *The father's role: Cross-cultural perspectives.* Hillsdale, NJ: Erlbaum.

Hodapp, R. M., & Mueller, E. (1982). Early social development. In B. B. Wolman et al. (Eds.), *Handbook of developmental psychology.* Englewood Cliffs, NJ: Prentice-Hall.

Hofer, M. A. (1981). *The roots of human behavior: An introduction to the psychobiology of early development.* San Francisco: W. H. Freeman.

Hoffman, L. W. (1989). Effects of maternal employment in the two-parent family. *American Psychologist, 44,* 283–292.

Hoffman, L. W. (1991). The influence of the family environment on personality: Accounting for sibling differences. *Psychological Bulletin, 110,* 187–203.

Hoffman, M. L. (1976). Empathy, role-taking, guilt, and development of altruistic motives. In T. Likona (Ed.), *Moral development: Current theory and research.* New York: Holt, Rinehart & Winston.

Hoffman, M. L. (1979). Development of moral thought, feeling, and behavior. *American Psychologist, 34,* 958–966.

Hoge, R. D. (1988). Issues in the definition and measurement of the giftedness construct. *Educational Researcher, 17,* 12–66.

Holland, A. J., Hall, A., Murray, R., Russell, G.F.M., & Crisp, A. H. (1984). Anorexia nervosa: A study of 34 twin pairs and one set of triplets. *British Journal of Psychiatry, 145,* 414–419.

Holland, J. L. (1975). *Vocational preference inventory (VPI).* Palo Alto, CA: Consulting Psychologists Press.

Holmes, R. H., & Rahe, R. H. (1967). The social readjustment rating scale. *Journal of Psychosomatic Research, 11,* 213–218.

Holstein, C. B. (1976). Irreversible, stepwise sequence in the development of moral judgment: A longitudinal study of males and females. *Child Development, 47,* 51–61.

Honzik, M. P. (1984). Life-span development. *Annual Review of Psychology, 35,* 309–331.

Horan, M. A., Hendriks, H.F.J., & Brouwer, A. (1990). Systems under stress: Infections agents and host defences. In M. A. Horan & A. Brouwer (Eds.), *Gerontology: Approaches to biomedical and clinical research.* London: Edward Arnold.

Horn, J. L. (1976). Human abilities: A review of research and theory in the early 1970's. In M. R. Rosenzweig & L. W. Porter (Eds.), *Annual review of psychology* (Vol. 27). Palo Alto, CA: Annual Reviews.

Horn, J. L., & Donaldson, G. (1976). On the myth of intellectual decline in adulthood. *American Psychologist, 31,* 701–717.

Horn, J. L., & Donaldson, G. (1980). Cognitive development in adulthood. In O. G. Brim, Jr., & J. Kagan (Eds.), *Constancy and change in human development.* Cambridge, MA: Harvard University Press.

Horn, J. M. (1983). The Texas adoption project. *Child Development, 54,* 268–275.

Horton, D. L., & Mills, C. B. (1984). Human leaning and memory. *Annual Review of Psychology, 35,* 361–394.

Hotvedt, M., & Mandel, J. (1982). Children of lesbian mothers. In J. Weinrich & B. Paul (Eds.), *Homosexuality: Social psychological and biological issues.* Beverly Hills, CA: Sage.

Howe, M. L. (1988). Measuring memory development in adulthood: A model-based approach to disentangling storage-retrieval contributions. In M. L. Howe & C. J. Brainerd (Eds.), *Cognitive development in adulthood: Progress in cognitive development research.* New York: Springer-Verlag.

Howe, M. L., & Brainerd, C. J. (Eds.). (1988). *Cognitive development in adulthood: Progress in cognitive development research.* New York: Springer-Verlag.

Howe, N.J.A. (1982). Biographical evidence and the development of outstanding individuals. *American Psychologist, 37,* 1071–1081.

Hoyer, W. J. (1985). Aging and the development of expert cognition. In T. M. Schlechter & M. P. Toglia (Eds.), *New directions in cognitive science.* Norwood, NJ: Ablex.

Hrncir, E. J. (1989). Children's play: The dynamic and spontaneous expression of the interface of emotion and cognition. *Child and Youth Care Quarterly, 18,* 171–175.

Hsu, L.Y.F. (1986). Prenatal diagnosis of chromosome abnormalities. In A. Milunsky (Ed.), *Genetic disorders and the fetus* (2nd ed.). New York: Plenum.

Hubel, D. H., & Wiesel, T. N. (1970). The period of susceptibility to the physiological effects of unilateral eye closure in kittens. *Journal of Physiology, 206,* 419–436.

Huesmann, L. R., & Eron, L. D. (1986). The development of aggression in children of different cultures: Psychological processes and exposure to violence. In L. R. Huesmann & L. D. Eron (Eds.), *Television and the aggressive child: A cross-national comparison.* Hillsdale, NJ: Erlbaum.

Huesmann, L. R., Eron, L. D., Lefkowitz, M. M., & Walder, L. O. (1984). The stability of aggression over time and generations. *Developmental Psychology, 20,* 1120–1134.

Hughes, R., Tingle, B. A., & Sawin, D. B. (1981). Development of empathic understanding in children. *Child Development, 52,* 122–128.

Hunt, C. E. (1991). Sudden infant death syndrome: The neurobehavioral perspective. *Journal of Applied Developmental Psychology, 12,* 185–188.

Hunt, E., & Agnoli, F. (1991). The Whorfian hypothesis: A cognitive psychology perspective. *Psychological Review, 98,* 377–389.

Hunt, J. M. (1964). The psychological basis for using pre-school enrichment as an antidote for cultural deprivation. *Merrill-Palmer Quarterly, 10,* 209–248.

Hunt, M. (1974). *Sexual behavior in the 1970's.* Chicago: Playboy Press.

Hurlock, E. B. (1964). *Child development* (4th ed.). New York: McGraw-Hill.

Hurrelmann, K. (1990). Parents, peers, teachers and other significant partners in adolescence. *International Journal of Adolescence and Youth, 2,* 211–236.

Hurst, J., & Shepard, J. (1986). The dynamics of plant closings: An extended emotional roller coaster ride. *Journal of Counseling and Development, 64,* 401–405.

Husén, T., & Tuijnman, A. (1991). The contribution of formal schooling to the increase in intellectual capital. *Educational Researcher, 20,* 17–25.

Huston, A. C., Watkins, B. Q., & Kunkel, D. (1989). Public policy and children's television. *American Psychologist, 44,* 424–433.

Huston, A. C., & Wright, J. C. (1983). Children's processing of television: The informative functions of formal features. In J. Bryant & D. R. Anderson (Eds.), *Children's understanding of television: Research on attention and comprehension* (pp. 35–68). New York: Academic Press.

Huston, A. C., Wright, J. C., Rice, M. L., Kerkman, D., & St. Peters, M. (1990). Development of television viewing patterns in early childhood: A longitudinal investigation. *Developmental Psychology, 26,* 409–420.

Huston-Stein, A., & Higgins-Trenk, A. (1978). Development of females from childhood through adulthood: Career and feminine role orientations. In P. B. Baltes (Ed.), *Lifespan development and behavior* (Vol. 1). New York: Academic Press.

Hutt, S. J., Lenard, H. G., & Prechtl, H.F.R. (1969). Psychophysiology of the newborn. In L. P. Lipsitt & H. W. Reese (Eds.), *Advances in child development and behavior.* New York: Academic Press.

Hyde, J. S. (1986). *Understanding human sexuality* (3rd ed.). New York: McGraw-Hill.

Hyde, J. S., Fennema, E., & Lamon, S. J. (1990). Gender differences in mathematics performance: A meta-analysis. *Psychological Bulletin, 107,* 139–155.

Hyde, J. S., Krajnik, M., & Skuldt-Niederberger, K. (1991). Androgyny across the life span: A replication and longitudinal follow-up. *Developmental Psychology, 27,* 516–519.

Hyde, S., & Linn, M. C. (1986). *The psychology of gender: Advances through meta-analysis.* Baltimore, MD: Johns Hopkins University Press.

Iennarella, R. S., Chisum, G. M., & Bianchi, J. (1986). A comprehensive treatment model for pregnant chemical users, infants and families. In I. J. Chasnoff (Ed.), *Drug use in pregnancy: Mother and child.* Boston: MTP Press.

Ihinger-Tallman, M. (1987). Sibling and stepsibling bonding in stepfamilies. In K. Pasley and M. Ihinger-Tallman (Eds.), *Remarriage and stepparenting: Current research and theory.* New York: Guilford Press.

Increase expected in AIDS in North America–UN agency. (1988, December 1). *The Edmonton Journal,* p. A2.

Ingram, D. (1991). A historical observation on "Why 'Mama' and 'Papa'?" *Journal of Child Language, 18,* 711–713.

Inhelder, B., & Piaget, J. (1958). *The growth of logical thinking from childhood to adolescence.* New York: Basic Books.

Inoff-Germain, G., Arnold, G. S., Nottelmann, E., D., Susman, E. J., Cutler, G. B., Jr., & Chrousos, G. P. (1988). Relations between hormone levels and observational measures of aggressive behavior of young adolescents in family interactions. *Developmental Psychology, 24,* 129–139.

Intons-Peterson, M. J. (1988). *Gender concepts of Swedish and American youth*. Hillsdale, NJ: Erlbaum.

Isaacson, L. E. (1986). *Career information in counseling and career development* (4th ed.). Boston: Allyn & Bacon.

Isabell, B. J., & McKee, L. (1980). Society's cradle: An anthropological perspective on the socialization of cognition. In J. Sants (Ed.), *Developmental psychology and society*. London: Macmillan.

Izard, C. E. (1977). Human emotions. New York: Plenum.

Izard, C. E., & Malatesta, C. Z. (1987). Perspectives on emotional development I: Differential emotions theory of early emotional development. In J. D. Osofsky (Ed.), *Handbook of infant development* (2nd ed.). New York: John Wiley.

Jacklin, C. N. (1989). Female and male: Issues of gender. *American Psychologist, 44,* 127–133.

Jacobson, J. L., & Wille, D. E. (1984). Influence of attachment and separation experience on separation distress at 18 months. *Developmental Psychology, 20,* 477–484.

Jacobson, S. W., Fein, G. G., Jacobson, J. L., Schwartz, P. M., & Dowler, J. K. (1985). Neonatal correlates of exposure to smoking, caffeine, and alcohol. *Infant and Behavior Development, 7,* 253–265.

Jacobson, S. W., & Kagan, J. (1979). Interpreting "imitative" responses in early infancy. *Science, 205,* 215–217.

Jacobvitz, R. S., Wood, M. R., & Albin, K. (1991). Cognitive skills and young children's comprehension of television. *Journal of Applied Developmental Psychology, 12,* 219–235.

James, W. (1892). *Psychology: The briefer course*. New York: Henry Holt.

James, W. (1950). *The principles of psychology*. New York: Dover. (Originally published by Henry Holt, 1890.)

Jarvik, L. F., Klodin, V., & Matsuyama, S. S. (1973). Human aggression and the extra Y chromosome: Fact or fantasy? *American Psychologist, 28,* 674–682.

Jean-Gilles, M., & Crittenden, P. M. (1990). Maltreating families: A look at siblings. *Family Relations, 39,* 323–329.

Jenkins, C. D., Zyzanski, S. J., & Rosenman, R. H. (1971). Progress toward validation of a computer-scored test of the type A coronary-prone behavior pattern. *Psychosomatic Medicine, 33,* 192–202.

Jensen, A. R. (1968). Social class, race, and genetics: Implications for education. *American Educational Research Journal, 5,* 1–42.

Jensen, W. A., et al. (1979). *Biology*. Belmont, CA: Wadsworth.

Jersild, A. T. (1963). *The psychology of adolescence* (2nd ed.). New York: Macmillan.

Johanson, D. J., & Shreeve, J. (1989). *Lucy's child*. New York: William Morrow.

Johnson, H. R., Myhre, S. A., Ruvalcaba, R.H.A., Thuline, H. C., & Kelley, V. C. (1970). Effects of testosterone on body image and behavior in Klinefelter's syndrome: A pilot study. *Developmental Medicine and Child Neurology, 12,* 454–460.

Johnson, J. E., & Yawkey, T. D. (1988). Play and integration. In T. D. Yawkey & J. E. Johnson (Eds.), *Integrative processes and socialization: Early to middle childhood*. Hillsdale, NJ: Erlbaum.

Johnson, J. H. (1986). *Life events as stressors in childhood and adolescence*. Beverly Hills, CA: Sage.

Johnson, M. K., Bransford, J. D., & Solomon, S. (1973). Memory for tacit implications of sentences. *Journal of Experimental Psychology, 98,* 203–205.

Johnson, R. D. (1962). Measurements of achievement in fundamental skills of elementary school children. *Research Quarterly, 33,* 94–103.

Johnston, W. B., & Packer, A. B. (1987). *Workforce 2000: Work and workers for the 21st century*. Indianapolis, IN: Hudson Institute.

Jones, E. (1957). *The life and work of Sigmund Freud* (Vol. 3). New York: Basic Books.

Jones, E. F., et al. (1986). *Teenage pregnancy in industrialized countries*. New Haven, CT: Yale University Press.

Jones, M. C. (1957). The later careers of boys who are early- or late-maturing. *Child Development, 28,* 113–128.

Jones, M. C. (1965). Psychological correlates of somatic development. *Child Development, 36,* 899–911.

Jones, M. C. (1974). Albert, Peter, and John B. Watson. *American Psychologist, 29,* 581–583.

Jones, W. H. (1979). Grief and involuntary career change: Its implications for counseling. *Vocational Guidance Quarterly, 27,* 196–201.

Jorgensen, S. R. (1991). Project taking charge: An evaluation of an adolescent pregnancy prevention program. *Family Relations, 40,* 373–380.

Joshi, P., Garon, L., & Lechasseur, S. (1984). Self-esteem and loneliness among unemployed women. *Psychological Reports, 54,* 903–906.

Joy, L. A., Kimball, M., & Zabrack, M. L. (1977, June). *Television exposure and children's aggressive behavior.* Paper presented at the annual meeting of the Canadian Psychological Association, Vancouver, British Columbia.

Jung, C. G. (1923). *Psychological types.* New York: Harcourt Brace Jovanovich.

Justice, E. (1985). Categorization as a preferred memory strategy: Developmental changes during elementary school. *Developmental Psychology, 21,* 1105–1110.

Juvonen, J. (1991). Deviance, perceived responsibility, and negative peer reactions. *Developmental Psychology, 27,* 672–681.

Kagan, J. S. (1976). Emergent themes in human development. *American Scientist, 64,* 186–196.

Kagan, J. S. (1978, August). The parental love trap. *Psychology Today,* pp. 54–61, 91.

Kagan, J. S., Kearsley, R. B., & Zelazo, P. R. (1977). The effects of infant day care on psychological development. *Educational Quarterly, 1,* 109–142.

Kagan, J., & Snidman, N. (1991). Temperamental factors in human development. *American Psychologist, 46,* 856–862.

Kahn, A., & Blum, D. (1982). Phenothiazines and sudden infant death syndrome. *Pediatrics, 70,* 75–78.

Kaitz, M., Meschulach-Sarfaty, O., Auerbach, J., & Eidelman, A. (1988). A reexamination of newborn's ability to imitate facial expressions. *Developmental Psychology, 24,* 3–7.

Kalat, J. W. (1981). *Biological psychology.* Belmont, CA: Wadsworth.

Kalish, R. A. (1981). *Death, grief, and caring relationships.* Pacific Grove, CA: Brooks/Cole.

Kalish, R. A. (1982). *Late adulthood: Perspectives on human development* (2nd ed.). Pacific Grove, CA: Brooks/Cole.

Kalish, R. A., & Reynolds, D. K. (1976). *Death and ethnicity: A psychocultural study.* Los Angeles: University of Southern California Press.

Kandel, D. B., & Logan, J. A. (1984). Patterns of drug use from adolescence to young adulthood: I. Period of risk for initiation, continued use, and discontinuation. *American Journal of Public Health, 74,* 660–666.

Kant, I. (1977). *Die metaphysic der sitten.* Frankfurt: Suhrkamp. (Originally published in 1797.)

Kanter, R. M. (1981). *Men and women of the corporation.* New York: Basic Books.

Kaplan, L. J. (1984). *Adolescence: The farewell to childhood.* New York: Simon & Schuster.

Kastenbaum, R. (1977). *Death, society, and human experience.* St. Louis: C. V. Mosby.

Kastenbaum, R. (1985). Dying and death: A lifespan approach. In J. E. Birren & K. W. Schaie (Eds.), *Handbook of the psychology of aging* (2nd ed.). New York: Van Nostrand Reinhold.

Kastenbaum, R., & Aisenberg, R. (1976). *The psychology of death.* New York: Springer-Verlag.

Katchadourian, H. (1987). *Fifty: Midlife in perspective.* New York: Freeman.

Kato, T. (1970). Chromosome studies in pregnant rhesus monkeys macaque given LSD-25. *Diseases of the Nervous System, 31,* 245–250.

Kavale, K., & Forness, S. (1985). *The science of learning disabilities.* San Diego, CA: College-Hill Press.

Kavale, K. A., Forness, S. R., & Lorsbach, T. C. (1991). Definition for definitions of learning disabilities. *Journal of Learning Disabilities, 14,* 257–266.

Kaye, K. (1977). Toward the origin of dialogue. In H. R. Schaffer (Ed.), *Studies in mother–infant interaction.* London: Academic Press.

Kazdin, A. E. (1989). Developmental psychopathology: Current research, issues, and directions. *American Psychologist, 44,* 180–187.

Keeling, R. P. (1987). Effects of AIDS on young Americans. *Medical Aspects of Human Sexuality, 21,* 22–33.

Kegan, R. (1982). *The evolving self: Problem and process in human development.* Cambridge, MA: Harvard University Press.

Kelly, J. R., & Westcott, G. (1991). *International Journal of Aging and Human Development, 32,* 81–89.

Kempe, R. S., & Kempe, C. H. (1984). *The common secret: Sexual abuse of children and adolescents.* New York: Freeman.

Kennell, J. H., Trause, M. A., & Klaus, M. H. (1975). Evidence for a sensitive period in the human mother. *Parent–Infant Interaction* (Ciba Foundation Symposium, new series) *33,* 87–102.

Kephart, W. K. (1950). Status after death. *American Sociological Review, 15,* 635–643.

Kessen, W. (1965). *The child.* New York: John Wiley.

Kiley, D. (1983). *The Peter Pan Syndrome: Men who have never grown up.* New York: Dodd, Mead.

Kinsey, A. C., Pomeroy, W. B., & Martin, C. E. (1948). *Sexual behavior in the human male.* Philadelphia: W. B. Saunders.

Kinsey, A. C, Pomeroy, W. B., Martin, C. E., & Gebhard, P. H. (1953). *Sexual behavior in the human female.* Philadelphia: W. B. Saunders.

Kirby, E. (1990, November 5). Last chance romance. *The Edmonton Journal,* p. C1.

Kirby, J. R., & Das, J. P. (1990). A cognitive approach to intelligence: Attention, coding, and planning. *Canadian Psychology, 31,* 320–331.

Kirk, S. (1979). *Educating exceptional children* (3rd ed.). Boston: Houghton Mifflin.

Klaus, M., & Kennell, J. (1983). *Bonding: The beginnings of parent–infant attachment* (rev. ed.). St. Louis: C. V. Mosby. (Originally published as *Maternal-infant bonding.*)

Klaus, M., Kreger, N., McAlpine, W., Steffa, M., & Kennell, J. (1972). Maternal attachment: Importance of the first post-partum days. *New England Journal of Medicine, 286,* 460–463.

Kleemeier, R. (1962). Intellectual changes in the senium. *Proceedings of the Social Statistics Section of the American Statistical Association, 1,* 290–295.

Kleinginna, P. R., Jr., & Kleinginna, A. M. (1988). Current trends toward convergence of the behavioristic, functional, and cognitive perspectives in experimental psychology. *The Psychological Record, 38,* 369–392.

Kline, D. W., & Schieber, F. (1985). Vision and aging. In J. E. Birren & K. W. Schaie (Eds.), *Handbook of the psychology of aging* (2nd ed.). New York: Van Nostrand Reinhold.

Kline, S. M. (1985). Achieving weight gain with anorexia and bulimic clients in a group setting. *Transactional Analysis Journal, 15,* 62–67.

Klocke, R. A. (1977). Influence of aging on the lung. In C. E. Finch and L. Hayflick (Eds.), *Handbook of the biology of aging.* New York: Van Nostrand Reinhold.

Knuppel, R. A., & Angel, J. L. (1990). Diagnosis of fetal-maternal hemorrhage. In R. D. Eden, F. H. Boehm, & M. Haire (Eds.), *Assessment and care of the fetus: Physiological, clinical, and medicolegal principles.* Norwalk, CT: Appleton & Lange.

Knutson, J. F. (1978). Child abuse as an area of aggression research. *Journal of Pediatric Psychology, 3,* 20–27.

Kogan, N. (1983). Stylistic variation in childhood and adolescence: Creativity, metaphor, and cognitive style. In P. H. Mussen (Ed.), *Handbook of child psychology* (4th ed.) (Vol. 3): *Cognitive development* (pp. 630–706) (J. H. Flavell & E. M. Markman, Eds.). New York: John Wiley.

Kohlberg, L. A. (1964). Development of moral character and moral ideology. In M. L. Hoffman & L. W. Hoffman (Eds.), *Review of child development research* (Vol. 1). New York: Russell Sage Foundation.

Kohlberg, L. A. (1966). Cognitive-development analysis of children's sex-role concepts and attitudes. In E. Maccoby (Ed.), *The development of sex differences.* Stanford, CA: Stanford University Press.

Kohlberg, L. A. (1969). Stage and sequence: The cognitive developmental approach to socialization. In D. Gosslin (Ed.), *Handbook of socialization theory and research.* Chicago: Rand McNally.

Kohlberg, L. A. (1978). Revisions in the theory and practice of moral development. *New Directions for Child Development, 2,* 83–87.

Kohlberg, L. A. (1980). *The meaning and measurement of moral development.* Worcester, MA: Clark University Press.

Kohlberg, L. (1984). *Essay on moral development.* Vol. 11: *The psychology of moral development.* New York: Harper & Row.

Kohlberg, L. A., & Candee, D. (1984). The relationship of moral judgment to moral action. In W. M. Kurtines & J. L. Gewirtz (Eds.), *Morality, moral behavior, and moral development* (pp. 52–73). New York: John Wiley.

Kolata, G. B. (1978). Behavioral teratology: Birth defects of the mind. *Science, 202,* 732–734.

Konner, M. (1982). Biological aspects of the mother–infant bond. In C. Parks & J. Stevenson-Hinde

(Eds.), *The place of attachment in human behavior*. New York: Basic Books.

Kopp, C. B., & Brownell, C. A. (1991). The development of self: The first 3 years. *Developmental Review, 11*, 195–196.

Kopp, C. B., & Kaler, S. R. (1989). Risk in infancy: Origins and implications. *American Psychologist, 44*, 224–230.

Koss, M. (1988). Hidden rape: Sexual aggression and victimization in a national sample of students in higher education. In A. Burgess (Ed.), *Rape and sexual assault* (Vol. 2). New York: Garland.

Kovacs, M. (1989). Affective disorders in children and adolescents. *American Psychologist, 44*, 209–215.

Krantz, D. S., Grunberg, N. E., Baum, A. (1985). Health psychology. *Annual Review of Psychology, 36*, 349–383.

Krauss, R. M., & Glucksberg, S. (1977). Social and nonsocial speech. *Scientific American, 236*, 100–105.

Kroupa, S. E. (1988). Perceived parental acceptance and female juvenile delinquency. *Adolescence, 23*, 143–155.

Kübler-Ross, E. (1969). *On death and dying*. New York: Macmillan.

Kübler-Ross, E. (1974). *Questions and answers on death and dying*. New York: Macmillan.

Kuder, F. (1977). *Activity, interests, and occupational choice*. Chicago: Science Research Associates.

Kuhn D. (1972). Mechanisms of change in the development of cognitive structures. *Child Development, 43*, 833–844.

Kuhn, D. (1984). Cognitive development. In M. H. Bornstein & M. E. Lamb (Eds.), *Developmental psychology: An advanced textbook* (pp. 133–180). Hillsdale, NJ: Erlbaum.

Kuhn, T. S. (1970). *The structure of scientific revolutions* (2nd ed., enl.). Chicago: University of Chicago Press.

Kurdek, L. A. (1991). Predictors of increases in marital distress in newlywed couples: A 3-year prospective longitudinal study. *Developmental Psychology, 27*, 627–636.

Kurtines, W., & Grief, E. B. (1974). The development of moral thought: Review and evaluation of Kohlberg's approach. *Psychological Bulletin, 81*, 453–470.

Kuziel-Perri, P., & Snarey, J. (1991). Adolescent repeat pregnancies: An evaluation study of a comprehensive service program for pregnant and parenting black adolescents. *Family Relations, 40*, 381–385.

Labouvie-Vief, G. (1980). Beyond formal operations: Uses and limits of pure logic in life-span development. *Human Development, 23*, 141–161.

Labouvie-Vief, G. (1986). Modes of knowledge and the organization of development. In M. L. Commons, L. Kohlberg, F. A. Richards, & J. Sinnott (Eds.), *Beyond formal operations 3: Models and methods in the study of adult and adolescent thought*. New York: Praeger.

Lachenmeyer, J. R., & Muni-Brander, P. (1988). Eating disorders in a nonclinical adolescent population: Implications for treatment. *Adolescence, 23*(90), 303–312.

Laczko, F. (1989). Between work and retirement: Becoming "old" in the 1980's. In B. Bytheway, T. Keil, P. Allatt, & A. Bryman (Eds.), *Becoming and being old: Sociological approaches to later life*. London: Sage.

Ladame, F., & Jeanneret, O. (1982). Suicide in adolescence: Some comments on epidemiology and prevention. *Journal of Adolescence, 5*, 355–366.

Lagercrantz, H., & Slotkin, T. A. (1986). The "stress" of being born. *Scientific American, 254*, 100–107.

Lamanna, M. A., & Riedmann, A. (1988). *Marriages and families: Making choices and facing change* (3rd ed.). Belmont, CA: Wadsworth.

Lamb, M. E. (1976a). Interactions between eight-month-olds and their fathers and mothers. In M. E. Lamb (Ed.), *The role of the father in child development*. New York: John Wiley.

Lamb, M. E. (1976b). Twelve-month-olds and their parents: Interaction in a laboratory playroom. *Developmental Psychology, 12*, 237–244.

Lamb, M. E. (1980). The development of parent–infant attachment in the first two years of life. In F. A. Pedersen (Ed.), *The father–infant relationship: Observational studies in the family setting*. New York: Holt, Rinehart & Winston.

Lamb, M. E. (Ed.). (1987). *The father's role: Cross-cultural perspectives*. Hillsdale, NJ: Erlbaum.

Lamb, M. E., Easterbrooks, M. A., & Holden, G. W. (1980). Reinforcement and punishment among preschoolers: Characteristics, effects, and correlates. *Child Development, 51*, 1230–1236.

Lamb, M. E., & Elster, A. B. (1985). Adolescent mother–infant–father relationships. *Developmental Psychology, 21,* 768–773.

Lamb, M. E., Frodi, M., Hwang, C., & Frodi, A. M. (1983). Effects of paternal involvement on infant preferences for mothers and fathers. *Child Development, 54,* 450–458.

Lambert, W. E. (1975). Culture and language as factors in learning and education. In A. Wolfgang (Ed.), *Education of immigrant students.* Toronto: Ontario Institute for Studies in Education.

Landesman, S., & Ramey, C. (1989). Developmental psychology and mental retardation: Integrating scientific principles with treatment practices. *American Psychologist, 44,* 409–415.

Landry, R. (1987). Additive bilingualism, schooling, and special education: A minority group perspective. *Canadian Journal for Exceptional Children, 3,* 109–114.

Langer, E. J., & Rodin, J. (1976). The effects of choice and enhanced personal responsibility for the aged. *Journal of Personality and Social Psychology, 34,* 191–198.

Langlois, J. H., Ritter, J. M., Roggman, L. A., & Vaughn, L. S. (1991). Facial diversity and infant preferences for attractive faces. *Developmental Psychology, 27,* 79–84.

Langlois, J. H., & Roggman, L. A. (1990). Attractive faces are only average. *Psychological Science, 1,* 115–121.

Langlois, J. H., Roggman, L. A., & Rieser-Danner, L. A. (1990). Infants' differential social responses to attractive and unattractive faces. *Developmental Psychology, 26,* 153–159.

Langlois, J. H., & Stephan, C. W. (1981). Beauty and the beast: The role of physical attractiveness in the development of peer relations and social behavior. In S. S. Brehm, S. M. Kassin, & F. X. Gibbons (Eds.), *Developmental social psychology.* New York: Oxford University Press.

Lapsley, D. K. (1990). Continuity and discontinuity in adolescent social cognitive development. In R. Montemayor, G. R. Adams, & T. P. Gullotta (Eds.), *From childhood to adolescence: A transitional period? (Advances in Adolescent Development,* Vol. 2). Newbury Park, CA: Sage.

La Rue, A., Dessonville, C., & Jarvik, L. F. (1985). Aging and mental disorders. In J. E. Birren &

K. W. Schaie (Eds.), *Handbook of the psychology of aging* (2nd ed.). New York: Van Nostrand Reinhold.

Laszlo, J. I. (1986). Development of perceptual motor abilities in children from 5 years to adults. In C. Pratt, A. F. Garton, W. E. Tunmer, & A. R. Nesdale (Eds.), *Research issues in child development.* Boston: Allen & Unwin.

Latané, R., & Darley, J. M. (1970). *The unresponsive bystander: Why doesn't he help?* New York: Appleton-Century-Crofts.

Lawton, M. P. (1976). The relative impact of congregate and traditional housing on elderly tenants. *Gerontologist, 16,* 237–242.

Lawton, M. P. (1981). Community supports for the aged. *Journal of Social Issues, 37,* 102–115.

Lazar, I., Darlington, R., Murray, H., Royce, J., & Snipper, A. (1982). Lasting effects of early education: A report from the Consortium for Longitudinal Studies. *Monographs of the Society for Research in Child Development, 47*(195).

Leaf, A. (1973, September). Getting old. *Scientific American, 299,* 44–53.

Leboyer, F. (1975). *Birth without violence.* New York: Random House.

Lee, V. E., Brooks-Gunn, J., & Schnur, E. (1988). Does Head Start work? A 1-year follow-up comparison of disadvantaged children attending Head Start, no preschool, and other preschool programs. *Developmental Psychology, 24,* 210–222.

Lefkowitz, M., Eron, L., Walder, L., & Huesmann, L. R. (1972). Television violence and child aggression: A follow-up study. In G. A. Comstock & E. A. Rubinstein (Eds.), *Television and social behavior* (Vol. 3). Washington, DC: U.S. Government Printing Office.

Lefrançois, G. R. (1973). *Of children* (1st ed.). Belmont, CA: Wadsworth.

Lefrançois, G. R. (1982). *Psychological theories and human learning.* Pacific Grove, CA: Brooks/Cole.

Lefrançois, G. R. (1983). *Psychology* (2nd ed.). Belmont, CA: Wadsworth.

Legerstee, M. (1991). Changes in the quality of infant sounds as a function of social and nonsocial stimulation. *First Language, 11,* 327–343.

Lehman, H. C. (1953). *Age and achievement.* Princeton, NJ: Princeton University Press.

Lenz, W. (1966). Malformations caused by drugs in pregnancy. *American Journal of Diseases in Children, 112*, 99–106.

Lerner, R. M. (1985). Individual and context in developmental psychology: Conceptual and theoretical issues. In J. R. Nesselroade & A. Von Eye (Eds.), *Individual development and social change: Explanatory analysis* (pp. 155–188). New York: Academic Press.

Lerner, R. M. (1987). The concept of plasticity in development. In J. J. Gallagher & C. T. Ramey (Eds.), *The malleability of children*. Baltimore: Brookes.

Lerner, R. M. (1991). Changing organism-context relations as the basic process of development: A developmental contextual perspective. *Developmental Psychology, 27*, 27–32.

Lerner, R. M., & Korn, S. J. (1972). The development of body-build stereotypes in males. *Child Development, 43*, 908–920.

Lerner, R. M., Lerner, J. V., Winelle, M., Hooker, K., Lenez, K., et al. (1986). Children and adolescents in their contexts: Tests of the goodness of fit model. In R. Plomin & J. Dunn (Eds.), *The study of temperament: Changes, continuities and challenges*. Hillsdale, NJ: Erlbaum.

Leslie, A. M. (1988). Some implications of pretense for mechanisms underlying the child's theory of mind. In J. W. Astington, P. L. Harris, & D. R. Olson (Eds.), *Developing theories of mind*. New York: Cambridge University Press.

Leslie, G. R. (1979). *The family in social context* (4th ed.). New York: Oxford University Press.

Lesser, H. (1977). *Television and the preschool child: A psychological theory of instruction and curriculum development*. New York: Academic Press.

Levine, R. A. (1987). Women's schooling, patterns of fertility, and child survival. *Educational Researcher, 16*, 21–27.

Levinson, D. J. (1977). Middle adulthood in modern society: A sociopsychological view. In G. Direnzo (Ed.), *Social character and social change*. Westport, CT: Greenwood Press.

Levinson, D. J. (1978). *The seasons of a man's life*. New York: Alfred A. Knopf.

Levinson, D. J. (1981). The midlife transition: A period in adult psychosocial development. In L. D. Steinberg (Ed.), *The life cycle: Readings in human development*. New York: Columbia University Press.

Levinson, D. J. (1986). A conception of adult development. *American Psychologist, 41*, 3–13.

Lévy-Leboyer, C., & Duron, Y. (1991). Global change: New challenges for psychology. *International Journal of Psychology, 26*, 575–583.

Lewin, R. (1975, September). Starved brains. *Psychology Today*, pp. 29–33.

Lewis, M., Sullivan, M. W., & Vasen, A. (1987). Making faces: Age and emotion differences in the posing of emotional expressions. *Developmental Psychology, 23*, 690–697.

Liben, L. (1975, April). *Perspective-taking skills in young children: Seeing the world through rose-colored glasses.* Paper presented at the meeting of the Society for Research in Child Development, Denver, CO.

Liberty, C., & Ornstein, P. A. (1973). Age differences in organization and recall: The effects of training in categorization. *Journal of Experimental Child Psychology, 15*, 169–186.

Lieberman, A. B. (1987). *Giving birth*. New York: St. Martin's Press.

Liebert, R. M., & Schwartzberg, N. S. (1977). Effects of mass media. In M. R. Rosenzweig & L. W. Porter (Eds.), *Annual review of psychology* (Vol. 28). Palo Alto, CA: Annual Reviews.

Liggins, G. C. (1988). The onset of labor: An historical review. In C. T. Jones (Ed.), *Research in perinatal medicine (VII): Fetal and neonatal development*. Ithaca, NY: Perinatology Press.

Light, L. L. (1991). Memory and aging: Four hypotheses in search of data. *Annual Review of Psychology, 42*, 333–376.

Lindemann, E. (1944). Symptomatology and management of acute grief. *American Journal of Psychiatry, 101*, 141–148.

Linn, M. C., & Hyde, J. S. (1989). Gender, mathematics, and science. *Educational Researcher, 18*, 17–27.

Lipsitt, L. P. (1982). Infant learning. In T. M. Field, A. Huston, H. C. Quay, L. Troll, & G. E. Finley (Eds.), *Review of human development*. New York: John Wiley.

Lipsitt, L. P., Engen, T., & Kaye, H. (1963). Developmental changes in the olfactory threshold of the neonate. *Child Development, 34*, 371–376.

Locke, J. (1699). *Some thoughts concerning education* (4th ed.). London: A. & J. Churchills.

Lockhart, A. S. (1980). Motor learning and motor development during infancy and childhood. In C. B. Corbin (Ed.), *A textbook of motor development*. Dubuque, IA: Brown.

Loehlin, J. C. (1985). Fitting heredity–environment models jointly to twin and adoption data from the California Psychological Inventory. *Behavior Genetics, 15,* 199–221.

Loehlin, J. C., Willerman, L., & Horn, J. M. (1988). Human behavior genetics. *Annual Review of Psychology, 39,* 101–133.

Loevinger, J. (1987). *Paradigms of personality.* New York: W. H. Freeman.

Long, J. (1989). A part to play: Men experiencing leisure through retirement. In B. Bytheway, T. Keil, P. Allatt, & A. Bryman (Eds.), *Becoming and being old: Sociological approaches to later life.* London: Sage.

Long, J., & Porter, K. L. (1984). Multiple roles of midlife women: A case for new directions in theory, research, and policy. In G. Baruch & J. Brooks-Gunn (Eds.), *Women in midlife.* New York: Plenum.

Long, L., & Long, T. (1983). *The handbook for latchkey children and their parents.* New York: Arbor House.

Lopata, H. Z. (1973). *Widowhood in an American city.* Cambridge, MA: Schenkman.

Lopata, H. Z. (1977). The meaning of friendship in widowhood. In L. Troll, J. Israel, & K. Israel (Eds.), *Looking ahead: A woman's guide to the problems and joys of growing older.* Englewood Cliffs, NJ: Prentice-Hall.

Lopata, H. Z. (1981). The meaning of friendship in widowhood. In L. D. Steinberg (Ed.), *The life cycle: Readings in human development.* New York: Columbia University Press.

Lopata, H. Z., & Barnewolt, D. (1984). The middle years: Changes and variations in social role commitments. In G. Baruch & J. Brooks-Gunn (Eds.), *Women in midlife.* New York: Plenum.

Lorenz, K. (1952). *King Solomon's ring.* London: Methuen.

Lowenthal, M. F., & Haven, C. (1981). Interaction and adaptation: Intimacy as a critical variable. In L. D. Steinberg (Ed.), *The life cycle: Readings in human development.* New York: Columbia University Press.

Lowery, C. R., & Settle, S. A. (1985). Effects of divorce on children: Differential impact on custody and visitation patterns. *Family Relations, 34,* 455–463.

Lozoff, B. (1989). Nutrition and behavior. *American Psychologist, 44,* 231–236.

Ludeman, K. (1981). The sexuality of the older person: Review of the literature. *Gerontologist, 21,* 203–308.

Luke, C. (1988). *Television and your child: A guide for concerned parents.* Toronto: Kagan & Woo.

Lunde, D. T., & Lunde, M. R. (1980). *The next generation: A book on parenting.* New York: Holt, Rinehart & Winston.

Lynn, D. B. (1974). *The father: His role in child development.* Pacific Grove, CA: Brooks/Cole.

Lynn, D. B. (1979). *Daughters and parents: Past, present and future.* Pacific Grove, CA: Brooks/Cole.

Maccoby, E. E., & Jacklin, C. N. (1974). *The psychology of sex differences.* Stanford, CA: Stanford University Press.

Maccoby, E. E., & Jacklin, C. N. (1980). Sex differences in aggression: A rejoinder and reprise. *Child Development, 51,* 964–980.

Macfarlane, A. (1975). Olfaction in the development of social preferences in the human neonate. In *Parent–infant interaction,* Proceedings of CIBA Foundation Symposium. Amsterdam: Elsevier.

Machida, S., & Holloway, S. D. (1991). The relationship between divorced mothers' perceived control over child rearing and children's postdivorce development. *Family Relations, 40,* 272–278.

Macklin, E. D. (1983). Nonmarital heterosexual cohabitation: An overview. In E. D. Macklin & R. H. Rubin (Eds.), *Contemporary families and alternative lifestyles: Handbook on research and theory* (pp. 49–74). Beverly Hills, CA: Sage.

MacMillan, D. L. (1982). *Mental retardation in school and society* (2nd ed.). Boston: Little, Brown.

MacMillan, D. L., & Meyers, C. E. (1979). Educational labeling of handicapped learners. In D. C. Berliner (Ed.), *Review of research in education* (Vol. 7). Washington, DC: American Educational Research Association.

Madsen, M. C. (1971). Developmental and cross-cultural differences in the cooperation and competitive behavior of young children. *Journal of Cross-Cultural Psychology, 2*, 365–371.

Madsen, M. C., & Lancy, D. F. (1981). Cooperative and competitive behavior: Experiments related to ethnic identity and urbanization in Papua New Guinea. *Journal of Cross-Cultural Psychology, 12*, 389–409.

Magnusson, D., & Backteman, G. (1978). Longitudinal stability of person characteristics: Intelligence and creativity. *Applied Psychological Measurement, 2*, 481–490.

Malina, R. M. (1990). Physical growth and performance during the transitional years (9 to 16). In R. Montemayor, G. R. Adams, & T. P. Gullotta (Eds.), *From childhood to adolescence: A transitional period?* (*Advances in Adolescent Development*, Vol. 2). Newbury Park, CA: Sage.

Malonebeach, E. E., & Zarit, S. H. (1991). Current research issues in caregiving to the elderly. *International Journal of Aging and Human Development, 32*, 103–114.

Mancini, J. A. (1984). Leisure lifestyles and family dynamics in old age. In W. H. Quinn & G. A. Hughston (Eds.), *Independent aging: Family and social systems perspectives* (pp. 58–71). Rockville, MD: Aspen.

Mandler, J. M. (1984). Representation and recall in infancy. In M. Moscovitch (Ed.), *Infant memory*. New York: Plenum.

Marcia, J. E. (1966). Development and validation of ego-identity status. *Journal of Personality and Social Psychology, 3*, 551–558.

Marcia, J. E. (1980). Identity in adolescence. In J. Adelson (Ed.), *Handbook of adolescent psychology*. New York: John Wiley.

Marcia, J. E., Friedman, M. L. (1970). Ego identity status in college women. *Journal of Personality, 38*, 249–269.

Markides, K., & Martin, H. (1979). A causal model of life satisfaction among the elderly. *Journal of Gerontology, 34*, 86–93.

Marland, S. P. (1972). *Education of the gifted and talented*. Washington, DC: U.S. Government Printing Office.

Marlatt, G. A., Baer, J. S., Donovan, D. M., & Kivlahan, D. R. (1988). Addictive behaviors: Etiology and treatment. *Annual Review of Psychology, 39*, 223–252.

Marsh, H. W. (1989). Sex differences in the development of verbal and mathematics constructs: The high school and beyond study. *American Educational Research Journal, 26*, 191–225.

Marsiglio, W. (1986). Teenage fatherhood: High school accreditation and educational attainment. In A. B. Elster & M. E. Lamb (Eds.), *Adolescent fatherhood*. Hillsdale, NJ: Erlbaum.

Marston, A. R., Jacobs, D. F., Singer, R. D., Widaman, K. F., & Little, T. D. (1988). Characteristics of adolescents at risk for compulsive overeating on a brief screening test. *Adolescence, 23*, 288–302.

Martin, J. P. (1978). Introduction. In J. P. Martin (Ed.), *Violence and the family*. New York: John Wiley.

Martin, N., & Jardine, R. (1986). Eysenck's contributions to behaviour genetics. In S. Modgil & C. Modgil (Eds.), *Hans Eysenck: Consensus and controversy*. Philadelphia: Falmer.

Maslow, A. H. (1970). *Motivation and personality* (2nd ed.). New York: Harper & Row.

Masters, J. C. (1979). Interpreting "imitative" responses in early infancy. *Science, 205*, 215.

Masters, W. H., & Johnson, V. E. (1966). *Human sexual response*. London: Churchill.

Masters, W. H., & Johnson, V. E. (1970). *Human sexual inadequacy*. Boston: Little, Brown.

Masters, W. H., Johnson, V. E., & Kolodny, R. C. (1988). *Crisis: Heterosexual behavior in the age of AIDS*. New York: Grove Press.

Matthews, K. A. (1984). Assessment of Type A: Anger and hostility in epidemiological studies of cardiovascular disease. In A. Ostfeld & E. Eaker (Eds.), *Measuring psychosocial variables in epidemiologic studies of cardiovascular disease*. Bethesda, MD: National Institutes of Health.

Mayer, N. K., & Tronick, E. Z. (1985). Mother's turn-giving signals and infant turn-taking in mother–infant interaction. In T. M. Field & N. A. Fox (Eds.), *Social perception in infants*. Norwood, NJ: Ablex.

Maykovich, M. K. (1976). Attributes versus behavior in extramarital sexual relations. *Journal of Marriage and the Family, 38*, 693.

Mazur, A. (1977). On Wilson's sociobiology. *American Journal of Sociology, 83*, 697–700.

McAdams, D. P. (1984). Love, power, and images of the self. In C. Z. Malatesta & C. E. Izard (Eds.), *Emotion in adult development* (pp. 159–174). Beverly Hills, CA: Sage.

McCabe, M. P. (1991). Influence of creativity and intelligence on academic performance. *The Journal of Creative Behavior, 25*, 116–122.

McCall, R. B., Applebaum, M. I., & Hogarty, P. S. (1973). Developmental changes in mental test performance. *Monographs of the Society for Research in Child Development, 38*(150).

McCartney, K., Bernieri, F., & Harris, M. J. (1990). Growing up and growing apart: A developmental meta-analysis of twin studies. *Psychological Bulletin, 107*, 226–237.

McCartney, K., & Jordan, E. (1990). Parallels between research on child care and research on school effects. *Educational Researcher, 19*, 21–27.

McClelland, D. C. (1973). Testing for competence rather than for "intelligence." *American Psychologist, 28*, 1–14.

McClelland, D., Constantian, C. S., Regalado, D., & Stone, C. (1978, June). Making it to maturity. *Psychology Today*, pp. 42–53, 114.

McCormick, M., Shapiro, S., & Starfield, B. (1984). High-risk young mothers: Infant mortality and morbidity in four areas in the United States, 1973–1978. *American Journal of Public Health, 74*, 18–23.

McCrae, R. R., & Costa, P. T. (1984). *Emerging lives: Enduring predispositions*. Boston: Little, Brown.

McCrae, R. R., & Costa, P. T. (1987). Validations of the five factor model of personality across instruments and observers. *Journal of Personality and Social Psychology, 52*, 81–90.

McGraw, M. B. (1943). *The neuromuscular maturation of the human infant*. New York: Columbia University Press.

McKay, J., Sinisterra, L., McKay, A., Gomez, H., & Lloreda, P. (1978). Improving cognitive ability in chronically deprived children. *Science, 200*, 270–278.

McKusick, V. A. (1986). *Mendelian inheritance in man* (7th ed.). Baltimore: Johns Hopkins University Press.

McNeill, D. (1970). *The acquisition of language: The study of developmental psycholinguistics*. New York: Harper & Row.

McTavish, D. G. (1971). Perceptions of old people: A review of research, methodologies and findings. *Gerontologist, 11*, 90–101.

Mead, M. (1970). Marriage in two steps. In H. A. Otto (Ed.), *The family in search of a future*. New York: Appleton-Century-Crofts.

Meadow, K. P. (1975). Development of deaf children. In E. M. Hetherington (Ed.), *Review of child development research* (Vol. 5). Chicago: University of Chicago Press.

Mednick, S. A. (1962). The associative basis of the creative process. *Psychological Review, 69*, 220–232.

Meikle, S., Peitchinis, J. A., & Pearce, K. (1985). *Teenage sexuality*. San Diego, CA: College-Hill Press.

Meissner, S. J. (1965). Parental interaction of the adolescent boy. *Journal of Genetic Psychology, 107*, 225–233.

Melican, G. J., & Feldt, L. S. (1980). An empirical study of the Zajonc-Markus hypothesis for achievement test score declines. *American Educational Research Journal, 17*, 5–19.

Meltzoff, A. N. (1988). Infant imitation after a 1-week delay: Long-term memory for novel acts and multiple stimuli. *Developmental Psychology, 24*, 470–476.

Meltzoff, A. N., & Moore, M. K. (1977). Imitation of facial and manual gestures by human neonates. *Science, 198*, 75–78.

Meltzoff, A. N., & Moore, M. K. (1979). Interpreting "imitative" responses in early infancy. *Science, 205*, 217–219.

Meltzoff, A. N., & Moore, M. K. (1983). Newborn infants imitate adult facial gestures. *Child Development, 54*, 702–709.

Meltzoff, A. N., & Moore, M. K. (1989). Imitation in newborn infants: Exploring the range of gestures imitated and the underlying mechanisms. *Developmental Psychology, 25*, 954–962.

Mercer, J. R. (1973). *Labeling the mentally retarded*. Berkeley: University of California Press.

Mercy killing: Act of love or selfishness? (1985, October 6). *Edmonton Journal*, p. B5.

Metzger, A. M. (1979–80). A methodological study of the Kübler-Ross stage theory. *Omega, 10,* 291–301.

Meyer, W. J. (1985). Summary, integration, and prospective. In J. B. Dusek (Ed.), *Teacher expectancies.* Hillsdale, NJ: Erlbaum.

Mielke, K. W. (1983). Formative research on appeal and comprehension in 3-2-1 CONTACT. In J. Bryant & D. R. Anderson (Eds.), *Children's understanding of television: Research on attention and comprehension* (pp. 241–264). New York: Academic Press.

Miller, B. (1979). Unpromised paternity: The lifestyles of gay fathers. In M. Levine (Ed.), *Gay men* (pp. 240–252). New York: Harper & Row.

Miller, B. C., & Dyk, P. H. (1991). Community of caring effects on adolescent mothers: A program evaluation case study. *Family Relations, 40,* 386–395.

Miller, G. A. (1956). The magical number seven, plus or minus two: Some limits on our capacity for processing information. *Psychological Review, 63,* 81–97.

Miller, J. B., & Lane, M. (1991). Relations between young adults and their parents. *Journal of Adolescence, 14,* 179–194.

Miller, L. B., & Bizzell, R. P. (1983). Long-term effects of four preschool programs: sixth, seventh, and eighth grades. *Child Development, 54,* 727–741.

Miller, S. A. (1981, April). *Certainty and necessity in the understanding of Piagetian concepts.* Paper presented at the Society for Research in Child Development Meetings, Boston, MA.

Mitchell, G. D., Arling, G. L., & Moller, G. W. (1967). Long term effects of maternal punishment on the behavior of monkeys. *Psychonomic Science, 8,* 209–210.

Miyawaki, K., Strange, W., Verbrugge, K., Liberman, A. M., Jenkins, J. J., & Fujimura, O. (1975). An effect of linguistic experience: The discrimination of [r] and [l] by native speakers of Japanese and English. *Perception & Psychophysics, 18,* 331–340.

Moenster, P. A. (1972). Learning and memory in relation to age. *Journal of Gerontology, 27,* 361–363.

Moerk, E. L. (1991). Positive evidence for negative evidence. *First Language, 11,* 219–251.

Moffitt, A. R. (1971). Consonant cue perception by 20–24 week old infants. *Child Development, 42,* 717–731.

Monachesi, E. D., & Hathaway, S. R. (1969). The personality of delinquents. In J. N. Butcher (Ed.), *MMPI: Research developments and clinical applications* (pp. 207–219). New York: McGraw-Hill.

Le monde au chevet de l'enfance menacée. (1990, September 29). *Le Monde,* p. 15.

Money, J. (1975). Counselling in genetics and applied behavior genetics. In K. W. Schaie, V. F Anderson, G. F. McClearn, & J. Money (Eds.), *Developmental human behavior genetics.* Lexington, MA: D. C. Heath.

Money, J. & Ehrhardt, A. A. (1968). Prenatal hormonal exposure: Possible effects on behavior in man. In R. P. Michael (Ed.), *Endocrinology and human behavior.* London: Oxford University Press.

Montemayor, R., & Flannery, D. J. (1990). Making the transition from childhood to early adolescence. In R. Montemayor, G. R. Adams, & T. P. Gullotta (Eds.), *From childhood to adolescence: A transitional period?* (*Advances in Adolescent Development,* Vol. 2). Newbury Park, CA: Sage.

Montessori, M. (1912). *The Montessori method.* New York: Frederick A. Stokes.

Moorcroft, W. H. (1989). *Sleep, dreaming, and sleep disorders.* Lanham, MD: University Press of America.

Moore, K. A. (1990). *Facts at a glance 1990.* Washington, DC: Child Trends.

Moore, R. C. (1986). *Childhood's domain: Play and place in child development.* London: Croom Helm.

Mor, V. (1985). Hospice and the elderly: Insights from the national hospice study. In G. L. Maddox & E. W. Busse (Eds.), *Aging: The universal human experience.* New York: Springer.

Morgan, B. S. (1981). A contribution to the debate on homogamy, propinquity, and segregation. *Journal of Marriage and the Family, 43,* 909–921.

Morganti, J. B., Nehrke, M. F., Hulicka, I. M., & Cataldo, J. R. (1988). Life-span differences in life satisfaction, self-concept, and locus of control. *International Journal of Aging and Human Development, 26,* 45–56.

Moriarty, A. (1990). Deterring the molester and abuser. Pre-employment testing for child and youth care workers. *Child and Youth Care Quarterly, 18,* 59–65.

Morin, S. F. (1988). AIDS: The challenge to psychology. *American Psychologist, 43*, 838–842.

Morrill, C. M., Leach, J. N., Shreeve, W. C., Radenaugh, M. R., & Linder, K. (1991). Teenage obesity. An academic issue. *International Journal of Adolescence and Youth, 2*, 245–250.

Morris, M. (1988). *Last-chance children: Growing up with older parents.* New York: Columbia University Press.

Morrison, E., Starks, K., Hyndman, C., & Ronzio, N. (1980). *Growing up sexual.* New York: D. Van Nostrand.

Morrison, J. R., & Stewart, M. A. (1973). The psychiatric status of the legal families of adopted hyperactive children. *Archives of Genetic Psychiatry, 28*, 888–891.

Morse, W. C. (1977). Serving the needs of children with behavior disorders. *Exceptional Children, 44*, 158–164.

Morsink, C. V. (1985). Learning disabilities. In W. H. Berdine & A. E. Blackhurst (Eds.), *An introduction to special education* (2nd ed.). Boston: Little, Brown.

Morton, J., & Johnson, M. H. (1991). CONSPEC and CONLERN: A two-process theory of infant face recognition. *Psychological Review, 98*, 164–181.

Moskowitz, B. A. (1978). The acquisition of language. *Scientific American, 239*, 92–108.

Mowat, F. (1952). *People of the deer.* Boston: Little, Brown.

Moynahan, E. D. (1973). The development of knowledge concerning the effect of categorization upon free recall. *Child Development, 44*, 238–245.

Mulhern, R. K., & Passman, R. H. (1979). The child's behavioral pattern as a determinant of maternal punitiveness. *Child Development, 15*, 417–423.

Mulhern, R. K. Jr., & Passman, R. H. (1981). Parental discipline as affected by the sex of the parent, the sex of the child, and the child's apparent responsiveness to discipline. *Developmental Psychology, 17*, 604–613.

Munns, K. (1981). Effects of exercise on the range of joint motion in elderly subjects. In E. L. Smith & R. C. Serfass (Eds.), *Exercise and aging: The scientific basis.* Hillside, NJ: Enslow.

Murdock, G. P. (1957). World ethnographic sample. *American Anthropologist, 59*, 676–688.

Murphy, C., Cain, W. S., Gilmore, M. M., & Skinner, R. B. (1991). Sensory and semantic factors in recognition memory for odors and graphic stimuli: Elderly versus young persons. *American Journal of Psychology, 104*, 161–192.

Murray, J. P. (1973, June). Television and violence: Implications of the Surgeon General's research program. *American Psychologist*, 472–478.

Murstein, B. I. (1976). *Who will marry whom? Theories and research in marital choice.* New York: Springer-Verlag.

Muss, R. E. (1988). Carol Gilligan's theory of sex differences in the development of moral reasoning during adolescence. *Adolescence, 23*, 229–243.

Mussen, P. H., Honzik, M. P., & Eichorn, D. H. (1982). Early adult antecedents of life satisfaction at age 70. *Journal of Gerontology, 37*, 316–322.

Muuss, R. E. (1975). *Theories of adolescence* (3rd ed.). New York: Random House.

Nadelson, C. C. (1990). Women leaders: Achievement and power. In R. A. Nemiroff & C. A. Colarusso (Eds.), *New dimensions in adult development.* New York: Basic Books.

Nadelson, C. C., & Nadelson, T. (1980). Dual-career marriages: Benefits and costs. In F. Pepitone-Rockwell (Ed.), *Dual-career couples.* Beverly Hills, CA: Sage.

Nagy, M. H. (1948). The child's theories concerning death. *Journal of Genetic Psychology, 73*, 3–27.

Nanpon, H. (1991). Les âges de la vie: La représentation des âges de l'existence par un groupe de jeunes étudiants. *Enfance, 45*, 205–219.

National Center for Health Statistics. (1985). *Annual summary of births, deaths, marriages, and divorces: U.S., 1984.* Hyattsville, MD: Public Health Service.

National Center for Health Statistics. (1987). *Advance report of final natality statistics, 1985.* Monthly vital statistics report (Vol. 36). Washington, DC: National Center for Health Statistics.

National Center for Health Statistics. (1990). Advance report of final marriage statistics, 1987. *Monthly vital statistics report* (Vol. 38). Hyattsville, MD: Public Health Service.

Neal, J. H. (1983). Children's understanding of their parents' divorces. In L. A. Kurdek (Ed.), *Children and divorce: New directions for child development* (pp. 3–14). San Francisco: Jossey-Bass.

Nealis, J. T. (1983). Epilepsy. In J. Umbriet (Ed.), *Physical disabilities and health impairment: An introduction* (pp. 74–85). Columbus, OH: Merrill.

Neiger, B. L., & Hopkins, R. W. (1988). Adolescent suicide: Character traits of high-risk teenagers. *Adolescence, 23*, 468–475.

Neisser, U. (1991). Two perceptually given aspects of the self and their development. *Developmental Review, 11*, 197–209.

Nelson, K. E. (1989). Strategies for first language teaching. In M. L. Rice & R. L. Schiefelbusch (Eds.), *Teachability of language*. Baltimore: Brookes.

Nesselroade, J. R., & Baltes, P. B. (1984). Sequential strategies and the role of cohort effects in behavioral development: Adolescent personality (1970–72) as a sample case. In S. A. Mednick, M. Harway, & K. M. Finello (Eds.), *Handbook of longitudinal research* (Vol. 1): *Birth and childhood cohorts* (pp. 55–87). New York: Holt, Rinehart & Winston.

Neugarten, B. L. (1964). *Personality in middle and late life*. New York: Lieber-Atherton.

Neugarten, B. L. (Ed.). (1968). *Middle age and aging: A reader in social psychology*. Chicago: University of Chicago Press.

Neugarten, B. (1973). Personality change in late life: A developmental perspective. In C. Eisdorfer & M. P. Lawton (Eds.), *The psychology of adult development and aging*. Washington, DC: American Psychological Association.

Neugarten, B. L. (1978). The wise of the young-old. In R. Gross, B. Gross, & S. Seidman (Eds.), *The new old: Struggling for decent aging*. New York: Doubleday-Anchor.

Neugarten, B. L., & Datan, N. (1981). The subjective experience of middle age. In L. D. Steinberg (Ed.), *The life cycle: Readings in human development*. New York: Columbia University Press.

Neugarten, B. L., & Weinstein, K. K. (1964). The changing American grandparents. *Journal of Marriage and the Family, 26*, 199–204.

Newcomb, M. D., & Bentler, P. M. (1988). *Consequences of adolescent drug use: Impact on the lives of young adults*. Newbury Park, CA: Sage.

Newcomb, M. D., & Bentler, P. M. (1989). Substance use and abuse among children and teenagers. *American Psychologist, 44*, 242–248.

Newman, B. M. (1982). Mid-life development. In B. B. Wolman et al. (Eds.), *Handbook of developmental psychology*. Englewood Cliffs, NJ: Prentice-Hall.

Newman, B. M., & Newman, P. R. (1983). *Understanding adulthood*. New York: Holt, Rinehart & Winston.

Newsweek (1969, January 6), p. 37.

Ng, S. H., Giles, H., & Moody, J. (1991). Information-seeking triggered by age. *International Journal of Aging and Human Development, 33*, 269–277.

Nock, S. L. (1979). The family life cycle: Empirical or conceptual tool? *Journal of Marriage and the Family, 41*, 15–26.

Nofsinger, M. M. (1990). *Children and adjustment to divorce: An annotated bibliography*. New York: Garland.

Nolan, C. Y. (1978). The visually impaired. In E. L. Meyen (Ed.), *Exceptional children and youth: An introduction*. Denver, CO: Love.

Norcia, A. M., & Tyler, C. W. (1985). Spatial frequency sweep VEP: Visual acuity during the first year of life. *Vision Research, 25*, 1399–1408.

Norton, A. J., & Moorman, J. E. (1987). Current trends in marriage and divorce among American women. *Journal of Marriage and the Family, 49*, 3–14.

Novak, L. (1972). Aging, total body potassium, fat-free mass, and cell mass in males and females between ages 18 and 85 years. *Journal of Gerontology, 27*, 438–443.

Nucci, L., Guerra, N., & Lee, J. (1991). Adolescent judgments of the personal, prudential, and normative aspects of drug use. *Developmental Psychology, 27*, 841–848.

Nunner-Winkler, G. (1984). Two moralities? A critical discussion of an ethic of care and responsibility versus an ethic of rights and justice. In W. M. Kurtines & J. L. Gewirtz (Eds.), *Morality, moral behavior, and moral development*. New York: John Wiley.

Nurmi, J. E. (1991). How do adolescents see their future? A review of the development of future orientation and planning. *Developmental Review, 11*, 1–59.

O'Brien, S. J., & Conger, P. R. (1991). No time to look back: Approaching the finish line of life's course. *International Journal of Aging and Human Development, 33*, 75–87.

O'Bryant, S. L. (1991). Older widows and independent lifestyles. *International Journal of Aging and Human Development, 32,* 41–51.

Oden, M. (1968). The fulfillment of promise: 40-year follow-up of the Terman gifted group. In R. S. Albert (Ed.) (1983). *Genius and eminence: The social psychology of creativity and exceptional achievement.* New York: Oxford University Press.

Oden, S. (1988). Alternative perspectives on children's peer relationships. In T. D. Yawkey & J. E. Johnson (Eds.), *Integrative processes and socialization: Early to middle childhood.* Hillsdale, NJ: Erlbaum.

Offer, D. O., & Offer, J. (1975). *From teenage to young manhood: A psychological study.* New York: Basic Books.

Offer, D. O., Ostrov, E., & Howard, K. (1981). *The adolescent: A psychological self-portrait.* New York: Basic Books.

Offer, D. O., Ostrov, E., & Howard, K. (1984). *Patterns of adolescent self-image.* San Francisco: Jossey-Bass.

Offer, D. O., Ostrov, E., Howard, H., & Atkinson, R. (1988). *The teenage world: Adolescents' self-image in ten countries.* New York: Plenum.

O'Leary, K. D. (1984). *Mommy, I can't sit still! Coping with hyperactive and aggressive children.* New York: New Horizon Press.

O'Leary, K. D., & Smith, D. A. (1991). Marital interactions. *Annual Review of Psychology, 42,* 191–212.

Olsho, L. W., Harkins, S. W., & Lenhardt, M. L. (1985). Aging and the auditory system. In J. E. Birren & K. W. Schaie (Eds.), *Handbook of the psychology of aging* (2nd ed.). New York: Van Nostrand Reinhold.

Olson, D. R. (1986). The cognitive consequences of literacy. *Canadian Psychology, 27,* 109–121.

Olson, G. M. (1981). The recognition of specific persons. In M. E. Lamb & L. R. Sherrod (Eds.), *Infant social cognition: Empirical and theoretical considerations.* Hillsdale, NJ: Erlbaum.

O'Neill, G. P. (1984). Some reflections on the integration of moderately mentally handicapped students (TMR) in Ontario schools. *Canadian Journal for Exceptional Children, 1,* 19–22.

O'Neill, N., & O'Neill, G. (1972). *Open marriage: A new life-style for couples.* New York: M. Evans.

Opper, S. (1977). Concept development in Thai urban and rural children. In P. R. Dasen (Ed.), *Piagetian psychology: Cross-cultural contributions.* New York: Gardner Press.

Ornstein, P. A., Baker-Ward, L., & Naus, M. J. (1988). The development of mnemonic skill. In F. E. Weinert & Perlmutter (Eds.), *Memory development: Universal changes and individual differences.* Hillsdale, NJ: Erlbaum.

Oster, H., Daily, L., & Goldenthal, P. (1989). Processing facial affect. In A. W. Young & H. D. Ellis (Eds.), *Handbook of research on face processing.* Amsterdam: North Holland.

Ovcharchyn, C. A., Johnson, H. H., & Petzel, T. P. (1981). Type A behavior, academic aspirations, and academic success. *Journal of Personality, 49,* 248–256.

Overton, W. F. (1973). On the assumptive base of the nature–nurture controversy: Additive versus interactive conceptions. *Human Development, 16,* 74–89.

Packard, V. (1968). *The sexual wilderness.* New York: Pocket Books.

Packard, V. (1983). *Our endangered children: Growing up in a changing world.* Boston: Little, Brown.

Page, E. B., & Grandon, G. M. (1979). Family configuration and mental ability: Two theories contrasted with U.S. data. *American Educational Research Journal, 16,* 257–272.

Paikoff, R. L., & Brooks-Gunn, J. (1991). Do parent–child relationships change during puberty? *Psychological Bulletin, 110,* 47–66.

Paley, V. G. (1984). *Boys and girls: Superheroes in the doll corner.* Chicago: University of Chicago Press.

Paley, V. G. (1986). *Mollie is three: Growing up in school.* Chicago: University of Chicago Press.

Pallas, A. M., Natriello, G., & McDill, E. L. (1989). The changing nature of the disadvantaged population: Current dimensions and future trends. *Educational Researcher, 18,* 16–22.

Palmore, E., & Cleveland, W. (1975). Aging, terminal decline, and terminal drop. *Journal of Gerontology, 31,* 76–81.

Paris, S. G., & Lindauer, B. K. (1976). The role of inference in children's comprehension and memory for sentences. *Cognitive Psychology, 8,* 217–227.

Paris, S. G., & Lindauer, B. K. (1982). Cognitive development in infancy. In B. B. Wolman et al. (Eds.), *Handbook of developmental psychology*. Englewood Cliffs, NJ: Prentice-Hall.

Parke, R. D. (1989). Social development in infancy: A 25-year perspective. In H. W. Reese (Ed.), *Advances in child development and behavior* (Vol. 21). New York: Academic Press.

Parke, R. D., & Ladd, G. W. (Eds.) (1989). *Family-peer relationships: Modes of linkage*. Hillsdale, NJ: Erlbaum.

Parkes, C. M. (1972). *Bereavement: Studies of grief in adult life*. New York: International University Press.

Parlee, M. B. (1984). Reproductive issues, including menopause. In G. Baruch & J. Brooks-Gunn (Eds.), *Women in midlife*. New York: Plenum.

Parnes, S. J., & Harding, H. E. (Eds.). (1962). *A sourcebook for creative thinking*. New York: Scribner's.

Parten, M. B. (1932). Social participation among preschool children. *Journal of Abnormal Social Psychology, 27*, 243–270.

Passman, R. H. (1974, September). *The effects of mothers and security blankets upon learning in children (Should Linus bring his blanket to school?)*. Paper presented at the annual meeting of the American Psychological Association, New Orleans, LA.

Passman, R. H. (1976). Arousal reducing properties of attachment objects: Testing the functional limits of the security blanket relative to the mother. *Developmental Psychology, 12*, 468–469.

Passman, R. H. (1977). Providing attachment objects to facilitate learning and reduce distress: Effects of mothers and security blankets. *Developmental Psychology, 12*, 25–28.

Passman, R. H. (1987). Attachments to inanimate objects: Are children who have security blankets insecure? *Journal of Consulting and Clinical Psychology, 55*, 825–830.

Passman, R. H., & Adams, R. E. (1982). Preferences for mothers and security blankets and their effectiveness as reinforcers for young children's behaviors. *Journal of Child Psychology and Psychiatry, 23*, 223–236.

Passman, R. H., & Blackwelder, D. E. (1981). Rewarding and punishing by mothers: The influence of progressive changes in the quality of their son's apparent behavior. *Developmental Psychology, 17*, 614–619.

Passman, R. H., & Erck, T. W. (1978). Permitting maternal contact through vision alone: Films of mothers for promoting play and locomotion. *Developmental Psychology, 14*, 512–516.

Passman, R. H., & Halonen, J. S. (1979). A developmental survey of young children's attachments to inanimate objects. *The Journal of Genetic Psychology, 134*, 165–178.

Passman, R. H., & Longeway, K. P. (1982). The role of vision in maternal attachment: Giving 2-year-olds a photograph of their mother during separation. *Developmental Psychology, 18*, 530–533.

Passman, R. H., & Weisberg, P. (1975). Mothers and blankets as agents for promoting play and exploration by young children in a novel environment: The effects of social and nonsocial attachment objects. *Developmental Psychology, 11*, 170–177.

Pattison, E. M. (1977). *The experience of dying*. Englewood Cliffs, NJ: Prentice-Hall.

Pavlov, I. P. (1927). *Conditional reflexes*. London: Oxford University Press.

Pawlik, K. (1991). The psychology of global environmental change: Some basic data and an agenda for cooperative international research. *International Journal of Psychology, 26*, 547–563.

Pearce, J. C. (1977). *Magical child: Rediscovering nature's plan for our children*. New York: Bantam Books.

Pearl, R., Bryan, T., & Herzog, A. (1990). Resisting or acquiescing to peer pressure to engage in misconduct: Adolescents' expectations of probable consequences. *Journal of Youth and Adolescence, 19*, 43–55.

Pearson, J. L., & Ferguson, L. R. (1989). Gender differences in patterns of spatial ability, environmental cognition, and math and English achievement in late adolescence. *Adolescence, 24*, 421–431.

Peck, R. C. (1968). Psychological developments in the second half of life. In B. L. Neugarten (Ed.), *Middle age and aging*. Chicago: University of Chicago Press.

Peplau, L. A. (1981). What homosexuals want in relationships. *Psychology Today, 15*, pp. 28–38.

Perlmutter, M. (1980). Development of memory in the preschool years. In R. Greene & T. D. Yawkey (Eds.), *Childhood development*. Westport, CT: Technomic.

Perlmutter, M. (1988). Cognitive potential throughout life. In J. E. Birren & V. L. Bengtson (Eds.), *Emergent theories of aging.* New York: Springer.

Petersen, A. C. (1988). Adolescent development. *Annual Review of Psychology, 39,* 583–607.

Peterson, C., & Peterson, R. (1986). Parent–child interaction and daycare: Does quality of daycare matter? *Journal of Applied Developmental Psychology, 7,* 1–15.

Peterson, G. W., Leigh, G. K, & Day, R. D. (1984). Family stress theory and the impact of divorce on children. *Journal of Divorce, 7,* 1–20.

Petro, S. J., Herrmann, D., Burrows, D., & Moore, C. M. (1991). Usefulness of commercial memory aids as a function of age. *International Journal of Aging and Human Development, 33,* 295–309.

Peverly, S. T. (1991). Problems with the knowledge-based explanation of memory and development. *Review of Educational Research, 61,* 71–93.

Pfeiffer, E. (1969). Sexual behavior in old age. In E. Pfeiffer & E. W. Busse (Eds.), *Behavior and adaptation in late life.* Boston: Little, Brown.

Pfeiffer, E., Verwoerdt, A., & Davis, G. C. (1972). Sexual behavior in middle life. *American Journal of Psychiatry, 128,* 1262–1267.

Phillips, D., McCartney, K., & Scarr, S. (1987). Child-care quality and children's social development. *Developmental Psychology, 23,* 537–543.

Piaget, J. (1932). *The moral judgment of the child.* London: Routledge & Kegan Paul.

Piaget, J. (1951). *Play, dreams and imitation in childhood.* New York: W. W. Norton.

Piaget, J. (1954). *The construction of reality in the child.* New York: Basic Books.

Piaget, J. (1961). The genetic approach to the psychology of thought. *Journal of Educational Psychology, 52,* 275–281.

Pill, C. J. (1990). Stepfamilies: Redefining the family. *Family Relations, 39,* 186–193.

Pinchbeck, I., & Hewitt, M. (1973). *Children in English society.* (Vol. 1). London: Routledge & Kegan Paul.

Pines, M. (1966). *Revolution in learning: The years from birth to six.* New York: Harper & Row.

Pines, M. (1975). In praise of the "invulnerables." *APA Monitor,* December, p. 7.

Pines, M. (1978, September). Invisible playmates. *Psychology Today,* pp. 38–42, 106.

Pines, M. (1979, January). Superkids. *Psychology Today,* pp. 53–63.

Pipes, P. L., Bumbals, J., & Pritkin, R. (1985). Collecting and assessing food intake information. In P. L. Pipes (Ed.), *Nutrition in infancy and childhood.* St. Louis: Times Mirror/Mosby College.

Pipp, S., & Haith, M. M. (1984). Infant visual responses: Which metric predicts best? *Journal of Experimental Child Psychology, 38,* 373–399.

Pitcher, E. G., & Schultz, L. H. (1983). *Boys and girls at play: The development of sex roles.* New York: Holt, Rinehart & Winston.

Placek, P. J. (1986). Commentary: Cesarean rates still rising. *Statistical Bulletin, 67,* 9.

Pleck, J. (1985). *Working wives/working husbands.* Beverly Hills, CA: Sage.

Plomin, R. (1987). Developmental behavioral genetics and infancy. In J. D. Osofsky (Ed.), *Handbook of infant development* (2nd ed.). New York: John Wiley.

Plomin, R. (1989). Environment and genes: Determinants of behavior. *American Psychologist, 44,* 105–111.

Pogrebin, L. C. (1980). *Growing up free: Raising your child in the 80's.* New York: McGraw-Hill.

Pogue-Geile, M. F., & Rose, R. J. (1985). Developmental genetic studies of adult personality. *Developmental Psychology, 21,* 547–557.

Polivy, J., & Herman, C. P. (1985). Dieting and binging: A causal analysis. *American Psychologist, 40,* 193–201.

Polson, B., & Newton, M. (1984). *Not my kid: A family's guide to kids and drugs.* New York: Arbor House.

Pool, I., & Moore, M. (1986). *Lone parenthood: Characteristics and determinants: Results from the 1984 family history survey.* Ottawa: Minister of Supply and Services (Housing, Family and Social Statistics Division).

Poon, L. W. (1985). Differences in human memory with aging: Nature, causes, and clinical implications. In J. E. Birren & K. W. Schaie (Eds.), *Handbook of the psychology of aging* (2nd ed.). New York: Van Nostrand Reinhold.

Pope, A. W., Bierman, K. L., & Mumma, G. H. (1991). Aggression, hyperactivity, and inattention-immaturity: Behavior dimensions associated with peer rejection in elementary school boys. *Developmental Psychology, 27*, 663–671.

Pope, H. G., Hudson, J. I., Jurgelun-Todd, D., & Hudson, M. S. (1984). Prevalence of anorexia nervosa and bulimia in three student populations. *International Journal of Eating Disorders, 2*, 75–85.

Post, G., & Crowther, J. H. (1985). Variables that discriminate bulimic from nonbulimic adolescent females. *Journal of Youth and Adolescence, 14*, 85–99.

Powell, M. B. (1991). Investigating and reporting child sexual abuse: Review and recommendations for clinical practice. *Australian Psychologist, 26*, 77–83.

Prado, W. (1958). *Appraisal of performance as a function of the relative-ego-involvement of children and adolescents.* Unpublished doctoral dissertation, University of Oklahoma, Norman, OK.

Preemies' diet seen key to progress. (1988, February 1). *Edmonton Journal*, p. C1.

Prendergast, J. M., & Armbrecht, H. J. (1990). The role of nutrition in ageing. In M. A. Horan & A. Brouwer (Eds.), *Gerontology: Approaches to biomedical and clinical research.* London: Edward Arnold.

Pressley, M., Forrest-Pressley, D., & Elliott-Faust, D. J. (1988). What is strategy instructional enrichment and how to study it: Illustrations from research on children's prose memory and comprehension. In F. E. Weinert & M. Perlmutter (Eds.), *Memory development: Universal changes and individual differences.* Hillsdale, NJ: Erlbaum.

Preyer, W. (1888–1889). *The mind of the child* (2 vols.). New York: Appleton-Century-Crofts. (First published in German, 1882.)

Pritchard, J., & MacDonald, P. (1984). *Williams obstetrics* (17th ed.). Englewood Cliffs, NJ: Prentice-Hall.

Putallaz, M., & Gottman, J. M. (1981). An interaction model of children's entry into peer groups. *Child Development, 52*, 986–994.

Quay, H. C. (1987). Intelligence. In H. C. Quay (Ed.), *Handbook of juvenile delinquency* (pp. 106–117). New York: John Wiley.

Quinlans have no regret—lawyer. (1983, March 19). *Edmonton Journal*, p. A2.

Quinn, R. P., Staines, G. L., & McCullough, M. (1974). *Job satisfaction: Is there a trend?* U.S. Department of Labor, Manpower Research Monograph No. 30. Washington, DC: U.S. Government Printing Office.

Raeburn, J. A. (1984). Mental handicap. In E. H. Emery & I. Pullen (Eds.), *Psychological aspects of genetic counseling.* New York: Academic Press.

Rahe, R. H. (1972). Subjects' recent life changes and their near-future illness susceptibility. In Z. J. Lipowski (Ed.), *Advances in psychosomatic medicine* (Vol. 8): *Psychosocial aspects of physical illness.* Basel, Switzerland: S. Karger.

Ramey, J. W. (1972). Emerging patterns of innovative behavior in marriage. *The Family Coordinator, 21*, 435–456.

Randhawa, B. S. (1991). Gender differences in academic achievement: A closer look at mathematics. *Alberta Journal of Educational Research, 37*, 241–257.

Rank, O. (1929). *The trauma of birth.* New York: Harcourt Brace Jovanovich.

Raskin, P. M. (1984). Procedures in research on identity status: Some notes on method. *Psychological Reports, 54*, 719–730.

Ratner, H. H., Padgett, R. J., & Bushey, N. (1988). Old and young adults' recall of events. *Developmental Psychology, 24*, 664–671.

Rawlings, G., Reynolds, E.O.R., Steward, A., & Strang, L. B. (1971). Changing prognosis for infants of very low birth weight. *The Lancet, 1*, 516–519.

Ray, W. J., & Ravizza, R. (1985). *Methods toward a science of behavior and experience* (2nd ed.). Belmont, CA: Wadsworth.

Rayna, S., Sinclair, H., & Stambak, M. (1989). Infants and physics. In H. Sinclair, M. Stambak, I. Lézine, S. Rayna, & M. Verba (Eds.), *Infants and objects: The creativity of cognitive development.* New York: Academic Press.

Rebok, G. W., & Balcerak, L. J. (1989). Memory self-efficacy and performance differences in young and old adults: The effect of mnemonic training. *Developmental Psychology, 25*, 714–721.

Recommended Dietary Allowances (9th ed.). (1980). Washington, DC: National Academy of Sciences.

Redmond, M. (1985). Attitudes of adolescent males toward adolescent pregnancy and fatherhood. *Family Relations, 34*, 337–342.

Reich, J. W., & Zautra, A. J. (1991). Analyzing the trait of routinization in older adults. *International Journal of Aging and Human Development, 32*, 161–180.

Reid, L. D., & Carpenter, D. J. (1990). Alcohol-abuse and alcoholism. In L. D. Reid (Ed.), *Opioids, bulimia, and alcohol abuse & alcoholism*. New York: Springer-Verlag.

Reissland, N. (1988). Neonatal imitation in the first hour of life: Observations in rural Nepal. *Developmental Psychology, 24*, 464–469.

Rescorla, L. (1991). Early academics: Introduction to the debate. *New Directions for Child Development, 53*, 5–11.

Rheingold, H. L. (1985). Development as the acquisition of familiarity. *Annual Review of Psychology, 36*, 1–17.

Rheingold, H. L., & Cook, K. V. (1975). The contents of boys' and girls' rooms as an index of parents' behavior. *Child Development, 46*, 459–463.

Rhodes, S. R. (1983). Age-related differences in work attitudes and behaviors: A review and conceptual analysis. *Psychological Bulletin, 93*, 328–367.

Rice, B. (1982, February). The Hawthorne defect: Persistence of a flawed theory. *Psychology Today*, pp. 71–74.

Rice, M. L. (1989). Children's language acquisition. *American Psychologist, 44*, 149–156.

Richardson, V., & Kilty, K. M. (1991). Adjustment to retirement: Continuity vs. discontinuity. *International Journal of Aging and Human Development, 33*, 151–169.

Ridley-Johnson, R., Surdy, T., & O'Laughlin, E. (1991). Parent survey on television violence viewing: Fear, aggression, and sex differences. *Journal of Applied Developmental Psychology, 12*, 63–71.

Riegel, K. F. (1970). The language acquisition process: A reinterpretation of selected research findings. In L. R. Goulet & P. B. Baltes (Eds.), *Life-span developmental psychology: Research and theory*. New York: Academic Press.

Riegel, K. F. (1972). Influence of economic and political ideologies on the development of developmental psychology. *Psychological Bulletin, 78*, 129–141.

Riegel, K. F. (1973a). Dialectic operations: The final period of cognitive development. *Human Development, 16*, 346–370.

Riegel, K. F. (1973b). Language and cognition: Some life-span developmental issues. *Gerontologist, 13*, 478–482.

Riegel, K. F. (1976). The dialectics of human development. *American Psychologist, 31*, 689–700.

Riegel, K. F., & Riegel, R. M. (1972). Development, drop, and death. *Developmental Psychology, 6*, 306–319.

Rimm, S. (1980). *The group inventory for finding creative talent*. Watertown, WI: Educational Assessment Services.

Rimmer, R. H. (1972). *Come live my life*. New York: Signet.

Rimmer, R. H. (1977). *Thursday, my love*. New York: Signet.

Ringler, N. M., Kennell, J. H., Harvella, R., Navojosky, B. J., & Klaus, M. H. (1975). Mother to child speech at two years: Effects of early postnatal contact. *Journal of Pediatrics, 86*, 141–144.

Ringwalt, C. L., & Palmer, J. H. (1989). Cocaine and crack users compared. *Adolescence, 24*, 851–859.

Rivera, G., & Regoli, R. (1987). Sexual victimization experiences of sorority women. *Sociology and Social Research, 72*, 39–42.

Roazen, P. (1975). *Freud and his followers*. New York: Alfred A. Knopf.

Roberts, P., & Newton, P. (1990). Levinsonian studies of women's adult development. *Psychology and Aging, 2*, 154–163.

Robinson, S. (1989). Caring for childbearing women: The interrelationship between midwifery and medical responsibilities. In S. Robinson & A. M. Thomson (Eds.), *Midwives, research and childbirth* (Vol. 1). New York: Chapman & Hall.

Rochat, P. (1989). Object manipulation and exploration in 2- to 5-month-old infants. *Developmental Psychology, 25*, 871–884.

Roche, A. F., Lipman, R. S., Overall, J. E., & Hung, W. (1979). The effects of stimulant medication on the growth of hyperkinetic children. *Pediatrics, 63*, 847–850.

Roethlisberger, S. J., & Dickson, W. J. (1939). *Management and the worker*. Cambridge, MA: Harvard University Press.

Roffwarg, H. P., Muzio, J. N., & Dement, W. C. (1966). Ontogenetic development of the human sleep-dream cycle. *Science, 152*, 604–619.

Rogers, C. R. (1951). *Client-centered therapy: Its current practice, its implications, and theory.* Boston: Houghton Mifflin.

Rolison, M. A., & Medway, F. J. (1985). Teachers' expectations and attributions for student achievement: Effects of label, performance, pattern, and special education intervention. *American Educational Research Journal, 22*, 561–573.

Rollins, B. C., & Feldman, H. (1981). Marital satisfaction over the family life cycle. In L. D. Steinberg (Ed.), *The life cycle: Readings in human development.* New York: Columbia University Press.

Roosa, M. W. (1991). Adolescent pregnancy programs collection: An introduction. *Family Relations, 40*, 370–372.

Roscoe, B., & Kruger, T. L. (1990). AIDS: Late adolescents' knowledge and its influence on sexual behavior. *Adolescence, 25*.

Rosengren, K. E., & Windahl, S. (1989). *Media matter: TV use in childhood and adolescence.* Norwood, NJ: Ablex.

Rosenkoetter, L. I., Huston, A. C., & Wright, J. C. (1990). Television and the moral judgment of the young child. *Journal of Applied Developmental Psychology, 11*, 123–137.

Rosenman, R. H., Brand, R. J., Jenkins, C. D., Friedman, M., Straus, R., & Wurm, M. (1975). Coronary heart disease in the western collaborative group study: Final follow-up experience of 8½ years. *Journal of the Medical Association, 233*, 872–877.

Rosenthal, R., & Jacobson, L. (1968a). *Pygmalion in the classroom: Teacher expectations and pupils' intellectual development.* New York: Holt, Rinehart & Winston.

Rosenthal, R., & Jacobson, L. (1968b). Teacher expectations for the disadvantaged. *Scientific American, 218*, 19–23.

Rosenthal, T. L., & Zimmerman, B. J. (1972). Modeling by exemplification and instruction in training conservation. *Developmental Psychology, 6*, 392–401.

Rosett, H. L., & Sander, L. W. (1979). Effects of maternal drinking on neonatal morphology and state regulation. In J. D. Osofsky (Ed.), *Handbook of infant development.* New York: John Wiley.

Ross, A. O. (1980). *Psychological disorders of children: A behavioral approach to theory, research, and therapy* (2nd ed.). New York: McGraw-Hill.

Ross, H. S. (1982). Establishment of social games among toddlers. *Developmental Psychology, 18*, 509–518.

Rossing, B. E. (1991). Patterns of informal incidental learning: Insights from community action. *International Journal of Lifelong Education, 10*, 45–60.

Rossman, I. (1977). Anatomic and body composition changes with aging. In C. Finch & L. Hayflick (Eds.), *Handbook of the biology of aging.* New York: Van Nostrand Reinhold.

Rothbart, M. K. (1982). The concept of difficult temperament: A critical analysis of Thomas, Chess, and Korn. *Merrill-Palmer Quarterly, 28*, 35–40.

Rothstein E. (1980, October 9). The scar of Sigmund Freud. *New York Review of Books*, pp. 14–20.

Rousseau, J. J. (1911). *Emile, or on education* (B. Foxley, Trans.). London: Dent. (Originally published 1762.)

Rovee-Collier, C. K. (1987). Learning and memory in infancy. In J. D. Osofsky (Ed.), *Handbook of infant development.* New York: John Wiley.

Rovee-Collier, C. K., Sullivan, M. W., Enright, M. L., Lucas, D., & Fagen, J. W. (1980). Reactivation of infant memory. *Science, 208*, 1159–1161.

Royal College of Psychiatrists (1987). *Drug scenes: A report on drugs and drug dependence by the Royal College of Psychiatrists.* London: Gaskell Press.

Rubin, J. Z., Provenzano, J. J., & Luria, Z. (1974). The eye of the beholder: Parents' views on sex of newborns. *American Journal of Orthopsychiatry, 44*, 512–519.

Rubin, K. H., Maioni, T. L., & Hornung, M. (1976). Free play behaviors in middle- and lower-class preschoolers: Parten and Piaget revisited. *Child Development, 47*, 414–419.

Rubin, L. B. (1978). *Women of a certain age: The midlife search for self.* New York: Harper.

Rubin, Z. (1970). Measurement of romantic love. *Journal of Personality and Social Psychology, 16*, 265–273.

Rubin, Z. (1980). *Children's friendships.* Cambridge, MA: Harvard University Press.

Rudel, R. G. (with J. M. Holmes & J. R. Pardes). (1988). *Assessment of developmental learning disorders: A neuropsychological approach.* New York: Basic Books.

Runco, M. A. (1986a). Flexibility and originality in children's divergent thinking. *The Journal of Psychology, 120,* 345–352.

Runco, M. A. (1986b). Maximal performance on divergent thinking tests by gifted, talented, and nongifted children. *Psychology in the Schools, 23,* 308–315.

Runco, M. A., & Albert, R. S. (1986). Exceptional giftedness in early adolescence and intrafamilial divergent thinking. *Journal of Youth and Adolescence, 15,* 335–344.

Russell, J. A. (1991). Culture and the categorization of emotions. *Psychological Bulletin, 110,* 426–450.

Ryan, E. B., Giles, H., Bartolucci, G., & Henwood, K. (1986). Psycholinguistic and social psychology components of communication by and with the elderly. *Language and Communication, 6,* 1–24.

Rybash, J. M., Hoyer, W. J., & Roodin, P. A. (1986). *Adult cognition and aging: Developmental changes in processing, thinking, and knowing.* New York: Pergamon.

Sagan, C. (1977). *The dragons of Eden.* New York: Ballantine Books.

Sagi, A., Ijzendoorn, M. H. Van, & Koren-Karie, N. (1991). Primary appraisal of the strange situation: A cross-cultural analysis of preseparation episodes. *Developmental Psychology, 27,* 587–596.

Salthouse, T. A. (1985). Speed of behavior and its implications for cognition. In J. E. Birren & K. W. Schaie (Eds.), *Handbook of the psychology of aging* (2nd ed.). New York: Van Nostrand Reinhold.

Salthouse, T. A., & Babcock, R. L. (1991). Decomposing adult age differences in working memory. *Developmental Psychology, 27,* 763–776.

Sameroff, A. J. (1968). The components of sucking in the human newborn. *Journal of Experimental Child Psychology, 6,* 607–623.

Sampson, J. P., Jr., & Reardon, R. C. (1990). Evaluating computer-assisted career guidance systems: Synthesis and implications. *Journal of Career Development, 17,* 143–149.

Sampson, J. P., Jr., Reardon, R. C., & Lenz, J. G. (1991). Computer-assisted career guidance: Improving the design and use of systems. *Journal of Career Development, 17,* 185–190.

Savin-Williams, R. C., & Small, S. A. (1986). The timing of puberty and its relationship to adolescent and parent perceptions of family interactions. *Developmental Psychology, 22,* 342–347.

Scanzoni, L. D., & Scanzoni, J. (1981). *Men, women, and change: A sociology of marriage and family* (2nd ed.). New York: McGraw-Hill.

Scarr, S. (1985). Constructing psychology: Making facts and fables for our times. *American Psychologist, 40,* 499–512.

Scarr, S., & Kidd, K. K. (1983). Developmental behavior genetics. In P. H. Mussen (Ed.), *Handbook of child psychology* (4th ed.) (Vol. 2): *Infancy and developmental psychobiology* (M. M. Haith & J. J. Campos, Eds.) (pp. 345–434). New York: John Wiley.

Scarr, S., & Salapatek, P. (1970). Patterns for fear development during infancy. *Merrill-Palmer Quarterly, 16,* 56–90.

Scarr, S., & Weinberg, R. A. (1983). The Minnesota adoption studies: Genetic differences and malleability. *Child Development, 54,* 260–267.

Scarr-Salapatek, S., & Williams, M. L. (1973). The effects of early stimulation on low-birth-weight infants. *Child Development, 44,* 94–101.

The "Scene" and the Skinheads. (1990, November 18). *Edmonton Journal,* p. E1.

Schaffer, H. R. (1966). The onset of fear of strangers and the incongruity hypothesis. *Journal of Child Psychology and Psychiatry, 7,* 95–106.

Schaffer, H. R. (1984). *The child's entry into a social world.* New York: Academic Press.

Schaie, K. W. (1965). A general model for the study of developmental problems. *Psychological Bulletin, 64,* 92–107.

Schaie, K. W. (Ed.). (1983a). *Longitudinal studies of adult psychological development.* New York: Guilford Press.

Schaie, K. W. (1983b). The Seattle longitudinal study: A 21-year exploration of psychometric intelligence in adulthood. In K. W. Schaie (Ed.), *Longitudinal studies of adult psychological development* (pp. 64–135). New York: Guilford Press.

Schaie, K. W. (1983c). What can we learn from the longitudinal study of adult psychological development? In K. W. Schaie (Ed.), *Longitudinal studies of adult psychological development* (pp. 1–19). New York: Guilford Press.

Schaie, K. W. (1986, December). Variability in cognitive function in the elderly: Implications for social participation. Paper presented at the Symposium on Phenotypic Variation in Populations: Relevance to Risk Assessment. Brookhaven National Laboratory, Upton, NY.

Schaie, K. W. (1988). Internal validity threats in studies of adult cognitive development. In M. L. Howe & C. J Brainerd (Eds.), *Cognitive development in adulthood: Progress in cognitive development research*. New York: Springer-Verlag.

Schaie, K. W., & Labouvie-Vief, G. (1974). Generational versus ontogenetic components of change in adult cognitive behavior: A fourteen year cross-sequential study. *Developmental Psychology, 10*, 305–320.

Schaie, K. W., Willis, S. L., Jay, G., & Chiuer, H. (1989). Structural invariance of cognitive abilities across the adult life span: A cross-sectional study. *Developmental Psychology, 25*, 652–662.

Schave, D., & Schave, B. (1989). *Early adolescence and the search for self: A developmental perspective*. New York: Praeger.

Scheiner, A. P., & McNabb, N. A. (1980). The child with mental retardation. In A. P. Scheiner & I. F. Abroms (Eds.), *The practical management of the developmentally disabled child*. St. Louis: C. V. Mosby.

Scher, J., & Dix, C. (1983). *Will my baby be normal? Everything you need to know about pregnancy*. New York: Dial Press.

Schiefelbusch, R. L., & McCormick, L. (1981). Language and speech disorders. In J. M. Kauffman & D. P. Hallahan (Eds.), *Handbook of Special Education*. Englewood Cliffs, NJ: Prentice-Hall.

Schlegel, A., & Barry, H., III. (1991). *Adolescence: An anthropological inquiry*. New York: Free Press.

Schmid, R. E., & Nagata, L. M. (1983). *Contemporary issues in special education*. New York: McGraw-Hill.

Schneider, D. J. (1991). Social cognition. *Annual Review of Psychology, 42*, 527–561.

Schneider, W., Borkowski, J. G., Kurtz, B. E., & Kerwin, K. (1986). Metamemory and motivation: A comparison of strategy use in German and American children. *Journal of Cross-Cultural Psychology, 17*, 315–336.

Schneider-Rosen, K., Braunwald, K. G., Carlson, V., & Cicchetti, D. (1985). Current perspectives in attachment theory: Illustration from the study of maltreated infants. In I. Bretherton & E. Waters (Eds.), *Growing points of attachment theory and research* (Monographs of the Society for Research in Child Development, 50, No. 209).

Schuller, T. (1989). Work-ending: Employment and ambiguity in later life. In B. Bytheway, T. Keil, P. Allatt, & A. Bryman (Eds.), *Becoming and being old: Sociological approaches to later life*. London: Sage.

Schultz, R., & Ewen, R. B. (1988). *Adult development and aging: Myths and emerging realities*. New York: Macmillan.

Schulz, D. A., & Rodgers, S. F. (1985). *Marriage, the family, and personal fulfillment* (3rd ed.). Englewood Cliffs, NJ: Prentice-Hall.

Schulz, R. (1985). Emotion and affect. In J. E. Birren & K. W. Schaie (Eds.), *Handbook of the psychology of aging* (2nd ed.). New York: Van Nostrand Reinhold.

Schumer, F. (1983). *Abnormal psychology*. Lexington, MA: D. C. Heath.

Schunk, D. H. (1984). Self-efficacy perspective on achievement behavior. *Educational Psychologist, 19*, 48–58.

Schwartzman, H. B. (1987). A cross-cultural perspective on child-structured play activities and materials. In A. W. Gottfried & C. C. Brown (Eds.), *Play interactions: The contribution of play materials and parental involvement to children's development*. Lexington, MA: D. C. Heath.

Scissons, E. H. (1985). *CareerScan: How to advance your career*. New York: Dembner Books.

Sears, P. S., & Barbee, A. H. (1977). Care and life satisfactions among Terman's gifted women. In J. C. Stanley, W. C. George, and C. H. Solano (Eds.), *The gifted and the creative: A fifty-year perspective*. Baltimore: Johns Hopkins University Press.

Sears, R. R., Maccoby, E. P., & Levin, H. (1957). *Patterns of child rearing*. New York: Harper & Row.

Sebald, H. (1984). *Adolescence: A social psychological analysis* (3rd ed.). Englewood Cliffs, NJ: Prentice-Hall.

Seelbach, W. C. (1984). Filial responsibility and the care of aging family members. In W. H. Quinn & G. A. Hughston (Eds.), *Independent aging: Family and social systems perspectives* (pp. 92–105). Rockville, MD: Aspen.

Seligman, M.E.P. (1975). *Helplessness: On depression, development, and death.* San Francisco: W. H. Freeman.

Selman, R. L. (1980). *The growth of interpersonal understanding.* New York: Academic Press.

Selman, R. L. (1981). The child as friendship philosopher. In S. R. Asher & J. M. Gottman (Eds.), *The development of children's friendships.* New York: Cambridge University Press.

Selye, H. (1974). *Stress without distress.* Philadelphia: J. B. Lippincott.

Seymour, D. (1971, November). Black children, black speech. *Commonweal*, p. 19.

Shanas, E. (1980). Older people and their families: The new pioneers. *Journal of Marriage and the Family, 42,* 9–15.

Shantz, C. U. (1975). The development of social cognition. In E. M. Hetherington (Ed.), *Review of child development research* (Vol. 5). Chicago: University of Chicago Press.

Shantz, C. U. (1983). Social cognition. In P. H. Mussen (Ed.), *Handbook of child psychology* (Vol. 3): *Cognitive Development* (J. H. Flavell & E. M. Markman, Eds.). New York: John Wiley.

Shedler, J., & Block, J. (1990). Adolescent drug use and psychological health: A longitudinal inquiry. *American Psychologist, 45,* 612–630.

Sheehy, G. (1976). *Passages: Predictable crises of adult life.* New York: E. P. Dutton.

Sheehy, G. (1981). *Pathfinders.* New York: Morrow.

Shepard, L. A., Smith, M. L., & Vojir, C. P. (1983). Characteristics of pupils identified as learning disabled. *American Educational Research Journal, 20,* 309–331.

Shepherd-Look, D. L. (1982). Sex differentiation and the development of sex roles. In B. B. Wolman et al. (Eds.), *Handbook of developmental psychology.* Englewood Cliffs, NJ: Prentice-Hall.

Sheppard, H. (1976). Work and retirement. In R. Binstock & E. Shanas (Eds.), *Handbook of aging and the social sciences.* New York: Van Nostrand Reinhold.

Sherman, M., & Key, C. B. (1932). The intelligence of isolated mountain children. *Child Development, 3,* 279–290.

Sherman, M., & Sherman, I. C. (1929). *The process of human behavior.* New York: W. W. Norton.

Shneidman, E. S. (1976). Death work and stages of dying. In E. Shneidman (Ed.), *Death: Current perspectives.* Palo Alto, CA: Mayfield.

Shotland, R. L., & Straw, M. K. (1976). Bystander response to an assault: When a man attacks a woman. *Journal of Personality and Social Psychology, 3,* 65–74.

Showers, C., & Cantor, N. (1985). Social cognition: A look at motivated strategies. *Annual Review of Psychology, 36,* 275–305.

Schreve, B. W., & Kunkel, M. A. (1991). Self-psychology, shame, and adolescent suicide: Theoretical and practical considerations. *Journal of Counseling and Development, 69,* 305–311.

Siegel, A. W., & White, S. H. (1982). The child study movement: Early growth and development of the symbolized child. In H. W. Reese (Ed.), *Advances in child development and behavior* (Vol. 17). New York: Academic Press.

Siegel, O. (1982). Personality development in adolescence. In B. B. Wolman et al. (Eds.), *Handbook of developmental psychology.* Englewood Cliffs, NJ: Prentice-Hall.

Siegler, R. S. (1989). Mechanisms of cognitive development. *Annual Review of Psychology, 40,* 353–379.

Siegler, R. S., & Liebert, R. M. (1972). Effects of presenting relevant rules and complete feedback on the conservation of liquid quantity task. *Developmental Psychology, 7,* 133–138.

Sigel, I. E. (1987). Does Hothousing rob children of their childhood? *Early Childhood Research Quarterly, 2,* 211–225.

Silverstein, F. S., & Johnston, M. V. (1990). Neurological assessment of children: The damaged child. In R. D. Eden, F. H. Boehm, & M. Haire (Eds.), *Assessment and care of the fetus: Physiological, clinical, and medicolegal principles*, Norwalk, CT: Appleton & Lange.

Silverstein, L. B. (1991). Transforming the debate about child care and maternal employment. *American Psychologist, 46,* 1025–1032.

Silvestri, G. T., & Lukasiewicz, J. M. (1989). Projections of occupational employment: 1988–2000. *Monthly Labor Review, 112*, 42–65.

Simmons, L. (1960). Aging in preindustrial societies. In C. Tibbitts (Ed.), *Handbook of social gerontology*. Chicago: University of Chicago Press.

Sinclair, D. (1989). *Human growth after birth* (5th ed.). New York: Oxford University Press.

Sinclair, H., Stambak, M., Lézine, I., Rayna, S., & Verba, M. (Eds.). (1989). *Infants and objects: The creativity of cognitive development.* New York: Academic Press.

Singer, J. L. (Ed.). (1973). *The child's world of make-believe: Experimental studies of imaginative play.* New York: Academic Press.

Singer, J. L., & Singer, D. G. (1983). Implications of childhood television viewing for cognition, imagination, and emotion. In J. Bryant & D. R. Anderson (Eds.), *Children's understanding of television: Research on attention and comprehension* (pp. 265–297). New York: Academic Press.

Singer, R. S. (1982). Childhood, aggression and television. *Television and Children, 5*, 57–63.

Singh, J. A., & Zingg, R. N. (1942). *Wolf-children and feral man.* New York: Harper & Row.

Skinner, B. F. (1953). *Science and human behavior.* New York: Macmillan.

Skinner, B. F. (1957). *Verbal behavior.* Englewood Cliffs, NJ: Prentice-Hall.

Skinner, B. F. (1961). *Cumulative record* (rev. ed.). New York: Appleton-Century-Crofts.

Skolnick, A. (1978, February). The myth of the vulnerable child. *Psychology Today*, pp. 56–60, 65.

Skolnick, A. (1981). Married lives: Longitudinal perspectives on marriage. In D. H. Eichorn, J. A. Clausen, N. Haan, M. P. Honzik, & P. H. Mussen (Eds.), *Present and past in middle life.* New York: Academic Press.

Slaby, A. E. (1989). Psychotropic and psychedelic emergencies. In A. J. Giannini & A. E. Slaby (Eds.), *Drugs of abuse.* Oradell, NJ: Medical Economics Books.

Sloan, D., Shapiro, S., & Mitchell, A. A. (1980). Strategies for studying the effects of the antenatal chemical environment on the fetus. In R. H. Schwarz & S. J. Yaffe (Eds.), *Drug and chemical risks to the fetus and newborn.* New York: Alan R. Liss.

Sloan, E. (1985). *Biology and women* (2nd ed.). New York: John Wiley.

Sloane, B. (1983). Health care: Physical and mental. In D. S. Woodruff & J. E. Birren (Eds.), *Aging: Scientific perspectives and social issues* (2nd ed.) (pp. 305–332). Pacific Grove, CA: Brooks/Cole.

Small, S. A., & Eastman, G. (1991). Rearing adolescents in contemporary society: A conceptual framework for understanding the responsibilities and needs of parents. *Family Relations, 40*, 455–462.

Smith, C. A. (1947). The effect of wartime starvation in Holland upon pregnancy and its product. *American Journal of Obstetrics and Gynecology, 53*, 599–608.

Smith, C. L. (1979). Children's understanding of natural language hierarchies. *Journal of Experimental Child Psychology, 27*, 437–458.

Smith, D. A., & Graesser, A. C. (1981). Memory for actions in scripted activities as a function of typicality, retention interval, and retrieval task. *Memory and Cognition, 9*, 550–559.

Smith, P. B., Weinman, M., & Malinak, L. R. (1984). Adolescent mothers and fetal loss, what is learned from experience? *Psychological Reports, 55*, 775–778.

Smoll, F. L., & Schutz, R. W. (1990). Quantifying gender differences in physical performance: A developmental perspective. *Developmental Psychology, 26*, 360–369.

Snyder, L. A., Freifelder, D., & Hartl, D. L. (1985). *General genetics.* Boston: Jones & Bartlett.

Snyderman, M., & Rothman, S. (1987). Survey of expert opinion on intelligence and aptitude testing. *American Psychologist, 42*, 137–144.

Solnick, R. E., & Corby, N. (1983). Human sexuality and aging. In D. S. Woodruff & J. E. Birren (Eds.), *Aging: Scientific perspectives and social issues* (2nd ed.) (pp. 202–224). Pacific Grove, CA: Brooks/Cole.

Sorensen, R. C. (1973). *Adolescent sexuality in contemporary America.* New York: William Collins.

Southall, D. P. (1988). Role of apnea in the sudden infant death syndrome: A personal view. *Pediatrics, 80*, 73–84.

Spearman, C. (1927). *The abilities of man.* New York: Macmillan.

Spellacy, W. N., Miller, S. J., & Winegar, A. (1986). Pregnancy after 40 years of age. *Obstetrics and Gynecology, 68,* 452–454.

Spence, A. P. (1989). *Biology of human aging.* Englewood Cliffs, NJ: Prentice-Hall.

Spitz, R. A. (1945). Hospitalism: An inquiry into the genesis of psychiatric conditions in early childhood. Part 1. *Psychoanalytic Studies of the Child, 1,* 53–74.

Spitz, R. A. (1954). Unhappy and fatal outcomes of emotional deprivation and stress in infancy. In I. Galdston (Ed.), *Beyond the germ theory.* Washington, DC: Health Education Council.

Springer, C., & Wallerstein, J. S. (1983). Young adolescents' responses to their parents' divorces. In L. A. Kurdek (Ed.), *Children and divorce: New directions for child development* (pp. 15–28). San Francisco: Jossey-Bass.

Springer, N. S. (1982). *Nutritional casebook on developmental disabilities.* New York: Syracuse University Press.

Spurlock, J. (1984). Black women in the middle years. In G. Baruch & J. Brooks-Gunn (Eds.), *Women in midlife.* New York: Plenum.

Sroufe, L., & Waters, E. (1976). The ontogenesis of smiling and laughter: A perspective on the organization of development in infancy. *Psychological Review, 83,* 173–189.

Sroufe, L., & Wunsch, J. (1972). The development of laughter in the first year of life. *Child Development, 43,* 1326–1344.

Stall, R. D., Coates, T. J., & Hoff, C. (1988). Behavioral risk reduction for HIV infection among gay and bisexual men. *American Psychologist, 43,* 878–885.

Stambak, M., Sinclair, H., Verba, M., Moreno, L., & Rayna, S. (1989). Infants and logic. In H. Sinclair, M. Stambak, I. Lézine, S. Rayna, & M. Verba (Eds.), *Infants and objects: The creativity of cognitive development.* New York: Academic Press.

Starr, R. H., Jr. (1979). Child abuse. *American Psychologist, 34,* 872–878.

Starr, R. H., Jr. (1982). A research-based approach to the prediction of child abuse. In R. H. Starr, Jr. (Ed.), *Child abuse prediction: Policy implications.* Cambridge, MA: Ballinger.

Starr, R. H., Jr., Dietrich, K. N., & Fischoff, J. (1981, April). *The contribution of children to their own abuse.* Paper presented at a meeting of the Society for Research in Child Development, Boston, MA.

Statistics Canada (1992). *Earnings of men and women: 1990.* Ottawa: Minister of Industry, Science and Technology.

Steenbarger, B. N. (1991). All the world is not a stage: Emerging contextualist themes in counseling and development. *Journal of Counseling and Development, 70,* 288–296.

Stein, S. B. (1983). *Girls and boys: The limits of nonsexist childrearing.* New York: Scribner's.

Stein, Z., Susser, M., Saenger, G., & Marolla, F. (1975). *Famine and human development: The Dutch hunger winter of 1944–1945.* New York: Oxford University Press.

Steinberg, L., & Silverberg, S. B. (1988). Influences on marital satisfaction during the middle stages of the family life cycle. *Journal of Marriage and the Family, 49,* 751–760.

Steiner, J. E. (1979). Human facial expressions in response to taste and smell stimulation. In H. Reese & L. Lipsitt (Eds.), *Advances in child development and behavior* (Vol. 13). New York: Academic Press.

Stern, C. (1956). Hereditary factors affecting adoption. In *A Study of Adoption Practices* (Vol. 2). New York: Child Welfare League of America.

Stern, D. N., Spieker, S., Barnett, R. K., & MacKain, K. (1983). The prosody of maternal speech: Infant age and context related changes. *Journal of Child Language, 10,* 1–15.

Stern, P. C. (1992). Psychological dimensions of global environmental change. *Annual Review of Psychology, 43,* 269–302.

Sternberg, R. J. (1984). A contextualist view of the nature of intelligence. *International Journal of Psychology, 19,* 307–334.

Sternberg, R. J. (1985). *Beyond IQ: A triarchic theory of human intelligence.* New York: Cambridge University Press.

Sternberg, R. J. (1986). *Intelligence applied: Understanding and increasing your intellectual skills.* New York: Harcourt Brace Jovanovich.

Sternberg, R. J., & Berg, C. (1987). What are theories of adult intellectual development theories of? In C. Schooler & K. W. Schaie (Eds.), *Cognitive functioning and social structure over the life course.* Norwood, NJ: Ablex.

Stevens-Long, J. (1990). Adult development: Theories past and future. In R. A. Nemiroff & C. A. Colarusso (Eds.), *New dimensions in adult development.* New York: Basic Books.

Stifter, C. A., & Fox, N. A. (1990). Infant reactivity: Physiological correlates of newborn and 5-month temperament. *Developmental Psychology, 26,* 582–588.

Stimpson, D., Neff, W., Jensen, L. C., & Newby, T. (1991). The caring morality and gender differences. *Psychological Reports, 69,* 407–414.

Stockman, J. A., III. (1990). Fetal hematology. In R. D. Eden, F. H. Boehm, & M. Haire (Eds.), *Assessment and care of the fetus: Physiological, clinical, and medicolegal principles.* Norwalk, CT: Appleton & Lange.

Stones, M. J., & Kozma, A. (1988). Physical activity, age, and cognitive/motor performance. In M. L. Howe & C. J. Brainerd (Eds.), *Cognitive development in adulthood: Progress in cognitive development research.* New York: Springer-Verlag.

Strangler, R. S., & Printz, A. M. (1980). DSM-III: Psychiatric diagnosis in a university population. *American Journal of Psychiatry, 137,* 937–940.

Stratton, P. (1988). Parents' conceptualization of children as the organizer of culturally structured environments. In J. Valsiner (Ed.), *Child development within culturally structured environments.* Vol. 1: *Parental cognition and adult–child interaction.* Norwood, NJ: Ablex.

Straus, M. A. (1980a). The marriage license as a hitting license: Evidence from popular culture, law, and social science. In M. A. Straus & G. T. Hotaling (Eds.), *The social causes of husband–wife violence.* Minneapolis: University of Minnesota Press.

Straus, M. A. (1980b). Wife-beating: How common and why? In M. A. Straus & G. T. Hotaling (Eds.), *The social causes of husband–wife violence.* Minneapolis: University of Minnesota Press.

Straus, M. A., & Gelles, R. (1986). Societal change and change in family violence from 1975 to 1985 as revealed by two national surveys. *Journal of Marriage and the Family, 48,* 465–479.

Strean, H. S. (1980). *The extramarital affair.* New York: Free Press.

Streissguth, A. P., Landesman-Dwyer, S., Martin, J. C., & Smith, D. W. (1980). Teratogen effects of alcohol in humans and laboratory animals. *Science, 209,* 353–361.

Strelau, J. (1989). Temperament risk factors in children and adolescents as studied in Eastern Europe. In W. B. Carey & S. C. McDevitt (Eds.), *Clinical and educational applications of temperament research.* Berwyn, PA: Swets North America.

Stuart, R. B. (1969). Critical reappraisal and reformulation of selected "mental health" programs. In L. A. Hamerlynck, P. O. Davidson, & L. E. Acker (Eds.), *Behavior modification and mental health services.* Calgary, Alta.: University of Calgary Press.

Super, D. E. (1957). *The psychology of careers.* New York: Harper & Row.

Super, D. E. (1974). Vocational maturity theory. In D. E. Super (Ed.), *Measuring vocational maturity for counseling and evaluation.* Washington, DC: National Vocational Guidance Association.

Super, D. E., & Hall, D. T. (1978). Career development: Exploration and planning. In M. R. Rosenzweig & L. W. Porter (Eds.), *Annual review of psychology* (Vol. 29). Palo Alto, CA: Annual Reviews.

Szewczuk, M. R., & Mackay, I. R. (1985). Cellular aspects of altered immune response in aging. In G. L. Maddox & E. W. Busse (Eds.), *Aging: The universal human experience.* New York: Springer.

Talbot, J. F., & Kaplan, R. (1991). The benefits of nearby nature for elderly apartment residents. *International Journal of Aging and Human Development, 33,* 119–130.

Tallmer, M., Formanek, R., & Tallmer, J. (1974). Factors influencing children's concepts of death. *Journal of Clinical Child Psychology, 3,* 17–19.

Tamir, L. (1982). *Men in their forties: The transition to middle age.* New York: Springer.

Tanner, J. M. (1955). *Growth at adolescence.* Springfield, IL: Thomas.

Tanner, J. M. (1975). Sequence, tempo and individual variation in the growth and development of boys and girls aged twelve to sixteen. In R. E. Grinder (Ed.), *Studies in adolescence* (pp. 502–522). New York: Macmillan.

Tavris, C., & Baumgartner, A. I. (1983, February). How would your life be different if you'd been born a boy? *Redbook*, p. 99.

Taylor, C. (1989). *Sources of the self.* Cambridge, MA: Harvard University Press.

Teahan, J., & Kastenbaum, R. (1970). Subjective life expectancy and future time perspective as predictors of job success in the "hard core unemployed." *Omega, 1,* 189–200.

Teenage pregnancy: The problem that hasn't gone away. (1981). The Alan Guttmacher Institute.

Television and your children. (1985). Ontario, Canada: TV Ontario, The Ontario Educational Communications Authority.

Telfer, M. A., Baker, D., Clark, G. R., & Richardson, C. E. (1968). Incidence of gross chromosomal errors among tall, criminal American males. *Science, 159,* 1249–1250.

Terkel, S. (1972). *Working.* New York: Random House.

Terman, L. M., assisted by B. T. Baldwin et al. (1925). *Genetic studies of genius* (Vol. 1). Stanford, CA: Stanford University Press.

Termine, N. T., & Izard, C. E. (1988). Infants' responses to their mothers' expressions of joy and sadness. *Developmental Psychology, 24,* 223–229.

Terrace, H. S. (1985). In the beginning was the "Name." *American Psychologist, 40,* 1011–1028.

Terry, R., & Coie, J. D. (1991). A comparison of methods for defining sociometric status among children. *Developmental Psychology, 27,* 867–880.

Thomas, A., & Chess, S. (1981). The role of temperament in the contribution of individuals to their development. In R. M. Lerner & N. A. Busch-Rossnagel (Eds.), *Individuals as producers of their development.* New York: Academic Press.

Thomas, A., Chess, S., & Birch, H. G. (1968). *Temperament and behavior disorders in children.* New York: New York University Press.

Thomas, A., Chess, S., & Birch, H.G. (1970). The origin of personality. *Scientific American, 223,* 102–109.

Thomas, A., Chess, S., & Korn, S. J. (1982). The reality of difficult temperament. *Merrill-Palmer Quarterly, 28,* 1–20.

Thomas, J. W. (1980). Agency and achievement: Self-management and self-regard. *Review of Educational Research, 50,* 213–240.

Thomas, R. M. (1992). *Comparing theories of child development* (3rd ed.). Belmont, CA: Wadsworth.

Thompson, R. F. (1975). *Introduction to physiological psychology.* New York: Harper & Row.

Thorndike, R. L., & Hagen, E. (1977). *Measurement and evaluation in psychology and education* (4th ed.). New York: John Wiley.

Thorndike, R. L., Hagen, E., & Sattler, J. M. (1985). *Revised Stanford-Binet intelligence scale* (4th ed.). Boston: Houghton Mifflin.

Thornton, A., & Freedman, D. (1983). The changing American family. *Population Bulletin, 38.* Washington, DC: Population Reference Bureau.

Thurstone, L. L. (1938). Primary mental abilities. *Psychometric Monographs, 1.* Chicago: University of Chicago Press.

Timiras, P. S. (1972). *Developmental physiology and aging.* New York: Macmillan.

Tittle, C. K. (1982). Career counseling in contemporary U.S. high schools. An addendum to Rehberg and Hotchkiss. *Educational Researcher, 11,* 12–18.

Tobin, S. S., & Kulys, R. (1981). The family in the institutionalization of the elderly. *Journal of Social Issues, 37,* 145–157.

Toffler, A. (1970). *Future shock.* New York: Random House.

Tolman, C. (1983). Further comments on the meaning of dialectic. *Human Development, 26,* 320–324.

Tomlin, A. M., & Passman, R. H. (1989). Grandmothers' responsibility in raising two-year olds facilitates their grandchildren's adaptive behavior: A preliminary intrafamilial investigation of mothers' and maternal grandmothers' effects. *Psychology and Aging, 4,* 119–121.

Toray, T., Coughlin, C., Vuchinich, S., & Patricelli, P. (1991). Gender differences associated with adolescent substance abuse: Comparisons and implications for treatment. *Family Relations, 40,* 338–344.

Torrance, E. P. (1966). Torrance's tests of creative thinking. *Norms technical manual.* Princeton, NJ: Personnel Press.

Torrance, E. P. (1974). *Torrance tests of creative thinking.* Lexington, MA: Ginn.

Torres, D. A. (1982). Youths and alcohol abuse: A continuing phenomenon. *Journal of Alcohol and Drug Education, 27,* 74–82.

Trawick-Smith, J. (1989). Play is not learning: A critical review of the literature. *Child and Youth Care Quarterly, 18,* 161–170.

Trehub, S. E., Schneider, B. A., Thorpe, L. A., & Judge, P. (1991). Observational measures of auditory sensitivity in early infancy. *Developmental Psychology, 27,* 40–49.

Trickett, P. K., Aber, J. L., Carlson, V., & Cicchetti, D. (1991). Relationship of socioeconomic status to the etiology and developmental sequelae of physical child abuse. *Developmental Psychology, 27,* 148–158.

Trickett, P. K., & Susman, E. J. (1988). Parental perceptions of child-rearing practices in physically abusive and nonabusive families. *Developmental Psychology, 24,* 270–276.

Trofatter, K. F., Jr. (1990). Fetal immunology. In R. D. Eden, F. H. Boehm, & M. Haire (Eds.), *Assessment and care of the fetus: Physiological, clinical, and medicolegal principles.* Norwalk, CT: Appleton & Lange.

Troll, L. E. (1982). *Continuations: Adult development and aging.* Pacific Grove, CA: Brooks/Cole.

Troll, L. E. (1985). *Early and middle adulthood* (2nd ed.). Pacific Grove, CA: Brooks/Cole.

Troll, L. E., Miller, S., & Atchley, R. C. (1979). *Families of later life.* Belmont, CA: Wadsworth.

Tronick, E. Z. (1989). Emotions and emotional communication in infants. *American Psychologist, 44,* 112–119.

Trost, J. (1981). Cohabitation in the Nordic countries: From deviant phenomenon to social institution. *Alternative Lifestyles, 4,* 401–427.

Tryon, R. C. (1949). Genetic differences in maze learning in rats. *Yearbook of the National Society for Studies in Education, 39,* 111–119.

Tsang, M. C. (1988). Cost analysis for educational policymaking: A review of cost studies in education in developing countries. *Review of Educational Research, 58,* 181–230.

Tuma, J. M. (1989). Mental health services for children. *American Psychologist, 44,* 188–195.

Turkheimer, E. (1991). Individual and group differences in adoption studies of IQ. *Psychological Bulletin, 110,* 392–405.

Turkheimer, E., & Gottesman, I. I. (1991). Individual differences and the canalization of human behavior. *Developmental Psychology, 27,* 18–22.

Turner, B. F., & Turner, C. B. (1991). Bem Sex-Role Inventory stereotypes for men and women varying in age and race among National Register psychologists. *Psychological Reports, 69,* 931–944.

Turner, B. L., II, Clark, W. C., Kates, R. W., Richards, J. F., Mathews, J. T. et al. (Eds.). (1991). *The earth as transformed by human action.* New York: Cambridge University Press.

Turner, R. J., & Sternberg, M. P. (1978). Psychosocial factors in elderly patients admitted to a psychiatric hospital. *Age and Ageing, 7,* 171–177.

U.S. Bureau of the Census. (1988). *Statistical abstracts of the United States, 1987* (108th ed.). Washington, DC: U.S. Government Printing Office.

U.S. Bureau of the Census. (1990). *Statistical Abstracts of the United States, 1990* (110th ed.). Washington, DC: U.S. Government Printing Office.

U.S. Bureau of the Census. (1991). *Statistical Abstracts of the United States, 1991* (111th ed.). Washington, DC: U.S. Government Printing Office.

U.S. Department of Commerce, Bureau of the Census. (1980). *Social indicators III: Selected data on social conditions and trends in the United States.* Washington, DC: U.S. Government Printing Office.

U.S. Department of Health and Human Services. (1981). *The health consequences of smoking: The changing cigarette; A report of the Surgeon General.* Washington, DC: U.S. Government Printing Office.

U.S. Department of Health and Human Services. (1986). *Health, United States, 1986.* DDH Publication No. PHS 87-1232. Washington, DC: U.S. Government Printing Office.

U.S. Department of Health and Human Services. (1988, September). *Monthly Vital Statistics Report* (Vol. 37, no. 6). Public Health Service. Centers for Disease Control. Washington, DC: U.S. Government Printing Office.

U.S. Department of Health and Human Services. (1989, February). *Monthly Vital Statistics Report* (Vol. 37, no. 11). Public Health Service. Centers for Disease Control. Washington, DC: U.S. Government Printing Office.

U.S. Department of Justice, Federal Bureau of Investigation. (1984). *Uniform crime reports for 1983.* Washington, DC: U.S. Government Printing Office.

U.S. Department of Labor. (1988, November). *Employment and earnings* (G. P. Green & R. K. Epstein, Eds.) (Vol. 35, no. 11). Washington, DC: Bureau of Labor Statistics.

Užgiris, I. C., Benson, J. B., Kruper, J. C., & Vasek, M. E. (1989). Contextual influences on imitative interactions between mothers and infants. In J. J. Lockman & N. L. Hazen (Eds.), *Action in social context: Perspectives on early development.* New York: Plenum.

Vaillant, G. E. (1977). *Adaptation to life.* Boston: Little, Brown.

Vaillant, G. E. (1978). Natural history of male psychological health: VI. Correlates of successful marriage and fatherhood. *American Journal of Psychiatry, 135,* 653–659.

Vaillant, G. E., & Milofsky, E. (1980). Natural history of male psychological health: IX. Empirical evidence for Erikson's model of the life cycle. *The American Journal of Psychiatry, 137,* 1348–1359.

Vaitenas, R., & Wiener, Y. (1977). Development, emotional, and interest factors in voluntary midcareer change. *Journal of Vocational Behavior, 11,* 291–304.

Valsiner, J. (1987). *Culture and the development of children's action: A cultural-historical theory of developmental psychology.* New York: John Wiley.

Vandell, D. L., & Ramanan, J. (1991). Children of the National Longitudinal Survey of Youth: Choices in after-school care and child development. *Developmental Psychology, 27,* 637–643.

Vandell, D. L., Wilson, K. S., & Buchanan, N. R. (1980). Peer interaction in the first year of life: An examination of its structure, content, and sensitivity to toys. *Child Development, 51,* 481–488.

Vandenberg, B. R. (1987). Beyond the ethology of play. In A. W. Gottfried & C. C. Brown (Eds.), *Play interactions: The contribution of play materials and parental involvement to children's development.* Lexington, MA: D. C. Heath.

Varga, D. (1991). The historical ordering of children's play as a developmental task. *Play and Culture, 4,* 322–333.

Verhaaren, P., & Connor, F. P. (1981). Physical disabilities. In J. M. Kauffman, & D. P. Hallahan (Eds.), *Handbook of special education* (pp. 248–289). Englewood Cliffs, NJ: Prentice-Hall.

Vinovskis, M. A. (1988). The historian and the life course: Reflections on recent approaches to the study of American family life in the past. In P. B. Baltes, D. L. Featherman, & R. M. Lerner (Eds.), *Life-span development and behavior* (Vol. 8). Hillsdale, NJ: Erlbaum.

Visher, E. B., & Visher, J. S. (1982). *How to win as a stepfamily.* New York: Dembner.

Visher, E. B., & Visher, J. S. (1988). *Old loyalties, new ties.* New York: Brunner/Mazel.

von Hofsten, C., & Lindhagen, K. (1979). Observations on the development of reaching for moving objects. *Journal of Experimental Child Psychology, 28,* 158–173.

Vorhees, C. V., & Mollnow, E. (1987). Behavioral teratogenesis: Long-term influences on behavior from early exposure to environmental agents. In J. D. Osofsky (Ed.), *Handbook of infant development.* New York: John Wiley.

Vygotsky, L. S. (1986). *Thought and language* (translated and revised by A. Kozulin). Cambridge, MA: MIT Press.

Waddington, C. H. (1975). *The evolution of an evolutionist.* Edinburgh: Edinburgh University Press.

Wadsworth, B. J. (1989). *Piaget's theory of cognitive and affective development* (4th ed.). New York: Longman.

Wakefield, J. F. (1991). The outlook for creativity tests. *The Journal of Creative Behavior, 25,* 184–193.

Walker, J. J. (1978). The gifted and talented. In E. L. Meyen (Ed.), *Exceptional children and youth: An introduction.* Denver, CO: Love.

Walker, L. J. (1988). The development of moral reasoning. In R. Vasta (Ed.), *Annals of child development* (Vol. 5). Greenwich, CT: JAI Press.

Wallach, M. A., & Kogan, N. (1965). *Modes of thinking in young children: A study of the creativity–intelligence distinction.* New York: Holt, Rinehart & Winston.

Wallerstein, J. S. (1989, January 23). Children after divorce: Wounds that don't heal. *The New York Times Magazine,* pp. 19–21, 41–44.

Wallerstein, J. S., & Kelly, J. B. (1974). The effects of parental divorce: The adolescent experience. In E. J. Anthony & C. Koupernik (Eds.), *The child in his family: Children at psychiatric risk* (Vol. 3). New York: John Wiley.

Wallerstein, J. S., & Kelly, J. B. (1975). The effects of parental divorce: Experiences of the preschool child. *Journal of the American Academy of Child Psychiatry, 14*, 600–616.

Wallerstein, J. S., & Kelly, J. B. (1976). The effects of parental divorce: Experiences of the child in later latency. *American Journal of Orthopsychiatry, 46*, 256–269.

Wallerstein, J. S., & Kelly, J. B. (1980). *Surviving the breakup: How children and parents cope with divorce.* London: Grant McIntyre.

Walsh, B. T. (1982). Endocrine disturbance in anorexia nervosa and depression. *Psychosomatic Medicine, 44*, 85–91.

Walsh, D. A., & Thompson, L. W. (1978). Age differences in visual sensory memory. *Journal of Gerontology, 33*, 383–387.

Walster, E., Aronsen, V., Abrahams, D., & Rottman, L. (1966). Importance of physical attractiveness in dating behavior. *Journal of Personality and Social Psychology, 4*, 508–516.

Ward, R. A. (1979). *The aging experience: An introduction to social gerontology.* Philadelphia: Lippincott.

Ward, S. K., Chapman, K., Cohn, E., White, S., & Williams, K. (1991). Acquaintance rape and the college social scene. *Family Relations, 40*, 65–71.

Warnes, A. M. (1985). Microlocational issues in housing for the elderly. In G. L. Maddox & E. W. Busse (Eds.), *Aging: The universal human experience.* New York: Springer.

Warren-Leubecker, A., & Bohannon, J. N. (1984). Intonation patterns in child-directed speech: Mother–father differences. *Child Development, 55*, 1379–1385.

Warshak, R. A., & Santrock, J. W. (1983). The impact of divorce in father-custody and mother-custody homes. The child's perspective. In L. A. Kurdek (Ed.), *Children and divorce: New directions for child development* (pp. 29–46). San Francisco: Jossey-Bass.

Washton, A. M. (1989). *Cocaine addiction: Treatment, recovery, and relapse prevention.* New York: W. W. Norton.

Wasserman, G. (1980). The nature and function of early mother–infant interaction. In B. L. Blum (Ed.), *Psychological aspects of pregnancy, birthing, and bonding.* New York: Human Sciences Press.

Waterman, A. S. (1984). Identity formation: Discovery or creation? *Journal of Early Adolescence, 4*, 329–341.

Waterman, A. S. (1988). Identity status theory and Erikson's theory: Commonalities and differences. *Developmental Review, 8*, 185–208.

Waters, E. (1980). Traits, relationships, and behavioral systems: The attachment construct and the organization of behavior and development. In K. Immelman, E. Barlow, M. Main, & L. Petrinovich (Eds.), *Development of behavior.* New York: Cambridge University Press.

Waters, E., Hay, D., & Richters, J. (1986). Infant–parent attachment and the origins of prosocial and antisocial behavior. In D. Olweus, J. Block, & M. Radke-Yarrow (Eds.), *Development of antisocial and prosocial behavior: Research, theories, and issues.* New York: Academic Press.

Watson, J. B. (1914). *Behavior: An introduction to comparative psychology.* New York: Holt, Rinehart & Winston.

Watson, J. B., & Rayner, R. (1920). Conditioned emotional reactions. *Journal of Experimental Psychology, 3*, 1–14.

Watts, W. D., & Wright, L. S. (1990). The relationship of alcohol, tobacco, marijuana, and other illegal drug use to delinquency among Mexican-American, black, and white adolescent males. *Adolescence, 25*, 171–181.

Webster, J. D., & Young, R. A. (1988). Process variables of the life review: Counseling implications. *International Journal of Aging and Human Development, 26*, 315–323.

Wegmann, R. (1991). How long does unemployment last? *The Career Development Quarterly, 40*, 71–81.

Weinberg, R. (1989). Intelligence and IQ. *American Psychologist, 44*, 98–104.

Weiner, B. (1980). *Human motivation.* New York: Holt, Rinehart & Winston.

Weininger, O. (1990). Play: For survival. In I. M. Doxey (Ed.), *Child care and education: Canadian dimensions.* Scarborough, Ont.: Nelson Canada.

Weis, D. L. (1983). "Open" marriage and multilateral relationships: The emergence of nonexclusive models of the marital relationship. In E. D. Macklin & R. H. Rubin (Eds.), *Contemporary families and alternative lifestyles: Handbook on research and theory* (pp. 194–215). Beverly Hills, CA: Sage.

Weisfeld, G. E. (1982). The nature–nurture issue and the integrating concept of function. In B. B. Wolman et al. (Eds.), *Handbook of developmental psychology*. Englewood Cliffs, NJ: Prentice-Hall.

Weiss, R. S. (1984). The impact of marital dissolution on income and consumption in single parent households. *Journal of Marriage and the Family, 46,* 115–127.

Weisskopf, M. (1987). Lead astray: The poisoning of America. *Discovery, 8,* 76–77.

Weitzman, L. J. (1985). *The divorce revolution: The unexpected social and economic consequences for women and children in America.* New York: Free Press.

Wellman, H. M. (1988). The early development of memory strategies. In F. E. Weinert & M. Perlmutter (Eds.), *Memory development: Universal changes and individual differences.* Hillsdale, NJ: Erlbaum.

Wellman, H. M., & Gelman, S. A. (1992). Cognitive development: Foundational theories of core domains. *Annual Review of Psychology, 43,* 337–375.

Wells, E., & Stryker, S. (1988). Stability and change in self over the life course. In P. B. Baltes, D. L. Featherman, & R. M. Lerner (Eds.), *Life-span development and behavior* (Vol. 8). Hillsdale, NJ: Erlbaum.

Welsh, G. S. (1980). *Welsh figure preference test.* Palo Alto, CA: Consulting Psychologists.

Werner, E. E., & Smith, R. S. (1982). *Vulnerable but invincible: A longitudinal study of resilient children and youth.* New York: McGraw-Hill.

Werry, J. S. (1972). The childhood psychoses. In H. C. Quay & J. S. Werry (Eds.), *Psychopathological disorders of childhood.* New York: John Wiley.

Wertham, F. (1954). *Seduction of the innocent.* New York: Holt, Rinehart & Winston.

Wertsch, J. V. (1985). *Vygotsky and the social formation of mind.* Cambridge, MA: Harvard University Press.

Wesley, F., & Wesley, C. (1977). *Sex-role psychology.* New York: Human Sciences Press.

Westoff, L. A., & Westoff, C. F. (1971). *From now to zero: Fertility, contraception and abortion in America.* Boston: Little, Brown.

White, B. L. (1985). *The first three years of life* (rev. ed.). Englewood Cliffs, NJ: Prentice-Hall.

Whiting, B. B. (1984). Problems of American middle-class women. In G. Baruch & J. Brooks-Gunn (Eds.), *Women in midlife.* New York: Plenum.

Whitney, E. N., & Hamilton, E.M.N. (1984). *Understanding nutrition* (3rd ed.). St. Paul, MN: West.

Whorf, B. L. (1941). The relation of habitual thought and behavior to language. In L. Spier (Ed.), *Language, culture and personality.* Salt Lake City: University of Utah Press.

Whorf, B. L. (1956). *Language, thought and reality.* New York: John Wiley.

Wilk, C. A. (1986). *Career women and childbearing: A psychological analysis of the decision process.* New York: Van Nostrand Reinhold.

Willemsen, E. (1979). *Understanding infancy.* San Francisco: W. H. Freeman.

Willerman, L. (1973). Activity level and hyperactivity in twins. *Child Development, 44,* 288–293.

Willerman, L. (1979). Effects of families on intellectual development. *American Psychologist, 34,* 923–929.

Williams, K., Haywood, K., & Vansant, A. (1991). Throwing patterns of older adults: A follow-up investigation. *International Journal of Aging and Human Development, 33,* 279–294.

Willig, A. (1985). A meta-analysis of selected studies on the effectiveness of bilingual education. *Review of Educational Research, 55,* 269–317.

Wilson, E. O. (1975). *Sociobiology: The new synthesis.* Cambridge, MA: Belknap.

Wilson, E. O. (1976). Academic vigilantism and the political significance of sociobiology. *Bio-science, 183,* 187–190.

Wilson, G. T., & Walsh, B. T. (1991). Eating disorders in DSM-IV. *Journal of Developmental Psychology, 100,* 362–365.

Wineburg, S. S. (1987). The self-fulfillment of the self-fulfilling prophecy: A critical appraisal. *Educational Researcher, 16,* 28–37.

Winn, M. (1985). *The plug-in drug* (rev. ed.). New York: Viking.

Winnicott, D. W. (1971). *Playing and reality*. New York: Basic Books.

Winsten, S. (1949). *Days with Bernard Shaw*. New York: Vanguard.

Witkin, H. A., et al. (1976). Criminality in XYY and XXY men. *Science, 193*, 547–555.

Wittrock, M. C. (1986). Students' thought processes. In M. C. Wittrock (Ed.), *Handbook of research on teaching* (3rd ed.). New York: Macmillan.

Wolff, P. H. (1963). Observations of the early development of smiling. In B. M. Foss (Ed.), *Determinants of infant behavior 2*. London: Methuen.

Wolff, P. H. (1966). The causes, controls, and organization of behavior in the neonate. *Psychological Issues, 5*(1)(Whole No. 17), 1–105.

Wolff, P. H. (1969). The natural history of crying and other vocalizations in early infancy. In B. Foss (Ed.), *Determinants of infant behavior 4*. London: Methuen.

Wolock, I., & Horowitz, B. (1984). Child maltreatment as a social problem: The neglect of neglect. *American Journal of Orthopsychiatry, 54*, 530–543.

Wood, B. S. (1981). *Children and communication: Verbal and nonverbal language development*. (2nd ed.). Englewood Cliffs, NJ: Prentice-Hall.

Wright, H. F. (1960). Observational child study. In P. H. Mussen (Ed.), *Handbook of research methods in child development*. New York: John Wiley.

Yamamoto, K. (1964). *Experimental scoring manual for Minnesota Tests of Creative Thinking and Writing*. Kent, OH: Bureau of Educational Research, Kent State University.

Yankelovich, D. (1972). *The changing values on campus*. New York: Washington Square Press.

Yankelovich, D. (1981). The meaning of work. In J. O'Toole, J. L. Scheiber, & L. C. Wood (Eds.), *Working, changes and choices* (pp. 33–34). New York: Human Sciences Press.

Yankelovich, D., & Lefkowitz, B. (1982). Work and American expectations. *National Forum, 62*, 3–5.

Yarrow, L. J., & Goodwin, M. S. (1973). The immediate impact of separation: Reactions of infants to a change in mother figures. In L. J. Stone, H. T. Smith, & L. B. Murphy (Eds.), *The competent infant: Research and commentary*. New York: Basic Books.

Yensen, R. (1975). On the measurement of happiness and its implications for welfare. In L. Levi (Ed.), *Emotions: Their parameters and measurements*. New York: Raven Press.

Zajonc, R. B. (1976). Family configuration and intelligence. *Science, 192*, 227–236.

Zajonc, R. B., & Markus, G. B. (1975). Birth order and intellectual development. *Psychological Review, 82*, 74–88.

Zani, B. (1991). Male and female patterns in the discovery of sexuality during adolescence. *Journal of Adolescence, 14*, 163–178.

Zeligs, R. (1974). *Children's experience with death*. Springfield, IL: Thomas.

Zigler, E., & Freedman, J. (1987). Early experience, malleability, and Head Start. In J. J. Gallagher & C. T. Ramey (Eds.), *The Malleability of children*. Baltimore: Brookes.

Zigler, E., & Hodapp, R. M. (1991). Behavioral functioning in individuals with mental retardation. *Annual Review of Psychology, 42*, 29–50.

Index

Boldfaced page numbers refer to boldfaced terms in the text.

Italicized page numbers refer to figures and illustrations.

Acknowledgments

Photo Credits